URDU

Practical Dictionary

Urdu–English / English–Urdu

URDU

Practical Dictionary

Urdu–English / English–Urdu

Daniel Krasa

Hippocrene Books, Inc.
New York

For information, address:
HIPPOCRENE BOOKS, INC.
171 Madison Ave.
New York, NY 10016
www.hippocrenebooks.com

Cataloging-in-Publication Data available from the Library of Congress.

ISBN-13: 978-0-7818-1340-2
ISBN-10: 0-7818-1340-9

Printed in the United States of America.

MIX
Paper from responsible sources
FSC® C011935
FSC
www.fsc.org

CONTENTS

PREFACE

This new Urdu-English/English-Urdu dictionary is designed to facilitate access to one of South Asia's most fascinating languages. Until now there was no practical mid-sized, commercially available dictionary of Urdu and English that includes both Urdu's genuine Nastaliq script and phonetic transcriptions that make it easier for learners of Urdu to pronounce the words correctly. In order to narrow this gap the present work has been compiled including more than 13,000 entries for Urdu and more than 9,000 entries for English, covering the vocabulary that one will come across most frequently in contact with Urdu speakers in everyday life as well as in modern literature and in the media. The book is meant both for non-Urdu speakers who are learning the language and for Urdu speakers who are able to read Urdu and wish to find an accurate translation or pronunciation for a specific word. The entries have been chosen on the basis of their frequencies and it has been attempted to keep the translations as exhaustive as possible. In a few cases words might have a number of meanings and thus several translations are given for a single entry.

The selected sources for the compilation of this dictionary include *Ferozsons Urdu-English Dictionary* and *English-Urdu Dictionary* (Lahore, Pakistan), *Concise Twenty-First Century Dictionary Urdu-English* (Delhi, India) as well as the *Oxford Urdu-English Dictionary* and *English-Urdu Dictionary* (Oxford, United Kingdom).

I express my sincere thanks to Monica Bentley and Barbara Keane-Pigeon, who have not only proofread the project but have also given me thorough guidance as well as valuable suggestions throughout the compilation of this dictionary. I am also thankful to Mr. Kamran Nadeem for his patient help, his precious input, and his fruitful assistance.

—Daniel Krasa

INTRODUCTION TO THE URDU LANGUAGE

Urdu is an Indo-Aryan language belonging to the wider family of Indo-European languages. It is spoken in Pakistan—where it is the national language as well as the *lingua franca*—and in many parts of India, where it is one of the twenty-two national languages scheduled in the constitution. There are between 60 and 70 million native speakers, but in Pakistan it is a compulsory subject in primary and medium schools, so that most of Pakistan's population of 196 million people speaks, writes, and reads Urdu. In India, Urdu is the co-official language in the states of Bihar, Jammu and Kashmir, Telangana, and Uttar Pradesh, as well as in the capital, Delhi.

The word "*Urdu*" is of Turkish origin, where it means a "military camp" and the historical development of the Urdu language is intimately linked to the emergence of Islam in the subcontinent. It was born around the 12th century, when Islamic conquerors from Afghanistan and present-day Iran settled temporarily in the area of Delhi. It is the city of Muradabad some 100 miles from Delhi that is generally referred to as the cradle of Urdu. Muslim soldiers spoke mainly Persian and Turkic languages, and it became necessary to create a common language for communication with the local people, who used dialects of Sanskrit-related Indo-Aryan languages. These dialects mingled with the languages of the new arrivals, absorbing many loanwords from Persian, Turkish, and through them, Arabic. Subsequently, this mixture of colloquial speeches developed into the main language of government of the Mughal Court and it was gradually transformed into a *lingua franca,* the common language, called until the early 20th century "Hindustani." Hindustan was the name of the Ganges Plain, the present-day territory encompassing Pakistan, Northern and Central India, as well as Bangladesh.

From the 13th to the 20th century, Hindustani was the cradle of a flourishing literature influenced by the Islamic-Oriental tradition and later by Hindu mythology. Following the emergence of a Hindu identity, Hindustani spoken by Hindus was characterized by a strong "de-Persianization" of its vocabulary, substituting words from Sanskrit. Subsequently, Hindustani ceased to exist and gave birth to two separate languages: Urdu and Hindi.

The differences between these two languages are cultural more than structural. They reflect religious and political differences to the extent that Urdu is usually associated with Islam and Hindi with Hinduism.

It is with the partition of India in 1947 and increased tensions between Muslims and Hindus that these two languages were considered radically different, although they actually are two variants of the same language.

Urdu is different from Hindi (nowadays the most widely spoken language of India) as it uses the Arabic-Persian alphabet called Nastaliq instead of the Devanagari alphabet that is used for Hindi. However, these languages have almost identical grammars, and have remained largely homogeneous, except for the standards used in intellectual, administrative, and religious backgrounds.

You will notice that speaking Urdu will open up doors to a world rich in history, culture, and adventure, and since Urdu und Hindi are not that different it will give you access to one of the largest linguistic communities of our planet!

TRANSCRIPTION & PRONUNCIATION

There are several transcription policies for Urdu and other Indo-Aryan languages, however in this book we adopted the transliteration system that is by far the most widely used in academic circles and thus is accepted by scholars at universities and institutes around the globe. Urdu verbs are always given in their infinitive form ending in -nā.

THE URDU ALPHABET

Urdu is written in the Nastaliq script, as shown below. Throughout this book, we have also provided the romanization for ease of use.

ا	a	ر	r	ق	q
ب	b	ڑ	ṛ	ک	k
پ	p	ز	z	گ	g
ت	t	ژ	ž	ل	l
ٹ	ṭ	س	s	م	m
ث	s	ش	š	ن	n
ج	j	ص	s	و	v
چ	c	ض	z	ہ	h
ح	ḥ	ط	t	ء	ʻ
خ	x	ظ	z	ی	y
د	d	ع	c	ے	ē
ڈ	ḍ	غ	ġ		
ذ	z	ف	f		

Numbers

0	۰	5	۵
1	۱	6	۶
2	۲	7	۷
3	۳	8	۸
4	۴	9	۹

URDU PRONUNCIATION GUIDE

Vowels

Letter	Urdu example	Approximate English equivalent
a	band	r**u**n, f**u**n
ā	āj	f**a**ther
ai	hai	p**ay**
au	aur	**oa**r
ē	ēk	*between* p**e**t *and* s**ai**d
i	zindah	h**i**t
ī	zanjīr	tr**ee**
ō	dō	*between Southern British* c**o**t *and* d**oo**r
u	gandum	p**u**t
ū	bhūt	m**oo**n

Consonants

Unlike the Urdu vowel system, consonants are more complex and mastering them requires additional information.

Retroflex consonants

There is an important contrast between dental and retroflex consonants in Urdu. In dental consonants the tongue touches the upper front teeth, whereas retroflex consonants are pronounced with the tongue turned back to the roof of your mouth. For example, set your mouth up to pronounce a normal English d, but then curl your tongue right up so that the bottom part of it touches the top part of your mouth. As you try to pronounce the original d, you will feel your tongue "flapping" forward. The three retroflex consonants are: ḍ, ṛ and ṭ.

Aspirated consonants

Urdu also distinguishes breathed or aspirated consonants from light or non-aspirated ones. Aspirated consonants are those pronounced with an audible expulsion of breath, a discernable, heavy puff of air. The aspirated consonants are marked by an h—written with the letter ھ— following them. They are: bh, ch, dh, ḍh, gh, jh, kh, ph, ṛh, th and ṭh. On the other hand non-aspirated consonants are pronounced far lighter than their English equivalents, with minimal breath. It is vital to emphasize the difference between aspirated and unaspirated consonants.

Nasalization

Urdu has several nasal sounds that affect the vowel preceding them, causing them to be pronounced through the nose. These nasal sounds are marked with the transcription letter ṁ. But even the consonants m and n can cause light nasalization when they stand in front of another consonant, for example: ambār "heap, pile."

Letter	Urdu example	Approximate English equivalent
b	bēṭā	**b**ox (*light*)
bh	bhūrā	**b**ox (*breathed*)
c	cōrī	**ch**urch (*light*)
ch	chōṭā	**ch**urch (*breathed*)
^{c}	^{c}īd	*a rasping sound that is pronounced deep in the back of the throat—unknown in English, most speakers ignore it or pronounce it like* ʻ
d	denā	**d**og (*light*)
dh	dhaniyā	**d**og (*breathed*)
ḍ	ḍākū	*like* **d** (*flapped*); *in the middle of a word it is often pronounced like a flapped* **r**

Letter	Urdu example	Approximate English equivalent
ḍh	ḍhōl	*like* **d** (*breathed*)
f	fauj	**f**at
g	garmī	**g**ive (*light*)
gh	ghar	**g**ive (*breathed*)
ġ	ġarīb	*a voiced velar* **ch** *as between Scottish English* lo**ch** *and the exclamation* U**gh**!*; many speakers ignore this sound and pronounce it like* **g**
h	havā	**h**at
ḥ	ḥāmil	*a voiceless strongly whispered* **h***, many speakers ignore it and pronounce it as the* **h** *in* **h**at
j	jāl	**j**et (*light*)
jh	jhūlā	**j**et (*breathed*)
k	kacrā	**k**ick (*light*)
kh	khiṛkī	**k**ick (*breathed*)
l	likhnā	**l**et
m	madad	**m**at
ṁ	maiṁ	*the vowel before is nasalised*
n	nīnd	**n**eed
p	pūrā	**p**et (*light*)
ph	phir	**p**et (*breathed*)
q	qaum	**k**ick*, but produced farther back in the throat*
r	ras	**r**at*, but rolled as in Scottish English or Italian*
ṛ	phēpṛā	butte**r***, as the American flapped* **r**
s	samundar	**s**it
š	šauhar	**sh**ine
t	tāp	**t**en (*light*)

Letter	Urdu example	Approximate English equivalent
th	thūknā	**t**en (*breathed*)
ṭ	ṭāng	*like* **t** (*flapped*)
ṭh	ṭhīk	*like* **t** (*breathed*)
v	vazīr	**w**ay
x	xarc	lo**ch**, *as in Scottish English*
y	yahāṁ	**y**es
z	zēvrāt	**z**ebra
ž	žālah	era**s**ure
‘	sā’ikil	*a so-called glottal stop that marks that the sounds before and after it are pronounced separately with a simple stop of the breath in between*

ABBREVIATIONS

adj.	adjective
adv.	adverb
art.	article
conj.	conjunction
interj.	interjection
n.	noun
n.f.	feminine noun
n.m.	masculine noun
num.	numeral
phr.	phrase
pl.	plural
pp.	postposition
prep.	preposition
pron.	pronoun
sing.	singular
v.	verb
v.i.	intransitive verb
v.t.	transitive verb

URDU-ENGLISH DICTIONARY

آ / ا alif

آبننا happen *v.i.* **ā bannā**
آبنوس African, dark-skinned person *n.m.* **ābnūs**
آبنوسی dark (*skin color*) *adj.* **ābnūsī**
اب now, presently *adv.* **ab**
آب water; splendor *n.m.* **āb**
آب باراں rain water *n.m.* **āb-ē-bārāṁ**
اب بھی even now, yet, as yet, still *adv.* **ab bhī**
آب پاشی irrigation *n.v.* **āb pāšī**
اب تب now and then, occasionally *adv.* **ab tab**
اب تک till now, yet *adv.* **ab tak**
آب چشم tears *n.m.* **āb-ē-cašm**
آب دوز submarine *n.m.* **āb dōz**
آب دیدہ in tears, weeping *adj.* **āb dīdah**
آب دیدہ ہونا be in tears, shed tears, cry *v.i.* **āb dīdah hōnā**
آب گیر pond; ditch *n.m.* **āb gīr**
آب مقطر distilled water *n.m.* **āb-ē-maqtar**
آب نقرہ quicksilver *n.m.* **āb-ē-naqrah**
اب ہی just now; instantly; already *adv.* **ab hī**
آب وہوا climate *n.f.* **āb-ō-havā**
ابا refusal, denial *n.m.* **ibā**
اباحت permission, leave *n.f.* **ibāḥat**
آباد populated *adj.* **ābād**
آبادی population *n.f.* **ābādī**
ابارنا release; deliver *v.t.* **ubārnā**
ابالنا boil *v.t.* **ubālnā**
آباؤاجداد ancestors, forefathers *n.m.* **ābā-ō-ajdād**
ابتدا beginning *n.f.* **ibtidā**
ابتدا میں in the beginning, at first *adv.* **ibtidā mēṁ**
ابتداء invention *n.m.* **ibtidā'**
ابتدائی primary *adj.* **ibtidā'ī**
ابتدائی تعلیم primary education *n.f.* **ibtidā'ī taᶜlīm**
ابتر ruined, spoiled *adj.* **abtar**

ruin, spoil *v.t.* **abtar karnā** اَبتر کرنا
destruction, ruin *n.f.* **abtarī** اَبتری
smile *n.m.* **ibtisām** اِبتسام
temptation; trial, misfortune *n.m.* **ibtilā** اِبتلا
cheerfulness *n.m.* **ibtihāj** اِبتہاج
the (Arabic) alphabet *n.m.* **abjad** اَبجد
eternity *n.m.* **abad** اَبد
for ever and ever *adj.* **abad-ul-ābād** اَبدالآباد
forever, eternally *adj.* **abadan** اَبداً
invention; publication *n.m.* **ibdāᶜ** اِبداع
change, exchange, substitution *n.m.* **ibdāl** اِبدال
cloud *n.m.* **abr** اَبر
cloudy *adj.* **abr ālūd** اَبر آلود
be cloudy *v.i.* **abr chānā** اَبر چھانا
release *n.m.* **ibrā** اِبرا
needle *n.f.* **abrah** اِبرہ
honor; dignity *n.f.* **ābrū** آبرو
disgrace, defame *v.t.* **ābrū utārnā** آبرو اتارنا
(raw) silk *n.m.* **abrēšam** ابریشم
water pot *n.m.* **abrīq** اِبریق
waterfall *n.m.* **ābšār / āb šār** آبشار / آب شار
abolition *n.m.* **ibtāl** اِبطال
further, most distant *adj.* **abᶜad** ابعد
confirmation; prolongation *n.m.* **abkā** ابکا
nausea, vomiting *n.f.* **ubkā'ī** اُبکائی
vomit *v.i.* **ubaknā** اُبکنا
boiled water *n.m.* **ublā pānī** اُبلا پانی
boil *v.i.* **ubalnā** اُبلنا
silly, stupid *adj.* **ablah** اَبلہ
blister *n.m.* **āblah** آبلہ
devil, Satan *n.m.* **iblīs** اِبلیس
son *n.m.* **ibn** اِبن
daughter *n.f.* **ibnat** اِبنت
suspicion; ambiguity; thumb *n.m.* **ibhām** اِبہام
greatness *n.f.* **ubhat** اُبہت
father *n.m.* **abū** ابو

paternal *adj.* **abvī** ابوی

irrigation *n.f.* **ābyārī** آبیاری

white *adj.* **abyaz** ابیض

light (*of little weight*) *adj.* / gratitude *n.m.* **abhār** ابھار

swelling *n.m.* **ubhār** اُبھار

raise, lift *v.t.* **ubhārna** اُبھارنا

rise, grow *v.i.* **ubharnā** اُبھرنا

you (*sing./pl.*) *pron.* **āp** آپ

flatter *v.t.* **āp āp karnā** آپ آپ کرنا

spontaneously *adv.* **āp hī āp** آپ ہی آپ

elder sister *n.f.* **āpā** آپا

disabled, crippled *adj.* **apāhaj** اپاہج

plan, scheme, measure, treatment *n.m.* **upā'ē** اُپائے

plan, scheme *v.t.* **upā'ē karnā** اُپائے کرنا

fault, crime *n.m.* **aparādh** اپرادھ

charge *v.t.* **aparādh lagānā** اپرادھ لگانا

April *n.m.* **aprail** اپریل

self; one another *pron.* **āppas** آپس

relationship *n.f.* **āppas dārī** آپس داری

mutually *pron.* **āppas mēṁ** آپس میں

disgrace, dishonor *n.m.* **apmān** اپمان

disgrace, dishonor *v.t.* **apmān karnā** اپمان کرنا

one's own, personal *adj.* **apnā** اپنا

each one, respective *adj.* **apnā apnā** اپنا اپنا

make something one's own *v.t.* **apnānā** اپنانا

kinship, friendship *n.f.* **apnāyat** اپنائیت

swell; become fat; be filled *v.i.* **apharnā** اپھرنا

operator *n.m.* **āpērēṭar** آپریٹر

descent, slope, decline *n.m.* **utār** اُتار

swallow, gulp down *v.i.* **utār jānā** اُتار جانا

disgrace, dishonor *v.t* **utār dēnā** اُتار دینا

take down; insert *v.t.* **utār lēnā** اُتار لینا

take down *v.t.* **utārnā** اُتارنا

house; tent *n.m.* **atāq** اتاق

tutor, instructor *n.m.* **atālīq** اتالیق

tuition; education *n.f.* **atāliqī** اتالیقی

obedience *n.m.* **ittibāᶜ** اِتباع
union, alliance *n.m.* **ittiḥād** اِتحاد
answer, reply; north *n.m.* **uttar** اُتر
descend, come down, drop *v.i.* **utarānā** اُترانا
northern *adj.* **uttarāhā** اُتراہا
day after tomorrow *n.* **atarsōṁ** اترسوں
alight, get down, descend *v.i.* **utarnā** اِترنا اترنا
fire, flame *n.f.* **ātaš** آتش
fireworks *n.m.* **ātaš bāzī** آتش بازی
volcano *n.m.* **ātaš fišāṁ** آتش فشاں
furious; passionate *adj.* **ātaš mizāj** آتش مزاج
hot *adj.* **ātašī** آتشی
conjunction, union; neighborhood *n.m.* **ittisāl** اِتصال
agreement; harmony *n.m.* **ittifāq** اتفاق
agree; harmonize *v.i.* **ittifāq bannā** اِتفاق بننا
be agreed; chance *v.i.* **ittifāq paṛnā** اِتفاق پڑنا
live in harmony, be on good terms *v.t.* **ittifāq rakhnā** اِتفاق رکھنا
by chance, unexpectedly *adv.* **ittifāq sē** اِتفاق سے
agree *v.t.* **ittifāq karnā** اِتفاق کرنا
be agreed *v.i.* **ittifāq hōnā** اِتفاق ہونا
accidentally, by chance *adv.* **ittifāqan** اتفاقاً
incidental *adj.* **ittifāqī** اِتفاقی
holiness, purity (*religious*) *n.m.* **ittiqā'** اِتقاء
destruction, ruin, loss *n.m.* **ittlāf** اِتلاف
highest, best *adj.* **uttam** اُتم
spirit, soul *n.m.* **ātmā** آتما
accomplishment, completion *n.m.* **itmām** اِتمام
as much as that, so many, so much *adj.* **utnā** اُتنا
as much as this, so many, so much *adj.* **itnā** اِتنا
exactly that much *adj.* **utnā hī** اُتنا ہی
as many as that, so many *adv.* **utnē** اُتنے
meanwhile *adv.* **itnē mēṁ** اِتنے میں
suspicion; accusation *n.m.* **ittihām** اِتہام
beat (someone) up *v.t.* **uttū banānā** اتو بنانا
Sunday *n.m.* **itvār** اتوار
abyss *n.m.* **athāh** اتھاہ

expenditure, expense, debit *n.m.* **uthāō** اتھاو
upset *adj.* **uthal puthal** اُتھل پتھل
shallow, low *adj.* **uthlā** اتھلا
upset *v.t.* **uthlānā** اتھلانا
move; be upset **v.i uthalnā** اتھلنا
flour *n.m.* **āṭā** آٹا
daily bread *n.f.* **āṭā dāl** آٹا دال
knead the dough *v.t.* **āṭā gūndhnā** آٹا گوندھنا
fit (into); fix *v.t.* **aṭānā** اٹانا
obstacle, hindrance *n.f.* **aṭak** اٹک
obstruct, hinder, impede *v.t.* **aṭkānā** اٹکانا
guess, supposition *n.f.* **aṭkal** اٹکل
shrewd *adj.* **aṭkal bāz** اٹکل باز
by guess, at random *adj.* **aṭkal sē** اٹکل سے
be kept stopped, be hindered *v.i.* **aṭaknā** اٹکنا
playful, merry *adj.* **aṭkhēl** اٹکھیل
playfulness *n.f.* **aṭkhēlī** اٹکھیلی
immovable; inevitable *adj.* **aṭal** اٹل
be contained, be held *v.i.* **aṭnā** اٹنا
rickshaw *n.m.* **āṭō rikšā** آٹو رکشا
eight *num.* **āṭh** آٹھ
restlessness *n.f.* **uṭh baiṭh** اُٹھ بیٹھ
jump up (suddenly) *v.i.* **uṭh baiṭhnā** اُٹھ بیٹھنا
take away *v.t.* **uṭhā lēnā** اُٹھا لینا
eighteen *num.* **aṭhārah** اٹھارہ
eighty-eight *num.* **aṭhāsī** اٹھاسی
rise, ascent; attitude; height *n.f.* **uṭhān** اُٹھان
lift, raise *v.t.* **uṭhānā** اُٹھانا
ninety-eight *num.* **aṭhānavē** اٹھانوے
fifty-eight *num.* **aṭhāvan** اٹھاون
twenty-eight *num.* **aṭhā'īs** اٹھائیس
seventy-eight *num.* **aṭhattar** اٹھتر
stutter *v.i.* **aṭhlānā** اٹھلانا
get up, rise, stand up *v.i.* **uṭhnā** اُٹھنا
mark, sign, trace; impression; effect, influence *n.m.* **asar** اثر
mark, affect, influence *v.t.* **asar karnā** اثر کرنا

have effect, be influenced *v.i.* **asar hōnā** اثر ہونا
sin *n.m.* **ism** اثم
middle, interim *n.m.* **asnā'** اثناء
marked, chosen *adj.* **asīr** اثیر
well-born, noble; genuine *adj.* **asīl** اثیل
sinner, liar *n.m.* **asīm** اثیم
today *adv.* **āj** آج
this day *adv.* **āj tak** آج تک
nowadays *adv.* **āj kal** آج کل
evade *v.t.* **āj kal karnā** آج کل کرنا
grandfather (paternal) *n.m.* **ājā** اجا
hire, lease, rental *n.m.* **ijārah** اِجارہ
deserted; ruined *adj.* **ujāṛ** اجاڑ
devastate, raze, demolish *v.t.* **ujāṛnā** اجاڑنا
squandering, destructive *adj.* **ujāṛū** اجاڑو
permission, leave *n.f.* **ijāzat** اِجازت
permit, allow *v.t.* **ijāzat dēnā** اِجازت دینا
bright, luminous *adj.* **ujāgar** اُجاگر
sunshine, daylight *n.m.* **ujālā** اُجالا
make bright; cleanse, polish *v.t.* **ujālnā** اُجالنا
ignorant, innocent, careless, foolish *adj.* **ajān** اجان
compulsion, constraint *n.m.* **ijbār** اِجبار
selecting, choosing *n.m.* **ijtibā** اِجتبا
congregation, assembly *n.m.* **ijtimā**ᶜ اِجتماع
gather *v.t.* **ijtimā**ᶜ **karnā** اجتماع کرنا
keeping aloof, avoiding, refraining *n.m.* **ijtināb** اِجتناب
endeavor, effort *n.m.* **ijtihād** اِجتہاد
worthy *adj.* **ajdār** اِجدار
stupid, ignorant; senseless *adj.* **ujaḍḍ** اُجڈ
reward, compensation *n.m.* **ajr** اجر
reward, recompense *v.t.* **ajr dēnā** اجر دینا
issue, issuing *n.m.* **ijrā'** اِجراء
issue *v.t.* **ijrā' karnā** اِجراء کرنا
reward; wages; fee *n.f.* **ujrat** اُجرت
desolate, ruined, wasted *adj.* **ujṛā** اُجڑا
in ruins, demolished, razed *adj.* **ujṛā pujṛā** اُجڑا پُجڑا

be razed; be shaved *v.i.* **ujaṛnā** اُجڑنا
be razed, fall into decay *v.i.* **ujaṛnā** اجڑنا
bright, luminous; clean; white *adj.* **ujlā** اجلا
brightness; whiteness; enlightenment *n.m.* **ujlāpan** اجلاپن
magnificence, glory *n.m.* **ijlāl** اجلال
assembly, council; agreement *n.m.* **ijmāᶜ** اجماع
result; summary *n.m.* **ijmāl** اِجمال
brief, summarized *adj.* **ijmālī** اِجمالی
foreign *adj.* **ajnabī** اجنبی
rent; fare; wages; reward *n.m.* **ajūrah** اجورہ
unconquered, invincible *adj.* **ajīt** اجیت
indigestible *adj.* **ajīran** اِجیرن
peep, spy; jump up *v.i.* **ujhaknā** اُجھکنا
high, lofty, superior *adj.* **ucc** اُچ
banished *adj.* **ucāṭ** اچاٹ
banish, drive away *v.t.* **ucāṭnā** اچاٹنا
pickle *n.m.* **acār** اچار
pronunciation, utterance, articulation *n.m.* **uccāran** اچارن
pronounce, utter *v.t.* **uccāran karnā** اچارن کرنا
height, elevation *n.f.* **uccān** اچان
rinse (one's mouth), gargle *v.t.* **acānā** اچانا
suddenly, by chance *adj.* **acānak** اچانک
proper, fitting, suitable *adj.* **ucit** اُچت
separate, divide *v.t.* **ucṭānā** اُچٹانا
be weary; be separated *v.i.* **ucaṭnā** اچٹنا
be pronounced, be uttered, be articulated *v.t.* **uccarnā** اچرنا
pick-pocket, swindler *n.m.* **ucakkā** اچکا
theft, swindling, defrauding *n.m.* **ucakkāpan** اچکاپن
lift up, raise up *v.t.* **uckānā** اچکانا
coat (*long*) *n.m.* **ackan** اچکن
immovable, motionless, firm *adj.* **acal** اچل
rinse (one's mouth), gargle *v.t.* **ācaman karnā** آچمن کرنا
wonder, astonishment *n.m.* **acambhā** اچنبھا
certain *adj.* **acūk** اچوک
good, well; really; indeed *adj.* **acchā** اچھا
wish, desire *n.f.* **icchā** اِچھا

cure, recover *v.t.* **acchā karnā** اچھا کرنا
say yes; call good *v.t.* **acchā kēhnā** اچھا کہنا
be fit, be pleasing *v.i.* **acchā lagnā** اچھا لگنا
throw up, toss up *v.t.* **uchālnā** اچھالنا
leap, bound *v.i.* **uchalnā** اچھلنا
suffocation, choking *n.m.* **ucchū** اچھو
untouched, pure *adj.* **achūtā** اچھوتا
enclosure, compound *n.f.* **iḥātah** اِحاطہ
surround, fence, enclose, limit, confine *v.t.* **iḥātah karnā** اِحاطہ کرنا
seclusion, retreat *n.m.* **iḥtijāb** احتجاب
protest *n.m.* **iḥtijāj** اِحتجاج
abstinence *n.m.* **iḥtirāz** اِحتراز
admiration, adoration, respect *n.m.* **iḥtirām** اِحترام
examination, inspection, control *n.m.* **iḥtisāb** اِحتساب
fortunate, prosperous *adj.* **iḥtizā** اِحتظا
probability, possibility, chance *n.m.* **iḥtimāl** اِحتمال
presume, suspect, guess *v.t.* **iḥtimāl karnā** اِحتمال کرنا
be likely, be probable *v.i.* **iḥtimāl hōnā** اِحتمال ہونا
probable, likely *adj.* **iḥtimālī** اِحتمالی
necessity, need, want; urgency *n.f.* **iḥtiyāj** اِحتیاج
caution, care, precaution *n.f.* **iḥtiyāt** اِحتیاط
carefully, cautiously *adv.* **iḥtiyāt sē** اِحتیاط سے
take precautions, care *v.t.* **iḥtiyāt karnā** اِحتیاط کرنا
carefully, cautiously *adv.* **iḥtiyātan** اِحتیاطاً
one *num.*; unity, oneness *n.m.* **aḥad** احد
unity, alliance; individuality *n.f.* **aḥdiyat** احدیت
perception, feeling *n.m.* **iḥsās** احساس
beneficence, favor; (good) deed *n.m.* **iḥsān** اِحسان
ungrateful, unthankful *adj.* **iḥsān farāmōš** اِحسان فراموش
be thankful, be grateful *v.t.* **iḥsān lēnā** اِحسان لینا
grateful, obliged *adj.* **iḥsān mand** اِحسان مند
gratitude, thankfulness *n.f.* **iḥsān mandī** اِحسان مندی
better, best *adj.* **aḥsan** احسن
red *adj.* **aḥmar** احمر
very foolish, stupid *adj.* **aḥmaq** احمق
befool, make a fool (of somebody) *v.t.* **aḥmaq banānā** احمق بنانا

foolishly, idiotically *adv.* **aḥmaqānah** احمقانہ
occasionally, sometimes *adv.* **aḥyānan** احیاناً
reviving, preserving *n.m.* **iḥiyā'** احیاء
brother *n.m.* **ax** اخ
newspaper; news *n.m.* **axbār** اخبار
news-writer, editor (*of a newspaper*) *n.m.* **axbār navīs** اخبار نویس
sister *n.f.* **uxt** اخت
conclusion, completion *n.m.* **ixtitām** اختتام
conclude, complete *v.t.* **ixtitām karnā** اختتام کرنا
star *n.m.* **axtar** اختر
astrologer *n.m.* **axtar šumār** اختر شمار
astrology *n.f.* **axtar šumārī** اختر شماری
invention, contrivance *n.m.* **ixtirāᶜ** اختراع
invent, contrive *v.t.* **ixtirāᶜ karnā** اختراع کرنا
abbreviation, synopsis *n.m.* **ixtisār** اختصار
abbreviate, abstract *v.t.* **ixtisār karnā** اختصار کرنا
specialty, characteristic *n.m.* **ixtisās** اختصاص
amity, concord, friendship, intimacy *n.m.* **ixtilāt** اختلاط
difference, discord *n.m.* **ixtilāf** اختلاف
obstruction, obstacle, hindrance *n.m.* **ixtilāl** اختلال
choice, option; authority, power; competency *n.m.* **ixtiyār** اختیار
choose, approve *v.t.* **ixtiyār karnā** اختیار کرنا
optional, voluntary *adj.* **ixtiyārī** اختیاری
grasp, capture *v.t.* **axaz karnā** اخذ کرنا
final, last *adj.* **āxir** • end *n.m.* **āxar** آخر
expulsion, extradition *n.m.* **ixrāj** اخراج
life after death, the afterworld *n.f.* **āxirat** آخرت
walnut *n.m.* **axrōṭ** اخروٹ
last, final *adj.* **āxirī** آخری
green *adj.* **axzar** اخضر
concealment, hiding *n.m.* **ixfā'** اخفاء
conceal, hide *v.t.* **ixfā' karnā** اخفاء کرنا
ember, spark of fire *n.m.* **axgar** اخگر
sincerity; affection *n.m.* **ixlās** اخلاص
sincere; affectionate *adj.* **ixlās mand** اخلاص مند
sincerity; affection *n.f.* **ixlās mandī** اخلاص مندی

righteous people *n.m.* **axyār** اخیار
last, final *adj.* **axīr** اخیر
grace, charm, elegance *n.f.* **adā** ادا
salutation, greeting *n.m.* **ādāb** آداب
address, designation, title *n.m.* **ādāb-ō-alqāb** آداب والقاب
best compliments, best respects *n.m.* **ādāb-ō-taslīmāt** آداب و تسلیمات
generous *adj.* **udār** ادار
generosity *n.f.* **udāratā** ادارتا
sad, depressed *adj.* **udās** اداس
sadness, depression *n.f.* **udāsī** اداسی
acting *n.f.* **adākārī** اداکاری
charge, levy, payment, due observance *n.f.* **adā'ēgī** ادائیگی
good manners, elegance *n.m.* **adab** ادب
behave politely *v.t.* **adab karnā** ادب کرنا
calamity, bad luck, misfortune *n.m.* **idbār** اِدبار
ginger *n.f.* **adrak** ادرک
alteration, commutation *n.m.* **adal badal** ادل بدل
interchange; commute *v.t.* **adlā badlā karnā** ادلا بدلا کرنا
Adam; man *n.m.* **ādam** آدم
cannibal *n.m.* **ādam xōr** آدم خور
man *n.m.* **ādmī** آدمی
civilize *v.t.* **ādmī banānā** آدمی بنانا
humanity *n.f.* **ādmiyat** آدمیت
light, moonlight *n.f.* **udōt** ادوت
writer *n.m.* **adīb** ادیب
half *adj.* **ādhā** آدھا
debt, credit; loan, advance *n.m.* **udhār** ادھار
take a loan, buy on credit *v.t.* **udhār lēnā** ادھار لینا
to that place, on that side, there *adv.* **udhar** ادھر
to this place, on this side, here *adv.* **idhar** اِدھر
here and there *adv.* **idhar udhar** اِدھر اُدھر
in the middle, in the midst *adv.* **adhar mēṁ** ادھر میں
immoral, sinful *adj.* **adharmī** اِدھرمی
vile, wretched *adj.* **adham** اِدھم
unraveling, unpicking *n.m.* **udhēṛ** اُدھیڑ
undo, unravel *v.t.* **udhēṛnā** ادھیڑنا

fire *n.m.* **āzar** آذر
obedience, submission; belief; confidence *n.m.* **izᶜān** اِذعان
injury, torment *n.f.* **aziyat** اذیت
agonizing *adj.* **aziyat xēz** اذیت خیز
hurt, injure, harm *v.t.* **aziyat dēnā** اذیت دینا
(right) across *adj.* **ārpār** آرپار
intentionally, deliberately *adv.* **irādatan** ارادةً
belief, faith; goodwill *n.m.* **irādat** ارادت
desire, intention, will *n.m.* **irādah** ارادہ
desire; intend, plan *v.t.* **irādah karnā** ارادہ کرنا
decorated, arranged *adj.* **ārāstah** آراستہ
rest, relief, comfort, tranquillity *n.m.* **ārām** آرام
comfortable *adj.* **ārām dēh** آرام دہ
relieve, comfort; cure, heal *v.t.* **ārām dēnā** آرام دینا
rest, relax *v.t.* **ārām karnā** آرام کرنا
place to rest, bedroom *n.f.* **ārām gāh** آرام گاہ
decoration *n.f.* **ārā'iš** آرائش
decorative, ornamental *adj.* **ārā'išī** آرائشی
one hundred million *num.* **arab** ارب
countless, numberless *adj.* **arab kharab** ارب کھرب
alliance, connection, affinity *n.m.* **irtibāt** ارتباط
death, demise *n.m.* **irtiḥāl** ارتحال
design, painting *n.m.* **irtisām** ارتسام
elevation, height, altitude; ascent *n.m.* **irtifāᶜ** ارتفاع
inheritance *n.m.* **irs** ارث
Urdu (*language*); army; army camp *n.m.* **urdū** اردو
royal camp; army camp *n.m.* **urdū-ē-mōᶜalla** اردوئے معلیٰ
order, give an order *v.t.* **ārḍar dēnā** آرڈر دینا
low-priced, cheap *adj.* **arzān** ارزان
low-price offer, cheapness *n.f.* **arzānī** ارزانی
desire, request *n.f.* **ārzū** آرزو
wish, desire, request *v.t.* **ārzū karnā** آرزو کرنا
wishing, eager, desirous *adj.* **ārzū mand** آرزو مند
lion *n.m.* **arslān** ارسلان
mirror *n.f.* **ārsī** آرسی
instruction, command *n.m.* **iršād** ارشاد

instruct, command *v.t.* **iršād farmānā** ارشاد فرمانا
earth, region, country *n.f.* **arz** ارض
earthly, regional, terrestrial *adj.* **arzī** ارضی
purple, violet *adj.* **arġavānī** ارغوانی
wish, desire, longing *n.m.* **armān** ارمان
saw (*large*) *n.m.* **ārah** آرہ
enemy, foe *n.m.* **arī** اری
saw (*small*) *n.f.* **ārī** آری
shelter, protection, refuge *n.f.* **āṛ** آڑ
horizontal, diagonal *adj.* **āṛā** آڑا
flight *n.f.* **uṛān** اڑان
fly (*aircraft, kite*) *v.t.* **uṛānā** اڑانا
forty-eight *num.* **aṛtālīs** اڑتالیس
thirty-eight *num.* **aṛtīs** اڑتیس
urad dal (*a dried legume*) *n.m.* **uṛad** اڑد
sixty-eight *num.* **aṛsaṭh** اڑسٹھ
flying *adj.* **uṛan** اڑن
fly *v.i.* **uṛnā** اڑنا
hindrance, obstruction *n.m.* **aṛangā** اڑنگا
peach *n.m.* **āṛū** آڑو
neighborhood *n.m.* **aṛōs-paṛōs** اڑوس پڑوس
two and a half *num.* **aṛhā'ī** اڑھائی
infinite, limitless *adj.* **az ḥadd** از حد
free, independent *adj.* **āzād** آزاد
set free *v.t.* **āzād karnā** آزاد کرنا
freedom, liberty, liberation *n.f.* **āzādī** آزادی
illness, disease; trouble *n.m.* **āzār** آزار
trouble, misery *n.f.* **āzārī** آزاری
from that, therefore *adv.* **azāṁ** ازاں
wedding, marriage *n.m.* **izdivāj** ازدواج
woe, grief, trouble *n.f.* **āzurdagī** آزردگی
sad, annoyed, troubled *adj.* **āzurdah** آزردہ
displease, annoy *v.t.* **āzurdah karnā** آزردہ کرنا
blue; blue-eyed *adj.* **azraq** ازرق
eternity *n.f.* **azal** ازل
eternal *adj.* **azalī** ازلی

test, experiment *v.* **āzmānā** آزمانا
test, trial, experiment *n.f.* **āzmā'iš** آزمائش
that; him, her *pron.* **us** • this, it *pron.* **is** اس
hope, expectation *n.f.* **ās** آس
adjacent, near, neighboring; on all sides *adj.* **ās pās** آس پاس
• on that, upon which, thereupon *adv.* **us par** اس پر
on this, upon this, hereupon; hence *adv.* **is par**
lose hope *v.t.* **ās tōṛnā** آس توڑنا
before, before that *adv.* **us sē pahlē** اس سے پہلے
after, afterwards, after that *adv.* **us kē baᶜd** اس کے بعد
therefore, hence *adv.* **is li'ē** اس لئے
in that, in it *pp.* **us mēṁ** • in this, into, in it *pp.* **is mēṁ** اس میں
for that reason *adv.* **is vajah sē** اس وجہ سے
foundation, base *n.f.* **asās** اساس
light; easy, simple *adj.* **āsān** آسان
lightness; easiness, simplicity *n.f.* **āsānī** آسانی
horse *n.m.* **asp** اسپ
steel *n.m.* **ispāt** اسپات
hospital *n.m.* **aspatāl** اسپتال
teacher, instructor; expert *n.m.* **ustād** استاد
stability, firmness *n.f.* **ustādgī** استادگی
standing (firmly), stable *adj.* **ustādah** استادہ
despotism, tyranny *n.m.* **istibdād** استبداد
exception, exemption *n.m.* **istisnā'** استثناء
acquisition, exploitation *n.m.* **istiḥsāl** استحصال
claim, right *n.m.* **istiḥqāq** استحقاق
firmness, strengthening, stability *n.m.* **istiḥkām** استحکام
expulsion, banishment *n.m.* **istixrāj** استخراج
request, desire *n.f.* **istidᶜā'** استدعاء
reasoning, argument *n.m.* **istidlāl** استدلال
repose, rest *n.f.* **istirāḥat** استراحت
wife; woman *n.f.* **istrī** استری
dropsy *n.f.* **istasqā** استسقا
referendum *n.m.* **istisvāb** استصواب
astonishment, surprise, wonder *n.m.* **istiᶜjāb** استعجاب
resignation *n.m.* **istiᶜfā'** استعفاء

colonization, settlement *n.m.* **isticmār** استعمار
colonialism *n.f.* **isticmāriyat** استعماریت
usage, use, application *n.m.* **isticmāl** استعمال
use, apply *v.t.* **isticmāl karnā** استعمال کرنا
benefit, gain, profit *n.m.* **istifādah** استفادہ
enquiry, investigation *n.m.* **istifhām** استفہام
uprightness, steadiness; persistency *n.f.* **istiqāmat** استقامت
welcoming (*of a person*), reception *n.m.* **istiqbāl** استقبال
welcome, receive *v.t.* **istiqbāl karnā** استقبال کرنا
settlement *n.m.* **istiqrār** استقرار
firmness, perseverence *n.m.* **istiqlāl** استقلال
perpetuity, continuance *n.m.* **istimrār** استمرار
perpetual, continual *adj.* **istimrārī** استمراری
strong, solid, stable *adj.* **ustuvārī** استواری
situation; residence (*far from home*) *n.m.* **asthān** استھان
stamp, postage *n.m.* **isṭāmp** اسٹامپ
station (*bus or railway*) *n.m.* **isṭēšan** اسٹیشن
lion; Leo (*Zodiac*) *n.m.* **asad** اسد
support, protection *n.m.* **āsrā** آسرا
sponge *n.m.* **isfanj** اسفنج
abortion *n.m.* **isqāṭ** اسقاط
school *n.m.* **iskūl** اسکول
scheme *n.f.* **iskīm** اسکیم
Islam *n.m.* **islām** اسلام
Islamic, pertaining to Islam *adj.* **islāmī** اسلامی
arms, weapons, armor *n.m.* **asliḥah** اسلحہ
armory, arsenal, magazine *n.m.* **asliḥah xānah** اسلحہ خانہ
manner, method, style *n.m.* **uslūb** اسلوب
name, denomination *n.m.* **ism** اسم
sky *n.m.* **āsmān** آسمان
celestial, heavenly *adj.* **āsmānī** آسمانی
diarrhea *n.m.* **ishāl** اسہال
black *adj.* **asvād** اسود
satisfied *adj.* **āsūdah** آسودہ
eighty *num.* **assī** اسی
evil spirit *n.m.* **āsēb** آسیب

prisoner *n.m.* **asīr** اسیر
hope, expectation *n.f.* **āšā** آشا
sign, mark; hint; wink *n.m.* **išārah** اشارہ
point out, hint *v.t.* **išārah karnā** اشارہ کرنا
publication *n.f.* **išāᶜat** اشاعت
suspicion, doubt, distrust *n.m.* **ištibāh** اشتباہ
partnership; company *n.m.* **ištirāk** اشتراک
comprising, inclusion *n.m.* **ištimāl** اشتمال
hunger, appetite *n.f.* **ištiha** اشتہا
peace, reconcilement *n.f.* **āšti** آشتی
daybreak, dawn *n.m.* **išrāq** اشراق
noble *adj.* **ašrāf** اشرف
Ashram (*Hindu center for religious training*) *n.m.* **āšram** آشرم
uneasiness, perturbation *adj.* **āšuftagī** آشفتگی
confused, distressed *adj.* **āšuftah ḥāl** آشفتہ حال
tear *n.m.* **ašk** اشک
evident, clear *adj.* **āškārā** آشکارا
verse, stanza *n.m.* **ašlōk** اشلوک
friend *n.f.* **āšnā** آشنا
bathing *n.m.* **ašnān** اشنان
friendship *n.f.* **āšnā'ī** آشنائی
blessing *n.f.* **ašīrbād** اشیرباد
firmness, determination *n.f.* **asālat** اصالت
personally; originally; completely *adv.* **asālatan** اصالتاً
persistence, stubborness *n.m.* **isrār** اصرار
expenditure, extravagence *n.m.* **isrāf** اصراف
stable *n.m.* **astabal** اصطبل
technical term *n.f.* **istilāḥ** اصطلاح
idiomatic, proverbial *adj.* **istilāḥī** اصطلاحی
root, origin *n.m.* **asl** اصل
in reality; in total *adv.* **aslan** اصلاً
correction, revision, reform *n.f.* **islāḥ** اصلاح
correct, revise, reform *v.t.* **islāḥ karnā** اصلاح کرنا
original, real, genuine *adj.* **aslī** اصلی
reality; purity; source *n.f.* **asliyat** اصلیت
noble, gentle *adj.* **asīl** اصیل

enlargement, increase, addition *n.f.* **azāfah** اضافہ
enlarge, increase *v.t.* **azāfah karnā** اضافہ کرنا
anxiety, restlessness *n.m.* **iztirāb** اضطراب
obedience, submission *n.f.* **itāᶜat** اطاعت
report, information, notice *n.f.* **itlāᶜ** اطلاع
application, usage *n.m.* **atlāq** اطلاق
satin *n.m.* **atlas** اطلس
satisfaction, contentment *n.m.* **itmīnān** اطمینان
saint *n.m.* **athar** اطہر
satisfy *v.t.* **itmīnān karnā** اطوار
discovery, revelation *n.m.* **azhār** اظہار
discover, reveal *v.t.* **azhār karnā** اظہار کرنا
trust, faith, confidence *n.m.* **iᶜtibār** اعتبار
trust, rely (upon), confide (in) *v.t.* **iᶜtibār karnā** اعتبار کرنا
trustworthy, reliable *adj.* **iᶜtibārī** اعتباری
moderation *n.m.* **iᶜtidāl** اعتدال
moderate *adj.* **iᶜtidāl pasand** اعتدال پسند
apology; mercy *n.m.* **iᶜtizār** اعتذار
protest, objection *n.m.* **iᶜtirāz** اعتراض
confession, admission *n.m.* **iᶜtirāf** اعتراف
faith, belief *n.f.* **iᶜtiqād** اعتقاد
believe *v.t.* **iᶜtiqād rakhnā** اعتقاد رکھنا
reliance, dependence *n.m.* **iᶜtimād** اعتماد
concern, alarm, anxiety *n.f.* **iᶜtinā'ī** اِعتنائی
wonder, miracle *n.m.* **iᶜjāz** اعجاز
glorification *n.m.* **iᶜzāz** اعزاز
proclamation *n.m.* **iᶜlān** اعلان
master, elder *n.m.* **āġā** آغا
origin, beginning *n.m.* **āġāz** آغاز
begin, start *v.t.* **āġāz karnā** آغاز کرنا
be started *v.i.* **āġāz hōnā** آغاز ہونا
embrace, bosom *n.f.* **āġōš** آغوش
benefit, gain *n.m.* **ifādah** افادہ
usefulness *n.f.* **ifādiyat** افادیت
horizon *n.m.* **āfāq** آفاق
sun *n.m.* **āftab** آفتاب

distress; fall *n.f.* **uftād** افتاد
helplessness *n.f.* **uftādagī** افتادگی
miserable, fallen, useless *adj.* **uftādah** افتادہ
opening, inauguration *n.m.* **iftitāḥ** افتتاح
honor, glory *n.m.* **iftixār** افتخار
uproar, tumult, disorder, panic *n.f.* **afrātafrī** افراتفری
abundance, excess *n.f.* **ifrāt** افراط
created, being born *adj.* **āfrīdah** آفریدہ
creation *n.f.* **āfrīniš** آفرینش
augmenting, increasing, adding *n.m.* **afzā** افزا
augmentation, increase *n.f.* **afzā'iš** افزائش
tale, fable, story *n.m.* **afsānah** افسانہ
officer *n.m.* **afsar** افسر
depression, melancholy *n.f.* **afsurdagī** افسردگی
sorrow *n.m.* **afsōs** افسوس
magic *n.m.* **afsūṁ** افسوں
magician; witch *n.m.* **afsūṁ sāz** افسوں ساز
breaking the fast (*during Ramadan*) *n.m.* **iftār** افطار
viper (*snake*) *n.m.* **afaʿī** افعی
Afghanistan *n.m.* **afġānistān** افغانستان
Afghani *adj.* **afġānī** افغانی
horizon *n.m.* **ufaq** افق
wounded, injured *adj.* **afgār** افگار
poverty *n.m.* **aflās** افلاس
rumor, gossip *n.m.* **afvāh** افواہ
spread a rumor *v.t.* **afvāh uṛānā** افواہ اڑانا
opium *n.f.* **afīm** افیم
addicted (to opium) *adj.* **afīmī** افیمی
lord, master *n.m.* **āqā** آقا
dwelling, abode *n.m.* **iqāmat** اقامت
luck, good fortune, prosperity *n.m.* **iqbāl** اقبال
confessor, one who confesses *n.m.* **iqbālī** اقبالی
quotation; selection *n.m.* **iqtibās** اقتباس
division *n.m.* **iqtisām** اقتسام
economic *adj.* **iqtisādī** اقتصادی
economy *n.m.* **iqtisādī nizām** اقتصادی نظام

economy *n.f.* **iqtisādiyāt** اقتصادیات
need, demand *n.m.* **iqtizā'** اقتضاء
action; attempt; decision; resolution *n.m.* **iqdām** اقدام
promise, pledge, consent *n.m.* **iqrār** اقرار
promise, pledge, consent *v.t.* **iqrār karnā** اقرار کرنا
confessor, one who confesses *n.m.* **iqrārī** اقراری
country, state, region *n.f.* **aqlīm** اقلیم
the United Nations (U.N.) *n.f.* **aqvām-ē-muttaḥidah** اقوام متحدہ
single, solitary, unique *adj.* **ikkā** اکا
harm, damage *n.m.* **akāj** اکاج
academy *n.f.* **akādamī** اکادمی
uproot, dislodge *v.t.* **ukhāṛna** اکھاڑنا
eighty-one *num.* **ikāsī** اکاسی
heaven, sky *n.m.* **ākāš** آکاش
ninety-one *num.* **ikānavē** اکانوے
fifty-one *num.* **ikāvan** اکاون
unit, single group *n.f.* **ikā'ī** اکائی
greatest *adj.* **akbar** اکبر
forty-one *num.* **iktālīs** اکتالیس
become tired (of), be bored *v.i.* **uktānā** اکتانا
attainment, acquiring (after hard work) *n.m.* **iktisāb** اکتساب
sufficiency, satisfaction, contentment *n.f.* **iktafā** اکتفاء
October *n.m.* **aktūbar** اکتوبر
thirty-one *num.* **iktīs** اکتیس
often, generally *adj.* **aksar** اکثر
(most) gracious, (most) merciful *adj.* **akram** اکرم
become stiff, become hard *v.i.* **akaṛnā** اکڑنا
provoke, raise, incite *v.t.* **uksānā** اکسانا
sixty-one *num.* **iksaṭh** اکسٹھ
food, diet *n.m.* **akl** اکل
seventy-one *num.* **ikhattar** اکہتر
twenty-one *num.* **ikkīs** اکیس
single, alone *adj.* **akēlā** اکیلا
fire; passion, lust *n.f.* **āg** آگ
set on fire, inflame *v.t.* **āg sulgānā** آگ سلگانا
catch fire *v.i.* **āg lagnā** آگ لگنا

آگا front, forepart *n.f.* **āgā**
اگاڑی front, forepart *n.f.* **agāṛī**
اُگانا cause to grow, produce (crops) *v.t.* **ugānā**
اگاہنا gather, collect, raise (funds) *v.t.* **ugāhnā**
آگاہی information, knowledge, intuition *n.f.* **āgāhī**
اگر if, in case, in the event of *conj.* **agar**
اگرَ front, foremost, chief *adj.* **agra**
اگرچہ although, though, even if *conj.* **agar cih**
اگست August *n.m.* **agast**
اگلا foremost, first, next, in front *adj.* **aglā**
اگلے سال next year *adv.* **aglē sāl**
اگم inaccessible, unattainable *adj.* **agam**
آگمن arrival, approach; source, origin *n.m.* **āgman**
اگوڑا front part (*of a house*) *n.m.* **agvaṛā**
آگے front, ahead; opposite; in the future *adv.* **āgē**
آگے آنا come forward *v.i.* **āgē ānā**
اگھاڑنا uncover, unveil, bare *v.t.* **ughāṛnā**
اگھانا be satisfied *v.i.* **aghānā**
اگھڑنا be unveiled, be exposed, be uncovered *v.i.* **ughaṛnā**
اگھوری filthy, foul *adj.* **aghōrī**
آل descendants *n.m.* **āl**
آلانا bring, fetch *v.t.* **ā lānā**
الاپچی cardamom *n.f.* **ilā'icī**
آلائش pollution, waste, trash *n.f.* **ālā'iš**
البیٹ turn, twist, bend *n.f.* **albēṭ**
التجا کرنا request *v.t.* **iltijā karnā**
التجاء request, petition *n.f.* **iltijā'**
التزام necessary, expedient *adj.* **iltizām**
التماس request, supplication, application *n.m.* **iltimās**
التواء adjournment, postponement *n.m.* **iltivā'**
التوائے جنگ truce *n.m.* **iltivā'-ē-jang**
اُلٹ inversion, reversal; transformation *n.f.* **ulaṭ**
اُلٹا inverse, reversed, upside down, topsy-turvy *adj.* **ulṭā**
اُلٹنا turn (over), upset, turn around *v.t.* **ulaṭnā**
اُلٹی طرف back side, reverse *n.f.* **ulṭī taraf**
الجبرا algebra *n.m.* **aljabrā**

complicate, confuse *v.t.* **uljhānā** الجھانا
confusion, entanglement *n.f.* **uljhan** الجھن
be entangled, be involved *v.i.* **ulajhnā** الجھنا
disbelief, atheism *n.m.* **ilḥād** الحاد
annexation, continuity *n.m.* **ilḥāq** الحاق
now, at present, at this time *adv.* **al-ḥāl** الحال
God be praised *int.* **al-ḥamdu-lillah** الحمد للہ
accusation, charge, allegation, blame *n.m.* **ilzām** الزام
laziness, inactiveness *n.m.* **ālas** آلس
be sleepy, be drowsy *v.i.* **ālsānā** آلسانا
lazy, inactive *adj.* **ālasī** آلسی
deception, duplicity *n.f.* **alsēṭ** السیٹ
briefly, in short *adv.* **al-ġarz** الغرض
whistle, flute *n.m.* **alġōzah** الغوزہ
thousand *num.* **alf** الف
alphabet *n.f.* **alif bē** الف بے
friendship, intimacy, love, affection *n.f.* **ulfat** الفت
show affection, make friends with *v.t.* **ulfat karnā** الفت کرنا
loose, separate, free; different; lonely *adj.* **alag** الگ
separately, individually *adv.* **alag alag** الگ الگ
divide, separate, remove, set free *v.t.* **alag karnā** الگ کرنا
separate, remove, get rid of *v.t.* **algānā** الگانا
Allah, God *n.m.* **Allāh** اللہ
banner *n.m.* **alam** الم
cupboard *n.f.* **almārī** الماری
diamond *n.m.* **almās** الماس
side; direction; length, extent *n.f.* **alang** النگ
leap, jump over *v.i.* **ulangnā** النگنا
tool, instrument *n.m.* **ālah** آلہ
inspiration, revelation *n.m.* **ilhām** الہام
owl; fool, idiot *n.m.* **ullū** الو
potato *n.m.* **ālū** آلو
plum *n.m.* **ālū buxārā** آلو بخارا
make a fool of *v.t.* **ullū banānā** الو بنانا
foolishness, silliness *n.m.* **ullūpan** الوپن
hidden, vanished, invisible, out of sight *adj.* **alōp** الوپ

soiled, foul, impure, polluted *adj.* **ālūdah** آلودہ
pollution *n.f.* **ālūdagī** آلودگی
mother *n.f.* **umm** اُم
mango *n.m.* **ām** آم
possession of authority, lordship; building *n.f.* **imārāt** امارات
dominant *adj.* **ammārah** امارہ
spiritual leader, spiritual guide (*especially in Islam*) *n.m.* **imām** امام
mother, mom *n.f.* **ammāṁ** اماں
immunity; security, protection *n.m.* **amān** امان
fit, go into *v.i.* **amānā** امانا
deposit, down payment *n.f.* **amānī** امانی
small unripe mango *n.f.* **ambiyā** امبیا
examination, trial, test *n.m.* **imtiḥān** امتحان
undergo an examination *v.t.* **imtiḥān dēnā** امتحان دینا
prolongation, protraction *n.m.* **imtidād** امتداد
mixing, mingling *n.m.* **imtizāj** امتزاج
prohibition, restraint, restriction *n.m.* **imtināᶜ** امتناع
prohibitive *adj.* **imtināᶜī** امتناعی
distinction, discrimination, discernment *n.m.* **imtiyāz** امتیاز
distinguish, discriminate *v.t.* **imtiyāz karnā** امتیاز کرنا
indestructible, ineffaceable; eternal *adj.* **amiṭ** امٹ
amchur (*mango seasoning*) *n.f.* **amcūr** اَمچور
arrival *n.f.* **āmad** آمد
income and expenses *n.f.* **āmad-ō-xarc** آمد و خرچ
coming and going, traffic *n.f.* **āmad-ō-raft** آمد و رفت
command, order; issue *n.m.* **amar** امر
nectar *n.m.* **amrit** امرت
guava *n.m.* **amrūd** امرود
today *adv.* **imrōz** اِمروز
dictatorship *n.f.* **āmiriyat** آمریت
(United States of) America *n.m.* **Amrikā** امریکا امریکا امریکا
American *adj.* **amrīkī** امریکی امریکی
this year *adv.* **imsāl** امسال
tonight *adv.* **imšab** امشب
possibility, eventuality *n.m.* **imkān** امکان

امکانی **imkānī** possible, eventual *adj.*
املی **imlī** tamarind, tamarind tree *n.f.*
آملیٹ **āmlēṭ** omelet *n.m.*
امن **amn** safety, security; peace *n.m.*
آمنا سامنا **āmnā sāmnā** encounter *n.m.*
اُمنگ **umang** ecstasy, elation, triumph *n.f.*
آمنے سامنے **āmnē sāmnē** opposite, face to face *adv.*
اُمیٹھنا **umēṭhnā** twist *v.t.*
اُمید **ummīd** hope, confidence, trust *n.f.*
اُمید رکھنا **ummīd rakhnā** hope, rely on, trust *v.t.*
اُمید ہونا **ummid hōnā** hope *v.i.*
امیدوار **ummīdvār** expecting, hopeful *adj.*
امیر **amīr** commander, ruler, governor, nobleman *n.m.*
امیر البحر **amīr-ul-baḥr** admiral *n.m.*
امین **amīn** trustee, guardian *n.m.* / trustworthy, faithful *adj.*
آمین **āmīn** so be it, amen *adv.*
ان **ann** grain; corn; food supply *n.m.*
آن **ān** time, moment *n.f.*
اُن **un** them, those *pron.*
اِن **in** these, them *pron.*
آن بان **ān bān** splendor, magnificence *n.f.*
اِن دنوں **in dinōṁ** nowadays, these days *adv.*
آنا **ānā** come, arrive *v.i.*
انا پرستی **anā parastī** egoism *n.f.*
آناً فاناً **ānan-fānan** every moment, immediately *adv.*
اناج **anāj** grain; corn *n.m.*
انادر **anādar** dishonor, disrespect *n.m.*
انادر کرنا **anādar karnā** dishonor, disrespect, insult *v.t.*
انار **anār** pomegranate *n.m.*
اناڑی **anāṛī** unskillful, inexperienced, awkward *adj.*
اناڑی پن **anāṛī pan** simplicity, ignorance; awkwardness *n.m.*
اناسی **unāsī** seventy-nine *num.*
انانیت **anāniyat** egoism *n.f.*
انبار **ambār** heap, pile *n.m.*
انبار خانہ **ambār xānah** storehouse, warehouse *n.m.*
انت **ant** end, completion, conclusion *n.f.*

انتالیس thirty-nine *num.* **untālīs**
انتخاب selection, choice, election *n.m.* **intixāb**
انتخاب کرنا select, choose, elect *v.t.* **intixāb karnā**
انتساب connection, relation; dedication *n.m.* **intisab**
انتشار spreading, dispersion; anxiety, confusion *n.m.* **intišār**
انتظار expectation, waiting *n.m.* **intizār**
انتظار دیکھنا be on the look out (for) *v.t.* **intizār dēkhnā**
انتظار کرنا expect, wait *v.t.* **intizār karnā**
انتظاری expectation, waiting *n.f.* **intizārī**
انتظام management, administration, organization *n.m.* **intizām**
انتظام دینا arrange, manage, organize *v.t.* **intizām dēnā**
انتظام رکھنا keep order *v.t.* **intizām rakhnā**
انتظام کرنا arrange, organize, put in order, manage *v.t.* **intizām karnā**
انتقال transfer, departure; death *n.m.* **intiqāl**
انتقال کرنا transfer, transport; die *v.t.* **intiqāl karnā**
انتقام revenge, vengeance, retaliation *n.m.* **intiqām**
انتقام لینا take revenge, retaliate *v.t.* **intiqām lēnā**
انتہا termination, completion, limit, end *n.f.* **intihā**
انتیس twenty-nine *num.* **untīs**
انٹ twist, entanglement *n.f.* **anṭ**
انٹنا be contained, fit (into) *v.i.* **anṭnā**
اُنٹوانا cram into *v.t.* **anṭvānā**
انٹی بایوٹک antibiotics *n.m.* **anṭī bāyōṭik**
انجام termination, conclusion, result *n.m.* **aṁjām**
انجام پانا be completed, be brought to an end *v.t.* **aṁjām pānā**
انجام دینا accomplish, finish *v.t.* **aṁjām dēnā**
انجان unknown, ignorant *adj.* **aṁjān**
انجانے unknowingly, ignorantly, unconsciously, unaware *adv.* **aṁjānē**
انجماد congealing, freezing *n.m.* **iṁjimād**
انجمن assembly, congregation, club, society *n.f.* **aṁjuman**
انجن engine, motor *n.m.* **injan**
انجیر fig, fig-tree *n.m.* **aṁjīr**
انجیل Bible, New Testament *n.m.* **iṁjīl**
انجینیر engineer *n.m.* **injīniyar**
انچ inch (= *2.54 cm*) *n.m.* **iṁc**
انچاس forty-nine *num.* **uṁcās**

انچائی height, elevation; stature; eminence *n.f.* **uṁcā'ī**
انحراف deflection; breaking (*of an alliance*) *n.m.* **inḥirāf**
انحراف کرنا deflect; break an alliance *v.t.* **inḥirāf karnā**
انخفاف lightness, brevity *n.m.* **inxifāf**
انخلال destruction, ruin *n.f.* **inxilāl**
انداز way, manner, method *n.m.* **andāz**
اندازاً by guess, roughly, approximately *adv.* **andāzan**
اندازہ guess, estimate *n.m.* **andāzah**
اندازہ کرنا guess, estimate *v.t.* **andāzah karnā**
اندام body, stature, figure *n.m.* **andām**
اندر inside *adv.* **andar**
اندر جانا enter, go inside *v.i.* **andar jānā**
اندر سے internally, from inside *adv.* **andar sē**
اندر کرنا drive in, bring in, put within *v.t.* **andar karnā**
اندرونی inward, internal, interior *adj.* **andarūnī**
اندوختہ gained, acquired *adj.* **andōxtah**
اندوہ grief, anxiety, trouble *n.m.* **andōh**
اندیش مند thoughtful, meditative, reflective *adj.* **andēš mand**
اندیشہ thought, consideration, reflection *n.m.* **andēšah**
اندیشہ کرنا think, consider, reflect *v.t.* **andēšah karnā**
اندھا blind *adj.* **andhā**
اندھاپن blindness, obscurity *n.m.* **andhāpan**
آندھی storm, whirlwind *n.f.* **āndhī**
اندھیر injustice, tyranny, inequity, lawlessness *n.m.* **andhēr**
اندھیر کرنا darken, dim; do wrong; tyrannize, oppress *v.t.* **andhēr karnā**
اندھیرا dark, hazy, dusky *adj.* **andhērā**
اندھیرا darkness, haziness, duskiness *n.m.* **andhērā**
اندھیری darkness *n.f.* **andhērī**
انڈا egg *n.m.* **anḍā**
انڈاکار oval, elliptical *adj.* / ellipse *n.m.* **anḍā kār**
انڈیا India *n.m.* **inḍiyā**
انڈیلنا pour out, empty, discharge *v.t.* **unḍēlnā**
انزال emission *n.m.* **inzāl**
اِنس man, mankind *n.m.* **iṁs**
اُنس attachment, friendship, love, affection, sympathy *n.m.* **uṁs**
انسان man, person, human being *n.m.* **insān**

humanity, human nature; politeness *n.f.* **insāniyat** انسانیت
fifty-nine *num.* **unsaṭh** انسٹھ
prevention *n.m.* **insidād** انسداد
answering machine *n.m.* **āṁsaring mašīn** آنسرنگ مشین
tear (*from eye*) *n.m.* **āṁṣū** آنسو
shed tears *v.i.* **āṁsū bhar ānā** آنسو بھر آنا
writing, composition, text, essay *n.f.* **inšā'** انشاء
God willing, perhaps, maybe *adv.* **inšā' allah** انشاء اللہ
justice, equity, fair play, impartiality *n.m.* **insāf** انصاف
performance, accomplishment *n.m.* **insirām** انصرام
printing, impression *n.m.* **intibā**[c] انطباع
reward, prize *n.m.* **in**[c]**ām** انعام
reflection *n.m.* **in**[c]**ikās** انعکاس
individuality, uniqueness *n.f.* **infirādī** انفرادی
dislocation (*of a bone*) *n.m.* **infikāk** انفکاک
contraction, shortening *n.m.* **inqibāz** انقباض
division, partition *n.m.* **inqisām** انقسام
expiration *n.m.* **inqizā** انقضاء
amputation *n.m.* **inqitā**[c] انقطاع
revolution; change, alteration *n.m.* **inqilāb** انقلاب
eye *n.f.* **ānkh** آنکھ
denial, refusal; decline *n.m.* **inkār** انکار
deny, refuse *v.t.* **inkār karnā** انکار کرنا
humbleness, modesty *n.m.* **inkisār** انکسار
value, appraise *v.i.* **ānknā** آنکنا
embrace, bosom *n.f.* **ankvār** انکوار
sprout, shoot *n.m.* **ankūrā** انکورا
esteem, adore *v.t.* **ānkhēṁ bichānā** آنکھیں بچھانا
look angry *v.t.* **ānkhēṁ nīlī pīlī karnā** آنکھیں نیلی پیلی کرنا
limb; organ; body *n.m.* **ank** انگ
coat *n.m.* **ankā** انگا
ember, spark, cinder *n.m.* **angārā** انگارا
English, Englishman *n.m.* **ankrēz** انگریز
English, British *adj.* **angrēzī** انگریزی
finger *n.f.* **ankušt** انگشت
yard, court, courtyard *n.m.* **āngan** آنگن

انگنائی inner-court, courtyard *n.f.* **angnā'ī**
انگوٹھا thumb; big toc *n.m.* **angūṭhā**
انگوٹھی ring (*jewelry*) *n.f.* **angūṭhī**
انگور grape *n.m.* **angūr**
انگیز exciting *adj.* **angēz**
انمول invaluable, inestimable, priceless, precious *adj.* **anmōl**
انمیل unmatched, heterogeneous, inharmonious *adj.* **anmēl**
اننّاس pineapple *n.m.* **anannās**
انہتر sixty-nine *num.* **unhattar**
انہدام demolition, destruction, extermination, annihilation *n.m.* **inhidām**
انہماک assiduity, assiduousness, abstractness *n.m.* **inhimāk**
انہیں them *pron.* **inhēṁ, unhēṁ**
انوٹھا uncommon, rare *adj.* **anūṭhā**
انور shining, brilliant, splendid *adj.* **anvar**
انوکھا uncommon, unusual, rare, extraordinary *adj.* **anōkhā**
انیس nineteen *num.* **unnīs**
اہانت contempt, scorn, insult *n.f.* **ihānat**
اہانت کرنا hate, disdain, affront *v.t.* **ihānat karnā**
اہتمام leadership, management, supervision *n.m.* **ihtimām**
آہستگی slowness, gentleness *n.f.* **āhistagī**
آہستہ slow; slowly, gently *adj./adv.* **āhistah**
اہل / people, citizen, inhabitant; member (*of a family*) *n.m.* **ahl**
capable, fit, worthy, competent *adj.*
اہلیت worth, capability, aptitude *n.f.* **ahliyat**
اہلیہ wife *n.f.* **ahilyah**
اہم important *adj.* **aham/ahm**
آہن iron *n.m.* **āhan**
آہن گر blacksmith *n.m.* **āhan gar**
آہنگ melody, sound, harmony, music *n.m.* **āhang**
اہیر herdsman *n.m.* **ahīr**
اہیر hunting *n.f.* **ahēr**
آؤ Come (here)! *interj.* **ā'ō**
آوارہ wanderer, vagabond *n.m.* **āvārah**
آوارہ مزاج careless, thoughtless *adj.* **āvārah mizāj**
آوارہ ہونا wander, be miserable *v.i.* **āvārah hōnā**
آواز sound, voice, cry, shout, echo *n.f.* **āvāz**

raise your voice, speak out *v.t.* **āvāz uṭhānā** آواز اٹھانا
call out, shout out *v.t.* **āvāz dēnā** آواز دینا
rumor, hearsay *n.f.* **avā'ī** اوائی
vagabond, dissolute *n.m.* **avbāš** اوباش
depravity, debauchery *n.f.* **avbāšī** اوباشی
up, on, high, above, upon *adv.* **ūpar** اوپر
from above; in addition to *adv.* **ūpar sē** اوپر سے
the one above, God *n.m.* **ūpar vālā** اوپر والا
refuge, place of concealment, hide-out *n.m.* **ōṭ** اوٹ
cause to boil, heat *v.t.* **auṭānā** اوٹانا
boil, evaporate *v.t.* **auṭnā** اوٹنا
summit, zenith, highest point *n.m.* **auj** اوج
ruined, desolate *n.m.* **ūjaṛ** اوجڑ
stomach, paunch *n.m.* **ōjh** اوجھ
screen; shelter, concealment *n.f.* **ōjhal** اوجھل
hide, screen *v.t.* **ōjhal karnā** اوجھل کرنا
be screened, be concealed, become invisible *v.i.* **ōjhal hōnā** اوجھل ہونا
empty; shallow; absurd *adj.* **ōchā** اوچھا
purple, grey, brown *adj.* **ūdā** اودا
more *adv.* / and, also *conj.* **aur** • side; direction; end, limit *n.f.* **ōr** اور
better *adj.* **aur acchā** اور اچھا
dew *n.f.* **ōs** اوس
sense, presence of mind *n.m.* **ausān** اوسان
average, medium *adj.* **ausat** اوسط
moderate, intermediate *adj.* **ausatī** اوسطی
employment, occupation, subsistence *n.f.* **auqāt basarī** اوقات بسری
subsist *v.t.* **auqat basarī karnā** اوقات بسری کرنا
vomit *v.i.* **ōkna** اوکنا
fault, defect, vice *n.m.* **augun** اوگن
rough, impassable, inaccessible *adj.* **aughat** اوگھٹ
first, foremost *adj.* **avval** اول
at first, in the first place *adv.* **avvalan** اولاً
wool *n.f.* **ūn** اون
camel *n.m.* **ūnṭ** اونٹ
female camel *n.f.* **ūnṭnī** اونٹنی
high, tall *adj.* **ūṁc** اونچ

high, elevated, tall *adj.* **ūṁca** اونچا

height, altitude, elevation, tallness *n.f.* **ūṁchā'ī** اونچائی

upset, overturn *v.t.* **aundhānā** اوندھانا

nap *n.f.* **aungh** اونگھ

feel drowsy, feel sleepy *v.i.* **ūnghnā** اونگھنا

woolen *adj.* **ūnī** اونی

delay, lateness *n.f.* **avēr** اویر

earring; pendant *n.m.* **āvēzah** آویزہ

ATM, cash machine *n.m.* **ē ṭī ēm** اے ٹی ایم

air conditioning, AC *n.f.* **ē sī** اے سی

verse (*of the Quran*) *n.f.* **āyat** آیت

sacrifice, selflessness; greatness *n.m.* **ēsār** ایثار

confirmation *n.m.* **ījāb** ایجاب

invention *n.m.* **ījād** ایجاد

invent *v.t.* **ījād karnā** ایجاد کرنا

annoyance, trouble; harm, pain *n.f.* **īzā** ایذا

annoy, trouble; injure, hurt, pain *v.t.* **īzā dēnā** ایذا دینا

annoying, troublesome *adj.* **īzā rasāṁ** ایذا رساں

Iran *n.m.* **īrān** ایران

Iranian *adj.* **īrānī** ایرانی

area code (*telephone*) *n.m.* **ēriyā kōḍ** ایریا کوڈ

spur (*for a horse*) *n.f.* **ēṛ** ایڑ

spur *v.t.* **ēṛ lagānā** ایڑ لگانا

heel *n.f.* **ēṛī** ایڑی

God *n.m.* **ēzēd** ایزد

divine, heavenly *adj.* **ēzdī** ایزدی

such, like this, so, of this sort *adj.* **aisā** ایسا

such and such, so and so; narrow-minded *adj.* **aisā taisā** ایسا تیسا

inferior, poor, indecent *adj.* **aisā vaisā** ایسا ویسا

standing, set up *adj.* **īstādah** ایستادہ

so to speak, like this, of such sort *adv.* **aisē hī** ایسے ہی

fulfillment *n.f.* **īfā'** ایفا'

only, single, sole, unique *adj.* / one *num.* **ēk** ایک

another, one more *adj.* **ēk aur** ایک اور

one more time *adv.* **ēk aur bār** ایک اور بار

once upon a time, at one time *adv.* **ēk bār** ایک بار

instantly, immediately; extremely *adv.* **ēk dām** ایک دام
alike, resembling, identical *adj.* **ēk sā** ایک سا
all together, all at once *adv.* **ēk sar** ایک سر
one-way ticket *n.m.* **ēk tarfah ṭikaṭ** ایک طرفہ ٹکٹ
secluded, isolated, lonely *adj.* **ēkānt** ایکانت
express mail *n.f.* **ikspres ḍāk** ایکسپریس ڈاک
envoy, ambassador *n.m.* **ēlcī** ایلچی
ambassadorship *n.m.* **ēlcī panā** ایلچی پنا
belief, faith, trust *n.m.* **īmān** ایمان
faithfully, honestly, conscientiously *adv.* **īmān sē** ایمان سے
faithful, conscientious, upright, trustworthy *adj.* **īmān dār** ایماندار
faithfulness, honesty, uprightness, trustworthiness *n.f.* **īmān dārī** ایمانداری
brick *n.f.* **īnṭ** اینٹ
twisting, tightening *n.f.* **ainṭh** اینٹھ
twist, turn, coil, tension *n.m.* **ainṭhan** اینٹھن
twist, wind, spin, squeeze *v.t.* **ainṭhnā** اینٹھنا
pull, drag, draw; scribble *v.t.* **aiṁcnā** اینچنا
firewood; fuel *n.m.* **indhan** ایندھن
doubt *n.m.* **aihām** ایہام
hall, gallery, chamber; palace *n.m.* **aivān** ایوان
doom; death *n.f.* **ā'ī** آئی
law, regulation, constitution, rules, custom, etiquette *n.m.* **ā'īn** آئین
in future, hereafter, next, subsequent *adj.* **ā'īndah** آئندہ
mirror *n.m.* **ā'īnah** آئینہ

bē ب

with, by, for, from, in, on *pp.* **ba** ب

by, with, of *pp.* **bā** با

polite, respectful *adj.* **bā adab** با ادب

pious, religious, faithful *adj.* **bā imān** با ایمان

sensible, discreet, courteous *adj.* **bā tamīz** با تمیز

modest, bashful *adj.* **bā ḥayā** با حیا

informed, warned *adj.* **bā xabar** با خبر

regular, formal, correct *adj.* **bā qāᶜēdah** با قاعدہ

notwithstanding, in spite of; although *conj.* **bā vujūd** با وجود

true, faithful *adj.* **bā vafā** با وفا

door, gate; section, chapter *n.m.* **bāb** باب

father, daddy *n.m.* **bābā** بابا

on account of, concerning, relating to *pp.* **bābat** بابت

father *n.m.* **bāp** باپ

ancestors, forefathers *n.m.* **bāp dādā** باپ دادا

speech, word, saying; conversation *n.f.* **bāt** بات

invent a story, invent a false excuse *v.t.* **bāt banānā** بات بنانا

put off, make excuses *v.t.* **bāt ṭālnā** بات ٹالنا

chit-chat, discourse *n.f.* **bāt cīt** بات چیت

converse, chat *v.t.* **bāt cīt karnā** بات چیت کرنا

assent, comply *v.t.* **bāt rakhnā** بات رکھنا

true to one's word, faithful to one's promise *adj.* **bāt kā pakkā** بات کا پکا

interrupt, cut one's speech short *v.t.* **bāt kāṭnā** بات کاٹنا

speak, talk *v.t.* **bāt karnā** بات کرنا

talkative *adj.* / talkative person *n.m.* **bātūnī** باتونی

weight *n.m.* / road, way, path *n.f.* **bāṭ** باٹ

musical instrument *n.m.* **bājā** باجا

millet *n.m.* **bājrā** باجرا

sound (*as a musical instrument*) *v.t.* **bājnā** باجنا

elder sister *n.f.* **bāji** باجی

wind, breeze *n.m.* **bād** باد

morning breeze *n.f.* **bād-ē-sabā** بادِ صبا

dust, whirlwind *n.m.* **bād gard** بادگرد

almond *n.m.* **bādām** بادام
sail *n.m.* **bādbān** بادبان
king, emperor, sovereign *n.m.* **bādšāh** بادشاہ
prince *n.m.* **bādšāh zādah** بادشاہ زادہ
imperial, royal *adj.* **bādšāhānah** بادشاہانہ
empire, kingdom *n.f.* **bādšāhat** بادشاہت
princess *n.f.* **bādšāh zādī** بادشاہزادی
royal *adj.* **bādšāhī** بادشاہی
king's court *n.f.* **bādšāhī ᶜadālat** بادشاہی عدالت
cloud *n.m.* **bādal** بادل
wine, spirits *n.m.* **bādah** بادہ
addicted to wine, drunkard *adj.* **bādah parast** بادہ پرست
wine-drinker *n.m.* **bādah nōš** بادہ نوش
obstacle, hurdle *n.f.* **bādhā** بادھا
time; burden, load *n.m.* **bār** بار
carrier, coolie *n.m.* **bār bardār** بار بردار
freight, cargo *n.f.* **bār bardārī** بار برداری
rain *n.m.* **bārān** باران
boar *n.m.* **bārāh** باراہ
cold, frigid *adj.* **bārid** بارد
rain *n.f.* **bāriš** بارش
May God bless you! *interj.* **bārak Allah!** بارک اللہ
court, palace *n.f.* **bārgāh** بارگاہ
twelve *num.* **bārah** بارہ
gunpowder *n.f.* **bārūd** بارود
creator, God *n.m.* **bāri** باری
thin, fine, subtle *adj.* **bārik** باریک
twelfth *adj.* **bārhavāṁ** بارھواں
fence, border *n.f.* **bāṛ** باڑ
enclosure, hedge *n.m.* **bāṛa** باڑا
rise, flood; increase, growth *n.f.* **bāṛh** باڑھ
hawk, falcon *n.m.* **bāz** باز
abstain, give up *v.i.* **bāz ānā** باز آنا
prevent, hold back *v.t.* **bāz rakhnā** باز رکھنا
cease, refrain *v.i.* **bāz rēhnā** باز رہنا
returning, retreat *n.f.* **baz gašt** بازگشت

market, bazaar *n.m.* **bāzār** بازار
belonging to the market *adj.* **bazārī** بازاری
layman, common man, ordinary person *n.m.* **bāzārī ādmī** بازاری آدمی
arm, shoulder *n.m.* **bāzū** بازو
armlet, bracelet *n.m.* **bāzū band** بازو بند
game, play, contest *n.f.* **bāzī** بازی
juggler *n.m.* **bāzī gar** بازی گر
jugglery *n.f.* **bāzī garī** بازی گری
stake, gamble, bet *v.t.* **bāzī lagānā** بازی لگانا
scent, smell, odor *n.m.* **bās** باس
easily *adv.* **ba'āsanī** باسانی
sixty-two *num.* **bāsaṭh** باسٹھ
basmati (*a kind of rice*) *n.m.* **bāsmatī** باسمتی
stale *adj.* **bāsī** باسی
resident, inhabitant *n.m.* **bāšindah** باشندہ
absurd, false, useless *adj.* **bātil** باطل
heart, mind; inside *n.m.* **bātin** باطن
internal, hidden *adj.* **bātinī** باطنی
reason, cause *n.m.* **bāᶜis** باعث
garden, park; orchard *n.m.* **bāġ** باغ
gardener *n.m.* **bāġbān** باغبان
gardening *n.f.* **bāġbānī** باغبانی
rebel, traitor *n.m.* / disloyal, rebellious *adj.* **bāġī** باغی
orchard, small garden *n.m.* **bāġīcah** باغیچہ
fabric; tissue *n.f.* **bāft** بافت
weaver *n.m.* **bāfindah** بافندہ
learned, instructed *adj.* **bāqir** باقر
remaining; perpetual, everlasting, eternal *adj.* **bāqī** باقی
remain, be left *v.i.* **bāqī rēhnā** باقی رہنا
remainder, remaining *n.m.* **bāqī māndah** باقی ماندہ
remnant, arrears *n.m.*. **bāqiyāt** باقیات
unmarried girl, virgin *n.f.* **bākirah** باکرہ
bridle, rein (*for a horse*) *n.f.* **bāg** باگ
hair; child, young person *n.m.* **bāl** بال
unanimously *adv.* **bil-ittēfāq** بالاتفاق
in brief, briefly *adv.* **bil-ijmāl** بالاجمال

intentionally, deliberately *adv.* **bil-irādah** بالارادہ

additional; external *adj.* **bālā'ī** بالائی

specially *adv.* **bi-ltaxsīs** بالتخصیص

explicitly, in detail *adv.* **bil-tafsīl** بالتفصیل

bucket *n.f.* **bālṭī** بالٹی

violently, forcibly *adv.* **bil-jabr** بالجبر

in short, in a word *adv.* **bil-jumlah** بالجملہ

happily, well, in a good manner *adv.* **bil-xair** بالخیر

pillow, cushion *n.f.* **bāliš** بالش

span *n.f.* **bālišt** بالشت

surely, certainly *adv.* **bil-zurūr** بالضرور

on the other hand, on the contrary *adv.* **bil-ᶜaks** بالعکس

generally, commonly *adv.* **bil-ᶜumūm** بالعموم

adult, mature *adj.* **bāliġ** بالغ

supposing, granted that *adv.* **bil-farz** بالفرض

at present, in fact, indeed *adv.* **bil-faᶜil** بالفعل

entirely *adv.* **bil-kul** بالکل

face to face, in person *adv.* **bil-mušāfah** بالمشافہ

opposite *adv.* **bil-muqābil** بالمقابل

earring *n.f.* **bālī** بالی

growth, development *n.f.* **bālīdagī** بالیدگی

pillow, cushion *n.f.* **bālīn** بالین

upper storey, terrace; roof *n.f.* **bām** بام

dress, garment; weaving *n.m.* **bānā** بانا

share, division *n.f.* **bānṭ** بانٹ

divide, distribute *v.t.* **bānṭnā** بانٹنا

barren, fruitless, unproductive *adj.* **bāṁjh** بانجھ

tie, fasten, bind *v.t.* **bāndhnā** باندھنا

bamboo *n.m.* **bāṁs** بانس

cry, shout *n.f.* **bāng** بانگ

lady, woman *n.f.* **bānō** بانو

ninety-two *num.* **bānavē** بانوے

founder, builder, composer, architect *n.m.* **bānī** بانی

lust (*sexually*) *n.f.* **bāh** باہ

out, outside; abroad, away *adv.* **bāhar** باہر

exit *n.m.* **bāhar jānē kā rāstā** باہر جانے کا رستا

mutually, together, with one another *adv.* **bāham** باہم
mutual *adj.* **bāhmī** باہمی
arm *n.m.* **bāhū** باہو
cook *n.m.* **bāvarcī** باورچی
kitchen *n.m.* **bāvarcī xānah** باورچی خانہ
mad, insane *adj.* **bā'ūlā** باؤلا
fifty-two *num.* **bāvan** باون
left *adj.* **bāyāṁ** بایاں
seller, dealer, merchant *n.m.* **bāya**c بایع
wind *n.f.* **bā'ī** بائی
twenty-two *num.* **bā'īs** بائیس
lion *n.m.* **babar** ببر
idol, statue, image; beloved one *n.m.* / dumb *adj.* **but** بت
worshipping *n.f.* **but parastī** بت پرستی
sculptor, carver *n.m.* **but tarāš** بت تراش
idol-temple, pagoda *n.m.* **but xānah** بت خانہ
idol-breaker, iconoclast *n.m.* **but šikan** بت شکن
idol-temple, pagoda *n.m.* **but kadah** بت کدہ
tell, explain, inform *v.t.* **batānā** بتانا
spend; pass *v.t.* **bitānā** بتانا
tell *v.t.* **batlānā** بتلانا
candle, wick, match, light *n.f.* **battī** بتی
headlights (*of a car*) *n.f.* **battiyāṁ** بتیاں
thirty-two *num.* **battīs** بتیس
twist *v.t.* **baṭnā** بٹنا
purse, wallet, small bag *n.m.* **baṭvā** بٹوا
collect, gather *v.t.* **baṭōrnā** بٹورنا
daughter *n.f.* **biṭiyā** بٹیا
set, install, place, *v.t.* **biṭhānā** بٹھانا
ring; play (*a musical instrument*); sound *v.t.* **bajānā** بجانا
in place of, instead *adv.* **bajā'ē** بجائے
passenger boat (*on a river*) *n.m.* **bajrā** بجرا
gravel *n.f.* **bajrī** بجری
besides, except *pp.* **bajuz** بجز
electricity *n.f.* **bijlī** بجلی
strike; sound *v.t.* **bajnā** بجنا

extinguish, put out *v.t.* **bujhānā** بجھانا
be extinguished, be relieved (*of hunger, thirst etc.*) *v.i.* **bujhnā** بجھنا
opinion, thought, idea *n.m.* **bicār** بچار
helpless, poor *adj.* **bicārah** بچارہ
save, protect *v.t.* **bacānā** بچانا
safety, escape *n.m.* **bacāō** بچاؤ
childhood, infancy *n.m.* **bacpan** بچپن
savings, surplus, gain *n.f.* **bacat** بچت
escape; be saved, be safe *v.i.* **bacnā** بچنا
child, infant *n.m.* **baccah** بچہ
spread, lay, scatter *v.t.* **bichānā** بچھانا
be parted, be separated *v.i.* **bichuṛnā** بچھڑنا
scorpion *n.m.* **bicchū** بچھو
established, confirmed, maintained *adj.* **baḥāl** بحال
maintain, uphold *v.t.* **baḥāl rakhnā** بحال رکھنا
reinstate, replace *v.t.* **baḥāl karnā** بحال کرنا
reinstatement, restoration *n.f.* **baḥālī** بحالی
argument, discussion, dispute *n.f.* **baḥas** بحث
argue, discuss, dispute *v.t.* **baḥas karnā** بحث کرنا
sea, ocean, gulf *n.m.* **baḥr** بحر
naval (*belonging to the sea*), nautical *adj.* **baḥrī** بحری
on account of, in favor of; regarding *adv.* **baḥaqq** بحق
by the order of, by authority of *adv.* **baḥukam** بحکم
in the capacity of, as *adv.* **baḥaiysiyat** بحیثیت
fever; passion *n.m.* **buxār** بخار
vent one's spleen, rage *v.t.* **buxār nikālnā** بخار نکالنا
luck, fate, fortune *n.m.* **baxt** بخت
lucky, fortunate *adj.* **baxtāvar** بختاور
share, lot, allotment *n.m.* **baxš** بخش
gift, reward; tip (*in a restaurant*) *n.f.* **baxšiš** بخشش
pardoner, giver, donor *n.m.* **baxšindah** بخشندہ
general, commander-in-chief; paymaster *n.m.* **baxšī** بخشی
avarice, stinginess *n.m.* **buxl** بخل
on the contrary *adv.* / contrary to, in opposition to *pp.* **baxilāf** بخلاف
well, thoroughly, in a good manner *adv.* **baxūbī** بخوبی
by oneself *adv.* **baxūd** بخود

بخوشی willingly, gladly, with pleasure *adv.* **bāxūšī**
بخیر safc and sound, in peace *adv.* **baxair**
بخیریت safely *adv.* **baxairiyat**
بخیل miserly, stingy *adj.* **baxīl**
بخیلی stinginess, avarice *n.f.* **baxīlī**
بد bad, evil *adj.* **bad**
بداختر unlucky, unfortunate *adj.* **bad axtar**
بدبخت unlucky, unfortunate *adj.* **bad baxt**
بدبختی misfortune *n.f.* **bad baxtī**
بدبو bad smell *n.f.* **bad bū**
بدتر worse *adj.* **bad tar**
بدحواس stupefied, confounded, bewildered *adj.* **bad ḥavās**
بددماغ proud; dissatisfied *adj.* **bad dimāġ**
بدرجہ according to *adv.* **badarjah**
بدزبان abusive, indecent; impertinent, rude *adj.* **bad zabān**
بدسلوکی ill treatment, misbehavior *n.f.* **bad sulūkī**
بدشکل ugly, bad looking *adj.* **bad šakl**
بدطینت evil-minded, malevolent *adj.* **bad tīnat**
بدقسمتی سے unfortunately *adv.* **bad qismatī sē**
بدکار evil, mean *adj.* **bad kār**
بدکاردا wicked, evil *adj.* **bad kirdār**
بدگمانی suspicion, mistrust *n.f.* **bad gumānī** • suspicious, distrustful *adj.* **bad gumān**
بدلحاظ disrespectful, impudent *adj.* **bad liḥāz**
بدمزاج ill-tempered, ill-natured *adj.* **bad mizāj**
بدمزگی tastelessness; displeasure *n.f.* **bad mazgī**
بدمعاش crook, a bad character *n.m.* **bad mᶜāš**
بدنام disreputable, infamous *adj.* **bad nām**
بدنامی defamation *n.f.* **bad nāmī**
بدنصیب unlucky, unfortunate *adj.* **bad nasīb**
بدنما ugly *adj.* **bad numā**
بدنیت dishonest, ill-intentioned *adj.* **bad niyyat**
بدنیتی dishonesty, ill-will *n.f.* **bad niyyatī**
بدہضمی indigestion *n.f.* **bad hazmī**
بدر outside; without *adv.* **badar** • full moon *n.m.* **badr**
بدرو drain, sewer *n.f.* **badarraū**
بدستور as usual, customarily *adv.* **badastūr**

innovation (*in a religious sense*), schism *n.f.* **bidaᶜat** بدعت
with difficulty *adv.* **badiqqat** بدقت
change, exchange, alteration *n.m.* **badal** بدل
revenge *n.m.* **badlā** بدلا
take revenge *v.t.* **badlā lēnā** بدلا لینا
change, exchange, alter *v.i.* **badalnā** بدلنا
cloud *n.f.* **badlī** بدلی
body; face *n.m.* **badan** بدن
by means of, through *adv.* **badaulat** بدولت
wickedness, badness *n.f.* **badī** بدی
abroad, foreign land *n.m.* **badēs** بدیس
foreigner *n.m.* **badēsī** بدیسی
wonderful, strange, rare *adj.* **badīᶜ** بدیع
Wednesday; rule, law *n.m.* **budh** بدھ
fool, stupid person *n.m.* **buddhū** بدھو
wisdom, intelligence *n.f.* **buddhī** بدھی
joke, fun *n.m.* **bazlah** بذلہ
• on, upon, above *pp.* / fruit *n.f.* / boon, blessing; choice *n.m.* **bar** بر
desert; land *n.m.* **barr**
continent *n.m.* **barr aᶜzam** بر اعظم
accomplish *v.t.* **bar lānā** بر لانا
openly, publicly *adv.* **bar milā** بر ملا
bad, evil; ugly *adj.* **burā** برا
equal, adequate *adj.* **barābar** برابر
equality, accuracy *n.f.* **barābarī** برابری
barat (*marriage procession*) *n.f.* **barāt** برات
brother *n.m.* **birādar** برادر
real brother, sibling *n.m.* **barādar-ē-ḥaqīqī** برادر حقیقی
brotherly, fraternal *adj.* **birādarānan** برادرانہ
fraternity, brotherhood *n.f.* **barādarī** برادری
dust, powder *n.m.* **burādah** برادہ
inflamed, enraged *adj.* **barāfruxtah** برافروختہ
flashing *adj.* **barrāq** براق
flash, splendor *n.f.* **barrāqī** براقی
balcony, verandah *n.m.* **barāmdah** برامدہ
excited, awakened *adj.* **barāngēxtah** برانگیختہ

for, for the sake of *adv.* **barā'ē** برائے
mischief, badness, wickedness *n.f.* **burā'ī** برائی
for God's sake, for mercy's sake *adv.* **barā'ē xudā** برائے خدا
ruined, deserted, wasted *adj.* **barbād** برباد
destruction, ruin, loss *n.f.* **barbādī** بربادی
use, apply *v.t.* **bartānā** برتانا
conduct, behavior, practice *n.m.* **bartā'ū** برتاؤ
excellent, superior, higher *adj.* **bartar** برتر
pot *n.m.* **bartan** برتن
happen, take place *v.i.* **baratnā** برتنا
tower, dome *n.m.* **burj** برج
Leo (*Zodiac*) *n.m.* **burj-ē-asad** برج اسد
exact, at once *adj.* **barjastah** برجستہ
dismissal, discharge, removal *n.f.* **barxāst** برخاست
removal, dismissal *n.f.* **barxāstgī** برخاستگی
endurance, patience, tolerance *n.f.* **bardāšt** برداشت
patient, tolerant *adj.* **burdbār** بردبار
patience, tolerance *n.f.* **burdbārī** بردباری
slave, captive *n.m.* **bardah** بردہ
year; rain *n.m.* **baras** برس
rainy season, monsoon *n.f.* **barsāt** برسات
rainy *adj.* **barsātī** برساتی
rain *v.i.* **barasnā** برسنا
Britain, Great Britain *n.m.* **Bartāniyah** برطانیہ
aside, apart *adv.* **bartaraf** برطرف
dismissal, discharge *n.f.* **bartarafī** برطرفی
snow, ice *n.f.* **barf** برف
snowy, icy, very cold *adj.* **barfānī** برفانی
iced, icy, very cold *adj.* **barfīlā** برفیلا
lightning, electricity *n.f.* **barq** برق
fixed, settled, established *adj.* **barqarār** برقرار
burqa, veil *n.m.* **burqa**ᶜ برقع
rainy season; rain *n.f.* **barkhā** برکھا
auspiciousness, blessings *n.f.* **barkāt** برکات
blessing, fortune; abundance, prosperity, increase *n.f.* **barkat** برکت
leaf *n.m.* **barg** برگ

rebellion *n.f.* **bargaštagī** برگشتگی
changed, reverted *adj.* **bargaštah** برگشتہ
rare, scarce; few, little *adj.* **birlā** برلا
demonstration, proof *n.m.* **burhān** برہان
angry *adj.* **barham** برہم
nakedness *n.f.* **barahangī** برہنگی
naked, nude, bare *adj.* **barahnah** برہنہ
brooch *n.m.* **brūc** بروچ
in time *adv.* **barvaqt** بروقت
fortunate, prosperous *adj.* **bar-ō-mand** برومند
acquitted, released, free *adj.* **barī** بری
biryani (*meat and rice dish*) *n.f.* **biryānī** بریانی
brake *n.m.* **brēk** بریک
nonsense, foolish talk *n.f.* / banyan tree *n.m.* **bāṛ** بڑ
great, big, large *adj.* **baṛā** بڑا
greatness *n.f.* **baṛā'ī** بڑائی
murmur, grumble *v.i.* **baṛbaṛānā** بڑبڑانا
enlarge, increase *v.t.* **baṛhānā** بڑھانا
increase *n.f.* **baṛhā'ī** بڑھائی
increase, growth *n.f.* **baṛhtī** بڑھتی
proceed, grow, increase *v.i.* **baṛhnā** بڑھنا
excellent, fine, nice, great *adj.* **baṛhiyā** بڑھیا
old lady, old woman *n.f.* **buṛhiyā** بڑھیا
goat *n.m./n.f.* **buz** بز
cowardly, timid *adj.* **buz dil** بزدل
great; aged, old (*person*); honorable *adj.* / old man; sage *n.m.* **buzurg** بزرگ
grandeur, reverence, nobleness *n.f.* **buzurgī** بزرگی
meeting, society, company *n.f.* **bazm** بزم
/ command, power, control, influence *n.m.* / sufficient, enough, no more *adj.* **bas** بس
• (That's) Enough! *interj.* / bus, coach *n.f.*
poisonous *adj.* **bis**
bus stop *n.m.* **bas isṭāp** بس اسٹاپ
bus station *n.m.* **bas isṭēšan** بس اسٹیشن
stop, desist *v.t.* **bas karnā** بس کرنا
forget *v.t.* **bisārnā** بسارنا
settle, found (a settlement) *v.t.* **basānā** بسانا

on account of *adv.* **basabab** بسبب
bedding, bed-roll *n.m.* **bistār** بستار
flower garden *n.m.* **bustān** بستان
bed *n.m.* **bistar** بستر
village, abode, colony *n.f.* **bastī** بستی
by all means *adv.* **basar-ō-cašm** بسروچشم
In the name of Allah! *interj.* **bismillah!** بسم اللہ
settle, dwell *v.t.* **basnā** بسنا
spring (*season*) *n.f.* **basant** بسنت
abundant, plenty, much *adv.* **bisyār** بسیار
shelter, lodging, abode *n.m.* **basērā** بسیرا
rest, lodge *v.t.* **basērā karnā** بسیرا کرنا
pleased, joyful, cheerful *adj.* **bašāš** بشاش
joyfulness, cheerfulness *n.f.* **bašāšat** بشاشت
man, human being *n.m.* **bašar** بشر
humanity, human nature *n.f.* **bašariat** بشریت
sight, vision; perception *n.f.* **basārat** بصارت
vision, insight *n.m.* **basar** بصر
sight, insight *n.f.* **basīrat** بصیرت
goose, duck *n.f.* **bat** بط
duck, duckling *n.f.* **batax** بطخ
by way of, in the manner of *adv.* **batarīq** بطریق
womb, belly, abdomen *n.m.* **batn** بطن
as, like *adv.* **bataur** بطور
after, afterwards, later on *adv.* **bād** بعد
certain, some, few *adv.* **ba^c^z** بعض
sometimes, often *adv.* **ba^c^z auqāt** بعض اوقات
far, distant, remote *adj.* **ba^c^īd** بعید
inconceivable *adj.* **ba^c^īd-ul-qiyās** بعیدالقیاس
rebellion, violence *n.f.* **baġāvat** بغاوت
malice, hatred *n.m.* **buġz** بغض
armpit; side *n.f.* / on one side *adv.* **baġal** بغل
carefully, watchfully *adv.* **baġaur** بغور
except, without, beside *adv.* **baġair** بغیر
eternity, perpetuity, immortality *n.f.* **bāqa** بقا
grain merchant, grocer, shopkeeper *n.m.* **baqqāl** بقال

to the extent of, according to *pp.* **baqadr** بقدر
plentiful, in abundance; abundantly, plentifully *adv.* **bakasrat** بکثرت
he-goat; fool *n.m.* **bakrā** بکرا
be scattered, be dispersed *v.i.* **bikharnā** بکھرنا
she-goat *n.f.* **bakrī** بکری
chatter, babble *v.i.* **bākna** بکنا
booking, reservation *n.f.* **buking** بکنگ
book, reserve *v.t.* **buking karnā** بکنگ کرنا
gossip, foolish talk *n.f.* **bakvās** بکواس
idle talker, gossiper *n.m.* **bakvāsī** بکواسی
scatter, disperse *v.t.* **bikhairnā** بکھیرنا
uproar, dispute, quarrel *n.m.* **bakhēṛā** بکھیڑا
deterioration, defect *n.m.* **bigāṛ** بگاڑ
deteriorate, spoil *v.i.* **bigāṛnā** بگاڑنا
heron, crane *n.m.* **baglā** بگلا
hypocrite *n.m.* **baglā bhagat** بگلا بھگت
• hole; bill, check, invoice *n.m.* / by, with *pp.* **bil** بل
twist, coil; strength, power, vigor *n.m.* **bal**
• without *pp.* **bilā** • male cat *n.m.* **billā** • evil spirit, misfortune *n.f.* **balā** بلا
bubble *n.m.* **bullā**
weeping, lamentation, wailing *n.m.* **bilāp** بلاپ
weep, lament, wail *v.i.* **bilāpnā** بلاپنا
eloquence, rhetoric *n.f.* **balāġat** بلاغت
call, summon, invite *v.t.* **bulānā** بلانا
regularly, constantly, without fail *adv.* **bilā nāġah** بلاناغہ
calling, summoning *n.m.* **balāvā** بلاوا
without reason *adv.* **bilā vajh** بلاوجہ
nightingale *n.f.* **bulbul** بلبل
bubble *n.m.* **bulbulah** بلبلہ
with regard to, regarding *pp.* **baliḥāz** بلحاظ
city, town *n.m.* **balad** بلد
phlegm *n.m.* **balġam** بلغم
phlegmatic *adj.* **balaġmī** بلغمی
but, moreover; on the contrary *conj.* **balkih** بلکہ
spear *n.m.* **ballam** بلم
high, elevated; great, sublime *adj.* **buland** بلند

brave, courageous *adj.* **buland ḥauslah** بلند حوصلہ
of high rank, of high position *adj.* **buland martabah** بلند مرتبہ
height, elevation *n.f.* **bulandī** بلندی
riot, mutiny *n.m.* **balvā** بلوا
powerful, strong *adj.* **balvān** بلوان
crystal, quartz *n.m.* **billaur** بلور
made of crystal, made of quartz *adj.* **billaurī** بلوری
oak tree, chestnut tree *n.m.* **balūt** بلوط
maturity; adolescence, puberty *n.m.* **bulūġ** بلوغ
churn, stir, shake *v.t.* **bilōnā** بلونا
cat *n.f.* **billī** بلی
eloquent, rhetoric *adj.* **balīġ** بلیغ
bomb *n.f.* **bam** بم
bombardment *n.f.* **bambārī** بمباری
with the help of, by means of *pp.* **bamadad** بمدد
to some extent *adv.* **bamartabah** بمرتبہ
together, along with *adv.* **bamaʿi** بمع
as, per, according to *pp.* **bamūjab** بموجب
forest, woods *n.m.* **ban** • without *pp.* / son *n.m.* **bin** بن
exile *n.m.* **ban bās** بن باس
become *v.i.* **ban jānā** بن جانا
wild man, ape *n.m.* **ban mānus** بن مانس
without *pp.* / basis, foundation; cause *n.f.* **binā** • prepared, made *adj.* **banā** بنا
ready-made *adj.* **banā banāyā** بنا بنایا
due to, on account of *pp.* **binābar** بنابر
therefore, keeping this in mind *adv.* **binābarēṁ** بنابریں
vegetation, flora *n.m.* **banāspatī** بناسپتی
build, construct, make, create, form *v.t.* **banānā** بنانا
perparation *n.m.* **banā'ō** بناؤ
construction, shape *n.f.* **banāvaṭ** بناوٹ
weaving, knitting *n.f.* **bināvaṭ** بناوٹ
daughter *n.f.* **bint** بنت
trade, commerce *n.m.* **banaj** بنج
wasteland *n.f.* **banjar** بنجر
closed, shut; barred, prevented *adj.* / dam, dike; joint, knuckle *n.m.* **band** بند
close, shut *v.t.* **band karnā** بند کرنا

earring *n.m.* **bundā** بندا

monkey, ape, baboon; port, harbor *n.m.* **bandar** بندر

port, harbor *n.m.* **bandar gāh** بندرگاہ

she-monkey *n.f.* **bandariyā** بندریا

bound (for) *adj.* / binding, prohibition *n.f.* **bandiš** بندش

devotion, service *n.f.* **bandagī** بندگی

servant *n.m.* **bandah** بندہ

management, arrangement, settlement *n.m.* **band-ō-basat** بندوبست

economy; arrangement *n.f.* **band-ō-basatī** بندوبستی

gun, rifle *n.f.* **bandūq** بندوق

load a gun *v.t.* **bandūq bharnā** بندوق بھرنا

shoot, fire *v.t.* **bandūq calānā** بندوق چلانا

shoot, fire *v.t.* **bandūq chōṛnā** بندوق چھوڑنا

shooter *n.m.* **bandūqcī** بندوقچی

bindee (*red dot worn by women on forehead*) *n.f.* **bindī** بندی

fastened, tied, shut *adj.* **bandhā** بندھا

binding, fastening *n.f.* **bandhātī** بندھائی

fastening, binding, imprisonment *n.m.* **bandhan** بندھن

waistcoat, short robe *n.f.* **banḍī** بنڈی

ridge (*of a house*) *n.f.* **banḍērī** بنڈیری

race, descendancy, lineage *n.m.* **baṁs** بنس

spoil, perish, expire, die *v.i.* **binasnā** بنسنا

flute; fishing hook *n.f.* **baṁsī** بنسی

Bengali *n.m./adj.* **bangālī** بنگالی

bungalow, summer-house *n.m.* **bangalah** بنگلہ

Bangladesh *n.m.* **Banglah Dēš** بنگلہ دیش

get something done *v.t.* **banvānā** بنوانا

cottonseed *n.m.* **binaulā** بنولا

man, human being *n.m.* **banī ādam** بنی آدم

Israelites, Jews *n.m.* **banī Isrā'īl** بنی اسرائیل

shopkeeper, grainseller *n.m.* **baniyā** بنیا

foundation, basis, origin *n.f.* **buniyād** بنیاد

good, better *adj.* **bah** بہ

in respect of, with relation to, in comparison with *pp.* **bah nisbat** بہ نسبت

value, price *n.f.* **bahā** بہا

brave, courageous, valiant *adj.* **bahādur** بہادر

bravery, heroism *n.f.* **bahādrī** بہادری
spring, bloom; youth *n.f.* **bahār** بہار
sweep, clean *v.t.* **buhārnā** بہارنا
broom *n.f.* **buhārī** بہاری
cause to flow, set afloat *v.t.* **bahānā** بہانا
plea, excuse *n.m.* **bahānah** بہانہ
make an excuse; pretend *v.t.* **bahānah karnā** بہانہ کرنا
flow, flood *n.m.* **bahā'ō** بہاؤ
well-being, welfare; health *n.f.* **bahbūdi** بہبودی
very; much, many *adv.* **bahut** بہت
all right, quite right *adv.* **bahut ṭhīk** بہت ٹھیک
very well, very good *adv.* **bahut xūb** بہت خوب
(too) much *adv.* **bahut sā** بہت سا
since a long time *adv.* **bahut muddat sē** بہت مدت سے
running; afloat *adv.* **bahtā** بہتا
abundance, excess, plenty *n.f.* **bahutāt** بہتات
better, excellent, superior *adj.* **bihtar** بہتر
seventy-two *num.* **bahattar** بہتر
improvement, advantage *n.f.* **bihtarī** بہتری
best, superior *adj.* **bihtarēṁ** بہترین
be paid *v.t.* **bahar pānā** بہر پانا
by all means, somehow or another *adv.* **bahar sūrat** بہر صورت
deaf; careless *adj.* **bahrā** بہرا
by all means; at any price *adv.* **bahar ḥāl** بہر حال
property, share, portion, profit, gain *n.m.* **baharah** بہرہ
actor *n.m.* **baharūpiyah** بہروپیہ
subscription, contribution, share, assessment *n.f.* **bihrī** بہری
female hawk, falcon; deaf woman *n.f.* **bahrī** بہری
paradise, heaven *n.f.* **bihišt** بہشت
mislead, deceive, cheat; seduce *v.t.* **bahkānā** بہکانا
seducing *adj.* **bahkānē vālā** بہکانے والا
be deceived, be misled, be deluded *v.i.* **bahaknā** بہکنا
amuse, entertain; divert *v.t.* **bahlānā** بہلانا
be amused, be entertained; be diverted *v.i.* **bahalnā** بہلنا
together, one with another *adv.* **baham** بہم
supply, provide *v.t.* **baham pahuṁcānā** بہم پہنچانا

sister *n.f.* **bahan/bahin/bēhn** بہن
flow, float, drift *v.i.* **bahnā** بہنا
brother-in-law (*sister's husband*) *n.m.* **bahnō'ī** بہنوئی
first sale (*of a shopkeeper*) *n.f.* **buhnī** بہنی
adopted sister *n.f.* **bhanēlī** بہنیلی
wife, bride; daughter-in-law *n.f.* **bahū** بہو
father's sister *n.f.* **bhūā** بہوا
ledger, diary *n.f.* **bahī** بہی
ledger *n.m.* **bahī khātā** بہی کھاتا
many, very much *adj.* **bahutērā** بہیترا
father *n.m.* / smell, odor *n.f.* **bū** بو
sister; lady *n.f.* **būbū** بوبو
marriage *n.m.* **bivāh** بواہ
sowing *n.f.* **bivā'ī** بوائی
strength, power, ability *n.m.* **būtā** بوتا
bottle *n.f.* **bōtal** بوتل
earthen vessel *n.f.* **būṭ** بوٹ
drugs; flowers; roots *n.f.* **būṭī** بوٹی
slice (of meat) *n.f.* **bōṭī** بوٹی
by reason of, for *pp.* **bavajah** بوجہ
understanding, comprehension, perception *n.f.* **būjh** • load, burden *n.m.* **bōjh** بوجھ
understand, comprehend, perceive, conceive, enquire *v.i.* **būjhnā** بوجھنا
(heavy) rain *n.f.* **bauchāṛ** بوچھاڑ
being, existence *n.f.* **būd** بود
residence, abode *n.f.* **būd-ō-bāš** بود و باش
weak, feeble; timid; dull *adj.* **bōdā** بودا
knowledge, understanding *n.m.* **bōdh** بودھ
• (canvas) bag, sack *n.m.* **bōrā** • sugar; powder *n.m.* **būrā** بورا
mad, insane *adj.* **baurā**
go mad, become crazy *v.i.* **baurānā** بورانا
be drowned; dive *v.i.* **būṛnā** • dip, steep, drench, immerse *v.t.* **bōṛnā** بوڑنا
old *adj.* **būṛhā** بوڑھا
old woman *n.f.* **būṛhi** بوڑھی
kiss, kissing *n.m.* **bōsah** بوسہ
kiss, give a kiss *v.t.* **bōsah dēnā** بوسہ دینا
kiss, get a kiss *v.t.* **bōsah lēnā** بوسہ لینا

بوسیدگی **bōsīdagī** *n.f.* rottenness, decay
بوسیدہ **bōsīdah** *adj.* rotten, decayed
بوش **bōš** *n.m.* pomp, splendor, magnificence
بوقلمون **būqalmūn** *adj.* colored (*of various colors*), checkered
بوک **bōk** *n.m.* he-goat, ram
بوکا **bōkā** *n.m.* basket; bucket
بوکنا **būknā** *v.t.* pound, grind, crush
بول **bōl** *n.m.* word, speech, conversation, utterance, voice
بول اٹھنا **bōl uṭhnā** *v.i.* speak out, cry out, exclaim
بول چال **bōl cāl** *n.f.* dialect, conversation, mode of speech
بول مارنا **bōl mārnā** *v.t.* taunt, ridicule
بولنا **bōlnā** *v.i./v.t.* speak, talk, say, tell, utter
بولنا چالنا **bōlnā calnā** *v.i.* converse, talk
بولی **bōlī** *n.f.* speech, language, dialect
بونا **baunā** *n.m.* dwarf
بوند **būnd** *n.f.* drop
بوند ٹپکنا **būnd ṭapaknā** *v.i.* trickle
بوندا باندی **būndā bāndī** *n.f.* rain (*a small amount*)
بونڈر **bavanḍar** *n.m.* whirlwind, storm
بونی **baunī** *n.f.* female dwarf
بے **bē** *pp.* without
بے آبرو **bē ābrū** *adj.* disgraced
بے اثر **bē asar** *adj.* without effect, inefficient
بے اختیاری **bē axtiyārī** *n.f.* helplessness
بے ادب **bē adab** *adj.* impolite, rude, insolent
بے ادبی **bē adabī** *n.f.* impoliteness, rudeness
بے اصل **bē asal** *adj.* incredible
بے اعتباری **bē iᶜtibārī** *n.f.* untrustworthiness, dishonesty
بے اعتدالی **bē iᶜtidālī** *n.f.* inequality
بے انتظامی **bē intizāmī** *n.f.* mismanagement
بے انتہا **bē intihā** *adj.* infinite, endless
بے اندازہ **bē andāzah** *adj.* immoderate
بے اندیشہ **bē andēšah** *adv.* thoughtlessly, fearlessly
بے انصاف **bē insāf** *adj.* unjust
بے انصافی **bē insāfī** *n.f.* injustice
بے ایمان **bē imān** *adj.* infidel, faithless, dishonest

بے ایمانی infidelity, dishonesty *n.f.* **bē imānī**
بے ایمانی کرنا act dishonestly, play false *v.t.* **bē imānī karnā**
بے باقی full payment, liquidation *n.f.* **bē bāqī**
بے باکی fearlessness *n.f.* **bē bākī**
بے بس helpless *adj.* **bē bas**
بے بہا invaluable *adj.* **bē bahā**
بی بی lady, madam; Miss (*form of address*) *n.f.* **bībī**
بے پردہ unveiled, immodest *adj.* **bē pardah**
بے پروا careless, thoughtless *adj.* **bē parvā**
بے تاب impatient, restless *adj.* **bē tāb**
بے تابی agitation, restlessness *n.f.* **bē tābī**
بے تال out of tune (*in music*) *adj.* **bē tāl**
بے تامل inconsiderate *adj.* **bē tāmmul**
بے تحاشا recklessly *adv.* **bē taḥāšā**
بے تقصیر innocent, faultless *adj.* **bē taqsīr**
بے تکلف frank *adj.* **bē takalluf**
بے تمیز indiscreet, silly *adj.* **bē tamīz**
بے جا misplaced, improper, unlawful, unreasonable, inaccurate *adj.* **bē jā**
بے جان lifeless, dead *adj.* **bē jān**
بے چارہ helpless, poor, miserable *adj.* **bē cārah**
بے چراغ dark; desolate *adj.* **bē carāġ**
بے چین restless, uneasy *adj.* **bē cain**
بے حال ruined; jobless, unemployed *adj.* **bē ḥāl**
بے حجاب shameless, immodest *adj.* **bē ḥijāb**
بے حد infinite, limitless *adj.* **bē ḥadd**
بے حواس senseless, distracted *adj.* **bē ḥavās**
بے حواسی insensibility, distraction *n.f.* **bē ḥavāsī**
بے حیا shameless, immodest *adj.* **bē ḥayā**
بے خبر careless, senseless *adj.* **bē xabar**
بے خود senseless, beside oneself *adj.* **bē xūd**
بے خودی senselessness *n.f.* **bē xūdī**
بے دل heartless, reluctant *adj.* **bē dil**
بے دماغ ill-tempered, impatient, easily provoked *adj.* **bē dimāġ**
بے دھڑک fearless *adj.* **bē dhaṛak**
بے ذوق tasteless *adj.* **bē zauq**
بے رحم cruel *adj.* **bē raḥm**

cruelty *n.f.* **bē raḥmī** بے رحمی
unemployed *adj.* **bē rōzgār** بے روزگار
disgusted, sick of *adj.* **bē zār** بے زار
mute *adj.* **bē zabān** بے زبان
undoubtedly, certainly *adv.* **bē šāibah** بے شائبہ
undoubtedly *adv.* **bē šak** بے شک
impatient, restless *adj.* **bē sabr** بے صبر
without honor, disgraced *adj.* **bē ᶜizzat** بے عزت
dishonor, disgrace, disrespect *n.f.* **bē ᶜizzatī** بے عزتی
unwise, stupid *adj.* **bē ᶜaql** بے عقل
causeless *adj.* **bē ᶜillat** بے علت
shameless *adj.* **bē ġairat** بے غیرت
thoughtless, contented *adj.* **bē fikr** بے فکر
innocent, faultless *adj.* **bē qusūr** بے قصور
unemployed; in vain, useless *adj.* **bē kār** بے کار
friendless *adj.* **bē kas** بے کس
innocent *adj.* **bē gunāh** بے گناہ
inhuman *adj.* **bē murauvat** بے مروت
unfortunate *adj.* **bē nasīb** بے نصیب
saltless; dull *adj.* **bē namak** بے نمک
unambitious, lazy *adj.* **bē himmat** بے ہمت
unskillful *adj.* **bē hunar** بے ہنر
senseless *adj.* **bē hōš** بے ہوش
senselessness, stupefaction *n.f.* **bē hōšī** بے ہوشی
faithless, treacherous *adj.* **bē vafā** بے وفا
foolish, ignorant *adj.* **bē vaqūf** بے وقوف
foolishness, silliness *n.f.* **bē vaqūfī** بے وقوفی
desert, wilderness *n.m.* **bayābān** بیابان
eighty-two *num.* **bayāsī** بیاسی
whiteness; notebook, account book *n.f.* **bayāz** بیاض
forty-two *num.* **bayālīs** بیالیس
statement, assertion, account, allegation, description, report *n.m.* **bayān** بیان
declare, assert, give an account of, describe, report *v.t.* **bayān karnā** بیان کرنا
bring forth, give birth to (*animals only*) *v.i.* **biyānā** بیانا
marriage, wedding *n.m.* **biyāh** بیاہ
marry *v.t.* **biyāh karnā** بیاہ کرنا

bring home a wife *v.t.* **biyāh lānā** بیاہ لانا
marry *v.t.* **biyāhnā** بیاہنا
house, abode; couplet, verse *n.f.* **bayt** بیت
treasury *n.m.* **bayt-ul-māl** بیت المال
pass away, pass over *v.i.* **bīt jānā** بیت جانا
happen, pass, elapse, expire *v.i.* **bītnā** بیتنا
son, child; boy *n.m.* **bēṭā** بیٹا
battery *n.f.* **baiṭrī** بیٹری
daughter *n.f.* **bēṭī** بیٹی
sit, sit down **v.i baiṭhnā** بیٹھنا
sitting; posture; seat, sitting place *n.f.* **baiṭhak** بیٹھک
assembly room, chamber hall, meeting place *n.m.* **baiṭhak xānah** بیٹھک خانہ
seed, germ; origin, source *n.m.* **bīj** بیج
sow seed *v.t.* **bīj bōnā** بیج بونا
sow seed *v.t.* **bīj ḍālnā** بیج ڈالنا
among, in, into, between *pp.* / middle, center; average *n.m.* **bīc** بیچ
intervention, arbitration, mediation, settlement *n.m.* **bīc bacā'ō** بیچ بچاؤ
in between *adv.* **bīc mēṁ** بیچ میں
sell *v.t.* **bēcnā** بیچنا
root, origin, foundation, lineage *n.f.* **bēx** بیخ
extirpator, exterminator *n.m.* **bēx kan** بیخ کن
extirpation, extermination, eradication *n.f.* **bēx kanī** بیخ کنی
cane, willow *n.f.* **bēd** • physician, doctor *n.m.* **baid** بید
watchful, wakeful, vigilant, awake *adj.* **bēdār** بیدار
fortunate, lucky *adj.* **bēdār baxt** بیدار بخت
wakefulness, alertness *n.f.* **bēdārī** بیداری
perforate, pierce, stab, wound *v.t.* **bēdhnā** بیدھنا
hostility, malice, hatred *n.m.* **bair** • brave, mighty, powerful *adj.* / hero *n.m.* **bīr** بیر
be hostile *v.t.* **bair paṛnā** بیر پڑنا
hate *v.t.* **bair rakhnā** بیر رکھنا
take revenge, retaliate *v.t.* **bair lēnā** بیر لینا
take revenge, retaliate *v.t.* **bair nikālnā** بیر نکالنا
waiter *n.m.* **bērā** بیرا
seclusion, renouncing (*the pleasures of the world*) *n.m.* **bairāg** بیراگ
ascetic, devotee *n.m.* **bairāgī** بیراگی
solitary, unpopulated *adj.* **bairān** بیران

بیرم feast, party *n.f.* **bēram**
بیرنگ map, sketch, plan *n.m.* **bīrang**
بیرون without *pp.* **bērūn**
بیرونی outer, external *adj.* **bērūni**
بیری enemy, adversary *n.m.* **bairā**
بیڑا enclosure, fence; siege *n.m.* **bēṛā**
بیڑی fetters; wedlock *n.f.* **bēṛī**
بیڑی ڈالنا put in fetters, put in chains *v.t.* **bēṛī ḍālnā**
بیزار angry, displeased *adj.* **bēzār**
بیزاری anger, displeasure *n.f.* **bēzārī**
بیس twenty *num.* **bīs**
بیسرا out of tune *adj.* **bēsurā**
بیسن gram-flour *n.m.* **bēsan**
بیسواں twentieth *adj.* **bisvāṁ**
بیش more, better; superior, excellent; delightful *adj.* **bēš**
بیش قیمت costly, precious *adj.* **bēš qīmat**
بیش وکم more or less *adv.* **bēš-ō-kam**
بیشتر better *adj.* **bēštar**
بیشہ forest; wilderness *n.m.* **bēšah**
بیشی increase, excess, surplus *n.f.* **bēšī**
بیضا white; bright *adj.* / sun *n.m.* **baizā**
بیضہ egg; testicle *n.m.* **baizah**
بیضوی oval, egg-shaped *adj.* **baizavī**
بیع sale, buying and selling *n.f.* **baiᶜ**
بیع کرنا sell, transfer *v.t.* **baiᶜ karnā**
بیک پیک backpack *n.m.* **baik paik**
بیکراں immense, infinite *adj.* **baikrāṁ**
بیگ bag *n.m.* **baig** • lord, master; speed, haste *n.m.* / quickly *adv.* **bēg**
بیگار compulsory labor *n.m.* **bēgār**
بیگانہ not related, strange, foreign *adj.* **bēgānah**
بیگم lady; queen *n.f.* **bēgam**
بیگن eggplant, brinjal *n.m.* **baigan**
بیگھا bigha (*measure of land equal to half an acre*) *n.m.* **bighā**
بیل bull, ox; fool *n.m.* **bail** • spade, mattock, shovel *n.m.* **bēl**
بیل دار embroidered, engraved *adj.* **bēl dār**
بیل کش farmer, peasant, villager *n.m.* **bēl kaš**

bullock cart *n.f.* **bail gāṛī** بیل گاڑی
donation, money for charity *n.m.* **bēlā** بیلا
small mattock, spade *n.m.* **bēlcah** بیلچہ
digger *n.m.* **bēldār** بیلدار
mattock, hoe *n.f.* **bēlak** بیلک
guardian, protector, preserver *n.m.* **bēlī** بیلی
fear, danger, risk *n.m.* **bīm** بیم
sick, ill *adj.* **bimār** بیمار
hospital *n.m.* **bimār xānah** بیمار خانہ
sickness, illness, disease *n.f.* **bimārī** بیماری
insurance, assurance *n.m.* **bīmah** بیمہ
sound, word *n.f.* **bīn** بین
among, between *pp.* **bayn** بین
clear, lucid, well-exposed *adj.* **bayyin** بین
international *adj.* **bayn-al-āqvāmī** بین الاقوامی
clearsighted *adj.* **bīnā** بینا
sight, vision *n.f.* **bīnā'ī** بینائی
band-aid *n.m.* **bainḍ ēḍ** بینڈ ایڈ
crooked, uncivilized; difficult, hard *adj.* **bēnḍā** بینڈا
bank *n.m.* **baink** بینک
aubergine, eggplant *n.m.* **baingan** بینگن
idle talk, absurdity, foolishness *n.f.* **bēhūdagī** بیہودگی
absurd, foolish, idle *adj.* **bēhūdah** بیہودہ
traffic, trade, business *n.m.* **byōpār** بیوپار
merchant, dealer, trader *n.m.* **byōpārī** بیوپاری
cut, shape, fashion *n.m.* **byōnt** بیونت
widow *n.f.* **bēvah** بیوہ
calling, correspondence; dealing, trade *n.m.* **byōhār** بیوہار
negotiate, deal with *v.t.* **byōhār karnā** بیوہار کرنا
lady; wife *n.f.* **bīvī** بیوی
sell; transfer *v.t.* **bēcnā** بیچنا
sister-in-law (*elder brother's wife*) *n.f.* **bhābhī** بھابھی
vapor, steam *n.f.* **bhāp** بھاپ
low tide *n.m.* **bhāṭā** بھاٹا
greens, vegetables *n.f.* **bhājī** بھاجی
load, burden, weight *n.m.* **bhār** بھار

heavy, weighty *adj.* **bhārī** بھاری
fare, freight, rent, hire, levy *n.m.* **bhāṛā** بھاڑا
part, share, division; fortune, destiny *n.f.* **bhāg** بھاگ
be unfortunate *v.i.* **bhāg phuṭnā** بھاگ پھوٹنا
be lucky, be fortunate *v.i.* **bhāg jāgnā** بھاگ جاگنا
flight, running, escape *n.f.* **bhāgaṛ** بھاگڑ
run away, flee, escape *v.i.* **bhāgnā** بھاگنا
glorious, divine *adj.* **bhāgvān** بھاگوان
point (*of an arrow/spear/lance*) *n.f.* **bhāl** بھال
spearman, lancer *n.m.* **bhālā bardār** بھالا بردار
bear *n.m.* **bhālū** بھالو
actress; (female) artist *n.f.* **bhān matī** بھان متی
be pleased, suit, fit *v.i.* **bhānā** بھانا
various, diverse *adj.* **bhānt bhānt** بھانت بھانت
nephew (*sister's son*) *n.m.* **bhāṁjā** بھانجا
niece (*sister's daughter*); hindrance, interruption, interference *n.f.* **bhāṁjī** بھانجی
pot, vessel *n.m.* **bhānḍā** بھانڈا
betray a secret *v.t.* **bhānḍā phōṛnā** بھانڈا پھوڑنا
price, rate, value *n.m.* **bhā'ō** بھاؤ
sister-in-law (*elder brother's wife*) *n.f.* **bhāvaj** بھاوج
brother, comrade, companion *n.m.* **bhā'ī** بھائی
brotherhood, fraternity *n.f.* **bhā'ī cārā** بھائی چارا
bring to a boil; provoke, enrage *v.t.* **bhabkānā** بھبکانا
boil, bubble, fume, be angry *v.i.* **bhabaknā** بھبکنا
threat, menace *n.f.* **bhabkī** بھبکی
demon, ghost *n.m.* **bhutnā** بھتنا
allowance (*for food*) *n.m.* **bhattah** بھتہ
nephew (*brother's son*) *n.m.* **bhatījā** بھتیجا
niece (*brother's daughter*) *n.f.* **bhatījī** بھتیجی
come in, enter *v.i.* **bhītar ānā** بھیتر آنا
corn, maize *n.m.* **bhuṭṭā** بھٹا
mislead, deceive *v.t.* **bhaṭkānā** بھٹکانا
stray, wander *v.i.* **bhaṭaknā** بھٹکنا
oven, fireplace *n.m.* **bhaṭṭhah** بھٹہ
with the current, down the river *adj.* **bhaṭyāl** بھٹیال
pleasure *n.f.* **bhajat** بھجت

hymn; worship *n.m.* **bhajan** بھجن
worship, say prayers *v.t.* **bhajan karnā** بھجن کرنا
be parched, be scorched *v.i.* **bhujnā** بھجنا
clumsy, awkward; stupid *adj.* **bhaddā** بھدا
good, happy, prosperous, lucky *adj.* **bhadar** بھدر
as much as, up to *adj.* **bhar** بھر
full, overflowing *adj.* **bharā** بھرا
crackling, crispy *adj.* **bhurburā** بھربھرا
stock, accumulation, stuffing, filling *n.f.* **bhartī** بھرتی
load, fill; recruit, enroll *v.t.* **bhartī karnā** بھرتی کرنا
suspicion, doubt, perplexity *n.m.* **bharam** بھرم
suspect *v.t.* **bharam karnā** بھرم کرنا
deceive, mislead *v.t.* **bharmānā** بھرمانا
suspicious *adj.* **bharmī** بھرمی
be filled, be full *v.i.* / fill, load *v.t.* **bharnā** بھرنا
hope, reliance, assurance, confidence, faith, belief *n.m.* **bharōsah** بھروسہ
give hope, reassure *v.t.* **bharōsah dēnā** بھروسہ دینا
wasp, hornet *n.f.* **bhiṛ** بھڑ
join, close, bring together *v.t.* **bhiṛānā** بھڑانا
joined, close, adjacent *adj.* **bhiṛā hū'ā** بھڑا ہوا
splendor, flash, blaze, show *n.f.* **bhaṛak** بھڑک
frighten, kindle, induce, incite, inflame *v.t.* **bhaṛkānā** بھڑکانا
break out, burst into flame, be very excited, be overheated *v.i.* **bhaṛaknā** بھڑکنا
come together, join *v.i.* **bhiṛnā** بھڑنا
flabby, loose *adj.* **bhus bhusā** بھس بھسا
eat up, devour *v.t.* **bhasaknā** بھسکنا
ashes *n.f.* **bhasm** بھسم
reduce to ashes, burn *v.t.* **bhasm karnā** بھسم کرنا
be reduced to ashes, be consumed entirely *v.i.* **bhasm hōnā** بھسم ہونا
beggar *n.m.* **bhikārī** بھکاری
deception, intimidation, misleading, delusion *n.m.* **bhakāvā** بھکاوا
stupid, foolish *adj.* **bhakvā** بھکوا
wet, soak *v.t.* **bhigānā** • drive off, chase away, defeat *v.t.* **bhagānā** بھگانا
devotee, pious man *n.m.* **bhagat** بھگت
act, mimic *v.t.* **bhagat khēlnā** بھگت کھیلنا
perform, dispose, complete, settle, adjust *v.t.* **bhugtānā** بھگتانا

بھگتائی devotion, religiousness *n.f.* **bhagtā'ī**
بھگتنا experience, suffer, bear *v.t.* **bhugatnā**
بھگوان God, supreme being *n.m.* **bhagvān**
بھگوڑا runaway, fugitive *n.m.* **bhigōṛā**
بھگونا wet, soak *v.t.* **bhigōnā**
بھلا well, good, healthy; wonderful; auspicious *adj.* **bhalā**
بھلانا cause to forget, try to forget, mislead *v.t.* **bhulānā**
بھلاوا deception, fraud, cheating *n.m.* **bhulāvā**
بھلائی goodness, excellence; welfare, prosperity, benefit *n.f.* **bhalā'ī**
بھلائی کرنا show kindness, do good *v.t.* **bhalā'ī karnā**
بھلکڑ forgetful, oblivious *adj.* **bhulakkaṛ**
بھنانا fry; boil; parch *v.t.* **bhunānā**
بھنبوڑنا gnaw, bite, devour *v.i.* **bhanbōṛnā**
بھنڈار storehouse, warehouse *n.m.* **bhanḍār**
بھنڈاری steward, storekeeper *n.m.* **bhanḍārī**
بھنڈی okra, lady's fingers, gumbo *n.f.* **bhinḍī**
بھنک hum *n.f.* **bhanak**
بھنگ hemp *n.f.* **bhang**
بھنگڑ hemp-addict; talkative person *n.m.* **bhangaṛ**
بھننا be fried; be boiled *v.i.* **bhunnā**
بھنوانا parch; fry; boil *v.t.*. **bhunvānā**
بھنور whirlpool; misfortune, grief *n.m.* **bhanvar**
بھنورا black bee *n.m.* **bhanvrā**
بھوبھل embers *n.m.* **bhūbhal**
بھوت demon, ghost, evil spirit *n.m.* **bhūt**
بھوت اتارنا exorcise *v.t.* **bhūt utārnā**
بھوت پریت ghosts *n.m.* **bhūt parēt**
بھوج eating; enjoying; feast, banquet *n.m.* **bhōj**
بھوجن food, meal, eating; enjoying *n.m.* **bhōjan**
بھوجی elder brother's wife *n.f.* **bhaujī**
بھور day-break, dawn, early morning *n.f.* **bhōr**
بھورا brown *adj.* **bhūrā**
بھوسی chaff, bran *n.f.* **bhūsī**
بھوک hunger, appetite *n.f.* **bhūk**
بھوک لگنا feel hungry *v.i.* **bhūk lagnā**
بھوکوں مرنا starve, die of hunger *v.i.* **bhūkōṁ marnā**

forgetfulness, negligence; mistake, fault, lapse *n.f.* **bhūl** بھول
labyrinth, puzzle, intricacies *n.f.* **bhūl bulaiyāṁ** بھول بھلیاں
simple; innocent, inexperienced *adj.* **bhōlā** بھولا
simplicity; innocence, inexperience *n.m.* **bhōlāpan** بھولاپن
forget, stray, miss, err *v.t.* **bhūlnā** بھولنا
land, country; earth, world; ground, site, place *n.f.* **bhūm** بھوم
earthquake *n.m.* **bhauncāl** بھونچال
astonished, amazed, aghast *adj.* **bhauncakkā** بھونچکا
silly, stupid *adj.* **bhōndū** بھوندو
bark; talk stupidly *v.i.* **bhaunknā** بھونکنا
thrust, drive in, pierce, stab *v.t.* **bhōnknā** بھونکنا
fry; parch; roast; burn; torment *v.t.* **bhūnnā** بھوننا
also, too, even, moreover, as well *adv.* **bhī** بھی
brother *n.m.* **bhayā** بھیا
fearful, frightful *adj.* **bhayānak** بھیانک
inward, internal *adj.* **bhītarī** بھیتری
meeting, visit; interview *n.f.* **bhēṭ** بھیٹ
sacrifice, offer *v.t.* **bhēṭ dēnā** بھیٹ دینا
meet, visit, come into contact *v.i.* **bhīṭnā** بھیٹنا
wet, damp *adj.* **bhījā** • brain *n.m.* **bhējā** بھیجا
send, dispatch *v.t.* **bhējnā** بھیجنا
secret, mystery *n.m.* **bhēd** بھید
find out a secret, solve a mystery *v.t.* **bhēd pānā** بھید پانا
give a clue *v.t.* **bhēd dēnā** بھید دینا
spy, quest for a secret *v.t.* **bhēd lēnā** بھید لینا
sheep *n.m.* **bhēṛ** • crowd, multitude; difficulty *n.m.* **bhīṛ** بھیڑ
crowd, bustle, mob *n.f.* **bhīṛ bhāṛ** بھیڑ بھاڑ
ram *n.m.* **bhēṛā** بھیڑا
shut, close, lock up *v.t.* **bhēṛnā** بھیڑنا
sheep *n.f.* **bhēṛī** بھیڑی
wolf *n.m.* **bhēṛiyā** بھیڑیا
appearance, resemblance, guise *n.m.* **bhēs** بھیس
disguise, change one's appearance *v.t.* **bhēs badalnā** بھیس بدلنا
charity, alms; begging *n.f.* **bhēkh** بھیک
beg *v.t.* **bhīkh māngnā** بھیک مانگنا
interview *n.f.* **bhēnṭ** بھینٹ

buffalo (*female*) *n.f.* **bhaiṁs** بھینس
buffalo (*male*) *n.m.* **bhaiṁsā** بھینسا
horrible, terrible *adj.* **bhayankar** بھینکر
squint-eyed *adj.* **bhēnkā** بھینگا
be wet, be damp *v.i.* **bhīnknā** بھینگنا

پ pē

پا **pā** leg; foot *n.m.*
پابند **pāband** bound, fettered *adj.*
پابند ہونا **pāband hōnā** be bound; conform to; observe *v.i.*
پابندی **pābandī** restraint, restriction, control *n.f.*
پابوسی **pābōsī** worship, adoration *n.f.*
پابوسی کرنا **pābōsī karnā** worship, adore *v.t.*
پاپ **pāp** sin, fault, crime, vice, guilt *n.m.*
پاپ کرنا **pāp karnā** commit a sin/crime *v.t.*
پاپا **pāpā** daddy, father; Pope *n.m.*
پاپڑ **pāpaṛ** papadum (*thin crispy bread made of pulse*) *n.m.*
پاپن **pāpan** wicked woman, criminal woman *n.f.*
پاپوش **pāpōš** slipper, shoe *n.f.*
پاپی **pāpī** sinner, criminal *n.f.*
پات **pāt** leaf *n.m.*
پاتال **pātāl** hell, abyss *n.m.*
پاٹنا **pāṭnā** roof, cover; fill up, irrigate *v.t.*
پاجامہ **pājāmah** loose cotton pants *n.m.*
پاجی **pājī** mean, low, base, vile, wicked *adj.*
پاجی پن **pājīpan** meanness, wickedness *n.m.*
پاداش **pādāš** reward, recompense *n.m.*
پادری **pādrī** clergyman, priest (*Catholic*) *n.m.*
پار **pār** opposite bank, opposite shore, other side; end *n.m.* / over, across, through *pp.*
پار کرنا **pār karnā** cross, ferry over; finish *v.t.*
پارا **pārā** mercury, quicksilver *n.m.*
پارچہ **pārcah** piece of cloth, clothing, dress *n.m.*
پارچہ دوز **pārcāh dōz** tailor, dressmaker *n.m.*
پارسا **pārsā** chaste, abstinent; holy, virtuous *adj.*
پارسال **pārsāl** last year *n.m./adv.*
پارسائی **pārsā'ī** chastity, abstinence, purity, holiness, virtue *n.f.*
پارسل **pārsal** parcel *n.m.*
پارسی **pārsī** Persian, Zoroastrian *n.m./adj.*
پارک **pārk** park *n.m.*

piece, bit, scrap, slice *n.m.* **pārah** پارہ
cause to fall, let fall *v.t.* **pāṛnā** پاڑنا
/ near, about, at, close, in the possession of *adv./pp.* **pās** پاس
custody; observance, consideration, watching, regard *n.m.*
come near to, reach *v.i.* **pās ānā** پاس آنا
sit near; get trained *v.i.* **pās baiṭhnā** پاس بیٹھنا
approximately, near, round about *adv.* **pās pās** پاس پاس
in consideration *adv.* **pās-ē-xātir** پاس خاطر
dice *n.m.* **pāsā** پاسا
throw dice *v.t.* **pāsā phēnknā** پاسا پھینکنا
gamble with dice *v.t.* **pāsā khēlnā** پاسا کھیلنا
watchman, guard *n.m.* **pāsbān** پاسبان
guarding, protection *n.f.* **pāsbānī** پاسبانی
passport *n.m.* **pāspōrṭ** پاسپورٹ
passport number *n.m.* **pāspōrṭ nambar** پاسپورٹ نمبر
old, ancient; past *adj.* **pāstān** پاستان
balance; small portion *n.m.* **pāsang** پاسنگ
broken to pieces, shattered *adj.* **pāš pāš** پاش پاش
pasha (*governor/nobleman*) *n.m.* **pāšā** پاشا
pure, clean, upright, holy, innocent, chaste *adj.* **pāk** پاک
pure, clean, unpolluted *adj.* **pāk sāf** پاک صاف
beautiful, lovely *adj.* **pāk sūrat** پاک صورت
purify, clean *v.t.* **pāk karnā** پاک کرنا
pure intention, good faith *n.f.* **pāk niyyat** پاک نیت
undefiled, pure, chaste *adj.* **pākbāz** پاکباز
purity, chastity, sincerity *n.f.* **pākbāzī** پاکبازی
chaste, modest, innocent *adj.* **pākdāman** پاکدامن
chastity, modesty, innocence *n.f.* **pākdāmnī** پاکدامنی
Pakistan *n.m.* **Pākistān** پاکستان
Pakistani *adj.* **Pākistānī** پاکستانی
deceit, wickedness, hypocrisy *n.m.* **pākhanḍ** پاکھنڈ
deceitful, hypocritical *adj.* **pākhanḍī** پاکھنڈی
cleanliness, purity *n.f.* **pākī** پاکی

پاکیزگی chasteness; neatness *n.f.* **pākīzagī**
پاکیزہ neat, clean, pure, chaste *adj.* **pākīzah**
پاگل mad, insane, crazy, foolish *adj.* / fool idiot, half-wit *n.m.* **pāgal**
پاگل خانہ lunatic asylum, madhouse *n.m.* **pāgal xānah**
پاگل ہونا be mad, go mad *v.i.* **pāgal hōnā**
پال dam, embankment *n.f.* **pāl**
پالا frost *n.m.* **pālā**
پالتو domestic (*for an animal*) *adj.* **pāltū**
پالغز slip, stumble, error *n.m.* **pālaġz**
پالک spinach *n.m.* **pālak**
پالکی sedan, palanquin *n.f.* **pālkī**
پالن bringing up, nourishing, breeding *n.m.* **pālan**
پالنا bring up, nourish, breed, protect, foster *v.t.* **pālnā**
پامال destroyed, ruined *adj.* **pāmāl**
پامالی destruction, ruin, devastation *n.f.* **pāmālī**
پامردی strength, resolution *n.f.* **pāmardī**
پان betel-leaf *n.m.* **pān**
پان لگانا prepare betel-leaf *v.i.* **pān lagānā**
پان والا betel-seller *n.m.* **pān vālā**
پانا get, obtain, find *v.t.* **pānā**
پانچ five *num.* **pāṁc**
پانچواں fifth *adj.* **pāṁcvāṁ**
پانچوں all five (*fingers etc.*) *adj.* **pāṁcōṁ**
پانڈے scholar, teacher, principle, schoolmaster *n.m.* **pāṇḍē**
پانی water; lustre, polish; modesty *n.m.* **pānī**
پانی آنا rain; be cloudy *v.i.* **pānī ānā**
پانی برسنا rain *v.i.* **pānī barasnā**
پانی بھرنا draw water; be humiliated, be ashamed *v.i.* **pānī bharnā**
پانی دینا water, irrigate *v.t.* **pānī dēnā**
پانی نکلنا ooze, leak *v.t.* **pānī nikalnā**
پاؤ quarter, fourth part *n.m.* **pā'ō**
پاؤں foot; leg; root, basis *n.m.* **pā'ōṁ**
پاؤں بھاری ہونا be pregnant *v.i.* **pā'ōṁ bhārī hōnā**
پاؤں پاؤں on foot *adj.* **pā'ōṁ pā'ōṁ**
پاؤں پسارنا stretch your legs; die *v.t.* **pā'ōṁ pasārnā**
پاؤں چومنا kiss one's feet, worship, honor (somebody) *v.t.* **pā'ōṁ cūmnā**

set foot, step in, enter *v.t.* **pā'ōṁ dharnā** پاؤں دھرنا
pound sterling *n.m.* **pā'ūnḍ** پاؤنڈ
extremity; conclusion, end *n.m.* **pāyāṁ** پایاں
leg; foot; foundation, support *n.m.* **pāyah** پایہ
foot; leg; foundation *n.m.* **pā'ē** پائے
coin *n.f.* **pā'ī** پائی
durable, steady, permanent *adj.* **pā'ēdār** پائیدار
stability, durability *n.f.* **pā'ēdārī** پائیداری
lower, beneath, under *adj./pp.* **pā'īṁ** پائیں
crust *n.m.* **papṛā** پپڑا
crust, incrustation *n.f.* **papṛī** پپڑی
eyelash *n.f.* **papnī** پپنی
eyelid *n.m.* **papōṭā** پپوٹا
papaya, papaya tree *n.m.* **papītā** پپیتا
good name, honor, reputation *n.f.* / leaf *n.m.* **pat** پت
disgrace *v.t.* **pat utārnā** پت اتارنا
autumn, fall *n.m.* **pat jhaṛ** پت جھڑ
• gallbladder; anger *n.m.* **pittā** • sign, symptom; address *n.m.* **patā** پتا
father *n.m.* **pitā**
leaf; card; banner, symbol *n.m.* **pattā** پتا
direct, point *v.t.* **patā dēnā** پتا دینا
dismiss, dispose, discharge *v.t.* **pattā kāṭnā** پتا کاٹنا
harass, annoy *v.t.* **pittā nikālnā** پتا نکالنا
leaf; letter *n.m.* **patr/pattar** پتر
letter, note *n.f.* **patrī** پتری
puppet, doll *n.m.* **putlā** • delicate, feeble, fine, lean, thin, narrow *adj.* **patlā** پتلا
pants, trousers *n.m.* **patlūn** پتلون
pupil (*of the eye*); small puppet, small doll *n.f.* **putlī** پتلی
kite *n.m.* **patang** پتنگ
fly a kite *v.t.* **patang uṛānā** پتنگ اڑانا
flying insect, moth; spark (*of fire*) *n.m.* **patangā** پتنگا
wife *n.f.* **patnī** پتنی
sign, symptom; address *n.m.* **patah** پتہ
leaf; share *n.f.* **pattī** پتی
pot, pan *n.m.* **patīlā** پتیلا
small pot, small pan, small kettle *n.f.* **patīlī** پتیلی

path, way, road, course *n.m.* **path** پتھ
stone, rock *n.m.* **patthar** پتھر
hail *v.i.* **patthar barasnā** پتھر برسنا
grit, gravel *n.f.* **pathrī** پتھری
stony, rocky, gritty *adj.* **patthrīlā** پتھریلا
large basket *n.m.* **piṭārā** پٹارا
small basket *n.f.* **piṭārī** پٹاری
crash; explosion *n.m.* **paṭāk** پٹاک
plank; bank (*of a canal or road*) *n.f.* **paṭṛī** پٹڑی
throw (on the ground), knock down, dash *v.t.* **paṭaknā** پٹکنا
bandage *n.f.* **paṭṭī** پٹی
dress, put a bandage on; blindfold *v.t.* **paṭṭī bāndhnā** پٹی باندھنا
seasoning, sprinkling; excitement *n.f.* **puṭh** پٹھ
comrade, follower, supporter *n.m.* **piṭhū** پٹھو
worshipper; priest (Hindu) *n.m.* **pujārī** پجاری
fifty *num.* **pacās** پچاس
eighty-five *num.* **pacāsī** پچاسی
digest; assimilate *v.t.* **pacānā** پچانا
ninety-five *num.* **pacānavē** پچانوے
watery, moist; soft, flabby *adj.* **pacpacā** پچپچا
fifty-five *num.* **pacpan** پچپن
regret, repent *v.t.* **pactānā** پچتانا
regret, repentance *n.m.* **pactāvā** پچتاوا
syringe, squirt *n.f.* **pickārī** پچکاری
be digested; be absorbed *v.i.* **pacnā** پچنا
mosaic (work) *n.f.* **pacī kārī** پچی کاری
twenty-five *num.* **paccīs** پچیس
dash down; overpower, overcome *v.t.* **pachāṛnā** پچھاڑنا
regret, repent *v.t.* **pachtānā** پچھتانا
seventy-five *num.* **pachattar** پچھتر
last, late; back; previous *adj.* **pichlā** پچھلا
last year *adv.* **pichlē sāl** پچھلے سال
west *n.m.* **pachham/pacchim** پچھم
ripeness, maturity; strength *n.f.* **puxtagī** پختگی
ripe, matured; wise; solid *adj.* **puxtah** پختہ
father *n.m.* **pidar/padar** پدر

پدرانہ paternal *adj.* **pidrānah**

پدری patrimonial, fatherly *adj.* **pidarī**

پدم lotus flower; a thousand billions *n.m.* **padam**

پذیر able, admitting, accepting, receiving *adj.* **pazīr**

پذیرائی acceptance, reception *n.f.* **pazīrā'ī**

پر • on, upon, above *pp.* / but still, however *conj.* / feather, wing *n.m.* **par**

پر full, complete *adj.* **pur**

پراٹھا paratha (*type of filled bread*) *n.m.* **parāṭhā**

پراگندہ scattered, dispersed; disturbed *adj.* **parāgandah**

پرانا old, ancient *adj.* **purānā**

پربت mountain, hill *n.m.* **parbat**

پرت layer; fold, ply *n.m.* **parat**

پرچانا tame *v.t.* **parcānā**

پرچم flag, banner; ensign (*military*) *n.m.* **parcam**

پرچہ slip, piece (*of paper*) *n.m.* **parcah**

پرچھائیں shadow, shade; reflection *n.f.* **parchā'īṁ**

پرخاش battle, war, conflict *n.m.* **parxāš**

پردادا great grandfather (*paternal*) *n.m.* **pardādā**

پردادی great grandmother (*paternal*) *n.f.* **pardādī**

پردازی completion; performance *n.f.* **pardāzī**

پردہ curtain *n.m.* **pardah**

پردہ کرنا conceal, hide oneself *v.t.* **pardah karnā**

پردیس foreign country *n.m.* **pardēs**

پردیسن stranger, foreigner *n.f.* **pardēsan**

پردیسی stranger, foreigner *n.m.* / foreign *adj.* **pardēsī**

پرزہ bit, piece, scrap (*of paper*) *n.m.* **purzah**

پرس asking, questioning, enquiry *n.f.* **purs** • purse *n.m.* **pars**

پرست worshipping, devoted *adj.* **parast**

پرستار worshipper *n.m.* **parastār**

پرستاری worship, service *n.f.* **parastārī**

پرستان fairyland *n.m.* **paristān**

پرستش worship, devotion *n.f.* **parastiš**

پرستش کرنا worship *v.t.* **parastiš karnā**

پرسش asking, questioning, enquiry *n.f.* **pursiš**

پرسوں the day before yesterday; the day after tomorrow *n.m.* **parsōṁ**

پرکھ inspection, test, trial, examination *n.f.* **parakh**

light *n.m.* **prakāš** پرکاش
spark *n.m.* **parkālah** پرکالہ
inspect, test, try, examine *v.t.* **parakhnā** پرکھنا
subdivision (*of a district*) *n.m.* **parganah** پرگنہ
extreme; next in order *adj.* **parlā** پرلا
drain, gutter, outlet (*of water*) *n.m.* **parnālah** پرنالہ
drain (*small*), gutter (*small*) *n.f.* **parnālī** پرنالی
great grandfather (*maternal*) *n.m.* **parnānā** پرنانا
great grandmother (*maternal*) *n.f.* **parnānī** پرنانی
bird *n.m.* **parind** پرند
bird *n.m.* **parindah** پرندہ
abstinence, forbearance *n.m.* **parhēz** پرہیز
abstain (from), avoid *v.t.* **parhēz karnā** پرہیز کرنا
care, concern, anxiety *n.f.* **parvā** پروا
flying, flight *n.f.* **parvāz** پرواز
true, just *adj.* **parvān** پروان
permission, order *n.f.* **parvānagī** پروانگی
warrant, licence; butterfly *n.m.* **parvānah** پروانہ
patron, nourisher, protector *n.m.* **parvar** پرور
brought up, fostered, nourished *adj.* **pirvardah** پروردہ
support, fostering, nourishment *n.f.* **parvariš** پرورش
bring up, support, nourish *v.t.* **parvariš karnā** پرورش کرنا
program *n.m.* **prōgrām** پروگرام
thread (*a needle*); string (*pearls*) *v.t.* **pirōnā** پرونا
beyond, further, at a distance *adv.* **parē** پرے
remain aside, keep a distance *v.i.* **parē rahnā** پرے رہنا
love, affection *n.f.* **prīt** پریت
beloved *adj.* **prītam** پریتم
troubled, worried, distressed, confused *adj.* **parēšān** پریشان
trouble, worry, distress, confusion *n.f.* **parēšānī** پریشانی
love, affection *n.m.* **prēm** پریم
fall, lie (down); happen *v.i.* **paṛnā** پڑنا
neighborhood, vicinity *n.m.* **paṛōs** پڑوس
neighbor *n.f.* **paṛōsan** پڑوسن
neighbor *n.m.* **paṛōsī** پڑوسی
educated *adj.* **paṛhā** پڑھا

teach, educate, instruct *v.t.* **paṛhānā** پڑھانا
teaching, education, instruction *n.f.* **paṛhā'ī** پڑھائی
read; learn, study *v.t.* **paṛhnā** پڑھنا
after, behind; then, therefore, hence, consequently *adv.* **pas** پس
remaining, left behind *adj.* **pas māndah** پس ماندہ
survivor *n.m.* **pas māndah** پس ماندہ
spread, stretch out, extend, expand *v.t.* **pasārnā** پسارنا
drive back *v.t.* **paspā karnā** پسپا کرنا
retreat *v.i.* **paspā hōnā** پسپا ہونا
defeat, retreat *n.f.* **paspā'ī** پسپائی
low, below; humble; mean *adj.* **past** پست
breast *n.f.* **pistān** پستان
pistachio *n.m.* **pistah** پستہ
lowness, inferiority; humility *n.m.* **pastī** پستی
son; boy; child *n.m.* **pisar** پسر
rib *n.f.* **paslī** پسلی
liked, chosen, preferred *adj.* / choice, liking, preference *n.f.* **pasand** پسند
like, choose, prefer *v.t.* **pasand karnā** پسند کرنا
liked, chosen, preferred *adj.* **pasandīdah** پسندیدہ
flea *n.m.* **pissū** پسو
sweat *n.m.* **pasīnah** پسینہ
sweat *v.i.* **pasīnah ānā** پسینہ آنا
back, support *n.f.* **pušt** پشت
bank, dyke *n.m.* **puštah** پشتہ
alliance *n.f.* **puštī** پشتی
wool, fur, hair *n.f.* **pašm** پشم
pashmina (*woolen shawl*) *n.m.* **pašmīnah** پشمینہ
beast, animal, cattle *n.m.* **pašū** پشو
repentant, penitent, sorrowful *adj.* **pašēmān** پشیمان
repent, regret *v.i.* **pašēmān hōnā** پشیمان ہونا
repentance, penitence *n.f.* **pašēmānī** پشیمانی
cooked, baked; ripe, mature *adj.* **pakkā** پکا
call, cry, shout *n.f.* **pukār** پکار
call, cry, shout *v.i.* **pukārnā** پکارنا
cook, bake; ripen *v.t.* **pakānā** پکانا
topaz *n.m.* **pukhrāj** پکھراج

hold, seizure, capture *n.f.* **pakaṛ** پکڑ

catch, arrest, hold, seize, capture *v.t.* **pakaṛnā** پکڑنا

ripen; be cooked, cook, boil *v.i.* **paknā** پکنا

pastry; fried food *n.m.* **pakvān** پکوان

pakora (*fried gram flour paste mixed with vegetables*) *n.m.* **pakōṛā** پکوڑا

foot *n.m.* **pag** پگ

footpath *n.f.* **pag ḍanḍī** پگ ڈنڈی

turban *n.f.* **pagṛī** پگڑی

disgrace, dishonor *v.t.* **pagṛī utārnā** پگڑی اتارنا

foolish, mad, crazy *adj.* **paglā** پگلا

moment, second *n.m.* **pal** • bridge *n.m.* **pul** پل

puppy, whelp *n.m.* **pillā** پلا

pulao (*dish of rice, meat, and spices*) *n.m.* **pulā'ō** پلاؤ

pepper *n.m.* **pilpil** پلپل

soft, flabby *adj.* **pilpilā** پلپلا

softness, flabbiness *n.f.* **pilpilāhaṭ** پلپلاہٹ

turn, turning; retreat; exchange *n.m.* **palṭā** پلٹا

eyelash; twinkling of an eye (*i.e. a moment*) *n.f.* **palak** پلک

bundle, parcel, package *n.m.* **pulandā** پلندا

bed, bedstead *n.m.* **palang** پلنگ

bed-cover *n.m.* **palang pōš** پلنگ پوش

ladle *n.f.* **palī** پلی

plate *n.f.* **plēṭ** پلیٹ

impure, unclean, polluted *adj.* **palīd** پلید

virtue, charity *n.m.* **pan** پن

water-mill *n.f.* **pan cakkī** پن چکی

shelter, refuge, protection *n.f.* **panāh** پناہ

give shelter, give protection *v.t.* **panāh dēnā** پناہ دینا

refugee *n.m.* **panāh gīr** پناہ گیر

religious division, sect; path, road, way *n.m.* **panth** پنتھ

Punjab *n.m.* **paṁjāb** پنجاب

Punjabi *adj.* **paṁjābī** پنجابی

rib; skeleton *n.m.* **paṁjar/piṁjar** پنجر

cage, trap *n.m.* **piṁjrā** پنجرا

claw; the five of *n.m.* **paṁjah** پنجہ

claw, pounce upon *v.t.* **paṁjah mārnā** پنجہ مارنا

pentangular (*having five angles*) *adj.* **paṁj gōšah** پنج گوشہ
meeting, council; court (*of arbitration*); jury *n.f.* **paṁcāyat** پنچایت
fifth *adj.* **paṁcam** پنچم
bird *n.m.* **paṁchī** پنچھی
advice, council *n.m.* **pand** پند
fifteen *num.* **pandrah** پندرہ
fifteenth *adj.* **pandrahvāṁ** پندرھواں
body; person; lump, ball (*of food*); village *n.m.* **piṇḍ** پنڈ
learned man, guru, teacher, Brahman *n.m.* **panḍit** پنڈت
calf (*of the leg*), leg, shin *n.f.* **piṇḍlī** پنڈلی
grocer; druggist *n.m.* **pansārī** پنساری
pencil *n.f.* **pansil** پنسل
wing; feather *n.m.* **pankh** پنکھ
fan, ventilator *n.m.* **pankhā** پنکھا
leaf (*of a flower*), petal *n.f.* **pankhṛī** پنکھڑی
cradle *n.m.* **pinghūṛā** پنگھوڑا
concealed, hidden, secret *adj.* **pinhāṁ** پنہاں
cheese *n.m.* **panīr** پنیر
mountain, hill, rock; difficult task, complicated problem *n.m.* **pahāṛ** پہاڑ
hike; climb a mountain *v.i.* **pahāṛōṁ par caṛhnā** پہاڑوں پر چڑھنا
mountaineer *n.m.* / hill, small mountain *n.f.* **pahāṛī** پہاڑی
mountain range *n.m.* **pahāṛī silsilah** پہاڑی سلسلہ
acquaintance, knowledge *n.f.* **pahcān** پہچان
watch; time; season *n.m.* **pahrā** پہرا
keep a watch *v.t.* **pahrā dēnā** پہرا دینا
put on clothes, wear *v.t.* **paharnā** پہرنا
flock (of cotton); beginning *n.m.* **pahal** پہل
begin *v.t.* **pahal karnā** پہل کرنا
first *adj.* **pahlā** پہلا
first class *n.m.* **pahlā darjah** پہلا درجہ
first name, Christian name *n.m.* **pahlā nām** پہلا نام
side, flank, wing *n.m.* **pahlū** پہلو
save oneself; keep aloof *v.t.* **pahlū bacānā** پہلو بچانا
athlete; wrestler; champion, hero *n.m.* **pahlvān** پہلوان
athleticism; wrestling; heroism *n.f.* **pahlvānī** پہلوانی
at first, first, in the first place, sooner, before *adv.* **pahlē** پہلے

at first, first of all *adv.* **pahlē pahal** پہلے پہل
cause to put on, dress *v.t.* **pahnānā** پہنانا
dress, clothing, garment *n.m.* **pahnāvā** پہناوا
arrival *n.f.* **pahuṁc** پہنچ
wrist, forearm *n.m.* **pahuṁcā** پہنچا
cause to arrive, transit, convey, conduct, accompany *v.t.* **pahuṁcānā** پہنچانا
arrive, reach *v.i.* **pahuṁcnā** پہنچنا
wear, dress, put on *v.t.* **pahannā** پہننا
enigma, riddle *n.f.* **pahēlī** پہیلی
toothless *adj.* **pōplā** پوپلا
son *n.m.* **pūt** پوت
grandson *n.m.* **pōtā** پوتا
book; clove of garlic *n.f.* **pōthī** پوتھی
worship, prayer *n.f.* **pūjā** پوجا
ask, inquire, question *v.t.* **pūchnā** پوچھنا
(young) plant *n.m.* **paudā** پودا
plant *v.t.* **paudā lagānā** پودا لگانا
mint *n.m.* **pōdīnah** پودینہ
peppermint *n.m.* **pōdīnah kā sat** پودینہ کا ست
full, whole, complete, entire *adj.* **pūrā** پورا
fill up, complete *v.t.* **pūrā karnā** پورا کرنا
east *n.m.* **pūrab** پورب
firm, strong, hard, stiff *adj.* **pōṛhā** پوڑھا
lie down, rest *v.i.* **pauṛhnā** پوڑھنا
crust, shell, skin, rind; layer; poppy *n.m.* **pōst** پوست
addicted (to opium) *adj.* **pōstī** پوستی
garment or coat made of fur or leather *n.f.* **pōstīn** پوستین
postcard *n.m.* **pōsṭ kārḍ** پوسٹ کارڈ
nourish, tame, rear *v.t.* **pōsnā** پوسنا
covering, dressed in *adj.* **pōš** پوش
dress, garment, clothes *n.f.* **pōšāk** پوشاک
dress, garments, clothes *n.f.* **pōšiš** پوشش
concealment, secrecy *n.f.* **pōšīdagī** پوشیدگی
concealed, hidden, covered *adj.* **pōšīdah** پوشیدہ
soft, hollow, spongy *adj.* **pūlā** پولا
police *n.m.* **pōlīs** پولیس

پولیس چوکی police post *n.f.* **pōlīs caukī**
پون air, wind *n.f.* **pavan** • three-quarters *adj.* **paun**
پونجی capital, funds, wealth; sum *n.f.* **pūṁjī**
پونچھ tail *n.f.* **pūṁch**
پونچھنا wipe, rub, dust *v.t.* **pōṁchnā**
پونگی flute, pipe *n.f.* **pōngī**
پے foot, footstep; mark, pursuit *n.m.* **pai**
پی husband, lover, darling, sweetheart *n.m./n.f.* **pī**
پی جانا drink, absorb *v.i.* **pī jānā**
پیا husband, sweetheart, lover *n.m.* **piyā**
پیار love, affection *n.m.* **piyār**
پیار کرنا love, caress *v.t.* **piyār karnā**
پیارا beloved, dear, loving *adj.* **piyārā**
پیاری beloved, pleasant *adj.* **piyārī**
پیاز onion *n.f.* **piyāz**
پیاس thirst *n.f.* **piyās**
پیاس لگنا be thirsty *v.i.* **piyās lagnā**
پیاسا thirsty *adj.* **piyāsā**
پیال straw, dried grass *n.f.* **payāl**
پیالہ cup, bowl *n.m.* **piyālah**
پیالی (small) cup, tea-glass *n.f.* **piyālī**
پیام message, news, intelligence *n.m.* **payām**
پیامبر messenger, prophet *n.m.* **payāmbar**
پیانا cause to drink; water, irrigate *v.t.* **piyānā**
پیپ pus; matter *n.m.* **pīp**
پیپا cask, barrel, butt *n.m.* **pīpā**
پیت love, affection *n.f.* **pīt**
پیتل brass, bronze *n.m.* **pītal**
پیتم husband, lover, sweetheart, most beloved *n.m.* **pītam**
پیٹ belly, stomach, womb, paunch; pregnancy; hunger *n.m.* **pēṭ**
پیٹ بجانا feel happy *v.t.* **pēṭ bajānā**
پیٹ بھر bellyful, full, satisfied (*with food*) *adj.* **pēṭ bhar**
پیٹ بھرنا fill one's belly, be satisfied *v.i.* **pēṭ bharnā**
پیٹ پالنا contrive, live decently *v.t.* **pēṭ pālnā**
پیٹ جلنا be very hungry *v.i.* **pēṭ jalnā**
پیٹ سے pregnant *adj.* **pēṭ sē**

starve one's self *v.t.* **pēṭ kāṭnā** پیٹ کاٹنا

hunger; maternal affection *n.f.* **pēṭ kī āg** پیٹ کی آگ

miscarry, abort *v.i.* **pēṭ girnā** پیٹ گرنا

pregnant *adj.* **pēṭ vālī** پیٹ والی

gas, petrol *n.m.* **paiṭrōl** پیٹرول

gas station, petrol station *n.m.* **paiṭrōl pamp** پیٹرول پمپ

back, the loins; back part; support *n.f.* **pīṭh** پیٹھ

support, aid *v.i.* **pīṭh par hōnā** پیٹھ پر ہونا

backbite *v.t.* **pīṭh pīchē kahnā** پیٹھ پیچھے کہنا

turn back, withdraw *v.t.* **pīṭh phērnā** پیٹھ پھیرنا

turn tail, run away *v.t.* **pīṭh dikhānā** پیٹھ دکھانا

gourd (*sweet*) *n.m.* **pēṭhā** پیٹھا

perplexity, deceit, trouble, complication, twist *n.f.* **pēc** پیچ

become difficult, become intricate, be entangled *v.i.* **pēc paṛnā** پیچ پڑنا

twisted, coiled, spiral, winding, intricate *adj.* **pēc dār** پیچ دار

twist, deceive *v.t.* **pēc dēnā** پیچ دینا

restlessness, distress, perplexity, agitation *n.m.* **pēc-ō-tāb** پیچ وتاب

be vexed, be distressed, be anxious *v.t.* **pēc-ō-tāb khānā** پیچ وتاب کھانا

colic pains, dysentery, diarrhea *n.f.* **pēciš** پیچش

twisting, winding, contortion *n.f.* **pēcīdgī** •پیچیدگی

twisted, coiled, complicated *adj.* **pēcīdah** •پیچیدہ

rear; pursuit, following; absence *n.m.* **pīchā** پیچھا

get rid of, get away from *v.t.* **pīchā chuṛānā** پیچھا چھڑانا

get rid of, be free *v.i.* **pīchā chūṭnā** پیچھا چھوٹنا

let alone, cease *v.t.* **pīchā chōṛnā** پیچھا چھوڑنا

follow, pursue *v.t.* **pīchā karnā** پیچھا کرنا

behind, in the rear, after, afterwards *adv.* **pīchē** پیچھے

persecute, torment *v.i.* **pīchē paṛnā** پیچھے پڑنا

behind, one after another, in succession *adv.* **pīchē pīchē** پیچھے پیچھے

surpass, leave behind *v.t.* **pīchē ḍālnā** پیچھے ڈالنا

keep back, fall back, lag behind *v.i.* **pīchē rahnā** پیچھے رہنا

filth; lavatory *n.m.* **paixānah** •پیخانہ

born, created, produced, invented *adj.* **paidā** پیدا

create, produce, invent, bring into existence *v.t.* **paidā karnā** پیدا کرنا

produce (*agricultural*); income, earning, profit *n.f.* **paidāvār** پیداوار

birth, creation; produce; earning, profit *n.f.* **paidā'iš** پیدائش

natural, innate, inborn, original *adj.* **paidā'išī** پیدائشی

on foot *adv.* / walking *adj.* / soldier (*infantry*) *n.m.* **paidal** پیدل

foot; footstep *n.m.* **pair** • Monday; priest, holy man *n.m.* **pīr** پیر

step, tread *v.t.* **pair dharnā** پیر دھرنا

footprint *n.m.* **pair kā nišān** پیر کا نشان

decorated, adorned *adj.* **pairāstah** پیراستہ

swimmer *n.m.* **pairāk** پیراک

swimming; swimmer *n.f.* **pairākī** پیراکی

cause to swim *v.t.* **pairānā** پیرانا

robe, vest, shirt (long) *n.m.* **pairāhan** پیراہن

press, crush, squeeze, grind *v.t.* **pērnā** پیرنا

swim, float *v.i.* **pairnā** پیرنا

follower, disciple *n.m.* **pairau** • turkey *n.m.* **pērū** پیرو

old age *n.f.* **pīrī** پیری

pain, suffering *n.f.* **pīṛ** • tree, plant, shrub *n.m.* **pēṛ** پیڑ

plant trees *v.t.* **pēṛ lagānā** پیڑ لگانا

(small) stool, seat; generation, genealogy, pedigree *n.f.* **pīṛhī** پیڑھی

generation after generation, from age to age *adv.* **pīṛhī dar pīṛhī** پیڑھی در پیڑھی

slipper, shoe *n.f.* **paizār** پیزار

look down upon, despair, condemn *v.i.* **paizār par marnā** پیزار پر مرنا

cut to bits, ruin, grind *v.t.* **pīs ḍālnā** پیس ڈالنا

coin; money, wealth *n.m.* **paisā** پیسا

spend money extravagantly *v.t.* **paisā uṛāna** پیسا اڑانا

sink money, invest money (*without return*) *v.t.* **paisā ḍabōnā** پیسا ڈبونا

take a bribe, waste money, embezzle *v.t.* **paisā khānā** پیسا کھانا

grind, bruise, powder; gnash (*teeth*) *v.t.* **pīsnā** پیسنا

money *n.m.* **paisē** پیسے

pay, give money *v.t.* **paisē dēnā** پیسے دینا

wealthy, rich *adj.* **paisē vālā** پیسے والا

before, in front of *adv.* / advanced, promoted *adj.* / front, fore-part *n.m.* **pēš** پیش

before this, formerly *adv.* **pēš azīṁ** پیش ازیں

come, come before, step forward; happen; behave *v.i.* **pēš ānā** پیش آنا

foresight, preparation (*in time*) *n.f.* **pēš bandī** پیش بندی

prudent, wise, provident *adj.* **pēš bīn** پیش بین

go forth; have effect *v.i.* **pēš jānā** پیش جانا

anticipation, alertness, activity *n.f.* **pēš qadamī** پیش قدمی
produce, present, submit *v.t.* **pēš karnā** پیش کرنا
urine *n.m.* **pīšāb/pēšāb** پیشاب
urinate *v.t.* **pēšāb karnā** پیشاب کرنا
forehead, brow; fate *n.f.* **pēšānī** پیشانی
before, formerly, prior *adv.* **pēštar** پیشتر
agent, deputy, manager *n.m.* **pēškār** پیشکار
present, tribute, offering *n.f.* **pēškaš** پیشکش
ancient; former *adj.* **pēšin** پیشن
foretelling, prophecy, prediction *n.f.* **pēšingō'ī** پیشنگوئی
trade, occupation, profession; custom, habit; practice *n.m.* **pēšah** پیشہ
artisan, workman, craftsman, tradesman *n.m.* **pēšah var** پیشہ ور
leader, guide; priest *n.m.* **pēšvā** پیشوا
leadership, guidance, supremacy; reception *n.f.* **pēšvā'ī** پیشوائی
welcome, receive *v.t.* **pēšvā'ī karnā** پیشوائی کرنا
presence; trial, advance *n.f.* **pēšī** پیشی
ancient; former; first *adj.* **pēšīnah** پیشینہ
ditch *n.m.* **paiġār** پیغار
message, news; mission *n.m.* **paiġām** پیغام
messenger, envoy, prophet *n.m.* **paiġāmbar** پیغامبر
mission, carrying a message *n.f.* **paiġāmbarī** پیغامبری
betel-leaf juice *n.f.* **pīk** پیک
battle, war; contest *n.f.* **paikār** پیکار
arrowhead *n.m.* **paikān** پیکان
packet *n.m.* **paikiṭ** پیکٹ
spitting pot, spittoon *n.m.* **pīkdān** پیکدان
face, countenance, appearance, portrait *n.f.* **paikar** پیکر
elephant; bishop (*in chess*) *n.m.* **pīl** پیل
yellow; pale *adj.* **pīlā** پیلا
yellowish *adj.* **pīlā sā** پیلا سا
yellowness; paleness *n.m.* **pīlāpan** پیلاپن
shove, push, press *v.t.* **pēlnā** پیلنا
promise, pledge, treaty, agreement *n.m.* **paimān** پیمان
cup, bowl (*used as a measure*) *n.m.* **paimānah** پیمانہ
measurement, survey *n.f.* **paimā'iš** پیمائش
pen *n.m.* **pēn** پین

drink; smoke *v.t.* **pīnā** • sharp, pointed *adj.* **painā** پینا
forty-five *num.* **paiṃtālīs** پینتالیس
thirty-five *num.* **paiṃtīs** پینتیس
pants, trousers *n.f.* **painṭ** پینٹ
palanquin, litter *n.f.* **pīnas** پینس
sixty-five *num.* **paiṃsaṭh** پینسٹھ
close together, successively *adv.* **paiham** پیہم
joined, fixed *adj.* **paivast** پیوست
junction, connection, adhesion *n.f.* **paivastgī** پیوستگی
joined, connected, attached *adj.* **paivastah** پیوستہ
patch, junction, addition *n.m.* **paivand** پیوند
patch *v.t.* **paivand lagānā** پیوند لگانا
patched, grafted *adj.* **paivandī** پیوندی
gate, entrance *n.m.* **phāṭak** پھاٹک
custody, imprisonment *n.f.* **phāṭak bandī** پھاٹک بندی
doorkeeper, gatekeeper *n.m.* **phāṭak dār** پھاٹک دار
plowshare *n.f.* **phāl** پھال
spring, jump, leap *n.m.* **phānd** پھاند
spring, jump, leap over *v.i./v.t.* **phāndnā** پھاندنا
noose, entrap, choke *v.t.* **phāṁsnā** پھانسنا
noose, loop; strangulation *n.f.* **phāṁsī** پھانسی
be hanged, be executed *v.t.* **phāṁsī pānā** پھانسی پانا
hang, strangle, execute *v.t.* **phāṁsī dēnā** پھانسی دینا
flake, slice, piece; a mouthful of *n.f.* **phānk** پھانک
mattock, spade, hoe *n.m.* **phā'ōṛā** پھاوڑا
shovel *n.f.* **phā'ōṛī** پھاوڑی
ornament, decoration *n.f.* **phaban** پھبن
fit, suit; look elegant *v.i.* **phabnā** پھبنا
aunt (father's sister) *n.f.* **phuptī** پھپتی
blister, bubble *n.m.* **phaphōlā** پھپھولا
single, unmatched *adj.* **phuṭ** • curse, malediction *n.m.* **phiṭ** پھٹ
curse *v.t.* **phiṭ phiṭ kārnā** پھٹ پھٹ کرنا
crack, fissure *n.m.* / cracked, broken, torn *adj.* **phaṭā** پھٹا
scold, curse *v.t.* **phiṭkārnā** پھٹکارنا
odd, separated, miscellaneous *adj.* **phuṭkal** پھٹکل
blot, stain, spot *n.f.* **phuṭkī** پھٹکی

be cracked, be broken, be burst; turn sour *v.i.* **phaṭnā** پھٹنا
jump, leap, hop; dance *v.i.* **phudaknā** پھدکنا
jump, hop *n.f.* **phudkī** پھدکی
again, then; afterwards; soon *adv.* **phir** پھر
come again, return *v.i.* **phir ānā** پھر آنا
still, however *adv.* **phir bhī** پھر بھی
over and over again *adv.* **phir phir** پھر پھر
trick *n.m.* **pharphand** پھر پھند
tricky, artful *adj.* **pharphandī** پھر پھندی
retract, withdraw; revoke *v.i.* **phir jānā** پھر جانا
cause to turn, whirl, wheel *v.t.* **phirānā** پھرانا
turning, rotation, circuit *n.m.* **phirā'ō** پھراؤ
activity, quickness, readiness, briskness *n.f.* **phurtī** پھرتی
act quickly, be quick *v.t.* **phurtī karnā** پھرتی کرنا
quick, active, smart *adj.* **phurtīlā** پھرتیلا
turn; walk about, wander; circulate, revolve *v.i.* **phirnā** پھرنا
flag, standard *n.m.* **pharairā** پھریرا
trembling, shivering *n.f.* **phurairī** پھریری
flutter, shake *v.t.* / flap *v.i.* **phaṛphaṛānā** پھڑ پھڑانا
flutter, shaking, agitation *n.f.* **phaṛphaṛāhaṭ** پھڑ پھڑاہٹ
fluttering, palpitation *n.f.* **phaṛak** پھڑک
cause to flutter, cause to vibrate *v.t.* **phaṛkānā** پھڑکانا
flutter, twitch, palpitate, vibrate *v.i.* **phaṛaknā** پھڑکنا
whispering *n.f.* **phus phus** پھس پھس
flabby, loose, spongy *adj.* **phusphusā** پھسپھسا
loosen, slacken *v.t.* **phaskānā** پھسکانا
become loose, become slack *v.i.* **phasaknā** پھسکنا
cause to slip *v.t.* **phislānā** • coax, flatter, seduce *v.i.* **phuslānā** پھسلانا
slipping *n.m.* **phislāhaṭ** پھسلاہٹ
slip; make an error *v.i.* **phisalnā** پھسلنا
be blown; be burnt *v.i.* **phuknā** پھکنا
fruit, produce; result *n.m.* **phal** پھل
reap the reward of *v.t.* **phal pānā** پھل پانا
cause to swell, fatten, inflate *v.t.* **phulānā** پھلانا
leap, spring *n.f.* **phalāng** پھلانگ

jump, spring, leap over *v.i./v.t.* **phalāngnā** پھلانگنا
fruitful *adj.* **phalit** پھلت
fireworks *n.f.* **phuljhaṛī** پھلجھڑی
prosper, bear fruit, thrive, have issue *v.i.* **phalnā** پھلنا
flourish *v.i.* **phalnā phūlnā** پھلنا پھولنا
flower garden; orchard; off-spring *n.f.* **phulvāṛī** پھلواڑی
cod; pod; loop *n.f.* **phalī** پھلی
scented oil *n.m.* **phulēl** پھلیل
net, noose, snare *n.m.* **phandā** پھندا
set a snare, entangle, knot, loop *v.t.* **phandā lagānā** پھندا لگانا
cause to jump, cause to leap *v.t.* **phandānā** پھندانا
cause to stick; cause to sink; snare, entrap *v.t.* **phaṁsānā** پھنسانا
be entangled; stick; sink *v.i.* **phaṁsnā** پھنسنا
pimple, boil *n.f.* **phuṁsī** پھنسی
hissing, hiss (*of a snake*) *n.m.* **phunkār** پھنکار
hiss (*as a snake*) *v.t.* **phunkārnā** پھنکارنا
grasshopper *n.m.* **phangā** پھنگا
aunt (*father's sister*) *n.f.* **phūphū** پھوپھو
fine rain, drizzle, fog *n.f.* **phuvār** پھوار
uncle (*husband of father's sister*) *n.f.* **phūphā** پھوپھا
rift, fend, split, breach, break, crack *n.f.* **phūṭ** پھوٹ
sow dissension, sow discord *v.t.* **phūṭ ḍālnā** پھوٹ ڈالنا
broken, burst, cracked *adj.* **phūṭā** پھوٹا
be broken, burst, break, crash *v.i.* **phūṭnā** پھوٹنا
bad luck, ill-fate *n.f.* **phūṭī qismat** پھوٹی قسمت
boil, sore, abscess *n.m.* **phōṛā** پھوڑا
eruption, small boil *n.m.* **phōṛā phuṁsī** پھوڑا پھنسی
straw *n.m.* **phūs** پھوس
rag, rubbish *n.m.* **phūsṛā** پھوسڑا
dregs, sediment *n.m.* **phōk** پھوک
flower, blossom *n.m.* **phūl** پھول
blossom *v.i.* **phūl ānā** پھول آنا
be delighted, be pleased *v.i.* **phūl jānā** پھول جانا
speak eloquently *v.t.* **phūl jhaṛnā** پھول جھڑنا
cauliflower *n.f.* **phūl gōbhī** پھول گوبھی
swelled, swollen; blossomed *adj.* **phūlā** پھولا

developed, bloomy, prosperous *adj.* **phūlā phalā** پھولا پھلا

blossom, flourish *v.i.* **phūlnā** پھولنا

hissing; snorting (*of a dog*) *n.f.* **phūṁ** پھوں

breath, blow, puff *n.f.* **phūnk** پھونک

blow up, destroy by fire, set fire *v.t.* **phūnk dēnā** پھونک دینا

blow up; inflame, set on fire *v.t.* **phūḍknā** پھونکنا

blow up; inflame, set on fire *v.t.* **phūnknā** پھونکنا

undisciplined, rude; uneducated *adj.* **phūhaṛ** پھوہڑ

stupidity, foolishness *n.m.* **phūhaṛ pan** پھوہڑپن

lung *n.m.* **phēpṛā** پھیپڑا

turning, turn, winding, twist *n.m.* **phēr** پھیر

turning, circuit, roll *n.m.* **phērā** پھیرا

change, interchange, alternation *n.f.* **phērā phērī** پھیرا پھیری

turn over, return, give back, twist *v.t.* **phērnā** پھیرنا

going round, circuit; hawking, begging *n.f.* **phērī** پھیری

hawk, beg *v.t.* **phērī karnā** پھیری کرنا

hawker, beggar *n.m.* **phērī vālā** پھیری والا

tasteless, pale, faint, light (*in color*), dull *adj.* **phīkā** پھیکا

spread, stretch, expand, multiply *v.t.* **phailānā** پھیلانا

spread, expansion, growth, length *n.m.* **phailā'ō** پھیلاؤ

be spread, be expanded, grow *v.i.* **phailnā** پھیلنا

foam, scum *n.m.* **phēn** پھین

foam, froth *v.i.* **phēnānā** پھینانا

rinse, wring out, squeeze *v.t.* **phīṁchā** پھینچنا

throw, cast, fling *n.f.* **phēnk** پھینک

throw away *v.t.* **phēnk dēnā** پھینک دینا

throw, cast, let fly; disregard, waste, spill, pour out *v.t.* **phēnknā** پھینکنا

tē ت

to, until, as far as, as long as, in order to *pp./adv./conj.* **tā** تا

heat; power; endurance, courage; fury *n.m.* **tāb** تاب

bright, luminous *adj.* **tāb dār** تاب دار

splendid, glittering, burning *adj.* **tābān** تابان

window; stove; chimney *n.m.* **tābdān** تابدان

summer, hot season *n.m.* **tābistān** تابستان

heat; grief, sorrow *n.f.* **tābiš** تابش

dependant, following, loyal *n.m.* **tābiᶜ** تابع

obedient, loyal *adj.* **tābiᶜdār** تابعدار

obedience, fidelity *n.f.* **tābiᶜdārī** تابعداری

followers, attendants *n.m.* **tābiᶜīn** تابعین

shining, luminous, bright *adj.* **tābindah** تابندہ

coffin *n.m.* **tābūt** تابوت

warmth, heat; fever *n.m.* **tāp** تاپ

warm oneself *v.i.* **tāpnā** تاپنا

penetration, impression *n.m.* **tā'asur** تأثر

crown *n.m.* **tāj** تاج

crowned head, emperor, king, prince *n.m.* **tājdār** تاجدار

merchant, trader *n.m.* **tājir** تاجر

king, prince *n.m.* **tājvar** تاجور

royalty, sovereignty *n.f.* **tājvarī** تاجوری

assault, attack, invasion *n.f.* **tāxt** تاخت

delay, postponement *n.m.* **tā'axur** تأخر

discipline *n.f.* **tādīb** تادیب

thread, wire, string *n.m.* **tār** تار

star; pupil (*of the eye*) *n.m.* **tārā** تارا

plunder, ruin, devastation *n.m.* **tārāj** تاراج

plunder, ruin, devastate *v.t.* **tārāj karnā** تاراج کرنا

leaving, abandoning *adj.* **tārik** تارک

date; epoch, era; history *n.f.* **tārīx** تاریخ

datewise, daily *adv.* **tārīx vār** تاریخ وار

dark, obscure *adj.* **tārīk** تاریک

darkness, obscurity *n.f.* **tārīkī** تاریکی

understanding, perception *n.f.* **tāṛ** تاڑ
understand, perceive *v.t.* **tāṛnā** تاڑنا
freshness *n.f.* **tāzgī** تازگی
fresh, new; happy *adj.* **tāzah** تازہ
be refreshed, be in good spirits *v.i.* **tāzah dam hōnā** تازہ دم ہونا
renew, refresh *v.t.* **tāzah karnā** تازہ کرنا
whip *n.m.* **tāziyānah** تازیانہ
brocade *n.m.* **tāš** تاش
look, glance; vine; grape *n.f.* **tāk** تاک
stare, look at *v.t.* **tāk lagānā** تاک لگانا
stare at, look at, peep *v.t.* **tāknā** تاکنا
in order to, so that, under the condition of *conj.* **tākih** تاکہ
stress, pressure, emphasis *n.f.* **tākīd** تاکید
urge, press *v.t.* **tākīd karnā** تاکید کرنا
emphatically, positively; strictly *adv.* **tākīdan** تاکیداً
emphatic, urgent; positive *adj.* **tākīdī** تاکیدی
thread, chord *n.m.* **tāgā** تاگا
thread, stitch *v.t.* **tāgnā** تاگنا
rhythm *n.f.* / pond, lake *n.m.* **tāl** تال
chime; beat (*musical*) *v.t.* **tāl dēnā** تال دینا
lock *n.m.* **tālā** تالا
lock up *v.t.* **tālā lagānā** تالا لگانا
tank, pond, reservoir (*of water*) *n.m.* **tālāb** تالاب
melancholy, grief, sorrow, torment *n.m.* **tā'alum** تالم
palate *n.m.* **tālū** تالو
key; clapping (*of hands*) *n.m.* **tālī** تالی
clap hands *v.t.* **tālī bajānā** تالی بجانا
applaud *v.t.* **tālī mārnā** تالی مارنا
compilation, composition *n.m.* **tālīf** تالیف
complete, whole, entire; full *adj.* **tām** تام
copper *n.m.* **tāmbā** تامبا
anger, darkness, irascibility *n.m.* **tāmas** تامس
hesitation, doubt, delay, disinclination, irresolution *n.m.* **tāmmul** تامل
consider, hesitate, doubt, reflect *v.t.* **tāmmul karnā** تامل کرنا
tune, note (*in music*) *n.f.* **tān** تان
play a tune; sing *v.t.* **tān uṛānā** تان اڑانا

heat, melt *v.t.* **tānā** تانا
copper *n.m.* **tānbā** تانبا
row, series *n.m.* **tāntā** تانتا
stretch, expand *v.t.* **tānnā** تاننا
heat; rage; passion *n.m.* **tā'ō** تاؤ
heat, melt *v.t.* **tā'ō dēnā** تاؤ دینا
be heated, be inflamed *v.t.* **tā'ō khānā** تاؤ کھانا
penalty, fine *n.m.* **tāvān** تاوان
fine *v.t.* **tāvān lagānā** تاوان لگانا
pay a penalty *v.t.* **tāvān dēnā** تاوان لینا
explanation, interpretation *n.f.* **tāvīl** تاویل
aunt (*wife of father's brother*) *n.f.* **tā'ī** تائی
aid, support, assistance *n.f.* **tā'īd** تائید
help, support, assist *v.t.* **tā'īd karnā** تائید کرنا
then; afterwards *adv.* **tab** تب
still, nevertheless *adv.* **tab bhī** تب بھی
till then, so long *adv.* **tab tak** تب تک
since that time, thereafter *adv.* **tab sē** تب سے
at that very moment, there and then *adv.* **tab hī** تب ہی
then indeed *adv.* **tab hī tō** تب ہی تو
transfer, change, exchange, alteration *n.m.* **tabādalah** تبادلہ
spoiled, ruined *adj.* **tabāh** تباہ
destruction, ruin *n.f.* **tabāhī** تباہی
change, modification *n.m.* **tabdīl** تبدیل
change, exchange, alter, transfer *v.t.* **tabdīl karnā** تبدیل کرنا
axe, hatchet *n.m.* **tabar** تبر
benediction, blessing *n.m.* **tabarruk** تبرک
cooling, refreshing *n.f.* **tabrīd** تبرید
smile *n.m.* **tabassum** تبسم
fever *n.f.* **tap** تپ
go down (*fever*) *v.i.* **tap utarnā** تپ اترنا
ague *n.m.* **tap-ē-larzah** تپ لرزہ
affection, cordiality, esteem *n.m.* **tapāk** تپاک
heat, warm *v.t.* **tapānā** تپانا
heat, warmth *n.f.* **tapiš** تپش
hot, warm *adj.* **tattā** تتا

dispersed, scattered *adj.* **tittar bittar** تتر بتر
lisp, stammer, stutter *v.i.* **tutlānā** تتلانا
butterfly; beautiful girl *n.f.* **titlī** تتلی
supplement, appendix *n.m.* **tatimmah** تتمہ
completion, accomplishment *n.f.* **tatmīm** تتمیم
wasp *n.m.* **tatayyā** تتیا
trinity (*in religion or astrology*) *n.f.* **taslīs** تثلیث
trade, commerce, business *n.f.* **tijārat** تجارت
trade *v.t.* **tijārat karnā** تجارت کرنا
mercantile, commercial *adj.* **tijāratī** تجارتی
transgression, deviation; surpassing *n.m.* **tajāvuz** تجاوز
pass, deviate; trespass *v.t.* **tajāvuz karnā** تجاوز کرنا
renewal *n.f.* **tajdīd** تجدید
trial, experiment, test *n.m.* **tajribah** تجربہ
practical knowledge, experience *n.f.* **tajribah kārī** تجربہ کاری
try, experiment, experience *v.t.* **tajurbah karnā** تجربہ کرنا
solitude, celibacy, bachelorhood *n.m.* **tajarrud** تجرد
separation, solitude *n.f.* **tajrīd** تجرید
analysis *n.f.* **tajzī** تجزی
curiosity; investigation *n.m.* **tajassus** تجسس
manifestation; splendor, brightness *n.f.* **tajallī** تجلی
dignity *n.m.* **tajammul** تجمل
resemblance, analogy *n.f.* **tajnīs** تجنیس
burial *n.m.* **tajhīz-ō-takfīn** تجہیز و تکفین
proposal, suggestion *n.f.* **tajvīz** تجویز
propose, suggest *v.t.* **tajvīz karnā** تجویز کرنا
you, thee *pron.* **tujh** تجھ
to you, to thee *pron.* **tujhē** تجھے
beneath, below, under *adv./pp.* **taḥt** تحت
movement, motion *n.m.* **taḥaruk** تحرک
record, writing, document, script *n.f.* **taḥrīr** تحریر
record, write, document *v.t.* **taḥrīr karnā** تحریر کرنا
recorded, documentary, in writing *adj.* **taḥrīrī** تحریری
movement, agitation *n.f.* **taḥrīk** تحریک
move *v.t.* **taḥrīk karnā** تحریک کرنا
applause, cheers *n.f.* **taḥsīn** تحسین

تحسین کرنا applaud, praise *v.t.* **taḥsīn karnā**
تحصیل gain, acquisition, collection *n.f.* **taḥsīl**
تحصیل کرنا gain, acquire, collect *v.t.* **taḥsīl karnā**
تحفظ preservation, conservation *n.m.* **taḥaffuz**
تحفہ gift, present *n.m.* / uncommon, rare *adj.* **tōḥfah**
تحقق verification, ascertainment *n.m.* **taḥaqquq**
تحقیر scorn, disdain, neglect *n.f.* **taḥqīr**
تحقیق investigation, search, inquiry *n.f.* **taḥqīq**
تحقیق کرنا investigate, inquire, verify *v.t.* **taḥqīq karnā**
تحقیقات investigation, search, inquiry *n.f.* **taḥqīqāt**
تحقیقی sure, certain *adj.* **taḥqīqī**
تحلیل digestion, dissolving *n.f.* **taḥlīl**
تحمل endurance, forbearance, patience *n.m.* **taḥammul**
تحمل کرنا endure, forbear, bear *v.t.* **taḥammul karnā**
تحمید praise (of God) *n.f.* **taḥmīd**
تحویل change, transfer *n.f.* **tahvīl**
تحویلدار trustee, treasurer *n.m.* **taḥvīldār**
تحیر amazement, wonder, astonishment *n.m.* **taḥayyur**
تخت throne *n.m.* **taxt**
تخت پر بٹھانا enthrone *v.t.* **taxt par biṭhānā**
تخت پر بیٹھنا sit on the throne, be king *v.i.* **taxt par baiṭhnā**
تخت نشینی coronation, accession to the throne *n.f.* **taxt našīnī**
تختہ board, plank; sheet (*of paper*) *n.m.* **taxtah**
تختہ سیاہ blackboard *n.m.* **taxtah siyāh**
تختۂ شطرنج chessboard *n.m.* **taxtah-ē-šatraṁj**
تختی tablet, small board *n.f.* **taxtī**
تخریب destruction, devastation *n.f.* **taxrīb**
تخصیص particularity, speciality *n.f.* **taxsīs**
تخفیف reduction, decrease; relief *n.f.* **taxfīf**
تخفیف کرنا reduce, decrease; relieve *v.t.* **taxfīf karnā**
تخلیہ privacy *n.m.* **taxliyah**
تخم seed, sperm; egg *n.m.* **tuxm**
تخمیناً nearly, about, by guess *adv.* **taxmīnan**
تخمینہ estimate, guess *n.m.* **taxmīnah**
تخمینی estimated *adj.* **taxmīni**

threat, intimidation *n.f.* **taxvīf** تخویف
fancy, supposition, imagination *n.m.* **taxayyul** تخیل
tradition *n.m.* **tadāvul** تداول
foresight, prudence *n.m.* **tadabbur** تدبر
opinion, advice; plan, proposal *n.f.* **tadbīr** تدبیر
scale, degree *n.f.* **tadrīj** تدریج
teaching, lecturing *n.f.* **tadrīs** تدریس
burial, interment *n.f.* **tadfīn** تدفین
doubt, perplexity, uncertainty *n.m.* **tazabzub** تذبذب
memoir *n.m.* **tazkirah** تذکرہ
moist, damp, wet, juicy *adj.* **tar** تر
completely wet *adj.* **tar batar** تر بتر
earth, ground; dust *n.m.* **turāb** تراب
eighty-three *num.* **tirāsī** تراسی
cut, cutting; shape, form *n.f.* **tarāš** تراش
cut, shave, shape *v.t.* **tarāšnā** تراشنا
song, melody; harmony, symphony *n.m.* **tarānah** ترانہ
ninety-three *num.* **tirānavē** ترانوے
freshness; humidity, moisture, dampness *n.f.* **tarāvaṭ** تراوٹ
grave, tomb *n.f.* **turbat** تربت
watermelon *n.m.* **tarbūz** تربوز
training, education, instruction *n.f.* **tarbiyat** تربیت
train, educate, instruct *v.t.* **tarbiyat karnā** تربیت کرنا
fifty-three *num.* **tirēpan** ترپن
presently, quickly, instantly *adv.* **turt** ترت
order, method, arrangement *n.f.* **tartīb** ترتیب
regularly, methodically *adv.* **tartīb vār** ترتیب وار
interpreter, translator *n.m.* **tarjumān** ترجمان
translation *n.m.* **tarjumah** ترجمہ
translate *v.t.* **tarjumah karnā** ترجمہ کرنا
preference, superiority *n.f.* **tarjīḥ** ترجیح
prefer *v.t.* **tarjīḥ dēnā** ترجیح دینا
across; slanting; perverse *adj.* **tirchā** ترچھا
side-glance *n.f.* **tirchī nazar** ترچھی نظر
mercy, pity, compassion *n.m.* **taraḥḥum** ترحم
hesitation, indecision, anxiety *n.m.* **taradud** تردد

تردید refutation, repelling *n.f.* **tardīd**
تردید کرنا refute, repel *v.t.* **tardīd karnā**
ترس fear, terror *n.m.* **tars**
ترساں fearful, afraid, timid *adj.* **tarsāṁ**
ترسانا tease *v.t.* **tarsānā**
ترسنا desire, long *v.i.* **tarasnā**
ترش sour, acidic; harsh *adj.* **turš**
ترش رو cynical, ill-humored *adj.* **turš rū**
ترشی sourness, acidity *n.f.* **turšī**
ترغیب strong desire, stimulation, temptation *n.f.* **tarġīb**
ترغیب دینا stimulate, excite; tempt *v.t.* **tarġīb dēnā**
ترقی promotion, progress *n.f.* **taraqqī**
ترک Turk *n.m.* **turk** • desertion, leaving *n.m.* **tark**
ترک وطن emigration *n.m.* **tark-ē-vatan**
ترکش quiver *n.m.* **tarkaš**
ترکہ bequest, legacy *n.m.* **tarkah**
ترکی Turk *n.m.* / Turkish *adj.* **turkī**
ترکیب plan, arrangement *n.f.* **tarkīb**
ترکیبی composed, planned; artificial *adj.* **tarkībī**
ترمیم amendment, revision, improvement, modification *n.f.* **tarmīm**
ترنگ wave; wham; mood *n.f.* **tarang**
تری wetness, moisture, dampness *n.f.* **tarī**
تریا female, woman; maid; wife *n.f.* **triyā**
تریسٹھ sixty-three *num.* **tirēsaṭh**
تڑپ restlessness, fury, outrageousness *n.f.* **taṛap**
تڑپانا agitate *v.t.* **taṛapānā**
تڑکا daybreak, dawn *n.m.* **taṛkā**
تزک pomp, splendor *n.m.* **tuzak**
تزکیہ purification *n.m.* **tazkiyah**
تزلزل commotion, agitation; earthquake *n.m.* **tazalzul**
تساہل negligence, carelessness, laziness *n.m.* **tasāhul**
تسبیح rosary, string of beads *n.f.* **tasbīḥ**
تسخیر capture, seizure (by force); sorcery, magic *n.f.* **tasxīr**
تسکین satisfaction, consolation, comfort *n.f.* **taskīn**
تسکین دینا pacify, calm, appease, soothe *v.t.* **taskīn dēnā**
تسلسل succession, sequence, series *n.m.* **tasalsul**

domination, sway, command *n.m.* **tasallut** تسلط
satisfaction, comfort, consolation, contentment *n.f.* **tasallī** تسلی
compliments, salutation *n.f.* **taslīm** تسلیم
leather strap *n.m.* **tasmah** تسمہ
strangle *v.t.* **tasmah khaiṁcnā** تسمہ کھینچنا
naming, nomination *n.m.* **tasmiyah** تسمیہ
facilitation, rendering easy *n.f.* **tašīl** تسہیل
similitude, resemblance *n.m.* **tašābuh** تشابہ
similitude, allegory, metaphor *n.f.* **tašbīh** تشبیہ
discrimination *n.m.* **tašaxxus** تشخص
diagnosis, verification, ascertainment *n.f.* **tašxīs** تشخیص
diagnose, verify *v.t.* **tašxīs karnā** تشخیص کرنا
hardship, severity *n.m.* **tašaddud** تشدد
consolidation *n.f.* **tašdīd** تشدید
explanation, exposition, interpretation *n.f.* **tašrīḥ** تشریح
honoring *n.f.* **tašrīf** تشریف
sit (down) *v.t.* **tašrīf rakhnā** تشریف رکھنا
come (in) *v.t.* **tašrīf lānā** تشریف لانا
depart, leave *v.i.* **tašrīf lē jānā** تشریف لے جانا
satisfaction, consolation *n.f.* **tašaffī** تشفی
formation, fabrication, organizing *n.f.* **taškīl** تشکیل
thirst; desire, longing *n.f.* **tišnagī** تشنگی
thirsty; desiring *adj.* **tišnah** تشنہ
proclamation *n.f.* **tašhīr** تشہیر
anxiety, confusion *n.f.* **tašvīš** تشویش
collision, conflict, clash *n.m.* **tasādum** تصادم
sacrifice, devotion; giving of alms *n.m.* **tasadduq** تصدق
attestation, verification *n.f.* **tasdīq** تصدیق
possession; use, expenditure *n.m.* **tasarruf** تصرف
use, spend *v.t.* **tasarruf karnā** تصرف کرنا
manifestation, explanation, clarification *n.f.* **tasrīḥ** تصریح
conjugation, inflection *n.f.* **tasrīf** تصریف
purification *n.m.* **tasfiyah** تصفیہ
crucifixion *n.f.* **taslīb** تصلیب
composition (*in literature*), writing *n.f.* **tasnīf** تصنیف
compile, write *v.t.* **tasnīf karnā** تصنیف کرنا

imagination, reflection; idea *n.m.* **tasavvur** تصور

imagine, meditate *v.t.* **tasavvur karnā** تصور کرنا

mysticism, contemplation *n.m.* **tasavvuf** تصوف

picture, portrait, photo, painting *n.m.* **tasvīr** تصویر

paint, draw, portray *v.t.* **tasvīr banānā** تصویر بنانا

paint, draw, portray, photograph *v.t.* **tasvīr kaimcnā** تصویر کھینچنا

contrast *n.m.* **tazādd** تضاد

mocking *n.f.* **tazḥīk** تضحیک

wastage, spoiling *n.f.* **tazīᶜ** تضیع

comparing, conforming; confronting *n.f.* **tatbīq** تطبیق

sanctification, purification *n.f.* **tathīr** تطہیر

injustice, oppression *n.m.* **tazallum** تظلم

acquaintance, introduction; custom; courtesy *n.m.* **taᶜāruf** تعارف

pursuit, chase *n.m.* **taᶜāqub** تعاقب

pursue, chase *v.t.* **taᶜāqub karnā** تعاقب کرنا

cooperation, assistance *n.m.* **taᶜāvun** تعاون

labor, toil; trouble *n.m.* **taᶜab** تعب

interpretation, explanation *n.f.* **taᶜbīr** تعبیر

astonishment, amazement *n.m.* **taᶜajjub** تعجب

number, enumeration *n.m.* **taᶜdād** تعداد

oppression, tyranny, violence *n.f.* **taᶜaddī** تعدی

objection, hindrance, obstacle *n.m.* **taᶜarruz** تعرض

explanation, description, definition; praise *n.f.* **taᶜrīf** تعریف

censure, punishment *n.f.* **taᶜzīr** تعزیر

falling in love, affection *n.m.* **taᶜaššaq** تعشق

idleness *n.m.* **taᶜattul** تعطل

holiday, vacation *n.f.* **taᶜtīl** تعطیل

respect, honor *n.f.* **taᶜzīm** تعظیم

honor *v.t.* **taᶜzīm karnā** تعظیم کرنا

stink, bad smell *n.m.* **taᶜaffun** تعفن

connection, relation; concern *n.m.* **taᶜalluq** تعلق

division (*of a province*), jurisdiction *n.m.* **taᶜalluqah** تعلقہ

learning, knowledge, study *n.m.* **taᶜallum** تعلم

teaching, instruction, education *n.f.* **taᶜlīm** تعلیم

compliance, execution, adherence *n.f.* **taᶜmīl** تعمیل

amulet *n.m.* **taᶜvīz** تعویذ

fixation; appointing, assigning *n.f.* **taᶜiyun** تعین
fixed, appointed *adj.* **taᶜiyunāt** تعینات
tub, bucket *n.m.* **taġār** تغار
food, nourishment *n.m.* **taġziah** تغذیہ
change, alteration *n.m.* **taġayyur** تغیر
boasting, glorying *n.m.* **tafāxur** تفاخر
difference; distance *n.m.* **tafāvut** تفاوت
investigation, inquiry, research *n.f.* **taftīš** تفتیش
investigate, inquire, research *v.t.* **taftīš karnā** تفتیش کرنا
rejoicing, amusement *n.f.* **tafrīḥ** تفریح
cheerfulness, amusement *n.f.* **tafrīḥ-ē-tabaᶜ** تفریح طبع
subtraction, division *n.f.* **tafrīq** تفریق
explanation, commentary *n.f.* **tafsīr** تفسیر
excellence, preference *n.f.* **tafzīl** تفضیل
reflection, meditation *n.m.* **tafakkur** تفکر
amusement, pastime *n.m.* **tafannun** تفنن
understanding *n.m.* **tafahhum** تفہم
instructing, teaching *n.f.* **tafhīm** تفہیم
entrusting *n.f.* **tafvīz** تفویض
demand, claim (*financial*) *n.m.* **taqāzā** تقاضا
distilling; dropping *n.m.* **taqātur** تقاطر
holiness, purity *n.m.* **taqaddus** تقدس
priority *n.m.* **taqaddum** تقدم
fate, destiny, luck, lot *n.f.* **taqdīr** تقدیر
purity *n.f.* **taqdīs** تقدیس
priority; performance, presentation *n.f.* **taqdīm** تقدیم
nearness, proximity, approach *n.m.* **taqarrub** تقرب
nomination, appointment *n.m.* **taqarrur** تقرر
function, occasion, ceremony, festival *n.f.* **taqrīb** تقریب
celebrate *v.t.* **taqrīb karnā** تقریب کرنا
nearly, about, approximately *adv.* **taqrīban** تقریباً
discourse, speech *n.f.* **taqrīr** تقریر
argumentative, talkative *adj.* **taqrīrī** تقریری
division, partition *n.f.* **taqsīm** تقسیم
divide, share *v.t.* **taqsīm karnā** تقسیم کرنا

fault, error, offense, crime, sin *n.f.* **taqsīr** تقصیر
faulty, guilty, criminal *adj.* **taqsīr vār** تقصیر وار
dissection *n.f.* **taqtīᶜ** تقطیع
dissect *v.t.* **taqtīᶜ karnā** تقطیع کرنا
imitation, copy, counterfeiting *n.f.* **taqlīd** تقلید
imitate, copy, counterfeit *v.t.* **taqlīd karnā** تقلید کرنا
abstinence, piety *n.f.* **taqvā** تقویٰ
strengthening, strength, support, aid *n.f.* **taqviyat** تقویت
fixing, adjusting; almanac, calendar *n.f.* **taqvīm** تقویم
pious, devout *adj.* **taqī** تقی
until, till, to, upto, while *pp.* **tak** • rhyme *n.f.* **tuk** تک
rhyme; agree with *v.t.* **tuk mēṁ tuk milānā** تک میں تک ملانا
piece, slice, chop (*of meat*) *n.m.* **tikkā** تکا
fatigue, tiredness *n.m.* **takān** تکان
be tired *v.i.* **thakān caṛhnā** تکھان چڑھنا
pride, arrogance *n.m.* **takabbur** تکبر
density, thickness *n.f.* **taksīf** تکثیف
contradiction, accusing (*of falsehood*) *n.f.* **takzīb** تکذیب
repetition; dispute, controversy *n.f.* **takrār** تکرار
repeat; dispute, quarrel, argue *v.t.* **takrār karnā** تکرار کرنا
respect, honor, reverence *n.f.* **takrīm** تکریم
breaking *n.m.* **takassur** تکسر
breaking (*into pieces*) *n.f.* **taksīr** تکسیر
ceremony, formality; etiquette *n.m.* **takalluf** تکلف
bother, take pains; be ceremonious *v.t.* **takalluf karnā** تکلف کرنا
difficulty, trouble, hardship, burden *n.f.* **taklīf** تکلیف
suffer *v.t.* **taklīf uṭhānā** تکلیف اٹھانا
trouble, annoy *v.t.* **taklīf dēnā** تکلیف دینا
take trouble *v.t.* **taklīf karnā** تکلیف کرنا
perfection, completion *n.m.* **takmilah** تکملہ
finishing, completion *n.f.* **takmīl** تکمیل
complete *v.t.* **takmīl karnā** تکمیل کرنا
look, gaze, watch, stare *v.t.* **taknā** تکنا
pillow, bolster *n.m.* **takiyah** تکیہ
lean, bolster, rely *v.t.* **takiyah lagānā** تکیہ لگانا

running *n.f.* **tag** تگ
bustle, toil, labor *n.f.* **tagāpū** تگاپو
sesame seed *n.m.* **til** • equal, like, similar *adj.* **tul** تل
cockroach *n.m.* **til caṭṭā** تل چٹا
put underneath, hide *v.t.* **tal karnā** تل کرنا
bottom; sole (*of a shoe*) *n.m.* **talā** تلا
search, investigation, quest *n.f.* **talāš** تلاش
seek, search, look for *v.t.* **talāš karnā** تلاش کرنا
search, investigation *n.f.* **talāšī** تلاشی
institute a search *v.t.* **talāšī lēnā** تلاشی لینا
recitation, reading (*of the Quran*) *n.f.* **tilāvat** تلاوت
counterfeiting, fraud, cheating *n.f.* **talbīs** تلبیس
sediment *n.f.* **talchaṭ** تلچھٹ
bitter, acidic, pungent, unpalatable *adj.* **talx** تلخ
ill-tempered *adj.* **talx mizāj** تلخ مزاج
sweet basil *n.f.* **tulsī** تلسی
favor, kindness *n.m.* **talattuf** تلطف
oblige, show kindness *v.t.* **talattuf karnā** تلطف کرنا
destruction, waste, ruin *n.m.* **talaf** تلف
destroy, waste, ruin *v.t.* **talaf karnā** تلف کرنا
pronunciation, utterance *n.m.* **talaffuz** تلفظ
religious instruction *n.f.* **talqīn** تلقین
tilak (*mark made by Hindus on forehead*) *n.m.* **tilak** تلک
discipleship, apprenticeship *n.m.* **talammuz** تلمذ
be agitated, be uneasy *v.i.* **tilmilānā** تلملانا
impatience, restlessness *n.f.* **tilmalī** تلملی
student, pupil, disciple, apprentice *n.m.* **talmīz** تلمیذ
sole (*of the foot*) *n.m.* **talvā** تلوا
flatter, coax *v.t.* **talvā sahlānā** تلوا سہلانا
sword *n.f.* **talvār** تلوار
under, beneath, below, down *pp./adv.* **talē** تلے
bottom; sole (*of a shoe*) *n.f.* **talī** • spleen, milt *n.f.* **tillī** تلی
you, thee *pron.* **tum** تم
show, entertainment, sight, amusement *n.m.* **tamāšā** تماشا
act (*in a play*); make fun of *v.t.* **tamāšā karnā** تماشا کرنا
funny thing; pretty sight *n.f.* **tamāšā kī bāt** تماشا کی بات

تماشا گاہ **tamāša gāh** theater *n.f.*
تمام **tamām** entire, whole, total, complete; finished, concluded; exact *adj.*
تمام شد **tamām šud** finished, completed *adj.*
تمام کرنا **tamām karnā** finish, complete, conclude *v.t.*
تمام و کمال **tamām-ō-kamāl** whole, entire, fully, completely, thoroughly *adj./adv.*
تمباکو **tambākū** tobacco *n.m.*
تمبو **tambū** tent *n.m.*
تمت **tammat** finished, completed *adj.*
تمتماہٹ **tamtamāhaṭ** glow, flush *n.f.*
تمثال **timsāl** resemblance *n.f.*
تمثیل **tamsīl** comparison, resemblance, similitude *n.f.*
تمدن **tamaddun** civilization, urbanization *n.m.*
تمرد **tamarrud** stubbornness, obstinacy; rebellion, disobedience *n.m.*
تمسخر **tamasxur** joking, buffoonery, fun *n.m.*
تمسک **tamassuk** bond, receipt; note *n.m.*
تمغہ **tamġah** medal, royal grant, diploma *n.m.*
تمکنت **tamkanat** majesty, dignity, honor, grandeur *n.f.*
تملق **tamalluq** caressing, flattering *n.m.*
تمن **tuman** brotherhood; troop, squadron; crowd *n.m.*
تمنا **tamannā** wish, desire *n.f.*
تمنا کرنا **tamannā karnā** wish, desire *v.t.*
تمنچہ **tamancah** pistol *n.m.*
تمہید **tamhīd** introduction, preface, preamble *n.f.*
تمہیں **tumhēṁ** to you, to thee *pron.*
تمیز **tamīz** discernment, judgment, discretion *n.m.*
تمیزدار **tamīzdār** judicious, discreet *adj.*
تمیز کرنا **tamīz karnā** distinguish, appreciate *v.t.*
تن **tan** body; person *n.m.*
تن پرور **tan parvar** self-indulgent, selfish *adj.*
تن پروری **tan parvarī** self-indulgence, selfishness *n.f.*
تن تنہا **tan tanhā** alone *adj.*
تن من **tan man** body and soul *n.m.*
تناسب **tanāsub** resemblance; proportion *n.m.*
تناسخ **tanāsux** transmigration; transformation *n.m.*
تناسل **tanāsul** generation, lineage *n.m.*
تناقض **tanāquz** contradiction, contrast, discrepancy *n.m.*

stressed *adj.* **tanā'ō zadah** تناوزده

eating *n.m.* **tanāvul** تناول

eat *v.t.* **tanāvul karnā** تناول کرنا

tambourine *n.m.* **tanbūrā** تنبورا

pay, salary, wages *n.f.* **tanxvāh** تنخواہ

active, fierce, hot; quick, rapid *adj.* **tund** تند

healthy *adj.* **tandurust** تندرست

cure *v.t.* **tandurust karnā** تندرست کرنا

health *n.f.* **tandurustī** تندرستی

diligence, attention *n.f.* **tandihī** تندہی

oven *n.m.* **tandūr** تندور

fall, decline, descent *n.m.* **tanazzul** تنزل

fall off, decline *v.i.* **tanazzul hōnā** تنزل ہونا

cancellation, revocation *n.m.* **tansīx** تنسیخ

dividing, division *n.f.* **tansīf** تنصیف

organization *n.f.* **tanzīm** تنظیم

prosperity, easy life *n.m.* **tanaᶜum** تنعم

breathing, respiration *n.m.* **tanaffus** تنفس

criticism, review *n.f.* **tanqīd** تنقید

criticize *v.t.* **tanqīd karnā** تنقید کرنا

weak, delicate, thin, fragile *adj.* **tunuk** تنک

straw; blade (*of grass*) *n.m.* **tinkā** تنکا

flutter, palpitate *v.i.* **tinaknā** تنکنا

narrow, tight, contracted *adj.* **tank** تنگ

poor; miserly *n.m.* **tank dast** تنگ دست

poverty, misery *n.f.* **tankdastī** تنگدستی

narrowness, tightness *n.f.* **tankī** تنگی

trunk (*of a tree*) *n.m.* **tanah** تنہ

alone, single, solitary *adj.* **tanhā** تنہا

loneliness, solitude *n.m.* **tanhā'ī** تنہائی

oven *n.m.* **tanūr** تنور

variety, diversity *n.m.* **tanavvōᶜ** تنوع

illumination, enlightenment *n.f.* **tanvīr** تنویر

surface, foundation, depth, layer *n.f.* **tah** تہ

plait by plait, layer by layer *adv.* **tah batah** تہ بتہ

pile (*one over another*), fold *v.t.* **tah batah karnā** تہ بتہ کرنا

plait *v.t.* **tah jamānā** تہ جمانا
cellar *n.m.* **tah xānah** تہ خانہ
fold up *v.t.* **tah karnā** تہ کرنا
there, there to *adv.* **tahāṁ** تہاں
fold, wrap *v.t.* **tahānā** تہانا
seventy-three *num.* **tēhattar** تہتر
spelling; orthography *n.f.* **tahajjī** تہجی
menace, threat *n.f.* **tahdīd** تہدید
civilization; politeness *n.f.* **tahzīb** تہذیب
civilized, educated, polite *adj.* **tahzīb yāftah** تہذیب یافتہ
triple, three-fold *adj.* **tihrā** تہرا
destroyed, ruined *adj.* **tahas nahas** تہس نہس
agony; panic *n.m.* **tahlukah/tahalkah** تہلکہ
false accusation, suspicion *n.f.* **tuhmat** تہمت
accuse *v.t.* **tuhmat lagānā** تہمت لگانا
congratulation, wishing *n.f.* **tahniyat** تہنیت
empty, vacant, void, vain *adj.* **tihī** تہی
poor, empty-handed *adj.* **tihī dast** تہی دست
womb; abdomen *n.m.* **tihī gāh** تہی گاہ
foolish, ignorant *n.m.* **tihī maġaz** تہی مغز
determination, preparation *n.m.* **tahiyyah** تہیہ
determine, prepare *v.t.* **tahiyyah karnā** تہیہ کرنا
then, in that case, therefore *adv.* **tō** تو
iron pan (*for making bread*) *n.m.* **tavā** توا
continuation, succession *n.m.* **tavātur** تواتر
civility, hospitality *n.f.* **tavāzuᶜ** تواضع
strong, robust, powerful, able *adj.* **tavālī** توالی
twin *n.m.* **tavām** توام
strong, robust, powerful *adj.* **tavānā** توانا
strength, power *n.f.* **tavānā'ī** توانائی
penitence, repentance *n.f.* **taubah** توبہ
gun, cannon *n.f.* **tōp** توپ
artillery; arsenal *n.m.* **tōp xānah** توپ خانہ
artilleryman, gunner *n.m.* **tōpcī** توپچی
conceal, cover *v.t.* **tōpnā** توپنا
mulberry *n.m.* **tūt** توت

care, consideration, attention, attentiveness *n.f.* **tavajjuh** توجہ
unity (*of God*) *n.m.* **tauḥīd** توحید
piousness, piety *n.m.* **tavvaruᶜ** تورع
break, rupture *n.m.* **tōṛ** توڑ
deficiency, scarcity *n.m.* **tōṛā** توڑا
pluck (*flowers*) *v.i.* **tōṛ lēnā** توڑلینا
break, tear, demolish *v.t.* **tōṛnā** توڑنا
conjunction *n.m.* **tavassul** توسل
horse, steed *n.m.* **tausan** توسن
mattress *n.f.* **tōšak** توشک
description *n.f.* **tausīf** توصیف
explanation, illustration *n.f.* **tauzīḥ** توضیح
increase, excess, surplus *n.f.* **taufīr** توفیر
(divine) guidance, help (*from God*); graciousness *n.f.* **taufīq** توفیق
hope, reliance, trust *n.f.* **tavaqquᶜ** توقع
delay, pause, rest, suspension *n.m.* **tavaqquf** توقف
delay, pause *v.t.* **tavaqquf karnā** توقف کرنا
vigilance, guardianship, keeping *n.f.* **tavaqī** توقی
strength, firmness *n.f.* **taukīd** توکید
weighing; weight *n.m.* **tōl** تول
affection, love; hope; attachment *n.m.* **tavalā** تولا
weigh; estimate *v.t.* **tōlnā** تولنا
towel *n.m.* **tauliyā** تولیا
birth; generation *n.f.* **taulīd** تولید
rich, wealthy, opulent *adj.* **tavangar** تونگر
suspicion; imagination *n.m.* **tavahhum** توہم
disgrace, defamation; contempt *n.f.* **tauhīn** توہین
ready, prepared, complete *adj.* **taiyār** تیار
make ready, prepare *v.t.* **taiyār karnā** تیار کرنا
readiness, preparation, arrangement *n.f.* **taiyārī** تیاری
relinquishment, abdication *n.m.* **tiyāg** تیاگ
leave, abandon, resign, give up *v.t.* **tiyāgnā** تیاگنا
renouncer; hermit *n.m.* **tiyāgī** تیاگی
butterfly *n.f.* **tītrī** تیتری
arrow *n.m.* **tīr** تیر

تیر انداز bowman, archer *n.m.* **tīr andāz**

تیر اندازی archery *n.f.* **tīr andāzī**

تیرا your, thy *pron.* **tērā**

تیراک swimmer *n.m.* **tairāk**

تیراکی swimming *n.f.* **tairākī**

تیرتھ holy spot, sacred place (*of pilgrimage*) *n.f.* **tīrath**

تیرتھ جاترا pilgrimage (*in Hinduism*) *n.f.* **tīrath jātrā**

تیرتھ کرنا go on pilgrimage *v.t.* **tīrath karnā**

تیرگی darkness, obscurity *n.f.* **tīragī**

تیرنا swim, float *v.i.* **tairnā**

تیرہ thirteen *num.* **tērah**

تیرہ dark, obscure *adj.* **tīrah**

تیرہ بخت unfortunate *adj.* **tīrah baxt**

تیرہ دل malicious *adj.* **tīrah dil**

تیرھواں thirteenth *adj.* **tērhavāṁ**

تیز sharp, pungent, acute; hot; keen; strong *adj.* **tēz**

تیز فہم intelligent *adj.* **tēz faham**

تیزی sharpness, pungency *n.f.* **tēzī**

تیس thirty *num.* **tīs**

تیسا such, so, in that manner *adj./adv.* **taisā**

تیسرا third *adj.* **tīsrā**

تیسواں thirtieth *adj.* **tīsvāṁ**

تیسی flax, linseed *n.f.* **tīsī**

تیغ dagger, sword *n.f.* **tēġ**

تیغ زن swordsman *n.m.* **tēġ zan**

تیکھا angry, passionate; sharp, pungent; spicy *adj.* **tīkhā**

تیل oil *n.m.* **tēl**

تیمار care, attention *n.m.* **tīmār**

تین three *num.* **tīn**

تین پانچ کرنا quarrel, dispute *v.t.* **tīn pāṁc karnā**

تینتالیس forty-three *num.* **taintālīs**

تینتیس thirty-three *num.* **taintīs**

تیندوا leopard *n.m.* **tēndū'ā**

تیور look, aspect *n.m.* **tēvar**

تیوہار festival *n.m.* **tē'ōhār**

twenty-three *num.* tē'īs تیس

was *v.i.* thā تھا

tap, slap; thumb *n.f.* thāp تھاپ

tap, beat *v.t.* thāpnā تھاپنا

flat dish (*made of brass or bronze*), tray *n.m.* thāl تھال

small flat dish, platter *n.f.* thālī تھالی

prop, support, maintain *v.t.* thāmnā تھامنا

locality, dwelling place *n.m.* thān تھان

police station *n.m.* thānah تھانہ

police officer *n.m.* thānah dār تھانہ دار

slap *n.f.* thappaṛ تھپڑ

slap; gust *n.m.* thapēṛā تھپیڑا

tremble, quiver, shake *v.i.* tharrānā تھرانا

tired, weary, exhausted *adj.* thakā تھکا

weariness, tiredness, exhaustion *n.f.* thakāvaṭ تھکاوٹ

be tired, be wearied, become weak *v.i.* thaknā تھکنا

land, place, spot, site *n.m.* thal تھل

stop, cease *v.i.* thamnā تھمنا

udder, teat *n.m.* than تھن

plaster, pile, heap *v.t.* thōpnā تھوپنا

little, less, few, scarce *adj.* thōṛā تھوڑا

more or less *adj.* thōṛā bahut تھوڑا بہت

little by little *adv.* / a little, very little *adj.* thōṛā thōṛā تھوڑا تھوڑا

lessen, reduce *v.t.* thōṛā karnā تھوڑا کرنا

very little *adj.* thōṛē sē thōṛā تھوڑے سے تھوڑا

spit *n.m.* thūk • mass, quantity, multitude *n.m.* thōk تھوک

defeat *v.t.* thūk lagānā تھوک لگانا

wholesale dealer (*in a village*) *n.m.* thōkdār تھوکدار

spit *v.i.* thūknā تھوکنا

theater *n.m.* thiyēṭar تھیٹر

large bag, sack *n.m.* thailā تھیلا

small bag, purse *n.f.* thailī تھیلی

ṭē ٹ

jump (over) *v.t.* **ṭāpnā** ٹاپنا
small island *n.m.* **ṭāpū** ٹاپو
sackcloth, canvas *n.m.* **ṭāṭ** ٹاٹ
embroidery *n.m.* **ṭāṭ bāfī** ٹاٹ بافی
stack (*of wood*); heap (*of grain, etc.*); evasion *n.f.* **ṭāl** ٹال
putting off, evasion; stalk *n.m.* **ṭāl maṭōl** ٹال مٹول
put off, evade *v.t.* **ṭāl maṭōl karnā** ٹال مٹول کرنا
putting off, evasion *n.m.* **ṭālā** ٹالا
put off, avoid, postpone; remove *v.t.* **ṭālnā** ٹالنا
small bell *n.f.* **ṭālī** ٹالی
crown (*of the head*), skull *n.f.* **ṭāṛṭ** ٹانٹ
share, valuation; weight *n.f.* **ṭānk** ٹانک
stitch; solder *n.m.* **ṭānkā** ٹانکا
stitch, cobble, solder, join, annex *v.t.* **ṭānknā** ٹانکنا
chisel; small hole, notch *n.f.* **ṭānkī** ٹانکی
stitch, sew; solder *v.t.* **ṭānkē lagānā** ٹانکے لگانا
leg *n.f.* **ṭāng** ٹانگ
hang up, suspend *v.t.* **ṭāng dēnā** ٹانگ دینا
leg; foot *n.f.* **ṭāngṛī** ٹانگڑی
hang up, suspend *v.t.* **ṭāngnā** ٹانگنا
tire *n.m.* **ṭāyar** ٹائر
toilet paper *n.m.* **ṭā'ilēṭ pēpar** ٹائلیٹ پیپر
family; household *n.f.* **ṭabbar** ٹبر
small hill, sandbank *n.m.* **ṭabbah** ٹبہ
leap, jump, spring, shoot *n.f.* **ṭappā** ٹپا
dripping *n.f.* **ṭapak** ٹپک
drip *v.i.* **ṭapak paṛnā** ٹپک پڑنا
dropping (*of rain*); falling (*of fruit*) *n.m.* **ṭapkā** ٹپکا
distil, cause to drip *v.t.* **ṭapkānā** ٹپکانا
dripping, distillation *n.m.* **ṭapkā'ō** ٹپکاؤ
drop, leak; be distilled *v.i.* **ṭapaknā** ٹپکنا
pony, small horse *n.m.* **ṭaṭṭū** ٹٹو
touch, feeling; search *n.f.* **ṭaṭōl** ٹٹول

touch, feel; search, investigate *v.t.* **ṭaṭōlnā** ٹٹولنا
ankle joint *n.m.* **ṭaxnah** ٹخنہ
grasshopper *n.m.* **ṭiḍḍā** ٹڈا
locust *n.f.* **ṭiḍḍī** ٹڈی
croak; chatter *v.i.* **ṭarrānā** ٹرانا
railway, train *n.f.* **ṭrēn** ٹرین
traveler's check *n.m.* **ṭraivalars cēk** ٹریولرس چیک
false tears, crocodile tears *n.m.* **ṭisvē** ٹسوے
weep, shed crocodile tears *v.t.* **ṭasvē bahānā** ٹسوے بہانا
sight, look *n.f.* **ṭak** • for a while, a little while *adv.* / little *adj.* **ṭuk** ٹک
gaze, stare *v.t.* **ṭak bāndhnā** ٹک باندھنا
station, stop at; lodge *v.t.* **ṭikānā** ٹکانا
abode, residence, lodging *n.m.* **ṭikā'ō** ٹکاؤ
ticket *n.m./n.f.* **ṭikaṭ** ٹکٹ
collision, striking, knocking *n.f.* **ṭakkar** ٹکر
collide, strike, knock *v.t.* **ṭakkar mārnā** ٹکر مارنا
piece, slice, part; a bit *n.m.* **ṭukṛā** ٹکڑا
mint *n.f.* **ṭaksāl** ٹکسال
true, genuine, pure *adj.* **ṭiksālī** ٹکسالی
idiomatic language *n.f.* **ṭiksālī zabān** ٹکسالی زبان
stay, lodge, remain, stop at *v.i.* **ṭiknā** ٹکنا
piece (of bread), small cake, wafer *n.f.* **ṭikkī** ٹکی
small cake; tablet *n.f.* **ṭikyā** ٹکیا
withdraw, move, go away *v.i.* **ṭalnā** ٹلنا
tomato *n.m.* **ṭamāṭar** ٹماٹر
twinkle, flicker *v.i.* **ṭimṭimānā** ٹمٹمانا
wrangling, quarrel, brawl *n.m.* **ṭanṭā** ٹنٹا
handless *adj.* **ṭunḍā** ٹنڈا
service, attendance *n.f.* **ṭahal** ٹہل
serve, attend *v.t.* **ṭahal karnā** ٹہل کرنا
maid servant *n.f.* **ṭahalnī** ٹہلنی
servant, attendant *n.m.* **ṭahalvā** ٹہلوا
twig, branch (*of a tree*) *n.f.* **ṭahnī** ٹہنی
hat, cap *n.m.* **ṭōp** ٹوپ
hat, cap *n.f.* **ṭōpī** ٹوپی
breach, fracture, break *n.f.* **ṭūṭ** ٹوٹ

rush in; fall upon *v.i.* **ṭūṭ paṛnā** ٹوٹ پڑنا
loss, deficiency *n.m.* **ṭōṭā** ٹوٹا
spell; charm *n.m.* **ṭōṭkā** ٹوٹکا
be broken, break, burst *v.i.* **ṭūṭnā** ٹوٹنا
hindrance, interruption *n.f.* **ṭōk** ٹوک
large basket *n.m.* **ṭōkrā** ٹوکرا
small basket *n.f.* **ṭōkrī** ٹوکری
challenge, question; prevent, stop *v.t.* **ṭōknā** ٹوکنا
quarter (*in a town*) *n.m.* **ṭōlā** ٹولا
society, crowd, group *n.m.* **ṭōlī** ٹولی
charm, fascination *n.m.* **ṭōnā** ٹونا
spying; search *n.f.* **ṭōh** ٹوہ
trace; investigate, find out *v.t.* **ṭōh lagānā** ٹوہ لگانا
television, TV *n.f.* **ṭī vī** ٹی وی
crooked, bent, awry *adj.* **ṭēṛhā** ٹیڑھا
bend, crook *v.t.* **ṭēṛhā karnā** ٹیڑھا کرنا
throb, throbbing; stitching *n.f.* **ṭīs** ٹیس
throb *v.t.* **ṭīs mārnā** ٹیس مارنا
prop, support, pillar *n.f.* **ṭēk** ٹیک
taxi *n.f.* **ṭaiksī** ٹیکسی
prop, support *v.t.* **ṭēknā** ٹیکنا
telephone *n.m.* **ṭailīfōn** ٹیلیفون
television *n.f.* **ṭailīvižan** ٹیلیویژن
windpipe, throat *n.m.* **ṭēnṭū'ā** ٹینٹوا
throttle, strangle, choke *v.t.* **ṭēnṭū'ā dabānā** ٹینٹوا دبانا
tennis *n.f.* **ṭainis** ٹینس
dignity, splendor, pomp *n.m.* **ṭhāṭh** ٹھاٹھ
mold; stamp *n.m.* **ṭhappā** ٹھپا
stamp, put a stamp on *v.t.* **ṭhappā lagānā** ٹھپا لگانا
crowd, herd, multitude *n.m.* **ṭhaṭ** ٹھٹ
joke, jest, fun *n.m.* **ṭhaṭā** ٹھٹا
joking, humor, mockery *n.f.* **ṭhaṭhōl** ٹھٹھول
joker, jester, funny person *n.m.* **ṭhaṭhē bāz** ٹھٹھے باز
kick *n.m.* **ṭhuḍḍā** ٹھڈا
chin *n.f.* **ṭhuḍḍī** ٹھڈی
crammed, stuffed; hard, solid *adj.* **ṭhas** ٹھس

abode, place, whereabouts *n.m.* **ṭhikānā** ٹھکانا
kick *v.t.* **ṭhukrānā** ٹھکرانا
swindler, cheat, robber *n.m.* **ṭhag** ٹھگ
be cheated, be robbed *v.i.* / cheat, rob *v.t.* **ṭhagnā** ٹھگنا
cheating, robbery, theft *n.f.* **ṭhagī** ٹھگی
tinkle, jingle *n.f.* **ṭhan ṭhan** ٹھن ٹھن
cold, chill *n.f.* **ṭhanḍ** ٹھنڈ
be cold *v.i.* **ṭhanḍ paṛnā** ٹھنڈ پڑنا
cold, chilled, cool *adj.* **ṭhanḍā** ٹھنڈا
cool, make cool; extinguish *v.t.* **ṭhanḍā karnā** ٹھنڈا کرنا
coldness, coolness *n.f.* **ṭhanḍak** ٹھنڈک
cold breath *n.f.* **ṭhanḍī sāṁs** ٹھنڈی سانس
sound, produce a sound; clink *v.t.* **ṭhankānā** ٹھنکانا
ring, resound; sob, whimper; clink *v.i.* **ṭhinaknā** ٹھنکنا
dwarfish, short, small *adj.* **ṭhingnā** ٹھنگنا
be fixed, be ascertained, be resolved *v.i.* **ṭhannā** ٹھننا
stop, bring to a halt *v.t.* **ṭhahrānā** ٹھہرانا
settlement; halt, stop; rest *n.m.* **ṭhahrā'ō** ٹھہراؤ
place, spot; residence *n.m.* **ṭhaur** ٹھور
chin *n.f.* **ṭhōṛī** ٹھوڑی
solid, compact; hard; heavy *adj.* **ṭhōs** ٹھوس
stumble *v.t.* **ṭhōkar khānā** ٹھوکر کھانا
hammer, beat, strike *v.t.* **ṭhōknā** ٹھوکنا
peck *v.t.* **ṭhōṁsnā** ٹھونسنا
seat, sitting place; support *n.m.* **ṭhiyā** ٹھیا
stopper, cork, plug *n.f.* **ṭhēpī** ٹھیپی
real, genuine; idiomatic *adj.* **ṭhēṭh** ٹھیٹھ
knock, blow, push *n.f.* **ṭhēs** ٹھیس
correct, accurate, right, true, exact *adj.* **ṭhīk** ٹھیک
alright, OK, okay *adv.* **ṭhīk ṭhāk** ٹھیک ٹھاک
correct, adjust, ascertain *v.t.* **ṭhīk karnā** ٹھیک کرنا
contract, work (*done by contract*) *n.m.* **ṭhēkah** ٹھیکہ
contractor *n.m.* **ṭhēkēdār** ٹھیکیدار
shove, push, move forward *v.t.* **ṭhēlnā** ٹھیلنا
pushcart, trolley *n.m.* **ṭhēlah** ٹھیلہ

sē ث

firm, fixed, stable, constant *adj.* **sābit** ثابت
remain firm, remain constant *v.i.* **sābit rahnā** ثابت رہنا
immovable, steady *adj.* **sābit qadam** ثابت قدم
prove, verify, confirm *v.t.* **sābit karnā** ثابت کرنا
splendid, shining, glittering *adj.* **sāqib** ثاقب
third person, arbitrator, mediator *n.m.* **sālis** ثالث
arbitration, mediation *n.f.* **sālisī** ثالثی
trinity *n.m.* **sālūs** ثالوث
second *adj.* / equal, match *n.m.* **sānī** ثانی
second (*unit of time*), moment *n.f.* **sāniyah** ثانیہ
constancy, permanence, stability, firmness *n.m.* **sabāt** ثبات
firmness, fixedness *n.m.* **sabt** ثبت
inscribe; subscribe *v.t.* **sabt karnā** ثبت کرنا
proof, testimony *n.m.* **subūt** ثبوت
evidence *n.m.* **subūt-ē-taḥrīrī** ثبوت تحریری
wealth, affluence *n.f.* **sarvat** ثروت
earth *n.m.* **sarā** ثریٰ
culture *n.f.* **saqāfat** ثقافت
cultural *adj.* **saqāfatī** ثقافتی
heaviness, burden, weight *n.f.* **saqālat** ثقالت
snow, ice *n.f.* **salj** ثلج
once more, again *adv.* **sum** ثم
fruit, produce; reward, result *n.m.* **samar** ثمر
value, price, cost *n.m.* **saman** ثمن
praise, applause *n.f.* **sanā** ثنا
reward *n.m.* **savāb** ثواب
robe *n.m.* **saub** ثوب
bull; Taurus (*Zodiac*) *n.m.* **saur** ثور

jīm ج

place, locality; seat *n.f.* **jā** جا
everywhere, here and there *adv.* **jā bajā** جا بجا
despotic *adj.* / despot, tyrant *n.m.* **jābir** جابر
caste, race, tribe, class, sort *n.f.* / born *adj.* **jāt** جات
pilgrimage *n.f.* **jātrā** جاترا
pilgrim *n.m.* **jātrī** جاتری
magic *n.m.* **jādū** جادو
charm, enchant *v.t.* **jādū karnā** جادو کرنا
magician, sorcerer *n.m.* **jādūgar** جادوگر
magic *n.f.* **jādūgarī** جادوگری
absorbent, attractive *adj.* **jāzib** جاذب
neighbor, partner (*in trade*) *n.m.* **jār** جار
broom *n.f.* **jārūb** جاروب
sweeper *n.m.* **jārōb kaš** جاروب کش
running, flowing, current *adj.* **jārī** جاری
carry on, continue *v.t.* **jārī rakhnā** جاری رکھنا
continue *v.i.* **jārī rahnā** جاری رہنا
begin, start; issue, introduce *v.t.* **jārī karnā** جاری کرنا
winter, coldness, cold *n.m.* **jāṛā** جاڑا
feel cold *v.i.* **jāṛā lagnā** جاڑا لگنا
spy *n.m.* **jāsūs** جاسوس
spying, espionage *n.f.* **jāsūsī** جاسوسی
awake, wake up, be awake, get up *v.i.* **jāgnā** جاگنا
net, snare, trap *n.m.* **jāl** جال
cobweb, spider's web *n.m.* **jālā** جالا
network *n.f.* **jālī** جالی
bowl, cup, glass, goblet *n.m.* **jām** جام
portmanteau *n.f.* **jāmdānī** جامدانی
comprehensive, collective *adj.* **jāmiᶜ** جامع
mosque (*for Friday's prayers*) *n.f.* **jāmiᶜ masjid** جامع مسجد
university *n.m.* **jāmiᶜah** جامعہ
life, soul, mind, spirit; energy, vigor; knowledge *n.f.* **jān** جان
save one's life *v.t.* **jān bacānā** جان بچانا

جان بخشی **jān baxšī** forgiveness, pardon *n.f.*
جان بلب **jān balab** dying *adj.*
جان پر کھیلنا **jān par khēlnā** risk one's life *v.t.*
جان پڑنا **jān paṛnā** seem, appear *v.i.*
جان پہچان **jān pahcān** acquaintance *n.f.*
جان نثار **jān nisār** devoted *adj.*
جانا **jānā** go, depart *v.i.*
جاناں **jānāṁ** mistress, beloved *n.m.*
جانب **jānib** towards *adv.*
جانباز **jānbāz** venturesome, daring *adj.*
جانچ **jāṁc** test, trial *n.m.*
جانچنا **jāṁcnā** try, test *v.t.*
جاندار **jāndār** animated, active, spirited *adj.*
جانشین **jā našīn** deputy, successor *n.m.*
جانشینی **jā našīnī** succession *n.f.*
جانفشانی **jānfišānī** zeal, devotion, diligence *n.f.*
جانکاری **jānkārī** knowledge *n.f.*
جاننا **jānnā** know, understand, recognize *v.t.*
جانور **jānvar** animal *n.m.*
جانی **jānī** vital, cordial, hearty *adj.*
جاہ **jāh** grandeur, dignity *n.m.*
جاہل **jāhil** illiterate, uneducated, ignorant *adj.*
جاہلیت **jāhlīt** illiteracy, ignorance *n.f.*
جاوداں **jāvidāṁ** eternal, everlasting, perpetual, immortal *adj.*
جاودانی **jāvdānī** eternity *n.f.*
جاوید **jāvīd** always, eternal *adj.*
جائداد **jā'ēdād** estate, property *n.m.*
جائز **jā'iz** lawful, legal; right, just *adj.*
جائزہ **jā'izah** review, examination *n.m.*
جائے پھل **jā'ē phal** nutmeg *n.m.*
جب **jab** when, as soon as, at the time *adv.*
جب تب **jab tab** now and then *adv.*
جب تک **jab tak** as long as, by that time, until *adv.*
جب جب **jab jab** whenever, at the very time *adv.*
جب سے **jab sē** since *adv.*
جب کبھی **jab kabhī** whenever, at the very time *adv.*

still, while *adv.* **jab kih** جب کہ
omnipotent, mighty *adj.* **jabbār** جبار
oppression, compulsion *n.m.* **jabr** جبر
oppress, compel *v.t.* **jabr karnā** جبر کرنا
forcibly, by force *adv.* **jabran** جبراً
omnipotence *n.m.* **jabrūt** جبروت
compulsory, forced *adj.* **jabrī** جبری
jaw *n.m.* **jabṛā** جبڑا
hill, mountain *n.m.* **jabal** جبل
nature, temperament, temper *n.m.* **jabillat** جبلت
natural *adj.* **jiblī** جبلی
robe, gown *n.m.* **jubbah** • forehead *n.f.* **jabah** جبہ
forehead *n.f.* **jabīṁ** جبیں
inform, point out, warn *v.t.* **jatānā** جتانا
plowing, cultivation *n.f.* **jutā'ī** جتائی
effort, endeavor, exertion *n.m.* **jatan** جتن
as much as, so much, so many *adv.* **jitnā** جتنا
body, figure, physique *n.m.* **jussah** جثہ
tested, tried, proved *adj.* **jacā** جچا
be estimated *v.i.* **jacnā** جچنا
grandfather *n.m.* **jadd** • endeavor, effort *n.f.* **jidd** جد
separate, different, distinct *adj.* **judā** جدا
separately, one by one *adv.* **judā judā** جدا جدا
separate, disunite, disjoin *v.t.* **judā karnā** جدا کرنا
contest, dispute *n.m.* **jidāl** جدال
separation, absence *n.f.* **judā'ī** جدائی
quarrel, battle, fighting *n.f.* **jadal** جدل
grandmother *n.f.* **jaddah** جدہ
effort, hard struggle, labor *n.f.* **jad-ō-jahad** جدوجہد
polar star; Capricorn (*Zodiac*) *n.m.* **jadī** • ancestral, paternal *adj.* **jaddī** جدی
modern, new, fresh *adj.* **jadīd** جدید
wherever, where, there *adv.* **jidhar** جدھر
leprosy *n.m.* **juzām** جذام
leper *n.m.* **juzāmī** جذامی
attraction, absorption *n.m.* **jazb** جذب
attract, absorb, draw *v.t.* **jazb karnā** جذب کرنا

be absorbed *v.i.* **jazb hōnā** جذب ہونا
passion, desire; rage, fury *n.m.* **jazbah** جذبہ
origin, root *n.m.* **jazr** جذر
drawing; base, foundation *n.m.* **jarr** جر
stocking, sock *n.m.* **jurrāb** جراب
courage, valor, bravery *n.m.* **jurāt** جرات
dare; presume *v.t.* **jurāt karnā** جرات کرنا
surgeon; anatomist *n.m.* **jarrāḥ** جراح
valiant, brave *adj.* **jarrār** جرار
drop; draft *n.m.* **jurᶜah** جرعہ
ring; multitude, crowd *n.m.* **jargah** جرگہ
crime, offense; guilt, fault *n.m.* **jurm** • body *n.m.* **jirm** جرم
commit a crime *v.t.* **jurm karnā** جرم کرنا
fine, penalty *n.m.* **jurmānah** جرمانہ
fine *v.t.* **jurmānah karnā** جرمانہ کرنا
valiant, brave *adj.* **jarī** جری
wounded *adj.* **jarīḥ** جریح
alone, separate, solitary *adj.* / newspaper; register, account book *n.m.* **jarīdah** جریدہ
root, origin, foundation *n.f.* **jaṛ** جڑ
destroy completely, ruin utterly *v.t.* **jaṛ kāṭnā** جڑ کاٹنا
be fixed, be joined, join *v.i.* **juṛnā** جڑنا
twins, pair *adj.* **juṛvāṁ** جڑواں
part, portion; ingredient *n.m.* / besides, except *pp.* **juz** جز
binding (*of a book*) *n.f.* **juz bandī** جزبندی
reward, compensation; retaliation *n.f.* **jazā** جزا
displeased, offended, angry *adj.* **jizbiz** جزبز
ebb, low tide *n.m.* **jazr** جزر
part, portion; ingredient *n.m.* **juzū** جزو
island *n.m.* **jazīrah** جزیرہ
peninsula *n.m.* **jazīrah numā** جزیرہ نما
tribute, poll-tax *n.m.* **jiziyah** جزیہ
whom, who, which, what, that *pron.* **jis** جس
whereupon *adv.* **jis par** جس پر
where, wherever *adv.* **jis jagah** جس جگہ
just as, according to *adv.* **jis taraḥ** جس طرح
boldness, courage *n.f.* **jasārat** جسارت

bulkiness, volume *n.f.* **jasāmat** جسامت
leap, jump, bound *n.f.* **jast** جست
search, quest, exploration *n.f.* **justjū** جستجو
body *n.m.* **jism** جسم
physical, corporeal *adj.* **jismānī** جسمانی
bulky, fat, corpulent *adj.* **jasīm** جسیم
festival, jubilee *n.m.* **jašn** جشن
counterfeit, forgery *n.m.* **ja^cl** جعل
forgery *n.f.* **ja^cl sāzī** جعل سازی
counterfeit, forged *adj.* **ja^clī** جعلی
geography *n.m.* **juġrāfiyah** جغرافیہ
oppression, violence, tyranny; injury *n.f.* **jafā** جفا
hardworking, energetic *n.m.* **jafākaš** جفاکش
oppressor, tyrant *n.m.* **jafāši^cār** جفاشعار
pair, couple *n.m.* **juft** جفت
bent, wrinkled *adj.* / wrinkle; buttock *n.m.* **juftah** جفتہ
tight *adj.* **jakaṛband** جکڑبند
fasten, tighten, tie *v.t.* **jakaṛnā** جکڑنا
epoch, period, age *n.m.* **jug** • universe; world, earth *n.m.* **jag** جگ
shining, glittering *adj.* **jag mag** جگ مگ
awaken, rouse (*from sleep*) *v.t.* **jagānā** جگانا
wit, humor, pun *n.f.* **jugat** • world *n.m.* **jagat** جگت
skillful, artful, clever *adj.* **jugtī** جگتی
liver; heart; mind; soul *n.m.* **jigar** جگر
heart-; liver-; intimate, closed; beloved, dear *adj.* **jigrī** جگری
glitter, shine, dazzle *v.i.* **jagmagānā** جگمگانا
glitter, splendor, dazzle *n.f.* **jagmagāhaṭ** جگمگاہٹ
firefly, glow-worm *n.m.* **jugnū** جگنو
place, spot, site *n.f.* **jagah** جگہ
everywhere *adv.* **jagah jagah** جگہ جگہ
trick, fraud, cheating *n.m.* **jul** • water *n.m.* **jal** جل
brightness, splendor, polish, lustre *n.f.* **jilā** • great, glorious *adj.* **jallā** جلا
purgative, purge *n.m.* **jullāb** جلاب
executioner *n.m.* **jallād** جلاد
polish *v.t.* **jilā dēnā** جلادینا

polisher *n.m.* **jilā kār** جلا کار
glory, majesty, grandeur *n.m.* **jalāl** جلال
glorious, majestic, illustrious *adj.* **jalālī** جلالی
animate, revive, give life *v.t.* **jilānā** • burn, inflame, light *v.t.* **jalānā** جلانا
weaver; fool, idiot *n.m.* **jullāha** جلاہا
splendor *n.f.* **jilā'ō** جلاؤ
skin; leather *n.f.* **jild** • at once, quickly, immediately *adv.* **jald** جلد
haste, agility; expedition *n.f.* **jald bāzī** جلد بازی
expeditious, hasty *adj.* **jald bāz** جلدباز
soon *adv.* / quickness, hurry, haste *n.f.* **jaldī** جلدی
quickly; urgently *adv.* **jaldī sē** جلدی سے
make haste, hurry *v.t.* **jaldī karnā** جلدی کرنا
meeting, assembly, party, committee *n.m.* **jalsah** جلسہ
inflammation, burning, heat *n.f.* **jalan** جلن
burn, be burnt; envy, be jealous *v.i.* **jalnā** جلنا
dropsy *n.m.* **jalandar** جلندر
procession, pomp *n.m.* **jalūs** جلوس
lustre, magnificence *n.m.* **jalvah** جلوہ
splendid, manifest, illustrious *adj.* **jalvah gar** جلوہ گر
apparent, evident *adj.* **jalī** جلی
jalebi (*deep-fried sweet dish*) *n.f.* **jalēbī** جلیبی
companion, colleague *n.m.* **jalīs** جلیس
great, glorious *adj.* **jalīl** جلیل
big, great, huge; much *n.m.* **jamm** جم
always, constantly *adv.* **jam jam** جم جم
vast multitude, big crowd *n.m.* **jam-ē-ġafīr** جم غفیر
sexual intercourse, copulation *n.m.* **jimāᶜ** جماع
society, company, assembly, association, group *n.f.* **jamāᶜat** جماعت
beauty, elegance, grace *n.m.* **jamāl** جمال
freeze *v.t.* **jamānā** جمانا
freezing *n.m.* **jamā'ō** جماؤ
yawning, gaping *n.f.* **jamā'ī** جمائی
yawn, gape *v.t.* **jamā'ī lēnā** جمائی لینا
rose-apple *n.m.* **jambū** جمبو
collection; total, sum *n.f.* **jamaᶜ** جمع
add, collect, gather, accumulate *v.t.* **jamaᶜ karnā** جمع کرنا

assemble, be collected, be added *v.i.* **jama^c hōnā** جمع ہونا
chief, leader *n.m.* **jama^cdār** جمعدار
Thursday *n.f.* **jumi^crāt** جمعرات
Friday *n.m.* **jum^cah** جمعہ
crowd, collection, multitude *n.f.* **jam^ciyat** جمعیت
crowd, multitude *n.m.* **jamghaṭ** جمگھٹ
camel *n.m.* **jamal** جمل
(the) whole, sum, total; phrase *n.m.* **jumlah** جملہ
become fixed, take root, be frozen *v.i.* **jamnā** جمنا
population, people *n.m.* **jumhūr** جمہور
republic, democracy *n.f.* **jumhūrī sultanat** جمہوری سلطنت
inactivity, deadlock *n.m.* **jamūd** جمود
all, whole, universal *adj.* **jamī^c** جمیع
altogether, universally *adv.* **jamī^can** جمیعا
beautiful, elegant *adj.* **jamīl** جمیل
demon, devil *n.m.* **jinn** جن
born, produced *adj.* **janā** جنا
Sir!, Your highness!, Your excellency! *interj.* **janāb** جناب
Respected sir!, Exalted sir!, Your excellency! *interj.* **janāb-ē-^cālī** جناب عالی
Dear sir! *interj.* **janāb-ē-man** جناب من
uncleanliness, pollution *n.f.* **janābat** جنابت
funcral *n.m.* **janāzah** جنازہ
inform; deliver (*a child*) *v.t.* **janānā** جنانا
midwife *n.f.* **janā'ī** جنائی
motion, movement, gesture *n.f.* **junbiš** جنبش
move, shake *v.t.* **junbiš dēnā** جنبش دینا
garden, paradise *n.f.* **jannat** جنت
trouble, difficulty *n.m.* **jaṁjāl** جنجال
sandalwood; big stone *n.m.* **jandal** جندل
kind, species, sort, class; sex, gender *n.f.* **jins** جنس
generic; sexual *adj.* **jinsī** جنسی
sexuality *n.f.* **jinsiyat** جنسیت
battle, war, combat, fight *n.f.* **jang** جنگ
wage war, combat, fight *v.t.* **jang karnā** جنگ کرنا
forest, wood, jungle *n.m.* **jangal** جنگل
fence, railing *n.m.* **janglā** جنگلا

savage, wild *adj.* **janglī** جنگلی
martial, warlike *adj.* **jangī** جنگی
fleet *n.m.* **jangī bēṛah** جنگی بیڑہ
warship *n.m.* **jangī jahāz** جنگی جہاز
birth; life, existence *n.m.* **janam** جنم
horoscope *n.f.* **janam pattrī** جنم پتری
birthday *n.m.* **janam din** جنم دن
give birth *v.t.* **janam dēnā** جنم دینا
south *n.m.* **janūb** جنوب
southern *adj.* **janūbī** جنوبی
January *n.f.* **janvarī** جنوری
insanity, madness *n.m.* **junūn** جنون
become insane, go mad *v.i.* **junūn hōnā** جنون ہونا
insane, mad *adj.* **junūnī** جنونی
jihad, holy crusade *n.m.* **jihād** جہاد
ship, vessel *n.m.* **jahāz** جہاز
sailor *n.m.* / naval, nautical *adj.* **jahāzī** جہازی
pirate *n.m.* **jahāzī ḍākū** جہازی ڈاکو
ignorance, illiteracy *n.f.* **jihālat** جہالت
world; where *n.m.* **jahāṁ** جہاں
experienced, widely traveled *adj.* **jahāṁdīdah** جہاندیدہ
world-subduing, world-conquering *adj.* **jahāngīr** جہانگیر
reason, motive, cause; direction, side *n.f.* **jihat** جہت
struggle, endeavor, effort *n.m.* **jahd** جہد
ignorance, stupidity *n.m.* **jahl** جہل
hell *n.m.* **jahannum** جہنم
hellish, infernal *adj.* **jahannumī** جہنمی
dowry *n.m.* **jahēz** جہیز
wherever, in whatsoever place, wheresoever *adv.* **jahīṁ** جہیں
who, what, which, that *pron.* **jō** جو
gambling *n.m.* **ju'ā** جوا
gamble *v.t.* **ju'ā khēlnā** جوا کھیلنا
reply, answer *n.m.* **javāb** جواب
reply, answer *v.t.* **javāb dēnā** جواب دینا
conversation, argument *n.m.* **javāb savāl** جواب سوال

call for an explanation *v.t.* **javāb talab karnā** جواب طلب کرنا
gambler *n.m.* **jū'ā bāz** جوا باز
counterpart, respondent *n.m.* **javābī** جوابی
generous, beneficient *adj.* **javād** جواد
corn, millet *n.f.* **jō'ār** • neighborhood, vicinity *n.m.* **jivār** جوار
gambler *n.m.* **jō'ārī** جواری
permission, permit; lawfulness, legitimacy *n.m.* **javāz** جواز
flame, fire, blaze; passion *n.f.* **jū'ālā** جوالا
volcano *n.m.* **jū'ālā mukhī** جوالا مکھی
/ youth, young adult, young man, young woman *n.m.* **javān** جوان
young, adolescent *adj.*
bravery, courage, heroism, manliness *n.f.* **javān mardī** جوان مردی
fortunate *adj.* **javān baxt** جوان بخت
brave, courageous; generous *adj.* **javān mard** جوان مرد
youth, adolescence, manhood *n.f.* **javānī** جوانی
jewels, gems *n.m.* **javāhir** جواہر
beauty, bloom; adolescence *n.m.* **jōban** جوبن
lustre, brilliance, light *n.f.* **jōt** جوت
shoe *n.m.* **jūtā** جوتا
astrology, astronomy *n.m.* **jōtiš** جوتش
astrologer, astronomer *n.m.* **jōtišī** جوتشی
plow, cultivate, yoke *v.t.* **jōtnā** جوتنا
shoe, slipper; pair of shoes *n.f.* **jōtī** جوتی
oppression, tyranny, violence *n.m.* **jaur** جور
wife, consort *n.f.* **jōrū** جورو
joint, link, patch; match, total, sum *n.m.* **jōṛ** جوڑ
patch, sum up, add *v.t.* **jōṛ lagānā** جوڑ لگانا
joining, connection, counterpart, match, pair, couple *n.m.* **jōṛā** جوڑا
join, unite, add, connect, patch *v.t.* **jōṛnā** جوڑنا
pair, couple; partner, mate *n.f.* **jōṛī** جوڑی
nut; nutmeg *n.m.* **jauz** جوز
Gemini (*Zodiac*) *n.m.* **jauzā** جوزا
boiling, heat; excitement, emotion, enthusiasm *n.m.* **jōš** جوش
boil *v.t.* **jōš dēnā** جوش دینا
roar, passion, excitement *n.m.* **jōš-ō-xarōš** جوش و خروش
boiling *adj.* **jōšāṁ** جوشاں

armor, armlet *n.m.* **jaušan** جوشن.
hunger, appetite *n.f.* **jūᶜ** جوع.
hungry *adj.* **jauᶜān** جوعان.
cavity, hollow *n.m.* **jauf** جوف.
troop *n.m.* **jauq** جوق.
risk, danger *n.f.* **jōkhōṁ** جوکھوں.
yoga; ascetic, hermit *n.m.* **jōg** جوگ.
yogi (*female*) *n.f.* **jōgin** جوگن.
yogi (*male*) *n.m.* **jōgī** جوگی.
strength (*of mind or body*) *n.f.* **jaulānī** جولانی.
July *n.f.* **jūlā'ī** جولائی.
louse *n.f.* / as, like, such as *adv./pp.* **jūṁ** جوں.
time, period, age *n.f.* / June *n.m.* **jūn** جون.
as long as, as far as *adj.* **jūṁ jūṁ** جوں جوں.
as it was, as in fact, the very same *adv.* **jūṁ kā tūṁ** جوں کا توں.
leech *n.f.* **jōnk** جونک.
jewel, gem, pearl; essence, nature, spirit; secret *n.m.* **jauhar** جوہر.
jeweler *n.m.* **jauharī** جوہری.
pond (*filled with rain*) *n.m.* **jauhaṛ** جوہڑ.
expect, look out for *v.t.* **jōhnā** جوہنا.
jasmine *n.f.* **jūhī** جوہی.
seeker, inquirer *n.m.* **jōyā** جویا.
seeker, inquirer *n.m.* **jō'indah** جوئندہ.
victory, triumph, conquest *n.f.* **jai** جے
life, soul, spirit, mind, conscience *n.m.* / sir, madam *interj.* **jī** جی
vomit; displease; take offense *v.t.* **jī burā karnā** جی برا کرنا
amuse oneself *v.t.* **jī bahlānā** جی بہلانا
be touched (with compassion), be deeply moved *v.i.* **jī bhar ānā** جی بھر آنا
G.P.O. (General Post Office) *n.m.* **jī. pī. ō.** جی پی او
long for, yearn for *v.i.* **jī tarasnā** جی ترسنا
fall in love *v.i.* **jī jānā** جی جانا
grieve, hurt *v.t.* **jī jalānā** جی جلانا
die *v.i.* **jī sē jānā** جی سے جانا
kill *v.t.* **jī sē mārnā** جی سے مارنا
desire *v.t.* **jī karnā** جی کرنا

like, love *v.i.* **jī lagnā** جی لگنا
kill, take someone's life *v.t.* **jī lēnā** جی لینا
feel nausea *v.i.* **jī matlānā** جی متلانا
come into the mind *v.i.* **jī mēṁ ānā** جی میں آنا
die *v.i.* **jī nikalnā** جی نکلنا
be discouraged *v.i.* **jī hārnā** جی ہارنا
cause to live, revive *v.t.* **jiyānā** جیانا
pocket *n.f.* **jēb** • breast, bosom; heart *n.f.* **jaib** جیب
pocket money *n.m.* **jēb xarc** جیب خرچ
pickpocket *v.t.* **jēb katarnā** جیب کترنا
watch *n.f.* **jēb ghaṛī** جیب گھڑی
tongue *n.f.* **jibh** جیبھ
silence, interrupt; hold one's tongue *v.t.* **jibh pakaṛnā** جیبھ پکڑنا
victory, gain, success *n.f.* **jīt** جیت
obtain victory *v.i.* **jīt hōnā** جیت ہونا
alive, living *adj.* **jītā** جیتا
living and healthy, alive and flourishing *adj.* **jītā jāgtā** جیتا جاگتا
win, conquer, overcome, beat *v.t.* **jītnā** جیتنا
for life, in a lifetime *adv.* **jītē jī** جیتے جی
live, enjoy a long life *v.i.* **jītē rahnā** جیتے رہنا
brother-in law (*husband's elder brother*) *n.m.* / eldest, first-born *adj.* **jēṭh** جیٹھ
eldest, highest, first-born, *adj.* **jēṭhā** جیٹھا
good, excellent *adj.* **jayyid** جید
cumin (*plant and seed*) *n.m.* **jīrā** جیرا
such as, according to, in this manner, which *adv.* **jaisā** جیسا
as well as *adv.* **jaisā taisā** جیسا تیسا
as though, whereas, as if *conj.* **jaisā kēh** جیسا کہ
somehow or another *adv.* **jaisē taisē** جیسے تیسے
as before, as it was *adv.* **jaisē kā taisā** جیسے کا تیسا
army *n.m.* **jaiš** جیش
jail, prison *n.m.* **jēl** جیل
jail, prison *n.m.* **jēl xānah** جیل خانہ
be bribed **v.i jīmnā** جیمنا
live, be alive, exist *v.i.* / living, life *n.m.* **jīnā** جینا
life, soul, being *n.m.* **jīv** جیو
astronomy, astrology *n.m.* **jyōtiš** جیوتش

astronomer, astrologer *n.m.* **jyōtišī** جیوتشی
lustre, radiance, splendor, flame *n.f.* **jyōtī** جیوتی
string, cord *n.f.* **jē'ōṛī** جیوڑی
life, existence, living, livelihood *n.m.* **jīvan** جیون
shrub, bramble *n.m.* **jhāṛ** جھاڑ
ease oneself *v.i.* **jhāṛ phirnā** جھاڑ پھرنا
purge *n.m.* **jhāṛā** جھاڑا
broom, whisk *n.f.* **jhāṛū** جھاڑو
sweep *v.t.* **jhāṛū dēnā** جھاڑو دینا
bush, underwood, forest, woods *n.f.* **jhāṛī** جھاڑی
foam, froth, scum *n.m.* **jhāg** جھاگ
frill, fringe *n.f.* **jhālar** جھالر
cover, conceal, screen *v.t.* **jhānpnā** جھانپنا
leaky, cracked, perforated *adj.* **jhāṁjhar** جھانجھر
deceive, trick, coax *v.t.* **jhāṁsnā** جھانسنا
deceiver, cheat; coaxer *n.m.* **jhāṁsū** جھانسو
peep, peeping, spying *n.f.* **jhānk** جھانک
peep, spy *v.t.* **jhānknā** جھانکنا
quick, sudden *adj.* **jhap** جھپ
quickly *adv.* **jhap sē** جھپ سے
spring, leap *n.f.* **jhapaṭ** جھپٹ
snatch, spring on, pounce upon *v.t.* **jhapaṭ lēnā** جھپٹ لینا
assault, attack, spring *n.m.* **jhapaṭṭā** جھپٹا
snatch, make a rush *v.t.* **jhapaṭṭā mārnā** جھپٹا مارنا
spring, pounce; run, walk fast, fly *v.i.* **jhapaṭnā** جھپٹنا
close your eyes, nap, doze *v.i.* **jhapaknā** جھپکنا
drowsiness; nap *n.f.* **jhapkī** جھپکی
take a nap, doze *v.t.* **jhapkī lēnā** جھپکی لینا
jerk, violent pull, shake, twitch *n.m.* **jhaṭkā** جھٹکا
jerk, shake, twitch *v.t.* **jhaṭaknā** جھٹکنا
falsify *v.t.* **jhuṭlānā** جھٹلانا
hesitation, shyness *n.f.* **jhijhak** جھجھک
hesitate, feel shy *v.t.* **jhijhaknā** جھجھکنا
cascade, waterfall *n.m.* **jharnā** جھرنا
wrinkle, fold *n.f.* **jhurrī** جھری
flame, heat; skirmish, fight *n.f.* **jhaṛap** جھڑپ

scold, rebuke *v.t.* **jhiṛaknā** جھڑکنا

scolding, rebuke, snappishness *n.f.* **jhiṛkī** جھڑکی

drop, fall off *v.i.* **jhaṛnā** جھڑنا

rain (*continuous*) *n.f.* **jhaṛī** جھڑی

rain (*continuously*) *v.i.* **jhaṛī lagnā** جھڑی لگنا

clean, white, shining *adj.* **jhak** جھک

bow, incline *v.t.* **jhukānā** جھکانا

storm, hurricane; sudden blast *n.m.* **jhakkaṛ** جھکڑ

bend, incline, stoop *v.i.* **jhuknā** جھکنا

passionate, talkative, wrathful *adj.* **jhakkī** جھکی

wrangling, quarrel, brawl *n.m.* **jhagṛā** جھگڑا

quarrel, wrangle *v.t.* **jhagṛā karnā** جھگڑا کرنا

dispute, quarrel, argue *v.i.* **jhagaṛnā** جھگڑنا

swing, rock a cradle, dangle *v.t.* **jhulānā** • be angry *v.i.* **jhallānā** جھلانا

singe, scorch, brand *v.t.* **jhulsānā** جھلسانا

glimpse; brightness *n.f.* **jhalak** جھلک

blister *n.m.* **jhalkā** جھلکا

cause to shine, polish *v.t.* **jhalkānā** جھلکانا

shine, glitter, flash *v.i.* **jhalaknā** جھلکنا

sparkle, flash, shimmer, glimmer, flicker *v.i.* **jhilmilānā** جھلملانا

fan, be soldered *v.i.* **jhalnā** جھلنا

glitter, shining *n.f.* **jhamak** جھمک

altercation, row, entanglement *n.m.* **jhamēlā** جھمیلا

quarrel, argument; difficulty, dilemma *n.m.* **jhanjhaṭ** جھنجھٹ

rattle, jingle *v.t.* **jhanjhanānā** جھنجھنانا

bush, underwood, clump of trees; swarm, flock, herd *n.m.* **jhunḍ** جھنڈ

flag, banner *n.m.* **jhanḍā** جھنڈا

small flag *n.f.* **jhanḍī** جھنڈی

jingle, rattle, tinkling, clinking *n.f.* **jhankār** جھنکار

lie, falsehood *n.m.* **jhūṭ** جھوٹ

tell a lie, lie *v.i.* **jhūṭ bōlnā** جھوٹ بولنا

liar *n.m.* **jhūṭ bōlnē vālā** جھوٹ بولنے والا

false *adj.* **jhūṭā** جھوٹا

squabbling, row, disturbance *n.f.* **jhauṛ** جھوڑ

swing, cradle *n.m.* **jhūlā** جھولا

swing, oscillate, sway; linger over *v.i.* **jhūlnā** جھولنا

wallet, sack, pouch, bag *n.f.* **jhōlī** جھولی
company, band, assembly *n.m.* **jhūmar** جھومر
sway, wave, rock *v.i.* **jhūmnā** جھومنا
hut, cottage *n.m.* **jhōnpṛā** جھونپڑا
nest (*of a bird*) *n.m.* **jhōṁjh** جھونجھ
cast, throw, toss *v.t.* **jhōnknā** جھونکنا
lake, pool *n.f.* **jhīl** جھیل
bear, endure, undergo *v.t.* **jhēlnā** جھیلنا
grieve, regret, lament *v.t.* **jhīnknā** جھینکنا
shrimp, prawn *n.m.* **jhīngā** جھینگا

cē چ

چابک horsewhip, whip *n.m.* / alert, active *adj.* **cābuk**

چابک دست nimble, active, alert, quick *adj.* **cābuk dast**

چابک سوار horserider, jockey *n.m.* **cābuk savār**

چابک مارنا whip, lash *v.t.* **cābuk mārnā**

چابکی agility, alertness; dispatch *n.f.* **cābukī**

چابنا chew, gnaw, crunch *v.t.* **cābnā**

چابی key *n.f.* **cābī**

چاپٹ bran, husk *n.f.* **cāpaṭ**

چاپڑ soil (*hard and stony*) *n.f.* **cāpaṛ**

چاپلوس flatterer *n.f.* **cāplūs**

چاپلوسی flattery *n.f.* **cāplūsī**

چاپلوسی کرنا flatter *v.t.* **cāplūsī karnā**

چاتر clever, skillful *adj.* **cātur**

چاٹ taste; relish *n.f.* **cāṭ**

چاٹنا taste, lick, lap, consume *v.t.* **cāṭnā**

چاچا uncle (*paternal*) *n.m.* **cācā**

چاچی aunt (*paternal*) *n.f.* **cācī**

چادر sheet; tablecloth *n.f.* **cādar**

چار four *num.* **cār**

چار بالش sofa, couch; large cushion *n.m.* **cār bāliš**

چار چشم faithless, untrustworthy *adj.* **cār cašm**

چار خانہ check, square *n.m.* **cār xānah**

چار دیواری enclosure, rampart, city-wall *n.f.* **cār dīvārī**

چار زانوں بیٹھنا squat *v.i.* **cār zānūṁ baiṭhnā**

چار مغز walnut *n.m.* **cār maġaz**

چارہ cure, remedy; resource *n.m.* **cārah**

چار و ناچار inevitable *adj.* **cār-ō-nācār**

چاشت morning; breakfast *n.m.* **cāšt**

چاشنی flavor; relish; syrup *n.f.* **cāšnī**

چاشنی دار tasty; sweet and sour *adj.* **cāšnī dār**

چاق active, alert; ready *n.m.* **cāq**

چاق وچوبند wealthy and vigorous; strong and healthy *adj.* **cāq-ō-cauband**

چاقو knife *n.m.* **cāqū**

چاک rent, slit, torn *adj.* **cāk**
چاک کرنا tear, rend, slit, split *v.t.* **cāk karnā**
چاکر servant *n.m.* **cākar**
چاکری service, employment *n.f.* **cākrī**
چاکلیٹ chocolate *n.m.* **cāklēṭ**
چال movement, motion; conduct, custom *n.f.* **cāl**
چال چلن character, conduct *n.m.* **cāl calan**
چالاک clever, smart, active; cunning *adj.* **cālāk**
چالاکی cleverness, smartness *n.f.* **cālākī**
چالان invoice, remittance *n.m.* **cālān**
چالیس forty *num.* **cālīs**
چانپنا press, squeeze *v.t.* **cānpnā**
چانٹا slap *n.m.* **cānṭā**
چاند moon; target *n.m.* **cānd**
چاند رات new moon *n.f.* **cānd rāt**
چاندنی moonlight *n.f.* **cāndnī**
چاندنی رات moonlit night *n.f.* **cāndnī rāt**
چاندی silver; wealth, profit *n.f.* **cāndī**
چاہ desire, love; need, wish *n.f.* / well, pit *n.m.* **cāh**
چاہت desire, longing; love *n.f.* **cāhat**
چاہنا wish, want, desire; love *v.t.* **cāhnā**
چاہیتا favorite, agreeable, desirable *adj.* **cāhītā**
چاہیئے must, should, ought; wanting; necessary *v.i.* **cāhī'ē**
چاول rice *n.m.* **cāval**
چائے دانی teapot *n.f.* **cā'ē dānī**
چائے tea (*mainly black tea*) *n.f.* **cā'ē**
چبانا chew, gnaw *v.t.* **cabānā**
چبلا childish, boyish, impolite *adj.* **cibilā**
چبلاپن childishness *n.m.* **cibilāpan**
چبوترہ terrace, platform *n.m.* **cabutrah**
چبھونا stick into *v.i.* **cubhōnā**
چپ silence, quietness, stillness *n.f.* **cup**
چپ چاپ silently, quietly, calmly *adv.* **cup cāp**
چپاتی chapati (*thin bread*) *n.f.* **capātī**
چپٹانا stick, paste, glue, attach *v.t.* **cipṭānā**

gluey, sticky, adhesive *adj.* **cipcipā** پچپچا
stickiness, adhesiveness *n.f.* **cipcipāhaṭ** پچپچاہٹ
greasy, oiled, oily *adj.* **cupṛī** چپڑی
stick, paste, glue, attach *v.t.* **cipkānā** چپکانا
stick, paste, adhere *v.i.* **cipaknā** چپکنا
quietly, silently *adv.* **cupkē cupkē** چپکے چپکے
shoe, slipper, sandals *n.f.* **cappal** چپل
pot lid *n.f.* **capnī** چپنی
oar, paddle *n.m.* **cappū** چپو
massage *n.f.* **cappī** چپی
mind, life, soul, heart *n.f.* / prostrate, lying on the back *adj.* **cit** چت
look, sight, glance *n.f.* **citvan** چتون
spot, stain *n.f.* **cittī** چتی
stained, spotted, speckled *adj.* **cittī dār** چتی دار
rag, tatter *n.m.* **cithṛā** چتھڑا
instantly, quickly *adv.* **caṭ** چٹ
instantly, quickly *adv.* **caṭ-paṭ** چٹ پٹ
rock *n.m.* **caṭān** چٹان
mat *n.f.* **caṭā'ī** چٹائی
tasty, spicy; pungent *adj.* **caṭpaṭā** چٹپٹا
restlessness *n.f.* **chaṭpaṭī** چٹپٹی
crack, crackle, split; speak rudely *v.i.* **caṭaxnā** چٹخنا
crack, crackle, split; speak rudely *v.i.* **caṭakna** چٹکنا
pinch *n.f.* **cuṭkī** چٹکی
pigtail, lock of hair (*as worn by Hindus*) *n.m.* **cuṭīyā** چٹیا
comb, dress the hair *v.t.* **cuṭīyā karnā** چٹیا کرنا
letter, note, order of demand *n.f.* **ciṭṭhī** چٹھی
postman *n.m.* **ciṭhī rasāṁ** چٹھی رساں
uncle (*father's brother*) *n.m.* **cacā** چچا
suck, suckle *v.t.* **cacōṛnā** چچوڑنا
aunt (*father's brother's wife*) *n.f.* **cacī** چچی
quarrel, strife, tumult, uproar *n.f.* **cax** چخ
lamp, light *n.m.* **cirāġ** چراغ
extinguish the light, switch off the lamp *v.t.* **cirāġ bujhānā** چراغ بجھانا
light, switch on the lamp *v.t.* **cirāġ rōšan karnā** چراغ روشن کرنا

چراگاہ **carāgāh** *n.f.* pasture, meadow
چرانا **carānā** *v.t.* graze, pasture
چرانا **curānā** *v.t.* rob, steal
چرب **carb** *adj.* fat, thick; oily, greasy
چرب زبانی **carb zabānī** *n.f.* eloquence, fine talk, elegant speech
چربی **carbī** *n.f.* grease, fat
چرچا **carcā** *n.m.* rumor, gossip, talk
چرچا کرنا **carcā karnā** *v.t.* spread a rumor, gossip, talk about
چرچرانا **carcarānā** *v.i.* crack, crackle, creak
چرخ **carx** *n.m.* wheel; sky
چرخہ **carxah** *n.m.* spinning wheel, reel
چرسہ **carsah** *n.m.* leather bucket
چرک **cirk** *n.m.* pus; dirt, filth
چرکا **carkā** *n.m.* wound, scratch
چرکیں **cirkīṁ** *adj.* dirty, filthy; foul
چرم **carm** *n.m.* leather, skin, hide
چرمی **carmī** *adj.* leathern, made of leather
چرن **caran** *n.m.* foot; feeding, grazing
چرنا **carnā** *v.t.* graze, eat grass
چرنا **cirnā** *v.i.* be torn, be split
چرند **carind** *n.m.* beast, quadruped
چرواہا **carvāhā** *n.m.* shepherd, herdsman
چڑا **ciṛā** *n.m.* cock-sparrow
چڑچڑا **ciṛciṛā** *adj.* cross, peevish
چڑچڑاہٹ **ciṛciṛāhaṭ** *n.f.* peevishness
چڑی **ciṛī** *n.f.* hen-sparrow
چڑیا **ciṛiyā** *n.f.* sparrow
چڑیا گھر **ciṛiyā ghar** *n.m.* zoo
چڑھانا **caṛhānā** *v.t.* cause to ascend, lift, uplift, raise
چڑھاؤ **caṛhā'ō** *n.m.* rise, increase, ascent
چڑھائی **caṛhā'ī** *n.f.* attack, assault, invasion; ascent, rise
چڑھنا **caṛhnā** *v.i.* rise, ascend, mount, climb
چسپاں **caspāṁ** *adj.* viscous, sticky, adhesive; coherent
چسپاں کرنا **caspāṁ karnā** *v.t.* paste, affix, join together
چشم **cašm** *n.f.* eye; look; expectation, hope
چشم پوشی **cašm pōšī** *n.f.* overlooking, pretending not to see

spectacles, glasses; wink, winking *n.f.* **cašmak** چشمک
spectacles, glasses; fountain, spring, source *n.m.* **cašmah** چشمہ
owl; fool, idiot *n.m.* **cuġad** چغد
tale-telling, story-telling *n.m.* **cuġl** چغل
backbiter, tale bearer *n.m.* **cuġl xōr** چغل خور
back-biting, tale-bearing *n.f.* **cuġlī** چغلی
backbite *v.t.* **cuġlī khānā** چغلی کھانا
screen *n.f.* **ciq** چق
flint *n.f.* **caqmāq** چقماق
beet, beetroot *n.m.* **cuqandar** چقندر
circular; wheel *n.m.* **cakkā** چکا
settle, adjust, finish, pay off (debt) *v.t.* **cukānā** چکانا
wheel (*potter's*); circle, circuit *n.m.* **cakkar** چکر
wide, broad; round, circular *adj.* **caklā** چکلا
cheating, trick, trickery *n.m.* **cakmah** چکمہ
embroidery, embroidered cloth *n.f.* **cikan** چکن
taste, relish; experience, suffer *v.t.* **cakhnā** چکھنا
• greasy, oily, glossy, slippery *adj.* **ciknā** چکنا
be settled, be finished, be adjusted *v.i.* **cuknā**
shatter, break into pieces *v.t.* **cuknā cūr karnā** چکنا چور کرنا
oiliness, greasiness *n.f.* **ciknāhaṭ** چکناہٹ
fat, oil, grease *n.f.* **ciknā'ī** چکنائی
clay *n.f.* **ciknī maṭṭī** چکنی مٹی
mill, millstone, grindstone *n.f.* **cakkī** چکی
peck; feed birds *v.t.* **cugnā** چگنا
pass away, die *v.i.* **cal basnā** چل بسنا
leave, depart, be off *v.t.* **cal dēnā** چل دینا
go away, be off *v.i.* **calā jānā** چلا جانا
• cause to move, impel, stir, drive *v.t.* **calānā** چلانا
scream, shout, roar, cry out *v.t.* **cillānā**
restless *adj.* **culbulā** چلبلا
restlessness *n.m.* **culbulāpan** چلبلاپن
restlessness *n.f.* **culbulāhaṭ** چلبلاہٹ
flowing, moving, going *adj.* **caltā** چلتا
chilam (*smoking pipe*) *n.f.* **cilam** چلم
wash basin, basin, sink *n.f.* **cilamcī** چلمچی

blind, screen *n.f.* **cilman** چلمن
character, behavior, conduct *n.f.* **calan** چلن
walk, go, move, flow *v.i.* **calnā** چلنا
handful *n.m.* **cullū** چلو
Let's go! *interj.* **calō** چلو
kiss *n.m.* **cummā** چما
cobbler, shoemaker *n.m.* **cammār** چمار
jasmine flower *n.f.* **cambēlī** چمبیلی
necklace *n.f.* **campā kalī** چمپا کلی
yellow, golden *adj.* **campa'ī** چمپئی
forceps, tongs, pincers *n.m.* **cimṭā** چمٹا
adhere, cling, stick to *v.i./v.t.* **cimaṭnā** چمٹنا
pincers, pinch *n.f.* **cimṭī** چمٹی
pinch *v.t.* **cimṭī kānṭā** چمٹی کانٹا
spoon *n.m.* **cammac** چمچ
spoon *n.m.* **camcah** چمچہ
spoonful *adj.* **camcah bhar** چمچہ بھر
small spoon *n.f.* **camcī** چمچی
skin, hide, leather *n.m.* **camṛā** چمڑا
glitter, brilliance, flash, glare *n.f.* **camak** چمک
glittering, shining, bright, brilliant *adj.* **camak dār** چمک دار
brilliance, splendor *n.f.* **camak damak** چمک دمک
speak lovingly, coax, soothe *v.t.* **cumkārnā** چمکارنا
polish, brighten *v.t.* **camkānā** چمکانا
shine, glitter, sparkle *v.i.* **camaknā** چمکنا
bat (*animal*) *n.f.* **cimgāḍar** چمگادڑ
flower bed, flower garden *n.m.* **caman** چمن
gardener *n.m.* **caman band** چمن بند
garden, meadow *n.m.* **caman zār** چمن زار
flower bed, garden *n.f.* **camnistān** چمنستان
chimney *n.f.* **cimnī** چمنی
kiss *n.f.* **cummī** چمی
gram, chickpea *n.m.* **canā** چنا
jasmine *n.f.* **cambīlī** چنبیلی
restless, moving, unsteady *adj.* **cancal** چنچل

few, some, little; how many, how much *adj.* **cand** چند
several, few, some *adj.* **cand ēk** چند ایک
temporary, transitory, for a few days *adj.* **cand rōzah** چند روزہ
so greatly, so much, so many *adv.* **candāṁ** چنداں
moon *n.m.* **candra** چندر
as beautiful as the moon *adj.* **candra mukhī** چندر مکھی
sandalwood, sandal tree *n.m.* **candan** چندن
contribution; subscription *n.m.* **candah** چندہ
pay a contribution; subscribe *v.t.* **candah dēnā** چندہ دینا
raise funds, collect subscriptions *v.t.* **candah karnā** چندہ کرنا
few, some, a little *adj.* / sometime, for sometime *adv.* **candē** چندے
crown *n.f.* **candyā** چندیا
be dazzled *v.i.* **cundhiyānā** چندھیانا
sound, healthy, good *adj.* **cangā** چنگا
spark (*of fire*) *n.f.* **cingārī** چنگاری
tray; flowerpot *n.f.* **cangēr** چنگیر
scream, screech *n.f.* **cinghāṛ** چنگھاڑ
trumpet (*like an elephant*), scream out *v.i.* **cinghāṛnā** چنگھاڑنا
choose, select, pick, pluck *v.t.* **cunnā** چننا
cause to select, cause to be picked, cause to be plucked *v.t.* **canvānā** چنوانا
emblem of sovereignty or royalty *n.m.* **canvar** چنور
small, young *adj.* **cunyā** چنیا
warble, chirp, sing, whistle *v.i.* **cahcahānā** چہچہانا
face; appearance, countenance *n.m.* **cēhrah** چہرہ
feature *n.m.* **cēhrah mōhrah** چہرہ مہرہ
chirp, warble, whistle *v.i.* **cahaknā** چہکنا
cheer; bustle, activity *n.f.* **cahal pahal** چہل پہل
coins, small change *n.m.* **chuṭṭē** چھوٹے
forty-four *num.* **cavālīs** چوالیس
wood, timber *n.f.* **cōb** چوب
rod, walking stick *n.f.* **cōb dastī** چوب دستی
wooden *adj.* **cōbī** چوبی
twenty-four *num.* **caubīs** چوبیس
open, wide open *adj.* **caupaṭ** چوپٹ
hip, buttock, bum, backside *n.m.* **cūtaṛ** چوتڑ
fourth *adj.* **cauthā** چوتھا

quarter, fourth part *n.f.* **cauthā'ī** چوتھائی
hurt, blow, bruise, injury, damage *n.f.* **cōṭ** چوٹ
be injured, suffer an injury *v.t.* **cōṭ khānā** چوٹ کھانا
wound, hurt *v.t.* **cōṭ karnā** چوٹ کرنا
be hurt, be wounded *v.i.* **cōṭ lagnā** چوٹ لگنا
pickpocket, thief *n.m.* **cōṭṭā** چوٹا
summit, peak, top *n.f.* **cōṭī** چوٹی
fourteen *num.* **caudah** چودہ
village chief, headman (*of a village*) *n.m.* **caudharī** چودھری
fourteenth *adj.* **caudhavāṁ** چودھواں
robber, thief, burglar *n.m.* **cōr** چور
powder, dust *n.m.* **cūrā** چورا
grind to powder, powder *v.t.* **cūrā cūrā karnā** چورا چورا کرنا
eighty-four *num.* **caurāsī** چوراسی
ninety-four *num.* **caurānavē** چورانوے
theft, robbery; stealth *n.f.* **cōrī** چوری
secretly, clandestinely *adv.* **cōrī cōrī** چوری چوری
steal, rob *v.t.* **cōrī karnā** چوری کرنا
bracelet *n.f.* **cūriyāṁ** چوریاں
broad, wide *adj.* **cauṛā** چوڑا
extensive, broad, wide *adj.* **cauṛā caklā** چوڑا چکلا
extension, breadth, width *n.f.* **cauṛā'ī** چوڑائی
bangle (*worn on the wrist*) *n.f.* **cūṛī** چوڑی
sweeper *n.m.* **cūṛhā** چوڑھا
chicken; young bird *n.m.* **cūzah** چوزہ
suck, absorb, drink, sip *v.t.* **cūsnā** چوسنا
cloak, overcoat *n.m.* **cūġah** چوغہ
crossroads, square *n.m.* **cauk** چوک
error, fault, mistake *n.f.* **cūk** چوک
door frame, threshold *n.f.* **caukhaṭ** چوکھٹ
husk (*of wheat, barley, etc.*) *n.m.* **cōkar** چوکر
bound, carriage *n.f.* **caukaṛī** چوکڑی
alert, cautious, careful, watchful *adj.* **caukas** چوکس
be cautious, be careful *v.i.* **caukas rahnā** چوکس رہنا
carefulness, watchfulness *n.f.* **caukasī** چوکسی

keep watch, look after *v.t.* **caukasī karnā** چوکسی کرنا

cautious, alert *adj.* **caukannā** چوکنا

err, fail, make a mistake, blunder, stumble *v.i.* **cūknā** چوکنا

quadliteral, four-sided *adj.* **caukōr** چوکور

post; small stool, small chair, frame (*to sit on*) *n.f.* **caukī** چوکی

watchman, guard *n.m.* **caukī dār** چوکی دار

bird food *n.m.* **cōgā** چوگا

polo (*sport*) *n.m.* **caugān** چوگان

quadruple, four times *adj.* **cauganā** چوگنا

pivot (*of a door*); tenon *n.m.* **cūl** چول

cloak; bridal gown *n.m.* **cōlā** چولا

waistcoat, small jacket *n.m.* **cōlī** چولی

kiss *n.m.* **cūmā** چوما

kiss *v.t.* **cūmnā** چومنا

like, such, as; because, how, which *pp./conj.* **cūṁ** چوں

fifty-four *num.* **cavvan** چون

chirping, squeaking *n.f.* **cūṁ cūṁ** چوں چوں

thirty-four *num.* **cauntīs** چونتیس

sixty-four *num.* **caunsaṭh** چونسٹھ

start up; bounce *v.i.* **caunk paṛnā** چونک پڑنا

whereas, that, since *conj.* **cūnkēh** چونکہ

funnel, tube *n.m.* **cōngā** چونگا

rat, mouse *n.m.* **cūhā** چوہا

seventy-four *num.* **cauhattar** چوہتر

small mouse, small rat *n.f.* **cūhiyā** چوہیا

mouse trap *n.m.* **cūhē dān** چوہیدان

viscosity, stickiness; glue *n.m.* **cēp** چیپ

stick together, paste, glue *v.t.* **cēpnā** چیپنا

spotted, speckled *adj.* **cītal** چیتل

tick *n.f.* **cīcṛī** چیچڑی

smallpox *n.f.* **cēcak** چیچک

scream, screech, shriek *n.f.* **cīx** چیخ

gathered, selected, picked *adj.* **cīdah** چیدہ

rend, tear, split, cut open *v.t.* **cīrnā** چیرنا

fig tree; pine tree *n.m.* **cīṛ** چیڑ
thing *n.f.* **cīz** چیز
furniture, goods *n.f.* **cīz bast** چیزبست
somewhat, little, something *adv.* **cīzē** چیزے
enigma, riddle *n.m.* **cīstān** چیستان
check *n.m.* **cēk** چیک
kite *n.f.* **cīl** چیل
disciple, follower, devotee, pupil *n.m.* **cailā** چیلا
cry, squeak, chirp; wrinkle, pucker *n.f.* **cīṁ** چیں
squeak *v.i.* **cīṁ bōlnā** چیں بولنا
chirp, chatter, grumble, cry out, murmur *v.t.* **cīṁ cīṁ karnā** چیں چیں کرنا
ease, comfort, rest, peace *n.m.* **cain** چین
make oneself comfortable *v.t.* **cain karnā** چین کرنا
China *n.m.* **cīn** چین
corn, bait, grain *n.m.* **cīnā** چینا
bruise *n.f.* **cīnṭ** چینٹ
Chinese *adj.* **cīnī** چینی
white sugar *n.f.* **cīnī** چینی
large ant *n.m.* **ciyūnṭā** چیونٹا
small ant *n.f.* **ciyūnṭī** چیونٹی
six *num.* **chē** چھ
impression, print, stamp *n.m.* **chāp** چھاپ
stamp *v.t.* **chāp lagānā** چھاپ لگانا
print, publish; stamp *v.t.* **chāpnā** چھاپنا
printer *n.m.* **chāpnē vālā** چھاپنے والا
printing press, press *n.m.* **chāpah xānah** چھاپہ خانہ
umbrella *n.m.* **chātā** چھاتا
chest, breast *n.f.* **chātī** چھاتی
lament, regret, repent *v.t.* **chātī pīṭnā** چھاتی پیٹنا
spread, cover, swarm *v.i.* **chā jānā** چھاجانا
buttermilk, whey *n.f.* **chāch** چھاچھ
peel, skin, rind *n.f.* **chāl** چھال
pimple, blister, pustule *n.m.* **chālah** چھالہ
betel-nut *n.f.* **chālyah** چھالیہ
shade, shadow; roof, thatched roof *n.f.* **chān** چھان
search, investigation, examination *n.f.* **chān bīn** چھان بین

roof, shade, spread, thatch *v.t.* **chānā** چھانا
selection; refuse; extraction *n.f.* **chānṭ** چھانٹ
select, choose, sort out; refuse *v.t.* **chānṭnā** چھانٹنا
sift, search, investigate, examine, filter *v.t.* **chānnā** چھاننا
shade, shadow *n.f.* **chā'ōṁ** چھاؤں
cantonment; barrack (*for soldiers*) *n.f.* **chā'ōnī** چھاؤنی
darkness, shade *n.f.* **chāyā** چھایا
beauty, grace, charm *n.f.* **chab** چھب
twenty-six *num.* **chabbīs** چھبیس
graceful, handsome *adj.* **chabīlā** چھبیلا
hidden, concealed *adj.* **chuppā/chippā** چھپا
hide, conceal, cover, close *v.t.* **chupānā/chipānā** چھپانا
printing, edition *n.f.* **chapā'ī** چھپائی
lizard *n.f.* **chupkalī** چھپکلی
fifty-six *num.* **chappan** چھپن
lurk; disappear, be absent *v.i.* **chupnā** چھپنا
roof, ceiling *n.f.* **chat** چھت
beehive *n.m.* **chattā** چھتا
umbrella *n.m.* **chatr/chattar** چھتر
small umbrella *n.f.* **chatrī** چھتری
thirty-six *num.* **chattīs** چھتیس
sixth *adj.* **chaṭā** چھٹا
littleness *n.m.* **chuṭāpā** چھٹاپا
release, exemption, liberty, leisure *n.m.* **chuṭkārā** چھٹکارا
be released, be acquitted, get rid of *v.t.* **chuṭkārā pānā** چھٹکارا پانا
• be acquitted, be discharged; be reduced, be cut into pieces *v.i.* **chaṭnā** چھٹنا
be released, be set free *v.i.* **chuṭnā**
holiday, leave, vacation *n.f.* **chuṭṭī** چھٹی
balcony, gallery *n.f.* **chajjā** چھجا
childish, petty, shallow *adj.* **chachōrā** چھچھورا
perforate *v.t.* **chidānā** چھدانا
long knife *n.f.* **churī** چھری
stab (*with a knife*) *v.t.* **churī mārnā** چھری مارنا
slim, thin; light *adj.* **charērā** چھریرا
alone, single, solitary; bachelor *adj.* **charā** چھڑا
set free, discharge, free *v.t.* **churānā** چھڑانا

sprinkling, watering *n.m.* **chiṛkā'ō** چھڑکاؤ

sprinkle, water *v.t.* **chiṛaknā** چھڑکنا

cane, walking stick *n.f.* **chaṛī** چھڑی

carriage, cart, vehicle ; draft *n.m.* **chakṛā** چھکڑا

fraud, trick, deception *n.m.* **chal** چھل

trickery, plot *n.m.* **chal bal** چھل بل

ring (*jewelry*) *n.m.* **challā** چھلا

bound, leap, jump *n.m.* **chalāng** چھلانگ

overflow *n.f.* **chalak** چھلک

crust, shell, bark, rind, husk *n.m.* **chilkā** چھلکا

husk, peel, be scratched, be peeled *v.t.* **chilkā utārnā** چھلکا اتارنا

spill *v.t.* **chalkānā** چھلکانا

be spilled, overflow *v.i.* **chalaknā** چھلکنا

sieve, strainer *n.f.* **chalnī** چھلنی

artful, treacherous, deceitful *adj.* **chalyā** چھلیا

seventy-six *num.* **chēhattar** چھہتر

dried date *n.m.* **chu'ārā** چھوارا

defilement, infection, contamination *n.f.* **chūt** چھوت

be infectious, be infected *v.i.* **chūt lagnā** چھوت لگنا

remission, leaving, separation, divorce *n.f.* **chūṭ** چھوٹ

little, small, short; young *adj.* **chōṭā** چھوٹا

smallness, littleness *n.f.* **chōṭā'ī** چھوٹائی

escape, be set free; be left *v.i.* **chūṭnā** چھوٹنا

holiday, vacation *n.f.* **chuṭṭī** چھوٹی

boy *n.m.* **chōrā** چھورا

girl *n.f.* **chōrī** چھوری

having left, omitting, except *adv.* **chōṛ** چھوڑ

leave behind, abandon *v.i.* **chōṛ jānā** چھوڑ جانا

let go, give up *v.t.* **chōṛ dēnā** چھوڑ دینا

give up, leave *v.i.* **chōṛnā** چھوڑنا

boy *n.m.* **chōkrā** چھوکرا

girl *n.f.* **chōkrī** چھوکری

peel, pare, skim, scrape *v.t.* **chōlnā** چھولنا

scraper *n.f.* **chōlnī** چھولنی

touch, feel; meddle with *v.t.* **chūnā** چھونا

dirt, excrement *n.f.* **chī chī** چھی چھی

sixty-six *num.* **chēyāsaṭh** چھیاسٹھ
eighty-six *num.* **chēyāsī** چھیاسی
forty-six *num.* **chēyālīs** چھیالیس
ninety-six *num.* **chēyānavē** چھیانوے
cloth-printer *n.m.* **chīpī** چھیپی
scatter, sprinkle *v.t.* **chīṭnā** چھیٹنا
diminution, decrease, decay *n.f.* **chīj** چھیج
decrease, decay, pine away *v.i.* **chījnā** چھیجنا
hole, opening *n.m.* **chēd** چھید
pierce, bore, perforate *v.t.* **chēdnā** چھیدنا
touch; irritation *n.f.* **chēṛ** چھیڑ
touch; irritate, molest, tease, make fun of *v.t.* **chēṛnā** چھیڑنا
bean; fop, coxcomb, dandy; handsome man *n.m.* **chailā** چھیلا
peel, pare, erase, scrap, scratch *v.t.* **chīlnā** چھیلنا
sprinkling, splash, light rain *n.m.* **chīnṭā** چھینٹا
sprinkle *v.t.* **chīnṭā dēnā** چھینٹا دینا
sprinkle *v.t.* **chīnṭā mārnā** چھینٹا مارنا
sprinkle, scatter *v.t.* **chīnṭnā** چھینٹنا
sneezing, sneeze *n.f.* **chīnk** چھینک
sneeze *v.t.* **chīnk mārnā** چھینک مارنا
sneeze *v.i.* **chīnknā** چھینکنا
snatch, wrench, pluck, rob *v.t.* **chīnnā** چھیننا
chisel, piercer *n.f.* **chēnī** چھینی

baṛī ḥē ح

doorkeeper *n.m.* **ḥājib** حاجب
need, necessity; hope; poverty *n.f.* **ḥājat** حاجت
needy; hoping; poor *adj.* **ḥājat mand** حاجت مند
pilgrim (*to Mecca*) *n.f.* **ḥājah** حاجہ
pilgrim (*to Mecca*) *n.m.* **ḥājī** حاجی
new, recent *adj.* **ḥādis** حادث
accident; incident, misfortune *n.m.* **ḥādisah/ḥādsah** حادثہ
contracted *adj.* **ḥāddah** حادہ
skillful, eminent, competent, intelligent *adj.* **ḥāziq** حاذق
difficult; ardent *adj.* **ḥārr** حار
obstruction *n.m.* **ḥārij** حارج
watchman, keeper, guard *n.m.* **ḥārris** حارس
envious, jealous *adj.* **ḥāsid** حاسد
besides, excepting *adv.* **ḥāšā** حاشا
God forbid!, By no means! *interj.* **ḥāšā Allah** حاشا اللہ
margin, border *n.m.* **ḥāšiyah** حاشیہ
produce, product; result; revenue, profit, gain *n.m.* **ḥāsil** حاصل
remainder, balance *n.m.* **ḥāsil tafrīq** حاصل تفریق
total, sum *n.m.* **ḥāsil jama**^{c} حاصل جمع
acquire, gain, collect *v.t.* **ḥāsil karnā** حاصل کرنا
briefly, in short *adv.* **ḥāsil kalām** حاصل کلام
present, ready *adj.* **ḥāzir** حاضر
regular, constant *adj.* **ḥāzir baš** حاضر باش
attend, wait on *v.i.* **ḥāzir rahnā** حاضر رہنا
bail *n.f.* **ḥāzir zamānat** حاضر ضمانت
present, produce; make ready *v.t.* **ḥāzir karnā** حاضر کرنا
omnipresent *adj.* **ḥāzir-ō-nāzir** حاضر و ناظر
town, city, village *n.m.* **ḥāzrah** حاضرہ
presence, attendance; breakfast *n.f.* **ḥāzrī** حاضری
audience *n.m.* **ḥāzrīn** حاضرین
• reciter (*of Holy Quran*); guardian, governer, preserver, protector *n.m.* **ḥāfiz** حافظ
memory *n.m.* **ḥāfizah**
barefooted *adj.* **ḥāfī** حافی

middle, center, mid *adj.* **ḥāq** حاق
resurrection; doomsday *n.m.* **ḥāqah** حاقہ
officer, ruler, commander, governor *n.m.* **ḥākim** حاکم
authoritatively, judicially *adv.* **ḥākimānah** حاکمانہ
state, condition; statement, case *n.m.* **ḥāl** حال
although, nonetheless *conj.* **ḥālānkih** حالانکہ
state, circumstance, condition *n.f.* **ḥālat** حالت
now, at present, soon *adv.* **ḥālī** حالی
sour, acid; sharp *adj.* **ḥāmiz** حامض
porter, carrier *n.m.* **ḥāmil** حامل
pregnant *adj.* **ḥāmilah/ḥāmla** حاملہ
supporter, protector, defender *n.m.* **ḥāmī** حامی
consent, promise *v.t.* **ḥāmī bharnā** حامی بھرنا
containing; comprehending *adj.* **ḥāvī** حاوی
wall, enclosure *n.m.* **ḥa'it** حائط
intervening, hindering *adj.* / obstacle, hinerance *n.m.* **ḥā'il** حائل
interrupt, disturb *v.i.* **ḥā'il hōnā** حائل ہونا
love, affection *n.f.* **ḥubb** حب
patriot *n.m.* **ḥubb-ul-vatan** حب الوطن
patriotism *n.f.* **ḥubb-ul-vatanī** حب الوطنی
bubble *n.m.* **ḥubāb/ḥabāb** حباب
prison, retention, imprisonment *n.f.* **ḥabs** حبس
suffocation *n.m.* **ḥabs-ul-nafas** حبس النفس
Abyssinia, Ethiopia *n.m.* **ḥabaš** حبش
Abyssinian, Ethiopian *n.m.* **ḥabašī** حبشی
rope, cord *n.f.* **ḥabl** حبل
grain, seed, berry *n.m.* **ḥabbah** حبہ
lover, beloved, sweetheart *n.m.* **ḥabīb** حبیب
final, permanent, decisive, definite *adj.* **ḥatmī** حتمی
as far as, until, up to, so that *conj./pp.* **ḥattā** حتی
pilgrimage (*to Mecca*) *n.m.* **ḥajj** حج
modesty, bashfulness; veil, curtain *n.m.* **ḥijāb** حجاب
barber, shaver, hairdresser *n.m.* **ḥajjām** حجام
argument, discussion *n.f.* **ḥujjat** حجت
argue, discuss *v.t.* **ḥujjat karnā** حجت کرنا
quarrelsome, argumentative *adj.* **ḥujjatī** حجتی

stone *n.m.* **ḥajar** حجر
small chamber, small room, cell, closet *n.m.* **ḥujrah** حجرہ
wisdom, intelligence, sense *n.m.* **ḥajjā** حجی
limit, boundary *n.f.* **ḥadd** حد
limit, bound *v.t.* **ḥadd bāndhnā** حد باندھنا
sharpness; fury, passion *n.f.* **ḥiddat** حدت
tradition, saying; Hadith *n.f.* **ḥadīs** حدیث
iron; helmet *n.m.* **ḥadīd** حدید
equality; comparison *n.m.* **ḥazā** حذا
caution *n.m.* **ḥazar** حذر
hot *adj.* **ḥarr** • free, well-born, noble *adj.* **ḥurr** حر
heat, warmth, burning; fever *n.f.* **ḥarārat** حرارت
watch, guard; arrest; custody *n.f.* **ḥirāsat** حراست
forbidden (*by Islam*), unlawful, prohibited *adj.* **ḥarām** حرام
corrupt person *n.m.* **ḥarām xōr** حرام خور
unlawful, illegitimate *adj.* **ḥarām zādah** حرام زادہ
illegitimacy *n.m.* **ḥarām zadgī** حرام زدگی
commit suicide *v.i.* **ḥarām maut marnā** حرام موت مرنا
illegal, illegitimate; wicked *adj.* / rascal, villain, bastard *n.m.* **ḥarāmī** حرامی
battle, war *n.f.* **ḥarb** حرب
cultivating, sowing *n.m.* **ḥars** حرث
interference, confusion, obstacle; farm *n.m.* **ḥarj** حرج
guard; refuge, shelter, asylum *n.m.* **ḥirz** حرز
eagerness, desire; greediness, avarice *n.f.* **ḥirs** حرص
ambitious, avaricious *adj.* **ḥirsī** حرصی
letter (*of alphabet*); particle *n.m.* **ḥarf** حرف
suffer disgrace *v.i.* **ḥarf ānā** حرف آنا
literary, word by word *adv.* **ḥarf baḥarf** حرف بحرف
criticism *n.f.* **ḥarf gīrī** حرف گیری
literally, letter by letter *adj.* **ḥarfan ḥarfan** حرفاً حرفاً
art, trade, skill, craft *n.f.* **ḥirfat** حرفت
profession, skill, craft, trade *n.m.* **ḥirfah** حرفہ
motion, movement; act *n.f.* **ḥarakat** حرکت
move, act *v.t.* **ḥarakat karnā** حرکت کرنا
sacred; forbidden *adj.* / enclosure, sanctuary *n.m.* / wife, concubine *n.f.* **ḥaram** حرم
seraglio (*women's living place*) *n.f.* **ḥaram sarā'ē** حرم سرائے

disappointment *n.m.* **ḥirmān** حرمان

chastity; dignity *n.f.* **ḥurmat** حرمت

respect *v.t.* **ḥurmat karnā** حرمت کرنا

disgrace *v.t.* **ḥurmat lēnā** حرمت لینا

freedom, liberty, liberation *n.f.* **ḥuriyyat** حریت

silk cloth *n.m.* **ḥarīr** حریر

silken; thin *adj.* **ḥarīrī** حریری

greedy; ambitious *adj.* **ḥarīs** حریص

enemy, rival, adversary *n.m.* **ḥarīf** حریف

burning, flame (*of fire*); warmth *n.f.* **ḥarīq** حریق

party, group *n.m.* **ḥazb** حزب

opposition *n.m.* **ḥazb ixtilāf** حزب اختلاف

precaution, foresight, prudence *n.m.* **ḥazm** حزم

grief, sadness, sorrow *n.m.* **ḥazn/ḥuzn** حزن

doubtful; sad; dull *adj.* **ḥazīn** حزین

feeling, sense, sensibility, sentiment *n.m.* **ḥiss** حس

• account, bill, check; counting, calculation *n.m.* **ḥisāb** حساب

according to, accordingly as *adv.* **ḥasāb**

render an account *v.t.* **ḥisāb dēnā** حساب دان

accounts, bookkeeping *n.f.* **ḥisāb kitāb** حساب کتاب

calculate *v.t.* **ḥisāb karnā** حساب کرنا

calculate *v.t.* **ḥisāb lagānā** حساب لگانا

accurate, correct, just; accountable *adj.* **ḥisābī** حسابی

emotional, sensible, sensitive *adj.* **ḥassās** حساس

incidentally, by chance *adv.* **ḥasb-ē-ittēfāq** حسب اتفاق

as follows, as given below *adv.* **ḥasb-ē-zail** حسب ذیل

as usual, usually *adv.* **ḥasb-ē-maᶜmūl** حسب معمول

pedigree, lineage; dynasty *n.m.* **ḥasb nasab** حسب نسب

envy, jealousy; malice *n.f.* **ḥasad** حسد

regret; desire *n.f.* **ḥasrat** حسرت

afflicted, grieved *adj.* **ḥasrat zadah** حسرت زدہ

cutting, curtailing *n.m.* **ḥasam** حسم

beauty, elegance *n.m.* **ḥusn** • beautiful, handsome *adj.* **ḥasan** حسن

benevolence, kindness *n.m.* **ḥasnah** حسنہ

envious, jealous *adj.* **ḥasūd** حسود

handsome, beautiful, elegant *adj.* **ḥasīn** حسین

joyful, happy *adj.* ḥašāš bašāš حشاش بشاش

meeting, gathering, congregation; doomsday, end of the world *n.m.* ḥašr حشر

insect; reptile *n.m.* ḥašrah حشره

violent *adj.* ḥašrī حشری

dignity; splendor, wealth *n.f.* ḥašmat حشمت

stuffing; rubbish, trash *n.m.* ḥašv حشو

hay, grass; hashish, marijuana *n.m.* ḥašīš حشیش

fort, fortress, castle, fortification *n.m.* ḥisār حصار

durability, firmness *n.m.* ḥasānat حصانت

siege, blockade *n.m.* ḥasr حصر

castle, fort, fortress, fortification *n.m.* ḥisn حصن

part, portion, division, share *n.m.* ḥissah حصه

partner, shareholder *n.m.* ḥissah dār حصه دار

partnership *n.f.* ḥissah dārī حصه داری

attainment, gain *n.m.* ḥusūl حصول

majesty, dignity, highness *n.f.* ḥazrat حضرت

presence; authority, court, your Honor *n.m.* ḥuzūr حضور

attendant *n.m.* / presence *n.f.* ḥuzūrī حضوری

wolf *n.m.* ḥatal حطل

pleasure, delight; flavor, taste *n.m.* ḥazz حظ

enjoy *v.t.* ḥazz uṭhānā حظ اٹھانا

safety, protection *n.f.* ḥifāzat حفاظت

guard, preserve *v.t.* ḥifāzat karnā حفاظت کرنا

memory; custody, preservation *n.m.* ḥifz حفظ

recite, learn by heart *v.t.* ḥifz karnā حفظ کرنا

precaution *n.m.* ḥifz-ē-mātaqaddum حفظ ماتقدم

assembly *n.m.* ḥafl حفل

guardian, protector *n.m.* ḥafīz حفیظ

justice, truth *n.m.* / just, right, true *adj.* ḥaqq حق

truth-loving, honest *adj.* ḥaqq pasand حق پسند

rightful *adj.* ḥaqq dār حق دار

grateful *adj.* ḥaqq šinās حق شناس

truly, really *adj.* ḥaqqā حقا

contempt, scorn, disdain, hatred *n.f.* ḥiqārat حقارت

bate; hate *v.t.* ḥiqārat karnā حقارت کرنا

true, perfect, divine *adj.* ḥaqqānī حقانی

truth, divinity *n.f.* **ḥaqqāniyat** حقانیت
shisha, hookah, water-pipe *n.m.* **ḥuqqah** حقہ
smoke *v.t.* **ḥuqqah pīnā** حقہ پینا
property, ownership; claim, right *n.f.* **ḥaqiyyat** حقیت
contemptible, despicable *adj.* **ḥaqīr** حقیر
truth, reality, fact *n.f.* **ḥaqīqat** حقیقت
in reality, truly *adv.* **ḥaqīqatan** حقیقتاً
actual, true, just *adj.* **ḥaqīqī** حقیقی
story, tale, narrative *n.f.* **ḥikāyat** حکایت
order, command; permission; jurisdiction *n.m.* **ḥukm** حکم
obedient *adj.* **ḥukm bardār** حکم بردار
break an order *v.t.* **ḥukm tōṛnā** حکم توڑنا
order, give an order *v.t.* **ḥukm dēnā** حکم دینا
rule, sovereignty *n.f.* **ḥukm rānī** حکم رانی
order, command *v.t.* **ḥukm karnā** حکم کرنا
warrant, decree *n.m.* **ḥukm nāmah** حکم نامہ
wisdom, knowledge; philosophy *n.f.* **ḥikmat** حکمت
policy, politics *n.f.* **ḥikmat ᶜamalī** حکمت عملی
government, sovereignty, authority, power *n.f.* **ḥukūmat** حکومت
govern, rule *v.t.* **ḥukūmat karnā** حکومت کرنا
philospher, sage *n.m.* **ḥakīm** حکیم
philosophical, wise *adj.* **ḥakīmānah** حکیمانہ
solution *n.m.* **ḥall** حل
dissolve; solve *v.t.* **ḥall karnā** حل کرنا
legal, lawful, according to Islamic law *adj.* **ḥalāl** حلال
slaughter (*in the religious way*) *v.t.* **ḥalāl karnā** حلال کرنا
sweetness, deliciousness; taste *n.f.* **ḥalāvat** حلاوت
oath, vow *n.f.* **ḥalaf** حلف
swear, take an oath *v.t.* **ḥalaf uṭhānā** حلف اٹھانا
throat *n.m.* **ḥalq** حلق
circle, ring *n.m.* **ḥalqah** حلقہ
slave, servant *n.m.* **ḥalqah bagōš** حلقہ بگوش
mildness, gentleness *n.m.* **ḥilm** حلم
halva (*a sweet dish*) *n.m.* **ḥalvā** حلوا
milk (*fresh and unboiled*) *n.m.* **ḥalīb** حلیب

حلیم **ḥalīm** *adj.* mild, gentle; human
حلیہ **ḥulyah** *n.m.* appearance; identity
حمار **ḥimār** *adj.* donkey
حماری **ḥimārī** *adj.* foolish, stupid
حماقت **ḥamāqat** *n.f.* foolishness, stupidity
حمال **ḥammāl** *n.m.* porter, carrier
حمام **ḥammām** *n.m.* bath, bathroom; Turkish bath
حمامہ **ḥammāmah** *n.m.* pigeon
حمایت **ḥimāyat** *n.f.* support, protection, defense
حمایت کرنا **ḥimāyat karnā** *v.t.* support, protect, defend
حمایتی **ḥimāyatī** *n.m.* protector, defender
حمایل **ḥamā'ēl** *n.f.* necklace made of flowers
حمت **ḥamat** *adj.* very hot, very warm; inky, black
حمد **ḥamd** *n.f.* praise, hymn (*religious*)
حمد کرنا **ḥamd karnā** *v.t.* praise (God)
حمق **ḥumq** *n.m.* stupidity, foolishness, ignorance
حمل **ḥaml** *n.m.* pregnancy; burden, load
حمل گرنا **ḥaml girnā** *v.i.* miscarry, abort
حملہ **ḥamlah** *n.m.* attack, assault
حملہ آور **ḥamlah āvar** *n.m.* attacker, assailant
حملہ کرنا **ḥamlah karnā** *v.t.* attack, assault
حمیت **ḥamīt** *n.f.* ardor, impetuosity
حمید **ḥamīd** *adj.* praised, glorious
حنان **ḥannān** *adj.* forgiving, kind, merciful
حنجرہ **ḥanjarah** *n.m.* throat; throttle
حوالات **ḥavālāt** *n.f.* lockup; trust, custody
حوالہ **ḥavālah** *n.m.* reference; charge, custody
حوالہ دینا **ḥavālah dēnā** *v.t.* refer, quote
حوالہ کرنا **ḥavālah karnā** *v.t.* make over; surrender
حوب **ḥōb** *n.m.* sin, fault; misfortune
حوت **ḥūt** *n.f.* Pisces (*Zodiac*)
حور **ḥūr** *n.f.* nymph, virgin of paradise, celestial bride
حوصلہ **ḥausalah** *n.m.* capacity, ambition; courage
حوصلہ مند **ḥausilah mand** *adj.* ambitious; courageous
حوض **ḥauz** *n.m.* reservoir, cistern, fountain
حویلی **ḥavēlī** *n.f.* house, mansion, dwelling

modesty, shyness; shame *n.f.* **ḥayā** حیا
life, existence *n.f.* **ḥayāt** حیات
modest, shy *adj.* **ḥayā dār** حیادار
since, where *adv.* **ḥais** حیث
lion *n.m.* **ḥaidar** حیدر
bewildered, perplexed *adj.* **ḥairān** حیران
surprise; worry *v.t.* **ḥairān karnā** حیران کرنا
confusion, distress, distraction *n.f.* **ḥairānā** حیرانی
astonishment, wonder *n.f.* **ḥairat** حیرت
stupefaction *n.f.* **ḥairat zadagī** حیرت زدگی
wonderstruck, aghast *adj.* **ḥairāt zadah** حیرت زدہ
court, enclosure *n.m.* **ḥītah** حیطہ
fraudulently, deceitfully *adv.* **ḥīlatan** حیلتاً
fraud, deceit, trick *n.m.* **ḥīlah** حیلہ
fraudulent, deceitful *adj.* **ḥīlah bāz** حیلہ باز
time, space, interval (*of time*), duration *n.m.* **ḥīn** حین
lifetime *n.f.* **ḥīn-ē-ḥayāt** حین حیات
animal, beast; idiot, halfwit *n.f.* **ḥaivān** حیوان
zoology *n.f.* **ḥaivāniyāt** حیوانات
brutal, beastly *adj.* **ḥaivānī** حیوانی
brutality, beastliness *n.f.* **ḥaivāniyyat** حیوانیت
living, alive *adj.* **ḥaiyy** حیّ

خ xē

conclusion, end *n.m.* **xātimah** خاتمہ
happy ending *n.m.* **xātimah bil-xair** خاتمہ بالخیر
end, die *v.i.* **xātimah hōnā** خاتمہ ہونا
lady, woman, madam *n.f.* **xātūn** خاتون
kite; falcon, eagle *n.f.* **xād** خاد
artful, cunning, deceiving *adj.* **xādiᶜ** خادع
servant, attendant *n.m.* **xādim** خادم
servant *n.f.* **xādimah** خادمہ
thorn, spine, bramble; jealousy *n.m.* **xār** خار
feel jealous, feel envious *v.t.* **xār khānā** خار کھانا
hedgehog *n.m.* **xār pušt** خارپشت
out of, excluded, rejected, outcast *adj.* **xārij** خارج
out of use *adj.* **xārij az istiᶜmāl** خارج از استعمال
senseless, foolish *adj.* **xārij az ᶜaql** خارج از عقل
out of the question, beside the point *adj.* **xārij az baḥs** خارج ازبحث
exclude, expel, cast off *v.t.* **xārij karnā** خارج کرنا
be excluded *v.i.* **xārij hōnā** خارج ہونا
externally, outwardly *adv.* **xārijan** خارجا
thorny *adj.* **xār dār** خاردار
itch *n.f.* **xāriš** خارش
itchy *adj.* **xārišī** خارشی
treasurer *n.m.* **xāzan** خازن
sister-in-law (*wife's sister*) *n.f.* **xāznah** خازنہ
mother-in-law (*husband's mother*) *n.f.* **xāš** خاش
particular, proper, private *adj.* **xas** خاص
especially, particularly *adv.* **xas kar** خاص کر
• noble, excellent, good, charming *adj.* **xāsah** خاصہ
habit, nature, manner, method *n.m.* **xāssah**
peculiarity *n.f.* **xāsiyyat** خاصیت
mind, soul, heart; thought *n.m.* **xātir** خاطر
satisfaction, tranquility *n.f.* **xātir jamaᶜ** خاطر جمع
satisfactory, tranquil *adj.* **xātir xavāh** خاطر خواه
king, emperor, sovereign *n.m.* **xāqān** خاقان

خاک xāk *n.f.* earth, dust, ashes
خاک اڑانا xāk uṛānā *v.t.* roam, wander; defame
خاکروب xākrōb *n.m.* sweeper
خاکسار xāksār *adj.* humble
خاکستری xākistarī *adj.* grey, ashen, pale
خاکہ xākah *n.m.* sketch, plan, draft
خاکہ اتارنا xākah utārnā *v.t.* trace
خاکی xākī *adj.* dusty, earthy
خال خال xāl xāl *adj.* occasionally, now and then *adv.* / very few, little, scarce
خالد xālid *adj.* everlasting
خالص xālis *adj.* pure, genuine, real, absolute, sincere
خالق xāliq *n.m.* God, creator
خالہ xālah *n.f.* aunt (*mother's sister*)
خالو xālū *n.m.* uncle (*husband of mother's sister*)
خالی xālī *n.m.* empty, vacant
خالی ہاتھ xālī hāth *adj.* penniless; unarmed
خام xām *adj.* raw, unripe, crude
خام خیالی xām xiyālī *n.f.* false notion, false imagination
خام ریش xām raiš *adj.* unwise; witty
خامہ xāmah *n.m.* pen
خاموش xāmōš *adj.* silent
خاموشی xāmōšī *n.f.* silence
خامی xāmī *n.f.* rawness, immaturity, imperfection
خان xān *n.m.* lord
خاندان xāndān *n.m.* family, dynasty
خانساماں xānsāmāṁ *n.m.* butler
خانقاہ xānqāh *n.f.* monastery, convent
خانگی xāngī *adj.* domestic, private
خانم xānum *n.m.* lady, woman, wife; princess
خانماں xānumāṁ *n.m.* household, house; family
خانہ xānah *n.m.* house, dwelling; chamber, room, compartment; column
خانہ آباد xānah ābād *adj.* prosperous
خانہ آبادی xānah ābādī *n.f.* prosperity
خانہ بدوش xānah badōš *n.m.* nomad, vagabond, wanderer, gypsy
خانہ جنگی xānah jangī *n.f.* civil war; domestic quarrel

mosque, temple, church; the Ka'aba *n.m.* **xānah-ē-xudā** خانہ خدا
ruin, destruction *n.f.* **xānah xarābī** خانہ خرابی
census *n.f.* **xānah šumārī** خانہ شماری
family *n.m.* **xānvādah** خانوادہ
east *n.m.* **xāvar** خاور
husband; lord, master *n.m.* **xāvand** خاوند
afraid, fearful *adj.* **xā'if** خائف
unfaithful; treacherous *adj.* **xā'in** خائن
news, report, information *n.f.* **xabar** خبر
cautious, careful, attentive, watchful *adj.* **xabar dār** خبر دار
inform, report, update *v.t.* **xabar dēnā** خبر دینا
messenger *n.m.* **xabar rasāṁ** خبر رساں
spy, informer *n.m.* **xabar gīr** خبر گیر
take care, look after *v.t.* **xabar gīrī karnā** خبر گیری کرنا
take care, look after; inquire *v.t.* **xabar lēnā** خبر لینا
be informed, have knowledge *v.i.* **xabar hōnā** خبر ہونا
madness, craziness, insanity *n.m.* **xabt** خبط
mad, crazy, insane *adj.* **xabtī** خبطی
wicked, evil, malignant *adj.* **xabīs** خبیث
learned, well-instructed *adj.* / knowing, wise, allah *n.m.* **xabīr** خبیر
end, conclusion *n.m.* / finished, ended, done *adj.* **xatm** ختم
finish *v.t.* **xatm karnā** ختم کرنا
end, be finished *v.i.* **xatm hōnā** ختم ہونا
circumcision *n.m.* **xatnah** ختنہ
shame, bashfulness *n.m.* **xijālat** خجالت
lucky, happy *adv.* **xajistah** خجستہ
ashamed *adj.* **xijl** خجل
modesty *n.m.* **xajlat** خجلت
mule *n.m.* **xacar** خچر
face, cheek *n.m.* **xadd** خد
God, creator *n.m.* **xudā** خدا
Goodbye!, Farewell! *interj.* **xudā ḥāfiz** خدا حافظ
God-worshipping, pious, devout *adj.* **xudā parast** خدا پرست
master, lord; husband *n.m.* **xudā vand** خداوند
O God!, O Lord! *interj.* **xudāyā** خدایا
divinity, godhead; world *n.f.* **xudā'ī** خدائی

doubt; fear, anxiety *n.m.* **xadšah** خدشہ
service, attendance; employment *n.f.* **xidmat** خدمت
serve, attend *v.t.* **xidmat karnā** خدمت کرنا
servant, attendant *n.m.* **xidmat gār** خدمت گار
attendance, service *n.f.* **xidmat gārī** خدمت گاری
servant *n.m.* **xidmat guzār** خدمت گزار
service *n.f.* **xidmat guzārī** خدمت گزاری
arrow *n.m.* **xadang** خدنگ
donkey *n.m.* **xar** خر
bad, ruined, spoiled, faulty *adj.* **xarāb** خراب
ruin, devastation *n.m.* **xarābah** خرابہ
mischief; badness *n.f.* **xarābī** خرابی
create mischief *v.t.* **xarābī ḍālnā** خرابی ڈالنا
snoring *n.m.* **xarrāṭā** خراٹا
snore *v.t.* **xarrāṭā bharnā** خراٹا بھرنا
snore *v.t.* **xarrāṭā mārnā** خراٹا مارنا
tax, tribute, duty *n.m.* **xirāj** خراج
tax, apply a tax *v.t.* **xirāj lagānā** خراج لگانا
polish *v.t.* **xarād caṛhānā** خراد چڑھانا
be polished *v.i.* **xarād caṛhnā** خراد چڑھنا
polisher, turner *n.m.* **xarādī** خرادی
millstonc, grinder, flour-mill *n.m.* **xarās** خراس
scratch *n.f.* **xarāš** خراش
absurdity, nonsense *n.f.* **xarāfāt** خرافات
talk nonsense; abuse (*verbally*) *v.t.* **xarāfāt buknā** خرافات بکنا
pace, gait *n.f.* **xarām** خرام
wasted, ruined, devastated *adj.* **xarb** خرب
melon *n.m.* **xarbūzah** خربوزہ
expenditure, expense *n.m.* **xarc** خرچ
spend, expend *v.t.* **xarc karnā** خرچ کرنا
be spent, be consumed, be used *v.i.* **xarc hōnā** خرچ ہونا
cost, expense *n.m.* **xarcah** خرچہ
extravagant *adj.* **xarcū** خرچو
bag *n.m.* **xurcīn** خرچین
snoring *n.m.* **xar xar** خر خر
snore *v.i.* **xarxarānā** خرخرانا

snoring; rough, uneven *adj.* **xar xarāhaṭ** خرخراہٹ

dispute, quarrel; tumult, riot *n.f.* **xarxašah** خرخشہ

small, little; young *adj.* **xurd** • wisdom, intellect, intelligence *n.f.* **xirad** خرد

wise, intelligent *adj.* **xirad mand** خرد مند

wisdom, intelligence *n.f.* **xirad mandī** خرد مندی

coward, pusillanimity *n.m.* **xardil** • mustard *n.m.* **xardal** خردل

proud; stupid, foolish *adj.* **xar dimāġ** خردماغ

small item, small thing *n.m.* **xurdah** خردہ

seller, hawker *n.m.* **xurdah farōš** خردہ فروش

bear *n.m.* **xirs** خرس

tent, pavilion *n.f.* **xargāh** خرگاہ

hare, rabbit *n.m.* **xargōš** خرگوش

happy, cheerful, delightful *adj.* **xurram** خرم

date *n.m.* **xurmā** خرما

barn; harvest *n.m.* **xurman** خرمن

issue, going out; assault, attack; rebellion *n.m.* **xurūj** خروج

buying, purchase *n.f.* **xarīd** خرید

customer, client, buyer *n.m.* **xarīdār** خریدار

go shopping, shop *v.t.* **xarīdārī karnā** خریداری کرنا

buy *v.t.* **xarīdnā** خریدنا

autumn *n.f.* **xarīf** خریف

autumn *n.f.* **xizān** خزاں

treasury, treasure *n.m.* **xazānah** خزانہ

autumnal *adj.* **xizānī** خزانی

infamy, disgrace *n.f.* **xizzī** • infamous, disgraced *adj.* **xazzī** خزی

treasury; magazine *n.m.* **xazīnah** خزینہ

damage, loss *n.m.* **xasārah** خسارہ

fatigue; wound; sickness *n.m.* **xastagī** خستگی

wounded; sick; poor *adj.* **xastah** خستہ

poor, needy *adj.* **xastah jān** خستہ جاں

grieved, afflicted, distressed *adj.* **xastah ḥāl** خستہ حال

brokenhearted *adj.* **xastah dil** خستہ دل

father-in-law *n.m.* **xusar/xusur** خسر

king *n.m.* **xusrau** خسرو

brick *n.f.* **xišt** خشت

dry, withered; cynical *adj.* / drought *n.f.* **xušk** خشک

خشکی dryness; cynicism *n.f.* **xuškī**
خشم anger, rage *n.m.* **xašm**
خشمگیں angry, enraged *adj.* **xašmgīṁ**
خشمناک furious *adj.* **xašmnāk**
خشنود satisfied, pleased *adj.* **xušnūd**
خشنودی contentment, pleasure *n.f.* **xušnūdī**
خشوع humiliation *n.f.* **xušūc**
خشیت fear, dread *n.f.* **xašiyyat**
خصلت nature *n.f.* **xaslat**
خصم husband; master; enemy *n.m.* **xasm**
خصوصاً especially, particularly *adv.* **xusūsan**
خصوصی special, peculiar; private, personal *adj.* **xusūsī**
خصوصیت speciality, peculiarity *n.f.* **xusūsiyyat**
خصومت enmity, strife, contention *n.f.* **xusūmat**
خضوع humility *n.m.* **xuzūc**
خط letter, script; line, streak; handwriting; beard, moustache *n.m.* **xatt**
خط استوا equator *n.m.* **xatt-ē-istivā**
خط بنانا shave, trim *v.i.* **xatt banānā**
خطا mistake, fault, omission *n.f.* **xatā**
خطا کرنا fail, commit a mistake *v.t.* **xatā karnā**
خطاب title, address; speech, lecture *n.m.* **xitāb**
خطاب کرنا address, deliver a speech *v.t.* **xltāb karnā**
خطا ہونا fail, err *v.i.* **xatā hōnā**
خطاوار defaulter; criminal *n.m.* **xatā vār**
خطبہ speech, address *n.m.* **xutbah**
خطر danger, hazard, risk, fear *n.m.* **xatar**
خطرناک dangerous, hazardous *adj.* **xatarnāk**
خطرہ danger, fear *n.m.* **xatrah**
خطہ region, district, zone, territory *n.m.* **xittah**
خطیب preacher, lecturer *n.m.* **xatīb**
خطیہ fault, sin *n.m.* **xittiyah**
خفا be angry *v.i.* **xafā/xifā**
خفت disgrace, shame *n.f.* **xift**
خفگی displeasure *n.f.* **xafgī**
خفی imperceptible, hidden, secret *adj.* **xafī**
خفیف light, trivial, insignificant *adj.* **xafīf**

خفیف ہونا feel ashamed *v.i.* **xafīf hōnā**
خفیفہ small, little *adj.* **xafīfah**
خفیہ hidden, disguised, secret *adj.* **xufyah**
خفیہ نویس spy *n.m.* **xufyah navīs**
خلا vacancy, emptiness *n.m.* **xalā**
خلاص freedom, release, discharge *n.m.* **xalās**
خلاص کرنا free, release, discharge *v.t.* **xalās karnā**
خلاصہ essence, extract, substance *n.m.* **xulāsah**
خلاصہ کرنا abridge, sum up *v.t.* **xulāsah karnā**
خلاصی freedom, discharge *n.f.* **xulāsī**
خلاصی پانا be released, be set free *v.t.* **xulāsī pānā**
خلاف contrary, in opposition *adj.* **xilāf**
خلافِ قاعدہ irregular *adj.* **xilāf qāᶜidah**
خلافِ قیاس absurd *adj.* **xilāf qiyās**
خلافِ ورزی کرنا disobey, oppose *v.t.* **xilāf-ē-varzī karnā**
خلاق God, creator *n.m.* **xalāq**
خلال toothpick *n.m.* **xilāl**
خلت intimacy *n.f.* **xullat**
خلجان uneasiness, restlessness *n.m.* **xalijān**
خلد paradise *n.m.* **xuld**
خلش interruption *n.f.* **xalaš**
خلط nature *n.m.* **xilt**
خلف successor, heir *n.m.* **xalaf**
خلف الصدق rightful heir *n.m.* **xalaf-ul-sidq**
خلق civility, hospitality; quality *n.m.* **xulq** • people, mankind *n.m.* **xalq**
خلقت people, mankind *n.f.* **xalqat**
خلقی natural, inherent *adj.* **xilqī**
خلل interruption; damage, injury *n.m.* **xalal**
خلل دماغ madness *n.m.* **xalal damāġ**
خلوص sincerity, purity; intimacy *n.f.* **xulūs**
خلیج bay, gulf *n.f.* **xalīj**
خلیفہ caliph *n.m.* **xalīfah**
خلیق polite, civil, kind *adj.* **xalīq**
خلیل intimate friend, sincere friend *n.m.* **xalīl**
خلیہ cell *n.m.* **xaliyah**
خم large jar, tin, pot *n.m.* **xum** • curl, curve, coil, fold *n.m.* **xam**

intoxication; headache *n.m.* **xumār** خمار
dumb, silent *adj.* **xamōš** خموش
silence, muteness *n.f.* **xamōšī** خموشی
stretching, gaping; retribution *n.m.* **xamyāzah** خمیازہ
crookedness *n.f.* **xamīdagī** خمیدگی
bent, crooked *adj.* **xamīdah** خمیدہ
leaven, yeast *n.m.* **xamīr** خمیر
ferment *v.t.* **xamīr uṭhānā** خمیر اٹھانا
bad spirit, devil *n.m.* **xannās** خناس
dagger *n.m.* **xanjar** خنجر
smiling, laughing, laughter *n.m.* **xandāṁ** خنداں
ditch, moat *n.m.* **xandaq** خندق
laughter, laugh, laughing *n.m.* / laughing *adj.* **xandah** خندہ
pig, swine, hog *n.m.* **xanzīr** خنزیر
cool, cold *adj.* **xunak** خنک
coldness, coolness, chilliness *n.f.* **xunakī** خنکی
habit, custom; disposition; nature *n.f.* **xū** خو
be habituated, develop a habit *v.i.* **xū paṛnā** خو پڑنا
habituate, accustom *v.t.* **xū ḍālnā** خو ڈالنا
dream; sleep *n.m.* **xvāb** خواب
dream *v.t.* **xvāb dēkhnā** خواب دیکھنا
delusion *n.m.* **xvāb-ō-xiyāl** خواب و خیال
bedroom *n.f.* **xvābgāh** خوابگاہ
asleep, sleeping; sleepy, drowsy *adj.* **xvābīdah** خوابیدہ
gentleman, governor, lord, master *n.m.* **xvājah** خواجہ
eunuch, hermaphrodite *n.m.* **xvājah sirā** خواجہ سرا
distressed, ruined *adj.* **xvār** خوار
distress, misery, hardship *n.f.* **xvārī** خواری
petitioner, applicant *n.m.* **xvāstgār** خواستگار
application *n.f.* **xvāstgārī** خواستگاری
tray *n.m.* **xvān** خوان
small tray *n.m.* **xvāncah** خوانچہ
vendor *n.m.* **xvāncah vālā** خوانچہ والا
literate, educated *adj.* **xvāndah** خواندہ
wishing, desiring *adj.* **xavāh** خواہ
wanting, desirous *adj.* **xavāhāṁ** خواہاں

خواہر sister *n.f.* **xvāhar**
خواہش desire, wish; passion *n.f.* **xvāhiš**
خواہش کرنا wish, long for *v.t.* **xvāhiš karnā**
خواہشمند desirous, willing *adj.* **xvāhišmand**
خوب pleasant, beautiful, good *adj.* **xūb**
خوبانی apricot *n.f.* **xūbānī**
خوبرو handsome, beautiful *adj.* **xūbrū**
خوبروئی beauty *n.f.* **xūbrū'ī**
خوبصورت handsome, beautiful *adj.* **xūbsūrat**
خوبصورتی beauty *n.f.* **xūbsūratī**
خوبی excellence, beauty; quality *n.f.* **xūbī**
خوجہ eunuch *n.m.* **xōjah**
خود self, own *adj.* **xūd** • helmet *n.m.* **xōd**
خودآرا self-conceited, proud *adj.* **xūd ārā**
خود بخود on one's own, by oneself *adj.* **xūd baxūd**
خود سر stubborn, arrogant, obstinate *adj.* **xūd sar**
خودغرض selfish *adj.* **xūd ġarz**
خودکشی suicide *n.f.* **xūd kušī**
خودکشی کرنا commit suicide *v.t.* **xūd kušī karnā**
خود مختاری independence, liberty *n.f.* **xūd muxtārī**
خودرو wild *adj.* **xūdrō**
خودی self respect; vanity, selfishness *n.f.* **xūdī**
خوراک food, provisions *n.f.* **xōrāk**
خورد small, little *adj.* **xūrd**
خوردبرد fraud, embezzlement *n.f.* **xūrdburd**
خوردبرد کرنا make away with, misappropriate *v.t.* **xūrdburd karnā**
خوردنی food, provisions, edible *n.f.* **xōrdanī**
خوردہ بیچنا retail *v.t.* **xūdah bēcnā**
خورشید sun *n.m.* **xūršīd**
خوش glad, happy *adj.* **xūš**
خوش اختر lucky, auspicious *adj.* **xūš axtar**
خوش اسلوب elegant, graceful *adj.* **xūš aslūb**
خوش آمدید Welcome! *interj.* **xūš āmdēd**
خوش آمدید کہنا welcome *v.t.* **xūš āmdēd kēhnā**
خوش خلق civil, polite *adj.* **xūš xalq**
خوش طبع cheerful, jolly *adj.* **xūš taba^c^**

please *v.t.* **xūš karnā** خوش کرنا
lucky, fortunate *adj.* **xūš nasīb** خوش نصیب
rejoice, be glad, be pleased *v.i.* **xūš hōnā** خوش ہونا
flattery *n.f.* **xūšāmad** خوشامد
flatterer *n.m.* **xūšāmdī** خوشامدی
fragrance, perfume, pleasant odor *n.f.* **xūšbū** خوشبو
fragrant, perfumed *adj.* **xūšbūdār** خوشبودار
prosperity, happiness *n.f.* **xūšḥālī** خوشحالی
pleasant, delicious *adj.* **xūšgavār** خوشگوار
pleased *adj.* **xūšnūd** خوشنود
pleasure, delight *n.f.* **xūšnūdī** خوشنودی
joy, happiness *n.f.* **xūšī** خوشی
meditation, deep thought *n.m.* **xauz** خوض
fear *n.m.* **xauf** خوف
terrified *adj.* **xauf zadah** خوف زدہ
be afraid of *v.t.* **xauf khānā** خوف کھانا
frightful *adj.* **xaufnāk** خوفناک
case, cover *n.m.* **xōl** خول
blood; murder, killing *n.m.* **xūn** خون
murder, kill *v.t.* **xūn karnā** خون کرنا
bloody *adj.* / murderer, assassin *n.m.* **xūnī** خونی
cucumber *n.m.* **xiyār** خیار
tailor *n.m.* **xaiyāt** خیاط
thought, idea *n.m.* **xayāl** خیال
imagine *v.t.* **xayāl bāndhnā** خیال باندھنا
regard, think, consider *v.t.* **xayāl karnā** خیال کرنا
ideal; imaginary *adj.* **xayālī** خیالی
embezzlement, dishonesty *n.f.* **xiyānat** خیانت
embezzle *v.t.* **xiyānat karnā** خیانت کرنا
welfare *n.m.* / safe, well, good *adj.* **xair** خیر
well-wisher *n.m.* **xair xvāh** خیر خواہ
charitable *adj.* **xairātī** خیراتی
darkness; dazzle; shamelessness *n.f.* **xīrgī** خیرگی
wicked *adj.* **xīrah** خیرہ
safety, health, welfare *n.f.* **xair-ō-ᶜāfiyat** خیروعافیت
happiness, welfare *n.f.* **xairiyat** خیریت

rising *adj.* **xēz** خیز
tent, pavilion *n.m.* **xaimah** خیمہ
camp *v.t.* **xaimah karnā** خیمہ کرنا
camping ground, encampment *n.m.* **xaimah gāh** خیمہ گاہ

dāl د

/ manner, custom; state, condition; fear, terror *n.m.* **dāb** داب
pressure, weight, force; control, check; impression *n.f.*
press, suppress, squeeze, snub *v.t.* **dābnā** دابنا
God; benefactor *n.m.* **dātā** داتا
toothbrush, twig used to brush one's teeth *n.m.* **dātan** داتن
darkness *n.m.* **dāj** داج
entering, penetrating *adj.* **dāxil** داخل
file, shelve *v.t.* **dāxil dāftar karnā** داخل دفتر کرنا
admit, include, enlist *v.t.* **dāxil karnā** داخل کرنا
admission, entrance, entry *n.m.* **dāxilah** داخلہ
inclusive, internal *adj.* **dāxilī** داخلی
ringworm; gift; justice, law, appeal *n.m.* **dād** داد
judge *n.m.* **dādgar** دادگر
grandfather (*paternal*) *n.m.* **dādā** دادا
grandmother (*paternal*) *n.m.* **dādī** دادی
home, house, abode, dwelling *n.m.* **dār** دار
cinnamon *n.f.* **dārcīnī** دارچینی
holder, possessor, sovereign, king *n.m.* **dārā** دارا
metropolis *n.m.* **dār-ul-imārāt** دارالامارات
capital *n.m.* **dār-ul-ḥukūmat** دارالحکومت
capital *n.m.* **dār-ul-xilāfah** دارالخلافہ
hospital *n.m.* **dār-ul-šafā'** دارالشفاء
remedy, medicine; alcoholic drink, wine *n.f.* **dārū** دارو
beard *n.f.* **dāṛhī** داڑھی
tale, story *n.f.* **dāstān** داستان
storyteller *n.m.* **dāstān-ē-gō** داستان گو
maidservant *n.f.* **dāsī** داسی
care, patronage *n.f.* **dāšt** داشت
concubine *n.f.* **dāštah** داشتہ
angel of death, death *n.m.* **dāᶜī ajal** داعی اجل
desire, wish *n.f.* **dāᶜiyah** داعیہ
stain, brand, mark, spot *n.m.* **dāġ** داغ
spotted *adj.* **dāġ dār** داغ دار

brand, mark *v.t.* **dāġ dēnā** داغ دینا
defame, stain *v.t.* **dāġ lagānā** داغ لگانا
burn (*with iron*); stigmatize *v.t.* **dāġnā** داغنا
curer, healer *n.m.* **dāfaᶜ** دافع
pulse, legumes, beans *n.m.* **dāl** دال
cinnamon *n.f.* **dāl cīnī** دال چینی
achieve success, avail *v.t.* **dāl galānā** دال گلانا
verandah *n.m.* **dālān** دالان
price, rate; net snare *n.m.* **dām** دام
settle the price *v.t.* **dām cukānā** دام چکانا
pay the price *v.t.* **dām dēnā** دام دینا
son-in-law *n.m.* **dāmād** داماد
beg, supplicate *v.t.* **dāman phailānā** دامن پھیلانا
to get rid of *v.t.* **dāman churānā** دامن چھڑانا
attached to; depending on *adj.* **dāman gīr** دامن گیر
charity, alms, donation *n.m.* / knowing, understanding *adj.* **dān** دان
wise, sage, learned *adj.* **dānā** دانا
wisdom, intelligence *n.f.* **dānā'ī** دانائی
tooth; tusk *n.m.* **dānt** دانت
extract a tooth *v.t.* **dānt ukhāṛnā** دانت اکھاڑنا
dentist *n.m.* **dānt banānē vālā** دانت بنانے والا
toothbrush, twig used to brush one's teeth *n.m.* **dāntan** دانتن
dentist *n.m.* **dāntōṁ kā ḍākṭar** دانتوں کا ڈاکٹر
opinion, view *n.f.* **dānist** دانست
knowingly *adv.* **dānistah** دانستہ
knowledge, wisdom; science *n.f.* **dāniš** دانش
learned *adj.* **dānišmand** دانشمند
learning, wisdom *n.f.* **dānišmandī** دانشمندی
grain; corn *n.m.* **dānah** دانہ
fortune, luck *n.m.* **dānah pānī** دانہ پانی
right (*hand/side*) *adj.* **dāhnā** داہنا
turn, opportunity *n.m.* **dā'ō** داؤ
ambush *n.m.* **dā'ō khāt** داؤگھات
get the opportunity, get a chance *v.t.* **dā'ō lagānā** داؤلگانا
God; judge; the sovereign *n.m.* **dāvar** داور
ambush; stratagem *n.m.* **dāōṁ** داوں

right (*hand/side*) *adj.* **dāyāṁ** دایاں
encircling, going round *adj.* **dā'ir** دائر
circle, circuit, ring *n.m.* **dā'irah** دائرہ
lasting, perpetual, eternal *adj.* **dā'im** دائم
continual, durable *adj.* **dā'imī** دائمی
nurse, midwife; maid *n.f.* **dāyah** دایہ
nurse, midwife; maid *n.f.* **dā'ī** دائی
on the right side, on the right hand *adj.* **dā'īn** دائیں
here and there, hither and thither *adv.* **dā'īn bā'īn** دائیں بائیں
bear *n.m.* **dubb** دب
be buried, be suppressed *v.i.* **dab jānā** دبا
press, suppress, squeeze; usurp *v.t.* **dabānā** دبانا
pressure,constraint; influence, strength *n.m.* **dabā'ō** دباؤ
press *v.t.* **dabā'ō ḍālnā** دباؤ ڈالنا
dignity, majesty *n.m.* **dabdabah** دبدبہ
suspense, doubt, uncertainty; dilemma *n.f.* **dubdhā** دبدھا
press down; stow away, hide *v.t.* **dabkānā** دبکانا
be covered, be concealed; crouch down *v.i.* **dubaknā** دبکنا
ambush *n.f.* **dabkī** دبکی
threaten *v.t.* **dabkī mārnā** دبکی مارنا
lean, thin, weak *adj.* **dublā** دبلا
be pressed down, be oppressed, be squeezed *v.i.* **dabnā** دبنا
ill-fashioned, crude, rough, rude *adj.* **dabang** دبنگ
seize, squeeze, pounce upon *v.t.* **dabōcnā** دبوچنا
silently, gently *adv.* **dabē pā'ōṁ** دبے پاؤں
clerk; writer *n.m.* **dabīr** دبیر
thick, stiff, strong *adj.* **dabīz** دبیز
liar, deceiver *n.m.* **dajjāl** دجال
smoke, steam *n.m.* **duxān** دخان
smoking *adj.* **duxānī** دخانی
steamer *n.m.* **duxānī jahāz** دخانی جہاز
daughter *n.f.* **duxtar** دختر
entrance, admission *n.m.* **daxl** دخل
admitted *adj.* **daxīl** دخیل
occupant *n.m.* **daxīl kār** دخیل کار
in, into, within *pp.* / door, gate *n.m.* / price, rate, value, tariff *n.f.* **dar** در

pearl *n.m.* **durr** در
import; income, return *n.f.* **dar āmad** درآمد
import and export; income and expenditure *n.f.* **darāmad barāmad** درآمد برآمد
come in, arrive at *v.i.* **dar ānā** درآنا
from door to door *adv.* **dar badar** دربدر
secretly *adv.* **dar pardah** درپردہ
pursue, follow *v.t.* **dar pē hōnā** درپے ہونا
under consideration, under trial *pp.* **dar pēš** درپیش
bell *n.f.* **darā** درا
long, tall, extended *adj.* **darāz** دراز
oppression, tyranny, injustice *n.f.* **darāz dastī** دراز دستی
length, tallness, extension *n.f.* **darāzī** درازی
sickle, hook (*for reaping*) *n.f.* **darāntī** درانتی
relating to, with regard to *pp.* **darbāb** درباب
house, court, hall *n.m.* **darbār** دربار
guard *n.m.* **darbāran** دربارن
courtier, something relating to the court *n.m.* **darbārī** درباری
guard, doorkeeper *n.m.* **darbān** دربان
writing *n.m.* **darj** درج
enter, insert, record, register *v.t.* **darj karnā** درج کرنا
dozen *n.f.* **darjan** درجن
grade, degree, class *n.m.* **darjah** درجہ
step by step *adv.* **darjah bah darjah** درجہ بہ درجہ
tree *n.m.* **daraxt** درخت
light, lighting *n.f.* **daraxiš** درخش
shining, brilliant *adj.* **daraxšāṁ** درخشاں
lustre, brilliancy, splendor *n.f.* **duraxšandagī** درخشندگی
shining, glittering; lucid *adj.* **duraxšandah** درخشندہ
application, appeal, petition, request *n.f.* **darxvāst** درخواست
request, apply *v.t.* **darxvāst karnā** درخواست کرنا
pain, ache; suffering; pity *n.m.* **dard** درد
painful; pitiable *adj.* **dard āmēz** درد آمیز
headache *n.m.* **dard-ē-sar** دردِ سر
painkiller *n.f.* **dard kī davā** درد کی دوا
compassionate; pitiful *adj.* **dard mand** دردمند
compassion, sympathy *n.f.* **dard mandī** دردمندی

painful *adj.* **dard nāk** دردناک

crack, flaw, seam *n.f.* **darz** درز

tailor *n.m.* **darzī** درزی

lesson, lecture *n.m.* **dars** درس

teach, give a lesson *v.t.* **dars dēnā** درس دینا

school, college, academy, institute *n.f.* **dars gāh** درس گاہ

right, correct, fit *adj.* **durust** درست

correct, rectify; arrange *v.t.* **durust karnā** درست کرنا

correction, correctness, soundness, accuracy *n.f.* **durustī** درستی

educational *adj.* **darsī** درسی

rigid, harsh, rough *adj.* **durušt** درشت

harshness, roughness, severity *n.f.* **duruštī** درشتی

appearance, seeing; interview (*with a religious teacher*) *n.f.* **daršan** درشن

required, wanted, necessary *adj.* **darkār** درکار

aside, apart *adv.* **darkinār** درکنار

monastery, shrine; palace *n.f.* **dargāh** درگاہ

bad treatment *n.f.* **durgat** درگت

pardon, forgive, excuse *v.t.* **dar guzar karnā** درگزر کرنا

money (*especially coins*) *n.m.* **daram** درم

remedy, cure, medicine *n.m.* **darmāṁ** درماں

misery, distress, ill-luck *n.f.* **darmāndgī** درماندگی

helpless, without remedy *adj.* **darmāndah** درماندہ

in the middle/course of, during, between, amid *adv./pp.* **darmiyāṁ** درمیاں

ferocious, fierce *adj.* **darindah** درندہ

delay, hesitation *n.m.* **dirang** درنگ

confused *adj.* **darham** درہم

confused, confounded; upset *adj.* **darham barham** درہم برہم

confuse, upset *v.t.* **darham barham karnā** درہم برہم کرنا

door, gate *n.m.* **darvāzah** دروازہ

knock at the door *v.t.* **darvāzah khaṭkhaṭānā** دروازہ کھٹکھٹانا

lie, falsehood *n.m.* **darōġ** دروغ

false swear, perjury *n.f.* **darōġ-ē-xalfī** دروغِ خلفی

liar *n.m.* **darōġ-ē-gō** دروغ گو

in, within, inside *pp.* **darōṁ** دروں

dervish, (*Sufi Muslim*) ascetic *n.m.* **darvēš** درویش

carpet *n.f.* **darī** دری
river *n.m.* **daryā** دریا
liberal, generous, frank *adj.* **daryā dil** دریا دل
enquiry, investigation; discovery *n.f.* **daryāft** دریافت
enquire, investigate; discover *v.t.* **daryāft karnā** دریافت کرنا
window *n.m.* **darīcah** دریچہ
torn *adj.* **darīdah** دریدہ
sigh; sorrow, regret, grief *n.m.* **darēġ** دریغ
grudge, dislike *v.t.* **darēġ karnā** دریغ کرنا
begging *n.m.* **daryūzah** دریوزہ
beggar *n.m.* **daryūzah gar** دریوزہ گر
thief, robber *n.m.* **duzd** دزد
theft, robbery *n.f.* **duzdī** دزدی
ten *num.* **das** دس
foreign country *n.m.* **disāvar** دساور
hand; purge *n.m.* **dast** دست
have diarrhea *v.i.* **dast ānā** دست آنا
purgative *n.m.* **dast āvar** دست آور
give up, withdraw from *v.t.* **dast bardār hōnā** دست بردار ہونا
renunciation, cession, withdrawal *n.f.* **dast bardāri** دست برداری
oppression, tyranny, violence *n.f.* **dast darāzī** دست درازی
craftsman, artisan, manufacturer *n.m.* **dast kār** دست کار
handwork, handicraft *n.f.* **dast kārī** دست کاری
patron, helper, protector *n.m.* **dast gīr** دست گیر
protection, aid, help, assistance *n.f.* **dast gīrī** دست گیری
handkerchief *n.m.* **dast māl** دست مال
turban *n.f.* **dastār** دستار
glove *n.m.* **dastānah** دستانہ
signature, note of hand, bond, certificate, document *n.f.* **dastāvēz** دستاویز
signature *n.m.* **dastaxat** دستخط
sign *v.t.* **dastaxat karnā** دستخط کرنا
quire (*of paper*), bundle; handle, pestle; squadron *n.f.* **dastah** دستہ
custom, rule, mode, fashion, usage; constitution *n.m.* **dastūr** دستور
commission, fee *n.f.* / constitutional, customary *adj.* **dastūrī** دستوری
by hand, per bearer *adj.* **dastī** دستی
procured, attained *adj.* **dastiyāb** دستیاب

December *n.m.* **disambar** دسمبر
tenth *adj.* **dasvāṁ** دسواں
jungle, forest, woods *n.m.* **dašt** دشت
enemy, rival, adversary, opponent *n.m.* **dušman** دشمن
enmity, hostility, rivalry *n.f.* **dušmanī** دشمنی
abuse *n.f.* **dušnām** دشنام
arduous, difficult *adj.* **dušvār** دشوار
difficulty *n.f.* **dušvārī** دشواری
blessing, benediction, prayer *n.f.* **duᶜā** دعا
feast, banquet; invitation, convocation *n.f.* **daᶜvat** دعوت
invite *v.t.* **daᶜvat dēnā** دعوت دینا
claim, charge, demand *n.m.* **daᶜvā** دعویٰ
establish a claim *v.t.* **daᶜvā jamānā** دعویٰ جمانا
treachery, deceit, fraud, delusion *n.m.* **daġā** دغا
treacherous, deceitful, insincere *adj.* **daġā bāz** دغا باز
treachery, cheating, deceitfulness *n.f.* **daġā bāzī** دغا بازی
deceive, cheat *v.t.* **daġā dēnā** دغا دینا
tumult, alarm *n.m.* **daġdaġā** دغدغا
office, department; record, register *n.m.* **daftar** دفتر
office worker, office manager *n.m.* / official *adj.* **daftarī** دفتری
repulsion, repelling *n.m.* **dafaᶜ** دفع
repel, ward off *v.t.* **dafaᶜ karnā** دفع کرنا
be repelled, be driven back *v.i.* **dafaᶜ hōnā** دفع ہونا
all at once, suddenly *adv.* **dafaᶜtan** دفعتاً
time; class; turn *n.f.* **dafᶜah** دفعہ
repulsion, prevention; cure, remedy *adj.* **dafᶜiyyah** دفعیہ
burial *n.m.* **dafn** دفن
bury *v.t.* **dafn karnā** دفن کرنا
be buried *v.i.* **dafn hōnā** دفن ہونا
bury *v.t.* **dafnānā** دفنانا
hidden treasure *n.m.* **dafīnah** دفینہ
angry, vexed, troubled; thin, slender *adj.* **diqq** دق
tease, vex, perplex *v.t.* **diqq karnā** دق کرنا
difficulty, trouble *n.f.* **diqqat** دقت
get into trouble, get into difficulty *v.i.* **diqqat mēṁ paṛnā** دقت میں پڑنا
subtle, fine, delicate *adj.* **daqīq** دقیق

minute; delicate question *n.m.* **daqīqah** دقیقہ
suffering, pain, ache, misery, distress *n.m.* **dukh** دکھ
bear trouble, suffer pain *v.t.* **dukh uṭhānā** دکھ اٹھانا
hurt, give pain *v.t.* **dukh dēnā** دکھ دینا
shop *n.f.* **dukān/dukkān** دکان
show, display, exhibit *v.t.* **dikhānā** • hurt, pain *v.t.* **dukhānā** دکھانا
small shop *n.m.* **dukāncah** دکانچہ
shopkeeper, trader; boss *n.m.* **dukāndār** دکاندار
business; shopkeeping *n.f.* **dukāndārī** دکانداری
show, display, exhibition *n.m.* **dikhāvā** دکھاوا
show, display, exhibition *n.m.* **dikhāvaṭ** دکھاوٹ
appear, be seen, come into sight *v.t.* **dikhā'ī dēnā** دکھائی دینا
misfortune, calamity *n.m.* **dukhṛā** دکھڑا
show, exhibit, display *v.t.* **dikhlānā** دکھلانا
south *n.m.* **dakkhin** دکھن
southern *adj.* **dakkhinī** دکھنی
unfortunate, afflicted *adj.* **dukhī** دکھی
hesitation, doubt, uncertainty *n.m.* **dugdā** دگدا
another, other *adj.* **digar** دگر
changed, altered *adj.* **digar gūṁ** دگرگوں
two-fold, double *adj.* **dugnā** دگنا
large number; herd, crowd, mob *n.m.* **dal** • heart; mind, soul *n.m.* **dil** دل
beloved *adj.* **dil ārā** دل آرا
beloved, sweetheart *n.m.* **dil ārām** دل آرام
cruel *adj.* **dil āzār** دل آزار
brave, courageous *adj.* **dil āvar** دل اور
bravery, heroism, valor *n.f.* **dil āvarī** دل اوری
clever, artful *adj.* **dil bāz** دل باز
attracted; in love *adj.* **dil bastah** دل بستہ
attractive *adj.* **dil band** دل بند
amuse, divert *v.t.* **dil bahlānā** دل بہلانا
pleasant, agreeable *adj.* **dil pazīr** دل پذیر
dishearten, disappoint *v.t.* **dil tōṛnā** دل توڑنا
desire to please *n.f.* **dil jō'ī** دل جوئی
interesting, pleasing *adj.* **dil casp** دل چسپ

interest *n.f.* **dil caspī** دل چسپی

amuse, please, make enjoy *v.t.* **dil xūš karnā** دل خوش کرنا

lover, sweetheart *n.f./n.m.* **dil dār** دل دار

sweetheart *n.m.* **dil rubā** دل ربا

heart-burning, moving, touching, affecting *adj.* **dil sōz** دل سوز

happy, glad, cheerful *adj.* **dil šād** دل شاد

brokenhearted, comfortless *adj.* **dil šikastah** دل شکستہ

charming, beautiful; deceptive, tricky, cunning *adj.* **dil farēb** دل فریب

brokenhearted, melancholic *adj.* **dil figār** دل فگار

attractive, lovely, alluring *adj.* **dil kaš** دل کش

amusement, merriment *n.f.* **dil lagī** دل لگی

bear in mind; keep something secret *v.t.* **dil mēṁ rakhnā** دل میں رکھنا

heart and mind; ambition *n.m.* **dil-ō-dimāġ** دل و دماغ

dear, beloved, sweetheart *adj.* **dulārā** دلارا

comfort, consolation *n.m.* **dilāsā** دلاسا

broker, salesman, agent *n.m.* **dallāl** دلال

direction, guidance, indication; proof, evidence *n.f.* **dalālat** دلالت

commission, brokerage *n.f.* **dalālī** دلالی

cause to give, assign *v.t.* **dilānā** دلانا

quilt *n.f.* **dulā'ī** دلائی

lovely, attractive, beloved *adj.* **dilbar** دلبر

kick (*with the hind legs*) *n.f.* **dulattī** دلتی

kick *v.t.* **dulattī mārnā** دلتی مارنا

satisfaction; security, assurance; peace *n.f.* **dil jama'ī** دلجمعی

poverty *n.m.* **daliddar** دلدر

poor *adj.* **daliddarī** دلدری

marsh, bog, swamp *n.m.* **daldal** دلدل

marshy, boggy, swampy *adj.* **daldalī** دلدلی

trot (*of a horse*) *n.f.* **dulkī** دلکی

grind, split *v.t.* **dulnā** دلنا

bridegroom *n.m.* **dulhā** دلہا

bride, wife *n.f.* **dulhan** دلہن

bucket, urn; Aquarius (*Zodiac*) *n.m.* **dalv** دلو

hearty; sincere *adj.* **dilī** دلی

pounded grain/pulse *n.m.* **daliyā** دلیا

daring, valiant, bold *adj.* **dalēr** دلیر
courageously, bravely, boldly *adv.* **dalērānah** دلیرانہ
bravery, boldness *n.f.* **dalērī** دلیری
dare, venture *v.t.* **dalērī karnā** دلیری کرنا
argument; reason; proof *n.f.* **dalīl** دلیل
argue *v.t.* **dalīl karnā** دلیل کرنا
breath; life, vitality; moment, time; blood *n.m.* / tail, end *n.f.* **dam** دم
artful, treacherous *adj.* **dam bāz** دم باز
pant, gasp; be exhausted *v.i.* **dam phūlnā** دم پھولنا
breathe one's last, die *v.t.* **dam tōṛnā** دم توڑنا
strong, vital *adj.* **dam dār** دم دار
put tail between legs (*dog*), run away, be subdued *v.t.* **dum dabānā** دم دبانا
false hope, deception; coaxing, soothing *n.m.* **dam dilāsā** دم دلاسا
concordant, harmonious, agreeable *adj.* **dam sāz** دم ساز
be deceived *v.t.* **dam khānā** دم کھانا
breathe, rest *v.t.* **dam lēnā** دم لینا
utter a word, speak *v.t.* **dam mārnā** دم مارنا
die, expire *v.i.* **dam nikalnā** دم نکلنا
wag tail (*dog*) *v.t.* **dum hilānā** دم ہلانا
brain, head; intellect *n.m.* **dimāġ** دماغ
refresh oneself *v.t.* **dimāġ tāzah karnā** دماغ تازہ کرنا
boring *adj.* **dimāġ xālī karnā** دماغ خالی کرنا
haughty, proud, arrogant *adj.* **dimāġ dār** دماغ دار
be haughty *v.i.* **dimāġ hōnā** دماغ ہونا
mental, intellectual *adj.* **dimāġī** دماغی
brain work *n.m.* **dimāġ kām** دماغی کام
lustre, brilliance, flash, glitter *n.f.* **damak** دمک
shine, glitter, glow *v.i.* **damaknā** دمکنا
asthma *n.m.* **damah** دمہ
day *n.m.* **din** دن
day by day *adv.* **din ba-din** دن بدن
waste time *v.t.* **din ginvānā** دن گنوانا
tooth *n.m.* **dandān** دندان
dentist *n.m.* **dandān sāz** دندان ساز
astonished, wonderstruck, surprised *adj.* **dang** دنگ
disturbance, riot, row, rebellion *n.m.* **dangā** دنگا

crowd, mob *n.m.* **dangal** دنگل
quarrelsome, disturbant *adj.* **dangalī** دنگلی
mean, low, vile *adj.* **danī** دنی
world *n.f.* **dunyā** دنیا
worldly *adj.* **dunyā dār** دنیا دار
worldliness *n.f.* **dunyā dārī** دنیا داری
worldly, belonging to the world *adj.* **dunyāvī** دنیاوی
worldly, belonging to the world *adj.* **dunyavī** دنیوی
ten *num.* **dah** • village *n.m.* **dēh** دہ
mouth, source *n.m.* **dahānah** دہانہ
fear, dread, awe *n.f.* **dahšat** دہشت
horrible, terrifying *adj.* **dahšat angēz** دہشت انگیز
villager; fool *n.m.* **dahqān** دہقان
rustic, boorish, primitive, rude *adj.* **dahqānī** دہقانی
burn, blaze *v.i.* **dahaknā** دہکنا
be frightened, be scared *v.i.* **dahal jānā** دہل جانا
threshold, porch, portico *n.f.* **dahlēz** دہلیز
tenth *adj.* **dahum** دہم
mouth *n.m.* **dahan** دہن
milk; squeeze out *v.t.* **duhnā** دہنا
curd, yogurt, thick milk *n.m.* **dahī** دہی
two *num.* **dō** دو
two-legged *adj.* **dō pāyah** دوپایہ
again, a second time, twice *adv.* **dōbārah** دوبارہ
face to face, in the presence of *adv.* **dō ba-dō** دوبدو
talk face to face *v.t.* **dō ba-dō kēhnā** دوبدو کہنا
meeting, visiting *adj.* **dō cār** دوچار
stitched, sewed *adj.* **dō xatah** دوختہ
two-colored *adj.* **dō rangī** دورنگی
kneel down *v.i.* **dō zānū hōnā** دوزانو ہونا
mutual, two-sided *adj.* **dō tarfah** دوطرفہ
double, two-fold *adj.* **dō gunā** دوگنا
double storied *adj.* **dō manzil** دومنزل
two-storied *adj.* **dō manzilah** دومنزلہ
bifold, double *adj.* **dō harā** دوہرا
medicine, remedy *n.f.* **davā** دوا

pharmacy, drugstore *n.m.* **davā xānah** دواخانہ
cure, treat *v.t.* **davā dārū karnā** دوا دارو کرنا
take medicine *v.t.* **davā khānā** دوا کھانا
undergo medical treatment *v.t.* **davā karnā** دوا کرنا
inkpot *n.f.* **davāt** دوات
medical treatment, cure, medicine *n.f.* **davā dārū** دوادارو
moving, revolving *adj.* **davvār** دوار
perpetuity, permanence *n.m.* **davām** دوام
running *adj.* **davān** دواں
again *adv.* **dōbāra** دوبارہ، پھر سے
veil, wrapper *n.m.* **dōpaṭṭah** دوپٹہ
noon, midday *n.f.* **dōpahar** دوپہر
déjeuner *n.m.* **dōpahar kā khānā** دوپہر کا کھانا
in the afternoon *adv.* **dōpahar kē ba^cd** دوپہر کے بعد
Gemini (*Zodiac*) *n.m.* **dō paikar** دوپیکر
doubled, bent *adj.* **dō tā** دوتا
double, two-fold *adj.* **dō cand** دوچند
smoke, vapor, haze *n.m.* **dūd** دود
race, tribe, family *n.m.* **dūdmāṁ** دودماں
milk *n.m.* **dūdh** دودھ
drink milk, suck *v.t.* **dūdh pīnā** دودھ پینا
milk *v.t.* **dūdh dōhnā** دودھ دوہنا
tea with milk *n.f.* **dūdh vālī cā'ē** دودھ والی چائے
milky; white; raw *adj.* **dūdhyā** دودھیا
• passing around, revolving, circulation; time, turn, circuit, course; reign *n.m.* **daur** دور
far, remote, distant *adj.* **dūr**
far-sighted, foreseeing *adj.* **dūr andēš** دور اندیش
far-sightedness, foresight *n.f.* **dūr andēšī** دور اندیشی
run away *v.i.* **dūr bhāgnā** دور بھاگنا
lifetime *n.f.* **daur-ē-ḥayāt** دور حیات
very far *adj.* **dūr darāz** دور دراز
remove, dispel, dispossess *v.t.* **dūr karnā** دور کرنا
time, age, period *n.m.* **daurān** دوران
telescope, spy-glass *n.m.* **dūrbīn** دوربین
tour, circuit *n.m.* **daurah** دورہ
go on tour *v.t.* **daurah karnā** دورہ کرنا

distance, remoteness *n.f.* **dūrī** دوری
run; incursion, attack, assault; struggle *n.f.* **dauṛ** دوڑ
toil hard, bustle *v.t.* **dauṛ dhūp karnā** دوڑ دھوپ کرنا
cause to run; drive, impel, speed *v.t.* **dauṛānā** دوڑانا
run *v.i.* **dauṛnā** دوڑنا
hell, inferno *n.m.* **dōzax** دوزخ
hellish, infernal *adj.* **dōzaxī** دوزخی
friend *n.m.* **dōst** دوست
friendship *n.f.* **dōst dārī** دوست داری
friendly *adv.* **dōstānah** دوستانہ
friendship, affection, love *n.f.* **dōstī** دوستی
second, next, other, else *adj.* **dūsrā** دوسرا
second class *n.m.* **dusrā darjah** دوسرا درجہ
shoulder; fault, blame *n.m.* **dōš** دوش
blame, accuse *v.t.* **dōš lagānā** دوش لگانا
blame *n.m.* **dōšan** دوشن
criminal *adj.* **dōšī** دوشی
virginity *n.f.* **dōšīzagī** دوشیزگی
buttermilk, curd *n.m.* **dōġ** دوغ
fortune, wealth; empire, kingdom, state *n.f.* **daulat** دولت
palace, mansion, house *n.m.* **daulat xānah** دولت خانہ
rich, wealthy, prosperous *adj.* **daulat mand** دولت مند
wealth, prosperity *n.f.* **daulat mandī** دولت مندی
double, two-fold *adj.* **dūnā** دونا
both *adj.* **dōnōḍ** دونوں
double *adj.* **dūhrā/dōhrā** دوہرا
repeat, revise *v.t.* **dōhrānā/dūhrānā** دوہرانا
milk *v.t.* **dōhnā** دوہنا
lamp *n.m.* **diyā** دیا
matchstick *n.f.* **diyā salā'ī** دیا سلائی
country, region, province, state *n.m.* **dīyār** دیار
honesty, piety, virtue *n.f.* **diyānat** دیانت
honest, just *adj.* **diyānat dār** دیانت دار
honesty *n.f.* **diyānat dārī** دیانت داری
preface, introduction, preamble *n.m.* **dībācah/dēbācah** دیباچہ
light, lamp, candle *n.m.* **dīpak** دیپک

sight, glance; show *n.f.* **dīd** دید
look, sight; interview *n.m.* **dīdār** دیدار
visible, worth seeing *adj.* **dīdānī** دیدنی
eye *n.m.* / seen *adj.* **dīdah** دیدہ
temple, church *n.f.* **dair** • delay, slowness *n.f.* **dēr** دیر
durable, lasting *adj.* **dēr pā** دیر پا
delayed, too late *adv.* **dēr sē** دیر سے
delay, postpone *v.t.* **dēr lagānā** دیر لگانا
be (too) late *v.i.* **dēr hōnā** دیر ہونا
old, ancient *adj.* **dērīnah** دیرینہ
country, region, territory *n.m.* **dēs** دیس
foreign country *n.m.* **dēsāvar** دیساور
native, local, indigenous; homemade *adj.* **dēsī** دیسی
country, region, territory *n.m.* **dēš** دیش
small kettle *n.f.* **dēġcah** دیغچہ
care, looking after *n.f.* **dēkh bhāl** دیکھ بھال
see, look, observe *v.t.* **dēkhnā** دیکھنا
look at, examine, inspect *v.t.* **dēkhnā bhālnā** دیکھنا بھالنا
other, another, else; again *adj.* **dīgar** دیگر
white ant *n.f.* **dīmak** دیمک
faith, religion (*mainly Islam*) *n.m.* **dīn** دین
convert *v.t.* **dīn mēṁ milānā** دین میں ملانا
give, grant, confer; offer; pay, allot *v.t.* **dēnā** دینا
religious, pious, faithful *adj.* **dīndār** دیندار
piety, religiosity *n.f.* **dīndārī** دینداری
religious, pious, faithful, virtuous *adj.* **dīnī** دینی
holy war, crusade *n.f.* **dīnī laṛā'ī** دینی لڑائی
village; countryside *n.m.* **dēhāt** دیہات
rural *adj.* / villager *n.m.* **dēhātī** دیہاتی
giant, monster, demon *n.m.* **dē'ō** دیو
God (*mainly in Hinduism*) *n.m.* **dēv** دیو
wall *n.f.* **dīvār** دیوار
bankruptcy *n.m.* **dēvālah** دیوالہ
Diwali (*Hindu festival*) *n.f.* **dīvālī** دیوالی
bankruptcy *n.m.* **dēvāliyah** دیوالیہ
(royal) court, tribunal; officer, secretary *n.m.* **dīvān** دیوان

premier, prime minister *n.m.* **dīvān-ē-aᶜlā** دیوان اعلیٰ

court, public hall *n.m.* **dīvān xānah** دیوان خانہ

mad, insane, crazy *adj.* **dīvānā** دیوانا

madness, insanity, lunacy *n.f.* **dīvānagī** دیوانگی

mad, insane, lunatic *n.f.* **dīvānah** دیوانہ

civil court; mad woman *n.f.* / mad, insane, lunatic *adj.* **dīvānī** دیوانی

half-god; good person *n.m.* **dēvtā** دیوتا

brother-in-law (*husband's younger brother*) *n.m.* **dēvāṛ** دیور

sister-in-law (*wife of husband's younger brother*) *n.f.* **dēvarānī** دیورانی

Goddess (*in Hinduism*) *n.f.* **Dēvī** دیوی

metal, mineral *n.f.* **dhāt** دھات

edge; sharpness; stream, current, line *n.f.* **dhār** دھار

sharp, edged *adj.* **dhār dār** دھار دار

line, linement, stripe, streak *n.f.* **dhārī** دھاری

roar, loud cry, thundering; gang (of robbers) *n.f.* **dhāṛ** دھاڑ

roar; attack, rob *v.t.* **dhāṛnā** دھاڑنا

pomp, glory, fame *n.f.* **dhāk** دھاک

thread *n.m.* **dhāgā** دھاگا

thread (a needle) *v.t.* **dhāgā ḍālnā** دھاگا ڈالنا

rice plant, paddy; mouth *n.m.* **dhān** دھان

raid, attack, assault *n.m.* **dhāvā** دھاوا

raid, attack, assault *v.t.* **dhāvā karnā** دھاوا کرنا

raid, attack, assault *v.t.* **dhāvā mārnā** دھاوا مارنا

spot, stain; bolt *n.m.* **dhabbah** دھبہ

smear, stain; bolt *v.t.* **dhabbah lagānā** دھبہ لگانا

vice, bad habit *n.f.* **dhat** دھت

get addicted to *v.i.* **dhat paṛnā** دھت پڑنا

abuse, drive away *v.t.* **dhatkarnā** دھت کرنا

narcotic plant, poison *n.m.* **dhatūrā** دھتورا

posture, attitude, shape *n.f.* **dhaj** دھج

strip (*of cloth*), rag, shred *n.f.* **dhajjī** دھجی

disgrace; tear to pieces *v.t.* **dhajjī uṛānā** دھجی اڑانا

time, age *n.m.* **dhar** دھر

axle *n.m.* **dhurā** دھرا

land, earth, soil, ground *n.f.* **dhartī** دھرتی

mushroom *n.m.* **dhartī kā phūl** دھرتی کا پھول

religion, faith (*mainly Hinduism*) *n.m.* **dharma/dharm** دھرم
navel; womb; beam *n.f.* **dharan** دھرن
place, put down; hold, keep; grasp; assume *v.t.* **dharnā** دھرنا
atheist, infidel; freethinker *n.m.* **dhariyah** دھریہ
body, trunk; drum *n.m.* **dhaṛ** دھڑ
successively, one after the other *adv.* **dhaṛā dhaṛ** دھڑا دھڑ
crash, rumble, roar *n.m.* **dhaṛākā** دھڑاکا
shock, push, jolt, jostle *n.m.* **dhakkā** دھکا
push, jostle, shove *v.t.* **dhakēlnā** دھکیلنا
tremble with fear, be frightened *v.i.* **dahalnā** دھلنا
explosion, crash *n.m.* **dhamākah** دھماکہ
sound (of footsteps); thumping, throbbing, threat *n.f.* **dhamak** دھمک
threaten, menace *v.t.* **dhamkānā** دھمکانا
palpitate, shake, flash, throb *v.i.* **dhamaknā** دھمکنا
threat, menace, intimidation *n.f.* **dhamkī** دھمکی
wealth, fortune, prosperity *n.m.* **dhan** • air, tone, keynote *n.f.* **dhun** دھن
Well done!, Bravo! *interj.* **dhan dhan** دھن دھن
mist, fog, haze *n.f.* **dhund** دھند
occupation, employment; business *n.m.* **dhandā** دھندا
dim, misty, foggy *adj.* **dhundlā** دھندلا
dimness, mistiness *n.m.* **dhundlāpan** دھندلاپن
rainbow *n.f.* **dhanak** دھنک
rich, wealthy *adj.* **dhanvān** دھنوان
wealthy, rich, fortunate *adj.* **dhanī** دھنی
coriander *n.m.* **dhaniyā** دھنیا
smoke *n.m.* **dhū'āṁ** دھواں
smoky *adj.* **dhū'āṁ dhār** دھواں دھار
chimney *n.m.* **dhū'āṁ kaš** دھواں کش
washerwoman *n.f.* **dhōban** دھوبن
washerman *n.m.* **dhōbī** دھوبی
sunlight, sunshine *n.f.* **dhūp** دھوپ
be sunny *v.i.* **dhūp paṛnā** دھوپ پڑنا
sunbathe *v.t.* **dhūp khānā** دھوپ کھانا
dhoti (*sarong worn around the waist*) *n.f.* **dhōtī** دھوتی
deceit, deception, delusion *n.m.* **dhōkā** دھوکا
imposture, cheat, fraud *n.f.* **dhōkā bāzī** دھوکا بازی

be deceived, be taken in *v.t.* **dhōkā khānā** دھوکا کھانا

deceive, cheat *v.t.* **dhōkā dēnā** دھوکہ دینا

thumb; slap *n.m.* **dhaul** • dust *n.f.* **dhūl** دھول

thumb; slap *v.t.* **dhūl lagānā** دھول لگانا

thumb; slap *v.t.* **dhūl mārnā** دھول مارنا

fame, pomp *n.f.* **dhūm** دھوم

make noise, create an uproar *v.t.* **dhūm macānā** دھوم مچانا

wash *v.t.* **dhōnā** دھونا

attention, thought, meditation, reflection, contemplation *n.m.* **dhiyān** دھیان

pay attention, take notice, contemplate *v.t.* **dhiyān dēnā** دھیان دینا

slow, soft, gentle, mild; lazy *adj.* **dhīmā** دھیما

slowly, softly, gently *adv.* **dhīmē dhīmē** دھیمے دھیمے

ḍāl ڈ

lake, pond *n.m.* **ḍābar** ڈابر
stopper, cork; arch, keystone *n.f.* **ḍāt** ڈاٹ
cork, put a stopper on; arch *v.t.* **ḍāt lagānā** ڈاٹ لگانا
be corked; be arched *v.i.* **ḍāt lagnā** ڈاٹ لگنا
swarm, herd, flock *n.f.* **ḍār** ڈار
jaw-tooth; grinder *n.f.* **ḍāṛh** ڈاڑھ
beard *n.f.* **ḍāṛhī** ڈاڑھی
post, mail *n.f.* **ḍāk** ڈاک
stamp, postage *n.m./n.f.* **ḍāk ṭikaṭ** ڈاک ٹکٹ
post office *n.m.* **ḍāk xānah** ڈاک خانہ
postage, postal charges *n.m.* **ḍāk kā xarc** ڈاک کا خرچ
postbox *n.m.* **ḍāk kā ḍibbā** ڈاک کا ڈبا
mail train, mail van *n.f.* **ḍāk gāṛī** ڈاک گاڑی
postman *n.m.* **ḍāk vālā** ڈاک والا
robbery, attack (*by robbers*) *n.m.* **ḍākā** ڈاکا
doctor, physician *n.m.* **ḍākṭar** ڈاکٹر
robber, bandit, pirate *n.m.* **ḍākū** ڈاکو
postman, courier *n.m.* **ḍākiyā** ڈاکیا
branch *n.f.* **ḍāl** ڈال
throw away, cast away, abandon *v.t.* **ḍāl dēnā** ڈال دینا
large lump, clod *n.m.* **ḍālā** ڈالا
dollar *n.m.* **ḍālar** ڈالر
put, put in, put on, pour; throw, cast, fling; drop, shed; miscarry *v.t.* **ḍālnā** ڈالنا
bough, branch *n.f.* **ḍālī** ڈالی
threat, menace; rebuke *n.f.* **ḍānṭ** ڈانٹ
threaten, menace; rebuke, scold *v.t.* **ḍānṭnā** ڈانٹنا
stick, staff, oar *n.m.* **ḍānḍ** ڈانڈ
landmark, boundary line *n.m.* **ḍānḍā** ڈانڈا
boatsman, rower *n.m.* **ḍānḍī** ڈانڈی
summit (*of a mountain*); highland *n.m.* **ḍāng** ڈانگ
homeless, wandering, lost; unsettled, unsteady *adj.* **ḍānvāṁ ḍōl** ڈانواں ڈول
wander around, be unsettled *v.i.* **ḍānvāṁ ḍōl phirnā** ڈانواں ڈول پھرنا
jealousy, envy *n.f.* **ḍāh** ڈاہ

directory *n.f.* **ḍā'irēkṭrī** ڈائریکٹری
witch *n.f.* **ḍā'in** ڈائن
strength, power, authority *n.f.* **ḍab** ڈب
small box *n.m.* **ḍibbā** ڈبا
deep *adj.* **ḍubā'ū** ڈباؤ
dip, dive, plunge *n.f.* **ḍubkī** ڈبکی
dip, immerse *v.t.* **ḍubkī dēnā** ڈبکی دینا
dive, plunge *v.t.* **ḍubkī lagānā** ڈبکی لگانا
drown, immerse, sink, flood *v.t.* **ḍubōnā** ڈبونا
small box *n.f.* **ḍibbī** ڈبی
rebuke, menace, threat *n.f.* **ḍapaṭ** ڈپٹ
ride quickly, gallop, rush; shout at, rebuke *v.t.* **ḍapṭānā** ڈپٹانا
big, large, monstrous, huge *adj.* **ḍapōl** ڈپول
stopper, cork *n.m.* **ḍaṭṭā** ڈٹا
stop, stay, contend *v.i.* **ḍaṭnā** ڈٹنا
fear, dread; awe *n.m.* **ḍar** ڈر
frighten, scare, terrify *v.t.* **ḍarānā** ڈرانا
frightful, dreadful, horrible, terrible, terrifying *adj.* **ḍarā'ōnā** ڈراونا
driver *n.m.* **ḍrā'īvar** ڈرائیور
timid, cowardly *adj.* **ḍarpōk** ڈرپوک
be frightened, be scared *v.t.* **ḍar khānā** ڈرکھانا
be afraid, fear, be frightened *v.i.* **ḍarnā** ڈرنا
bite, sting *v.t.* **ḍasnā** ڈسنا
embezzle; gulp, swallow *v.i.* **ḍakār jānā** ڈکار جانا
bellow, belch *v.t.* **ḍakār lēnā** ڈکار لینا
robber, pirate *n.f.* **ḍakait** ڈکیت
robbery *n.f.* **ḍakaitī** ڈکیتی
step out *v.i.* **ḍig bharnā** ڈگ بھرنا
degree (*academic*) *n.f.* **ḍigrī** ڈگری
degree-holder *n.m.* **ḍigrī dār** ڈگری دار
trembling, tottering *adj.* **ḍagmag** ڈگمگ
tremble, totter, stagger, *v.i.* **ḍagmagānā** ڈگمگانا
small lump *n.f.* **ḍalī** ڈلی
upper-arm; penalty, fine, punishment *n.m.* **ḍanḍ** ڈنڈ
receive a penalty, pay a fine *v.i.* **ḍanḍ bharnā** ڈنڈ بھرنا

club, staff, rod *n.m.* **ḍanḍā** ڈنڈا
sting, bite *n.m.* **ḍank** ڈنک
sting, bite *v.t.* **ḍank mārnā** ڈنک مارنا
kettledrum, drumstick *n.m.* **ḍankā** ڈنکا
become famous *v.t.* **ḍankā bajnā** ڈنکا بجنا
witch *n.f.* **ḍanknī** ڈنکی
dip, dive, plunge, immersion *n.m.* **ḍōb** ڈوب
dip, immerse *v.t.* **ḍōb dēnā** ڈوب دینا
drown, sink, be immersed *v.i.* **ḍūbnā** ڈوبنا
seed-vessel (*for poppy seeds*) *n.m.* **ḍōḍā** ڈوڈا
string, rope *n.f.* **ḍōr** ڈور
thread, cord *n.f.* **ḍōrī** ڈوری
bucket *n.m.* **ḍōl** ڈول
move, shake, swing, sway *v.i.* **ḍōlnā** ڈولنا
sedan, palanquin *n.f.* **ḍōlī** ڈولی
spoon; canoe, boat *n.m.* **ḍōngā** ڈونگا
small spoon; small boat *n.f.* **ḍōngī** ڈونگی
wooden spoon *n.f.* **ḍō'ī** ڈوئی
residence, dwelling, tent *n.m.* **ḍērah** ڈیرہ
one and a half *num.* **ḍēṛh** ڈیڑھ
dentist *n.m.* **ḍēnṭisṭ** ڈینٹسٹ
boasting, vaunting; pride *n.f.* **ḍīng** ڈینگ
boast, brag *v.t.* **ḍīng mārnā** ڈینگ مارنا
one and a half *num.* **ḍē'ōṛhā** ڈیوڑھا
threshold, porch, entrance *n.f.* **ḍē'ōṛhī** ڈیوڑھی
doorkeeper, watchman *n.m.* **ḍē'ōṛhī dār** ڈیوڑھی دار
encouragement, confidence, comfort *n.m.* **ḍhāras** ڈھارس
animate; comfort *v.t.* **ḍhāras bandhānā** ڈھارس بندھانا
slope, mold, mode, fashion *n.f.* **ḍhāl** ڈھال
mold, cast, form; pour out, spill *v.t.* **ḍhālnā** ڈھالنا
pull down, break, demolish *v.t.* **ḍhānā** ڈھانا
cover, hide *v.t.* **ḍhānpnā** ڈھانپنا
plan, sketch, model, frame *n.m.* **ḍhāncah** ڈھانچہ
cover, conceal, hide *v.t.* **ḍhānknā** ڈھانکنا
two and half *num.* **ḍhā'ī** ڈھائی

shape, manner, fashion, position *n.m.* **ḍhab** ڈھب
nut, screw *n.f.* **ḍhibrī** ڈھبری
impudence, shamelessness, obstinacy *n.f.* **ḍhiṭā'ī** ڈھٹائی
slope, declinity *n.m.* **ḍhalān** ڈھلان
cause to mold; level *v.t.* **ḍhalānā** ڈھلانا
slope, slant, declivity *n.m.* **ḍhalvān** ڈھلوان
proclamation, announcement *n.m.* **ḍhanḍhōrā** ڈھنڈھورا
behavior, manner *n.m.* **ḍhang** ڈھنگ
cattle *n.m.* **ḍhōr** ڈھور
large drum *n.m.* **ḍhōl** ڈھول
small drum *n.f.* **ḍhōlak** ڈھولک
small drum *n.f.* **ḍhōlkī** ڈھولکی
transport, carry *v.t.* **ḍhōnā** ڈھونا
four and a half *num.* **ḍhōṁcā** ڈھونچا
search *n.f.* **ḍhūnḍ** ڈھونڈ
search, seek, look for *v.t.* **ḍhūnḍnā** ڈھونڈنا
deceit, trick *n.m.* **ḍhōng** ڈھونگ
deceitful, tricky *adj.* **ḍhōngyā** ڈھونگیا
stubborn, obstinate; forward; daring *adj.* **ḍīṭh** ڈھیٹ
pile, heap, accumulation *n.m.* / much, many, abundant; enough *adj.* **ḍhēr** ڈھیر
fall down, die, be killed *v.i.* **ḍhēr hō jānā** ڈھیر ہوجانا
delay, loseness, slack *n.f.* **ḍhīl** ڈھیل
slackness, looseness, laziness *n.m.* **ḍhēlāpan** ڈھیلاپن

zāl ذ

ذابح **zābiḥ** *n.m.* butcher, slaughterer
ذات **zāt** *n.f.* nature, essence, soul, substance; self; body
ذات الریہ **zāt-ul-riyah** *n.m.* pneumonia
ذات بھائی **zāt bhā'ī** *n.m.* kinsman
ذات پات **zāt pāt** *n.f.* tribe, caste, lineage
ذاتی **zātī** *adj.* private, personal; natural, real, essential; material
ذاکر **zākir** *adj.* remembering, grateful
ذاہل **zāhil** *adj.* careless, forgetful
ذائقہ **zā'iqah** *n.m.* taste, relish
ذائقہ دار **zā'iqah dār** *adj.* tasty, savory, flavorful
ذائقہ لینا **zā'iqah lēnā** *v.t.* taste, relish
ذبح **zabaḥ** *n.m.* slaughter, sacrifice
ذبح کرنا **zabaḥ karnā** *v.t.* slaughter, sacrifice
ذبح ہونا **zabaḥ hōnā** *v.i.* be slaughtered, be sacrificed
ذبیح **zabīḥ** *adj.* slaughtered, sacrificed
ذخیرہ **zaxīrah** *n.m.* provision, stock, store, treasure
ذخیرہ کرنا **zaxīrah karnā** *v.t.* store, stock
ذرا **zarā** *adj.* just, rather; a bit, a little
ذرا سا **zarā sā** *adj.* a bit, a little; short; a little while
ذراع **zirāᶜ** *n.m.* yard, cubit; forearm
ذریت **zurriyat** *n.f.* race, lineage, descent
ذریعہ **zarīᶜah** *n.m.* source, way, method
ذقن **zaqan** *n.m.* chin
ذکا **zakā** *n.m.* sharpness (of mind)
ذکاوت **zakāvat** *n.f.* intelligence; purity
ذکر **zikr** *n.m.* remembrance, memory; mention
ذکر کرنا **zikr karnā** *v.t.* recite, mention
ذکی **zakī** *adj.* wise, clever, intelligent; acute
ذل **zill** *n.m.* gentleness, ease; method, mode
ذلت **zillat** *n.f.* disgrace, insult
ذلیل **zalīl** *adj.* base, mean; disgraceful
ذمہ **zimmah** *n.m.* charge, duty, obligation, trust, responsibility

trustee, assignee *n.m.* **zimmah dār** ذمہ دار

charge, trust, obligation, responsibility, liability *n.f.* **zimmah dārī** ذمہ داری

make over; deliver in trust *v.t.* **zimmah karnā** ذمہ کرنا

take charge, take upon oneself *v.t.* **zimmah lēnā** ذمہ لینا

infidel, non-Muslim (*living in an Islamic country*) *n.m.* **zimmī** ذمی

blamable, culpable *adj.* **zamīm** ذمیم

crime, sin, fault *n.m.* **zanb** ذنب

intelligence, wits *n.f.* **zihānat** ذہانت

acuteness; sagacity, understanding; wit *n.m.* **zēhn** ذہن

think, consider *v.t.* **zēn laṛānā** ذہن لڑانا

intelligent, intellectual, ingenious *adj.* **zahīn** ذہین

having, possessing, endowed with *adj.* **zū** ذو

glorious, splendid *adj.* **zū-ul-jalāl** ذوالجلال

intelligent *adj.* **zī šaᶜūr** ذی شعور

sensible; wise *adj.* **zī hōš** ذی ہوش

rē ر

syrup, molasses *n.f.* **rāb** راب

conjunction, connection, union, bond, liaison *n.m.* **rābitah** رابطہ

night *n.f.* **rāt** رات

the whole night *adv.* **rāt bhar** رات بھر

be late at night *v.t.* **rāt bhīgnā** رات بھیگنا

day and night *adv.* **rāt din** رات دن

dinner, supper *n.m.* **rāt kā khānā** رات کا کھانا

at night, during the night *adv.* **rāt kō** رات کو

midnight *n.m.* **rāt kē bārah bajē** رات کے بارہ بجے

just for one night *adv.* **rāt kī rāt** رات کی رات

pension, stipend, allowance (*for food*) *n.m.* **rātib** راتب

stipendiary (*one who receives a fixed allowance*) *n.m.* **rātib xōr** راتب خور

during the night *adv.* **rātōṁ rāt** راتوں رات

government, sovereignty, reign, kingdom, dominion, royalty *n.m.* **rāj** راج

dominion, kingdom *n.m.* **rāj pāṭ** راج پاٹ

royal court *n.m.* **rāj darbār** راج دربار

princess *n.f.* **rāj dulārī** راج دلاری

palace; metropolis, capital *n.f.* **rāj dhānī** راج دھانی

reign, rule, govern *v.t.* **rāj karnā** راج کرنا

throne, enthronement *n.f.* **rāj gaddī** راج گدی

goose *n.m.* **rāj haṁs** راج ہنس

king, monarch *n.m.* **rājah** راجہ

rest, repose, comfort, ease *n.f.* **rāḥat** راحت

caravan *n.m.* **rāḥilah** راحلہ

merciful, compassionate *adj.* **rāḥim** راحم

quarrel, dispute, tumult *n.f.* **rāṛ** راڑ

secret, mystery *n.m.* **rāz** راز

betray a secret *v.t.* **rāz fāš karnā** راز فاش کرنا

trusty, confident, faithful *adj.* **rāz dār** رازدار

intimate friend, close friend *n.m.* **rāzdān** رازدان

God; cherisher, sustainer *n.m.* **rāziq** رازق

adoptability, suitability *n.f.* / head, top, summit, peak *n.m.* **rās** راس

principle, capital (*money*); stock *n.m.* **rās-ul-māl** راس المال

Zodiac *n.m.* **rās manḍal** راس منڈل
true, correct, just *adj.* **rāst** راست
truthful, honest, righteous, upright *adj.* **rāst bāz** راست باز
path, way, road *n.m.* **rāstah** راستہ
guide, show the way *v.t.* **rāstah dikhānā** راستہ دکھانا
wait for, watch for *v.t.* **rāstah dēkhnā** راستہ دیکھنا
uprightness, honesty *n.f.* **rāstī** راستی
firm, constant, sincere, staunch, durable *adj.* **rāsix** راسخ
pious, religious, orthodox *adj.* **rāšid** راشد
happy, satisfied; willing, wishing *adj.* **rāzī** راضی
please, satisfy *v.t.* **rāzī karnā** راضی کرنا
compromise *n.m.* **rāzī nāmah** راضی نامہ
agree *v.i.* **rāzī hōnā** راضی ہونا
shepherd *n.m.* **rāʿī** راعی
inclined, fond of, willing, wishing, desirous *adj.* **rāġib** راغب
writer, correspondent *n.m.* **rāqim** راقم
ashes *n.f.* **rākh** راکھ
ashtray *n.f.* **rākh dānī** راکھ دانی
rider *n.m.* **rākib** راکب
raga (*a musical tune*); music, song, melody *n.m.* **rāg** راگ
music and having fun *n.m.* **rāg rang** راگ رنگ
singer; musician *n.f.* **rāgī** راگی
saliva, spittle *n.f.* **rāl** رال
thigh *n.f.* **rān** ران
rejected, expelled *adj.* **rāndah** راندہ
cook, prepare food *v.t.* **rāndhnā** راندھنا
widow; prostitute *n.f.* **rānḍ** رانڈ
queen, princess *n.f.* **rānī** رانی
path, way, road *n.m.* **rāh** راہ
guide, show the way *v.t.* **rāh batānā** راہ بتانا
toll, toll duty *n.m.* **rāh dārī** راہ داری
highwayman; robber *n.m.* **rāh zan** راہ زن
road, way, path *n.m.* **rāh guzar** راہ گزر
traveller *n.m.* **rāh gīr** راہ گیر
monk, priest (*Christian*) *n.m.* **rāhib** راہب
traveller *n.m.* **rāhrau** راہرو

guide, conductor, leader *n.m.* **rāhnumā** راہنما
guidance *n.f.* **rāhnumā'ī** راہنمائی
traveller, passenger *n.m.* **rāhī** راہی
historian, narrator *n.m.* **rāvī** راوی
customary, current, common, usual *adj.* **rā'ij** رائج
enforce, make current *v.t.* **rā'ij karnā** رائج کرنا
prevail, be en vogue *v.i.* **rā'ij hōnā** رائج ہونا
opinion, judgment, advice *n.f.* **rā'ē** رائے
mustard seed; small particle *n.f.* **rā'ī** رائی
judge; advice, give consent *v.t.* **rā'ē dēnā** رائے دینا
make a mountain out of a molehill *v.t.* **rā'ī kā pahāṛ banānā** رائی کا پہاڑ بنانا
fruitless, vain, useless *adj.* **rā'igāṁ** رائیگاں
syrup, extract, juice *n.m.* **rubb** • god, lord, master *n.m.* **rabb** رب
interest (*on money*) *n.m.* **ribā** • robbing, ravishing *adj.* **rubā** ربا
godly, divine *adj.* **rabbānī** ربانی
connection, relation *n.m.* **rabt** ربط
quarter, fourth part *n.m.* **ruba**ᶜ ربع
Oh my God!, Oh my goodness! *interj.* **rabbanā** ربنا
spring (*season*) *n.f.* **rabī**ᶜ ربیع
season *n.f.* **rut** رت
rank, stair; honor, dignity *n.m.* **rutbah** رتبہ
jewel, gem, precious stone *n.m.* **ratan** رتن
chariot, fourwheeled carriage *n.m.* **rath** رتھ
repetition *n.f.* **raṭ** رٹ
repeat, reiterate, recite; memorize *v.i.* **raṭnā** رٹنا
optimism *n.f.* **rajā'iyat** رجائیت
registration *n.f.* **rajisṭarī** رجسٹری
return, coming back *n.f.* **raj**ᶜ**at** رجعت
man *n.m.* **rajal** رجل
purslain *n.m.* **rajilah** رجلہ
dominion (*by a king*) *n.m.* **rajvāṛā** رجواڑا
inclination, appeal; reference; return *n.f.* **rujū**ᶜ رجوع
turn, return; incline, refer to, appeal *v.t.* **rujū**ᶜ **karnā** رجوع کرنا
discarded, deprived, outcast *adj.* **rajīm** رجیم
please, enchant, charm *v.t.* **rijhānā** رجھانا
celebrate; decorate, stain with henna *v.t.* **racānā** رچانا

marching, departure; death *n.f.* **riḥlat** رحلت
die *v.t.* **riḥlat karnā** رحلت کرنا
mercy, pity, kindness *n.m.* **raḥm** • womb *n.m.* **riḥm** رحم
merciful, compassionate, kindhearted *adj.* **raḥm dil** رحم دل
feel pity *v.t.* **raḥm khānā** رحم کھانا
most merciful *adj.* **raḥmān** رحمان
mercy, pity, kindness *n.f.* **raḥmat** رحمت
merciful, kind *adj.* **raḥīm** رحیم
mercifulness, kindness *n.f.* **raḥīmī** رحیمی
side, direction, face *n.m.* **rux** رخ
change sides; be inattentive; become angry *v.t.* **rux badalnā** رخ بدلنا
turn the face; march toward; attend to *v.t.* **rux karnā** رخ کرنا
goods, property; furniture; apparel *n.m.* **raxt** رخت
cheek, face; complexion; aspect *n.m.* **ruxsār** رخسار
brilliance, splendor, rays (*of light*) *n.m.* **raxš** رخش
dazzling, bright *adj.* **raxšāṁ** رخشاں
leave, departure; permission, license *n.f.* **ruxṣat** رخصت
casual leave *n.f.* **ruxsat-ē-ittifāqī** رخصت اتفاقی
dismiss, give leave, permit *v.t.* **ruxsat dēnā** رخصت دینا
see off, bid farewell *v.t.* **ruxsat karnā** رخصت کرنا
take leave, depart *v.i.* **ruxsat hōnā** رخصت ہونا
gap, hole, notch, slit, crack, fracture *n.m.* **raxnah** رخنہ
put obstacles in the way, obstruct *v.t.* **raxnah ḍālnā** رخنہ ڈالنا
pick holes; criticize *v.t.* **raxnah nikālnā** رخنہ نکالنا
rejection, opposition; vomiting *n.m.* **radd** رد
reject, oppose; vomit *v.t.* **radd karnā** رد کرنا
be returned, be rejected *v.i.* **radd hōnā** رد ہونا
change, alteration *n.f.* **radd-ō-badal** ردوبدل
dispute, discussion, criticism *n.f.* **radd-ō-qadaḥ** ردوقدح
rejected, inferior, worthless *adj.* **radī/raddī** ردی
meanness, baseness *n.f.* **razālat** رذالت
vile, mean; of low background *adj.* **razīl** رذیل
vine, vineyard; grape *n.m.* **raz** رز
food; support, subsistence *n.m.* **rizq** رزق
battle, war, combat *n.m.* **razm** رزم
battlefield *n.f.* **razm gāh** رزم گاہ

juice; spirit, essence *n.m.* / arriving, reaching *adj.* **ras** رس
juicy, liquid; tasteful *adj.* **ras bharā** رس بھرا
rasgulla (*cheese-based syrupy sweet dish*) *n.m.* **ras gullā** رس گلا
rope, cable *n.m.* **rassā** • quick (*in understanding*), clever *adj.* **rasā** رسا
(divine) mission, prophethood *n.f.* **risālat** رسالت
magazine, pamphlet; cavalry, herd (*of horses*) *n.m.* **risālah** رسالہ
access, entrance, approach; wisdom, skill *n.f.* **rasā'ī** رسائی
doomsday, day of judgement, resurrection *n.f.* **rustaxēz** رستخیز
free, safe, liberated *adj.* **rastgār** رستگار
hero, brave man *n.m.* **rustam** رستم
path, way, road *n.m.* **rastah** رستہ
provision, supply, income *n.f.* **rasad** رسد
due; proportionate, gradual *adj.* **rasadī** رسدی
custom, usage; model, plan *n.f.* **rasm** رسم
custom, usage *n.m.* **rasm-ō-rivāj** رسم و رواج
customary, ordinary, usual, common; formal *adj.* **rasmī** رسمی
string, cord, rope *n.f.* **rasan** رسن
rope dancer *n.m.* **rasan bāz** رسن باز
drip, leak, ooze *v.i.* **risnā** رسنا
infamous, disgraced, degraded *adj.* **rusvā** رسوا
infamy, disgrace, dishonor *n.f.* **rusvā'ī** رسوائی
influence, friendship *n.m.* **rasūx** رسوخ
win influence, gain influence *v.t.* **rasūx ḥāsil karnā** رسوخ حاصل کرنا
prophet, messenger *n.m.* **rasūl** رسول
tumor, swelling *n.f.* **rasaulī** رسولی
cook *n.m.* **rasōyā** رسویا
kitchen, cooking place *n.f.* **rasō'ī** رسوئی
string, cord *n.f.* **rassī** رسی
receipt, acknowledgment *n.f.* **rasīd** رسید
arrival; ripeness, maturity *n.f.* **rasīdagī** رسیدگی
arrived, received; ripe, mature *adj.* **rasīdah** رسیدہ
juicy; luxurious *adj.* **rasīlā** رسیلا
instruction, teaching *n.f.* **rašādat** رشادت
relationship, kinship, connection; string, thread, line *n.m.* **rištah** رشتہ
relation, kinsman *n.m.* **rištah dār** رشتہ دار

relationship *n.f.* **ristah dārī** رشتہ داری
guidance; rectitude, piety, dutifulness *n.m.* **rušd** رشد
jealousy, envy *n.m.* **rašk** رشک
envy, feel jealous *v.t.* **rašk karnā** رشک کرنا
bribe *n.f.* **rišvat** رشوت
bribe *v.t.* **rišvat dēnā** رشوت دینا
saint, sage, poet, religious person (*among Hindus*) *n.m.* **rišī** رشی
righteous, pious, dutiful *adj.* **rašīd** رشید
pleasure, contentment; approval, permission *n.f.* **rizā** رضا
fostering *n.f.* **razāᶜat** رضاعت
volunteer *n.m.* **rizā kār** رضا کار
willing, agreeing, permitting *adj.* **rizā mand** رضامند
quilt, coverlet *n.f.* **razā'ī** رضائی
paradise, pleasure *n.m.* **rizvān** رضوان
paradise, heaven *n.m.* **rizvān kadah** رضوان کدہ
wet, moist; tender; fresh, green *adj.* **ratb** رطب
celebrated *adj.* **ratb-ul-lisān** رطب اللسان
wet and dry, evil and good *n.m.* **ratb-ō-yābas** رطب ویابس
moisture, dampness, humidity *n.f.* **rutūbat** رطوبت
public, common people *n.f.* **riᶜāyā** رعایا
partiality; remission; indulgence *n.f.* **riᶜāyat** رعایت
awe, fear *n.m.* **ruᶜab** رعب
awe-inspiring *adj.* **ruᶜab dār** رعب دار
thunder *n.m.* **raᶜd** رعد
shaking, tremor *n.m.* **raᶜšah** رعشہ
palsied *adj.* **raᶜšah dār** رعشہ دار
lovely, graceful *adj.* **raᶜnā** رعنا
loveliness, grace, beauty *n.f.* **raᶜnā'ī** رعنائی
pride, arrogance, haughtiness *n.f.* **raᶜūnat** رعونت
desire, inclination, wish *n.f.* **raġbat** رغبت
desire, be inclined, wish *v.t.* **raġbat karnā** رغبت کرنا
friendship, companionship *n.f.* **rifāqat** رفاقت
accompany, befriend *v.t.* **rifāqat karnā** رفاقت کرنا
contentment, welfare, enjoying life *n.f.* **rifāh** رفاہ
public good, public welfare *n.f.* **rifāh xalā'iq** رفاہ خلائق
public good, public welfare *n.f.* **rifāh ᶜām** رفاہ عام

going, leaving, motion *n.f.* **raft** رفت

pace, speed; going *n.f.* **raftār** رفتار

gone, departed, deceased *adj.* **raftah** رفتہ

gradually, step by step *adv.* **raftah raftah** رفتہ رفتہ

raising, height, elevation *n.m.* **rafaᶜ** رفع

deciding, finishing, settling *n.m.* **rafaᶜ dafaᶜ** رفع دفع

dispose, settle; pardon *v.t.* **rafaᶜ dafaᶜ karnā** رفع دفع کرنا

remove; settle *v.t.* **rafaᶜ karnā** رفع کرنا

height, elevation; dignity, eminence *n.f.* **rifᶜat** رفعت

benevolence, kindness, courtesy *n.m.* **rafaq** رفق

darning, mending *n.m.* **rafū** رفو

run away, abscond *v.i.* **rafū cakkar hōnā** رفو چکر ہونا

darn, mend *v.t.* **rafū karnā** رفو کرنا

darner *n.m.* **rafūgar** رفوگر

elevated, high, exalted *adj.* **rafīᶜ** رفیع

companion, friend, ally *n.m.* **rafīq** رفیق

accomplice *n.m.* **rafīq-ē-jurm** رفیق جرم

rivalry *n.f.* **raqābat** رقابت

dancer *n.m.* **raqqās** رقاص

area, enclosure *n.m.* **raqbah** رقبہ

subtleness, thinness, softness *n.f.* **riqqat** رقت

dance, dancing *n.m.* **raqs** رقص

letter, note, piece of paper *n.m.* **ruqᶜah** رقعہ

number, mark, figure, sum *n.f.* **raqm** رقم

save (*money*) *v.t.* **raqm bacānā** رقم بچانا

mark, note, write, state *v.t.* **raqm karnā** رقم کرنا

competitor, rival *n.m.* **raqīb** رقیب

liquid; thin, fine, subtle *adj.* **raqīq** رقیق

kindhearted *adj.* **raqīq-ul-qalb** رقیق القلب

care, care-taking *n.m.* **rakh rakhā'ō** رکھ رکھاؤ

accept, take; employ, engage *v.t.* **rakh lēnā** رکھ لینا

stirrup; train *n.f.* **rakāb** رکاب

companion *n.m.* **rakāb dār** رکاب دار

small dish *n.f.* **rakābī** رکابی

prevention, hindrance *n.f.* **rukā'ō** رکاؤ

hindrance, obstacle *n.m.* **rukāvaṭ** رکاوٹ

roughness, dryness; indifference, carelessness *n.f.* **rukhā'ī** رکھائی

blood *n.m.* **rakt** رکت

rickshaw *n.m.* **rikšā** رکشا

pillar, support *n.m.* **rukn** رکن

place, put; pledge; hold, keep *v.t.* **rakhnā** رکھنا

stop, hinder; rest, wait *v.i.* **ruknā** رکنا

guard, watchman, keeper *n.m.* **rakhvālā** رکھوالا

care, protection, watch *n.f.* **rakhvālī** رکھوالی

fine, thin, shallow *adj.* **rakīk** رکیک

strong, steady, firm, stable *adj.* **rakīn** رکین

vein, artery *n.f.* **rag** رگ

surgeon *n.m.* **rag zan** رگ زن

constitution, nature *n.m.* **rag-ō-rēšah** رگ وریشہ

friction, rubbing *n.f.* **ragaṛ** رگڑ

rub, scour, grind, grate *v.t.* **ragaṛnā** رگڑنا

sandy, desert-like *adj.* **rēgistānī** ریگستانی

mixture, combination *n.m.* **ralā** رلا

mixed, combined *adj.* **ralā milā** رلا ملا

make someone cry, cause to weep *v.t.* **rulānā** رلانا

terror; scare *n.m.* **ram** رم

sound of rain *n.f.* **rim jhim** رم جھم

fortune-teller, astrologer *n.m.* **rammāl** رمال

pomegranate *n.m.* **rummān** رمان

sign, hint, symbol; secret, riddle, enigma *n.f.* **ramz** رمز

geomancy; fortune-telling *n.m.* **ramal** رمل

roam, rove, wander *v.i.* **ramnā** رمنا

battle, war, combat *n.m.* **ran** رن

grief, pain, sorrow *n.m.* **ranj** رنج

grieve, feel sorrow *v.t.* **ranj karnā** رنج کرنا

grief, displeasure *n.m.* **ranjiš** رنجش

grieved, sorrowful, displeased; offended *adj.* **ranjīdah** رنجیدہ

displease, offend *v.t.* **ranjīdah karnā** رنجیدہ کرنا

skeptic, free-thinker *n.m.* **rind** رند

plane, level *v.t.* **randah phērnā** رندہ پھیرنا

prostitute *n.f.* **ranḍī** رنڈی

color, dye, paint, pigment *n.m.* **rang** رنگ
painter, artist *n.m.* **rang āmēz** رنگ آمیز
painting, coloring *n.f.* **rang āmēzī** رنگ آمیزی
paint, varnish *v.t.* **rang bharnā** رنگ بھرنا
dye, color, varnish *v.t.* **rang dēnā** رنگ دینا
appearance, mode, aspect, style *n.m.* **rang ḍhang** رنگ ڈھنگ
dyer *n.m.* **rang rēz** رنگ ریز
color, dye, hue; design *n.f.* **rangat** رنگت
orange (*fruit*) *n.m.* **rangtarā** رنگترا
colored *adj.* **rangdār** رنگدار
bright, airy, lively, merry *adj.* **rangīlā** رنگیلا
colored, painted *adj.* **rangīn** رنگین
lively, jolly, merry *n.m.* **rangīn mizāj** رنگین مزاج
path, road *n.m.* **rah** رہ
remain, stay *v.i.* **rah jānā** رہ جانا
released *adj.* **rihā** رہا
remaining *adj.* **rahā sahā** رہا سہا
set free, free, release *v.t.* **rihā karnā** رہا کرنا
residence, dwelling *n.f.* **rahā'iš** رہائش
freedom, liberation, release *n.f.* **rihā'ī** رہائی
priesthood *n.f.* **ruhbāniyyat** رہبانیت
mortgage, pledge *n.m.* **rihn/rahn** رہن
mortgage, pledge *v.t.* **rahin rakhnā** رہن رکھنا
live, exist; stay, remain *v.i.* **rahnā** رہنا
guide *n.m.* **rahnumā** رہنما
guidance *n.f.* **rahnumā'ī** رہنمائی
inhabitant, resident *n.m.* **rahnē vālā** رہنے والا
horse *n.m.* **rahvār** رہوار
face, surface *n.m.* **rū** • going, proceeding *adj.* / flow, stream, current *n.m.* **rau** رو
face to face, in presence of *adv.* **rū ba-rū** روبرو
acquainted, known *adj.* **rū šinās** روشناس
acquaintance *n.f.* **rū šināsī** روشناسی
right, just, lawful *adj.* **ravā** روا
custom, usage, practice *n.f.* **rivāj** رواج
be customary, be current usage *v.i.* **rivāj pānā** رواج پانا
introduce, make customary *v.t.* **rivāj dēnā** رواج دینا

customary, current, traditional *adj.* **rivājī** رواجی
approval, consent, toleration *n.f.* **ravādārī** رواداری
hair, wool, fur *n.m.* **rō'āṁ** رواں
going, running, moving *adj.* **ravāṁ** رواں
departure, setting out; dispatch *n.f.* **ravāngī** روانگی
departed, dispatched *adj.* **ravānā** روانہ
dispatch *v.t.* **ravānah karnā** روانہ کرنا
set out, depart *v.i.* **ravānah hōnā** روانہ ہونا
flow, fluency *n.f.* **ravānī** روانی
story, tale, narrative, legend *n.f.* **rivāyat** روایت
traditional *adj.* **rivāyatī** روایتی
fox *n.m.* **rōbāh** روباہ
stratagem; trick, cunningness; hypocrisy *n.f.* **rōbāh bāzī** روباہ بازی
face, countenance, appearance, picture, feature *n.m.* **rūp** روپ
disfigure, deface *v.t.* **rūp bigāṛnā** روپ بگاڑنا
silvered, silvery, made of silver *adj.* **rūpahlā** روپہلا
hiding, concealed *adj.* **rū pōš** روپوش
abscond oneself, hide, conceal *v.i.* **rū pōš hōnā** روپوش ہونا
rupee (*currency in Pakistan and India*), money *n.m.* **rūpayah/rūpiyah** روپیہ
bread, loaf, roti (*a traditional bread*) *n.f.* **rōṭī** روٹی
bake a loaf of bread *v.t.* **rōṭī pakānā** روٹی پکانا
baker *n.m.* **rōṭī pakānē vālā** روٹی پکانے والا
bread and clothes (*i.e. the basic needs*) *n.m.* **rōṭī kapṛā** روٹی کپڑا
be offended, be displeased *v.i.* **rūṭhnā** روٹھنا
soul, spirit, life *n.f.* **rūḥ** روح
pleasing, exhilarating *adj.* **rūḥ afzā** روح افزا
die, breathe one's last *v.t.* **rūḥ parvāz karnā** روح پرواز کرنا
spiritual *adj.* **rūḥānī** روحانی
spirituality *n.f.* **rūḥāniyyat** روحانیت
stream, current, channel *n.m.* **rūd/rōd** رود
riverbed, channel *n.m.* **rūd xānah** رود خانہ
channel, big canal *n.m.* **rūdbār** رودبار
favor, partiality *n.f.* **rū riᶜāyat** رورعایت
daily, every day *adv.* **rōz** • day *n.m.* **rōz/rūz** روز
daily, day by day *adj.* **rōz ba-rōz** روز بروز

daily, every day *adj.* **rōz marrah** روزمرہ
hole, window *n.m.* **rōzan/rauzan** روزن
diary, daily account book *n.m.* **rōz nāmcah** روزنامچہ
fast *n.m.* **rōzah** روزہ
keep a fast *v.t.* **rōzah rakhnā** روزہ رکھنا
break a fast *v.t.* **rōzah khōlnā** روزہ کھولنا
daily food, daily allowance, daily sustenance *n.m.* **rōzī** روزی
daily wages, daily earnings *n.m.* **rōzīnah** روزینہ
village *n.m.* **rōstā** روستا
villager, peasant *n.m.* **rōstā'ī** روستائی
behavior, manner, method, custom, mode *n.f.* **raviš** روش
bright, clear, shining *adj.* **raušan/rōšan** روشن
ventilator, skylight *n.m.* **raušan dān** روشن دان
enlightened, broad-minded *adj.* **raušan dil** روشن دل
intelligent, wise *adj.* **raušan dimāġ** روشن دماغ
conscientious, enlightened *adj.* **raušan zamīr** روشن ضمیر
wise, sensible *adj.* **raušan qiyās** روشن قیاس
lit, light, illuminate *v.t.* **raušan karnā** روشن کرنا
famous, renowned *adj.* **rōšnās** روشناس
light, brightness; ink *n.f.* **raušanā'ī/rōšnā'ī** روشنائی
light, illumination, brightness; eyesight *n.f.* **rōšnī** روشنی
garden; tomb, mausoleum *n.m.* **rauzah** روضہ
paradise, heaven *n.m.* **rōzah-ē-rizvān** روضہ رضوان
oil, butter, grease *n.m.* **rauġan** روغن
greasy, buttered, oily *adj.* **rauġanī** روغنی
obstacle, hinderance, restraint, prevention, check *n.f.* **rōk** روک
prevention, restraint *n.f.* **rōk thām** روک تھام
hinderance, obstacle, obstruction *n.f.* **rōk ṭōk** روک ٹوک
dry, plain, harsh *adj.* **rūkhā** روکھا
cash *n.m.* **rōkaṛ** روکڑ
cash-book *n.f.* **rōkaṛ bahī** روکڑ بہی
stop, withhold, detain, prevent, interrupt, block *v.t.* **rōknā** روکنا
sickness, illness, disease; defect *n.m.* **rōg** روگ
sick, ill, unhealthy *adj.* **rōgī** روگی
handkerchief, napkin *n.m.* **rūmāl** رومال
Roman; Turkish *adj.* **rūmī** رومی

cry, weep, mourn, shed tears *v.i.* **rōnā** رونا
cry, weep (*bitterly*) *v.t.* **rōnā pīṭnā** روناپیٹنا
trample, tread down *v.t.* **raundnā** روندنا
brightness, beauty, elegance *n.f.* **raunaq** رونق
small hair *n.m.* **raungaṭā** رونگٹا
dream, vision *n.m.* **rōyā** رویا
appearance, resemblance; sight *n.f.* **rōyat/rūyat** رویت
conduct, behavior, custom, manner *n.m.* **ravaiyah** رویہ
face *n.m.* **rū'ē** روئے
cotton *n.f.* **rū'ī** روئی
growth, vegetation *n.f.* **rō'īdagī** روئیدگی
hypocrisy *n.m.* **riyā** ریا
state, dominion, rule, government *n.f.* **riyāsat** ریاست
devotion; abstinence, discipline; training, labor *n.f.* **riyāzat** ریاضت
worship, meditate *v.t.* **riyāzat karnā** ریاضت کرنا
worshipping, being devotional *adj.* **riyāzatī** ریاضتی
mathematics *n.f.* **riyāzī** ریاضی
mathematician *n.m.* **riyāzī dāṁ** ریاضی داں
hypocritical, deceitful *adj.* **riyākār** ریاکار
hypocrisy *n.f.* **riyākārī** ریاکاری
sand, dust *n.f.* **rēt** • ceremony, rite; habit, custom *n.f.* **rīt** ریت
sandy *adj.* **rētlā** ریتلا
be pleased, be delighted *v.i.* **rījhnā** ریجھنا
bear *n.m.* **rīch** ریچھ
air, wind *n.f.* **rīḥ** ریح
mortar, plaster; Urdu (*language*) *n.m.* / mixed, scattered; molded *adj.* **rēxtah** ریختہ
radio *n.m.* **rēḍiyō** ریڈیو
radiator *n.m.* **rēḍiyēṭar** ریڈییٹر
backbone *n.f.* **rīṛh** ریڑھ
shedding, pouring, dropping, scattering *adj.* **rēz** ریز
change, small coins *n.f.* **rēz gārī** ریز گاری
scrap, bit, piece *n.f.* **rēzgī** ریزگی
particle, scrap, bit, piece *n.m.* **rēzah** ریزہ
break into pieces *v.t.* **rēzah rēzah karnā** ریزہ ریزہ کرنا
equality; copying *n.f.* **rīs** ریس

restaurant *n.m.* **rēstōrān** ریستوران
beard *n.f.* **rīš** ریش
silk *n.m.* **rēšam** ریشم
silken *adj.* **rēšmī** ریشمی
fiber *n.m.* **rēšah** ریشہ
fibrous *adj.* **rēšah dār** ریشہ دار
line, mark; fate, destiny *n.f.* **rēkhā** ریکھا
sand *n.f.* **rēg** ریگ
desert, sandy place *n.m.* **rēgistān** ریگستان
carriage; railway, train *n.f.* **rēl** ریل
railway, train *n.f.* **rēlgāṛī** ریل گاڑی
shove, push, cram *v.t.* **rēlnā** ریلنا
railways *n.f.* **rēlvē** ریلوے
night *n.f.* **rain** رین
cook, prepare food *v.t.* **rīndhnā** ریندھنا
bray (*as a donkey*), bellow (*as a buffalo*) *v.i.* **rēnknā** رینکنا
crawl, creep *v.i.* **rēngnā/rīngnā** رینگنا
flock (*of sheep or goats*) *n.m.* **rēvaṛ** ریوڑ
rhubarb *n.m.* **rēvand** ریوند
leader, chief, head (*of a department*) *n.m.* **ra'īs** رئیس

zē ز

born of *adj.* **zā** زا
offspring; birth; food, provisions *n.m.* **zād** زاد
birthplace, nativeland *n.m.* **zād būm** زادبوم
travelling expenses, provisions (*for a journey*) *n.m.* **zād-ē-rāh** زادراہ
born of *adj.* **zādah** زادہ
/ bitterly (weeping) *adv.* / lamentation, groan, groaning *n.m.* **zār** زار
afflicted, wounded, aggrieved *adj.*
bitterly *adv.* **zār zār** زار زار
weak, emaciated *adj.* **zār-ō-nizār** زار و نزار
crying, groaning, wailing *n.f.* **zārī** زاری
old, grey-haired *adj.* **zāl** زال
thigh; knee; lap *n.m.* **zānū** زانو
devotee; ascetic, hermit *n.m.* **zāhid** زاہد
devotion *n.f.* **zāhidī** زاہدی
angle, corner *n.f.* **zāviyah** زاویہ
horoscope *n.m.* **zā'icah** زائچہ
redundant, superfluous, exceeding *adj.* **zā'id** زائد
pilgrim *n.f.* **zā'ir** زائر
deficient, failing, vanishing, perishing *adj.* **zā'il** زائل
language, tongue *n.f.* **zabān** زبان
eloquent; fluent (*in a language*) *adj.* **zabān āvar** زبان آور
stammer, lisp, stutter *v.i.* **zabān tutlānā** زبان تتلانا
poet; linguist *n.m.* **zabān dān** زبان دان
abusive (*verbally*) *adj.* **zabān darāz** زبان دراز
abuse, call names *v.t.* **zabān darāzī karnā** زبان درازی کرنا
well-known, famous, on tongue of everybody *adj.* **zabān zad xalā'iq** زبان زد خلائق
famous, renowned *adj.* **zabān zadah** زبان زدہ
talk, say a few words *v.t.* **zabān hilānā** زبان ہلانا
flame, blaze *n.m.* **zabānah** زبانہ
verbal, oral *adj.* **zabānī** زبانی
stronger, superior, greater, above, on top *adj.* **zabar** زبر
strong, powerful, vigorous; violent *adj.* **zabardast** زبردست
forcibly, violently *adv.* **zabardastī sē** زبردستی سے

bad, wicked, evil *adj.* **zabūn** زبون
vice, wickedness, evilness *n.f.* **zabūnī** زبونی
nonsense, foolish talk *n.f.* **zaṭal** زٹل
gossip, talk nonsense, tell false stories *v.t.* **zaṭal mārnā** زٹل مارنا
gossiper, idle-talker *n.f.* **zaṭallī** زٹلی
glass *n.m.* **zujāj** زجاج
threatening, scolding, forbidding *n.f.* **zajar** زجر
vexed, teased *adj.* **zic** زچ
vex, tease, annoy *v.t.* **zic karnā** زچ کرنا
Saturn (*planet*) *n.m.* **zuḥal** زحل
trouble, pain; uneasiness (*of mind*) *n.f.* **zaḥmat** زحمت
uneasy, unwell *adj.* **zaḥmatī** زحمتی
wound, sore, cut *n.f.* **zaxm** زخم
wounded, injured *adj.* **zaxmī** زخمی
target; range; striking, beating *n.f.* **zad** زد
beating, thrashing *n.f.* **zad-ō-kōb** زد وکوب
struck, beaten *adj.* **zadah** زدہ
gold, money, wealth *n.f.* **zar** زر
purchased *adj.* **zar xarīd** زر خرید
pollen *n.f.* **zar-ē-gul** زرِ گل
cash, ready money *n.f.* **zar-ē-naqd** زر نقد
agriculture, cultivation *n.f.* **zarāᶜat** زراعت
agriculturist, cultivator *n.f.* **zarāᶜat pēšah** زراعت پیشہ
till, cultivate *v.t.* **zarāᶜat karnā** زراعت کرنا
brocade *n.f.* **zar baft** زربفت
fertile, productive, rich (*soil*) *adj.* **zarxēz** زرخیز
yellow; pale *adj.* **zard** زرد
apricot *n.f.* **zard ālū** زرد الو
yellow color *n.f.* **zard rang** زرد رنگ
yellowish *adj.* **zard sā** زرد سا
turn pale *v.i.* **zard hō jānā** زرد ہو جانا
embroidery *n.f.* **zar dōzī** زردوزی
yellowness, paleness *n.f.* **zardī** زردی
splendid, glittering, gaudy *adj.* **zarq barq** زرق برق
goldsmith *n.f.* **zar gar** زرگر
golden *adj.* **zarrīṁ** زریں

golden rule *n.f.* **zarrīṁ usūl** زریں اصول
golden opportunity *n.m.* **zarrīṁ mauqᶜah** زریں موقعہ
ugly, deformed *adj.* **zišt** زشت
ugliness *n.f.* **zištī** زشتی
saffron *n.f.* **zaᶜfarān** زعفران
yellow, saffron-colored *adj.* **zaᶜfarānī** زعفرانی
assertion, presumption *n.f.* **zaᶜm** زعم
jump, leap, spring *n.f.* **zaġand** زغند
defeat, repulse *n.m.* **zak** زک
be defeated, suffer a loss *v.t.* **zak uṭhānā** زک اٹھانا
defeat, humiliate *v.t.* **zak dēnā** زک دینا
zakat (*charity given by Muslims*) *n.f.* **zakāt** زکات
cold, rheum, catarrh *n.m.* **zukām** زکام
catch a cold *v.i.* **zukām hōnā** زکام ہونا
pure, pious, virtuous *adj.* **zakī** زکی
earthquake *n.f.* **zalzalah** زلزلہ
curl, lock (*of hair*) *n.f.* **zulf** زلف
rein, bridle *n.f.* **zamām** زمام
time *n.m.* **zamān** زمان
time, age, period, season *n.m.* **zamānah** زمانہ
emerald *n.m.* **zumurrud** زمرد
group, troop *n.m.* **zumrah** زمرہ
winter *n.m.* **zamistān/zamastān** زمستان
time *n.m.* **zaman** زمن
earth, ground, soil, land *n.f.* **zamīn** زمین
underground *n.f.*. **zamīn dōz** زمین دوز
landlord *n.m.* **zamīndār** زمیندار
woman, wife *n.f.* **zan** زن
fornication, adultery *n.f.* **zinā** زنا
rape *n.f.* **zinā bil-jabr** زنا بالجبر
fornicator, adulterer *n.f.* **zinā kār** زنا کار
fornication, adultery *n.f.* **zinā kārī** زنا کاری
female, feminine *adj.* **zanānah** زنانہ
hornet, wasp *n.f.* **zambūr** زنبور
bag, purse; wallet; basket *n.f.* **zanbīl** زنبیل
chain *n.f.* **zanjīr** زنجیر

eunuch *n.f.* / castrated *adj.* **zanxah** زنخہ
jail, prison *n.f.* **zindān** زندان
prisoner, captive *n.f.* **zindānī** زندانی
life, living, existence *n.f.* **zindagī** زندگی
alive, living *adj.* **zindah** زندہ
cheerful, lively, hilarious *adj.* **zindah dil** زندہ دل
cheerfulness, liveliness *n.f.* **zindah dilī** زندہ دلی
live *v.i.* **zindah rahnā** زندہ رہنا
bring to life *v.t.* **zindah karnā** زندہ کرنا
rust *n.f.* **zang** زنگ
rusty *adj.* **zang ālūdah** زنگ آلودہ
become rusty *v.i.* **zang lagnā** زنگ لگنا
rusty, rust-colored *adj.* **zangārī** زنگاری
life, living, existence *n.f.* **zindagānī** زنگانی
never, on no account, by no means *adv.* **zim̈hār** زنہار
childbirth, giving birth *n.f.* **zih** زہ
devotion, abstinence, continence *n.m.* **zuhd** زہد
poison *n.m.* **zahr** زہر
poisoned *adj.* **zahr ālūdah** زہر آلودہ
do something by force, do something unwillingly *v.t.* **zahr mār karnā** زہر مار کرنا
poison *v.t.* **zahr dēnā** زہر دینا
bile; gall bladder *n.m.* **zahrah** • Venus (*planet*) *n.f.* **zuhrah** زہرہ
poisonous *adj.* **zahrīlā** زہریلا
Excellent!, Bravo! *interj.* **zihē** زہے
decline, fall, decay *n.m.* **zavāl** زوال
couple, pair *n.m.* **zauj** زوج
wife *n.f.* **zaujah** زوجہ
quickly, soon, suddenly *adv.* **zūd** زود
strength, force, power *n.m.* **zōr** زور
strong, powerful *adj.* **zōr āvar** زور آور
strengthen, stress, press, force, compel *v.t.* **zōr dēnā** زور دینا
strong; loud *adj.* / strongly; loudly *adv.* **zōr sē** زور سے
powerful, strong, robust *adj.* **zōr mand** زور مند
excess, surplus, abundance; increase *n.f.* **ziyādatī** زیادتی
too much, more, excessive; moreover *adj./adv.* **ziyādah** زیادہ
most, more, much more *adj.* **ziyādah tar** زیادہ تر

add, increase *v.t.* **ziyādah karnā** زیادہ کرنا
pilgrimage *n.f.* **ziyārat** زیارت
go on a pilgrimage *v.t.* **ziyārat karnā** زیارت کرنا
shrine, place of pilgrimage *n.m.* **ziyārat gāh** زیارت گاہ
damage, injury, harm; loss *n.f.* **ziyāṁ** زیاں
beauty, grace, elegance *n.f.* **zēb** زیب
beautiful, graceful, elegant *adj.* **zēbā** زیبا
ornament, decoration, adorning *n.f.* **zēbā'iš** زیبائش
ornamental, decorated, elegant *adj.* **zēbā'išī** زیبائشی
olive *n.m.* **zaitūn** زیتون
below, under *pp.* / inferior, lower *adj.* **zēr** زیر
mixed, upside down, topsy-turvy *adj.* **zēr-ō-zabar** زیر وزبر
intelligent, wise *adj.* **zīrak** زیرک
intelligence, wisdom *n.f.* **zīrakī** زیرکی
cumin seed; pollen *n.f.* **zīrah** زیرہ
life, existence *n.f.* **zīst** زیست
saddle *n.f.* **zīn** زین
decoration; beauty, elegance *n.f.* **zīnat** زینت
ladder, flight of stairs *n.m.* **zīnah** زینہ
jewel, ornament *n.m.* **zēvar** زیور
jewelry *n.f.* **zēvrāt** زیورات

ژ že

nonsense; obscene talk, indecent speech *n.m.* **žāž** ژاژ
idle talk; obscene talk *n.f.* **žāž xā'ī** ژاژ خائی
hail; dew, frost *n.m.* **žālah** ژالہ
hailstorm *n.f.* **žālah bārī** ژالہ باری
hail *v.t.* **žālah bārī hōnā** ژالہ باری ہونا
deep, penetrating *adj.* **žarf** ژرف
perplexity, distress, entanglement *n.f.* **žōlīdagī** ژولیدگی
entangled, intricate *adj.* **žōlīdah** ژولیدہ
perplexed, distressed *adj.* **žōlīdah ḥāl** ژولیدہ حال
fierce, terrible, ferocious *adj.* **žiyān** ژیان

sīn س

like, so, as, resembling *pp.* **sā** سا
elk, deer *n.m.* **sābar** سابر
former, prior, preceding *adj.* **sābiq** سابق
above-mentioned, afore-mentioned *adj.* **sābiq-uz-zikr** سابق الذکر
as usual *adv.* **sābiq dastūr** سابق دستور
formerly, previously, in the past *adv.* **sābiq mēṁ** سابق میں
formerly, previously *adv.* **sābiqan** سابقاً
friendship, acquaintance *n.m.* **sābiqah** سابقہ
come in contact with, become acquainted with *v.i.* **sābiqah paṛnā** سابقہ پڑنا
seven *num.* **sāt** سات
cheat; tricks; hesitation *n.f.* **sāt pāṁc** سات پانچ
cheat, trick on; be in doubt, hesitate *v.t.* **sāt pāṁc karnā** سات پانچ کرنا
preserve, keep carefully *v.t.* **sāt pardōṁ mēṁ rakhnā** سات پردوں میں رکھنا
abroad, far away, over the seven seas *adj.* **sāt samundar pār** سات سمندر پار
goblet, wine cup *n.m.* **sātgīn** ساتگین
seventh *adj.* **sātvāṁ** ساتواں
all seven *adj.* **sātōṁ** ساتوں
/ together *adv.* / society, company, troop, herd *n.m.* **sāth** ساتھ
with, along, next (to) *pp.*
join, cooperate, help *v.t.* **sāth dēnā** ساتھ دینا
live together *v.i.* **sāth rahnā** ساتھ رہنا
together *adv.* **sāth sāth** ساتھ ساتھ
accompany, walk side by side *v.i.* **sāth sāth calnā** ساتھ ساتھ چلنا
comrade, companion, associate *n.m.* **sāthī** ساتھی
sixty *num.* **sāṭh** ساٹھ
adorer, prostrater *n.m.* / adoring, prostrating *adj.* **sājid** ساجد
lover, sweetheart; husband *n.m.* **sājan** ساجن
share, partnership *n.m.* **sājhā** ساجھا
magician, enchanter *n.m.* **sāḥir** ساحر
magically *adv.* **sāḥir sē** ساحر سے
witch, enchantress *n.f.* **sāḥirah** ساحرہ
magic, enchantment, sorcery *n.f.* **sāḥirī** ساحری
seashore, coast, beach *n.m.* **sāḥil** ساحل

manufacture, fabrication, construction *n.m.* **sāxt** ساخت
made (of), formed (*artificially*) *adj.* **sāxtah** ساختہ
simplicity, plainness *n.m.* **sādagī** سادگی
blank, simple, plain *adj.* **sādah** سادہ
simple, artless; uneducated *n.m.* **sādah dil** سادہ دل
simple; stupid, simpleton *adj.* **sādah lauḥ** سادہ لوح
silliness; stupidity *n.f.* **sādah lauḥī** سادہ لوحی
plain, simple; white *adj.* **sādī** سادی
Sadhu (a Hindu monk), ascetic, hermit *n.m.* **sādhū** سادھو
plenty *suffix/adj.* / juice; worth, value; strength; excellence *n.f.* **sār** سار
pure, excellent; all, whole, entire *adj.* **sārā** سارا
camel driver *n.m.* **sār bān** ساربان
crane, heron *n.m.* **sāras** سارس
thief, plunderer *n.m.* **sāriq** سارق
accomplish, bring to an end *v.t.* **sārnā** سارنا
saree, sari (*a woman's dress*) *n.f.* **sāṛī** ساڑی
saz (*a musical instrument*) *n.m.* **sāz** ساز
conspiracy, intrigue, plot *n.f.* **sāz bāz** سازباز
conspiracy, intrigue, plot *n.f.* **sāziš** سازش
conspiratorial, fraudulent, collusive *adj.* **sāzišī** سازشی
suitable, favorable, agreeing *adj.* **sāz gār** سازگار
mother-in-law *n.f.* **sās** ساس
moment, time, minute *n.m.* **sāᶜat** ساعت
forearm *n.f.* **sāᶜid** ساعد
endeavorer, energetic person *n.m.* **sāᶜī** ساعی
goblet, wine-cup *n.m.* **sāġar** ساغر
lower leg *n.f.* **sāq** ساق
fallen, dropped *n.m.* **sāqit** ساقط
sweetheart, lover, beloved *n.m.* **sāqī** ساقی
reputation; credit, trust; goodwill *n.f.* **sākh** ساکھ
silent, quiet, mute, resting *adj.* **sākit** ساکت
inhabitant *n.m.* / quiet, tranquil *adj.* **sākin** ساکن
vegetables, herbs *n.m.* **sāg** ساگ
teakwood, teak tree *n.m.* **sāgvān** ساگوان
sago *n.m.* **sāgū dānah** ساگودانہ
year *n.m.* **sāl** سال

year by year *adv.* **sāl ba-sāl** سال بسال
all year round, all through the year *adv.* **sāl bhar** سال بھر
old, aged *adj.* **sāl xūrdah** سال خوردہ
birthday *n.m.* **sāl girah** سال گرہ
last year *n.m.* **sāl guzaštah** سال گزشتہ
calendar *n.m.* **sāl nāmah** سال نامہ
brother-in-law (*sister's husband*) (*also an abuse*) *n.m.* **sālā** سالا
leader, chief, commander *n.m.* **sālār** سالار
yearly, annual *adj.* **sālānah** سالانہ
devotee; traveler *n.m.* **sālik** سالک
safe, sound; whole, full *adj.* **sālim** سالم
hypocrisy, trick, fraud, deceit *n.f.* **sālūs** سالوس
sister-in-law (*wife's sister*) *n.f.* **sālī** سالی
luggage, baggage; furniture *n.m.* **sāmān** سامان
hearer, listener *n.m.* **sāmiᶜ** سامع
hearing, listening *n.m.* **sāmiᶜah** سامعہ
front; opposite, facing, confronting *n.m.* **sāmnā** سامنا
confront, encounter, oppose *v.t.* **sāmnā karnā** سامنا کرنا
in front, before, opposite *adv.* **sāmnē** سامنے
exalted, sublime, high *adj.* **sāmī** سامی
grindstone *n.m.* **sān** سان
snake, cobra *n.m.* **sānp** سانپ
snake charmer *n.m.* **sānp vālā** سانپ والا
evening, nightfall *n.m.* **sāṁjh** سانجھ
truth, reality *n.f.* **sāṁc** سانچ
mold, matrix (*pl.* matrices) *n.m.* **sāṁcah** سانچہ
mold *v.t.* **sāṁcah mēṁ ḍhālnā** سانچہ میں ڈھالنا
event, incident, happening *n.m.* **sāniḥah** سانحہ
bull, stallion *n.m.* **sānḍ** سانڈ
dromedary, camel *n.f.* **sānḍnī** سانڈنی
breath, sigh *n.m./n.f.* **sāṁs** سانس
be suffocated *v.i.* **sāṁs ruknā** سانس رکنا
breathe, inhale *v.t.* **sāṁs lēnā** سانس لینا
exhale *v.t.* **sāṁs nikālnā** سانس نکالنا
dark-colored *adj.* **sānvlā** سانولا
moneylender, banker *n.m.* **sāhūkār** ساہوکار

canopy, thatched roof *n.m.* **sā'ibān** سائبان
applicant, petitioner; beggar *n.m.* **sā'il** سائل
scientific *adj.* **sā'insdāṁ** سائنسداں
shade, shadow; shelter, protection *n.m.* **sāyah** سایہ
shady *adj.* **sāyah dār** سایہ دار
size *n.m.* **sā'iz** سائیز
groom *n.m.* **sā'is** سائیس
bicycle *n.f.* **sā'ikil** سائیکل
God; master, lord *n.m.* **ṣā'īn** سائیں
whistle *v.t.* **sā'ēn sā'ēn karnā** سائیں سائیں کرنا
all, total, whole, entire, every *adj.* **sab** سب
first of all *adv.* **sab sē pahlē** سب سے پہلے
everything *adj.* **sab kuch** سب کچھ
reason, cause *n.m.* **sabab** سبب
praising, glorifying *adj.* **subḥān** سبحان
God be blessed!, Heavens be praised! *interj.* **subḥān Allah** سبحان اللہ
basket *n.m.* **sabad** سبد
green, unripe; flourishing *adj.* **sabz** سبز
greenish *adj.* **sabz sā** سبز سا
greenness, greenery; vegetables *n.m.* **sabzah** سبزہ
meadow, pasture, lawn *n.m.* **sabzah zār** سبزہ زار
vegetable; greenness *n.f.* **sabzī** سبزی
greengrocer *n.m.* **sabzī farōš** سبزی فروش
vegetable market *n.m.* **sabzī manḍī** سبزی منڈی
lesson, unit, lecture *n.m.* **sabaq** سبق
teach, give a lesson *v.t.* **sabaq dēnā** سبق دینا
take a lesson *v.t.* **sabaq lēnā** سبق لینا
superiority, excellence, leading *n.f.* **sabqat** سبقت
excel, surpass *v.t.* **sabqat lē jānā** سبقت لے جانا
light, delicate *adj.* **subuk/sabuk** سبک
relieved *adj.* **subuk dōš** سبکدوش
relieve *v.t.* **subuk dōš karnā** سبکدوش کرنا
lightness, delicacy; sobbing *n.f.* **subkī** سبکی
sob *v.t.* **subkiyāṁ lēnā** سبکیاں لینا
jar, pitcher; pot *n.m.* **sabū** سبو
road, way, path; mode, manner *n.f.* **sabīl** سبیل

march, leap, bound *n.m.* **sapāṭā** سپاٹا
betel-nut *n.m.* **supārī** سپاری
army *n.m.* **sipāh** سپاہ
soldier *n.m.* **sipāhī** سپاہی
military, soldier-like *adj.* **sipāhiyānah** سپاہیانہ
shield *n.m.* **sipar** سپر
charge, care, trust *n.f.* **supurd** سپرد
place in charge, consign, entrust *v.t.* **supurd karnā** سپرد کرنا
dream *n.m.* **sapnā** سپنا
commander-in-chief, general *n.m.* **sipah sālār** سپہ سالار
sky; sphere *n.m.* **sipahr** سپہر
snake-charmer, snake-catcher *n.m.* **sapērā** سپیرا
essence, strength, power *n.m.* / true, right, real *adj.* **sat** ست
sitar (*a musical instrument*) *n.m.* **sitār** • covering, concealing *adj.* **sattār** ستار
sitar-player *n.m.* **sitār navāz** ستار نواز
star *n.m.* **sitārah** ستارہ
be lucky *v.i.* **sitārah camaknā** ستارہ چمکنا
astronomer; astrologer *n.m.* **sitārah šinās** ستارہ شناس
astronomy; astrology *n.f.* **sitārah šināsī** ستارہ شناسی
eighty-seven *num.* **satāsī** ستاسی
trouble, torment, tease, harm *v.t.* **satānā** ستانا
ninety-seven *num.* **satānavē** ستانوے
fifty-seven *num.* **sattāvan** ستاون
praise *n.m.* **sitā'iš/satā'iš** ستائش
twenty-seven *num.* **sattā'is** ستائیس
seventy-seven *num.* **satattar** ستتر
seventy *num.* **sattar** • concealing, covering *n.m.* **satr** ستر
seventeen *num.* **satrah** سترہ
seventeenth *adj.* **satrahvāṁ** سترھواں
injustice, oppression, tyranny *n.m.* **sitam** ستم
oppressor, tyrant *n.m.* **sitam gar** ستم گر
oppression, tyranny *n.f.* **sitam garī** ستم گری
September *n.m.* **sitambar** ستمبر
pillar, column *n.m.* **sutūn/satūn** ستون
virtuous, chaste *adj.* **sutī** ستی

be ruined, be destroyed *v.i.* **satiyānās hōnā** ستیاناس ہونا
ruin, destruction *n.m.* **satiyānās** ستیاناس
ruin, destroy *v.t.* **satiyānās karnā** ستیاناس کرنا
conflict, battle, combat, fight *n.m.* **satēz** ستیز
passive resistance *n.m.* **sattiyah girah** ستیہ گرہ
clean, neat, tidy, clear *adj.* **suthrā** ستھرا
cleanliness, tidiness, clearness *n.m.* **suthrā'ī** ستھرائی
be distracted, be restless *v.i.* **saṭpaṭānā** سٹپٹانا
ornamentation, decoration *n.f.* **saj dhaj** سج دھج
adoring, bowing (*while praying*) *adj.* **sajjād** سجاد
prayer carpet *n.m.* **sajjādah** سجادہ
adorn, decorate *v.t.* **sajānā** سجانا
decoration, arrangement *n.m.* **sajāvaṭ** سجاوٹ
sweetheart, lover, beloved, husband *n.m.* **sajan** سجن
point out, explain *v.t.* **sujhānā** سجھانا
true, right, genuine *adj.* / truth *n.m.* / indeed, really, truly *adv.* **sac** سچ
really, truly *adv.* **sac muc** سچ مچ
true, real, honest *adj.* **saccā** سچا
truth, reality, honesty, purity *n.f.* **saccā'ī** سچائی
cloud *n.m.* **saḥāb** سحاب
enchantment, magic, sorcery *n.m.* **saḥr** سحر
liberality, generosity *n.f.* **saxāvat** سخاوت
strong, hard, stiff; strict, severe *adj.* **saxt** سخت
reproach, scold *v.t.* **saxt sust kahnā** سخت سست کہنا
hardness, strictness, cruelty *n.f.* **saxtī** سختی
use force, oppress *v.t.* **saxtī karnā** سختی کرنا
speech, talk, language *n.m.* **saxun/suxan** سخن
eloquent; talking *adj.* **saxun pardāz** سخن پرداز
critic *n.m.* **saxun cīṁ** سخن چیں
skilled in language, eloquent *adj.* / poet; scholar *n.m.* **saxun dān** سخن دان
orator, public speaker *n.m.* **saxun sāz** سخن ساز
poetry *n.m.* **saxun gō'ī** سخن گوئی
liberal, generous *adj.* **saxī** سخی
wall, barrier, obstacle, hinderance *n.m.* **sadd** سد
always, ever *adv.* **sadā** سدا

intelligence, consciousness *n.m.* **sudh** سدھ
commonsense, presence of mind *n.m.* **sudh budh** سدھ بدھ
leave, set out, depart *v.i.* **sidhārnā** سدھارنا
train, tame *v.t.* **sadhānā** سدھانا
pretty, well-shaped, graceful *adj.* **saḍaul** سڈول
• secret, mystery *n.m.* **sirr** • head, top, chief, leader; sir *n.m.* **sar** سر
head, skull, top *n.m.* **sir**
exalted, promoted *adj.* **sar afrāz** سرافراز
arrangement, preparation *n.m.* **sar anjām** سرانجام
manage, arrange, provide *v.t.* **sar anjām dēnā** سرانجام دینا
brave, heroic, valiant *adj.* **sar bāz** سرباز
openly, in public *adv.* **sar-ē-bāzār** سربازار
entirely, wholly, completely *adv.* **sar ba-sar** سربسر
be spoiled *v.t.* **sir par caṛhānā** سرپرچڑھانا
patron, guardian *n.m.* **sar parast** سرپرست
chairman, president *n.m.* **sar paṁc** سرپنچ
cover, lid *n.m.* **sar pōš** سرپوش
mourn, lament *v.t.* **sir pīṭnā** سرپیٹنا
bow (one's head) *v.t.* **sir jhukānā** سرجھکانا
fountain, spring, source *n.f.* **sar cašmah** سرچشمہ
agreement *n.m.* **sar xat** سرخط
general, commander (*of an army*) *n.m.* **sar xail** سرخیل
commander, ringleader *n.m.* **sar dār** سردار
at present, immediately *adv.* **sar-ē-dast** سردست
department, office *n.m.* **sar rištah** سررشتہ
region, territory, country *n.f.* **sar zamīn** سرزمین
rebellion *n.f.* **sar zōrī** سرزوری
early in the evening, evening *adj.* **sar-ē-šām** سرشام
annoy, tease *v.t.* **sir khānā** سرکھانا
beheaded *adj.* **sir kaṭā** سرکٹا
conquer, achieve, accomplish *v.t.* **sar karnā** سرکرنا
confounded, perplexed; straying *adj.* **sar gardāṁ** سرگرداں
confusion, perplexity, distress *n.f.* **sar gardānī** سرگردانی
zealous, ardent *adj.* **sar garm** سرگرم
zeal, earnestness *n.f.* **sar garmī** سرگرمی

commander, ringleader, chief *n.m.* **sar garōh** سرگروه
narrative, story *n.f.* **sar guzašt** سرگزشت
whispering *n.f.* **sar gōšī** سرگوشی
drunk, intoxicated *adj.* **sar mast** سرمست
address; superscription *n.m.* **sar nāmah** سرنامہ
destiny, fate *n.m.* **sar navišt** سرنوشت
be ashamed *v.t.* **sir nīcā karnā** سرنیچا کرنا
end, top, tip, point, arrowhead *n.m.* **sirā** سرا
illusion, mirage *n.m.* **sarāb** سراب
lamp, candle; sun *n.m.* **sirāj** سراج
entirely, from the beginning to the end *adv.* **sarāsar** سراسر
confusion, perplexity, consternation *n.f.* **sarāsīmagī** سراسیمگی
confused, perplexed *adj.* **sarāsīmah** سراسیمہ
trace, track, search *n.m.* **surāġ** سراغ
detective, spy *n.m.* **surāġ rasāṛ** سراغ رساں
praise, admire *v.t.* **sarāhnā** سراہنا
contagion, infection *n.f.* **sirāyat** سرایت
inn, caravan *n.m.* **sarā'ī** سرائے
manager, supervisor, head (*of a department*) *n.m.* **sarbarāh** سربراہ
management, supervision *n.f.* **sarbarāhī** سربراہی
hidden, closed, shut *adj.* **sarbastah** سربستہ
exalted, glorious, eminent *adj.* **sarbuland** سربلند
exaltation, glory, eminence *n.f.* **sarbulandī** سربلندی
sealed, locked *adj.* **sarbamuhr** سربمہر
chief, leader *n.m.* **sar tāj** سرتاج
border, frontier, boundary *n.m.* **sarḥadd** سرحد
red *adj.* **surx** سرخ
successful, victorious *adj.* **surx rū** سرخ رو
success, fame, respect *n.f.* **surx rū'ī** سرخ روئی
reddish *adj.* **surx sā** سرخ سا
redness; blood *n.f.* **surxī** سرخی
reddish *adj.* **surxī mā'il** سرخی مائل
cold, cool *adj.* **sard** سرد
cold-blooded; cool-tempered *adj.* **sard mizāj** سرد مزاج
coldness *n.f.* **sard mahrī** سرد مہری
cold, coldness, chilliness; winter *n.f.* **sardī** سردی

happening, occurrence *n.m.* **sarzad** سرزد
happen, occur *v.i.* **sarzad hōnā** سرزد ہونا
frenzy, delirium *n.m.* **sarsām** سرسام
verdant, flourishing, prosperous *adj.* **sarsabz** سرسبز
rustle; creep *v.i.* **sarsarānā** سرسرانا
mustard *n.f.* **sarsōṁ** سرسوں
brimful; drunk *adj.* **saršār** سرشار
nature, temperament *n.f.* **sarišt** سرشت
tear (*from eye*) *n.m.* **sarašk** سرشک
crab; cancer; Cancer (*Zodiac*) *n.m.* **sartān** سرطان
rapidity, haste *n.m.* **suraᶜt** سرعت
chief, head, ringleader *n.m.* **sarġanah** سرغنہ
cough *n.m.* **surfah** سرفہ
theft, robbery *n.m.* **sarqah** سرقہ
government; lord, master *n.m.* **sarkār** سرکار
official, of the government *adj.* **sarkārī** سرکاری
tipsy, drunk; proud, arrogant *adj.* **sarkarāṁ** سرگراں
refractory, rebellious *adj.* **sarkaš** سرکش
rebellion, insurrection *n.f.* **sarkašī** سرکشی
vinegar *n.m.* **sirkah** سرکہ
punishment *n.f.* **sar kōbī** سرکوبی
winter, cold season *n.m.* **sarmā** سرما
capital, stock *n.m.* **sarmāyah** سرمایہ
capitalist *n.m.* **sarmāyah dār** سرمایہ دار
wintery *adj.* **sarmā'ī** سرمائی
eternal, everlasting *adj.* **sarmad** سرمد
tunnel; mine *n.m.* **surang** سرنگ
pillow; head (*of bed or tomb*) *n.m.* **sarhānah** سرہانہ
joy, pleasure *n.m.* **surūr** • leader, chief, master, lord *n.m.* **sarvar** سرور
leadership *n.f.* **sarvarī** سروری
angel; voice from heaven *n.m.* **sarōš** سروش
concern; relation *n.m.* **sar-ō-kār** سروکار
throne; couch *n.m.* **sarīr** سریر
glue; starch *n.m.* **sarēš** سریش
quick, nimble; ready *adj.* **sarīᶜ** سریع
melodious, harmonious *adv.* **surīlā** سریلا

rotten, putrid, stinking *adj.* **saṛā** سڑا
bad smell, stink, rottenness *n.f.* **saṛānd** سڑاند
sixty-seven *num.* **saṛsaṭh** سڑسٹھ
road, street *n.f.* **saṛak** سڑک
decompose, rot, decay, go bad *v.i.* **saṛnā** سڑنا
worthless, rotten *adj.* **saṛyal** سڑیل
punishment *n.f.* **sazā** سزا
punish *v.t.* **sazā dēnā** سزا دینا
suitable, liable *adj.* **sazā vār** سزا وار
loose, lazy, slack, idle *adj.* **sust** سست
relax, slow down *v.t.* **sust karnā** سست کرنا
cheap *adj.* **sastā** سستا
rest, lie down *v.t.* **sastānā** سستانا
cheapness *n.f.* **sastā'ī** سستائی
father-in-law *n.m.* **susar** سسر
father-in-law (*also an abuse*) *n.m.* **susrā** سسرا
house of one's father-in-law *n.m.* **susrāl** سسرال
mother-in-law (*also an abuse*) *n.f.* **susrī** سسری
sob, sigh, gasp *v.i.* **sisaknā** سسکنا
sobbing, sighing *n.f.* **siskī** سسکی
sob *v.i.* **siskī bharnā** سسکی بھرنا
surface, platform *n.f.* **sataḥ** سطح
flat; superficial *adj.* **saṭḥī** سطحی
line, row, rank *n.f.* **satar** سطر
force, power, authority *n.f.* **satvat** سطوت
prosperity, auspiciousness, fortune *n.f.* **saᶜādat** سعادت
lucky, prosperous, fortunate *adj.* **saᶜādat mand** سعادت مند
lucky, auspicious *adj.* **saᶜd** سعد
endeavor, attempt, effort *n.f.* **saᶜī** سعی
embassy *n.m.* **sifārat** سفارت
embassy *n.m.* **sifārat xānah** سفارت خانہ
recommendation *n.f.* **sifāriš** سفارش
recommend *v.t.* **sifāriš karnā** سفارش کرنا
commendatory *adj.* **safārišī** سفارشی
murderer, butcher, killer *n.m.* **saffāk** سفاک
earthenware; tile *n.m.* **sifāl** سفال

bored, pierced, perforated *adj.* **siftah** سفتہ
travel, journey *n.m.* **safar** سفر
traveling expenses *n.m.* **safar xarc** سفر خرچ
travel, go on a journey *v.t.* **safar karnā** سفر کرنا
passport *n.m.* **safar nāmah** سفر نامہ
ignoble, mean, contemptible *adj.* **siflah** سفلہ
lower, inferior *adj.* **siflī** سفلی
powder *n.m.* **safūf** سفوف
white, blank *adj.* **safēd** سفید
fortunate, lucky *adj.* **safēd baxt** سفید بخت
whitish *adj.* **safēd sā** سفید سا
whiteness *n.f.* **safēdī** سفیدی
whiten, whitewash *v.t.* **safēdī karnā** سفیدی کرنا
ambassador, envoy *n.m.* **safīr** سفیر
ship, vessel, boat *n.m.* **safīnah** سفینہ
bathroom, public bath *n.m.* **saqāvah** سقاوہ
hell *n.m.* **saqar** سقر
error, mistake *n.m.* **saqat** سقط
ceiling, roof *n.m.* **saqf** سقف
flaw, defect, fault *n.m.* **suqm** سقم
water-carrier *n.m.* **saqqah** سقہ
weak, sick, ailing *adj.* **saqīm** سقیم
Sikh (*a disciple of Guru Nanak*) *n.m.* **sikh** سکھ
ease, comfort, relief *n.m.* **sukh** سکھ
get rest, get relief *v.t.* **sukh pānā** سکھ پانا
live comfortably *v.i.* **sukh sē rahnā** سکھ سے رہنا
dry *adj.* **sukhā** سکھا
dry, make dry *v.t.* **sukhānā** • teach, instruct *v.t.* **sikhānā** سکھانا
power, strength, ability *n.f.* **sakat** سکت
teach, instruct *v.t.* **sikhlānā** سکھلانا
be roasted, be parched *v.i.* **siknā** • can, be able to *v.i.* **saknā** سکنا
coin *n.m.* **sikkah** سکہ
silence, quietness *n.f.* **sukūt** سکوت
scooter *n.m.* **skūṭar** سکوٹر
silence, quietness *n.m.* **sukūn** سکون
residence, dwelling *n.f.* **sukūnat** سکونت

سکے small change *n.m.* **sikkē**

سکھی happy, glad *adj.* **sukhī**

سکیڑنا shrink, shrivel, tighten *v.i.* **sukaṛnā**

سگ dog *n.m.* **sag**

سگ شکاری hound, hunting dog *n.m.* **sag-ē-šikārī**

سگا real; full; own *adj.* **sagā**

سگا بھائی real brother *n.m.* **sagā bhā'ī**

سگائی betrothal *n.f.* **sagā'ī**

سگریٹ cigarette *n.f.* **sigrēṭ**

سگریٹ پینا smoke (a cigarette) *v.t.* **sigrēṭ pīnā**

سگنل traffic lights *n.m.* **signal**

سل stone, rock *n.f.* **sil**

سلاح arms, weaponry *n.f.* **silāḥ**

سلاخ iron bar *n.m.* **salāx**

سلاست simplicity, plainness *n.f.* **salāsat**

سلام salutation, compliment; peace *n.m.* **salām**

سلام دینا send compliments *v.t.* **salām dēnā**

سلام کرنا greet, salute *v.t.* **salām karnā**

سلام لینا return the compliments *v.t.* **salām lēnā**

سلامت well, sound, healthy, safe *adj.* **salāmat**

سلامت روی moderation; good management *n.f.* **salāmat ravī**

سلامتی safety, peace, well-being, health *n.f.* **salāmatī**

سلامی salutation, reception *n.f.* **salāmī**

سلانا get (something) stitched, cause to sew *v.t.* **silānā**

سلانا put to sleep, lull *v.t.* **sulānā**

سلائی sewing, stitching *n.f.* **silā'ī**

سلائی large needle *n.f.* **salā'ī**

سلب seizing (*forcibly*), plunder *n.m.* **salb**

سلجھانا disentangle, unfold, unravel *v.t.* **suljhānā**

سلجھنا be disentangled, be unfolded, be unraveled *v.i.* **sulajhnā**

سلسلہ series, succession, chain *n.m.* **silsilah**

سلسلہ وار consecutive, serial *adj.* **silsilah vār**

سلطان sultan, emperor, king, sovereign, monarch *n.m.* **sultān**

سلطانہ empress, queen *n.f.* **sultānah**

سلطانی regal, royal *adj.* **sultānī**

سلطنت sultanate, empire, kingdom *n.f.* **saltanat**

olden days, past, former times *n.m.* **salaf** سلف
thread; wire *n.f.* **silk** سلک
light, inflame, kindle *v.t.* **sulgānā** سلگانا
be sewn, be stitched *v.i.* **silnā** سلنا
road, way; mode, conduct; civility *n.m.* **sulūk** سلوک
treat kindly, befriend *v.t.* **sulūk karnā** سلوک کرنا
salted; tasteful *adj.* **salōnā** سلونا
simple, easy; plain *adj.* **salīs** سلیس
manners, etiquette; method, mode *n.m.* **salīqah** سلیقہ
well-mannered, discrete *adj.* **salīqah dār** سلیقہ دار
mild, moderate; considerate *adj.* **salīm** سلیم
hoof *n.m.* **sum** • poison *n.m.* **samm** سم
time, season *n.m.* **samā** سما
society, assembly, congress, club, association *n.m.* **samāj** سماج
solicitation, entreaty; flattery *n.f.* **samājat** سماجت
be contained, fit (into) *v.i.* **samānā** سمانا
heaven, sky, the firmament *n.m.* **samā'** سماء
heavenly, celestial *adj.* **samāvī** سماوی
side; direction, way, path *n.f.* **simt/samt** سمت
shrinking, contracting *n.f.* **simaṭ** سمٹ
shrink, be contracted *v.i.* **simaṭnā** سمٹنا
understanding, comprehension; knowledge *n.f.* **samajh** سمجھ
understanding, comprehension *n.f.* **samajh būjh** سمجھ بوجھ
make someone understand, describe, explain, instruct *v.t.* **samjhānā** سمجھانا
wise, intelligent *adj.* **samajhdār** سمجھدار
understand, perceive *v.i./v.t.* **samajhnā** سمجھنا
agreement, mutual understanding *n.m.* **samjhautā** سمجھوتا
hearing, listening *n.m.* **sama**ᶜ سمع
fish; Pisces (*Zodiac*) *n.f.* **samak** سمک
jasmine *n.f.* **saman** سمن
sea, ocean *n.m.* **samundar** سمندر
weasel, marten; sable *n.m.* **samūr** سمور
samosa (*a filled savory pie*) *n.m.* **samōsā** سموسا
together with, along with *adj.* **samēt** سمیت
gather, collect, scrape *v.t.* **samēṭnā** سمیٹنا
insensible, numb, paralyzed *adj.* **sun** • age, period, time; year *n.m.* **sinn** سن

سناتن **sanātan** perpetual, eternal *adj.*
سنار **sunār** goldsmith *n.m.*
سنان **sanān** head of a spear; grinder *n.m.*
سنانا **sunānā** cause to hear, tell, speak, proclaim, announce *v.t.*
سنبھالنا **sambhālnā** support, sustain, maintain, hold up *v.t.*
سنبھل کر **sambhal kar** carefully *adv.*
سنبھلنا **sambhalnā** be supported; recover; be cautious; be firm *v.i.*
سنت **sant** monk; saint, devotee *n.m.*
سنت **sunnat** Sunna (*religious practice according to prophet Muhammed*) *n.m.*
سنتری **santrī** sentinel, watchman *n.m.*
سنجاب **sanjāb** squirrel; ermine, fur *n.f.*
سنجاف **sanjāf** border, fringe *n.f.*
سنجوگ **sanjōg** connection, cohesion, union *n.m.*
سنجیدگی **sanjīdagī** solemnity, gravity *n.f.*
سنجیدہ **sanjīdah** considerate; grave, serious *adj.*
سند **sanad** certificate, testimonial, credential *n.f.*
سندر **sundar** beautiful, handsome *adj.*
سندری **sundarī** beauty *n.m.*
سنڈر **sanḍar** stout, strong *adj.*
سنسار **saṁsār** world, universe *n.m.*
سنسناہٹ **saṁsanāhaṭ** whiz, simmering, hissing, twinkling *n.f.*
سنک **sanak** madness, insanity *n.f.*
سنکنا **sinaknā** blow (nose) *v.i.*
سنگ **sang** stone; weight *n.m.*
سنگ تراش **sang tarāš** sculptor *n.m.*
سنگ دل **sang dil** cruel, merciless *adj.*
سنگ مرمر **sang-ē-marmar** marble *n.m.*
سنگار **singār** decoration, ornament *n.m.*
سنگار کرنا **singār karnā** dress; decorate, adorn *v.t.*
سنگارنا **singārnā** dress; decorate, adorn *v.t.*
سنگترہ **sangtarah** orange (*fruit*) *n.m.*
سنگم **sangam** meeting, union, junction; confluence (*of rivers*) *n.m.*
سنگین **sangīn** stony; weighty, heavy *adj.*
سنگین جرم **sangīn jurm** capital crime *n.m.*

lion *n.m.* **singh** سنگھ

throne *n.m.* **singhāsan** سنگھاسن

cause to smell *v.t.* **sunghānā** سنگھانا

listen, hear *v.t.* **sunnā** سننا

year; era *n.m.* **sanh** سنہ

golden *adj.* **sunahrā** سنہرا

preparation, arrangement *n.f.* **sanvār** سنوار

prepare, arrange *v.t.* **sanvārnā** سنوارنا

Sunni *adj.* **sunnī** سنی

ascetic (*a Hindu monk*) *n.m.* **sannyāsī** سنیاسی

Saturday *n.m.* **sanīcar** سنیچر

cinema *n.m.* **sinēmā** سنیما

triangle *n.m.* / triangular *adj.* **sēh gōšah** سہ گوشہ

support, aid, help, assistance *n.m.* **sahārā** سہارا

support, help, assist *v.t.* **sahārā dēnā** سہارا دینا

bear, tolerate, endure, be patient *v.t.* **sahārnā** سہارنا

good luck; love-making; happiness (*in a marriage*) *n.m.* **suhāg** سہاگ

become a widow *v.i.* **suhāg ujaṛnā** سہاگ اجڑنا

nuptial night, wedding night *n.f.* **suhāg rāt** سہاگ رات

agreeable, charming, pleasant *adj.* **suhānā** سہانا

easy, simple *adj.* **sahaj** سہج

garland worn during a wedding ceremony *n.m.* **sēhrā** سہرا

easy, simple *adj.* **sahl** سہل

make easy, facilitate *v.t.* **sahl karnā** سہل کرنا

rub gently, tickle, caress *v.t.* **sahlānā** سہلانا

share, portion; fear *n.m.* **sahm** سہم

fear, be afraid *v.i.* **sahamnā** سہمنا

bear, tolerate, endure *v.i.* **sahnā** سہنا

mistake, error *n.f.* **sahv** سہو

erroneously, by mistake *adv.* **sahvan** سہواً

ease, facility *n.f.* **suhūlat** سہولت

That's correct!, That's right! *interj.* **sahī bāt hai** سہی بات ہے

female friend, girlfriend *n.f.* **sahēlī** سہیلی

• hundred *num.* **sau** • therefore, so, so that, hence *conj./adv.* **sō** سو

direction, side *n.f.* **sū**

• one and a quarter *num.* / more, in addition *adv.* **savā** سوا
except, besides, save, but *conj./adv.* **sivā**
taste; relish, pleasure, delight; blackness *n.m.* **savād** سواد
rider, horseman *n.m.* **savār** سوار
welcome, reception *n.m.* **svāgat** سواگت
welcome, receive *v.t.* **svāgat karnā** سواگت کرنا
question, application, request *n.m.* **sū'āl/savāl** سوال
ask, question *v.t.* **sū'āl karnā** سوال کرنا
petitioner, inquirer, beggar *n.m.* **sū'ālī** سوالی
master, lord; husband *n.m.* **svāmī** سوامی
acting, disguise *n.m.* **savāng** • imitation, mockery, farce *n.m.* **svāng** سوانگ
actor, imitator, mimic *n.m.* **savāngī** سوانگی
one and a quarter *num.* **savāyā** سوایا
except, save, but *conj.* **sivā'ē** سوائے
yarn, thread; wire *n.m.* **sūt** سوت
made of cotton *adj.* **sūtī** سوتی
not real; belonging to someone else *adj.* **sautēlā** سوتیلا
step-brother *n.m.* **sautēlā bhā'ī** سوتیلا بھائی
suitcase *n.m.* **sūṭkēs** سوٹ کیس
swell, inflame; rise *v.i.* **sūjnā** سوجنا
perception, vision *n.f.* **sūjh** سوجھ
perceive, be perceptible, come to mind *v.i.* **sūjhnā** سوجھنا
thought, reflection, attention *n.f.* **sōc** سوچ
consideration; caution *n.m.* **sōc bicār** سوچ بچار
think, reflect *v.t.* **sōcnā** سوچنا
burning, combustion *n.f.* **sōxtagī** سوختگی
burnt, scorched *adj.* **sōxtah** سوختہ
profit, gain, interest *n.m.* **sūd** سود
usurer *n.m.* **sūd xōr** سود خور
profitable, beneficial *adj.* **sūd mand** سود مند
insanity, madness; trade, business, bargaining, marketing *n.m.* **saudā** سودا
traffic; goods, ware *n.m.* **saudā sulf** سودا سلف
merchant, tradesman *n.m.* **saudāgar** سوداگر
commerce, trade *n.f.* **saudāgarī** سوداگری
melancholic; mad, insane *adj.* **saudā'ī** سودائی

soda *n.m.* **sōḍā** سوڈا

hero, warrior *n.m.* **sūr** سور

pig, swine, boar, hog *n.m.* **sū'ar** سوَر

hole *n.m.* **surāx** سوراخ

bore, make hole *v.t.* **surāx karnā** سوراخ کرنا

chapter; sign, vestige *n.f.* **sūrat** سورت

sun *n.m.* **sūraj** سورج

heaven, paradise; sky *n.m.* **svarg** سورگ

heavenly, celestial, divine *adj.* **svargī** سورگی

brave, valiant, bold *adj.* **sūrmā** سورما

burning, heat; passion *n.m.* **sōz** سوز

burning, flaming *adj.* **sōzāṁ** سوزاں

rarity, curiosity *n.f.* **sūġāt** سوغات

dry, parched, withered *adj.* **sūkhā** سوکھا

dry, wither *v.i.* **sūkhnā** سوکھنا

lamentation, mourning, affliction, grief *n.m.* **sōg** سوگ

mourn, grieve *v.t.* **sōg karnā** سوگ کرنا

sorrowful, mourning *adj.* **sōg vār** سوگ وار

oath *n.m.* **saugand** سوگند

swear, take an oath *v.t.* **saugand khānā** سوگند کھانا

sorrowful, afflicted *adj.* **sōgı** سوگی

sixteen *num.* **sōlah** سولہ

gibbet, gallows *n.f.* **sūlī** سولی

hang, execute *v.t.* **sūlī caṛhānā** سولی چڑھانا

hang, execute *v.t.* **sūlī dēnā** سولی دینا

sixteenth *adj.* **sōlhavāṁ** سولھواں

Monday *n.m.* **sōmvār** سوموار

gold *n.m.* / sleep *v.i.* **sōnā** سونا

hand over, entrust *v.t.* **saunpnā** سونپنا

dry ginger *n.m.* **sōnṭh** سونٹھ

trunk (*of an elephant*) *n.m.* **sūnḍ** سونڈ

anise seed, fennel *n.m.* **saunf** سونف

smell; inhale *v.t.* **sūnghnā** سونگھنا

golden *adj.* **sōnahlā** سونہلا

deep red *adj.* **sūhā** سوہا

سوہان file *n.m.* **sōhān**
سوہان روح troublesome, painful, annoying *adj.* **sōhān-ē-rūḥ**
سوہن friend; lover *n.m.* / pleasing, charming *adj.* **sōhan**
سوہنا shine, be beautiful, be handsome *v.i.* / handsome, beautiful, lovely *adj.* **sōhnā**
سوہنی charming, pleasing *adj.* **sōhanī**
سوء bad, evil *adj.* **sū'**
سویرا morning, dawn, daybreak *n.m.* **savērā**
سوئی needle *n.f.* **sū'ī**
سوئی پرونا thread a needle *v.t.* **sū'ī pirōnā**
سے with, from, by, of, at, since, to, through, than, out of *pp.* **sē**
سی ڈی CD *n.f.* **sī ḍī**
سیاح traveler, pilgrim *n.m.* **sayyāḥ**
سیاحت journey, voyage, pilgrimage *n.f.* **siyāḥat**
سیادت dominion, rule, sovereignty *n.f.* **siyādat**
سیار wanderer, traveler *n.m.* **sayyār**
سیارہ planet *n.m.* **sayyārah**
سیاست politics; administration *n.f.* **siyāsat**
سیاست دان politician *n.m.* **siyāsat dān**
سیاق accounts, arithmetic, enumeration *n.m.* **siyāq**
سیال flowing, fluid, liquid *adj.* **sayyāl**
سیانا wise, clever, artful *adj.* **siyānā**
سیاہ black, dark *adj.* **siyāh**
سیاہ بخت unlucky, unfortunate *adj.* **siyāh baxt**
سیاہ کار wicked, criminal, tyrannical *adj.* **siyāh kār**
سیاہی ink; blackness, darkness *n.f.* **siyahī**
سیب apple *n.m.* **sēb**
سیپ shell *n.f.* **sīp**
سیٹ seat, place *n.f.* **sīṭ**
سیٹی whistle *n.f.* **sīṭī**
سیٹی بجانا whistle *v.t.* **sīṭī bajānā**
سیٹھ merchant; banker *n.m.* **sēṭh**
سیج bed, couch *n.f.* **sēj**
سیخ spit, skewer *n.f.* **sīx**
سید lord, master, prince, ruler, head, chief *n.m.* **saiyyid**
سیدھ directness, straightness, aim *n.f.* **sīdh**
سیدھا direct, straight, forward, simple, right *adj.* **sīdhā**

simplicity, straightness; honesty *n.m.* **sīdhā pan** سیدھاپن

straighten *v.t.* **sīdhā karnā** سیدھا کرنا

full, saturated, satisfied *adj.* **sēr** • walk, stroll; excursion *n.m.* **sair** سیر

satisfied, contented *adj.* **sēr cašm** سیر چشم

walk, stroll *v.t.* **sair karnā** سیر کرنا

irrigated, watered *adj.* **sērāb** سیراب

irrigate, water *v.t.* **sērāb karnā** سیراب کرنا

ladder, staircase, step *n.f.* **sīṛhī** سیڑھی

lead (*metal*) *n.m.* **sīsah** سیسہ

sword *n.f.* **saif** سیف

rosary, beads; curse *n.f.* **saifī** سیفی

learn, acquire knowledge *v.t.* **sīkhnā** سیکنا

second *n.m.* **sēkanḍ** سیکنڈ

dampness, moisture *n.f.* **sīl** • flow, flowing, current; flood *n.m.* **sail** سیل

flood, torrent, inundation *n.m.* **sailāb** سیلاب

walking, going *adj.* **sailānī** سیلانی

silver *n.f.* **sīm** سیم

forehead, face, countenance *n.m.* **sīmā** سیما

silvery, of silver; white *adj.* **sīmīṁ** سیمیں

army, forces *n.f.* **sēnā** • sew, stitch *v.t.* **sīnā** سینا

forty-seven *num.* **saiṁtālīs** سینتالیس

thirty-seven *num.* **saiṁtīs** سینتیس

irrigation, watering *n.f.* **sīṁc** سینچ

irrigate, water *v.t.* **sīṁcnā** سینچنا

vermilion, red lead *n.m.* **sēndūr** سیندور

horn *n.m.* **sīng** سینگ

chest, breast *n.m.* **sīnah** سینہ

tray *n.f.* **sīnī** سینی

service, attendance *n.f.* **sēvā** سیوا

seam; sewing, darning *n.f.* **sīvan** سیون

šīn ش

masterpiece *n.m.* **šāh kār** شاہ کار

youth, young man *n.m.* **šābb** شاب

Bravo!, Well done!, Excellent! *interj.* **šābāš** شاباش

applaud, praise, encourage *v.t.* **šābāš dēnā** شاباش دینا

praise, applause *n.f.* **šābāšī** شاباشی

branch (of tree), bough, twig, horn, cutting *n.f.* **šāx** شاخ

branchy, horned *adj.* **šāx dār** شاخ دار

orchard, garden (*full of trees*) *n.f.* **šāxsār** شاخسار

noise, row; difficulty, dilemma *n.m.* **šāxsānah** شاخسانہ

bough, branch (*of tree*); yoke *n.m.* **šāxah** شاخہ

happy, glad, cheerful *n.m.* **šād** شاد

happy, cheerful *adj.* **šād dil** شاد دل

happy, contented *adj.* **šād kām** شاد کام

make someone glad, delight, rejoice *v.t.* **šād kārnā** شاد کرنا

fresh, verdant, succulent *adj.* **šādāb** شاداب

freshness, succulence *n.f.* **šādābī** شادابی

pleased, cheerful *adj.* **šādāṛ** شاداں

happy, pleased, gay *adj.* **šādmāṛ** شادماں

pleasure, delight, merriment, rejoicing *n.f.* **šādmānī** شادمانی

marriage, wedding, festivity; delight, pleasure, joy *n.f.* **šādī** شادی

wed, marry, celebrate a wedding *v.t.* **šādī karnā** شادی کرنا

rarely, seldomly *adv.* / seldom, uncommon, abnormal *adj.* **šāz-ō-nādir** شاذونادر

commentator *n.m.* **šāriḥ** شارح

legislator; main road, highway *n.m.* **šāriᶜ** شارع

thoroughfare *n.m.* **šāriᶜ-ē-ᶜām** شارع عام

clever, sly, cunning *adj.* **šātir** شاطر

poet *n.m.* **šāᶜir** شاعر

poetess *n.f.* **šāᶜirah** شاعرہ

poetry *n.f.* **šāᶜirī** شاعری

advocate, mediator *n.m.* **šāfiᶜ** شافع

healer *n.m.* / healing, curing *adj.* **šāfī** شافی

troublesome, difficult; tragic *adj.* **šāqq** شاق

thankful, grateful *adj.* **šākir** شاکر

شاکی **šākī** complaining *adj.*
شاگرد **šāgird** pupil, disciple, scholar *n.m.*
شاگردی **šāgirdī** apprenticeship, learning, studying *n.f.*
شال **šāl** shawl *n.f.*
شام **šām** evening *n.f.*
شام کا کھانا **šām kā khānā** dinner, supper *n.m.*
شام کو **šām kō** in the evening *adv.*
شامت **šāmat** bad luck, misfortune *n.f.*
شامل **šāmil** included, joined, annexed, involved *adj.*
شامل کرنا **šāmil karnā** include, join, attach *v.t.*
شامیانہ **šāmiyānah** canopy, pavilion *n.m.*
شان **šān** business, affair; condition, state, position; dignity, grace *n.f.*
شان دار **šān dār** splendid, grand, pompous *adj.*
شان و شوکت **šān-ō-šaukat** splendor, pomp, show, glory *n.f.*
شانہ **šānah** shoulder; comb *n.m.*
شاہ **šāh** shah, king, prince, sovereign, monarch *n.m.*
شاہ راہ **šāh-ē-rāh** highway, public road *n.f.*
شاہ زادہ **šāh zādah** prince *n.m.*
شاہانہ **šāhānah** royal, imperial, kingly *adj.*
شاہد **šāhid** witness *n.m.*
شاہزادی **šāh zādī** princess *n.f.*
شاہنشاہ **šāhinšāh** emperor *n.m.*
شاہنشاہی **šāhinšāhī** royal, imperial *adj.*
شاہی **šāhī** reign, sovereignty, dominion *n.f.*
شاہین **šāhīn** falcon *n.m.*
شاور **šāvar** shower *n.m.*
شایان **šāyān** suitable, fit, worthy *adj.*
شائبہ **šā'ibah** doubt, suspicion *n.m.*
شاید **šāyad** perhaps, possibly, probably *adv.*
شائستگی **šā'istagī** politeness, good manners, decency *n.f.*
شائستہ **šā'istah** polite, courteous, gentle *adj.*
شائستہ مزاج **šā'istah mizāj** mild, well-tempered *adj.*
شائع **šā'iᶜ** published, revealed, broadcasted *adj.*
شائع کرنا **šā'iᶜ karnā** publish, issue, broadcast *v.t.*
شائق **šā'iq** desirous, fond, longing; zealous *adj.*
شب **šab** night *n.f.*

youth, youthfulness *n.m.* **šabāb** شباب
shepherd *n.m.* **šubān** شبان
by night *adv.* / nightly, nocturnal *adj.* **šabānah** شبانہ
resemblance, similarity *n.f.* **šabāhat** شباہت
voice, sound, noise, song; word *n.m.* **šabd** شبد
dew *n.f.* **šabnam** شبنم
doubt, suspicion, uncertainty *n.m.* **šubah** شبہ
picture, image, portrait *n.f.* **šabīh** شبیہ
bat *n.m.* **šappar** شپر
quickly, soon *adv.* / hasty, speedy, quick *adj.* **šitāb** شتاب
camel *n.m.* **šutur** شتر
camel-driver *n.m.* **šutur bān** شتربان
wicked *adj.* **šutur ġumzah** شتر غمزہ
brave, courageous *adj.* **šujāᶜ** شجاع
bravery, courage *n.f.* **šajāᶜit** شجاعت
tree, plant *n.m.* **šajar** شجر
field map *n.m.* **šujarah** شجرہ
person, individual, being *n.m.* **šaxs** شخص
personal *adj.* **šaxsī** شخصی
personality, individuality; nobility *n.f.* **šaxsiyyat** شخصیت
severity, difficulty; violence, vehemence *n.f.* **šiddat** شدت
strong; violent *adj.* **šadīd** شدید
pure, clean, bright *adj.* **šuddh** شدھ
evil, wickedness *n.f.* **šarr** شر
raise a quarrel *v.t.* **šarr uṭhānā** شر اٹھانا
wine, liquor, spirit, alcoholic beverage, drink *n.f.* **šarāb** شراب
drink liquor, drink wine *v.t.* **šarāb pīnā** شراب پینا
tavern *n.m.* **šarāb xānah** شراب خانہ
wet, soaked *adj.* **šarābōr** شرابور
drunkard *n.m.* **šarābī** شرابی
mischief, wickedness *n.f.* **šarārat** شرارت
spark, flash *n.m.* **šarārah** شرارہ
nobility, politeness *n.f.* **šarāfat** شرافت
partnership *n.f.* **šarākat** شراکت
participate *v.t.* **šarākat karnā** شراکت کرنا
drinking; drink, beverage *n.m.* **šurb** شرب

syrup; lemonade; drink (*sweet*) *n.m.* **šarbat** شربت
condition, agreement, term *n.f.* **šart** شرط
legally *adv.* **šarᶜan** شرعاً
lawful, religious, dogmatic *adj.* **šaraᶜī** شرعی
dignity, honor, excellence *n.m.* **šaraf** شرف
east *n.m.* **šarq** شرق
eastern, oriental *adj.* **šarqī** شرقی
infidelity; polytheism; paganism; company, society *n.m.* **širk** شرک
partnership, company, society *n.f.* **širkat** شرکت
shame; modesty, bashfulness *n.f.* **šarm** شرم
ashamed, abashed *adj.* **šarm sār** شرمسار
shame, disgrace; bashfulness *n.f.* **šarmindagī** شرمندگی
ashamed, abashed, embarrassed *adj.* **šarmindah** شرمنده
modest, bashful *adj.* **šarmīlā** شرمیلا
beginning, start, commencement *n.m.* **šurūᶜ** شروع
begin, start, commence *v.t.* **šurūᶜ karnā** شروع کرنا
artery *n.f.* **širyān** شریان
body *n.m.* / naughty, mischievous, wicked *adj.* **šarīr** شریر
Sharia (*Islamic law*); justice *n.f.* **šarīᶜat** شریعت
noble, honorable, eminent, illustrious; gentle *adj.* **šarīf** شریف
custard apple *n.m.* **šarīfah** شریفہ
partner, participant, associate, colleague *n.m.* **šarīk** شریک
get attended, include *v.t.* **šarīk karnā** شریک کرنا
aim *n.f.* **šast** شست
aim at *v.t.* **šast bāndhnā** شست باندھنا
washed, cleaned, polished *adj.* **šustah** شستہ
six *num.* **šaš** شش
hexagonal *adj.* **šaš pahlū** شش پہلو
throughout the world *n.f.* **šaš jihat** شش جہت
confounded, astonished, perplexed *adj.* **šaš dar** شش در
river; riverbank *n.m.* **šatt** شط
chess *n.f.* **šatranj** شطرنج
chess player *n.m.* **šatranj bāz** شطرنج باز
habit, custom, method, manner *n.m.* **šiᶜār** شعار
habitual, customary *adj.* **šiᶜārī** شعاری
rays (*of the sun*), sunshine *n.f.* **šuᶜaᶜ** شعاع

radiant, radial *adj.* **šuᶜāᶜī** شعاعی
conjuration, juggling *n.m.* **šuᶜbadah** شعبدہ
conjurer, juggler *n.m.* **šuᶜbadah bāz** شعبدہ باز
section, branch, part, department, division *n.m.* **šuᶜbah** شعبہ
hair *n.m.* **šaᶜr** • verse, couplet; poetry *n.m.* **šiᶜr** شعر
flame, blaze *n.m.* **šuᶜlah** شعلہ
ablaze, aflame *adj.* **šuᶜlah-ē-zan** شعلہ زن
intellect, wisdom *n.m.* **šuᶜūr** شعور
Shiite *adj.* **šiᶜī** شعی
jackal *n.m.* **šaġāl** شغال
ardor, zeal, enthusiasm *n.m.* **šaġaf** شغف
employment, occupation *n.m.* **šuġl/šaġl** شغل
restoration (*of health*), healing, cure, recovery *n.f.* **šifā/šafā** شفا
be healed, be cured *v.i.* **šifā pānā** شفا پانا
hospital, clinic *n.m.* **šifā xānah** شفا خانہ
cure, heal *v.t.* **šifā dēnā** شفا دینا
be healed, be cured *v.i.* **šifā hōnā** شفا ہونا
recommendation; entreaty *n.f.* **šafāᶜt** شفاعت
recommend, mediate *v.t.* **šafāᶜt karnā** شفاعت کرنا
transparent, clear *adj.* **šaffāf** شفاف
peach *n.m.* **šaftālū** شفتالو
twilight, dawn *n.f.* **šafaq** شفق
kindness, favor, affection *n.f.* **šafaqat** شفقت
advocate, patron *n.m.* **šafīᶜ** شفیع
kind, affectionate, compassionate, merciful *adj.* **šafīq** شفیق
half, piece, part *n.f.* **šiqq** • cleaving, splitting, crack, fissure *n.m.* **šaqq** شق
misery, disgrace *n.f.* **šaqāvat** شقاوت
doubt, hesitation, suspicion *n.m.* **šakk** شک
doubt, suspect *v.t.* **šakk karnā** شک کرنا
without a doubt, doubtless *adv.* **šakk kē baġair** شک کے بغیر
hunting, chase, game *n.m.* **šikār** شکار
hunt *v.t.* **šikār karnā** شکار کرنا
go hunting, hunt *v.t.* **šikār khēlnā** شکار کھیلنا
hunter *n.m.* **šikārī** شکاری
hunting dog, hound *n.m.* **šikārī kuttā** شکاری کتا
complaint *n.f.* **šikāyat** شکایت

شکایت کرنا complain *v.t.* **šikāyat karnā**
شکر thanks, gratitude, gratefulness *n.m.* **šukr**
شکر sugar *n.f.* **šakar/šakkar**
شکرقندی sweet potato *n.f.* **šakar qandī**
شکر کرنا thank *v.t.* **šukr karnā**
شکرگزار thankful, grateful *adj.* **šukr guzār**
شکریا Thank you!, Thanks! *interj.* **šukriyā**
شکرہ falcon, hawk *n.m.* **šikrah**
شکست defeat, loss *n.f.* **šikast**
شکست خوردہ defeated *adj.* **šikast xūrdah**
شکست دینا defeat *v.t.* **šikast dēnā**
شکستگی breaking, brokenness, breakage, fracture *n.f.* **šikastagī**
شکستہ broken *adj.* **šikastah**
شکستہ خاطر afflicted; offended *adj.* **šikastah xātir**
شکل figure, form, shape *n.f.* **šakl**
شکل بگاڑنا disfigure; disgrace *v.i.* **šakl bigāṁnā**
شکل بنانا shape, form, give a shape *v.t.* **šakl banānā**
شکم belly, paunch *n.m.* **šikam**
شکن fold, wrinkle, plait, crease *n.f.* **šikan**
شکن ڈالنا fold, crease *v.t.* **šikan ḍālnā**
شکوہ complaint, accusation *n.f.* **šikvah**
شکوہ grandeur, dignity *n.f.* **šIkōh**
شکوہ کرنا complain *v.t.* **šikvah karnā**
شکی suspicious, doubtful, skeptical *adj.* **šakkī**
شکیب patience, tolerance *n.f.* **šikēb**
شکیبا patient, tolerant *adj.* **šikēbā**
شکیل handsome, well-shaped *adj.* **šakīl**
شگاف fissure, rent, crack *n.m.* **šigāf**
شگفتگی pleasure, delight; blooming; exhilaration *n.f.* **šiguftagī**
شگفتہ expanded, blooming *adj.* **šiguftah**
شگفتہ خاطر cheerful, happy, delighted *adj.* **šiguftah xātir**
شگن omen *n.m.* **šugun**
شگوفہ blossom, bud *n.m.* **šigūfah**
شگون omen *n.m.* **šagūn**
شلوار trousers, loose pants *n.m.* **šalvār**
شلوار قمیض shalwar qameez (*a traditional costume*) *n.f.* **šalvār qamīz**

counting, numbering, calculation *n.m.* **šumār** شمار
count, number *v.t.* **šumār karnā** شمار کرنا
counting, enumeration *n.f.* **šumārī** شماری
north *n.m.* **šamāl/šimāl** شمال
northern *adj.* **šamālī** شمالی
sun *n.m.* **šams** شمس
solar *adj.* **šamsī** شمسی
sword *n.f.* **šamšēr** شمشیر
swordsman *n.m.* **šamšēr zan** شمشیر زن
lamp, candle, lantern *n.m.* **šamaᶜ** شمع
inclusion *n.f.* **šamūliyat** شمولیت
fragrance, perfume, odor *n.f.* **šamīm** شمیم
identification, recognition *n.f.* **šināxt** شناخت
recognise, identify *v.t.* **šināxt karnā** شناخت کرنا
ID card *n.m.* **šināxtī kārḍ** شناختی کارڈ
intelligent, knowing; familiar *adj.* **šināsā** شناسا
royal; great, large *adj.* **šah** شہ
witness, evidence; martyrdom *n.f.* **šahādat** شہادت
give evidence *v.t.* **šahādat dēnā** شہادت دینا
honey *n.m.* **šahd** شہد
bee *n.f.* **šahad kī makkhī** شہد کی مکھی
month *n.m.* **šahr** • city, town *n.m.* **šahr/šahar** شہر
exile, expulsion, banishment *n.m.* **šahr badr** شہر بدر
exile, banish *v.t.* **šahr badr karnā** شہر بدر کرنا
city-walls, fortification, rampart *n.f.* **šahr-ē-panāh** شہر پناہ
cemetery, graveyard *n.m.* **šahr-ē-xamōšaṁ** شہر خموشاں
fame, celebrity; rumor *n.f.* **šuhrat** شہرت
reputation, fame; rumor *n.m.* **šuhrah** شہرہ
citizen, townsman *n.m.* **šahrī** شہری
civics, people; cultivating *n.f.* **šaharyāt** شہریات
prince, king; despotic ruler *n.m.* **šaharyār** شہریار
nationality, citizenship *n.f.* **šahriyat** شہریت
clarion, flute, pipe *n.f.* **šahnā'ī** شہنائی
lust, sexual desire *n.f.* **šahvat** شہوت
lustful, desirous *adj.* **šahvat parast** شہوت پرست
martyr *n.m.* **šahīd** شہید

bright; fast, brisk; mischievous, insolent, shameless *adj.* **šōx** شوخ
mischief, playfulness, humor *n.f.* **šōxī** شوخی
make noise *v.t.* **šōr macānā** شور مچانا ♦ noise, cry, outcry *n.m.* **šōr** شور
soup, broth *n.m.* **šōrbā** شوربا
confusion, disturbance, tumult *n.f.* **šōriš** شورش
niter, saltpeter *n.m.* **šōrah** شوره
noise, turbulance, uproar *n.m.* **šōr-ō-ġul** شوروغل
disturbed, dejected *adj.* **šōrīdah** شوریده
part, piece, particle *n.m.* **šōšah** شوشہ
taste; ardor, zeal, eagerness; fondness, affection, desire *n.m.* **šauq** شوق
with pleasure, willingly *adv.* **šauq sē** شوق سے
fond of, eager, desirous *adj.* **šauqīn** شوقین
eagerly, fondly *adv.* **šauqiyah** شوقیہ
magnificence, dignity; power, might *n.f.* **šaukat** شوکت
black; unfortunate, unlucky *adj.* **šūm** شوم
husband *n.m.* **šauhar** شوہر
sheikh, chief, leader *n.m.* **šaix** شیخ
fool, rogue *n.m.* **šaix cillī** شیخ چلی
lover; mad man *n.m.* / madly in love, deeply in love *adj.* **šaidā** شیدا
lion, tiger; hero *n.m.* **šēr** • milk *n.m.* **šīr** شیر
lion *n.m.* **šēr babar** شیر ببر
management, organization; stitching (*in a book*) *n.m.* **šīrāzah** شیرازه
lioness, tigress *n.f.* **šērnī** شیرنی
syrup; juice; molasses *n.m.* **šīrah** شیره
sweet, pleasant, gentle *adj.* **šīrīṁ** شیریں
sweetness *n.f.* **šīrīnī** شیرینی
glass house, crystal place *n.m.* **šīš maḥal** شیش محل
glass, crystal; bottle, flask *n.m.* **šīšah** شیشہ
small glass, small bottle *n.f.* **šīšī** شیشی
Satan, devil *n.m.* **šaitān** شیطان
mischief, wickedness *n.f.* / wicked, devilish, diabolical *adj.* **šaitānī** شیطانی
Shia (*an Islamic sect*), followers of Hazrat Ali *n.m.* **šīʿah** شیعہ
mad (of love), in love *adj.* **šēftah** شیفتہ
be (madly) in love *v.i.* **šēftah hōnā** شیفتہ ہونا
grief, lamentation, mourning *n.m.* **šēvan** شیون

svād ص

patient, enduring *adj.* **sābir** صابر

soap *n.m.* **sāban/sābun** صابن

soap *n.m.* **sābūn** صابون

master, lord, ruler, officer; companion; Mister (Mr.), sir *n.m.* **sāḥib** صاحب

polite *adj.* **sāḥib-ē-axlāq** صاحب اخلاق

fortunate, lucky *adj.* **sāḥib-ē-iqbāl** صاحب اقبال

emperor, king *n.m.* **sāḥib-ē-taj-ō-taxt** صاحب تاج و تخت

intelligent *adj.* **sāḥib-ē-tamīz** صاحب تمیز

handsome *adj.* **sāḥib-ē-jamāl** صاحب جمال

host, master of the house *n.m.* **sāḥib-ē-xānah** صاحب خانہ

pious man, good fellow **n.m sāḥib-ē-dil** صاحب دل

selfish *adj.* **sāḥib-ē-ġarz** صاحب غرض

perfect, excellent, skillful *adj.* **saḥib kamāl** صاحب کمال

lady *n.f.* **saḥibah** صاحبہ

proceeding, on-going; issued, passed, arrived *adj.* **sādir** صادر

issue, pass (*an order*) *v.t.* **sādir karnā** صادر کرنا

be issued, be enacted; proceed *v.i.* **sādir hōnā** صادر ہونا

true, sincere, faithful *adj.* **sādiq** صادق

truthful *adj.* **sādiq-ul-qaul** صادق القول

lightning, thunderbolt *n.m.* **sāᶜiqah** صاعقہ

clean, clear, pure, bright; innocent *adj.* / clearly, entirely *adv.* **sāf** صاف

open-hearted, frank, sincere *adj.* **sāf dil** صاف دل

clear, transparent *adj.* **sāf šaffāf** صاف شفاف

be frank, be straightforward *v.t.* **sāf sāf karnā** صاف صاف کہنا

clean, clear *v.t.* **sāf karnā** صاف کرنا

clear, pure *adj.* **sāfī** صافی

virtuous, chaste, righteous *adj.* **sāliḥ** صالح

silent, mute; inanimate; irrational *adj.* **sāmit** صامت

right, straight (*to the point*), well-aimed *adj.* **sā'ib** صائب

morning, dawn *n.f.* **sabāḥ** صباح

beauty, gracefulness, elegance *n.f.* **sabāḥat** صباحت

morning, dawn, daybreak *n.f.* **subḥ** صبح

early (*in the morning*), at dawn *adv.* **subḥ dam** صبح دم

dawn (*of the day*) *n.f.* **subḥ sādiq** صبح صادق
time before dawn *n.f.* **subḥ kāzib** صبح کاذب
dawn *v.i.* **subḥ hōnā** صبح ہونا
patience *n.m.* **sabr** صبر
have patience, wait *v.t.* **sabr karnā** صبر کرنا
patience, forbearance *n.f.* **sabūrī** صبوری
beautiful, handsome *adj.* **sabīḥ** صبیح
friendship, companionship *n.f.* **saḥābit** صحابت
librarian, bookseller *n.m.* **saḥāf** صحاف
journalist, editor *n.m.* **saḥāfī** صحافی
companionship, company, fellowship *n.f.* **suḥbat** صحبت
keep company, cohabit *v.t.* **suḥbat rakhnā** صحبت رکھنا
health *n.f.* **siḥḥat** صحت
curative, healthy *adj.* **siḥḥat baxš** صحت بخش
recover *v.t.* **siḥḥat pānā** صحت پانا
desert; wilderness *n.m.* **saḥrā** صحرا
bedouin *n.m.* **saḥrā našīn** صحرا نشین
of the desert; wild *adj.* **saḥrā'ī** صحرائی
courtyard *n.m.* **saḥn** صحن
true, right, correct *adj.* **saḥīḥ** صحیح
safe and sound *adj.* **saḥīḥ sālim** صحیح سالم
correct, rectify *v.t.* **saḥīḥ karnā** صحیح کرنا
book, volume; page *n.m.* **saḥīfah** صحیفہ
hundred *num.* **sad** صد
sound, tone, noise; echo *n.f.* **sadā** صدا
presidentship, chairmanship, chancellorship *n.f.* **sadārat** صدارت
truth, honesty, fidelity *n.f.* **sadāqat** صداقت
breast, chest; chief *n.m.* **sadr** صدر
supreme court *n.f.* **sadr ᶜadālat** صدر عدالت
president *n.m.* **sadr-ē-majlis** صدر مجلس
president *n.m.* **sadr našīn** صدر نشین
shell; pearl *n.f.* **sadaf** صدف
truth, sincerity *n.m.* **sidq** صدق
alms, sacrifice; favor, grace *n.m.* **sadqah** صدقہ
shock, blow; accident, calamity *n.m.* **sadmah** صدمہ

suffer a shock, suffer a blow *v.t.* **sadmah uṭhānā** صدمہ اٹھانا
give a blow, hurt *v.t.* **sadmah pahumcānā** صدمہ پہنچانا
hundreds, many *adj.* **sadhā** صدہا
century, centenary *n.f.* **sadī** صدی
friend *n.m.* **sadīq** • just, true, sincere *adj.* **siddīq** صدیق
pureness, clearness *n.f.* **sarāḥat** صراحت
evidently, clearly *adv.* **sarāḥatan** صراحتاً
road, path, way *n.f.* **sirāṭ** صراط
right way *n.m.* **sirāt-ē-mustaqīm** صراط مستقیم
banker, money-changer *n.m.* **sarrāf** صراف
bank, exchange (*of foreign currencies*) *n.m.* **sarrāfah** صرافہ
banking, money-changing; discount *n.f.* **sarrāfī** صرافی
• only, mere *adj.* / purely, exclusively *adv.* **sirf** صرف
expenditure, cost; change *n.m.* **sarf**
spend *v.t.* **sarf karnā** صرف کرنا
grammar *n.f.* **sarf-ō-naḥū** صرف و نحو
expense; profit, advantage; economy *n.m.* **sarfah** صرفہ
economically *adv.* **sarfah sē** صرفہ سے
be economical, economize *v.t.* **sarfah karnā** صرفہ کرنا
etymologist, grammarian *n.m.* **sarfī** صرفی
evident, apparent, manifest *adj.* **sariḥ** صریح
hardship, difficulty *n.f.* **saᶜūbat** صعوبت
ascent, mounting, climbing *n.m.* **suᶜūd** صعود
smallness *n.m.* **saġir** صغر
minor *n.m.* **saġīr san** صغر سن
minority *n.f.* **saġīr sanī** صغر سنی
small, inferior *adj.* **saġīr** صغیر
childhood, infancy *n.f.* **saġīrī** صغیری
series, order, rank, line *n.f.* **saff** صف
pure, clean, brilliant; sincere *adj.* **safā** صفا
cleanliness, neatness, purity *n.f.* **safā'ī** صفائی
cleanse, clean, purify *v.t.* **safā'ī karnā** صفائی کرنا
page; surface *n.m.* **safḥah** صفحہ
zero *n.m.* **sifar/sifr** صفر
pure, just, righteous *adj.* **safī** صفی
firmness, hardness, severity *n.f.* **salābat** صلابت

advice, counsel; concord, treaty *n.f.* **salāḥ** صلاح
advise, counsel *v.t.* **salāḥ dēnā** صلاح دینا
adviser, counsellor *n.m.* **salāḥ dēnē vālā** صلاح دینے والا
adviser, counsellor *n.m.* **salāḥ kār** صلاح کار
take advice, consult *v.t.* **salāḥ karnā** صلاح کرنا
virtue, integrity *n.f.* **salāḥiyyat** صلاحیت
legitimate *adj.* **sulbī** صلبی
peace, truce, reconciliation *n.f.* **sulḥ** صلح
make a truce, come to terms *v.t.* **sulḥ karnā** صلح کرنا
reward, compensation, recompense *n.m.* **silah** صلہ
prayer (*by Muslims*) *n.f.* **salāt** صلواۃ
cross, crucifix *n.f.* **salīb** صلیب
deaf *adj.* **summ** صم
pure, unmixed; sincere *adj.* **samīm** صمیم
skillful, expert *adj.* **sannāᶜ** صناع
art, trade, skill, industry *n.f.* **sanāᶜt** صناعت
sandalwood *n.m.* **sandal** صندل
box, trunk *n.m.* **sandūq/sundūq** صندوق
artistic; industrial *adj.* **sanᶜatī** صنعتی
kind, sort, species *n.f.* **sinf** صنف
idol *n.m.* **sanam** صنم
temple (*where idols are kept*), pagoda *n.m.* **sanam kadah** صنم کدہ
pine tree *n.m.* **sanōbar** صنوبر
province *n.m.* **sūbah** صوبہ
governor *n.m.* **sūbah dār** صوبہ دار
voice, sound *n.f.* **saut** صوت
form, figure, shape *n.f.* **sūrat** صورت
acquaintance *n.f.* **sūrat āšnāʾī** صورت آشنائی
plan, manage *v.t.* **sūrat karnā** صورت کرنا
painter; sculptor *n.m.* **sūrat gar** صورت گر
sufi (*a Muslim mystic*) *n.m.* / wise *adj.* **sūfī** صوفی
fury, violence; impetuosity *n.f.* **saulat** صولت
fasting *n.m.* **saum** صوم
hunter, fowler; fisherman *n.m.* **saiyyād** صیاد
preservation, guarding, keeping *n.f.* **siyānat** صیانت

صید game, prey, quarry *n.f.* **said**

صید افگن hunter *n.m.* **said afgan**

صیغہ گردانا conjugate *v.t.* **sīġah gardānnā**

صیقل burnish, polishing *n.f.* **saiqal**

صیقل کرنا burnish *v.t.* **saiqal karnā**

صیہون Zion *n.m.* **saihūn**

صیہونی Zionist *adj.* **saihūnī**

صیہونیت Zionism *n.f.* **saihūniyat**

zvād ض

strict, punctual *adj.* / governor, master *n.m.* **zābit** ضابط

regularity, conformity *n.f.* **zābitagī** ضابطگی

ordinance, rule, law, code *n.m.* **zābitah** ضابطہ

civil procedure code *n.m.* **zābitah-ē-dīvānī** ضابطہ دیوانی

criminal procedure code *n.m.* **zābitah-ē-faujdāri** ضابطہ فوجداری

surety, bail; sponsor *n.m.* **zāmin** ضامن

security; surety, bail *n.f.* **zāminī** ضامنی

lost, destroyed, perished *adj.* **zā'ic** ضائع

be destroyed, be wasted *v.i.* **zā'ic hōnā** ضایع کرنا

lose, destroy, waste *v.t.* **zā'ic karnā** ضائع کرنا

check, control; guarding; confiscation, seizure *n.m.* **zabt** ضبط

control; confiscate, seize *v.t.* **zabt karnā** ضبط کرنا

be confiscated, be seized *v.i.* **zabt hōnā** ضبط ہونا

confiscation, seizure *n.f.* **zabtī** ضبطی

thickness, bulkiness, corpulence *n.f.* **zaxāmat** ضخامت

thick, bulky, corpulent *adj.* **zaxīm** ضخیم

contrary, opposite; stubbornness, persistence *n.f.* **zidd** ضد

despite, out of opposition (to) *pp.* **zidd par** ضد پر

persist, persevere; contradict *v.t.* **zidd karnā** ضد کرنا

stubborn; perverse, naughty *adj.* **ziddī** ضدی

injury, harming *n.m.* **zirār** ضرار

blow, striking, beating, violence, injury *n.f.* **zarb** ضرب

proverb, saying *n.f.* **zarb-ul-masal** ضرب المثل

multiply *v.t.* **zarb dēnā** ضرب دینا

give a blow, strike *v.t.* **zarb lagānā** ضرب لگانا

injury, damage; loss, ruin *n.m.* **zarar** ضرر

injure, damage *v.t.* **zarar pahuṁcānā** ضرر پہنچانا

harmful, injurious *adj.* **zarar rasāṁ** ضرر رساں

urgent, unavoidable, necessary *adj.* / Of course!, Sure! *interj.* **zarūr** ضرور

need, necessity *n.f.* **zarūrat** ضرورت

necessarily, essentially *adj.* **zarūratan** ضرورتاً

necessary *adj.* **zarūrī** ضروری

weakness *n.m.* **zucf** ضعف

weak, old, feeble *n.m.* **za^cīf** ضعیف
weakness, old age, feebleness *n.f.* **za^cīfī** ضعیفی
error, fault; vice *n.f.* **zalālat** ضلالت
part, district, division *n.m.* **zila^c** ضلع
surety, guarantee, bail; security *n.f.* **zamānat** ضمانت
by the way, incidentally *adv.* **zimnan** ضمناً
implicative, collateral *adj.* **zimnī** ضمنی
mind, heart, thought, conscience *n.f.* **zamīr** ضمیر
addition, appendix *n.m.* **zamīmah** ضمیمہ
light, sunlight *n.f.* **zau** ضو
light, brilliancy *n.f.* **ziyā** ضیا
feast, banquet; entertainment *n.f.* **ziyāfat** ضیافت
feast; entertain *v.t.* **ziyāfat karnā** ضیافت کرنا
lion *n.m.* **zaiġam** ضیغم
stranger; guest *n.m.* **zaif** ضیف
anguish, melancholy, anxiety *n.f.* **zīq** ضیق

tōē ط

sweet, agreeable *adj.* **tāb** طاب
printer; seal *n.m.* **tābi^c** طابع
happening, occurring *adj.* **tārī** طاری
overcome, overshadow *v.i.* **tārī hōnā** طاری ہونا
river basin; bowl, vessel, cup *n.m.* **tās** طاس
devotion, obedience, submission *n.f.* **tā^cat** طاعت
violent, rebellious *adj.* **tāġī** طاغی
arch, niche *n.m.* **tāq** طاق
accomplish, make an expert *v.t.* **tāq karnā** طاق کرنا
be accomplished, be efficient *v.i.* **tāq hōnā** طاق ہونا
ability; power, force, strength, might *n.f.* **tāqat** طاقت
powerful, strong, forceful *adj.* **tāqatvar** طاقتور
seeker, enquirer; candidate *n.m.* **tālib** طالب
student *n.m.* **tālib-ē-^cilm** طالب علم
rising, arising, appearing *adj.* / fortune, prosperity *n.m.* **tāli^c** طالع
fortunate, wealthy *adj.* **tāli^c mand** طالع مند
fortune, wealth *n.f.* **tāli^c mandī** طالع مندی
covetous, greedy, desirous *adj.* **tāmi^c** طامع
pious, pure, chaste *adj.* **tāhir** طاہر
peacock *n.m.* **tā'ūs** طاؤس
bird *n.m.* **tā'ir** طائر
medicine (*the science*) *n.f.* **tibb** طب
medical practice *n.f.* **tabābat/tibābat** طبابت
cook *n.m.* **tabbāx** طباخ
slap *n.m.* **tabāṁcah** طبانچہ
nature, temper; print, impression, edition *n.f.* **taba^c** طبع
selfmade, original *adj.* **taba^c zād** طبع زاد
print *v.t.* **taba^c karnā** طبع کرنا
natural, physical, constitutional *adj.* **taba^cī** طبعی
fold, layer; cover; tray *n.m.* **tabaq** طبق
storey, floor *n.m.* **tabaqah** طبقہ
drum *n.m.* **tabl/tabal** طبل
tambourine *n.m.* **tablah** طبلہ

طبی medical *adj.* **tibbī**
طبی علاج medical treatment *n.m.* **tibbī ʿilāj**
طبیب physician, doctor *n.f.* **tabīb**
طبیعت health, nature, temperament, constitution *n.f.* **tabīʿat**
طبیعت آنا fall in love, be fond (of) *v.i.* **tabīʿ'at ānā**
طبیعت بہلانا divert, amuse *v.t.* **tabīʿat bahlānā**
طبیعت علیل ہونا be indisposed *v.i.* **tabīʿat ʿalīl hōnā**
طبیعت لگنا take interest (in), be attached (to) *v.i.* **tabīʿat lagnā**
طبیعی natural, innate; physical *adj.* **tabīʿī**
طرار eloquent *adj.* **tarrār**
طرارہ sharpness, quickness *n.m.* **tarrārah**
طراری sharpness, quickness *n.f.* **tarrārī**
طراوت freshness; dampness, moisture *n.f.* **tarāvat**
طرب joy, pleasure *n.f.* **tarab**
طرح manner, mode; plan *n.f.* **tarḥ**
طرح دار graceful, well-shaped *adj.* **tarḥ dār**
طرز form, manner, fashion *n.f.* **tarz**
طرف side, direction; margin; corner *n.f.* **taraf**
طرفدار partial *adj.* **tarafdār**
طرفداری partiality *n.f.* **tarafdārī**
طرفداری کرنا side with, take sides *v.t.* **tarafdārī karnā**
طرفہ wonderful, extraordinary *adj.* **turfah**
طریق way, path; manner *n.m.* **tarīq**
طریقت way, path, mode, rule *n.f.* **tarīqat**
طریقہ custom, rite, manner *n.m.* **tarīqah**
طشت large basin, cup, bowl *n.m.* **tašt**
طشتری small plate *n.m.* **taštarī**
طعام food; eating *n.m.* **taʿām**
طعم taste, savor, flavor *n.m.* **taʿam**
طعن blame, reproach *n.m.* **taʿn**
طعن زنی taunting, reproaching; sarcasm, irony *n.f.* **taʿn zanī**
طعن و تشنیع taunt, reproach *n.f.* **taʿn-ō-tašnīʿ**
طعنہ blame, reproach *n.m.* **taʿnah**
طعنہ مارنا taunt, reproach *v.t.* **taʿnah mārnā**
طغیانی flood, inundation, overflow *n.f.* **tuġyānī**

infant, child; young animal *n.m.* **tifl** طفل
infantile, childish *adj.* **tiflānah** طفلانہ
parasite *n.f.* **tufailī** طفیلی
dew *n.f.* **tall** طل
gold *n.m.* **tilā** طلا
gilder *n.m.* **tilā sāz** طلا ساز
divorce *n.f.* **talāq** طلاق
divorce *v.t.* **talāq dēnā** طلاق دینا
golden *adj.* **talā'ī** طلائی
desire, wish, demand; search, enquiry *n.f.* **talab** طلب
desire, ask for, seek, enquire *v.t.* **talab karnā** طلب کرنا
student, pupil *n.m.* **talabah** طلبہ
magic; talisman *n.m.* **tilism** طلسم
magical, mystical *adj.* **tilismātī** طلسماتی
magical, mystical *adj.* **talismī** طلسمی
appearance, face, aspect *n.f.* **talᶜat** طلعت
sunrise *n.m.* **tulūᶜ-ē-āftāb** طلوع آفتاب
rise *v.i.* **tulūᶜ hōnā** طلوع ہونا
avaricious, greedy *adj.* **tammāᶜ** طماع
slap *n.f.* **tamāncah** طمانچہ
consolation, satisfaction; rest, repose *n.f.* **tamāniyat** طمانیت
pomp, show, grandeur *n.m.* **tamtarāq** طمطراق
greediness, avarice *n.f.* **tamaᶜ** طمع
allure, tempt *v.t.* **tamaᶜ dēnā** طمع دینا
pistol *n.m.* **tamancah** طمنچہ
playful *adj.* **tannāz** طناز
tamboura (*an Asian guitar*) *n.m.* **tambūr** طنبور
sarcastically, ironically, jokingly *adv.* **tanzan** طنزاً
sound, noise; vanity, pride *n.m.* **tantanah** طنطنہ
purity, purification, cleanliness, ablution *n.f.* **tahārat** طہارت
purity, purification *n.m.* **tuhr** طہر
pure *adj.* **tahūr** طہور
going-round, turning *n.m.* **tavāf** طواف
go round, turn round *v.t.* **tavāf karnā** طواف کرنا
length, excess *n.f.* **tavālat** طوالت
whore *n.f.* **tavā'if** طوائف

manner, condition, state, mode, conduct *n.m.* **taur** طور
manner, practice *n.m.* **taur tarīqah** طور طریقہ
parrot *n.m.* **tōtā** طوطا
obedience *n.m.* **tauᶜ** طوع
storm, hurricane; wind *n.m.* **tūfān** طوفان
stormy, windy *adj.* **tūfānī** طوفانی
necklace, collar *n.m.* **tauq** طوق
length *n.m.* **tūl** طول
longitude *n.m.* **tūl-ul-balad** طول البلد
lengthen *v.t.* **tūl dēnā** طول دینا
long, tall *adj.* **tavīl** طویل
fold, roll up *v.t.* **tai karnā** طے کرنا
airplane *n.m.* **tayyārah** طیارہ
good, agreeable *adj.* **tayyib** طیب
perfume, odor, essence *n.f.* **tīb** طیب
bird *n.m.* **tair** طیر
anger, rage; passion *n.f.* **taiš** طیش
be enraged, become angry *v.i.* **taiš ānā** طیش آنا
nature, disposition *n.f.* **tīnat** طینت

zōē ظ

tyrant, oppressor *n.m.* **zālim** ظالم
cruel *adj.* **zālimānah** ظالمانہ
apparent, evident *adj.* **zāhir** ظاہر
showy, formal *adj.* **zāhir dār** ظاہر دار
formality, ceremony *n.f.* **zāhir dārī** ظاہر داری
make a show; pretend *v.t.* **zāhir dārī baratnā** ظاہر داری برتنا
show, reveal, exhibit; pretend *v.t.* **zāhir karnā** ظاہر کرنا
seemingly, apparently, evidently *adv.* **zāhir mēṁ** ظاہر میں
be visible, be apparent, appear *v.i.* **zāhir hōnā** ظاہر ہونا
apparently, evidently, visibly *adv.* **zāhiran** ظاہرا
external *adj.* **zāhirī** ظاہری
wise; hilarious, witty, humorous *n.m.* **zarāf** ظراف
wisdom; wit, humor *n.f.* **zarāfat** ظرافت
ingenuity, politeness; vase *n.m.* **zarf** ظرف
polite; wise; witty *adv.* **zarīf** ظریف
victory, triumph *n.m.* **zafar** ظفر
victorious (*in war*) *adj.* **zafar mauj** ظفر موج
victorious (*as a person*) *adj.* **zafar yāb** ظفریاب
shadow; shade, protection *n.m.* **zill** ظل
oppression, injustice *n.m.* **zulm** ظلم
oppress, tyrannize *v.t.* **zulm karnā** ظلم کرنا
darkness *n.f.* **zulmat** ظلمت
presumption, suspicion; wrong impression *n.m.* **zann** ظن
presume, suspect *v.t.* **zann karnā** ظن کرنا
supposed, suspected *adj.* **zannī** ظنی
midday, noon *n.m.* **zuhr** • back *n.f.* **zahr** ظہر
visibility, appearance, manifestation *n.m.* **zuhūr** ظہور
assistant, associate, ally *n.m.* **zahīr** ظہیر

ᶜain ع

عابد **ᶜābid** *n.m.* worshipper, devotee
عاج **ᶜāj** *n.m.* ivory
عاجز **ᶜājiz** *adj.* incapable, unable, helpless, weak
عاجزانہ **ᶜājzānah** *adv.* humbly; helplessly
عاجزی **ᶜājizī** *n.f.* inability, helplessness
عاجزی کرنا **ᶜājizī karnā** *v.t.* implore, supplicate
عاجل **ᶜājil** *adj.* hasty, speedy
عادت **ᶜādat** *n.f.* habit, custom, practice
عادت پڑنا **ᶜādat paṛnā** *v.i.* get used (to)
عادت کرنا **ᶜādat karnā** *v.t.* adopt a habit
عادتاً **ᶜādatan** *adv.* habitually, by habit
عادل **ᶜādil** *adj.* just, upright, righteous
عادی **ᶜādī** *adj.* habitual, accustomed
عار **ᶜār** *n.f.* shame, disgrace
عار ہونا **ᶜār hōnā** *v.i.* feel ashamed
عارض **ᶜāriz** *n.m.* cheek; incident, happening
عارض ہونا **ᶜāriz hōnā** *v.i.* befall, happen
عارضہ **ᶜārizah** *n.m.* sickness, disease, disorder; impediment
عارضی **ᶜārizī** *adj.* accidental; casual
عارف **ᶜārif** *adj.* wise; devout, pious
عاری **ᶜārī** *adj.* free (from), void (of)
عاریت **ᶜāriyyat** *n.f.* loan
عاریتاً **ᶜāriyatan** *adv.* on loan
عاریتی **ᶜāriyyatī** *adj.* borrowed, lent
عازم **ᶜāzim** *adj.* bound (for), intending
عاشق **ᶜāšiq** *n.m.* lover
عاشق مزاج **ᶜāšiq mizāj** *adj.* amorous
عاشق ہونا **ᶜāšiq hōnā** *v.i.* fall in love, be in love
عاشقانہ **ᶜāšiqānah** *adj.* amorous
عاشقی **ᶜāšiqī** *n.m.* love, courtship
عاصف **ᶜāsif** *n.m.* heavy storm of wind, stormy day
عاصی **ᶜāsī** *adj.* sinful; rebellious; criminal
عاطفت **ᶜātifat** *n.f.* kindness

safety, welfare; health *n.f.* ᶜ**āfiyat** عافیت
disobedient, rebellious, stubborn *adj.* ᶜ**āqq** عاق
end, termination, conclusion *n.m.* ᶜ**āqibat** عاقبت
wise, sensible *adj.* ᶜ**āqil** عاقل
wisely *adv.* ᶜ**āqilānah** عاقلانہ
learned, intelligent *adj.* ᶜ**ālim** • world, universe *n.m.* ᶜ**ālam** عالم
wisely *adv.* ᶜ**ālimānah** عالمانہ
global, universal *adj.* ᶜ**ālimī** عالمی
high, elevated; excelled *adj.* ᶜ**ālī** عالی
distinguished, of high rank *adj.* ᶜ**ālī jah** عالی جاہ
sharp-witted *adj.* ᶜ**ālī dimāġ** عالی دماغ
magnificent, splendid *adj.* ᶜ**ālī šān** عالی شان
ambitious *adj.* ᶜ**ālī hamrah** عالی ہمراہ
public, general, common *adj.* ᶜ**ām** عام
royal, imperial; rich *adj.* ᶜ**āmirah** عامرہ
worker *n.m.* ᶜ**āmil** عامل
common, general; whole, entire *adj.* ᶜ**āmmah** عامہ
common *adj.* ᶜ**āmī** عامی
vicious, faulty, infamous *adj.* ᶜ**ā'ib** عائب
happening, referring (to) *adj.* ᶜ**ā'id** عائد
levy *v.t.* ᶜ**ā'id karnā** عائد کرنا
cloak *n.f.* ᶜ**abā** عبا
worship, prayer *n.f.* ᶜ**ibādat** عبادت
worship, pray *v.t.* ᶜ**ibādat karnā** عبادت کرنا
composition; style, phraseology, diction *n.f.* ᶜ**ibārat** عبارت
vain, idle, useless; absurd *adj.* ᶜ**abas** عبث
servant, slave *n.m.* ᶜ**abd** عبد
warning; example *n.f.* ᶜ**ibrat** عبرت
exemplary *adj.* ᶜ**ibrat numā** عبرت نما
passing (over), crossing *n.m.* ᶜ**ubūr** عبور
reproof, rebuke, reproach *n.m.* ᶜ**itāb** عتاب
ancient *adj.* ᶜ**atīq** عتیق
museum *n.m.* ᶜ**ajā'ib ghar** عجائب گھر
wonderful, astonishing; rare *adj.* / wonder *n.m.* ᶜ**ajab** عجب
weakness *n.m.* ᶜ**ajz** عجز
speed, haste *n.f.* ᶜ**ujlat** عجلت

marvel, miracle *n.m.* **ᶜajūbah** عجوبہ
strange *adj.* **ᶜajīb** عجیب
justice, law; court of justice *n.m.* **ᶜadālat** عدالت
judicial *adj.* **ᶜadālatī** عدالتی
enmity, hostility *n.f.* **ᶜadāvat** عداوت
number *n.m.* **ᶜadad** عدد
justice *n.m.* **ᶜadl** عدل
non-existence, discontinuance *n.m.* **ᶜadam** عدم
enemy, adversary *n.m.* **ᶜadū** عدو
alike, equal, equivalent; just *adj.* **ᶜadīl** عدیل
pain, agony, anguish *n.m.* **ᶜazāb** عذاب
apology, excuse *n.m.* **ᶜuzr** عذر
maid, virgin; Virgo (*Zodiac*) *n.f.* **ᶜazrā** عذرا
Arabia; Arabs *n.m.* **ᶜarab** عرب
Arabian, Arabic *adj.* **ᶜarabī** عربی
roof; sky *n.m.* **ᶜarš** عرش
dockyard, deck *n.m.* **ᶜaršah** عرشہ
time, duration, period *n.m.* **ᶜarsah** عرصہ
request, petition *n.f.* **ᶜarz** عرض
application, petition *n.f.* **ᶜarzī** عرضی
alias *n.m.* **ᶜurf** عرف
knowledge, wisdom; science *n.m.* **ᶜirfān** عرفان
juice; spirit, essence *n.m.* **ᶜaraq** عرق
ascension, rising; height, elevation *n.m.* **ᶜurūj** عروج
bride; marriage, wedding *n.f.* **ᶜurūs** عروس
naked, bare, nude *adj.* **ᶜuryān** عریان
nakedness, nudity *n.f.* **ᶜuryānī** عریانی
broad, wide *adj.* **ᶜarīz** عریض
petition, application *n.m.* **ᶜarīzah** عریضہ
excellence; glory *n.m.* **ᶜizz** عز
mourning, lamenting; condolence *n.f.* **ᶜazā** عزا
honor, glory, respect *n.f.* **ᶜizzat** عزت
insult, disgrace *v.t.* **ᶜizzat bigāṛnā** عزت بگاڑنا
dismissal *n.m.* **ᶜazl** عزل
retirement, retiring *n.f.* **ᶜuzlat** عزلت
determination, resolution, ambition *n.m.* **ᶜazm** عزم

dear, beloved, precious, worthy *adj.* **ᶜazīz** عزیز
determination, resolution *n.f.* **ᶜazīmat** عزیمت
soldier *n.m.* **ᶜaskarī** عسکری
pleasure, enjoyment *n.f.* **ᶜišrat** عشرت
love *n.m.* **ᶜišq** عشق
lover *n.f.* **ᶜišq bāz** عشق باز
coquetry *n.m.* **ᶜišvah** عشوہ
coquetry *n.f.* **ᶜišvah garī** عشوہ گری
club, staff; scepter *n.m.* **ᶜasā** عصا
nerve; muscle *n.m.* **ᶜasab** عصب
bigotry, prejudice *n.f.* **ᶜasabiyyat** عصبیت
time, age *n.m.* **ᶜasr** عصر
afternoon tea *n.m.* **ᶜasrānah** عصرانہ
chastity; defence, protection *n.f.* **ᶜismat** عصمت
sin, violation (of law) *n.m.* **ᶜisyān** عصیان
muscle *n.m.* **ᶜuzlah** عضلہ
limb, joint *n.m.* **ᶜuzū** عضو
favor; gift, present *n.f.* **ᶜatā** عطا
bestow, confer *v.t.* **ᶜatā karnā** عطا کرنا
druggist; perfumer *n.m.* **ᶜattār** عطار
Mercury (*planet*) *n.m.* **ᶜattārad** عطارِد
amateur *n.m.* **ᶜatā'ī** عطائی
perfume, fragrance *n.m.* **ᶜitr/ᶜatr** عطر
thirst *n.f.* **ᶜataš** عطش
kindness, affection *n.m.* **ᶜatf** عطف
grant, assignment *n.m.* **ᶜatiyyah** عطیہ
greatness, magnificence *n.f.* **ᶜazmat** عظمت
great, magnificent; high *adj.* **ᶜazīm** عظیم
splendid, dignified *adj.* **ᶜazīm-ul-šān** عظیم الشان
chastity, modesty *n.f.* **ᶜiffat** عفت
forgiveness, pardon *n.m.* **ᶜafū** عفو
forgive, pardon *v.t.* **ᶜafū karnā** عفو کرنا
stinking; rottenness; infection *n.f.* **ᶜafūnat** عفونت
chaste, modest *adj.* **ᶜafīf** عفیف
eagle *n.m.* **ᶜuqāb** عقاب
behind, after *adj.* **ᶜaqab** عقب

end, conclusion, accomplishment *n.f.* **ᶜuqbā** عقبیٰ
knot *n.m.* **ᶜaqd** عقد
knot; wed *v.t.* **ᶜaqd karnā** عقد کرنا
knot; difficult task, problem *n.m.* **ᶜuqdah** عقدہ
scorpion; Scorpio (*Zodiac*) *n.m.* **ᶜaqrab** عقرب
wisdom; sense, intellect; reason; opinion *n.m.* **ᶜaql** عقل
wise, intelligent *adj.* **ᶜaql mand** عقل مند
wisdom, intelligence *n.f.* **ᶜaql mandī** عقل مندی
intellectual, rational, mental *adj.* **ᶜaqlī** عقلی
punishment; torture *n.f.* **ᶜuqūbat** عقوبت
faith, belief *n.f.* **ᶜaqīdat** عقیدت
creed, doctrine *n.m.* **ᶜaqīdah** عقیدہ
barren, childless *adj.* **ᶜaqīm** عقیم
reflection; shadow *n.m.* **ᶜaks** عکس
reflect *v.t.* **ᶜaks ḍālnā** عکس ڈالنا
reflective *adj.* **ᶜaksī** عکسی
cure, treatment *n.m.* **ᶜilāj** علاج
cure, treat (*medical*) *v.t.* **ᶜilāj karnā** علاج کرنا
separation *n.f.* **ᶜalāḥidagī** علاحدگی
separate, apart *adj.* **ᶜalāḥidah** علاحدہ
jurisdiction, region, division, area *n.m.* **ᶜilāqah** علاقہ
ailment *n.f.* **ᶜalālat** علالت
omniscient, all-knowing *adj.* **ᶜallām** علام
mark, sign; symptom *n.f.* **ᶜalāmat** علامت
learned, wise *adj.* **ᶜallāmah** علامہ
openly, publicly *adv.* **ᶜalāniyah** علانیہ
besides, in addition (to) *adv.* **ᶜilāvah** علاوہ
besides this, in addition to this, moreover *adv.* **ᶜilāvah azīṁ** علاوہ ازیں
fault, defect, bad habit *n.f.* **ᶜillat** علت
faulty, imperfect *adj.* **ᶜillatī** علتی
knowledge, science *n.m.* **ᶜilm** • standard, banner, ensign *n.m.* **ᶜalam** علم
ethics; literature *n.m.* **ᶜilm-ē-adab** علم ادب
theology *n.m.* **ᶜilm-ē-ilahī** علم الٰہی
minerology *n.m.* **ᶜilm-ē-jamādāt** علم جمادات
philosophy *n.m.* **ᶜilm-ē-ḥikmat** علم حکمت
chemistry *n.m.* **ᶜilm-ē-kīmiyā** علم کیمیا

علم معدنیات minerology *n.m.* **ᶜilm-ē-maᶜdaniyāt**
علم ہندسہ geometry *n.m.* **ᶜilm-ē-hindsah**
علمی scientific; literary *adj.* **ᶜilmī**
علمیت learning, scholarship *n.m.* **ᶜilmiyyat**
علو sublimity, eminence *adj.* **ᶜuluv**
علی high; sublime, eminent *adj.* **ᶜalī**
علیل indisposed, sick, ill; weak *adv.* **ᶜalīl**
علیم learned, wise *adj.* **ᶜalīm**
عم uncle (*father's brother*) *n.m.* **ᶜamm**
عماد pillar; confidence, trust *n.m.* **ᶜimād**
عمارت building, edifice *n.f.* **ᶜimārat**
عمامہ turban *n.m.* **ᶜimāmah**
عمداً on purpose, intentionally, deliberately *adv.* **ᶜamadan**
عمدگی greatness, excellence *n.f.* **ᶜumdagī**
عمر age, life, lifetime *n.f.* **ᶜumr**
عمق depth *n.m.* **ᶜumuq**
عمل action, effect *n.m.* **ᶜamal**
عمل داری rule, government *n.f.* **ᶜamal dārī**
عمل درآمد process, action *n.m.* **ᶜamal dar āmad**
عمل درآمد کرنا act upon, enforce *v.t.* **ᶜamal dar āmad karnā**
عملہ staff, personnel *n.m.* **ᶜamalah**
عملی practical *adj.* **ᶜamlī**
عموم common, general, universal *adj.* **ᶜumūm**
عموماً generally, commonly *adv.* **ᶜumūman**
عمومی common, normal *adj.* **ᶜumūmī**
عمیق deep, profound *adj.* **ᶜamīq**
عمیم full, complete; universal *adj.* **ᶜamīm**
عناد enmity; obstinacy, stubbornness *n.m.* **ᶜinād**
عنب grape *n.m.* **ᶜinab**
عند near, before, with *pp.* **ᶜind**
عندلیب nightingale *n.f.* **ᶜandalīb**
عندیہ intention; viewpoint, opinion *n.m.* **ᶜindiyah**
عنصر origin, element *n.m.* **ᶜunsar**
عنصری original, elementary *adj.* **ᶜunsurī**
عنفوان beginning, start *n.m.* **ᶜunfuvān**
عنکبوت spider *n.f.* **ᶜankabūt**

heading, title *n.m.* **ᶜunvān** عنوان

promise, agreement, obligation; time, season; mandate *n.m.* **ᶜahd** عہد

break one's promise *v.t.* **ᶜahd tōṛnā** عہد توڑنا

promise, make a vow *v.t.* **ᶜahd karnā** عہد کرنا

treaty, charter *n.m.* **ᶜahd nāmah** عہد نامہ

agreement, treaty *n.m.* **ᶜahd-ō-paimān** عہد وپیمان

designation, status; employment; duty office; administration *n.m.* **ᶜuhdah** عہدہ

officer, official *adj.* **ᶜuhdah dār** عہدہ دار

public, common people *n.m.* **ᶜavām** عوام

public, mankind *n.m.* **ᶜavām-ul-nās** عوام الناس

wife; lady, woman *n.f.* **ᶜaurat** عورت

recompense, reward; retaliation, revenge *n.m.* **ᶜivaz** عوض

pay a compensation *v.t.* **ᶜivaz dēnā** عوض دینا

take revenge *v.t.* **ᶜivaz lēnā** عوض لینا

cunning, sly *adj.* **ᶜayyār** عیار

cunningness, slyness *n.f.* **ᶜayyārī** عیاری

luxurious *adj.* **ᶜayyāš** عیاش

luxury *n.f.* **ᶜayyāšī** عیاشی

family, household *n.m.* **ᶜayāl** عیال

clear, evident, apparent *adj.* **ᶜayān** عیاں

sin, defect, vice, fault *n.m.* **ᶜaib** عیب

criticism *n.f.* **ᶜaib jū'ī** عیب جوئی

festival, holiday *n.f.* **ᶜīd** عید

Christian *n.m.* **ᶜīsā'ī** عیسائی

Christ, Jesus *n.m.* **ᶜīsā** عیسی

pleasure, delight *n.m.* **ᶜaiš** عیش

eye; eyesight; fountain, spring *n.f.* **ᶜain** عین

spectacles, glasses, goggles *n.f.* **ᶜainak** عینک

ġain غ

cave, cavern *n.m.* **ġār** غار
ravage, devastation, plunder *n.f.* **ġārat** غارت
ravage, spoil, plunder *v.t.* **ġārat karnā** غارت کرنا
raider, plunderer *n.m.* **ġārat gar** غارت گر
pillage, destruction *n.f.* **ġārat garī** غارتگری
hero, conqueror *n.m.* **ġāzī** غازی
usurper, plunderer *n.m.* **ġāzib** غاصب
negligent, neglectful, inattentive *adj.* **ġāfil** غافل
overcoming, overpowering *adj.* **ġālib** غالب
overcome, overpower *v.t.* **ġālib karnā** غالب کرنا
probably, apparently *adv.* **ġāliban** غالبا
dear, precious, expensive *adj.* **ġālī** غالی
small carpet *n.m.* **ġālīcah** غالیچہ
absent, vanished, invisible *adj.* **ġā'ib** غائب
utmost, highest, extreme *adj./adv.* **ġāyat** غایت
dust; sorrow, grief *n.m.* **ġubār** غبار
dusty *adj.* **ġubār ālūdah** غبار آلودہ
be in a bad mood; take revenge *v.t.* **ġubār nikālnā** غبار نکالنا
balloon *n.m.* **ġubārah** غبارہ
cheating, fraud, embezzlement *n.m.* **ġabn** غبن
dull, weak (*in mind*); imprudent; forgetful *adj.* **ġabī** غبی
treacherous, disloyal *adj.* **ġaddār** غدار
treachery, disloyalty *n.f.* **ġaddārī** غداری
rebellion, mutiny, riot *n.f.* **ġadar** غدر
food, diet *n.f.* **ġizā** غذا
provision, nutrition *n.f.* **ġizā'iyat** غذائیت
west *n.m.* **ġurb** غرب
gargle *n.m.* **ġarārah** غرارہ
gargle *v.t.* **ġarārah karnā** غرارہ کرنا
roar, growl; frown *v.t.* **ġurrānā** غرانا
poverty; humility *n.f.* **ġurbat** غربت
poor, impoverished *adj.* **ġurbat zadah** غربت زدہ
western *adj.* **ġarbī** غربی

غرض intention, object, aim, purpose *n.f.* **ġaraz**
غرق drowned, immersed *adj.* **ġarq**
غروب sunset *n.m.* **ġurūb**
غروب آفتاب sunset *n.m.* **ġurūb-ē āftāb**
غروب ہونا set (*the sun*) *v.i.* **ġurūb hōnā**
غرور pride, haughtiness, vanity *n.m.* **ġarūr**
غریب poor, needy; humble; strange *adj.* **ġarīb**
غریبانہ humbly *adv.* **ġarībānah**
غریبی poverty; humility *n.f.* **ġarībī**
غریق drowned, immersed *adj.* **ġarīq**
غزال gazelle *n.m./n.f.* **ġazāl**
غزل ghazal (*lyric poem*) *n.m.* **ġazal**
غسل bathing *n.m.* **ġusl**
غسل خانہ bathroom, toilet *n.m.* **ġusl xānah**
غش faint, fainting, swoon *n.m.* **ġaš**
غشی swoon, fainting *n.f.* **ġašī**
غصب violence, force, oppression *n.m.* **ġasb**
غصہ anger, fury, rage *n.m.* **ġussah**
غصیلا angry, furious *adj.* **ġusīlā**
غضب violence, oppression *n.m.* **ġazab**
غضب ناک angry, furious *adj.* **ġazab nāk**
غضنفر champion, hero; lion *n.m.* **ġazanfar**
غفار merciful *adj.* **ġaffār**
غفر pardon, forgiveness *n.m.* **ġafr**
غفران pardon, forgiveness *n.m.* **ġufrān**
غفلت negligence, carelessness *n.f.* **ġaflat**
غفور forgiving, merciful *adj.* **ġafūr**
غل noise, outcry *n.m.* **ġul**
غلاظت dirt, filth *n.f.* **ġilāzat**
غلاف cover, case *n.f.* **ġilāf**
غلام slave *n.m.* **ġulām**
غلامی slavery *n.f.* **ġulāmī**
غلبہ victory, conquest; superiority *n.m.* **ġalabah**
غلط wrong, false, incorrect *adj.* **ġalat**
غلط فہمی misunderstanding *n.f.* **ġalat fahmī**
غلطی mistake, error *n.f.* **ġalatī/ġaltī**

غلطی کرنا err, make a mistake *v.t.* **ġalatī karnā**
غلغلہ tumult, noise *n.m.* **ġulġulah**
غلہ corn; grain *n.m.* **ġallah**
غلو excess, exaggeration *n.f.* **ġulū**
غلیظ dirty, filthy; obscene *adj.* **ġalīz**
غم grief, sorrow *n.m.* **ġam/ġamm**
غم خواری condolence, sympathy *n.f.* **ġam khvārī**
غم زدہ afflicted, grieved *adj.* **ġam zadah**
غمگین sad, sorrowful *adj.* **ġam gīn**
غم ناک sorrowful, woeful *adj.* **ġam nāk**
غماز backbiter *n.m.* **ġammāz**
غمازی backbiting *n.f.* **ġammāzī**
غمی grief, sorrow, mourning *n.f.* **ġamī**
غنچہ blossom, bud, rosebud *n.m.* **ġuncah**
غنڈہ vagabond, rascal *n.m.* **ġunḍah**
غنودگی drowsiness *n.f.* **ġanūdgī**
غنی rich, wealthy *adj.* **ġanī**
غنیم enemy, adversary *n.m.* **ġanīm**
غنیمت plunder; prize; boon, blessing *n.f.* **ġanīmat**
غور meditation, reflection, deep thought *n.m.* **ġaur**
غور کرنا reflect, consider, think *v.t.* **ġaur karnā**
غوطا مارنا dip, dive, plunge *v.t.* **ġōtah mārnā**
غوطہ dip, dive, plunge *n.m.* **ġōtah**
غوغا noise, uproar *n.m.* **ġauġā**
غوغائی noisy *adj.* **ġaugā'ī**
غوک frog *n.m.* **ġūk**
غول crowd, mob, gang, troop *n.m.* **ġōl**
غیاث assistance, aid *n.f.* **ġiyās**
غیب concealed, invisible, absent, mysterious *adj.* **ġaib**
غیبت slander *n.f.* **ġībat**
غیبت کرنا slander *v.t.* **ġībat karnā**
غیبی absent *adj.* **ġaibī**
غیر without, beside, except, save *pp./adv.* **ġair**
غیر آباد uninhabited *adj.* **ġair ābād**
غیر حاضر absent *adj.* **ġair ḥāzir**

غیر حاضری absence *n.f.* **ġair ḥāzirī**
غیر دلچسپ boring, dull *adj.* **ġair dilcasp**
غیر ذمہ داری irresponsibility *n.f.* **ġair zimmah dārī**
غیر متأثر ineffective *adj.* **ġair mutā'ssir**
غیر متناسب unproportional *adj.* **ġair mutanāsib**
غیر محدود unlimited, boundless, indefinite *adj.* **ġair maḥdūd**
غیر مستعمل not in use, new *adj.* **ġair mustaᶜmal**
غیر مشروط unconditional *adj.* **ġair mašrūt**
غیر مطلب unwanted, undesirable *adj.* **ġair matlub**
غیر معلوم unknown *adj.* **ġair maᶜlūm**
غیر معمولی unusual, uncommon *adj.* **ġair maᶜmūlī**
غیر مکمل imperfect, incomplete *adj.* **ġair mukammal**
غیر ممکن impossible *adj.* **ġair mumkin**
غیر مناسب unsuitable *adj.* **ġair munāsib**
غیر واجب unreasonable, wrong, improper *adj.* **ġair vājib**
غیرت shame; bashfulness, modesty; envy *n.f.* **ġairat**
غیرت کھانا feel ashamed *v.t.* **ġairat khānā**
غیرت مند bashful, modest *adj.* **ġairat mand**
غیر معتبر incredible; unreliable, deceitful *adj.* **ġair muᶜatabir**
غیریت strangeness *n.f.* **ġairiyyat**

fē ف

opening *n.m./adj.* **fātiḥ** فاتح

weak, idle, unsound *adj.* **fātir** فاتر

sinful, unchaste *adj.* **fājir** فاجر

obscene, shameless, impudent, indecent *adj.* **fāḥiš** فاحش

whore, prostitute *n.f.* **fāḥišah** فاحشہ

dove *n.f.* **fāxtah** فاختہ

excellent, honorable *adj.* **fāxir** فاخر

splendid, elegant *adj.* **fāxrah** فاخرہ

horseman *n.m.* **fāris** فارس

Persia *n.m.* **fārs** فارس

Persian *adj.* **fārsī** فارسی

free, disengaged, unoccupied *adj.* **fāriġ** فارغ

ruining, breaking, violating *adj.* **fāsix** فاسخ

corrupt, vicious, wicked, perverse *adj.* **fāsidah** فاسدہ

impious *adj.* **fāsiq** فاسق

apparent, manifest, notorious *n.m.* **fāš** فاش

distance, space, interval *n.m.* **fāsilah** فاصلہ

superfluous, abundant; accomplished *adj.* **fāzil** فاضل

talented, highly educated *adj.* **fāzil-ē-ajall** فاضل اجل

doer, operator; agent; subject *n.m.* **fāᶜil** فاعل

starvation; fasting *n.m.* **fāqah** فاقہ

starve; fast *v.t.* **fāqah karnā** فاقہ کرنا

omen, foresight *n.f.* **fāl** فال

spare, surplus, extra *adj.* **fāltu** فالتو

color, complexion *n.m.* **fām** فام

lantern, candlestick *n.m.* **fānūs** فانوس

mortal, perishable, transitory; inconsistent *adj.* **fānī** فانی

gain, profit, benefit, advantage *n.m.* **fā'idah** فائدہ

profitable, advantageous *adj.* **fā'idah mand** فائدہ مند

liberal, beneficent *adj.* **fā'iz** فائض

superior, excelling *adj.* **fā'iq** فائق

Very well!, Bravo! *interj.* **fabiha** فبہا

victory, success *n.f.* **fatḥ** فتح

فتح پانا be victorious, succeed *v.t.* **fatḥ pānā**

فتح مند victorious, triumphant *adj.* **fatḥ mand**

فتح مندی victory, triumph *n.f.* **fatḥ mandī**

فتنہ revolt, mutiny; mischief *n.m.* **fitnah**

فتنہ اٹھانا cause mischief, cause disturbance *adj.* **fitnah uṭhānā**

فتنہ انگیز mischievous, quarrelsome, turbulent *adj.* **fitnah angēz**

فتور defect, disorder; riot *n.m.* **futūr**

فتوری riotous, contentious; deceitful, treacherous *adj.* **futūrī**

فتویٰ fatwa (*religious judgment/sentence delivered by Islamic leader*) *n.m.* **fatvā**

فتیلہ wick *n.m.* **fatīlah**

فجر dawn, daybreak, early morning *n.f.* **fajr**

فحش indecent, frivolous, obscene *adj.* **fuḥš**

فخر boast, pride, glory *n.m.* **faxr**

فخریہ boastfully, proudly *adv.* **faxriyyah**

فدا devotion; sacrifice *n.m.* / devoted *adj.* **fidā**

فدا کرنا sacrifice, devote (oneself) *v.t.* **fidā karnā**

فدا ہونا be sacrificed, die (for) *v.i.* **fidā hōnā**

فدائی courageous, valiant *adj.* **fidā'ī**

فر pomp, grace, dignity *n.m.* **far/farr**

فراخ wide, extensive, ample, large *adj.* **farāx**

فراخ دل generous, open-hearted *adj.* **farāx dil**

فراخی wideness, largeness; prosperity *n.f.* **farāxī**

فرار flight, absconding *n.m.* **firār**

فراز high, aloft *adj.* / ascent, height, elevation *n.m.* **farāz**

فرازی highness, exaltation *n.f.* **farāzī**

فراست perception, discernment; penetration, understanding *n.f.* **firāsat**

فراغت repose, leisure *n.f.* **farāġat**

فراق separation; anxiety *n.m.* **firāq**

فراموش forgotten, neglected *adj.* **farāmōš**

فراموش کرنا forget *v.t.* **farāmōš karnā**

فراہم collected, gathered *adj.* **farāham**

فراہم کرنا collect, gather; deliver *v.t.* **farāham karnā**

فراہمی collection *n.f.* **farāhamī**

فراواں abundant, copious, opulent *adj.* **farāvāṁ**

فراوانی abundance, plentifulness *n.f.* **firāvānī**

فربہ fat, plump, stout *adj.* **farbah**
فربہی fatness, plumpness *n.f.* **farbahī**
فرتوت very old *adj.* **fartūt**
فرج fridge, refrigerator *n.m.* **frij**
فرجام end, conclusion *n.m.* **farjām**
فرح pleasure, joy *n.f.* **faraḥ**
فرحاں cheerful, joyful, merry *adj.* **farḥaṁ**
فرحت pleasure, cheerfulness, joy *n.f.* **farḥat**
فرحت افزاء amusing, entertaining *adj.* **farḥat afzā'**
فرحت بخش refreshing, pleasant *adj.* **farḥat baxš**
فرخ lucky, fortunate *adj.* **farrux**
فرخندہ happy, fortunate *adj.* **farxandah**
فرد individual *adj.* / list; sheet (of paper); fragment, verse *n.m.* **fard**
فردوس paradise, heaven; garden *n.m.* **firdaus**
فرزانگی wisdom, intellect *n.f.* **farzānagī**
فرزانہ intelligent, wise *adj.* **farzānah**
فرزند child *n.m.* **farzand**
فرس horse *n.m.* **faras**
فرستادہ messenger, ambassador, envoy *n.m.* / sent *adj.* **firistādah**
فرسنگ league *n.m.* **farsang**
فرسودگی decay, wear, tear *n.f.* **firsudgī**
فرسودہ spoiled, rotten, torn *adj.* **farsūdah**
فرش floor, pavement *n.m.* **farš**
فرشتہ angel, prophet, messenger *n.m.* **farištah**
فرصت leisure, rest, leave *n.f.* **fursat**
فرض duty, responsibility *n.m.* **farz**
فرض کرنا impose (a duty); suppose, assume *v.t.* **farz karnā**
فرضا for instance *adv.* **farzan**
فرضی incumbent, indispensable, imperative, supposed, nominal *adj.* **farzī**
فرط abundance, excess, predominance *n.f.* **fart**
فرعونی arrogance; tyranny oppression, despotism *n.f.* **firᶜaunī**
فرفر fluently, quickly *adv.* **farfar**
فرق difference, distinction *n.m.* **farq**
فرقت separation, distinction *n.f.* **furqat**
فرقہ sect, tribe, class *n.m.* **firqah**

order, command *n.m.* **farmān** فرمان
obedient *adj.* **farmān ravā** فرمان روا
order, command; say, declare *v.t.* **farmānā** فرمانا
order, command *n.f.* **farmā'iš** فرمائش
ordered, desired *adj.* **farmā'išī** فرمائشی
order, command *v.t.* **farmā'iš karnā** فرمائش کرنا
Europe *n.m.* **farang** فرنگ
Europe *n.m.* **farangistān** فرنگستان
European, white (*skin color*) *adj.* **farangī** فرنگی
dictionary, vocabulary, glossary *n.f.* **farhang** فرہنگ
under, down, below *pp.* **farō/firō** فرو
suppress *v.t.* **farō karnā** فرو کرنا
omission, overlooking *n.f.* **farō guzāšt** فروگزاشت
weak, humble, poor, worthless *adj.* **farō māyah** فرومایہ
subside; be extinguished *v.i.* **farō hōnā** فرو ہونا
humility *n.f.* **firōtī** فروتی
sale, disposal *n.f.* **farōxt** فروخت
sell *v.t.* **farōxt karnā** فروخت کرنا
sold *adj.* **farūxtah** فروختہ
descending, alighting; stopping, halting *n.m.* / down, beneath *adv.* **farōd** فرود
February *n.f.* **farvarī** فروری
luminous, shining *adj.* **furōzāṁ** فروزاں
vendor, seller *n.m.* **farōšindah** فروشندہ
indirect; additional *adj.* **furūʿī** فروعی
illumination, brightness, light *n.m.* **farōġ** فروغ
illuminate; promote *v.t.* **farōġ dēnā** فروغ دینا
omit, leave out, overlook *v.t.* **farō guzāštī karnā** فروگزاشتی کرنا
complaint, case, charge, suit *n.f.* **faryād** فریاد
complain, file a suit, sue *v.t.* **faryād karnā** فریاد کرنا
complaint *n.f.* **faryādī** فریادی
trick, fraud, deceit *n.m.* **farēb** فریب
tricky, deceitful *adj.* **farēb āmēz** فریب آمیز
deceive, cheat *v.t.* **farēb dēnā** فریب دینا
pretend, play a trick *v.t.* **farēb karnā** فریب کرنا
dishonest, deceitful, insincere *adj.* / cheat, impostor *n.f.* **farēbī** فریبی

unique, singular, incomparable *adj.* **farīd** فرید
in love, charmed, fascinated *adj.* / lover *n.m.* **farēftah** فریفتہ
be fascinated, fall in love *v.i.* **farēftah hōnā** فریفتہ ہونا
order; section, division, department *n.m.* **farīq** فریق
quarrel, riot, disturbance, brawl *n.m.* **fasād** فساد
quarrelsome, rebellious *adj.* **fasādī** فسادی
fiction, tale; romance *n.m.* **fasānah** فسانہ
spreading, scattering, diffusing *adj.* **fišāṁ** فشاں
eloquence, pure language *n.f.* **fasāḥat** فصاحت
chapter, part, section, division; season *n.f.* **fasl** فصل
spring (*season*) *n.f.* **fasl-ē-bahār** فصل بہار
autumn, fall *n.f.* **fasl-ē-xarīf** فصل خریف
spring (*season*) *n.f.* **fasl-ē-rabīᶜ** فصل ربیع
harvest *v.t.* **fasl kāṭnā** فصل کاٹنا
eloquent *adj.* **fasīḥ** فصیح
rampart, city wall *n.f.* **fasīl** فصیل
atmosphere; open space *n.f.* **fazā** فضا
leaving, refuse; reminder; redundance *n.m.* **fuzlah** فضلہ
useless, needless, futile; exuberant *adj.* **fuzūl** فضول
extravagant *adj.* **fuzūl xarc** فضول خرچ
excellence, perfection *n.f.* **fazīlat** فضیلت
nature, creation, form *n.f.* **fitrat** فطرت
natural; wise *adj.* **fitratī** فطرتی
verb; work, action, deed *n.m.* **fiᶜil** فعل
practically, in fact, indeed *adv.* **fiᶜilan** فعلاً
lost, gone; astonished; pale *adj.* **faqq** فق
poverty *n.m.* **faqr** فقر
sentence, phrase *n.m.* **fiqrah** فقرہ
simply, merely, only *adv.* **faqat** فقط
theology, knowledge (*of Islamic laws*) *n.f.* **fiqah/fiqh** فقہ
lost, absent *adj.* **faqīd** فقید
unique, incomparable, matchless *adj.* **faqīd-ul-misāl** فقیدالمثال
beggar; worshipper, saint *n.m.* **faqīr** فقیر
poverty, beggary; humility (*in a religious way*) *n.f.* **faqīrī** فقیری
idea, thought, opinion *n.m./n.f.* **fikr** فکر
think, consider, reflect *v.t.* **fikr karnā** فکر کرنا

thoughtful; sad, sorrowful *adj.* **fikr mand** فکر مند
wounded, sore; confused, distracted *adj.* **figār** فگار
deliverance; happiness; prosperity *n.f.* **falāḥ** فلاح
adversity, misfortune *n.f.* **falākat** فلاکت
flannel *n.f.* **falālīn** فلالین
such one, such thing, so and so, a certain one *n.m.* **fulān** فلان
philosophy *n.m.* **falsafah** فلسفہ
philosopher *n.m.* **falsafī** فلسفی
philosophical *adj.* **falsafiyānah** فلسفیانہ
pepper *n.f.* **filfil** فلفل
sky, heaven *n.m.* **falak** فلک
heavenly *adj.* **falakī** فلکی
film *n.f.* **film/filim** فلم
wick, fuse, torch *n.m.* **falītah** فلیتہ
art, craft; skill *n.m.* **fann** فن
artist (*male*) *n.m.* **fann kār** فن کار
artist (*female*) *n.f.* **fann kārah** فن کارہ
mortality *n.f.* **fanā** فنا
perish, die *v.i.* **fanā hōnā** فنا ہونا
list, index, inventory *n.f.* **fihrist** فہرست
understanding, comprehension *n.m.* **fahm** فہم
instruction, explanation; warning *n.f.* **fahmā'iš** فہمائش
instruct, explain; warn *v.t.* **fahmā'iš karnā** فہمائش
understood; intelligent, wise *adj.* **fahmīdah** فہمیدہ
spring, fountain *n.m.* **favvārah** فوارہ
death *n.f.* **faut** فوت
take a photo *v.t.* **fōṭō khaiṁcnā** فوٹو کھینچنا
take a photo *v.t.* **fōṭō lēnā** فوٹو کھینچنا، فوٹو لینا
photo *n.m.* **fōṭō** فوٹو، تصویر
photographer *n.m.* **fōṭōgrāfar** فوٹوگرافر
army *n.f.* **fauj** فوج
navy *n.f.* **fauj-ē-baḥrī** فوج بحری
land forces *n.f.* **fauj-ē-bar** فوج بر
criminal court; criminal case *n.f.* **fauj dārī** فوج داری
military *adj.* **faujī** فوجی

soldier *n.m.* **faujī sipāhī** فوجی سپاہی
immediately, at once *adv.* **fauran** فوراً
purse, bag; tax, revenue *n.m.* **fōtah** فوطہ
superiority, excellence, loftiness; summit; altitude *n.m.* **fauq** فوق
preference; superiority, excellence *n.f.* **fauqiyyat** فوقیت
steel *n.m.* **faulād** فولاد
made of steel *adj.* **faulādī** فولادی
telephone *n.m.* **fōn** فون
phone, call *v.t.* **fōn karnā** فون کرنا
per, for, by, in, into, among *pp.* / defect, fault *n.f.* **fī** فی
now, presently *adv.* **fīl-ḥāl** فی الحال
nowadays *adv.* **fī zamānah** فی زمانہ
liberal *adj.* **faiyyāz** فیاض
ribbon, tape *n.m.* **fītah** فیتہ
victorious *adj.* **fīrōz** فیروز
victorious, prosperous *adj.* **fīrōz mand** فیروز مند
turquoise (*gem*) *n.m.* **fīrōzah** فیروزہ
turquoise (*color*) *adj.* **fīrōzī** فیروزی
fee *n.f.* **fīs** فیس
fashion *n.m.* **faišan** فیشن
decision; division, separation *n.m.* / decided, settled *adj.* **faisal** فیصل
decide *v.t.* **faisal karnā** فیصل کرنا
settlement, arbitration; decision *n.m.* **faislah** فیصلہ
judicial decision *n.m.* **faislah-ē-ᶜadālat** فیصلۂ عدالت
settle, decide *v.t.* **faisalah karnā** فیصلہ کرنا
bounty, abundance, liberality *n.m.* **faiz** فیض
public good *n.m.* **faiz-ē-ᶜām** فیض عام
benefited, blessed *adj.* **faiz yāb** فیض یاب
beneficence, generosity *adj.* **faizān** فیضان
fax *n.m.* **faiks** فیکس
elephant *n.m.* **fīl** فیل
elephant driver *n.m.* **fīl bān** فیل بان
turkey *n.m.* **fīl murġ** فیل مرغ
/ philosopher; crooked person *n.m.* **failsūf** فیلسوف
intelligent, wise; crooked, cunning *adj.*

ق qāf

large plate; vessel, case, frame *n.f.* / space, interval *n.m.* **qāb** قاب
/ holding, occupying, seizing, possessing *adj.* **qābiz** قابض
holder, occupant, occupier *n.m.*
worthy, deserving; capable *adj.* **qābil** قابل
credible, trustworthy *adj.* **qābil-ē-iᶜtibār** قابلِ اعتبار
pitiable *adj.* **qābil-ē-afsōs** قابلِ افسوس
transferable *adj.* **qābil-ē-intiqāl** قابلِ انتقال
praiseworthy *adj.* **qābil-ē-taᶜrīf** قابلِ تعریف
answerable *adj.* **qābil-ē-javāb** قابلِ جواب
pardonable *adj.* **qābil-ē-muᶜāfī** قابلِ معافی
be competent, deserve *v.i.* **qābil hōnā** قابل ہونا
midwife *n.f.* **qābilah** قابلہ
capacity, capability, possibility, ability, accomplishment *n.f.* **qābiliyyat** قابلیت
power, command, authority *n.m.* **qābū** قابو
fatal, deadly *adj.* / murderer, assassin *n.m.* **qātil** قاتل
potent, powerful *adj.* **qādir** قادر
goose; duck *n.f.* **qāz** قاز
distributor *n.m.* **qāsim** قاسم
slice; eyebrow *n.f.* **qāš** قاش
messenger, envoy *n.m.* **qāsid** قاصد
failing, unable, deficient *adj.* **qāsir** قاصر
judge, magistrate *n.m.* **qāzī** قاضی
decisive, final, definite; sharp, cutting *adj.* **qātiᶜ** قاطع
custom, rule, system; base, basis *n.m.* **qāᶜidah** قاعدہ
caravan *n.m.* **qāfilah** قافلہ
rhyme *n.m.* **qāfiyah** قافیہ
cardamom *n.m.* **qāqulah** قاقلہ
model, mold, form, frame *n.m.* **qālib** قالب
tapestry *n.m.* **qālīcah** قالیچہ
woolen carpet *n.m.* **qālīn** قالین
statue, figure *n.f.* **qāmat** قامت
contented, satisfied *n.m.* **qāniᶜ** قانع
law, rule, regulation *n.m.* **qānūn** قانون

legislate, make laws *v.t.* **qānūn banānā** قانون بنانا
lawyer *n.m.* **qānūn dān** قانون دان
legislator *n.m.* **qānūn gō** قانون گو
legally, lawfully, by law *adv.* **qānūnan** قانوناً
legal, lawful, constitutional *adj.* **qānūnī** قانونی
leader *n.m.* **qā'id** قائد
confessing, agreeing, convinced *adj.* **qā'il** قائل
convince *v.t.* **qā'il karnā** قائل کرنا
erect, standing, established, firm *adj.* **qā'im** قائم
firmness, durability *n.f.* **qā'imī** قائمی
defect, trouble, deficiency *n.f.* **qabāḥat** قباحت
baseness; deformity *n.m.* **qubḥ** قبح
grave, tomb *n.f.* **qabr** قبر
graveyard, cemetery *n.m.* **qabristān** قبرستان
contraction, possession, seizure; constipation *n.m.* **qabz** قبض
receipt, acquittance, acknowledgement *n.m.* **qabz-ul-vasūl** قبض الوصول
grip, hold; possession *n.m.* **qabzah** قبضہ
before, beforehand *adv.* / previous, preliminary *adj.* **qabl** قبل
before this, prior to this *adv.* **qabal az vaqt** قبل از وقت
dome, arch *n.m.* **qubbah** قبہ
consent, assent, approbation, admission *n.m.* **qabūl/qubūl** قبول
bad, vile, detestable, shameful; ugly, deformed *adj.* **qabīḥ** قبیح
race, tribe; category, species, class, sort *n.m.* **qabīl** قبیل
tribe, clan, family *n.m.* **qabīlah** قبیلہ
battle, fighting, murder *n.m.* **qitāl** قتال
murder, killing, homicide, slaughter, massacre *n.m.* **qatl** قتل
famine, dearth, scarcity *n.m.* **qaḥt** قحط
famine, drought *n.f.* **qaḥt sālī** قحط سالی
stature, height, size *n.m.* **qadd** قد
antiquity *n.f.* **qadāmat** قدامت
conservative *adj.* **qadāmat pasand** قدامت پسند
tall, high *adj.* **qadd āvar** قدآور
goblet, bowl *n.m.* **qadaḥ** قدح
dignity, respect, value, rank, merit, honor *n.f.* **qadr** قدر
nature, ability; force, authority; divine power *n.f.* **qudrat** قدرت

قدرتی **qudratī** natural; divine *adj.*
قدرومنزلت **qadr-ō-manzilat** dignity, rank *n.f.*
قدرے **qadrē** somewhat, to some extent, a little *adv.*
قدرے قدرے **qadrē qadrē** little by little *adv.*
قدسی **qudsī** holy *adj.*
قدسیہ **qudsiyah** holy, celestial *adj.*
قدم **qadam** foot; footstep, pace *n.m.*
قدوقامت **qadd-ō-qāmat** stature, figure, posture *n.m.*
قدیم **qadīm** old, ancient *adj.*
قدیمی **qadīmī** old, ancient; former *adj.*
قرابت **qarābat** nearness, affinity; relationship *n.f.*
قرابتی **qarābatī** related to, akin, relative *adj.*
قرات **qirāt** reading, recitation, utterance, pronunciation *n.f.*
قرار **qarār** stability (of mind), rest, quietness, peace; settlement, agreement *n.m.*
قرار پانا **qarār pānā** be quiet; be determined; receive *v.t.*
قرارداد **qarār dād** agreement, resolution, settlement *n.m.*
قرار واقعی **qarār vaqā'ī** positively, rightly, accurately *adv.*
قرآن **qur'ān** Quran *n.m.*
قرآن شریف **qur'ān šarīf** Holy Quran *n.m.*
قرب **qurb** vicinity, nearness *n.m.*
قربان **qurbān** sacrifice, offering *n.m.*
قربان گاہ **qurbān gāh** altar *n.f.*
قربانی **qurbānī** sacrifice *n.f.*
قربت **qurbat** relationship, nearness, intimacy *n.m.*
قرحہ **qarḥah** sore, wound *n.m.*
قرض **qarz** debt, loan *n.m.*
قرض خواہ **qarz xvāh** creditor *n.m.*
قرض دار **qarz dār** debtor *n.m.* / indebted *adj.*
قرضہ **qarzah** debt, loan *n.m.*
قرطاس **qirtās** paper *n.m.*
قرق **qurq** embargo; confiscation, seizure *n.m.*
قرنائی **qarnā'ī** trumpet *n.f.*
قرنفل **qaranfal** clove *n.m.*
قریب **qarīb** near, nearby, adjacent, next (to) *adj.* / almost *adv.*
قریباً **qarīban** nearly, approximately, shortly *adv.*
قریبی **qarībī** near, adjacent; akin, relative; intimate *adj.*

order, context; analogy *n.m.* **qarīnah** قرینہ
village, town *n.m.* **qaryah** قریہ
robber; pirate *n.m.* **qazzāq** قزاق
division, kind, sort, part *n.f.* **qism** قسم
oath *n.m.* **qasam** قسم
swear, take an oath *v.t.* **qasam khānā** قسم کھانا
fate, destiny, luck, fortune, lot *n.f.* **qismat** قسمت
fortunately, luckily, by chance *adv.* **qismat sē** قسمت سے
fortunate, lucky *adj.* **qismat vālā** قسمت والا
sharer, partner; distributor, divider *n.m.* **qasīm** قسیم
butcher *n.m.* **qassāb** قصاب
merciless *adj.* / butcher *n.m.* **qasā'ī** قصائی
small town, village *n.m.* **qasbah** قصبہ
intention, wish, desire *n.m.* **qasd** قصد
intend; pursue; resolve *v.t.* **qasd karnā** قصد کرنا
intentionally, deliberately *adv.* **qasdan** قصداً
palace, mansion, citadel *n.m.* **qasr** قصر
government house *n.m.* **qasr-ē-ḥukūmat** قصر حکومت
story, tale *n.m.* **qissah** قصہ
defect, error, fault, sin *n.m.* **qusūr** قصور
guilty, faulty *adj.* **qusūr vār** قصور دار
poem, ode *n.m.* **qasīdah** قصیدہ
destiny, fate *n.f.* **qazā** قضا
case, quarrel, dispute, debate *n.m.* **qaziyah** قضیہ
line, row, rank, order, series; train *n.m.* **qitār/qatār** قطار
stand in a line, form a queue *v.t.* **qatār bāndhnā** قطار باندھنا
pivot, pole; polar star *n.m.* **qutb** قطب
South Pole, Antarctic *n.m.* **qutb-ē-junūbī** قطب جنوبی
North Pole, Arctic *n.m.* **qutb-ē-šimālī** قطب شمالی
polar *adj.* **qutbī** قطبی
drop, very small quantity *n.m.* **qatrah** قطرہ
cutting, segment, portion; shape, style *n.m.* **qata^c** قطع
abandon, desert, cut off all connections *v.t.* **qata^c-ē-ta^clluq karnā** قطع تعلق کرنا
plot, piece, part, fragment *n.m.* **qit^cah/qat^cah** قطعہ
final, complete, decisive, conclusive *adj.* **qata^cī** قطعی
sitting; kneeling *n.m.* **qa^cdah** قعدہ

قعر **qaʿr** *n.m.* abyss, bottom, depth
قفس **qafas** *n.m.* cage; network, lattice
قفل **qufl** *n.m.* lock, bolt
قلابہ **qulābah** *n.m.* hook, buckle
قلاش **qallāš** *adj.* poor; shameless, shrewd, malicious
قلب **qalb** *n.m.* heart; mind, soul, intellect
قلبی **qalbī** *adj.* cordial; hearty
قلعہ **qilʿah/qalʿah** *n.m.* fort, castle
قلعی **qalaʿī** *n.f.* tin
قلعی گر **qalaʿī gar** *n.m.* tinsmith, tinner
قلفی **qulfī** *n.f.* kulfi (*a sort of ice-cream*)
قلق **qalaq** *n.m.* discomfort, anxiety; regret, grief
قلم **qalam** *n.m.* pen; reed
قلم رو **qalam rau** *n.f.* empire, kingdom; jurisdiction
قلم کرنا **qalam karnā** *v.t.* cut off, prune, behead
قلمی **qalmī** *adj.* handwritten
قلندر **qalandar** *n.m.* hermit, monk
قلہ **qullah** *n.m.* top, peak, summit (*of a mountain*)
قلی **qulī** *n.m.* coolie, porter, laborer
قمار **qimār** *n.m.* dice
قمار باز **qimār bāz** *n.m.* gambler
قمار بازی **qimār bāzī** *n.f.* gambling
قماش **qumāš** *n.m.* household items; kind manners
قمچی **qamcī** *n.f.* whip, rod, twig
قمر **qamar** *n.m.* moon
قمرا **qamrā** *n.m.* moonlight
قمری **qamarī** *adj.* lunar
قمری **qumrī** *n.m.* turtledove
قمیض **qamīz** *n.m.* shirt
قناعت **qanāʿat** *n.f.* contentment, tranquility
قند **qand** *n.m.* sugar
قندیل **qindīl** *n.f.* candle, lamp
قنوت **qanūt** *n.f.* obedience (*to God*), devotion, piety
قنوط **qunūt** *n.f.* despair
قنوطیت **qunūtiyyat** *n.f.* frustration, pessimism

law *n.m.* **qanūn** قنون
strict, avenging *adj.* / deity, god *n.m.* **qahhār** قہار
severity; calamity; fury *n.m.* **qahr** قہر
by force *adv.* **qahran** قہراً
burst, loud laughter *n.m.* **qahqahah** قہقہہ
burst into laughter *v.t.* **qahqahah mārnā** قہقہہ مارنا
coffee *n.m.* **qahvah** قہوہ
coffee-house *n.m.* **qahvah xānah** قہوہ خانہ
grammar *n.m.* **qavāʿid** قواعد
singer, musician *n.m.* **qavvāl** قوال
qawwali (*a music style*) *n.f.* **qavvālī** قوالی
justice *n.m.* **qavām** قوام
food; livelihood *n.f.* **qūt** قوت
power, strength, vigor, energy *n.f.* **quvvat** قوت
power of attraction *n.f.* **quvvat-ē-jāzibah** قوت جاذبہ
physical strength *n.f.* **quvvat-ē-jismānī** قوت جسمانی
mental power, memory *n.f.* **quvvat-ē-ḥāfizah** قوت حافظہ
power of the heart, power of the mind *n.f.* **quvvat-ē-dil** قوت دل
korma (*a meat curry*) *n.m.* **qōrmah** قورمہ
bow, arc; Sagittarius (*Zodiac*) *n.f.* **qaus** قوس
rainbow *n.f.* **qaus-ē-quzaḥ** قوس قزح
curved, bow-shaped *adj.* **qausī** قوسی
word, saying, speech; promise, consent *n.m.* **qaul** قول
give one's word, promise *v.t.* **qaul dēnā** قول دینا
nation; tribe, caste, sect, race *n.m.* **qaum** قوم
national; tribal, racial *adj.* **qaumī** قومی
national government *n.f.* **qaumī ḥukūmat** قومی حکومت
national assembly *n.f.* **qaumī majlis** قومی مجلس
nationality, citizenship *n.f.* **qaumiyyat** قومیت
consul, envoy *n.m.* **qaunsal** قونصل
strong, powerful, solid, firm *adj.* **qavī** قوی
strong-hearted, strong-minded *adj.* **qavī dil** قوی دل
strong, mighty, robust *adj.* **qavī haikal** قوی ہیکل
vomiting, vomit *n.f.* **qai** قے
feel nausea; be sick (of) *v.i.* **qai ānā** قے آنا
vomit *v.t.* **qai karnā** قے کرنا

قیاس supposition, presumption, guess *n.m.* **qiyās**
قیاس کرنا suppose, conceive, guess *v.t.* **qiyās karnā**
قیاسا by conjecture, by analogy *adv.* **qiyāsan**
قیاسی imaginary *adj.* **qiyāsī**
قیافہ guess; countenance, likeness, appearance, mode, look *n.m.* **qiyāfah**
قیام stay, settlement, standing, residence *n.m.* **qiyām**
قیام کرنا stay, put up, halt *v.t.* **qiyām karnā**
قیامت resurrection; doomsday *n.f* / huge, great, extreme, excessive *adj.* **qiyāmat**
قید confinement, imprisonment, restraint; obstacle; obligation *n.f.* **qaid**
قید خانہ prison, jail *n.m.* **qaid xānah**
قید رکھنا keep in custody *v.t.* **qaid rakhnā**
قید کرنا imprison, captivate *v.t.* **qaid karnā**
قیدی prisoner *n.m.* **qaidī**
قیصر Caesar, emperor, sovereign *n.m.* **qaisar**
قیل word, speech *n.m.* **qīl**
قیل وقال controversy; dialogue, chit chat, conversation *n.f.* **qīl-ō-qāl**
قیلولہ midday nap, siesta *n.m.* **qāilūlah**
قیم true, correct; erect, standing *adj.*. **qaiyyim**
قیمت price, value, cost, worth *n.f.* **qīmat**
قیمت چکانا settle the price *v.t.* **qīmat cukānā**
قیمت لگانا fix a price *v.t.* **qīmat lagānā**
قیمتاً on payment *adv.* **qīmatan**
قیمتی valuable, costly, expensive *adj.* **qīmatī**
قیمہ minced meat *n.m.* **qīmah**
قینچی scissors *n.f.* **qaiṁcī**
قینچی کرنا prune, trim *v.t.* **qaiṁcī karnā**
قیوم permanent, everlasting *adj.* **qayūm**

کـ kāf

of, belonging, concerning *pp.* **kā** کا

pigeon-house, dove-cage *n.f.* **kābuk** کابک

bolt *n.m.* **kāblah** کابلہ

nightmare *n.m.* **kābūs** کابوس

writer, calligrapher; copyist, clerk *n.m.* **kātib** کاتب

spin, twist *v.t.* **kātnā** کاتنا

account, account-book; pit *n.m.* **khātah** کھاتہ

bedstead, sofa, couch *n.f.* **khāṭ** کھاٹ

cut, cutting, incision, wound, clip; section, separation, deduction *n.f.* **kāṭ** کاٹ

cut, clip; deduct; correct *v.t.* **kāṭ chānṭ kārnā** کاٹ چھانٹ کرنا

cut off, hew, amputate *v.t.* **kāṭ ḍālnā** کاٹ ڈالنا

bite *v.t.* **kāṭ khānā** کاٹ کھانا

wound, cut; contradict *v.t.* **kāṭ karnā** کاٹ کرنا

cut, clip, saw, bite, sever, cleave; eliminate *v.t.* **kāṭnā** کاٹنا

wood, timber *n.m.* **kāṭh** کاٹھ

puppet, doll; toy *n.f.* **kāṭh putlī** کاٹھ پتلی

fool, stupid person, half-wit *n.m.* **kāṭh kā ullū** کاٹھ کا الو

bier, coffin *n.f.* **kāṭh kī ghōṛī** کاٹھ کی گھوڑی

wood, timber; frame, shape, structure; saddle *n.f.* **kaṭhī** کاٹھی

itch *n.f.* **khāj** کھاج

business, affair, action *n.m.* **kāj** کاج

kohl (*black eye cosmetic*) *n.m.* **kājal** کاجل

apply kohl *v.t.* **kājal lagānā** کاجل لگانا

cashew-nut *n.m.* **kājū** کاجو

upper story, balcony; place, villa; tower *n.m.* **kāx** کاخ

timid, cowardly *adj.* **kādar** کادر

cotton cloth *n.f.* **khādī** کھادی

liar *n.m.* **kāzib** کاذب

/ action, affair, work, operation, profession, labor, business, function, duty *n.m.* **kār** کار
automobile, motor-car *n.f.*

useful, serviceable *adj.* **kār āmad** کار آمد

obedient, dutiful *adj.* **kār band** کاربند

cartridge *n.m.* **kārtūs** کارتوس

embroidery *n.f.* **kār cōbī** کار چوبی

factory, workshop, garage; laboratory *n.m.* **kār xānah** کارخانہ

war, battle, conflict *n.m.* **kār zār** کارزار

worker, agent *n.m.* **kār kun** کارکن

workshop *n.f.* **kār gāh** کارگاہ

effective, efficient *adj.* **kār gar** کارگر

salty, brackish *adj.* **khārā** کھارا

workmanship; action, policy; trick *n.f.* **kārastānī** کارستانی

manager, agent, officer, representative *n.m.* **kārindah** کارندہ

caravan *n.m.* **kārvāṁ** کارواں

inn, caravan serai *n.f.* **kārvāṁ sarā'ē** کارواں سرائے

business, trade; employment, occupation, profession *n.m.* **kārōbār** کاروبار

businessman, trader *n.m.* **kārōbārī** کاروباری

fatal, deadly *adj.* **kārī** کاری

fatal wound *n.m.* **kārī zaxm** کاری زخم

skill, workmanship *n.f.* **kārī garī** کاری گری

canal, aqueduct, water course *n.m.* **kārēz** کاریز

workman, artist, laborer *n.m.* **kārīgar** کاریگر

bay, creek *n.f.* **khāṛī** کھاڑی

endive *n.f.* **kāsnī** کاسنی

cup, goblet, bowl; plate *n.m.* **kāsah** کاسہ

May it so happen!, God grant! *interj.* **kāš** کاش

house, residence *n.m.* **kāšānah** کاشانہ

cultivation, field *n.f.* **kāšt** کاشت

cultivator, farmer *n.m.* **kāšt kār** کاشت کار

cultivation, agriculture *n.f.* **kāšt kārī** کاشت کاری

cultivate *v.t.* **kāšt karnā** کاشت کرنا

discoverer, exposer, revealer, detective *n.m.* **kāšif** کاشف

suppressing (one's anger) *adj.* **kāzim** کاظم

paper; leaf *n.m.* **kāğaz** کاغذ

infidel, idolater *n.m.* / impious, infidel *adj.* **kāfir** کافر

evaporate, disappear *v.i.* **kāfūr hō jānā** کافور ہوجانا

sufficient, enough *adj.* / coffee *n.f.* **kāfī** کافی

elder brother; uncle (*father's brother*) *n.m.* **kākā** کاکا

curl, lock *n.f.* **kākul** کاکل

aunt (*father's sister*) *n.f.* **kākī** کاکی

کاگ **kāg** crow, raven *n.m.*
کھال **khāl** skin, hide; bellows; river, canal, creek *n.f.*
کال **kāl** time, season, age; death; famine *n.m.*
کھال اتارنا **khāl utārnā** peel, skin *v.t.*
کالا **kālā** black, dark *adj.*
کالا منہ **kālā muṁh** defamed, disgraced, sinful *adj.*
کالبد **kālbud** body, frame, structure, form *n.m.*
کالک **kālak/kālik** blackness, darkness *n.f.*
کالک کا ٹیکا **kālak kā ṭīkā** black spot, stain; disgrace *n.m.*
کالک کا ٹیکا لگنا **kālak kā ṭīkā lagnā** defame, disgrace *v.i.*
کالی آندھی **kālī āndhī** hurricane *n.f.*
کالی زبان **kālā zabān** inauspicious *adj.*
کام **kām** action, act, task; occupation, profession; use, need, purpose *n.m.* work, business;
کام آنا **kām ānā** be of use, be used *v.i.*
کام تمام کرنا **kām tamām karnā** finish, accomplish *v.t.*
کام چور **kām cōr** shirker, idler *n.m.*
کام خانہ **kām xānah** factory *n.m.*
کام کاج **kām kāj** labor, industry, activity *n.m.*
کام کرنا **kām karnā** work *v.t.*
کامران **kāmrān** lucky, fortunate; successful *adj.*
کامرانی **kāmrānī** success; happiness; luck *n.f.*
کامل **kāmil** accomplished, perfect, complete *adj.*
کاملہ **kāmilah** accomplished, perfect complete *adj.*
کامنی **kāmnī** charming, loving *adj.*
کامیاب **kāmyāb** successful, victorious, prosperous *adj.*
کامیابی **kāmyābī** success, victory, prosperity *n.f.*
کان **kān** ear *n.m.* / mine, quarry *n.f.*
کان کا کچا **kān kā kaccā** credulous *adj.*
کان کن **kān kan** miner *n.m.*
کان کنی **kān kanī** mining *n.f.*
کھانا **khānā** eat, consume; suffer, endure *v.t.*
کانا **kānā** one-eyed *adj.*
کانا پھوسی **kānā phūsī** whispering *n.f.*
کانا پھوسی کرنا **kānā phūsī karnā** whisper *v.t.*
کانپ اٹھنا **kāṁp uṭhnā** shiver from fear *v.i.*

shiver, tremble *v.i.* **kāṁpnā** کانپنا
fork; thorn; bait, hook *n.m.* **kānṭā** کانٹا
prick a thorn *v.i.* **kānṭā cubhnā** کانٹا چبھنا
glass *n.f.* **kāṁc** کانچ
tray, basket *n.m.* **khāṁcā** کھانچا
shoulder *n.m.* **kāndhā** کاندھا
sugar *n.m.* **khānḍ** کھانڈ
cough *v.i.* **khāṁsnā** کھانسنا
cough *n.f.* **khāṁsī** کھانسی
cough *v.i.* **khāṁsī ānā** کھانسی آنا
grass, straw, hay *n.m.* **kāh** کاہ
anxiety; decline, decay, diminution *n.f.* **kahiš** کاہش
lazy, indolent *adj.* **kāhil** کاہل
laziness, indolence *n.f.* **kāhilī** کاہلی
priest; magician, wizard *n.m.* **kāhan** کاہن
greenness *n.f.* **kāhī** کاہی
for what?, why? *adv.* **kāhē kō** کاہے کو
extravagant *adj.* **khā'ū uṛā'ō** کھاؤ اڑاؤ
digging, searching, research, enquiry *n.f.* **kāviš** کاوش
body; appearance; person *n.m.* **kāyā** کایا
world, universe *n.f.* **kā'ināt** کائنات
ditch, trench, drain *n.f.* **khā'ī** کھائی
stingy; clever, cunning *adj.* **kā'iyāṁ** کائیاں
scooter *n.m.* **kā'inēṭik** کائینیٹک
hump *n.m.* **kub** • when? *adv.* **kab** کب
hump-backed *adj.* **kubā** کبا
kabab (*roasted meat*) *n.m.* **kabāb** کباب
roast; burst *v.t.* **kabāb karnā** کباب کرنا
liver; heart *n.m.* **kabid** کبد
greatness, grandeur; pride, dignity *n.m.* **kibr** کبر
old age *n.f.* **kibar** کبر
greatness, magnificence, pride *n.m.* **kibriyā** کبریا
sulphur *n.f.* **kibrīt** کبریت
pigeon *n.m.* **kabūtar** کبوتر
dark blue, azure *adj.* **kabūd** کبود
grief, affliction *n.f.* **kabīdagī** کبیدگی

afflicted, grieved *adj.* **kabīdah** کبیدہ
large, immense, great *adj.* **kabīr** کبیر
sometimes, rarely, seldom, ever *adv.* **kabhī** کبھی
sometimes, occasionally, at times, now and then *adv.* **kabhī kabhī** کبھی کبھی
never *adv.* **kabhī nahīṁ** کبھی نہیں
become fat *v.i.* **kuppā hōnā** کپا ہونا
cotton, cotton-plant *n.f.* **kapās** کپاس
destroy; finish, exhaust, absorb, use up *v.t.* **khapānā** کھپانا
sale, demand, consumption *n.f.* **khapat** کھپت
cloth, clothes, dress *n.m.* **kapṛā** کپڑا
clothes *n.m.* **kapṛē** کپڑے
take off (clothes) *v.t.* **kapṛē utārnā** کپڑے اتارنا
put on (clothes), wear *v.t.* **kapṛē pahannā** کپڑے پہننا
shiver, tremble *v.i.* **kapkapānā** کپکپانا
shivering, trembling *n.f.* **kapkapī** کپکپی
dog *n.m.* **kuttā** کتا
book, writing *n.f.* **kitāb** کتاب
bookworm, studious person *n.m.* **kitāb kā kīṛā** کتاب کا کیڑا
writing, calligraphy *n.f.* **kitābat** کتابت
inscription, motto *n.m.* **kitābah** کتابہ
linen *n.m.* **katān/kattān** کتان
cause to spin, get spun *v.t.* **katānā** کتانا
library *n.m.* **kutub xānah** کتب خانہ
bookseller *n.m.* **kutub farōš** کتب فروش
inscription *n.m.* **katbah** کتبہ
cause to be cut *v.t.* **katrānā** کترانا
cutting out, deduction *n.f.* **katar bēvant** کتربیونت
cut, trim *v.t.* **katarnā** کترنا
scissors *n.f.* **katarnī** کترنی
how much?, how many? *adv.* **kitnā** کتنا
how many? *adv.* **kitnē** کتنے
ledger, account book *n.f.* **khataunī** کھتونی
bitch *n.f.* **kuttī** کتی
bitch *n.f.* **kuttiyā** کتیا
sound, rattling *n.f.* **khaṭ khaṭ** کھٹ کھٹ

کھٹا sour, acid *adj.* **khaṭṭā**
کھٹا ہونا turn sour *v.i.* **khaṭṭā hōnā**
کٹار sword, dagger *n.m.* **kaṭār**
کٹار مارنا stab *v.t.* **kaṭār mārnā**
کٹاری small dagger *n.f.* **kaṭārī**
کھٹاس sourness, acidity *n.f.* **khaṭās**
کٹانا cause to cut, cause to bite *v.t.* **kaṭānā**
کٹاؤ cut, cutting *n.m.* **kaṭā'ō**
کٹائی harvest time, reaping season; cutting (of crops) *n.f.* **kaṭā'ī**
کٹر cruel, merciless, pitiless *adj.* **kaṭṭar**
کھٹکا knocking; fear, peril; suspicion *n.m.* **khaṭkā**
کھٹکھٹانا knock (at the door) *v.t.* **khaṭkhaṭānā**
کٹکٹانا grate (one's teeth); suffer distress *v.t.* **kiṭkiṭānā**
کھٹکنا sound, rattle; clash *v.i.* **khaṭaknā**
کٹہرا railing, wooden frame, wooden cage *n.m.* **kaṭahrā**
کٹوانا cause to cut, cause to bite *v.t.* **kaṭvānā**
کٹورا cup, goblet, bowl *n.m.* **kaṭōrā**
کھٹیا bedstead *n.f.* **khaṭyā**
کٹھ پتلی puppet; girl *n.f.* **kaṭh putlī**
کٹھن difficult, hard, arduous *adj.* **kaṭhin**
کثافت density, thickness *n.f.* **kasāfat**
کثرت abundance, excess; multitude, majority *n.f.* **kasrat**
کثرت سے abundantly, plentifully *adv.* **kasrat sē**
کثرت کام overwork *n.m.* **kasrat kām**
کثیر abundant, numerous; many, much *adj.* **kasīr**
کج curved, crooked, bent; perverse *adj.* **kaj**
کج خلق ill-tempered, rough, rude *adj.* **kaj xulq**
کج رفتار perverse, unprincipled; irregular *adj.* **kaj raftār**
کج فہم stupid *adj.* **kaj fahm**
کھجانا scratch, itch, tickle; irritate, feel itchy *v.t./v.i.* **khujānā**
کجلانا smolder; become mildewed *v.i.* **kajlānā**
کھجور date; date tree *n.f.* **khajūr**
کچا immature, raw, unripe, crude *adj.* **kaccā**
کچا تخمینہ rough estimate *n.m.* **kaccā taxmīnah**

full, crowded, packed, crammed *adj.* **khacā khac** کھچا کھچ
cram, stuff *v.t.* **khacā khac bharnā** کھچا کھچ بھرنا
pull, drag; tightness, tenseness; attraction *n.m.* **khicā'ō** کھچاؤ
rubbish, trash, litter *n.m.* **kacrā** کچرا
crush, trample *v.t.* **kucalnā** کچلنا
be drawn, be pulled, be attracted *v.i.* **khicnā** کھچنا
court, court of justice *n.f.* **kacahrī** کچہری
hold a court *v.t.* **kacahrī karnā** کچہری کرنا
mango pickle *n.m.* **kacūmar** کچومر
any, anything, some, something, few, a little *adj.* **kuch** کچھ
nearly, almost, somewhat *adv.* **kuch kuch** کچھ کچھ
nothing *adv.* **kuch nahīṁ** کچھ نہیں
house, retreat *n.f.* **kad** کد
bridegroom *n.m.* **kad xudā** کد خدا
marriage, wedding *n.f.* **kad xudā'ī** کد خدائی
hoe, spade, pick, axe *n.m.* **kudāl** کدال
mattock *n.f.* **kudālī** کدالی
cause to dig; engrave *v.t.* **khudānā** کھدانا
digging; engraving *n.f.* **khudā'ī** کھدائی
house, home; place *n.m.* **kadah** کدہ
foulness, muddiness, impurity; resentment *n.f.* **kudūrat** کدورت
where?, where to? *adv.* **kidhar** کدھر
pit, ditch, crack *n.m.* **khaḍ** کھڈ
cavity, pit *n.m.* **khaḍḍā** کھڈی
lie *n.m.* **kizb** کذب
hoof *n.m.* **khur** کھر
power, strength *n.m.* / deaf *adj.* **karr** کر
pure, genuine, honest, straight-forward *adj.* **kharā** کھرا
purity, honesty *n.m.* **kharāpan** کھراپن
hard, thick, stiff, rigid *adj.* **karārā** کرارا
nobility; excellence; generosity *n.f.* **karāmat** کرامت
dislike, disgust, aversion, abhorrence *n.f.* **karāhat** کراہت
groan, sigh, moan *v.i.* **karāhnā** کراہنا
rent, hire, fare *n.m.* **kirāyah** کرایہ

rent, hire *v.t.* **kirāyah par caṛhānā** کرایہ پرچڑھانا
hire *v.t.* **kirāyah par lēnā** کرایہ پرلینا
hirer; tenant *n.m.* **kirāyah dār** کرایہ دار
billion *num.* **kharab** کھرب
grief, pain, anguish *n.m.* **karb** کرب
shirt, tunic, waistcoat *n.m.* **kurtah** کرتہ
action, deed; bad deed *n.f.* **kartūt** کرتوت
bodice, small shirt, blouse; underwear *n.f.* **kurtī** کرتی
sword *n.f.* **kiric** کرچ
scrape, scratch *v.t.* **khuracnā** کھرچنا
rigid, insensible, harsh, solid *n.f.* **karaxt** کرخت
deed, action, manner *n.m.* **kirdār** کردار
rough, rugged, uneven, wrinkled *adj.* **khurdarā** کھردرا
God *n.m.* **kird gār** کردگار
card *n.m.* **kārḍ** کرڈ
chair, stool, seat *n.f.* **kursī** کرسی
miracle, wonder *n.m.* **kirišmah/karašmah** کرشمہ
rubbish, trash; sweeping *n.f.* **karkaṭ** کرکٹ
rough, wrinkled *adj.* **khurkhurā** کھرکھرا
sandy, gritty *adj.* **kirkirā** کرکرا
brittle, crispy *adj.* **kurkurā** کرکرا
vulture; arrow *n.m.* **kargas** (گدھ) کرگس
loom *n.m.* **kargah** کرگہ
mortar *n.m.* **kharal** کھرل
kindness, favor, grace *n.m.* **karam** کرم
act, deed, fate, destiny *n.m.* **karm** کرم
worm *n.m.* **kirm** کرم
silkworm *n.m.* **kirm pīlah** کرم پیلہ
ray, beam, sunbeam *n.f.* **kiran** کرن
do, make, act, perform; effect *v.t.* **karnā** کرنا
globe, sphere; region *n.m.* **kurrah** کرہ
cause to do, cause to perform *v.t.* **karvānā** کروانا
side, sideway *n.f.* **karvaṭ** کروٹ
rage, anger; passion; resentment *n.m.* **krōdh** کرودھ
ten million *num.* **karōṛ** کروڑ
millionaire *n.m.* **karōṛ patī** کروڑپتی

show and pomp, magnificence *n.f.* **karr-ō-farr** کروفر
grocrery; spices *n.m.* **kiryānah** کریانہ
investigation, search *n.f.* **kurēd** کرید
scratch, scrape *v.t.* **kurēdnā** کریدنا
bitter gourd *n.m.* **karēlā** کریلا
merciful, bountiful, gracious, generous, liberal *adj.* **karīm** کریم
rustle, rattle, knock *v.i.* **khaṛkhaṛānā** کھڑکھڑانا
rustling, rattling, knocking *n.f.* **khaṛkhaṛāhaṭ** کھڑکھڑاہٹ
standing, erect, upright *adj.* **khaṛā** کھڑا
bracelet, anklet; ring *n.m.* / strong, stiff, hard, harsh *adj.* **kaṛā** کڑا
stand *v.i.* **khaṛā hōnā** کھڑا ہونا
crash *n.m.* **kaṛākā** کڑاکا
cauldron *n.m.* **kaṛāh** کڑاہ
frying pan *n.f.* **kaṛāhī** کڑاہی
large spoon *n.m.* **kaṛchā** کڑچھا
laddle spoon *n.f.* **kaṛchī** کڑچھی
crash, crack *n.f.* **kaṛak** کڑک
crackle, thunder, roar *v.i.* **kaṛaknā** کڑکنا
window *n.f.* **khiṛkī** کھڑکی
bitter, acrid, sharp, harsh *adj.* **kaṛvā** کڑوا
taste bitter *v.i.* **kaṛvā lagnā** کڑوا لگنا
bitterness, acridity *n.f.* **kaṛvāhat** کڑواہٹ
rafter, fetter, ring; handcuff *n.f.* **kaṛī** کڑی
muscular, robust; bony *adj.* **kaṛyal** کڑیل
grieve; envy; pity *v.i.* **kuṛhnā** • be drawn, be extracted, be boiled *v.i.* **kaṛhnā** کڑھنا
curry *n.f.* **kaṛhī** کڑھی
scorpion *n.m.* **kuzdum** کزدم
cousin *n.m./n.f.* **kazin** کزن
• strength, tightness, straightness; person, man; somebody, anybody *n.m.* **kas** کس
who?, whom?; what?, which? *pron.* **kis**
everybody *n.m.* **kas-ō-nā-kas** کس وناکس
laziness; indisposition *n.f.* **kasālat** کسالت
farmer, cultivator; peasant *n.m.* **kisān** کسان
profession, trade, business, employment *n.m.* **kasab** کسب
earn, acquire, gain *v.t.* **kasab karnā** کسب کرنا
musk *n.f.* **kastūrī** کستوری

customs *n.m.* **kasṭam** کسٹم
breach, loss; fraction; deficiency; affliction *n.f.* **kasr** کسر
whispering *n.f.* **khusar phusar** کھسر پھسر
measles *n.f.* **khasrā** کھسرا
exercise; practice, habit *n.f.* **kasrat** کسرت
athlete *n.m.* / athletic *adj.* **kasratī** کسرتی
vowel *n.m.* **kasrah** کسرہ
pain, ache, affliction *n.f.* **kasak** کسک
slip away, abscond *v.i.* **khisak jānā** کھسک جانا
remove, move away *v.t.* **khiskānā** کھسکانا
laxity, slowness, indolence, indisposition *n.m.* **kasal** کسل
restlessness *n.f.* **kasmasāhaṭ** کسمساہٹ
tighten, tie, bind *v.t.* **kasnā** کسنا
pluck, pull, tear, scratch *v.t.* **khasōṭnā** کھسوٹنا
touchstone; test, examination; proof *n.f.* **kasauṭī** کسوٹی
test, examine; prove *v.t.* **kasvaṭī par parakhnā** کسوٹی پر پرکھنا
solar eclipse *n.m.* **kusūf** کسوف
anyone, someone *pron.* **kisī** کسی
anyhow, somehow *adv.* **kisī tarah̤** کسی طرح
a little, to some extent *adv.* **kisī qadr** کسی قدر
someone or the other *adv.* **kisī nah kisī** کسی نہ کسی
ashamed, humiliated; bashful *adj.* **khisyānā** کھسیانا
thick; impure *adj.* **kasīf** کسیف
bitter, pungent *adj.* **kasēlā** کسیلا
drawing, pulling, carrying, enduring *adj.* **kaš** کش
expanding, opening *adj.* **kušā** کشا
opening, displaying, expanding, solving *adj.* **kušād** کشاد
expansion, latitude, extension, openness *n.f.* **kušādagī** کشادگی
expanded, vast, extensive, spacious *adj.* **kušādah** کشادہ
frank, open-hearted, generous *adj.* **kušādah dil** کشادہ دل
discovery *n.m.* **kašāf** کشاف
struggle *n.f.* **kašākaš** کشاکش
opening, expansion, enlargement *n.f.* **kušā'iš** کشائش
massacre, bloodshed *n.m.* **kušt-ō-xūn** کشت و خون
slain, killed *adj.* **kuštah** کشتہ

کشتی wrestling *n.f.* **kuštī** • boat *n.f.* **kištī/kaštī**
کشتی باز wrestler *n.m.* **kuštī bāz**
کشتی بان boatman *n.m.* **kištī bān**
کشتی لڑنا wrestle *v.t.* **kuštī laṛnā**
کشش attraction, allurement, drawing *n.f.* **kašiš**
کشش ثقل gravity *n.f.* **kašiš-ē-siql**
کشف revelation, manifestation; opening; solution *n.m.* **kašf**
کشفی revealed, manifest *adj.* **kašfī**
کشمش raisins, currants, dried grapes *n.f.* **kišmiš**
کشنیز (دھنیہ) coriander *n.m.* **kašnīz**
کشور climate; country, region, territory *n.f.* **kišvar**
کشیدگی resentment, tension, displeasure *n.f.* **kašīdagī**
کشیدہ drawn, extended; contracted *adj.* **kašīdah**
کشیدہ خاطر annoyed, defected, displeased *adj.* **kašīdah xātir**
کف froth, spittle, scum, foam *n.m.* **kaf**
کف دست palm (of the hand) *n.m.* **kaf-ē-dast**
کفارہ atonement, penitence *n.m.* **kafārah**
کفارہ دینا atone (for) *v.t.* **kafārah dēnā**
کفالت pledge; pawn; security *n.f.* **kafālat**
کفایت sufficiency, abundance; economy, thrift; profit *n.f.* **kifāyat**
کفایت سے economically, frugally *adv.* **kifāyat sē**
کفایت شعار economical, frugal, thrifty *adj.* **kifāyat šiᶜār**
کفایت شعاری economy, frugality, thrift *n.f.* **kifāyat šiᶜārī**
کفایتی cheap, economical, frugal, thrifty *adj.* **kifāyatī**
کفایہ sufficient, reasonable *adj.* **kifāyah**
کفر infidelity; atheism, paganism *n.m.* **kufr**
کفران infidelity; ingratitude *n.m.* **kufrān**
کفران نعمت ingratitude, thanklessness *n.m.* **kufrān-ē-niᶜmat**
کفش shoe, slipper *n.f.* **kafiš**
کفش دوز shoemaker, cobbler *n.m.* **kafiš dōz**
کفن shroud; coffin *n.m.* **kafan**
کفو kin, family, caste, brotherhood *n.m.* **kufū**
کفور ungrateful *adj.* **kafūr**
کفیل surety, guarantee; security *n.m.* **kafīl**

کفیل ہونا **kafīl hōnā** *v.i.* stand surety
ککڑ **kukkaṛ** *n.m.* cock
ککڑی **kakṛī** *n.f.* cucumber • **kukṛī** *n.f.* hen; maize
کل **kal** *n.f.* tomorrow; yesterday; ease, comfort, relief; machine; lock, trigger / **kul** *adj.* all, entire, whole • *n.m.* wrangle, quarrel / *adj.* soft, low, sweet
کھل جانا **khul jānā** *v.i.* open; be free
کھلا **khulā** *adj.* open; loose; vast
کلا **kallā** *n.m.* head; jaw; cheek; fine art, skill
کھلاڑی **khilāṛī** *adj.* playful, sportive
کلام **kalām** *n.m.* word, speech, discourse, conversation
کلام کرنا **kalām karnā** *v.t.* talk, speak, discuss, quarrel, argue
کلاں **kalāṁ** *adj.* large, great, big
کھلانا **khilānā** *v.t.* feed, give to eat; cause to play
کلاہ **kulāh** *n.m.* hat, cap; crown
کلائی **kalā'ī** *n.f.* wrist, forearm
کلب **kalb** *n.m.* dog
کلبلانا **kulbalānā** *v.i.* itch; fidget, writhe; grumble
کلبلاہٹ **kulbalāhaṭ** *n.f.* restlessness, fidgeting; itchiness
کھلبلی **khalbalī** *n.f.* hurry, agitation, alarm, tumult, panic, commotion, disorder
کھلبلی ڈالنا **khalbalī ḍālnā** *v.t.* create panic, create confusion
کلبہ **kulbah** *n.m.* cottage, hut; cell
کلپانا **kalpānā** *v.t.* oppress, afflict
کلپنا **kalapnā** *v.i.* be afflicted, grieve
کلچہ **kulcah** *n.m.* kulcha (*type of bread*)
کلر **kallar** *adj.* unproductive, barren
کلس **kalas** *n.m.* spire, dome, peak, pinnacle
کلغی **kalġī** *n.f.* plume, crest
کلف **kalaf** *n.m.* pimple; starch; dye; padlock
کلفت **kulfat** *n.f.* trouble, affliction, distress
کلک **kalk** *n.f.* reed; pen
کلکل **kalkal** *n.m.* wrangling, quarreling
کلکل کرنا **kalkal karnā** *v.t.* wrangle, quarrel
کلمۃ الحق **kalmat-ul-ḥaqq** *n.m.* truth
کھلنا **khilnā** *v.i.* blossom, bloom, flower; laugh • **khulnā** *v.i.* be opened, be open, come loose, unravel
کلنک **kalank** *n.m.* stigma, accusation, scandal

کلہاڑا **kulhāṛā** *n.m.* axe, hatchet

کلہاڑی **kulhāṛī** *n.f.* small axe

کلہم **kulluhum** *n.m.* all of them, the whole

کلوخ **kulūx** *n.m.* clod (of dirt); brick

کلوگرام **kilōgrām** *n.m.* kilogram

کلول **kalōl** *n.f.* wantonness, play, diversion

کلومیٹر **kilūmīṭar** *n.m.* kilometer

کھلونا **khilaunā** *n.m.* toy

کلی **kullī** *n.f.* gargling / *adj.* universal, entire, whole, general, common •

kalī *n.f.* bud, blossom

کھلیان **khalyān** *n.m.* granary, barn

کلیان **kalyān** *n.m.* welfare, prosperity; happiness; success

کلیجہ **kalējah** *n.m.* liver; heart; courage; mind, spirit

کلید **kalīd** *n.f.* key, index

کلیسہ **kalīsah** *n.m.* church, cathedral

کلیم **kalīm** *n.f.* speaker, interlocutor

کلیہ **kulliyah** *n.m.* formula, rule, principle

کھم **kham** *n.m.* pillar, post, column

کم **kam** *adj.* less, few, little, rare, seldom, deficient

کم بخت **kam baxt** *adj.* unlucky, unfortunate

کم بختی **kam baxtī** *n.f.* ill-luck, misfortune; mishap

کم بختی کا مارا **kam baxtī kā mārā** *adj.* distressed, wretched; accused

کم تر **kam tar** *adj.* less, smaller, lowly

کم ترین **kam tarīn** *adj.* least; humble

کم خرچ **kam xarc** *adj.* economical, frugal, thrifty

کم ذات **kam zāt** *adj.* vile, base

کم سن **kam san** *adj.* young, minor

کم سِنی **kam sinī** *n.f.* youth, minority

کم عقل **kam ᶜaql** *adj.* stupid, foolish, ignorant

کم عمر **kam ᶜumr** *adj.* young, minor

کم کرنا **kam karnā** *v.t.* diminish, lessen, reduce

کم وبیش **kam-ō-bēš** *adv.* more or less

کم یاب **kam yāb** *adj.* rare, scarce

کم یابی **kam yābī** *n.f.* rarity, scarcity

کما حقہ **kamā ḥaqqah** *adv.* as it should be, in a proper manner, exactly, properly

کمار **kumār** *n.m.* prince; son

کماری princess; daughter; virgin *n.f.* **kumārī**
کمال excellence, perfection; completion, conclusion *n.m.* **kamāl**
کمال حاصل کرنا attain perfection *v.t.* **kamāl ḥāsil karnā**
کمان bent, curved; flexible, elastic *adj.* / bow, arch; Sagittarius (*Zodiac*) *n.f.* **kamān**
کمان چڑھنا be victorious *v.i.* **kamān caṛhnā**
کمان دار archer, bowman *n.m.* **kamān dār**
کمانا earn, acquire, get, accumulate; work *v.t.* **kamānā**
کماؤ laborious, working *adj.* **kamā'ū**
کمائی earnings, income, gain, profit; work, performance *n.f.* **kamā'ī**
کھمبا pillar, post, column *n.m.* **khambā**
کمبل blanket *n.m.* **kambal**
کمپنی company *n.f.* **kampanī**
کمتی scant, little, less *adj.* **kamtī**
کمتی بڑھتی more or less *adv.* **kamtī baṛhtī**
کمر waist, loins *n.f.* **kamar**
کمر بستہ ready, prepared; armed *adj.* **kamar bastah**
کمر توڑنا dismay, disappoint, discourage *v.t.* **kamar tōṛnā**
کمرہ room, chamber, apartment *n.m.* **kamrah**
کمزور weak, powerless, feeble *adj.* **kamzōr**
کمزوری weakness, debility *n.f.* **kamzōrī**
کمک aid, assistance, help *n.f.* **kumak**
کمل lotus *n.m.* **kamal**
کملی small blanket *n.f.* **kamlī**
کمہار potter *n.m.* **kumhār**
کمی deficiency, loss, reduction, diminution, decrease, deficit *n.f.* **kamī**
کمی بیشی decrease and increase, profit and loss *n.f.* **kamī bēšī**
کمیت quantity, number *n.f.* **kammiyyat**
کمیشن discount; commission *n.f.* **kamīšan**
کمین low; mean, wicked *adj.* / ambush *n.f.* **kamīn**
کمین گاہ ambush *n.f.* **kamīn gāh**
کن • side, corner *n.m.* **kan** • what?, which?; who?, whom? *pron.* **kin**
making, doing *adj.* **kun**
کن ماننا be grateful *v.i.* **kun mānnā**
کنارا bank, shore, coast; edge, side, border *n.m.* **kinārā**
کنارا کش ہونا retire, keep aloof *v.i.* **kinārā kaš hōnā**
کناری lace; hem *n.f.* **kinārī**

along the shore, by the side of *adv.* **kinārē kinārē** کنارے کنارے
indirectly, metaphorically *adv.* **kināyitan** کنایتاً
metaphor, allusion, hint, taunt *n.m.* **kināyah** کنایہ
family, tribe, brotherhood *n.m.* **kumbah** کنبہ
throat *n.m.* / by heart *adv.* **kanṭh** کنٹھ
necklace *n.f.* **kanṭh mālā** کنٹھ مالا
corner *n.m.* **kuṁj** کنج
gypsy; nomad tribe *n.m.* **kaṁjar** کنجر
greengrocer, fruit seller, vegetable seller *n.m.* **kuṁjṛā** کنجڑا
sparrow *n.m.* **kuṁjašk** کنجشک
miser, niggard *n.m.* **kaṁjūs** کنجوس
stinginess *n.f.* **kaṁjūsī** کنجوسی
key *n.f.* **kuṁjī** کنجی
blunt, slow, dull *adj.* **kund** کند
foolish, stupid, dull *adj.* **kund zihn** کند ذہن
log; block *n.m.* **kundā** کندا
pure gold *n.m.* **kundan** کندن
engraved, carved *adj.* **kandah** کندہ
engraver, carver *n.m.* **kandah kār** کندہ کار
engraving, carving, inscription *n.f.* **kandah kārī** کندہ کاری
engrave, carve *v.t.* **kandah karnā** کندہ کرنا
shoulder *n.m.* **kandhā** کندھا
portion, part, piece, section *n.m.* **khanḍ** کھنڈ
tank, pool, reservoir *n.m.* **kunḍ** کنڈ
hook *n.m.* **kunḍā** کنڈا
curl, coil; ring, circle; earring *n.m.* **kunḍal** کنڈل
circle, ringlet, coil *n.f.* **kunḍlī** کنڈلی
dividing, breaking, cutting *n.m.* **khunḍan** کھنڈن
canister, tin *n.m.* **kanistar** کنستر
stone, gravel, pebble *n.m.* **kankar** کنکر
jingle, clink *v.i.* **khanaknā** کھنکنا
flying a kite *n.m.* **kankavvā** کنکوا
poor, miserable; bankrupt *adj.* **kangāl** کنگال
rinse, wash, clean *v.t.* **khangālnā** کھنگالنا
poverty; bankruptcy *n.f.* **kangālī** کنگالی
millet *n.f.* **kangnī** کنگنی

comb *n.m.* **kanghā** کنگھا
small comb *n.f.* **kanghī** کنگھی
comb *v.t.* **kanghī karnā** کنگھی کرنا
maker, manufacturer *n.m.* **kunindah** کنندہ
bachelor, unmarried man *n.m.* **kuṁvārah** کنوارہ
maid, unmarried girl, virgin, miss *n.f.* **kuṁvārī** کنواری
well *n.m.* **kuṁvāṁ** کنواں
prince; child, son *n.m.* **kuṁvar** کنور
lotus; heart *n.m.* **kaṁval** کنول
• who, what, which; that, as, for, because, if, whether *pron./conj.* **kih/kē** کہ
small, little; slender; mean *adj.* **kih**
where?, where to? *adv.* **kahāṁ** کہاں
from where? *adv.* **kahāṁ sē** کہاں سے
cause to be said, be called *v.t.* **kahānā** کہانا
story, tale, fable *n.f.* **kahānī** کہانی
proverb, saying *n.f.* **kahāvat** کہاوت
fog, mist *n.m.* **kuhr** کہر
weeping, crying, lamentation *n.m.* **kuhrām** کہرام
cave, den *n.m.* **kahaf** کہف
Milky Way, galaxy *n.f.* **kahkašāṁ** کہکشاں
be called, cause to say *v.t.* **kahlānā** کہلانا
saying, proverb *n.f.* **kahan** • ancient, old *adj.* **kuhan** کہن
aged, old *adj.* **kuhan sāl** کہن سال
old age *n.f.* **kuhan sālī** کہن سالی
say, tell *v.t.* **kahnā** کہنا
obey (an order) *v.t.* **kahnā mānnā** کہنا ماننا
old, ancient *adj.* **kuhnah** کہنہ
elbow *n.f.* **kuhnī** کہنی
somewhere, anywhere, wherever *adv.* **kahīṁ** کہیں
from anywhere *adv.* **kahīṁ sē** کہیں سے
here and there, in some place *adv.* **kahīṁ kahīṁ** کہیں کہیں
somewhere or the other *adv.* **kahīṁ nah kahīṁ** کہیں نہ کہیں
nowhere *adv.* **kahīṁ nahīṁ** کہیں نہیں
lane, street *n.f.* **kū** • to, for, at, on *pp.* **kō** کو
shoulder *n.m.* **khavvā** کھوا
crow *n.m.* **kavvā** کوا

کواڑ **kivāṛ** *n.m.* shutter; door, gate, entrance
کوب **kōb** *adj.* beating, pounding
کھوپڑی **khōpṛī** *n.f.* skull, cranium
کوتاہ **kōtāh** *adj.* small, little, short, brief
کوتاہ بین **kōtāh bīn** *adj.* shortsighted; imprudent, indiscreet
کوتاہ نظر **kōtāh nazar** *adj.* shortsighted
کوتاہی **kōtāhī** *n.f.* smallness, deficiency; negligence, irresponsibility, failure
کوتاہی کرنا **kōtāhī karnā** *v.t.* fail, neglect
کوتوال **kōtvāl** *n.f.* chief police officer
کوتوالی **kōtvālī** *n.f.* chief police station
کھوٹ **khōṭ** *n.f.* adulteration, alloy, impurity, falsehood, fault
کوٹ **kōṭ** *n.m.* enclosure, fortification, fort, castle
کھوٹ ملانا **khōṭ milānā** *v.t.* alloy
کھوٹا **khōṭā** *adj.* impure, defective; false, fraudulent, counterfeit
کوٹنا **kūṭnā** *v.t.* beat, pound, thrash; break into pieces
کھوٹی کھری کہنا **khōṭī kharī kahnā** *v.t.* abuse
کوٹھڑی **kōṭhṛī** *n.f.* cell, small room, cabin, closet
کھوج **khōj** *n.f.* trace, search, enquiry, quest
کھوج نکالنا **khōj nikālnā** *v.t.* track (down)
کھوجنا **khōjnā** *v.t.* search, seek, enquire, investigate
کوچ **kūc** *n.m.* departure, decampment; march
کوچ کرنا **kūc karnā** *v.t.* depart, march; die
کوچک **kōcak** *adj.* small, little
کوچہ **kūcah** *n.m.* lane, narrow street
کوچہ بکوچہ **kūcah ba-kūcah** *adv.* from lane to lane, everywhere
کوچی **kūcī** *n.f.* (paint)brush
کودک **kōdak** *n.m.* child, youth, youngster
کودن **kōdan/kaudan** *adj.* foolish, stupid; dull
کھودنا **khōdnā** *v.t.* dig, excavate; carve, engrave
کودنا **kūdnā** *v.i.* leap, jump; rejoice
کوڈ **kōḍ** *n.m.* code
کور **kōr** *n.m.* margin, edge, border, side / blind *adj.*
کور بختی **kōr baxtī** *n.f.* misfortune, calamity
کور چشم **kōr cašm** *adj.* blind
کورا **kōrā** *adj.* fresh, new, unused

کورنش salutation, adoration *n.f.* **kōrniš**
کورنش بجانا salute, pay respect *v.t.* **kōrniš bajānā**
کوڑا whip, lash *n.m.* **kōṛā**
کوڑاکرکٹ rubbish, dirt *n.m.* **kūṛā karkaṭ**
کوڑا مارنا whip, lash *v.t.* **kōṛā mārnā**
کوڑی score *n.f.* **kōṛī**
کوڑی بھر very little *adj.* **kauṛī bhar**
کوڑھ leprosy *n.f.* **kōṛh**
کوڑھی leprous *adj.* / leper *n.m.* **kōṛhī**
کوز hump *n.m.* **kūz**
کوزہ jug, pot, cup *n.m.* **kūzah**
کوس kettledrum, drum *n.m.* **kōs**
کوسا curse *n.m.* **kōsa**
کوسنا curse, abuse *v.t.* **kōsnā**
کوسوں دور very far, far away *adj.* **kōsōṁ dūr**
کوش dictionary; treasure *n.m.* **kōš**
کوشش attempt, effort, endeavor *n.f.* **kōšiš**
کوشش کرنا attempt, try *v.t.* **kōšiš karnā**
کوفت beating, torture; trouble; grief, anguish *n.f.* **kōft**
کوفتہ ground, beaten, pounded *adj.* **kōftah**
کوفی coffee *n.f.* **kōfī**
کوکھ womb, belly, abdomen *n.f.* **kōkh**
کوکب star, constellation *n.m.* **kaukab**
کوکنا cry, shriek, sob, wail *v.i.* **kūknā**
کولا side, wall; corner *n.m.* **kōlā**
کھولنا boil *v.i.* **khaulnā** • open, untie, unlock, loosen, reveal *v.t.* **khōlnā**
کولی embrace *n.f.* **kaulī**
کومل mild, tender, soft, sweet, delicate *adj.* **kōmal**
کوملتا tenderness, softness *n.f.* **kōmalnā**
کون who?, which? *pron.* / being, existence; universe, worlds *n.m.* **kaun**
کون سا which?, what?, what sort of? *pron.* **kaun sā**
کھونا lose, waste *v.t.* **khōnā**
کونا corner, angle; side *n.m.* **kōnā**
کونپل young shoot, bud, sprout *n.f.* **kōnpal**
کھونٹا pin, peg, nail; support *n.m.* **khūnṭā**
کونچی brush *n.f.* **kuṁcī**

flash (of lightning); brightness *n.f.* **kaund** کوند

flash, glare, lighten *v.i.* **kaundnā** کوندنا

corner, angle *n.m.* **kōnah** کونہ

angular, cornered *adj.* **kōnē dār** کونے دار

mountain; hill *n.m.* **kōh** کوہ

volcano *n.m.* **kōh-ē-ātaš fišāṁ** کوہ آتش فشاں

hump *n.m.* **kōhān** کوہان

mountains, mountainous area, highland *n.m.* **kōhistān** کوہستان

mountaineer, highlander *n.m.* / mountainous, hilly *adj.* **kōhistānī** کوہستانی

elbow *n.f.* **kōhnī** کوہنی

armchair *n.f.* **kōhnī dār kursī** کوہنی دار کرسی

boatsman *n.m.* **khivaiyyā** کھویا

poetry, poem *n.f.* **kavītā** کویتا

coal, charcoal *n.m.* **kō'ēlah** کوئلہ

any, anyone, anybody; some, somebody, something *pron.* **kō'ī** کوئی

Don't mention it!, You're welcome! *interj.* **kō'ī bāt nahīṁ!** کوئی بات نہیں

no one, nobody *pron.* **kō'ī nahīṁ** کوئی نہیں

how many *pron.* **kaē** کے

through, by means of *pp.* **kē zarīᶜah** کے ذریعہ

what?, which? *pron.* **kyā** کیا

What's up?!; Excellent!, Well done! *interj.* **kyā bāt hai!** کیا بات ہے

It goes without saying!,
Who knows!, Maybe! *interj.* **kyā jānē!** کیا جانے

Excellent!, Wonderful!, Well done! *interj.* **kyā xūb!** کیا خوب

flowerbed *n.f.* **kyārī** کیاری

field, battlefield *n.m.* **khēt** کھیت

reap (a field) *v.i.* **khēt kāṭnā** کھیت کاٹنا

kettle *n.f.* **kētlī** کیتلی

agriculture, farming *n.f.* **khētī** کھیتی

agriculture, farming *n.f.* **khētī bāṛī** کھیتی باڑی

mud, dirt, mire *n.f.* **kīcaṛ** کیچڑ

deceit, fraud, treachery *n.m.* **kaid** کید

rice pudding *n.f.* **khīr** کھیر

cucumber *n.m.* **khīrā** کھیرا

insect, worm *n.m.* **kīṛā** کیڑا

insect, ant, worm, leech *n.f.* **kīṛī** کیڑی

کھیس grinning *n.f.* **khīs**

کیس hair (*on head*) *n.f.* **kēs**

کیسا how?, in what manner?, what sort of?, why? *pron.* **kaisā?**

کیسر saffron *n.m.* **kēsar**

کیسری deep orange-yellow *adj.* / lion *n.m.* **kēsrī**

کیسہ purse, bag; pocket *n.m.* **kīsah**

کیش religion, faith, sect *n.m.* **kēš**

کیف exhilaration, intoxication *n.m.* **kaif**

کیفر revenge, vengeance; punishment *n.m.* **kaifar**

کیفی drunk, intoxicated *adj.* **kaifī**

کیفیت circumstance, condition; relation; nature, quality, mode *n.f.* **kaifiyyat**
narrative, story, account, explanation, remark; situation, state,

کیکڑا crab; cancer *n.m.* **kēkṛā**

کھیل play, game, sport, fun, trick *n.m.* **khēl**

کیل nail, spike, peg, pin, wedge *n.f.* **kīl**

کیل کانٹا equipment, tools *n.m.* **kīl kānṭā**

کیلا banana *n.m.* **kēlā** • peg, nail, bolt *n.f.* **kīlā**

کھیلنا play, gamble, sport, perform *v.i./v.t.* **khēlnā**

کیلنا nail, pin, fasten; charm a snake *v.t.* **kīlnā**

کیلی screw, nail; key; pivot, axis *n.f.* **kīlī**

کیمیا chemistry, alchemy *n.f.* **kīmiyā**

کیمیا بنانا chemist, alchemist; deceiver *n.m.* **kīmiyā gar**

کیمیا گری chemistry, alchemy *n.f.* **kīmiyā garī**

کھینا row, punt *v.t.* **khēnā**

کھینچ pull, attraction, drawing, holding; aversion *n.f.* **khaiṁc**

کھینچا تانی struggle, fight *n.f.* **khaiṁcā tānī**

کھینچنا draw, pull, drag, tighten *v.t.* **khaiṁcnā**

کیندر center of circle, pole *n.m.* **kēndr**

کینڈا mold, rough plan; sample *n.m.* **kainḍā**

کینسر cancer *n.m.* **kainsar**

کینہ malice, grudge, enmity, hatred *n.m.* **kīnah**

کینہ ور malicious, insincere, deceitful *adj.* **kīnah var**

کینیڈا Canada *n.m.* **kainēḍā**

کینیڈین Canadian *adj.* **kainēḍiyan**

کھیوا fare (*for a ferry or boat*) *n.m.* **khaivā**

why? *pron.* **kyōṁ?** کیوں

why not? *phr.* **kyōṁ nahīṁ?** کیوں نہیں

boatsman *n.m.* **khēvan hār** کھیون ہار

how?, why?, what for? *pron.* **kyōṁkar?** کیونکر

because, since, for *conj.* **kyōṁkih/kyōṁkē** کیونکہ

many, several, some *adj.* **ka'ī** کئی

few, some *adj.* **ka'ī ēk** کئی ایک

repeatedly, often, again and again, several times *adv.* **ka'ī bār** کئی بار

گ gāf

pregnant (*used for animals*) *adj.* **gābhan** گابھن

carrot *n.f.* **gājar** گاجر

rubbish, worthless stuff *n.f.* **gājar mūlī** گاجر مولی

sediment, dirt *n.f.* **gād** گاد

mud; clay *n.m.* **gārā** گارا

knead clay *v.t.* **gārā karnā** گارا کرنا

guard; ward *n.m.* **gārad** گارد

drive (into), bury, sink, plant, pitch, hide *v.t.* **gāṛnā** گاڑنا

car, cart, carriage, coach, motorcar, train, bus *n.f.* **gāṛī** گاڑی

carter, coachman *n.m.* **gāṛī bān** گاڑی بان

drive (a vehicle) *v.t.* **gāṛī calānā** گاڑی چلانا

garage *n.m.* **gāṛī xānah** گاڑی خانہ

drive (a vehicle), yoke *v.t.* **gāṛī hānknā** گاڑی ہانکنا

thick, dense, coarse, strong; close *adj.* **gāṛhā** گاڑھا

be good friends *v.i.* **gāṛhī channā** گاڑھی چھننا

water vessel, pitcher *n.m.* **gāgar** گاگر

cheek *n.m.* **gāl** گال

flake *n.m.* **gālā** گالا

abuse *n.f.* **gālī** گالی

abuse, call names *v.t.* **gālī dēnā** گالی دینا

be abused *v.t.* **gālī khānā** گالی کھانا

abuse, brawl *n.f.* **gālī gālōc** گالی گلوچ

foot; step, pace *n.m.* **gām** گام

sing *v.t.* **gāna** • song *n.m.* **gānā** گانا

knot; bundle, parcel; joint *n.f.* **gāṁṭh** گانٹھ

be knotted *v.i.* **gāṁṭh paṛhnā** گانٹھ پڑھنا

careful with money; rich, wealthy *adj.* **gāṁṭh kā pūrā** گانٹھ کا پورا

tie (a knot), fasten, join *v.t.* **gāṁṭhnā** گانٹھنا

perfumer, perfume-seller *n.m.* **gāndhī** گاندھی

place; time *n.f.* / sometimes, frequently *adv.* **gāh** گاہ

customer, buyer *n.m.* **gāhak** گاہک

once, sometimes *adv.* **gāhē** گاہے

bull, ox *n.m.* **gā'ō** گاؤ

large pillow, boister *n.m.* **gā'ō takyah** گاؤتکیہ
embezzlement *n.f.* **gā'ōghap** گاؤگھپ
fool *n.m.* **gā'ōdī** گاؤدی
village *n.m.* **gā'ōṁ** گاؤں
singer; musician *n.m.* **gāyak** گایک
cow *n.f.* **gā'ē** گائے
calf *n.m.* **gā'ē kā bichṛā** گائے کا بچھڑا
beef *n.m.* **gā'ē kā gōšt** گائے کا گوشت
gossip, chat *n.f.* **gap** گپ
chitchat, idle talk *n.f.* **gap šap** گپ شپ
cave *n.f.* **guphā** گپھا
plight, condition, state; tune *n.f.* **gat** گت
cardboard *n.m.* **gattā** گتا
cudgel; wooden sword *n.m.* **gatkā** گتکا
knot, riddle, puzzle *n.f.* **gutthī** گتھی
manual, handbook *n.m.* **guṭkā** گٹکا
bundle, package; clove *n.m.* **gaṭṭhā** گٹھا
small bundle, parcel, packet *n.f.* **guṭharī** گٹھڑی
bundle, pack (up) *v.t.* **guṭharī bāndhnā** گٹھڑی باندھنا
seed, clove; stone *n.f.* **guṭhlī** گٹھلی
be joined, be connected *v.i.* **gaṭhnā** گٹھنا
knotty; strong, robust *adj.* **gaṭhīlā** گٹھیلا
elephant *n.m.* **gaj** گج
garland, necklace *n.m.* **gajrā** گجرا
mortar *n.m.* **gac** گچ
cluster, bunch *n.m.* **guchā** گچھا
plump, soft *adj.* **gudgudā** گدگدا
beggar *n.m.* **gadā** گدا
melted, dissolved *adj.* **gudāz** گداز
beggar *n.m.* **gadāgar** گداگر
begging *n.f.* **gadāgarī** گداگری
begging; poverty *n.f.* **gadā'ī** گدائی
muddy, foul, dirty *adj.* **gadlā** گدلا
muddiness *n.m.* **gadlā pan** گدلاپن
cushion, seat; throne *n.f.* **gaddī** گدی

dethrone *v.t.* **gaddī sē utārnā** گدی سے اتارنا

cushion, bedding *n.m.* **gadēlā** گدیلا

vulture *n.m.* **gidh** گدھ

ass, donkey; fool *n.m.* **gadhā** گدھا

stupidity, foolishness *n.m.* **gadhā pan** گدھاپن

intermingled, mixed, disordered *adj.* **gaḍ maḍ** گڈ مڈ

shepherd *n.m.* **gaḍaryā** گڈریا

kite *n.f.* **guḍḍī** گڈی

maker, workman; desire; strength *n.m.* / if, in the event *adv.* **gar** گر

gram *n.m.* **grām** گرام

great; dear, precious, revered; respectable *adj.* **girāmī** گرامی

costly, precious, dear; heavy *adj.* **girāṁ** گراں

fall, drop, lower, shed *v.t.* **girānā** گرانا

dearness, dearth, scarcity *n.f.* **girānī** گرانی

cat *n.f.* **gurbah** گربہ

thundering, roaring *n.f.* **garaj** گرج

church *n.m.* **girjā** گرجا

thunder, roar *v.i.* **garajnā** گرجنا

about, near, behind *adv.* **gird** • dust *n.f.* **gard** گرد

dusty, dirty *adj.* **gard ālūdah** گرد آلودہ

vicinity *n.f.* **gird-ē-navāḥ** گرد نواح

on every side, on all sides, all round *n.m.* **girdā gird** گرداگرد

turning, revolving *n.f.* **gardān** گردان

turn, revolve *v.t.* **gardānnā** گرداننا

revolution; misfortune *n.f.* **gardiš** گردش

neck *n.f.* **gardan** گردن

kidney *n.m.* **gurdah** گردہ

heavens, firmament *n.m.* **gardūṁ** گردوں

axe *n.m.* **gurz** گرز

seizure, capture, grasp, hold; criticism *n.f.* **girift** گرفت

criticize *v.t.* **girft karnā** گرفت کرنا

arrested, seized, captured *adj.* / prisoner *n.m.* **giriftār** گرفتار

arrest, capture *v.t.* **giriftār karnā** گرفتار کرنا

be arrested; fall in love *v.i.* **giriftār hōnā** گرفتار ہونا

arrest, seizure, capture *n.f.* **giriftārī** گرفتاری

arrested, seized, caught *adj.* **giriftah** گرفتہ

wolf *n.m.* **gurg** گرگ
experienced, veteran *adj.* **gurg-ē-bārāṁ dīdah** گرگ باراں دیدہ
servant *n.m.* **gurgā** گرگا
shoe, slipper *n.f.* **gurgābī** گرگابی
lizard, chameleon *n.m.* **girgaṭ** گرگٹ
hot, warm *adj.* **garm/garam** گرم
great demand, great sale *n.f.* **garm bāzārī** گرم بازاری
zeal; warmth, affection *n.f.* **garm jōšī** گرم جوشی
lukewarm *adj.* **garm sard** گرم سرد
garam masala (*a spice blend*), seasoning *n.m.* **garm masālā** گرم مسالا
summer, hot season *n.m.* **garmā** گرما
hot; fresh *adj.* **garma garm** گرما گرم
be hot; be excited; be angry; heat *v.i./v.t.* **garmānā** گرمانا
heat, warmth; summer, hot season *n.f.* **garmī** گرمی
fall, drop, tumble, collapse, sink *v.i.* **girna** گرنا
knot, joint; knuckle *n.m.* **girah** گرہ
knotted, joined *adj.* **girah dār** گرہ دار
eclipse (*of the sun or moon*); spot *n.m.* **grahn** گرہن
guru, tutor, teacher *n.m.* **gurū** • pledge; pawn; mortgage *n.m.* **girau** گرو
group, party, band (of people), company *n.m.* **garōh** گروہ
pledged, pawned, mortgaged *adj.* **girvī** گروی
admiring, attraction, attachment *n.f.* **girvīdagī** گرویدگی
attracted, fascinated, attached *adj.* **girvīdah** گرویدہ
weeping *adj.* **giriyāṁ** گریاں
collar; neck *n.m.* **girēbān** گریبان
hold (by the collar); accuse *v.t.* **girēbān pakaṛnā** گریبان پکڑنا
deviation; flight, escape *n.f.* **gurēz** گریز
weeping lamentation *n.m.* **giryah** گریہ
weep, lament *v.t.* **giryah-ō-zārī karnā** گریہ وزاری کرنا
raw sugar *n.m.* **guṛ** گڑ
request (*humbly*), beseech *v.i.* **giṛgiṛānā** گڑگڑانا
bustle, disorder, confusion *n.m.* **gaṛbaṛ** گڑبڑ
enter, penetrate; be buried *v.i.* **gaṛnā** گڑنا
waterpot *n.m.* **gaṛvā** گڑوا
doll *n.f.* **guṛiyā** گڑیا
castle, fort *n.m.* **gaṛh** گڑھ

گڑھا hole, pit, cavity *n.m.* **gaṛhā**
گڑھی small fort, fortification *n.f.* **gaṛhī**
گزارش request, petition; representation *n.f.* **guzāriš**
گزارش کرنا request; represent *v.t.* **guzāriš karnā**
گزارنا pass by; die *v.i.* **guzarnā**
گزارہ living, subsisting; toll, passage *n.m.* **guzārah**
گزر passage, pass *n.f.* **guzar**
گزر عام thoroughfare, public road *n.f.* **guzar-ē-ᶜām**
گزر نامہ passport *n.m.* **guzar nāmah**
گزرنا pass (*die*); elapse *v.i.* **guzarnā**
گزشتہ past, elapsed, gone, left *adj.* **guzaštah**
گزند injury; loss *n.m.* **gazand**
گزیر escape; remedy *n.m.* **guzīr**
گزین choosing *adj.* **guzīn**
گسائیں saint, priest (*Hindu*) *n.m.* **gusā'īṁ**
گستاخ rude, arrogant *adj.* **gustāx**
گستاخی rudeness, arrogance; disrespect *n.f.* **gustāxī**
گستر spreading, scattering *adj.* **gustar**
گشت walk, stroll, tour *n.m.* **gašt**
گشتی circulating, patroling *adj.* **gaštī**
گفت و شنید debate, talk, discussion *n.f.* **guft-ō-šunīd**
گفتار speech, discourse, saying *n.f.* **guftār**
گفتگو dialogue, conversation *n.f.* **guftgū**
گفتہ proverb, saying, maxim *n.m.* **guftah**
گل rose, flower *n.m.* **gul** • clay, mud, earth *n.f.* **gil**
گل اندام delicate, slender, beautiful *adj.* **gul andām**
گل پھولنا blossom *v.i.* **gul phūlnā**
گل چیں gardener, florist *n.m.* **gul chīṁ**
گل چھڑے اڑانا enjoy life, live a luxurious life *v.t.* **gul chaṛē uṛānā**
گل دان flowerpot *n.m.* **gul dān**
گل دستہ bouquet *n.m.* **gul dastah**
گل دم nightingale *n.f.* **gul dam**
گل زار garden *n.m.* **gul zār**
گل کاری embroidery *n.f.* **gul kārī**
گل لالہ tulip; poppy flower *n.m.* **gul-ē-lālah**
گل مہندی balsam *n.f.* **gul mahndī**

be extinguished, go out (*light*) *v.i.* **gul hōnā** گل ہونا
throat, neck; collar *n.m.* **galā** گلا
cut someone's throat, kill; oppress *v.t.* **galā kāṭnā** گلا کاٹنا
rose *n.m.* **gulāb** گلاب
rosy, rose-colored *adj.* **gulābī** گلابی
glass *n.m.* **gilās** گلاس
soluble *adj.* **galā'ū** گلاؤ
flower garden *n.m.* **gulšan** گلشن
citron *n.m.* **galgal** گلگل
gulgula (*a fried sweet cake*) *n.m.* **gulgulā** گلگلا
melt, dissolve *v.i.* **galnā** گلنا
herd, flock, drove *n.m.* **galla** گلہ
squirrel *n.f.* **gulahrī** گلہری
throat, neck *n.m.* **gulū** گلو
necktie; shawl *n.m.* **gulū band** گلوبند
lane, alley, road, street, pathway *n.f.* **galī** گلی
gulli danda (*a game resembling tip-cat*) *n.f.* **gullī ḍanḍā** گلی ڈنڈا
lane, narrow street *n.m.* **galī kūcah** گلی کوچہ
lost, missing *adj.* **gum** گم
astray, lost, abandoned *adj.* **gum rāh** گم راہ
depravity, deviation, seduction *n.f.* **gum rāhī** گم راہی
agent, representative *n.m.* **gumāštah** گماشتہ
doubt, distrust, suspicion *n.m.* **gumān** گمان
probability *n.m.* **gumān-ē-ġālib** گمان غالب
doubt, suspect, suppose *v.t.* **gumān karnā** گمان کرنا
deep, thoughtful, serious *adj.* **gambhīr** گمبھیر
flowerpot *n.m.* **gamlah** گملہ
virtue, quality, excellence *n.m.* **gun** گن
praise *v.t.* **gun gānā** گن گانا
sugarcane *n.m.* **gannā** • time; turn, fold *n.m.* **gunā** گنا
sin, fault, crime *n.m.* **gunāh** گناہ
criminal, sinner, culprit *n.m.* **gunāh gār** گناہ گار
dome, arch *n.m.* **gumbad** گنبد
pickaxe *n.f.* **gēntī** • numbering, counting, calculation *n.f.* **gintī** گنتی
number, count, calculate *v.t.* **gintī karnā** گنتی کرنا

گنتی کے **gintī kē** few *adj.*
گنج **gaṁj** treasury, heap, markct, granary; baldness *n.m.*
گنج بخش **gaṁj baxš** generous, extravagant *adj.*
گنجا **gaṁjā** bald *adj.*
گنجان **guṁjān** dense, thick *adj.*
گنجان آباد **guṁjān ābād** densely populated *adj.*
گنجائش **guṁjā'iš** accommodation, capacity *n.f.*
گنجور **gaṁjūr** treasurer *n.m.*
گنجینہ **gaṁjīnah** treasure, magazine *n.m.*
گند **gand** stink, smell; filth *n.f.*
گندگی **gandagī** stink, rottenness, filth, dirt *n.f.*
گندم **gandum** wheat *n.m.*
گندہ **gandah** stinking, filthy, foul, dirty *adj.*
گندھک **gandhak** sulphur *n.f.*
گندھنا **gandhnā** be plaited; be kneaded *v.i.*
گندھی **gandhī** perfumer *n.m.*
گنڈا **gunḍā** scoundrel, rascal *n.m.* / wicked *adj.*
گنڈاسا **ganḍāsā** axe, sickle *n.m.*
گنگا **gangā** Ganges River *n.f.*
گنگنانا **gunganānā** sing softly, hum *v.i.*
گننا **ginnā** reckon, count, consider *v.t.* / count, calculate, number *v.i.*
گنوار **ganvār** villager, countryman *n.m.*
گنوانا **ganvānā** waste, lose, throw away, get rid of *v.t.*
گنی **gunī** skillful, talented; virtuous *adj.*
گہرا **gahrā** deep, profound *adj.*
گہرائی **gahrā'ī** depth, deepness *n.f.*
گہنا **gahnā** ornament, jewel; pawn; mortgage *n.m.*
گہوارہ **gahvārah** swing, cradle *n.m.*
گو **gū** excrement, filth *n.m.* • **gō** saying, telling *adj.*
گو کہ **gō kih** although, however, as if *adv.*
گومگو **gōmagō** hesitation, reluctance *n.m.*
گوارا **gavārā** acceptable, bearable; palatable, tasty *adj.*
گوارا کرنا **gavārā karnā** bear, endure, tolerate; digest *v.t.*
گوالا **gvālā** cowherd, milkman *n.m.*
گوالن **gvālan** milkmaid *n.f.*

گواہ witness *n.m.* **gavāh**
گواہ چشم دید eyewitness *n.m.* **gavāh-ē-cašm dīd**
گواہی evidence, testimony *n.f.* **gavāhī**
گوبھی cauliflower *n.m.* **gōbhī**
گوجر cowherd *n.m.* **gūjar**
گود lap; embrace *n.f.* **gōd**
گودام warehouse, storehouse *n.m.* **gūdām**
گودڑ rags (*old clothes*), rubbish *n.m.* **gūdaṛ**
گودہ pulp, pap, kernel *n.m.* **gūdah**
گور tomb, grave *n.f.* **gōr**
گورا fair, white (*skin color*) *adj.* **gōrā**
گورستان graveyard *n.m.* **gōristān**
گوش ear *n.m.* **gōš**
گوشت meat, flesh *n.m.* **gōšt**
گوشت خور carnivorous *n.m.* **gōšt xōr**
گوشہ corner, angle *n.m.* **gōšah**
گوشہ گیر retired, secluded *adj.* **gōšah gīr**
گوشہ نشین retired, recluse *adj.* **gōšah našīn**
گوشہ نشینی privacy, retirement, solitude *n.f.* **gōšah našīnī**
گول round, circular *adj.* **gōl**
گول سا roundish *adj.* **gōl sā**
گولا ball; cannonball, bomb *n.m.* **gōlā**
گولائی roundness *n.f.* **gōlā'ī**
گولی pill; ball; bullet *n.f.* **gōlī**
گولی چلانا fire, open firing *v.t.* **gōlī calānā**
گولی لگنا be shot *v.i.* **gōlī lagnā**
گولی مارنا shoot at *v.t.* **gōlī mārnā**
گوں color, tint; kind, mode *n.m.* **gūṁ**
گوناگوں various, varied *adj.* **gūnā gūṁ**
گونج echo, resounding *n.f.* **gūṁj**
گونجنا echo, resound *v.i.* **gūṁjnā**
گوند gum; glue *n.m.* **gōnd**
گونگا dumb, speechless, mute *adj.* **gūngā**
گونہ mode, manner, kind, form; color *n.m.* **gūnah**
گوہ lizard *n.f.* **gōh**

gem, pearl, jewel *n.m.* **gauhar** گوہر
singer; musician *n.m.* **gavayyā** گویا
speaking, eloquent *adj.* / as if, though *adv.* **gōyā** گویا
eloquence *n.f.* **gōyā'ī** گویائی
speaking, spoken, talking, talked *adj.* **gō'ī** گوئی
went, gone *v.i.* **gayā** گیا
worthless, useless *adj.* **gayā guzrā** گیا گزرا
eleven *num.* **gyārah** گیارہ
eleventh *adj.* **gyāravāṁ** گیارھواں
knowledge, intelligence, intellect, wisdom, understanding *n.m.* **giyān** گیان
acquire (spiritual) knowledge *v.i.* **giyān hōnā** گیان ہونا
sage, philosopher, wiseman *n.m.* **giyāni** گیانی
grass *n.f.* **giyāh** گیاہ
song, hymn *n.m.* **gīt** گیت
Bhagadvad Gita (*a religious book of the Hindus*) *n.f.* **gītā** گیتا
world, universe *n.m.* **gētī** گیتی
jackal; coward *n.m.* **gīdaṛ** گیدڑ
cowardly, timid; stupid *adj.* **gīdī** گیدی
taking, holding, covering, conquering *adj.* **gīr** گیر
gas *n.m.* **gais** گیس
lock; long hair *n.m.* **gēsū** گیسو
simpleminded, silly, stupid *adj.* **gēglā** گیگلا
simplemindedness, stupidity *n.m.* **gēglāpan** گیگلاپن
accompany, go along with *v.i.* **gail jānā** گیل جانا
comrade *n.m.* **gail vālā** گیل والا
wet, moist, damp *adj.* **gīlā** گیلا
wet *v.t.* **gīlā karnā** گیلا کرنا
humidity, wetness, dampness *n.m.* **gīlāpan** گیلاپن
large ball *n.f.* **gēnd** گیند
bowl *v.t.* **gēnd dēnā** گیند دینا
rhinoceros *n.m.* **gēṇḍā** گینڈا
world, universe *n.m.* **gaihāṁ** گیہاں
wheaten, made of wheat *adj.* **gēhvāṁ** گیہواں
wheat *n.m.* **gēhūṁ** گیہوں
ambush; stratagem *n.f.* **ghāt** گھات

lay an ambush, lurk *v.i.* **ghāt mēṁ baiṭhnā** گھات میں بیٹھنا
landing place, quay, wharf; mountain pass; loss *n.m.* **ghāṭ** گھاٹ
loss, deficiency *n.m.* **ghāṭā** گھاٹا
lose, suffer a loss *v.t.* **ghāṭ uṭhānā** گھاٹا اٹھانا
valley, pass *n.f.* **ghāṭī** گھاٹی
grass *n.f.* **ghās** گھاس
straw, weed *n.m.* **ghās phūs** گھاس پھوس
cut the grass *v.t.* **ghās kāṭnā** گھاس کاٹنا
old; experienced *adj.* **ghāgh** گھاگھ
petticoat *n.m.* **ghāghrā** گھاگھرا
oil press; sugar mill *n.f.* **ghānī** گھانی
wound, cut, sore *n.m.* **ghā'ō** گھاؤ
wounded, hurt *adj.* **ghā'il** گھائل
worry; be confused, be embarrassed *v.i.* **ghabrānā** گھبرانا
confusion, agitation *n.f.* **ghabrāhaṭ** گھبراہٹ
Don't worry! *interj.* **ghabrā'ō mat!** گھبراؤ مت
dark, obsure, hidden *adj.* **ghup** گھپ
cloudiness; cloud *n.f.* **ghaṭā** گھٹا
reduce, decrease, diminish, subtract, lessen *v.t.* **ghaṭānā** گھٹانا
reduction, decrease *n.m.* **ghaṭā'ō** گھٹاؤ
knee *n.m.* **ghuṭnā** • decrease, abate, fall; happen *v.i.* **ghaṭnā** گھٹنا
inferior, cheap *adj.* **ghaṭiyā** گھٹیا
house, home, abode *n.m.* **ghar** گھر
household, family, dynasty *n.f.* **gharānā** گھرانا
family, household, home *n.m.* **ghar bār** گھربار
be surrounded, be besieged *v.i.* **ghirnā** گھرنا
pulley; wheel *n.f.* **ghirnī** گھرنی
wife *n.f.* **ghar vālī** گھروالی
domestic, tame *adj.* **gharēlū** گھریلو
horse *n.m.* **ghuṛ** گھڑ
horse race *n.f.* **ghuṛ dauṛ** گھڑ دوڑ
stable *n.f.* **ghuṛ sāl** گھڑسال
pitcher, jar, pot *n.m.* **ghaṛā** گھڑا
invention; workmanship *n.f.* **ghaṛat** گھڑت
frown, rebuke *n.f.* **ghaṛkī** گھڑکی
forge, form, make, fabricate, work, invent *v.t.* **ghaṛnā** گھڑنا

moment; watch, clock *n.f.* **gharī** گھڑی
whispering *n.f.* **ghusaṛ phusaṛ** گھسڑ پھسڑ
penetrate, enter, rush in *v.i.* **ghusnā** گھسنا
grass-cutter *n.m.* **ghasyārah** گھسیارا
drag, haul, pull *v.t.* **ghasīṭnā** گھسیٹنا
insert, cram, thrust *v.t.* **ghusēṛnā** گھسیڑنا
short petticoat *n.f.* **ghagrī** گھگری
mixed; melted *adj.* **ghul mil** گھل مل
mixture; melting; softness *n.f.* **ghulāvaṭ** گھلاوٹ
melt, be dissolved; suffer *v.i.* **ghulnā** گھلنا
encircle, circulate, turn round *v.t.* **ghumānā** گھمانا
battle, force; mob, crowd *n.m.* **ghamsān** گھمسان
pride, arrogance *n.m.* **ghamanḍ** گھمنڈ
proud, arrogant *adj.* **ghamanḍī** گھمنڈی
disgust, dislike, hatred; nausea *n.f.* **ghin** گھن
clouds; sky *n.m.* **ghan** گھن
be disgusted; feel nauseous *v.i.* **ghin ānā** گھن آنا
thick, close; much, many *adj.* **ghanā** گھنا
bell; clock *n.m.* **ghanṭā** گھنٹا
clock tower *n.m.* **ghanṭā ghar** گھنٹا گھر
gong, bell *n.f.* **ghanṭī** گھنٹی
ring the bell *v.t.* **ghanṭī bajānā** گھنٹی بجانا
knot; button; tag *n.f.* **ghunḍī** گھنڈی
rinse; mix, shake *v.t.* **ghanghōlnā** گھنگولنا
dense; terrible *adj.* **ganghōr** گھنگھور
awful, horrible *adj.* **ghōr** گھور
stare at, look at *v.i.* **ghūrnā** گھورنا
horse *n.m.* **ghōṛā** گھوڑا
mare *n.f.* **ghōṛī** گھوڑی
milkman, cowherd *n.m.* **ghōsī** گھوسی
melt, dissolve, stir *v.t.* **ghōlnā** گھولنا
rotation *n.m.* **ghūm** گھوم
wander, travel; revolve, rotate, turn, bend *v.i.* **ghūmnā** گھومنا
draft, gulp *n.m.* **ghūnṭ** گھونٹ
shock, blow (*with the fist*) *n.m.* **ghūṁsā** گھونسا
give a blow *v.t.* **ghūṁsā mārnā** گھونسا مارنا

nest *n.m.* **ghōṁslah** گھونسلہ

veil *n.m.* **ghūngaṭ** گھونگٹ

ghee (*clarified butter*) *n.m.* **ghī** گھی

pumpkin, gourd *n.m.* **ghiyā** گھیا

enclosing, circuit, circle, surrounding *n.m.* **ghēr** گھیر

siege, blockade *n.m.* **ghērā** گھیرا

surround, encircle, enclose; blockade, besiege, lay seige *v.t.* **ghērnā** گھیرنا

lām ل

no, not, without *adv.* **lā** لا

necessary, essential, inevitable *adj.* **lā budī** لا بدی

remediless, incurable *adj.* **lā davā** لا دوا

unperishable, eternal *adj.* **lā zavāl** لا زوال

inevitable, unavoidable *adj.* **lā bud** لا بد

profit, gain, interest, produce, advantage; welfare *n.m.* **lābh** لابھ

leg; kick *n.f.* **lāt** لات

kick; spurn *v.t.* **lāt mārnā** لات مارنا

pillar; minaret; lord, governor, chief *n.f.* **lāṭ** لاٹ

staff; minaret; pillar, column *n.f.* **lāṭh** لاٹھ

stick, club, cudgel *n.f.* **lāṭhī** لاٹھی

incomparable, unmatched *adj.* **lā sānī** لاثانی

modesty, bashfulness; shame *n.f.* **lāj** لاج

silenced, speechless; matchless *adj.* **lā javāb** لاجواب

silence *v.t.* **lā javāb karnā** لاجواب کرنا

azure; gem *n.m.* **lājvard** لاجورد

sky-blue, azure *adj.* **lājvardī** لاجوردی

helpless, compelled, disabled *adj.* **lā cār** لاچار

helplessness, inability; poverty *n.f.* **lā cārgī** لاچارگی

helplessness, inability; poverty *n.f.* **lā cārī** لاچاری

useless, fruitless, unprofitable, unproductive *adj.* **lā ḥāsil** لا حاصل

touching, adhering, joining *adj.* **lāḥiq** لاحق

insoluble; difficult *adj.* **lā ḥal** لاحل

rent free *adj.* **lā xirāj** لا خراج

load, burden *n.f.* **lād** لاد

load, pile, heap *v.t.* **lādna** لادنا

doubtless, undoubtedly, unquestionably *adv.* **lā raib** لاریب

necessary, compulsory *adj.* **lāzim** لازم

necessary, inevitable *adj.* **lāzimī** لازمی

imperishable, eternal, everlasting *adj.* **lā zavāl** لازوال

dead body, corpse *n.f.* **lāš** لاش

useless, vain; absurd *adj.* **lā tā'il** لاطائل

incurable, without remedy *adj.* **lā ᶜilāj** لا علاج

لاعلم **lā ʿilm** ignorant, unaware *adj.*
لاغر **lāġar** lean, thin; emaciated *adj.*
لاغری **lāġarī** leanness, thinness *n.f.*
لاف **lāf** self-praise, vanity, boasting; falsehood *n.f.*
لاکھ **lākh** hundred thousand *num.*
لاکلام **lā kalām** speechless *adj.*
لاگ **lāg** enmity, grudge, ill-feeling *n.f.*
لاگت **lāgat** cost, expenditure *n.f.*
لاگو **lāgū** adhering, attached *adj.*
لال **lāl** red; angry, enraged *adj.* / son; dear, darling *n.m.*
لالٹین **lālṭain** lantern *n.f.*
لالچ **lālac** avarice, greed; ambition; selfishness *n.m.*
لالچی **lālcī** avaricious, greedy *adj.*
لالہ **lālah** tulip; poppy flower *n.m.*
لالی **lālī** redness; reputation, honor *n.f.*
لام **lām** brigade *n.m.*
لامحالہ **lā maḥālah** surely, certainly, definitely *adv.*
لامذہب **lā mazhab** irreligious, secular *adj.*
لامسہ **lāmisah** touch, feeling *n.f.*
لامکان **lā makān** homeless *adj.*
لانا **lāna** bring, fetch *v.i.*
لاولد **lā valad** childless; issue-less *adj.*
لایزال **lā yazāl** endless, eternal *adj.*
لایزال **lāyazāl** everlasting *adj.*
لایعنی **lā yaʿnī** absurd, insignificant, meaningless *adj.*
لائق **lā'iq** worthy, deserving, suitable, capable *adj.*
لایموت **lā yamūt** deathless, immortal *adj.*
لب **lab** lip *n.m.*
لباس **libās** dress, apparel, costume *n.m.*
لبھانا **lubhānā** seduce, allure, charm, attract *v.t.*
لپ **lap** handful *n.f.*
لپائی **lipā'ī** plastering *n.f.*
لپٹ **lapaṭ** flame, glow; scent *n.f.*
لپٹنا **lipaṭnā** cling, adhere, embrace *v.i.*
لپڑ **lappaṛ** slap, blow *n.m.*

لپک **lapak** *n.f.* spring, flash, bounce
لپکنا **lapakna** *v.i.* jump, leap, rush, snatch (at)
لپیٹ **lapēṭ** *n.f.* fold, wrapping, coating, bandage; coil, entanglement
لپیٹنا **lapēṭna** *v.t.* fold, wrap, twist, entangle
لت **lat** *n.f.* bad habit, vice
لت پت **lat pat** *adj.* wet, moist, soaked
لتا **lattā** *n.m.* rag, scrap (*of cloth*)
لتاڑنا **latāṛnā** *v.t.* insult, spurn, treat with contempt
لٹ **laṭ** *n.f.* lock of hair, tangled hair
لٹانا **luṭānā** *v.t.* plunder, squander, spend lavishly
لٹکانا **laṭkānā** *v.t.* hang, suspend
لٹکن **laṭkan** *n.m.* pendulum, pendant
لٹکنا **laṭaknā** *v.i.* hang, delay, dangle
لٹنا **luṭnā** *v.i.* be looted, be sacked, be robbed
لٹو **laṭṭū** *n.m.* top; plummet
لٹیرا **luṭērā** *n.m.* plunderer, robber, gangster
لٹھ **laṭh** *n.m.* club, stick
لجا **lajjā** *n.f.* shame, modesty, bashfulness
لجاجت **lajājat** *n.f.* importunity, entreaty
لجانا **lajānā** *v.i.* be ashamed
لچا **luccā** *adj.* shameless; mean, wicked, corrupt / vagabond; wicked person *n.m.*
لچر **lacar** *adj.* meaningless; weak, loose
لچک **lacak** *n.f.* softness, elasticity, flexibility
لچک دار **lacak dār** *adj.* soft, elastic, flexible
لچھن **lacchan** *n.m.* mode, habit, manner; condition; action; sign, mark
لچھمی **lachmī** *n.f.* beauty; wealth
لحاظ **liḥāz** *n.m.* regard, respect; glance, observation, consideration, attention
لحد **laḥad** *n.f.* grave, tomb
لحظہ **laḥzah** *n.m.* moment; glance
لحم **laḥm** *n.m.* flesh, meat
لحن **laḥn** *n.f.* melody, note, sound
لخت **laxt** *n.m.* piece, part, bit, portion
لڈو **laḍḍū** *n.m.* laddoo (*a dessert*)
لذت **lazzat** *n.f.* taste, flavor, relish; joy, pleasure
لذیذ **lazīz** *adj.* sweet; delicious, tasteful, tasty, savory

shivering, trembling *adj.* **larzāṁ** لرزاں

trembling, quaking *n.f.* **larziš** لرزش

tremble, shake, quake *v.i.* **laraznā** لرزنا

earthquake *n.m.* **larzah** لرزہ

string, rope, thread, chain; series *n.m.* **laṛ** لڑ

quarrelsome *adj.* **laṛākā** لڑاکا

quarrel, fight, battle, war *n.f.* **laṛā'ī** لڑائی

go to war *v.i.* **laṛā'ī par jānā** لڑائی پر جانا

declare war, decide (to go to) war *v.t.* **laṛā'ī ṭhānnā** لڑائی ٹھاننا

battlefield *n.m.* **laṛā'ī kā maidān** لڑائی کا میدان

son, boy *n.m.* **laṛkā** لڑکا

boyhood, childhood *n.m.* **laṛakpan** لڑکپن

stagger, totter; stammer, stutter *v.i.* **laṛkhaṛānā** لڑکھڑانا

daughter, girl *n.f.* **laṛkī** لڑکی

struggle, fight, quarrel *v.i./v.t.* **laṛnā** لڑنا

string, link *n.f.* **laṛī** لڑی

roll (over), topple (over); lie down *v.i.* **luṛhaknā** لڑھکنا

necessity, compulsion *n.m.* **lazūm** لزوم

stickiness *n.m.* **las** لس

talkative, eloquent, fluent *adj.* **lassān** لسان

tongue; language, dialect, speech *n.f.* **lisān** لسان

lassi (*buttermilk-based drink*) *n.f.* **lassī** لسی

army; camp *n.m.* **laškar** لشکر

military *adj.* **laškarī** لشکری

grace, elegance, deliciousness, fineness *n.f.* **latāfat** لطافت

taste, beauty, grace, courtesy *n.m.* **lutf** لطف

fine, delicious, delicate, courteous, elegant *adj.* **latīf** لطیف

pleasantry, joke *n.m.* **latīfah** لطیفہ

joker, jester, witty person *n.m.* **latīfah gō** لطیفہ گو

spittle, saliva; viscosity *n.m.* **luᶜāb** لعاب

viscous, slimy *adj.* **luᶜāb dār** لعاب دار

play, playing, game, sport *n.m.* **laᶜb** لعب

doll, puppet *n.f.* **laᶜbat/luᶜbat** لعبت

ruby *n.m.* **laᶜl** لعل

cursing, abuse *n.f.* **laᶜn** لعن

curse, abuse *n.f.* **la^cnat** لعنت
cursed, abused *adj.* **la^cnatī** لعنتی
detested, abominable *adj.* **la^cīn** لعین
up to, to the end *adv.* **laġāyat** لغایت
dictionary; tongue; speech, language *n.f.* **luġat** لغت
slip, tottering; ambiguity *n.f.* **laġziš** لغزش
absurd, foolish; false *adj.* **laġv** لغو
literal, verbal *adj.* **luġvī** لغوی
literal meaning, verbal meaning *n.m.* **laġvī ma^cnī** لغوی معنی
attached, enclosed, included; wrapped, folded *adj.* **laff** لف
eloquent *adj.* **laffāz** لفاظ
eloquence *n.f.* **laffāzī** لفاظی
envelope, cover, enclosure *n.m.* **lifāfah** لفافہ
word, phrase, saying *n.m.* **lafz** لفظ
literally, word by word *adj.* **lafz bah lafz** لفظ بہ لفظ
literally, explicitly, distinctly *adv.* **lafzan** لفظاً
literal, explicit, distinct *adj.* **lafzī** لفظی
surname, title *n.m.* **laqab** لقب
wise man *n.m.* **luqmān** لقمان
mouthful, morsel, bit *n.m.* **luqmah** لقمہ
paralysis *n.m.* **laqvah** لقوہ
paralytic *adj.* **laqvah zadah** لقوہ زدہ
varnish *n.m.* **luk** لک
millionaire *n.m.* **lakh pati** لکھ پتی
get written, cause to write, dictate *v.t.* **likhānā** لکھانا
writing *n.f.* **likhā'ī** لکھائی
log, beam *n.m.* **lakkaṛ** لکڑ
timber, wood; stick, staff *n.f.* **lakṛī** لکڑی
write *v.t.* **likhnā** لکھنا
education *n.f.* **likhnā paṛhnā** لکھنا پڑھنا
stammering, stuttering *n.f.* **luknat** لکنت
line, streak, stripe *n.f.* **lakīr** لکیر
draw a line, mark a boundary *v.t.* **lakīr khaiṁcnā** لکیر کھینچنا
up to, near, until, as far as *pp.* **lag** لگ
about, nearly, almost, approximately *adv.* **lag bhag** لگ بھگ
constantly, continually, successively *adv.* **lagā tār** لگاتار

bridle, rein *n.f.* **lagām** لگام
bridle, curb, control, check *v.t.* **lagām dēnā** لگام دینا
rent, land revenue *n.m.* **lagān** لگان
apply, fix, attach, join; appoint, employ *v.t.* **lagānā** لگانا
relation, connection, adherence *n.m.* **lagā'ō** لگاؤ
wife; woman *n.f.* **lugā'ī** لگائی
affection, attachment, longing, desire, craze *n.f.*. **lagan** لگن
begin to; be applied, be attached, be connected; touch, feel; seem; *v.i.* **lagnā** لگنا
covet, long for, desire; excite *v.i.* **lalcānā** للچانا
calling, shouting, cry; challenge *n.f.* **lalkār** للکار
call, shout, cry; challenge *v.t.* **lalkārnā** للکارنا
For God's sake!, By God! *interj.* **lillah** للہ
long, tall *adj.* **lambā** لمبا
prolong, lengthen *v.t.* **lambā karnā** لمبا کرنا
length *n.f.* **lambā'ī** لمبائی
very long, very tall *adj.* **lambōtrā** لمبوترا
moment, minute *n.m.* **lamḥah** لمحہ
brightness, glow, flash *n.m.* **lamᶜah** لمعہ
pour, spill, over-turn *v.t.* **lunḍhānā** لنڈھانا
anchor *n.m.* **langar** لنگر
cast an anchor *v.t.* **langar ḍālnā** لنگر ڈالنا یا لگانا
lame, crippled, disabled *adj.* **langṛā** لنگڑا
lameness, disability *n.f.* **langṛā'ī** لنگڑائی
tongue; tone, sound, voice; accent, dialect *n.m.* **laḥjah** لہجہ
therefore, for this reason, consequently *adv.* **lihazā** لہذا
wave, movement; excitement, emotion *n.f.* **lahar/lahr** لہر
odd; merry, emotional, fantastic *adj.* **lahrī** لہری
striped *adj.* **lahriyā** لہریا
garlic *n.m.* **lahsan/lahsun** لہسن
glitter, brilliance, flash, blaze *n.f.* **lahak** لہک
glitter, flash, blaze, shine *v.i.* **lahaknā** لہکنا
splendid, glittering, glistening *adj.* **lahakīlā** لہکیلا
bloom, flourish, grow *v.t.* **lahlahānā** لہلہانا
skirt, petticoat *n.m.* **lahangā** لہنگا
play, sports *n.m.* **lahv** • blood *n.m.* **lahū** لہو
covered with blood, bloodstained *adj.* **lahū luhān** لہولہان

play, sports, amusement, pastime *n.m.* **lahv-ō-laᶜb** لہو ولعب
hot wind *n.f.* **lū** • flame; attachment, desire *n.f.* **lau** لو
desire, be in devotion *v.t.* **lau lagānā** لو لگانا
avarice, greediness *n.m.* **lōbh** لوبھ
greedy *adj.* **lōbhī** لوبھی
loot, plunder; robbery *n.f.* **lūṭ** لوٹ
come back, return *v.i.* **lauṭ ānā** لوٹ آنا
go back *v.i.* **lauṭ jānā** لوٹ جانا
booty, looted items; robbery *n.m.* **lūṭ kā māl** لوٹ کا مال
return, send back *v.t.* **lauṭānā** لوٹانا
• loot, rob, plunder *v.t.* **lūṭnā** • return, go back; turn over *v.i.* **lauṭnā** لوٹنا
roll, toss; sprawl, lie down; be charmed *v.i.* **lōṭnā**
impurity, contamination, pollution *n.m.* **laus** لوث
flexibility, softness; starch, stickiness *n.m.* **lōc** لوچ
starchy; soft, flexible *adj.* **lōc dār** لوچ دار
eye *n.m.* **lōcan** لوچن
plank, table, board *n.f.* **lauḥ** لوح
epitaph *n.f.* **lauḥ-ē-qabar** لوح قبر
lullaby *n.f.* **lōrī** لوری
almond *n.m.* **lauz** لوز
people *n.m.* **lōg** لوگ
pearl *n.m.* **lō' lō'** لؤلؤ
fox *n.m.* **lōmaṛ** لومڑ
vixen, fox *n.f.* **lōmaṛī** لومڑی
salt *n.m.* **lūn/lavan** لون
boy, lad; slave *n.m.* **launḍā** لونڈا
maid, servant *n.f.* **launḍī** لونڈی
girl; daughter *n.f.* **launḍyā** لونڈیا
iron *n.m.* **lōhā/lauhā** لوہا
ironsmith, blacksmith *n.m.* **lōhār** لوہار
firm, strong, hard, rigid *adj.* **lōhā laṭh** لوہا لٹھ
blanket *n.f.* **lō'ī** لوئی
tune, air, melody; taste, desire *n.f.* **la'ē** لے
fetch, bring *v.i.* **lē ānā** لے آنا
receive, take back, extort *v.t.* **lē lēnā** لے لینا
worth, ability, capability, capacity *n.f.* **liyāqat** لیاقت

band-aid, plaster, ointment *n.m.* **lēp** لیپ
evasion, delay *n.f.* **lait-ō-laᶜll** لیت و لعل
liter *n.m.* **līṭar** لیٹر
lie down, rest *v.i.* **lēṭnā** لیٹنا
stingy, miserly *adj.* **līcaṛ** لیچڑ
• dressed; finished, ready *adj.* / spring; vinegar *n.m.* **lais** لیس
gum, plaster; stickiness *n.f.* **lēs**
sticky, glutinous *adj.* **lais dār** لیس دار
mark, path, trace *n.f.* **līk** لیک
but, yet, however, still *conj.* **lēkin** لیکن
night *n.f.* **lail** لیل
night and day *n.m.* **lail-ō-nahār** لیل ونہار
sport; play, performance *n.f.* **līlā** • lamb *n.m.* **lēlā** لیلا
night *n.f.* **lailat** لیلۃ
lamp *n.m.* **laimp** لیمپ
lemon, lime *n.m.* **līmūṁ** لیموں
receiving, taking *n.m.* **lēn** لین
traffic, trade *n.m.* **lēn dēn** لین دین
trade, carry on business *v.t.* **lēn dēn karnā** لین دین کرنا
take, receive, draw, buy *v.t.* **lēnā** لینا
filth *n.f.* **lēṁḍī** لینڈی
be very proud *v.i.* **lēṁḍī tar hōnā** لینڈی تر ہونا
for (the sake of), on account of, instead of *pp./adv.* **li'ē** لئے

mīm م

that, what, whatsoever, which, as far as, as much as *pp.* **mā** ما
following, that follows *adj.* **mā baᶜd** ما بعد
rest, remainder *n.m.* **mā baqā** ما بقا
in the meantime, between, during *pp.* **mā bain** ما بین
subordinate, inferior, dependent *adj.* **mā taḥat** ما تحت
earlier, aforesaid, bygone *adj.* **mā taqqadum** ما تقدم
environment, surroundings *n.m.* **mā ḥaul** ما حول
until, while *pp.* **mā dām** ما دام
besides, moreover *pp.* **mā dūn** ما دون
rich, wealthy *adj.* **māl dār** مالدار
besides, beyond, over and above *adj./adv.* **mā varā** ماورا
recourse; fixed abode; focus (of) *n.f.* **mā'ab** ماب
defeat *n.f.* **māt** مات
outdo, confound, beat *v.t.* **māt karnā** مات کرنا
mother; smallpox *n.f.* **mātā** ماتا
parents *n.m.* **mātā pitā** ماتاپتا
mourning, grief *n.m.* **mātam** ماتم
condolence *n.f.* **mātam pursī** ماتم پرسی
console *v.t.* **mātam pursī karnā** ماتم پرسی کرنا
mourner; mourning *n.m.* **mātam dār** ماتم دار
mourning *n.f.* **mātam dārī** ماتم داری
lament, mourn *v.t.* **mātam karnā** ماتم کرنا
mourning, mournful *adj.* **mātamī** ماتمی
forehead, head; top, summit *n.m.* **māthā** ماتھا
jar, vat *n.m.* **māṭ** ماٹ
glorious, honorable *adj.* **mājid** ماجد
glorious, honorable *adj.* **mājidah** ماجدہ
incident, occurrence *n.m.* **mājrā** ماجرا
matches *n.f.* **mācis** ماچس
source, origin *n.m.* **māxaz** ماخذ
source *n.m.* **mā'axiz** ماخذ
taken, seized; involved, accused *adj.* **māxūz** ماخوذ
mother *n.f.* **mādar** مادر

innate, inborn, natural *adj.* **mādar zād** مادرزاد
motherly, maternal *adj.* **mādrī** مادری
mother-tongue *n.f.* **mādrī zabān** مادری زبان
matter, substance, subject *n.m.* **māddah** مادہ
materialist *n.m.* **māddah parast** مادہ پرست
materialism *n.f.* **māddah parastī** مادہ پرستی
material, natural *adj.* **māddī** مادی
mare *n.f.* **mādiyān** مادیان
materialism, substance *n.f.* **māddiyat** مادیت
beating, striking, stroke *n.f.* / serpent, snake *n.m.* **mār** مار
beat, strike; embezzle *v.i.* **mār baiṭhnā** مار بیٹھنا
drive away *v.t.* **mār bhagānā** مار بھگانا
be beaten *v.i.* **mār paṛnā** مار پڑنا
be slain, be killed *v.i.* **mār jānā** مار جانا
kill, murder *v.t.* **mār ḍālnā** مار ڈالنا
slay, kill; usurp *v.t.* **mār rakhnā** مار رکھنا
knock down; kill *v.t.* **mār girānā** مار گرانا
work hard, toil, try one's best *v.t.* **mārā mār karnā** مارا مار کرنا
March (*month*) *n.m.* **mārc** مارچ
kill, beat to death *v.t.* **mār dēnā** مار دینا
brand *n.m.* **mārkah** مارکہ
rob, plunder *v.t.* **mār lānā** مار لانا
beat, strike, punish; drive away; kill, slaughter, murder *v.t.* **mārnā** مارنا
for, for the sake of, on account of *pp.* **mārē** مارے
starch, gruel *n.f.* **māṛī** ماڑی
flesh, meat *n.m.* **mās** ماس
above-mentioned, preceding, that precedes *adj.* **mā sabaq** ماسبق
tasteless *adj.* **māsax** ماسخ
focus *n.f.* **māsikah** ماسکہ
What God desires! *interj.* **māšā' Allah!** ماشاء اللہ
be fickle, be indecisive *v.i.* **māšah tōlah hōnā** ماشہ تولہ ہونا
sour milk *n.m.* **māzar** ماضر
past *n.f.* **māzī** ماضی
what it contains *n.m.* **mā fīhā** ما فیہا
last, prior; before, preceding *adj.* **mā qabl** ماقبل
above-mentioned *adj.* **mā qabal-ul-zikr** ماقبل الذکر

ماکول edible *adj.* **mākūl**
مال string, garland *n.f.* / wealth, stock, property, goods, merchandise *n.m.* **māl**
مال حصہ داری joint stock *n.m.* **māl-ē-ḥissah dārī**
مال خانہ storehouse, warehouse *n.m.* **māl xānah**
مال ضامن surety *n.m.* **māl zāmin**
مال گذار tenant; landholder *n.m.* **māl guzār**
مال گذاری land revenue, assessment (*of revenue*), rent (*for land*) *n.f.* **māl guzārī**
مال مارنا rob, swindle *v.t.* **māl mārnā**
مال ور rich *adj.* **māl vār**
مالا rosary, chaplet, garland *n.f.* **mālā**
مالا مال full, replete, abundant *adj.* **mālā māl**
مالا مال کرنا enrich, heap up, fill *v.t.* **mālā māl karnā**
مالاینحل insoluble, inextricable *adj.* **mā lā yanḥal**
مالا کلام indescribable, inexpressible *adj.* **mā lā kalām**
مالایطاق intolerable, unbearable *adj.* **mā lā yutāq**
مالش rubbing, massage; shampooing *n.f.* **māliš**
مالش کرنا rub, massage; shampoo *v.t.* **māliš kārnā**
مالک master, owner, proprietor *n.m.* **mālik**
مالکی royal *adj.* **mālkī**
مالکیت possession, proprietorship *n.f.* **mālkiyat**
مالن gardener *n.f.* **mālan/mālin**
مالوف familiar, customary, dear *adj.* **mālūf**
مالی gardener *n.m.* / financial *adj.* **mālī**
مالی پیشکار accountant *n.m.* **mālī pēškār**
مالی سال financial year *n.m.* **mālī sāl**
مالیت cost, value *n.f.* **māliyat**
ماما uncle (*maternal*) *n.m.* / mother, mom, mommy *n.f.* **māmā**
مامتا maternal love *n.f.* **māmtā**
مامن place of security, place of freedom *n.m.* **māmān**
مامور ordered, commanded, determined *adj.* **māmūr**
مامور ہونا be appointed, be entrusted *v.i.* **māmūr hónā**
ماموں uncle (*maternal*) *n.m.* **māmūṁ**
مامون secure, safe; constant, firm *adj.* **māmūn**
مامی aunt (*maternal*) *n.f.* **māmī**
ماں mother *n.f.* **māṁ**
مان honor, regard, respect *n.m.* **mān**

ماں باپ parents *n.m.* **māṁ bāp**

مان رکھنا honor, respect *v.t.* **mān rākhnā**

مانجنا cleanse, scrub *v.t.* **māṁjnā**

مانجھی boatman, sailor *n.m.* **māṁjhī**

ماند dim, faded, faint *adj.* **mānd**

ماند پڑجانا become dim, be faded, be faint *v.i.* **mānd pāṛ jānā**

ماندگی weariness, fatigue *n.f.* **māndagī**

مانڈ paste, starch (*made of rice flour*) *n.m.* **mānḍ**

مانڈنا knead, rub, flatten *v.t.* **mānḍnā**

مانڈی starch (*made of rice flour*) *n.f.* **mānḍī**

مانس man, human being *n.m.* **mānus/mānas**

مانع impediment, hindrance, obstacle, prohibition *n.m.* **māniᶜ**

مانع ہونا be prohibited, prevent, hinder, object (to) *v.i.* **māniᶜ hónā**

مانگ parting (of hair) *n.f.* **māng**

مانگ اجڑنا become a widow *v.i.* **māng ujaṛnā**

مانگ بھری married woman, wife *n.f.* **māng bharī**

مانگ جلی widow *n.f.* **māng jalī**

مانگ لینا borrow *v.t.* **māng lēnā**

مانگنا beg, ask for, require, demand; pray; borrow *v.t.* **māngnā**

ماننا accept, agree; confess, admit; suppose, believe; obey *v.t.* **mānnā**

مانند like, resembling *adj.* **mānind**

مانوس intimate, familiar, associated *adj.* **mānūs**

ماہ moon; month *n.m.* **māh**

ماہ بماہ monthly, every month *adv.* **māh ba-māh**

ماہ تاب moonshine, moonlight *n.m.* **māh tāb**

ماہ جبیں moon-faced, beautiful *adj.* **māh jabīṁ**

ماہِ رواں current month *n.m.* **māh-ē-ravāṁ**

ماہِ شمسی solar month *n.m.* **māh-ē-šamsī**

ماہِ قمری lunar month *n.m.* **māh-ē-qamrī**

ماہر well-acquainted (*with an art*), familiar (with), expert, competent *adj.* **māhir**

ماہرِ ریاضیات mathematician *n.m.* **māhir-ē-riyāziyāt**

ماہرِ طبعیات physicist *n.m.* **māhir-ē-tabiᶜyāt**

ماہرِ علمِ ارضیات geologist *n.m.* **māhir-ē-arziyāt**

ماہرِ علمِ تاریخ historian *n.m.* **māhir-ē-ᶜilm-ē-tārīx**

ماہرِ علمِ جغرافیہ geographer *n.m.* **māhir-ē-ᶜilm-ē-juġrāfiyah**

ماہر علم حیوانات **māhir-ē-ᶜilm-ē-ḥaivānāt** zoologist *n.m.*
ماہر علم کیمیا **māhir-ē-ᶜilm-ē-kīmiyā** chemist *n.m.*
ماہر لسانیات **māhir-ē-lisāniyāt** linguist, philologist *n.m.*
ماہر نفسیات **māhir-ē-nafsiyāt** psychologist *n.m.*
ماہواری **māhvārī** monthly *adv.*
ماہواری **māhvārī** menstruation *n.f.*
ماہی **māhī** fish *n.f.*
ماہی بے آب **māhī bē āb** restless, uneasy *adj.*
ماہی گیر **māhī gīr** fisherman *n.m.*
ماہی گیری **māhī gīrī** fishing *n.f.*
ماہیانہ **māhiyānah** monthly pay *n.m.*
ماہیت **māhiyat** essence, nature *n.f.*
ماء **mā'** water *n.m.*
ماوا **māvā** curd, condensed milk; substance, essence; abode, dwelling, residence *n.m.*
ماوشما **mā-ō-šumā** everybody *n.m.*
ماؤف **mā'ūf** afflicted *adj.*
ماومن **mā-ō-man** self-praise, pride, egoism *n.f.*
مایا **māyā** illusion, delusion, mirage, show *n.f.*
مائع **mā'iᶜ** liquid, fluid *n.m.*
مائل **mā'il** inclined, bent; fond, desirous *adj.*
مائل کرنا **mā'il karnā** bend, persuade *v.t.*
مایہ **māyah** fund, wealth, capital, stock *n.m.*
مایہ دار **māyah dār** capitalist *n.m.*
مایوس **māyūs** hopeless, desperate, disappointed *adj.*
مایوس کرنا **māyūs kārnā** disappoint *v.t.*
مایوسی **māyūsī** despair, disappointment, hopelessness *n.f.*
مائی **mā'ī** mother, mom, mommy *n.f.*
مآل **mā'al** end, termination; consequence, result *n.m.*
مباح **mubāḥ** lawful, just; allowed, permissible *adj.*
مباحثہ **mubāḥasah** debate, dispute, contest; investigation *n.m.*
مباحثہ کرنا **mubāḥasah kārnā** discuss, dispute, argue *v.t.*
مبادا **mubādā** be it not so, God forbid, by no means *adv.*
مبادرت **mubādarat** haste *n.f.*
مبادلہ **mubādalah** exchange; retaliation *n.m.*
مبارز **mubāriz** warrior, soldier *n.m.*
مبارزت **mubārazat** battle, war, fight, combat *n.f.*

Congratulations! *interj.* / auspicious, blessed, happy, fortunate *adj.* **mubārāk** مبارک

Congratulations!, Good wishes! *interj.* **mubārāk bād!** مبارک باد

congratulate *v.t.* **mubārāk bād kahnā** مبارک باد کہنا

congratulations, blessing *n.f.* **mubārāk bādī** مبارک بادی

congratulate, bless *v.t.* **mubārāk bādī dēnā** مبارک بادی دینا

auspiciousness, blessing *n.f.* **mubārākī** مبارکی

exaggeration *n.m.* **mubālaġah** مبالغہ

exaggerate *v.t.* **mubālaġah karnā** مبالغہ کرنا

glorying, boasting; arrogance *n.f.* **mubāhāt** مباہات

mutual care *n.m.* **mubāhalah** مباہلہ

commencement; subject, principle *n.m.* **mubtadā** مبتدا

beginner, novice, young student *n.m.* **mubtadī** مبتدی

base, mean, contemptible *adj.* **mubtazal** مبتذل

involved, entangled, affected *adj.* **mubtalā** مبتلا

inquiry, discussion, dispute *n.m.* **mabḥas** مبحث

beginning, origin, source *n.m.* **mabdā** مبدا

altered, changed, exchanged *adj.* **mubaddal** مبدل

expended, conferred, bestowed *adj.* **mabzūl** مبذول

free, exempted; innocent *adj.* **mubarrā** مبرا

cooled *adj.* **mubarrad** مبرد

inevitable; urgent; tight, firm *adj.* **mubram** مبرم

spread out, expanded, stretched *adj.* **mabsūt** مبسوط

observer *n.m.* **mubassir** مبصر

abolishing, annihilating, annulling *adj.* **mubtil** مبطل

created; sent *adj.* **mabᶜūs** مبعوث

sum, quantity *n.m.* **mablaġ** مبلغ

based, founded *adj.* **mabni** مبنی

hidden, indistinct; occult *adj.* **mubham** مبہم

astonished, amazed, stupefied *adj.* **mabhūt** مبہوت

clear, manifest, evident *adj.* **mubīn** مبین

/ opinion, view; doctrine; sect; thought; advice; vote *n.f.* **mat** مت
do not, don't *adv.*

change one's views *v.t.* **mat phirnā** مت پھرنا

give advice, counsel *v.t.* **mat dēnā** مت دینا

advice, counsel, opinion, belief, thought *n.m.* **matā** متا

متابعت **mutāba^cat** *n.f.* submission, obedience
متاثر **mutā'assir** *adj.* impressed, touched, affected
متاخر **mutā'axir** *adj.* following, succeeding
متاسف **mutā'assif** *adj.* repentant, regretful, sorrowful
متاسفانہ **mutā'assifānah** *adv.* regretfully; impressively
متاع **matā^c** *n.f.* goods, valuables
متامل **mutā'ammil** *adj.* contemplating, meditative, thoughtful
متانت **matānat** *n.f.* firmness, solidity
متبادر **mutabādir** *adj.* making haste
متبادل **mutabādil** *adj.* alternate, alternative
متبادلہ **mutabādilah** *adj.* reciprocal, mutual
متبحر **mutabaḥḥir** *adj.* learned, educated
متبرک **mutabarrak** *adj.* holy, sacred, blessed
متبسم **mutabassim** *adj.* smiling
متبع **muttabi^c** *n.m.* follower, disciple
متبوع **matbū^c** *adj.* followed, obeyed
مستثنیٰ **mustasnā** *adj.* excluded, excepted, omitted, selected
متجلی **mutajallā** *adj.* bright, splendid
متحد **muttaḥid** *adj.* united
متحرک **mutaḥarrik** *adj.* moveable, moving, moved
محترم **mutaḥarrim** *adj.* respected, revered
متحقق **mutaḥaqqaq** *n.m.* verifier, researcher / *adj.* verified, true, certain
متحقق کرنا **mutaḥaqqaq karnā** *v.t.* verify, prove
متحمل **mutaḥammil** *adj.* patient, enduring, passive, considerate
متحیر **mutḥaiyyir** *adj.* astonished, amazed, wondering
متخاصم **mutaxāsim** *adj.* hostile, contending
متخلص **mutaxallis** *adj.* pure, free
متخیل **mutaxaiyyil** *adj.* imagining, suspecting
متداول **mutadāval** *adj.* customary, common, current, in use
متدین **mutadaiyyin** *adj.* religious, orthodox, pious
متذبذب **mutazabzib** *adj.* hesitating, anxious
متذکرہ **mutazakkirah** *adj.* mentioned, referred, stated
مترادف **mutarādif** *adj.* continued, consecutive, successive
متراکب **mutarākib** *n.m.* associate, companion
مترتب **mutarattab** *adj.* arranged, compiled

مترجم translator, interpreter *n.m.* **mutarjim** • translated *adj.* **mutarjam**
مترحم merciful, pitiful, kind *adj.* **mutaraḥḥim**
متردد hesitating, anxious, perplexed *adj.* **mutaraddid**
مترقب expecting, watching, observing *adj.* **mutaraqqib**
مترقبہ expected *adj.* **mutarqqabah**
مترنم singing, melodious *adj.* **mutarannim**
متروک abolished, obsolete, rejected, abandoned *adj.* **matrūk**
متروک الاستعمال not in use, unused, obsolete *adj.* **matrūk-ul-isti^cmāl**
متزلزل shaken, shaky *adj.* **mutazalzal**
متساوی equal, straight, parallel, right *adj.* **mutasāvī**
متسلط absolute, despotic *adj.* **mutasallit**
متسلم consigned, delivered *adj.* **mutasallam**
متسلی satisfied, comforted *adj.* **mutasalī**
متسم branded, stigmatized *adj.* **mutassam**
متشابہ alike, similar, resembling *adj.* **mutašābih**
متشدد violent; hard, strict *adj.* **mutašaddid**
متشرع orthodox, religious, pious *adj.* **mutašarri^c**
متشکل resembling, alike, similar *adj.* **mutašakkil**
متشکی doubtful, suspicious *adj.* **mutašakkī**
متصادم colliding, clashing *adj.* **mutasadim**
متصرف extravagant *adj.* **mutasarrif**
متصل adjoining, near, touching, continual, successive *adj.* **muttasil**
متصور imagined, conceived, reflected, considerate *adj.* **mutasavvar**
متضاد opposite, contrary *adj.* **mutazād**
متضرب inclusive *adj.* **mutazarrib**
متعارف widely known, self-evident *adj.* **muta^caraf**
متعاقب following, subsequent, successive, pursuing *adj.* **muta^cāqib**
متعال lofty, high, great, sublime *adj.* **muta^cāl**
متعجب astonished, amazed, surprised *adj.* **muta^cajjib**
متعدد several, many, various *adj.* **muta^caddad**
متعذر objector *n.m.* **mu^ctazir**
متعصب partial, prejudiced; superstitious *adj.* **muta^cassib**
متعفن stinking, rotten, putrid *adj.* **muta^caffin**
متعلق belonging to, connected with, attached to, concerning *adj.* **muta^calliq**
suspended, hanging;

متعلم scholar *n.m.* **mutaᶜallim**
متعین appointed, determined, fixed *adj.* **mutaᶜaiyyan**
متعین کرنا appoint, determine, fix *v.t.* **mutaᶜaiyyan karnā**
متغالب victorious *adj.* **muttaġāllib**
متغیر changing, changed, altered *adj.* **mutaġaiyyar**
متفرق miscellaneous, separated *adj.* **mutafarraq**
متفق agreeing, consenting *adj.* **muttafiq**
متفق ہونا agree upon, consent *v.i.* **muttafiq hōnā**
متفکر anxious, worried, thoughtful; serious *adj.* **mutafakkir**
متفکر ہونا worry, be worried *v.i.* **mutafakkir hōnā**
متقدم ancient; anterior; precedent *adj.* **mutaqaddim**
متقی sober, temperate; pious *adj.* **muttaqī**
متکبر proud, arrogant, disdainful *adj.* **mutakabbir**
متکلم speaking *adj.* **mutakallim**
متلاشی searcher, explorer, inquirer *n.m.* **mutalāšī**
متلذذ relishing *adj.* **mutalazziz**
متلون variable, inconstant, changeable *adj.* **mutalavvin**
متلی sickness, nausea *n.f.* **matlī**
متمتع enjoying *adj.* **mutamattiᶜ**
متمنی wishing, desiring, hoping *adj.* **mutamannī**
متمول rich, wealthy *adj.* **mutamavvil**
متنازع disputed, contested *adj.* **mutanāzaᶜ**
متناسب similar *adj.* **mutanāsib**
متناقص opposite, contrary *adj.* **mutanāqis**
متنبہ cautious, wakeful, aware *adj.* **mutanabbah**
متبنی adopted child *n.m.* **mutabannā**
متبنی کرنا adopt a child *v.t.* **mutabannā karnā**
متنفر offensive *adj.* **mutanaffir**
متنفس living being, person, individual; animal *n.m.* **mutanaffis**
متواتر successively, repeatedly, constantly *adv.* **mutavātir**
متوازن balanced *adj.* **mutavāzzin**
متوازی parallel *adj.* **mutavāzī**
متواضع complimenting, entertaining *n.m.* **mutavāziᶜ**
متوالا intoxicated, drunk *adj.* **matvālā**
متوجہ attentive, favorable *adj.* **mutavajjih**

attend to, favor *v.i.* **mutavajjih hōnā** متوجہ ہونا
average, moderate *adj.* **mutavassit** متوسط
related, adjoining *adj.* **mutavassil** متوصل
inhabitant, native *n.m.* **mutavattin** متوطن
deceased, dead *adj.* **mutavaffī** متوفی
hopeful, expecting *adj.* **mutavaqqiᶜ** متوقع
trusting; resigned *adj.* **mutavakkil** متوکل
trustee, kinsman, guardian *n.m.* **mutavallī** متولی
date, day *n.f.* **mitī** متی
churn, stir, knead *v.t.* **mathnā** متھنا
be erased, be swept away *v.i.* **miṭ jānā** مٹ جانا
erase, destroy, efface *v.t.* **miṭānā** مٹانا
pea *n.f.* **maṭar** مٹر
stroll, leisure walk *n.f.* **maṭar gašt** مٹرگشت
flirtation, flirtatious glance *n.f.* **maṭak** مٹک
wink, twinkle *v.t.* **maṭkānā** مٹکانا
wink, twinkle *v.i.* **maṭaknā** مٹکنا
be erased, be cancelled, be expired *v.i.* **miṭna** مٹنا
hut, temple, pagoda *n.m.* **maṭṭh** مٹھ
handful, bundle *n.m.* **muṭṭhā** مٹھا
slow, lazy, sluggish *adj.* **maṭṭhā** مٹھا
pleasantness, sweetness *n.f.* **maṭhās** مٹھاس
confectionery, candy *n.f.* **miṭā'ī** مٹھائی
darling, sweetheart; parrot *n.m.* **miṭṭhū** مٹھو
earth, clay, soil *n.f.* **miṭṭī** • fist *n.f.* **muṭṭhī** • kiss *n.f.* **miṭṭhī** مٹھی
a handful *adj.* **muṭṭhī bhar** مٹھی بھر
kiss *v.t.* **miṭṭhī lēnā** مٹھی لینا
instance, likeness, example *n.f.* **misāl** مثال
quote, give an example *v.t.* **misāl dēnā** مثال دینا
bladder *n.m.* **masānah** مثانہ
affirmative, positive, established, proved *adj.* **musbat** مثبت
proverb *n.f.* **masal** مثل
similar, like, resembling *adj.* **misl** مثل
for instance, for example *adv.* **masalan** مثلاً
triple, triangular, trilateral *adj.* **musallas** مثلث
duplicate, double, second *adj.* / copy *n.m.* **musannā** مثنیٰ

authorized, legal, lawful, licensed *n.m.* **majāz** مجاز

lawfully *adv.* **majāzan** مجازاً

figurative, illusive *adj.* **majāzī** مجازی

power, strength, capacity, authority *n.f.* **majāl** مجال

striving *adj.* **mujāhid** مجاہد

crusaders, Islamic fighters *n.m.* **mujāhidīn** مجاہدین

forced, compelled, oppressed, helpless *adj.* **majbūr** مجبور

force, compel, oppress *v.t.* **majbūr karnā** مجبور کرنا

by force, compulsorily, necessarily *adv.* **majbūran** مجبوراً

force, compulsion, helplessness *n.f.* **majbūrī** مجبوری

assembled, congregated *adj.* **mujtamaᶜ** مجتمع

recent, modern *adj.* **mujaddid** مجدد

absorbed, attracted *adj.* **majzūb** مجذوب

nonsense, foolishness *n.f.* **majzūb kī baṛ** مجذوب کی بڑ

single, alone, solitary *adj.* **mujarrad** مجرد

solitude, bachelorship *n.f.* **mujarradī** مجردی

criminal, offender, felon *n.m.* **mujrim** مجرم

convict, find guilty *v.t.* **mujrim ṭhahrānā** مجرم ٹھہرانا

injured, wounded, hurt *adj.* **majrūḥ** مجروح

injure, wound, hurt *v.t.* **majrūḥ karnā** مجروح کرنا

embodied, physical; solid *adj.* **mujassam** مجسم

polished, bright *adj.* **mujallā** مجلا

bound *adj.* **mujallad** مجلد

convention, assembly, association, board, committee, party, company *n.f.* **majlis** مجلس

town hall *n.m.* **majlis xānah** مجلس خانہ

literary institute *n.f.* **majlis-ē-ᶜilmī** مجلس علمی

social, civil *adj.* **majlisī** مجلسی

multitude, meeting, gathering, crowd; collection *n.m.* **majmaᶜ** مجمع

briefly, in short *adv.* **mujmalan** مجملاً

collection, assembly *n.m.* **majmūᶜah** مجموعہ

aggregate, collected *adj.* **majmūᶜī** مجموعی

mad (*with love*); insane *n.m.* **majnūn** مجنون

lazy, idle, slow, useless, passive; unknown *adj.* **majhūl** مجہول

prescribed, prepared *adj.* **mujavvazah** مجوزہ

hollow, empty, vacant *adj.* **mujavvaf** مجوف

noble, glorious, exalted *adj.* **majīd** مجید

from me, to me, me *pron.* **mujh sē** مجھ سے
me, to me *pron.* **mujhē** مجھے
platform, stage *n.f.* **macān** مچان
excite, commit, raise, stir up, cause, produce *v.t.* **macānā** مچانا
wink, blink *v.t.* **mickānā** مچکانا
agreement, bond, note *n.m.* **mucalkah** مچلکہ
be stubborn *v.i.* **macalnā** مچلنا
be caused, be produced; break out *v.i.* **macnā** مچنا
mosquito *n.m.* **macchar** مچھر
fish *n.f.* **machlī** مچھلی
fish *v.t.* **machlī pakaṛnā** مچھلی پکڑنا
fish *v.t.* **machlī kā šikār karnā** مچھلی کا شکار کرنا
monkey; clown *n.m.* **machandar** مچھندر
fishmonger, fisherman *n.m.* **machvā** مچھوا
regard, respect; help *n.m.* **muḥābā** محابا
front, face; opposite *n.m.* **muḥāz** محاذ
battlefield *n.m.* **muḥāz-ē-jang** محاذ جنگ
warrior, fighter *n.m.* **muḥārib** محارب
accountant, financial examiner *n.m.* **muḥāsib** محاسب
calculation, account, accountancy *n.m.* **muḥāsabah** محاسبہ
check accounts *v.t.* **muḥasabah karnā** محاسبہ کرنا
besieging *adj.* **muḥāsir** محاصر
siege, blockade *n.m.* **muḥāsarah** محاصرہ
give up a siege *v.t.* **muḥāsarah uṭhānā** محاصرہ اٹھانا
besiege, blockade *v.t.* **muḥāsarah karnā** محاصرہ کرنا
protector, keeper, guard, guardian *n.m.* **muḥāfiz** محافظ
preservation, protection, custody *n.f.* **muḥāfazat** محافظت
impossible, absurd *adj.* **muḥal** محال
idiom, proverb *n.m.* **muḥāvarah** محاورہ
lover; friend *n.m.* **muḥibb** محب
patriot *n.m.* **muḥibb-ul-vatan** محب الوطن
love, affection, friendship *n.f.* **muḥabbat/maḥabbat** محبت
loving, affectionate, friendly *adj.* **muḥabbat āmēz** محبت آمیز
love *v.t.* **muḥabbat karna** محبت کرنا
prison, jail *n.m.* **maḥbas** محبس
beloved *n.m.* **maḥbūb** محبوب

محبوبہ **maḥbūbah** *n.f.* darling, beloved, sweetheart
محبوبی **maḥbūbī** *n.m.* loveliness, love, affection
محبوس **maḥbūs** *n.m.* prisoner, captive
محتاج **muḥtāj** *adj.* needy, poor
محتاج کرنا **muḥtāj karnā** *v.t.* make poor, impoverish
محتاجی **muḥtājī** *n.f.* want, need, poverty
محترم **muḥtarim** *n.m.* respecting, honoring
محتسب **muḥtasib** *n.m.* police inspector
محتشم **muḥtašim** *adj.* eminent, strong, powerful
محجور **maḥjūr** *adj.* forbidden
محدث **muḥaddis** *n.m.* narrator, relator, believer
محدود **maḥdūd** *adj.* limited, bound
محدود کرنا **maḥdūd karnā** *v.t.* limit, confine
محذوب **maḥzūb** *adj.* omitted, cut off
محراب **miḥrāb** *n.f.* arch, niche, shelf
محرابی **miḥrābī** *adj.* arched
محرر **muḥarrir** *n.m.* clerk, writer
محرق **muḥriq** *adj.* inflamed, burning
محرک **muḥarrik** *adj.* moving
محروم **maḥram** *n.m.* spouse; intimate friend
محزون **maḥzūn** *adj.* grieved, sad, afflicted
محسن **muḥsin** *adj.* beneficent, generous
محسوب **maḥsūb** *adj.* calculated, counted, numbered
محسود **maḥsūd** *adj.* envied; hated
محسوس **maḥsūs** *adj.* felt, perceived
محسوس کرنا **maḥsūs karnā** *v.t.* feel, perceive
محشر **maḥšar** *n.m.* resurrection day
محصور **maḥsūr** *adj.* besieged, surrounded
محصور کرنا **maḥsūr karnā** *v.t.* besiege
محصول **maḥsūl** *n.m.* tax, duty, toll
محصول لگانا **maḥsūl lagānā** *v.t.* levy a tax, levy a duty
محصولی **maḥsūlī** *adj.* taxable, dutiable
محض **maḥz** *adj.* mere, absolute, pure, simple
محضر **maḥzar** *n.m.* petition, application, attestation
محظوظ **maḥzūz** *adj.* cheerful, pleased, delighted
محفل **maḥfil** *n.f.* assembly, congregation, congress

safe, guarded, protected, preserved *adj.* **maḥfūz** محفوظ
safe, safe locker *n.m.* **mahfūz lākar** محفوظ لاکر
philosopher, researcher, scholar *n.m.* **muḥaqqiq** محقق
firm, strong, fortified *adj.* **muḥkam** محکم
court, tribunal *n.m.* **maḥkamah** محکمہ
subject, subordinate *n.m.* **maḥkūm** محکوم
palace, mansion *n.m.* **maḥall** محل
quarter (*of town*), district *n.m.* **muḥallah** محلہ
neighbor, resident (*of the same district*) *n.m.* **muḥallah dār** محلہ دار
worthy, praised, praiseworthy *adj.* **maḥmūd** محمود
labor, industry; toil *n.f.* **miḥnat** محنت
hardworking *adj.* **miḥnat kaš** محنت کش
hardworking, industrious *adj.* **miḥnatī** محنتی
charmed, absorbed, fascinated *adj.* **maḥv** محو
charm, fascinate; erase, efface *v.t.* **maḥv karnā** محو کرنا
axis *n.m.* **maḥvar** محور
fascination *n.f.* **maḥviyyat** محویت
surrounding, encircling; comprehending *adj.* / circumference *n.m.* **muḥīt** محیط
surround, encircle *v.i.* **muḥit ḥōna** محیط ہونا
enmity, hostility *n.f.* **muxāsamat** مخاصمت
speaker *n.m.* **muxātib** مخاطب
address *v.t.* **muxātib karnā** مخاطب کرنا
abbreviated, abridged; alleviated, light *adj.* **muxaffaf** مخافف
enemy, opponent, adversary *n.m.* / opposite, adverse *adj.* **muxālif** مخالف
opposition, rebellion, disagreement *n.f.* **muxālafat** مخالفت
oppose, rebel, resist, disagree *v.t.* **muxālafat karnā** مخالفت کرنا
reporter; spy, informer *n.m.* **muxbir** مخبر
report; spy *v.t.* **muxbirī karnā** مخبری کرنا
/ independent; authorized, empowered, selected *adj.* **muxtār** مختار
attorney, delegate *n.m.*
general manager *n.m.* **muxtār-ē-ᶜām** مختار عام
director, manager *n.m.* **muxtār-ē-kār** مختار کار
authorize, empower *v.t.* **muxtār karnā** مختار کرنا
power of attorney *n.m.* **muxtār nāmah** مختار نامہ
independence; power, authority *n.f.* **muxtārī** مختاری
specific, appropriate; peculiar *adj.* **muxtass** مختص

مختصر concise, brief, abridged, abbreviated *adj.* **muxtasar**
مختصر کرنا abbreviate, abridge *v.t.* **muxtasar karnā**
مختصراً briefly, in short *adv.* **muxtasaran**
مختلف different, diverse, various *adj.* **muxtalif**
مخدوم lord, master *n.m.* **maxdūm**
مخدومہ miss, lady *n.f.* **maxdūmah**
مخروطی conical, tapered *adj.* **maxrūtī**
مخزن treasury, magazine, storehouse, granary *n.m.* **maxzan**
مخزن العلوم encyclopedia *n.m.* **maxzan-ul-ᶜulūm**
مخصوص specified, special, particular *adj.* **maxsūs**
مخفی hidden, secret *adj.* **maxfī**
مخل intruding, disturbing *adj.* / intruder, disturber *n.m.* **muxill**
مخلص pure, sincere, true, real *adj.* / escape, release, salvation *n.f.* **muxlis**
مخلصانہ faithfully, sincerely *adv.* **muxlisānah**
مخلوط mixed, blended; confused *adj.* **maxlūt**
مخلوق creature, creation *n.f.* **maxlūq**
مخمصہ dilemma, perplexity *n.m.* **maxmasah**
مخمل velvet *n.m.* **maxmal**
مخمور drunk, intoxicated *adj.* **maxmūr**
مخنث effeminate *adj.* / eunuch *n.m.* **muxannas**
مخیر liberal, charitable, bountiful *adj.* **muxaiyyir**
مد • wine; honey; intoxication, pleasure; pride, arrogance; madness *n.f.* **mad**
extension, flood-tide *n.m.* **madd**
مداح praiser *n.m.* **maddāḥ**
مداحی praising, commending *adj.* **maddāḥī**
مداخلت access, admission; interference, interruption, intervention *n.f.* **mudāxalat**
مدار circumference, orbit; dependence *n.m.* **madār**
مدار المہام prime minister *n.m.* **madār-ul-mahām**
مدارات hospitality, courtesy, politeness *n.f.* **mudārāt**
مداری juggler, monkey-dancer *n.m.* **madārī**
مدافعت self-defense, repulsion *n.f.* **mudāfaᶜat**
مدام eternally, permanently, everlasting, always *adv.* **mudām**
مدامی eternal, perpetual *adj.* **mudāmī**
مداوا۔ مداومت remedy, cure, treatment, healing *n.m.* **mudāvā**
مداوات remedy, cure, treatment, healing *n.f.* **mudāvāt**
مدت interval, length (of time), duration, long period (of time) *n.f.* **muddat**

long period of time *n.f.* **muddat-ē-madīd** مدت مدید

help, support, aid, assistance *n.f.* **madad** مدد

help, support, aid, assist *v.t.* **madad karnā** مدد کرنا

helper, assistant, protector, auxiliary *n.m.* **madad gār** مددگار

professor, teacher, master, lecturer *n.m.* **mudarris** مدرس

school, college, academy, university *n.m.* **madrasah** مدرسہ

teachership, professorship, lectureship *n.f.* **mudarrisī** مدرسی

aim, object, meaning; desire, wish *n.m.* **muddaᶜā** مدعا

defendant, accused *n.m.* **muddaᶜā ᶜalaih** مدعا علیہ

joined, merged, doubled; concealed *adj.* **mudġam** مدغم

tomb, burial place *n.m.* **madfan** مدفن

buried *adj.* **madfūn** مدفون

well-argued, reasonable *adj.* **mudallal** مدلل

proud, fastidious, conceited; foolish *adj.* **mudammiġ** مدمغ

senseless, unconscious *adj.* **madhōš** مدہوش

insensibility, senselessness *n.f.* **madhōšī** مدہوشی

ebb and tide, flux and reflux *n.m.* **mudd-ō-jazr** مدوجزر

round, circular *adj.* **mudavvar** مدور

long, extensive *adj.* **maddīd/madīd** مدید

editor, director, administrator, principle, headmaster *n.m.* **mudīr** مدیر

indebted, involved in debt *adj.* **madyūn** مدیون

sweet, melodious *adj.* **madhur** مدھر

medium, temperate, moderate *adj.* **maddham** مدھم

lessen, reduce, moderate *v.t.* **maddham karnā** مدھم کرنا

taste, relish; joke, wit, pleasantry; mockery *n.m.* **mazāq** مذاق

funny, witty, humorous *adj.* **mazāqiyah** مذاقیہ

slaughterhouse; altar *n.m.* **mazbaḥ** مذبح

masculine, male *adj.* **muzakkar** مذکر

mentioned, related *adj.* **mazkūr** مذکور

censure, blame; satire; contempt *n.f.* **mazammat** مذمت

blamed; contemptible *adj.* **mazmūm** مذموم

religion, faith, sect *n.m.* **mazhab** مذہب

religious *adj.* **mazhabī** مذہبی

religiousness *n.f.* **mazhabiyat** مذہبیت

die *v.i.* **mar jānā** مر جانا

dead *adj.* **marā** مرا

return, recourse *n.f.* **murāja^cat** مراجعت
desire; intention, object, aim *n.f.* **murād** مراد
achieve an objective *v.t.* **murād ḥāsil karnā** مراد حاصل کرنا
desirous, needy *adj.* **murād mand** مراد مند
synonymous *adj.* **murādif** مرادف
take a vow *v.t.* **murād mānnā** مراد ماننا
desirable; understood, implied *adj.* **murādī** مرادی
regard, reflection, consideration, view *n.m.* **murā^cāt** مراعات
appeal *n.m.* **murāfa^cah** مرافعہ
meditation, templation, observation *n.m.* **murāqabah** مراقبہ
mediate, observe, supervise *v.t.* **murāqabah karnā** مراقبہ کرنا
square *adj.* **murabba^c** مربع
arranged, attached, connected *adj.* **marbūt** مربوط
• confection; preserve, fruit jam *n.m.* **murabbā** مربی
patron, guardian, protector *n.m.* **murabbī**
jar, vessel *n.m.* **martabān** مرتبان
degree, dignity, rank; change *n.m.* **martabah** مرتبہ
high, elevated *adj.* **murtafa^c** مرتفع
guilty, committing *adj.* **murtakib** مرتکب
pawned, pledged, deposited *adj.* **murtahan** مرتہن
refuge, asylum *n.m.* **marja^c** مرجع
fade, wither, pine; feel faint *v.i.* **murjhānā** مرجھانا
hot, spicy; strong *adj.* **mirch** • pepper, chili pepper *n.f.* **mirc** مرچ
Hello!, Welcome! *interj.* **marḥabā!** مرحبا
stage; journey; difficulty *n.m.* **marḥalah** مرحلہ
mercy, favor, kindness, pity, compassion *n.f.* **marḥamat** مرحمت
grant, bestow, confer *v.t.* **marḥamat karnā** مرحمت کرنا
deceased, dead, late *adj.* **marḥūm** مرحوم
man, male; person; husband; hero *n.m.* **mard** مرد
impure, polluted; ugly *adj.* **mardār** مردار
manliness, heroism, bravery *n.f.* **mardānagī** مردانگی
man, gentleman *n.m.* **mardum** مردم
cannibal *n.m.* **mardum xōr** مردم خور
census *n.f.* **mardum šumarī** مردم شماری
homicide, murder *n.f.* **mardum kašī** مردم کشی
gloominess, dismalness, melancholy; death *n.f.* **murdanī** مردنی

dead; weak *adj.* **murdah** مردہ
hopeless, lifeless *adj.* **murdah dil** مردہ دل
rejected, excluded, abandoned *adj.* **mardūd** مردود
son of nobleman, prince *n.m.* **mirzā** مرزا
prophet, apostle, angel *n.m.* **mursal** مرسل
instructor, religious teacher, spiritual guide *n.m.* **muršid** مرشد
sickness, disease *n.m.* **maraz** مرض
choice, assent; pleasure *n.f.* **marzī** مرضی
moist, damp, wet *adj.* **martūb** مرطوب
terrified, frightened *n.m.* **marᶜūb** مرعوب
cock, fowl, bird *n.m.* **murġ** مرغ
water fowl, wild duck *n.f.* **murġābī** مرغابی
pasture, meadow *n.m.* **murġazar** مرغزار
favorite, desirable, lovely, desired *adj.* **marġūb** مرغوب
hen, chicken, poultry *n.f.* **murġī** مرغی
contented, happy, pleasant *adj.* **muraffah** مرفہ
tomb, grave; bed *n.f.* **marqad** مرقد
written, described, mentioned *adj.* **marqūm** مرقوم
mixture, compound *n.m.* / mixed, compounded, combined *adj.* **murakkab** مرکب
horse; camel; vehicle *n.m.* **markab** مرکب
mix, compound, combine *v.t.* **murakkab karnā** مرکب کرنا
center, middle *n.m.* **markaz** مرکز
central *adj.* **markazī** مرکزی
death *n.f.* **marg** • deer *n.m.* **mirg** مرگ
burning ground (*used for Hindu cremations*) *n.m.* **marghaṭ** مرگھٹ
pipe, flute *n.f.* **murlī** مرلی
play the pipe, play the flute *v.t.* **murlī bajānā** مرلی بجانا
repair, mending *n.f.* **murammat** مرمت
repair, mend; beat up *v.t.* **murammat karnā** مرمت کرنا
marble *n.m.* **marmar** مرمر
death; destruction, ruin *n.m.* **maran** مرن
die, expire; cease, fade *v.i.* **marnā** مرنا
pawned, pledged, mortgaged *n.m.* **marhūn** مرہون
pearl *n.m.* **marvārīd** مروارید
humanity, generosity *n.f.* **muravvat** مروت

مروج **muravvaj** *adj.* current, customary, in vogue
مرور **murūr** *n.m.* passing, elapsing, transition; traffic
مروڑ **marōṛ** *n.f.* twist, turn
مروڑنا **marōṛnā** *v.t.* twist, turn, writhe
مری **marī** *n.f.* plague
مرید **maryad** *n.m.* obeyer, follower, disciple
مریض **marīz** *n.m.* patient, sick person
مڑنا **muṛnā** *v.i.* turn, turn back, bend, become turned
مڑھنا **maṛhnā** *v.t.* cover, spread, coat, case
مزا کرنا **mazā karnā** *v.t.* enjoy oneself
مزاج **mizāj** *n.m.* temperament, nature, mood, humor, disposition; pride
مزاج دار **mizaj dār** *adj.* conceited, proud
مزاحمت **muzāḥamat** *n.f.* obstacle, prevention, impediment, opposition
مزار **mazār** *n.m.* grave, tomb; shrine
مزارع **muzāriᶜ** *n.m.* agriculturist, cultivator
مزد **muzd** *n.f.* reward, compensation, salary, wages
مزدور **mazdūr/muzdūr** *n.m.* laborer, worker; carrier, porter
مزدوری **mazdūrī/muzdūrī** *n.f.* labor, work; wages, pay
مزرع **mazraᶜ** *n.m.* field
مزہ **mazah** *n.m.* taste, flavor; deliciousness
مزہ لوٹنا **mazah lūṭnā** *v.t.* enjoy, revel
مزید **mazīd** *adj.* increased, further / *n.f.* addition, increase, advantage / *adv.* moreover
مزیدار **mazēdār** *adj.* delicious, tasteful, flavorful
مزین **muzayyan** *adj.* adorned, decorated
مژدہ **muždah** *n.m.* good news
مس **mas** *n.m.* touch • **mis** *n.m.* copper
مساحت **misāhat** *n.f.* geometry; measurement, dimension; survey
مساعد **musāᶜid** *adj.* assisting, helping
مسافت **masāfat** *n.f.* distance, space
مسافر **musāfir** *n.m.* passenger, traveler
مسافر خانہ **musāfir xānah** *n.m.* rest house, inn, motel, hotel
مسافری **musāfirī** *n.f.* journey, traveling
مسالا **masālā** *n.m.* ingredients; spices
مسالا چائے **masālā cā'ē** *n.f.* chai tea
مسام **masām** *n.m.* pore

crematorium *n.m.* **masān** مسان
equality, equation, evenness *n.f.* **musāvāt** مساوات
equal, even, neutral, parallel *adj.* **musāvī** مساوی
intoxicated, drunk; lustful *adj.* **mast** مست
contractor; tenant *n.m.* **mustājir** مستاجر
lease, contract *n.f.* **mustājirī** مستاجری
intoxicated, drunk; lustful *adj.* **mastānah** مستانہ
granted, acceptable, agreeable *adj.* **mustajāb** مستجاب
virtuous, laudable *adj.* **mustaḥsan** مستحسن
worthy, deserving, rightful *adj.* **mustaḥiqq** مستحق
be entitled *v.i.* **mustaḥiqq hōnā** مستحق ہونا
rejected, turned down, returned *adj.* **mustaradd** مسترد
mason; carpenter; blacksmith; artisan *n.m.* **mistarī** مستری
borrowed *adj.* **mustaᶜār** مستعار
lend *v.t.* **mustaᶜār dēnā** مستعار دینا
borrow *v.t.* **mustaᶜār lēnā** مستعار لینا
prompt, ready, prepared *adj.* **mustaᶜidd** مستعد
promptness, readiness *n.m.* **mustaᶜiddī** مستعدی
resigned *adj.* **mustaᶜfī** مستعفی
used, in use, employed, applied *adj.* **mustaᶜmal** مستعمل
drowned, immersed, absorbed *adj.* **mustaġraq** مستغرق
independent, rich *adj.* **mustaġnī** مستغنی
benefitting, gaining *adj.* **mustafīd** مستفید
future *n.m.* **mustaqbil** مستقبل
permanent, consistent *adj.* **mustaqil** مستقل
straight, right, direct, faithful *adj.* **mustaqīm** مستقیم
forehead *n.m.* **mastak** مستک
genuine, certified; supported, approved *adj.* **mustanad** مستند
liable, worthy, fit, deserving *adj.* **mustaujib** مستوجب
concealed, covered, hidden *adj.* **mastūr** مستور
straight, even, plane, equal *adj.* **mustavī** مستوی
intoxication, drunkenness; lust *n.f.* **mastī** مستی
mosque *n.f.* **masjid** مسجد
worshipped *adj.* **masjūd** مسجود
purifying, washing (*prior to prayer*) *n.m.* **mašḥ** مسح

مسحور **mashūr** enchanted, bewitched *adj.*
مسخر **musaxxar** subdued, conquered *adj.*
مسخرہ **masxarah** buffoon, joker, clown, fool *n.m.*
مسدود **masdūd** shut, closed *adj.*
مسرت **masarrat** happiness, joy, pleasure *n.f.*
مسرف **musrif** extravagant *adj.*
مسرور **masrūr** glad, happy, delighted *adj.*
مسروقہ **masrūqah** stolen, robbed *adj.*
مسطح **musattah** plain, even, level *adj.*
مسعود **masᶜūd** happy, fortunate *adj.*
مسقف **musaqqaf** roofed, ceilinged *adj.*
مسکرانا **muskurānā** smile, grin *v.i.*
مسکراہٹ **muskurāhaṭ** smile, grin *n.f.*
مسکن **maskan** residence, dwelling *n.m.*
مسکہ **maskah** butter *n.m.*
مسکین **miskīn** poor, miserable *adj.*
مسکینی **miskīnī** poverty *n.f.*
مسلح **musallah** armed *adj.*
مسلسل **musalsal** successive, serial, linked, connected *adj.*
مسلط **musallat** conquered; conquering *adj.*
مسلک **maslak** routine, rule, practice; way, track *n.m.*
مسلم **muslim** Muslim *n.m.*
مسلم **musallam** preserved; whole, entire *adj.*
مسلمان **musalmān** Muslim *n.m.*
مسلمانی **musalmānī** Muslim, Islamic *adj.*
مسلنا **masalnā** rub, bruise, crush *v.t.*
مسلوب **maslūb** seized, deprived *adj.*
مسمات **musammāt** lady *n.f.*
مسمار **mismār** ruined, demolished, destroyed *adj.*
مسموع **masmūᶜ** heard, listened to, audible *adj.*
مسموم **masmūm** poisoned *adj.*
مسمی **musammā** named, called, entitled *adj.*
مسند **masnad** throne, chair, seat *n.f.*
مسہری **masahrī** mosquito net *n.f.*
مسہل **mushil** laxative, purgative *adj.*
مسواک **misvāk** toothbrush (*used in the countryside*) *n.m.*

draft, sketch, manuscript *n.m.* **masavvadah** مسودہ
Christ *n.m.* **masīḥ** مسیح
problem *n.m.* **masa'lah** مسئلہ
similarity, resemblance *n.f.* **mušābahat** مشابہت
signified, indicated *adj.* **mušār** مشار
proficient *adj.* **muššāq** مشاق
smell, smelling *n.f.* **mašām** مشام
observer *n.m.* **mušāhid** مشاہد
observation *n.m.* **mušāhadah** مشاہدہ
renowned person, famous person *n.m.* **mušāhīr** مشاہیر
consultation *n.f.* **mušāvarat** مشاورت
likened, assimilated *adj.* **mušabbah** مشبہ
fistful, handful; blow *n.f.* **mušt** مشت
ambiguous, suspect, obscure *adj.* **muštabah** مشتبہ
common *n.m.* **muštarak** مشترک
purchaser, buyer; Jupiter (*planet*) *n.m.* **muštarī** مشتری
flaming, inflamed *adj.* **mušta**ᶜ**il** مشتعل
comprising, containing, including *adj.* **muštamil** مشتمل
proclaimed, announced *adj.* **muštahir** مشتہر
strong, robust *adj.* **muštaṇḍā** مشٹنڈا
explained *adj.* **mušarraḥ** مشرح
exalted, honored *adj.* **mušarraf** مشرف
exalt, honor *v.t.* **mušarraf karnā** مشرف کرنا
east *n.f.* **mašriq** مشرق
eastern, oriental *adj.* **mašriqī** مشرقی
drink, beverage *n.m.* **mašrūb** مشروب
explained, above-mentioned *adj.* **mašrūḥ** مشروح
conditionally *adv.* **mašrūtan** مشروطا
legal, lawful, legitimate *adj.* **mašrū**ᶜ مشروع
torch, lantern *n.f.* **maš**ᶜ**al** مشعل
employment, engagement *n.m.* **mašġalah** مشغلہ
employed, occupied, busy *adj.* **mašgūl** مشغول
kind, affectionate, dear *adj.* **mušfiq** مشفق
kindly, affectionately *adv.* **mušfiqānah** مشفقانہ
exercise, practice *n.f.* **mašq** مشق

exercise, practice *v.t.* **mašq karnā** مشق کرنا
trouble, toil, pain, distress *n.f.* **mašaqqat** مشقت
practical *adj.* **mašqī** مشقی
musk *n.m.* **mušk** مشک
musky *adj.* **mušk bār** مشک بار
hard, difficult, intricate *adj.*/ difficulty, hardship, intricacy *n.f.* **muškil** مشکل
with difficulty *adv.* **muškil sē** مشکل سے
grateful, thankful; thanked, praised *adj.* **maškūr** مشکور
doubtful, uncertain, ambiguous *adj.* **maškūk** مشکوک
musky; black *adj.* **muškiṁ** مشکیں
fragrant, perfumed *adj.* **mašmūm** مشموم
proved, attested *adj.* **mašhūd** مشہود
well-known, famous, noted, reputed, celebrated *adj.* **mašhūr** مشہور
reputation, notoriety *n.f.* **mašhūrī** مشہوری
consultation, counsel, advice; conspiracy, plot *n.f.* **mašvarat** مشورت
consultation, counsel, advice; conspiracy, plot *n.m.* **mušvarah** مشورہ
take advice, consult *v.t.* **mušvarah karnā** مشورہ کرنا
disturbed, uneasy, perplexed, confused *adj.* **mušavvaš** مشوش
walking, going *n.f.* **maši** مشی
will, wish; pleasure *n.f.* **mašiyyat** مشیت
vanity, pride *n.f.* **mašīxat** مشیخت
counselor, adviser; senator *n.m.* **mušīr** مشیر
machine *n.f.* **mašīn** مشین
mechanical *adj.* **mašīnī** مشینی
companion, comrade, associate *n.m.* **masāḥib** مصاحب
companionship, society, company *n.f.* **musāḥabat** مصاحبت
shaking hands *n.m.* **musāfaḥah** مصافحہ
shake hands, join hands *v.t.* **musāfaḥah karnā** مصافحہ کرنا
reconciliation, pacification, compromise *n.f.* **musālaḥat** مصالحت
reconcile, compromise, make peace *v.t.* **musālaḥat karnā** مصالحت کرنا
book; page *n.m.* **musḥaf** مصحف
source, origin *n.m.* **masdar** مصدر
attested, verified, authenticated *adj.* **musaddaqah** مصدقہ
authenticated, proved, true, genuine *adj.* **masdūr** مصدور
obstinate, persisting *adj.* **musirr** مصر

مصرف **masraf** *n.m.* expense, expenditure, cost, charge • **musrif** *adj.* prodigal, wasteful
مصروف **masrūf** *adj.* expended, employed, engaged, busy, occupied
مصطلح **mustalaḥ** *adj.* idiomatic, phraseological / *n.m.* phrase, idiom, technical term
مصعون **mas^cūn** *adj.* protected, guarded, preserved
مصفا **musaffā** *adj.* clarified, pure, clean
مصفی **masaffī** *adj.* purifying, refining, cleaning, clarifying
مصلح **musliḥ** *n.m.* adviser, reformer, mediator
مصلحت **maslaḥat** *n.f.* expedience, convenience; advice, counsel; policy
مصلحت بیں **maslaḥat bīṁ** *adj.* prudent, wise
مصلحت کرنا **maslaḥat karnā** *v.t.* advise, consult
مصلحتاً **maslaḥatan** *adv.* expediently, advisedly
مصلوب **maslūb** *adj.* crucified
مصلیٰ **musallā** *n.m.* prayer rug
مصمت **musammat** *adj.* silenced, quieted
مصمم **musammam** *adj.* determined, fixed, firm
مصمم ارادہ **musammam irādah** *n.m.* decision, determination, resolution
مصنف **musannaf** *adj.* composed, written • **musannif** *n.m.* author, composer, writer
مصنوعہ **masnū^cah** *adj.* formed, created, constructed, invented; artificial
مصنوعی **masnū^cī** *adj.* artificial, fabricated, counterfeit, false
مصور **musavvir** *n.m.* painter, drawer; photographer; sculptor • **musavvar** *adj.* painted, illustrated; printed; formed
مصوری **musavvirī** *n.f.* painting, drawing; photography
مصیبت **musībat** *n.f.* misfortune, disaster, calamity, misery, trouble
مصیبت زدہ **musībat zadah** *adj.* unfortunate, miserable
مضارع **muzāri^c** *adj.* resembling
مضاعف **muzā^caf** *adj.* doubled, multiplied
مضاف **muzāf** *adj.* added, annexed
مضافات شہر **muzāfāt-ē-šahr** *n.f.* outskirts (*of a city*), suburbs
مضائقہ **muzā'iqah** *n.m.* harm, distress; significance, consequence
مضبوط **mazbūt** *adj.* strong, firm, fixed, durable
مضبوطی **mazbūtī** *n.f.* strength, durability, solidity
مضحک **muzḥik** *adj.* ridiculous, funny
مضحکہ **mazḥakah** *n.m.* humor, fun, pleasantry, pun
مضحکہ اڑانا **mazḥakah uṛānā** *v.t.* make fun, tell jokes
مضحکہ خیز **mazḥakah xēz** *adj.* ridiculous

pernicious, hurtful, noxious *adj.* **muzir** مضر
injury, hurt, harm, damage *n.f.* **mazarrat** مضرت
injured, hurt, harmed, wounded *adj.* **mazrūb** مضروب
distressed, agitated, embarrassed, restless *adj.* **muztarr** مضطر
agitated, afflicted, uneasy, confused, troubled *adj.* **muztarib** مضطرب
distractedly, confusedly, uneasily *adv.* **muztaribānah** مضطربانہ
weak, idle, exhausted *adj.* **muzmaḥill** مضمحل
concealed; conceived, imagined *adj.* **muzmar** مضمر
added, accumulated, joined *adj.* **mazmūm** مضموم
content, sense, meaning, subject *n.m.* **mazmūn** مضمون
past, bygone *adj.* **mazā** مضیٰ
Let bygones be bygones! *interj.* **mazā mā mazā!** مضیٰ ما مضیٰ
suitable; like, equal, corresponding, alike, identical *adj.* **mutābiq** مطابق
conform, suit, coincide *v.i.* **mutābiq hōnā** مطابق ہونا
conformity, equality, coincidence, analogy, similarity *n.f.* **mutābaqat** مطابقت
compare with, make like *v.t.* **mutābiq karnā** مطابق کرنا
consideration, study, reading *n.m.* **mutālaᶜah** مطالعہ
joking, joke, pleasantry *n.m.* **mutāyabah** مطایبہ
kitchen *n.m.* **matbax** مطبخ
press, printing press, printing house *n.m.* **matbaᶜ** مطبع
cooked, boiled *adj.* **matbūx** مطبوخ
printed, pressed; agreeable, acceptable *adj.* **matbūᶜ** مطبوع
printed, pressed, published *adj.* **matbūᶜah** مطبوعہ
rain; rainy season *n.m.* **matar** مطر
male singer; male musician; male artist *n.m.* **mutrib** مطرب
female singer; female musician; female artist *n.f.* **mutribah** مطربہ
prosperous, current, flowing *adj.* **mutrid** مطرد
rejected, dejected *adj.* **matrūḥ** مطروح
reproached, blamed *adj.* **matᶜūn** مطعون
intention, desire, wish, object, aim, motive, purpose *n.m.* **matlab** مطلب
meaning, sense; interest; petition;
have a concern, have a motive, be interested *v.t.* **matlab rakhnā** مطلب رکھنا
have a concern, mean *v.i.* **matlab hōna** مطلب ہونا
selfish *adj.* **matlabī** مطلبی
horizon, east, place of the rising sun *n.m.* **matlaᶜ** مطلع

مطلع notified, informed, aware *adj.* **muttala^c**
مطلع کرنا inform *v.t.* **muttala^c karnā**
مطلق absolute, universal, altogether, entire, total *adj.* **mutlaq**
مطلق العنان free, absolute, independent *adj.* **mutlaq-ul-^cinān**
مطلقاً entirely, absolutely, altogether *adv.* **mutlaqan**
مطلقہ divorced woman *n.f.* **mutallaqah**
مطلوب desired, demanded, required, intended *adj.* **matlūb**
مطمئن quiet, tranquil; secure, satisfied, safe *adj.* **mutma'in**
مطہر cleansed, purified *adj.* **mutahhar** • cleansing, purifying *adj.* **mutahhir**
مطول long, prolonged, lengthy *adj.* **mutavval**
مطیر raining, dropping *adj.* **matīr**
مطیع obedient, submissive *adj.* **mutī^c**
مظاہر helping, assisting *adj.* **muzāhir**
مظاہرہ demonstration *n.m.* **muzāharah**
مظفر successful, victorious *adj.* **muzaffar**
مظلم dark, black; mysterious *adj.* **muzlim**
مظلمہ oppression, tyranny, injustice *n.m.* **muzlimah**
مظلوم oppressed *adj.* **mazlūm**
مظلومی oppression, tyranny *n.f.* **mazlūmī**
مظہر • exhibiting, displaying *adj.* / exhibitor, player, actor *n.m.* **muzhir**
theater, stage *n.m.* **mazhar**
مع with, together, along with *pp.* **ma^c**
مع ہذا with this, in addition, besides *adv.* **ma^c hazā**
معاً all at once, at the same time, instantly, along with, together *adv.* **ma^can**
معادل equal, equivalent *adj.* **mu^cādal**
معادلت justice, equality *n.f.* **mu^cādalat**
معارض opponent, adversary *n.m.* **mu^cāriz**
معارضہ opposition, rivalry, contradiction *n.m.* **mu^cārizah**
معاش livelihood, subsistence, income; property *n.f.* **ma^cāš**
معاشرت society *n.f.* **mu^cāšarat**
معاشرتی social *adj.* **mu^cāšaratī/mu'ašarti**
معاشرہ society *n.m.* **mu^cāšarrah**
معاشی economical *adj.* **ma^cašī**
معاشیات economics, economy *n.f.* **ma^cāšiyyāt**
معاضد helper, assistant *n.m.* **ma^cāzid**
معاضدت help, assistance, support *n.f.* **ma^cāzidat**

benevolence, kindness *n.f.* **muᶜātafat** معاطفت

pardoned, forgiven, excused *adj.* **muᶜāf** معاف

pardon, forgive, excuse *v.t.* **muᶜāf karnā** معاف کرنا

Sorry!, I'm sorry! *interj.* **muᶜāf kījiē!** معاف کیجئے

exemption, remission, pardon *n.f.* **muᶜāfī** معافی

punishing *adj.* **muᶜāqib** معاقب

punishment, chastisement *n.f.* **muᶜāqabat** معاقبت

physician, doctor *n.m.* **muᶜālij** معالج

curing, healing; treatment, remedy *n.m.* **muᶜālajah** معالجہ

cure, heal, treat, apply remedy (to) *v.t.* **muᶜālajah karnā** معالجہ کرنا

dealing, affair, matter, cause, suit, transaction, contract business, concern, negotiation, *n.m.* **muᶜāmalah** معاملہ

deal (with), treat *v.t.* **muᶜāmalah karnā** معاملہ کرنا

obstinate, stubborn, disobedient, rebellious, hostile *adj.* **muᶜānid** معاند

enmity, conflict *n.f.* **muᶜānadat** معاندت

contractor, ally *n.m.* **muᶜāhid** معاہد

contract, agreement *n.m.* **muᶜāhadah** معاہدہ

returning, coming back *n.f.* **muᶜāvadat** معاودت

retaliation, revenge; substitution, exchange, remuneration *n.m.* **muᶜāvazah** معاوضہ

helper, assistant *n.m.* **muᶜāvin** معاون

help, aid, assistance *n.f.* **muᶜāvanat** معاونت

help, assist *v.t.* **muᶜāvanat karnā** معاونت کرنا

inspection, examination *n.m.* **muᶜāyanah** معاینہ

inspect, examine *v.t.* **muᶜāyanah karnā** معاینہ کرنا

inspection, sight, view *n.m.* **muᶜāyanah** معائینہ

mosque, church, temple (*any place of worship*) *n.m.* **muᶜabad** معبد

accustomed, habituated, customary *adj.* **muᶜtād** معتاد

reliable, trustworthy, credible, confidential *adj.* **muᶜtabar** معتبر

reliance, confidence, trustworthiness *n.f.* **muᶜtabarī** معتبری

numbered, computed *adj.* **muᶜtadd** معتد

temperate, moderate, tolerable, mild *adj.* **muᶜtadil** معتدل

temper, moderate *v.t.* **muᶜtadil karnā** معتدل کرنا

opposing, objecting, resisting *adj.* **muᶜtariz** معترض

object, obstruct, impede *v.i.* **muᶜtariz hōnā** معترض ہونا

acknowledging, confessing *adj.* **muᶜtarif** معترف

separatist, dissenter *n.m.* **muᶜtazil** معتزل

infidel, atheist *n.m.* **muᶜtazilī** معتزلی
preserved; relying (on) *adj.* **muᶜtasim** معتصم
believer, follower, adherent *n.m.* **muᶜtaqid** معتقد
trustworthy, reliable, confidential *adj.* **muᶜtamad** معتمد
cursed, oppressed, persecuted *adj.* **maᶜtūb** معتوب
miracle *n.m.* **muᶜjizah** معجزہ
prompt, without delay, hasty, expedient *adj.* **muᶜajjal** معجل
counted, numbered *adj.* **muᶜaddad** معدد
justice, equity, rectitude *n.f.* **maᶜdalat** معدلت
mine *n.m.* **maᶜdan/maᶜdin** معدن
mineral *adj.* **maᶜdanī** معدنی
stomach, paunch *n.m.* **miᶜdah** معدہ
annihilate *v.t.* **maᶜdūm karnā** معدوم کرنا
numbered, counted *adj.* **maᶜdūd** معدود
very few *adj.* **maᶜdūd-ē-cand** معدود چند
non-existent, annihilated, extinct *adj.* **maᶜdūm** معدوم
punished, tormented; prevented, hindered *adj.* **muᶜazzab** معذب
excuse, apology; plea *n.f.* **maᶜzirat** معذرت
excused, excusable *adj.* **maᶜzūr** معذور
excuse *v.t.* **maᶜzūr rakhnā** معذور رکھنا
naked, bare, bald *adj.* **muᶜarrā** معرا
ladder, ascent *adj.* **miᶜrāj** معراج
meeting-place; happening, occurrence, occasion *n.m.* **maᶜriz** معرض
knowledge, science, skill, revelation *n.f.* **maᶜrifat** معرفت
noun *n.m.* **maᶜrifah** معرفہ
fight; battlefield *n.m.* **maᶜrikah** معرکہ
representation; petition *n.f.* **maᶜrūz** معروض
petition, application; representation *n.m.* **maᶜrūzah** معروضہ
famous, notorious, noted, celebrated *adj.* **maᶜrūf** معروف
honored, esteemed, honorable, revered *adj.* **muᶜazzaz** معزز
deposed, dismissed, degraded *adj.* **maᶜzūl** معزول
dismiss, discharge, disgrace, degrade *v.t.* **maᶜzūl karnā** معزول کرنا
be dismissed *v.i.* **maᶜzūl hōnā** معزول ہونا
dismissal, deposition *n.f.* **maᶜzūlī** معزولی
difficult, arduous, hard *adj.* **muᶜassir** • poor, needy *adj.* **muᶜsir** معسر
difficult, hard *adj.* **maᶜsūr** معسور

beloved, sweetheart *n.m.* **ma^cšūq** معشوق
lovely, fascinating *adj.* **ma^cšūqānah** معشوقانہ
loveliness *n.f.* **ma^cšūqī** معشوقی
defended, innocent; preserved; simple *adj.* **ma^csūm** معصوم
innocence, simplicity *n.f.* **ma^csūmiyat** معصومیت
disobedience, defection, sin *n.f.* **ma^csiyat** معصیت
perfumed, fragrant *adj.* **mu^cattar** معطر
suspended, disengaged, unemployed, jobless *adj.* **mu^cattal** معطل
suspend, abolish, dismiss, detain *v.t.* **mu^cattal karnā** معطل کرنا
suspension, dismissal *n.f.* **mu^cattalī** معطلگی
inclined, turned; connected, appended *adj.* **ma^ctūf** معطوف
honored, respected, exalted *adj.* **mu^cazzam** معظم
reasonable, plausible, probable, understandable *adj.* **ma^cqūl** معقول
reasonableness, probability, plausibility *n.f.* **ma^cqūliyat** معقولیت
inverted, reversed *adj.* **ma^ckūs** معکوس
suspended, pending, hanging *adj.* **mu^callāq** معلق
teacher, instructor, tutor, master *n.m.* **mu^callim** معلم
indisposed, diseased, distempered, sick, affected *adj.* **ma^clūl** معلول
known, evident, apparent *adj.* **ma^clūm** معلوم
know, understand, find out, discover, learn *v.t.* **ma^clūm karnā** معلوم کرنا
it seems *adv.* **ma^clūm hōtā hai** معلوم ہوتا ہے
seem, appear, be known, be discovered *v.i.* **ma^clūm hōnā** معلوم ہونا
information, knowledge *n.f.* **ma^clūmāt** معلومات
exalted, elevated, high, sublime *adj.* **mu^callā** معلی
teaching, instruction, tutorship *n.f.* **mu^callimī** معلمی
mason, builder; architect *n.m.* **mi^cmār** معمار
masonry; architecture; building *n.f.* **mi^cmārī** معماری
aged, blessed with a long life *adj.* **mu^cammar** معمر
riddle, enigma, puzzle, crossword *n.m.* **mu^cammah** معمہ
solve a puzzle *v.t.* **mu^cammah ḥal karnā** معمہ حل کرنا
inhabited, populated; full, abundant; cultivated *adj.* **ma^cmūr** معمور
cultivation; population; fullness, abundancy *n.f.* **ma^cmūrī** معموری
habit, custom, practice *n.m.* / governed, established; made, prepared *adj.* **ma^cmūl** معمول
menstruation *n.m.* **ma^cmūl kē din** معمول کے دن
customary, common, ordinary *adj.* **ma^cmūlī** معمولی
dedicated *adj.* **ma^cnūn** معنون

real, essential, significant *adj.* **maᶜnavī** معنوی
meaning, significance, indication, sense; reality *n.f.* **maᶜnī/maᶜnā** معنی
interpret, explain *v.t.* **maᶜnī dēnā** معنی دینا
imply, mean *v.t.* **maᶜni rakhnā** معنی رکھنا
agreed, stipulated, promised, established, resolved, certain *adj.* **maᶜhūd** معہود
crooked, bent *adj.* **maᶜvajj** معوج
assistance, aid, favor, protection *n.m.* **maᶜūn** معون
assistance, aid, help *n.f.* **maᶜūnat** معونت
touchstone, standard, criteria *n.m.* **miᶜyār** معیار
company, association *n.f.* **maᶜiyyat** معیت
livelihood, subsistence *n.f.* **maᶜišat** معیشت
fixed, appointed, established, certified *adj.* **muᶜaiyyan** معین
assistant, aide, helper *n.m.* **muᶜīn** معین
fix, appoint, establish *v.t.* **muᶜaiyyan karnā** معین کرنا
infamous; defective; improper, indecent *adj.* **maᶜyūb** معیوب
error, delusion, deception, fallacy *n.m.* **muġālatah** مغالطہ
mislead, delude *v.t.* **muġālatah dēnā** مغالطہ دینا
mislead, delude *v.t.* **muġālatah ḍālnā** مغالطہ ڈالنا
contrary, adverse, reverse *adj.* **muġāyar** مغایر
exchange, disagreement, repugnance *n.f.* **muġāyarat** مغایرت
west *n.m.* **maġrib** مغرب
westernized *adj.* **maġrib zadah** مغرب زدہ
western, occidental *adj.* **maġribī** مغربی
westernization *n.f.* **maġribiyyat** مغربیت
immersed, sunk, dipped *adj.* **muġarraq** مغرق
proud, arrogant, haughty *adj.* **maġrūr** مغرور
pride, arrogance, haughtiness *n.f.* **maġrūrī** مغروری
brain, intellect; marrow; kernel, pith *n.m.* **maġz** مغز
bother, get on one's nerves *v.t.* **maġz cāṭnā** مغز چاٹنا
talkative *adj.* **maġz caṭ** مغز چٹ
distract, tease; worry *v.t.* **maġz khānā** مغز کھانا
chatter, brag, bother *v.t.* **maġz kē kīṛē uṛānā** مغز کے کیڑے اڑانا
feel distracted *v.t.* **maġz uṛānā** مغز اڑانا
edging, border, hem *n.f.* **maġzī** مغزی
bathed *adj.* **maġsil** مغسل
washed, bathed *adj.* **maġsūl** مغسول

pardon, remission, absolution, deliverance *n.f.* **maġfirat** مغفرت
pardoned, forgiven; dead, deceased *adj.* **maġfūr** مغفور
Mughal *n.m.* **muġal** مغل
hard, rigorous, severe *adj.* **muġallaz** مغلظ
abusive language, abuse *n.f.* **muġallazāt** مغلظات
obscure, intricate *adj.* **muġlaq** مغلق
conquered, overcome, subdued *adj.* **maġlūb** مغلوب
choleric, short-tempered *adj.* **maġlūb-ul-ġazab** مغلوب الغضب
overcome, subdue *v.t.* **maglūb karnā** مغلوب کرنا
humility; pressure; obedience *n.f.* **maġlūbiyat** مغلوبیت
obscured, hidden *adj.* **maġlūq** مغلوق
Mughal *adj.* **muġliyyah** مغلیہ
defective, faulty; wicked *adj.* **maġmūz** مغموز
sad, grieved, sorrowful, mournful *adj.* **maġmūm** مغموم
male singer; musician *n.m.* **muġannī** مغنی
female singer *n.f.* **muġanniyah** مغنیہ
boasting, arrogance *n.f.* **mufāxarat** مفاخرت
separation, alienation, forsaking *n.f.* **mufāraqat** مفارقت
free of charge, gratis *adj.* **muft** مفت
parasite *n.m.* **muft xōr** مفت خور
free of charge, gratis *adv.* **muft mēṁ** مفت میں
key *n.f.* **miftāḥ** مفتاح
honored, glorified *adj.* **muftaxar** مفتخر
tricky, liar *adj.* **muftarī** مفتری
investigated, inquired *adj.* **muftaqad** مفتقد
captured, taken, conquered *adj.* **maftūḥ** مفتوح
tempted, fascinated, charmed, mad (*of love*) *adj.* **maftūn** مفتون
mufti (*Muslim priest or lawmaker*) *n.m.* **muftī** مفتی
honored, dignified *adj.* **mufaxxar** مفخر
exhilarating, refreshing, stimulating *adj.* **mufarriḥ** مفرح
solitary, single, simple *adj.* **mufrad** مفرد
solitary, alone, single *adj.* **mufardah** مفردہ
separated *adj.* **mufarraz** مفرز
excessive, vast, transcendent *adj.* **mufrit** مفرط
fugitive, escaped *adj.* **mafrūr** مفرور
spread; carpeted *adj.* **mafrūš** مفروش

supposed, granted *adj.* **mafrūz** مفروض
hypothesis *n.m.* **mafrūzah** مفروضہ
mischievous *adj.* **mufsid** مفسد
mischief *n.m.* **mufsid pan** مفسدپن
mischievously *adv.* **mufsidānah** مفسدانہ
riot, tumult, uproar, disturbance *n.m.* **mafsadah** مفسدہ
commentator *n.m.* **mufassir** مفسر
detailed, explained, elaborated *adj.* / fully, in detail *adv.* **mufassal** مفصل
describe in detail *v.t.* **mufassal likhnā** مفصل لکھنا
obedient, submissive *adj.* **munqād** منقاد
missed, lost, extinct *adj.* **mafqūd** مفقود
careful, thinking, thoughtful *adj.* **mufakkir** مفکر
insolvent, bankrupt, poor, penniless *adj.* **muflis** مفلس
impoverish *v.t.* **muflis karnā** مفلس کرنا
bankruptcy, poverty *n.f.* **muflisī** مفلسی
paralytic *adj.* **maflūj** مفلوج
unfortunate, distressed, indigent, destitute *adj.* **maflūk** مفلوک
understood, comprehended *adj.* / meaning, sense *n.m.* **mafhūm** مفہوم
ceded, entrusted, consigned, resigned *adj.* **mufavvazah** مفوضہ
useful, beneficial, advantageous, profitable *adj.* **mufīd** مفید
opposite, opposing, confronting *adj./pp.* **muqābil** مقابل
opposition, confronting, encounter, collision, competition *n.m.* **muqābalah** مقابلہ
oppose, confront, compete *v.t.* **muqābalah karnā** مقابلہ کرنا
slaughter, carnage; battle, conflict *n.m.* **muqātalah** مقاتلہ
connection, conjunction *n.f.* **muqāranat** مقارنت
disconnection, cutting off, separation *n.m.* **muqātaᶜah** مقاطعہ
word, speech, discourse, talk *n.m.* **maqāl** مقال
book, article, discourse *n.m.* **maqālah** مقالہ
place, site; dwelling, abode; occasion, opportunity, situation *n.m.* **maqām** مقام
local *adj.* **maqāmī** مقامی
tomb, mausoleum *n.m.* **maqbarah** مقبرہ
captured, seized *adj.* **maqbūzah** مقبوضہ
accepted, admitted, received *adj.* **maqbūl** مقبول
popular *adj.* **maqbūl-ē-ᶜām** مقبول عام
killed, murdered *adj.* **maqtūl** مقتول
quantity, measure, size, dimension, number, amount, rate *n.f.* **miqdār** مقدار

destiny, fate *n.m.* **muqaddar** مقدر

holy, sacred *adj.* **muqaddas** مقدس

prior, antecedent, preceeding, first; superior *adj.* **muqaddam** مقدم

case, lawsuit; preface, preamble *n.m.* **muqaddamah** مقدمہ

power, means, resources, capacity *n.m.* **maqdūr** مقدور

scissors *n.f.* **miqrāz** مقراض

admitted, approximate *adj.* / relative; friend *n.m.* **muqarrab** مقرب

established, fixed, appointed, employed *adj.* **muqarrar** مقرر

portion; fate, destiny *n.m.* / divided *adj.* **maqsūm** مقسوم

intention, object, purpose, plan *n.m.* **maqsad** مقصد

object, intent, aim *n.m.* / intended, proposed *adj.* **maqsūd** مقصود

distilled *adj.* **muqattar** مقطر

locked, bolted *adj.* **muqaffal** مقفل

oppressed, disturbed *adj.* **maqhūr** مقہور

saying, maxim, motto *n.m.* **maqūlah** مقولہ

strengthening, invigorating *adj.* **maqavvī** مقوی

imprisoned, confined *adj.* **muqaiyyad** مقید

stationed, residing *adj.* **muqīm** مقیم

mouth; face *n.m.* **mukh** مکھ

fist; blow, thump *n.m.* **mukkā** مکا

cunning, artful, deceitful *adj.* **makkār** مکار

fraud, cheating, deceitfulness *n.f.* **makkārī** مکاری

dialogue *n.m.* **mukālamah** مکالمہ

house, home *n.m.* **makān** مکان

school, academy; office *n.m.* **maktab** مکتب

written *adj.* **maktūb** مکتوب

crest, crown *n.m.* **mukaṭ** مکٹ

fraud, cheating, deceit *n.m.* **makr** مکر

repeatedly, again *adv.* **mukarrar** مکرر

respected, revered, noble, venerable *adj.* **mukarram** مکرم

deny, refuse *v.i.* **mukarnā** مکرنا

hated, hateful, abhorred *adj.* **makrūh** مکروہ

mouth; face; appearance *n.m.* **mukhṛā** مکھڑا

large spider *n.m.* **makṛā** مکڑا

spider *n.f.* **makṛī** مکڑی

spider's web, cobweb *n.m.* **makṛī kā jālā** مکڑی کا جالا

cubic *adj.* **mukaᶜab** مکعب
careful, carefully executed; elaborate *adj.* **mukallaf** مکلف
perfect, accomplished, complete *adj.* **mukammal** مکمل
butter *n.m.* **makkhan** مکھن
large ant *n.m.* **makōṛā** مکوڑا
fly *n.f.* **makhnī** مکھی
miser, stingy person *n.m.* **makhnī cūs** مکھی چوس
chief, headman *n.m.* **mukhiyā** مکھیا
corn, maize *n.f.* **maka'ī** مکئی
crocodile, alligator *n.m.* / but, except, moreover, however, unless, still *conj.* **magar** مگر
cheerful, glad, happy, pleased *adj.* **magan** مگن
mullah (*religious judge or priest*) *n.m.* **mullā** ملا
agreement, concord, reconciliation *n.m.* **milāp** ملاپ
sailor, boatman, mariner *n.m.* **mallāḥ** ملاح
inspection, consideration, view, regard *n.m.* **mulāḥazah** ملاحظہ
employee, servant, attendant *n.m.* **mulāzim** ملازم
service, duty, employment *n.f.* **mulāzamat** ملازمت
interview, conversation; visit, meeting *n.f.* **mulāqāt** ملاقات
visitor *n.m.* **mulāqātī** ملاقاتی
sadness, grief, anguish, displeasure *n.m.* **malāl** ملال
reproach, rebuke, blame *n.f.* **malāmat** ملامت
join, mix, bring together, attach, unite *v.t.* **milānā** ملانا
soft, tender, gentle, mild *adj.* **mulā'im** ملائم
softness, tenderness, gentleness, mildness *n.f.* **mulā'imat** ملائمت
rubbish, dirt, debris *n.m.* **malbah** ملبہ
clothes, garment, suit *n.m.* / dressed *adj.* **malbūs** ملبوس
religion, sect, belief, faith; society *n.f.* **millat** ملت
petitioner, applicant *n.m.* **multajī** ملتجی
applying, requesting *adj.* **multamis** ملتمس
postponed, delayed, adjourned *adj.* **multavī** ملتوی
joined, added, annexed *adj.* **mulḥaq** ملحق
considered, regarded *adj.* **malḥūz** ملحوظ
criminal, accused, convicted *adv.* **mulzam** ملزم
cursed, accused *adj.* **malᶜūn** ملعون
named, entitled *adj.* **mulaqqab** ملقب

ملک • king, monarch, sovereign *n.m.* **malik** • country, region, territory *n.m.* **mulk**
property, possession, belonging *n.f.* **milk**

ملکِ فرس Persia *n.m.* **mulk-ē-fars**

ملکہ queen *n.f.* **malikah**

ملکی proprietory *adj.* / farmer; landlord *n.m.* **milkī** • national; political, civil *adj.* **mulkī**

ملمع coated, plated *adj.* **mulammaᶜ**

ملمع کرنا coat, plate *v.t.* **mulammaᶜ karnā**

ملنا meet, be united, be mixed, be joined *v.i.* **milnā**

ملنا tread, trample; rub *v.t.* **malnā**

ملنی meeting, reception *n.f.* **milnī**

ملوانا cause to be joined, cause to be united *v.t.* **milvānā**

ملول sad, dejected; tired, weary *adj.* **malūl**

ملی national *adj.* **mallī**

ملیح salty; charming, pleasing *adj.* **malīḥ**

ملین filthy, foul *adj.* **malīn**

ممات death *n.f.* **mamat**

مماثل similar, alike *adj.* **mumāsil**

مماس tangent, touching *n.m.* **mamās**

ممانعت prohibition, restriction *n.f.* **mumānaᶜat**

ممتا affection, attachment, tenderness *n.f.* **mamtā**

ممتاز exalted, distinguished, illustrious, dominant *adj.* **mumtāz**

ممتحن examiner, tester *n.m.* **mumtaḥin**

ممد protector *n.m.* **mumidd**

ممدوح praised, celebrated *adj.* **mamdūḥ**

ممسک miserly, stingy *adj.* **mumsik**

ممکن possible, feasible *adj.* **mumkin**

مملکت kingdom *n.f.* **mamlakat**

مملوکہ possessed *adj.* **mamlūkah**

ممنوع prohibited, forbidden *adj.* **mamnūᶜ**

ممنون thankful, grateful; obliged *adj.* **mamnūn**

من from, of, on, out of *pp.* **min** • heart, mind, soul, spirit *n.m.* **man**

من جملہ completely, totally *adv.* **min jumlah**

من موجی conceited *adj.* **man maujī**

منا darling; pet *n.m.* **munnā**

منادی proclamation *n.f.* **manādī**

منادی کرنا proclaim *v.t.* **manādī karnā**

minaret; watch-tower; light house *n.m.* **manārah** مناره
convenient, proper, suitable, reasonable *adj.* **munāsib** مناسب
convenience, suitability, relevancy, consistency *n.f.* **munāsibat** مناسبت
discussion, dispute, contest *n.m.* **munāzarah** مناظره
profits, benefits *n.m.* **munāfi**[c] منافع
hypocrite; atheist, infidel *n.m.* **munāfiq** منافق
hypocrisy *n.f.* **munāfaqat** منافقت
conciliate, persuade, reason (with) *v.i.* **manānā** منانا
pulpit *n.m.* **minbar** منبر
fountain, source, origin *n.m.* **manba**[c] منبع
• obligation; favor, kindness; entreaty *n.f.* **minnat** منت
vow, promise; acknowledgment *n.f.* **mannat**
make a vow *v.t.* **mannat mānnā** منت ماننا
chosen, selected, elected *adj.* **muntaxab** منتخب
charm; sacred verse, sacred text *n.m.* **mantar** منتر
incantation; exorcism, sorcery *n.m.* **mantar jantar** منتر جنتر
counselor, adviser, minister *n.m.* **mantarī/mantrī** منتری
disposed, dispersed, diffused, scattered *adj.* **muntašir** منتشر
expected, awaited *adj.* **muntazar** • expecting, waiting *adj.* **muntazir** منتظر
manager, superintendent *n.m.* **muntazim** منتظم
transferred, carried, transported *adj.* **muntaqqal** منتقل
minute *n.m.* **minaṭ** منٹ
astrologer; astronomer *n.m.* **munajjim** منجم
frozen, iced, frigid *adj.* **munjamid** منجمد
dependent, restricted *adj.* **munḥasir** منحصر
bent, curved *adj.* **munḥanī** منحنی
unfortunate, unlucky *adj.* **manḥūs** منحوس
slow, dull, mild *adj.* **mandā** مندا
temple, pagoda *n.m.* **mandir** مندر
ring *n.f.* **mundrī** مندری
circle, sphere *n.m.* **manḍal** منڈل
hover around, fly around *v.i.* **manḍlānā** منڈلانا
group, assembly, company *n.f.* **manḍlī** منڈلی
market, mart *n.f.* **manḍī** منڈی
stage; floor, storey (*of a house*); lodging, house *n.f.* **manzil** منزل
rank; dignity *n.f.* **manzilat** منزلت

floor, storey; dignity *n.m.* **manzilah** منزلہ

threaded, linked, attached, connected *adj.* **munsalik** منسلک

betrothed, related, allied *adj.* **mansūb** منسوب

cancelled, abolished, erased *adj.* **mansūx** منسوخ

cancellation, abolition *n.f.* **mansūxī** منسوخی

allusion, principle, motive, desire, intention; source, origin *n.m.* **manšā'** منشاء

diploma; charter; mandate *n.m.* **manšūr** منشور

clerk, secretary; writer; teacher *n.m.* **munšī** منشی

post, rank, office *n.m.* **mansab** منصب

official position, government post *n.m.* **mansab-ē-sarkārī** منصب سرکاری

judge, arbitrator *n.m.* / just, fair *adj.* **munsif** منصف

justly, fairly *adv.* **munsifānah** منصفانہ

appointed, nominated; fixed, erected, established *adj.* **mansūb** منصوب

project, scheme, plan, design, determination, intention *n.m.* **mansūbah** منصوبہ

determine, plan; resolve, contrive, conspire *v.t.* **mansūbah bāndhnā** منصوبہ باندھنا

planning *n.f.* **mansūbah bandī** منصوبہ بندی

triumphant, victorious; protected, defended *adj.* **mansūr** منصور

manifested, declared *adj.* **mansūs** منصوص

mixed, united, joined *adj.* **munzam** منضم

logic, reasoning *n.f.* **mantiq/mantaq** منطق

zone, belt *n.m.* **mintaqah** منطقہ

Zodiac *n.m.* **mintaqat-ul-burūj** منطقۃ البروج

sight, aspect, look, scene, view; landscape; face *n.m.* **manzar** منظر

regular, fixed; annexed, added; arranged, organized *adj.* **munnazzam** منظم

organize *v.t.* **munnazzam karnā** منظم کرنا

seen, visible; admired, approved, accepted, admitted, chosen *adj.* **manzūr** منظور

permission, approval *n.f.* **manzūrī** منظوری

poetic; metrical *adj.* **manzūm** منظوم

prohibition, prevention, refusal *n.m.* **manaᶜ** منع

prohibit, forbid, prevent, refuse *v.t.* **manaᶜ karnā** منع کرنا

be forbidden, be prohibited *v.i.* **manaᶜ hōnā** منع ہونا

destroyed, extinct, annihilated *adj.* **munaᶜdim** منعدم

attending, paying attention (to) *adj.* **manaᶜtif** منعطف

held, bound; convened, celebrated *adj.* **munaᶜqid** منعقد

inverted, reversed, inverse, upside down, topsy-turvy *adj.* **munaᶜkis** منعکس

liberal, generous, beneficent *adj.* **munᶜim** منعم

disturbed, miserable, sad *adj.* **munaġaz** منغض
wide, ample, extended *adj.* **munfarijah** منفرجہ
single, solitary, separate, unique; isolated; odd *adj.* **munfarid** منفرد
separated, divided *adj.* **munfasil** منفصل
advantage; profit, gain *n.f.* **manfaᶜat** منفعت
afflicted; abashed, ashamed *adj.* **munfaᶜil** منفعل
negative; rejected; subtracted, deducted *adj.* **manfī** منفی
glory, virtue, praise *n.f.* **manqabat** منقبت
divided *adj.* **munqasim** منقسم
painted, printed, colored *adj.* **munaqqaš** منقش
expired, completed, finished *adj.* **munqazī** منقضی
broken, cut off; finished, extinct *adj.* **munqatiᶜ** منقطع
upside down, inverted *adj.* **munqalib** منقلب
engraved, carved; painted *adj.* **manqūš** منقوش
imperfect, unfinished, deficient *adj.* **manqūs** منقوص
dotted, spotted *adj.* **manqūtah** منقوطہ
translated, narrated, related; copied, transferred *adj.* **manqūl** منقول
transferable, movable *adj.* **manqūlah** منقولہ
denying, rejecting, sceptical *adj.* **munkir** منکر
deny, disown *v.t.* **munkir hōnā** منکر ہونا
broken; miserable; poor *adj.* **munkasir** منکسر
discovered, disclosed, displayed, revealed, published *adj.* **munkašif** منکشف
beggar; borrower *n.m.* **mangtā** منگتا
stubborn; careless *adj.* **mangrā** منگرا
Tuesday *n.m.* **mankal** منگل
Mars (*planet*); pleasure, happiness *n.m.* / lucky, fortunate *adj.* **mangal** منگل
betrothal *n.f.* **mangnī** منگنی
betroth *v.t.* **mangnī karnā** منگنی کرنا
send for, call for, ask for, order *v.t.* **mangvānā** منگوانا
mouth; face; presence, aspect; opening; capacity, ability, strength *n.m.* **muṁh** منہ
express displeasure *v.t.* **muṁh burā banānā** منہ برا بنانا
be displeased, make faces, frown *v.i.* **muṁh bigaṛnā** منہ بگڑنا
fully, completely *adv.* **muṁh bhar kē** منہ بھر کے
fill one's mouth; bribe *v.t.* **muṁh bharnā** منہ بھرنا
abusive; fearless *adj.* **muṁh phaṭ** منہ پھٹ
be astonished; look at; hope; look stupid *v.t.* **muṁh taknā** منہ تکنا

kiss; caress *v.t.* **muṁh cūmnā** منہ چومنا
show one's face, appear *v.t.* **muṁh dikhāṇā** منہ دکھانا
beg to, request; bite *v.t.* **muṁh ḍālnā** منہ ڈالنا
oral, verbal *adj.* **muṁh zabānī** منہ زبانی
headstrong, obstinate *adj.* **muṁh zōr** منہ زور
disgrace, bring disgrace *v.t.* **muṁh kālā karnā** منہ کالا کرنا
be disgraced *v.i.* **muṁh kālā hōnā** منہ کالا ہونا
confront, turn one's face, regard; tackle *v.t.* **muṁh karnā** منہ کرنا
speak; reveal; abuse *v.t.* **muṁh khōlnā** منہ کھولنا
be familiar (with), be on good terms (with) *v.t.* **muṁh lagānā** منہ لگانا
bite; feed; silence *v.t.* **muṁh mārnā** منہ مارنا
ask for, request *v.t.* **muṁh māngnā** منہ مانگنا
deducted, subtracted *adj.* **miṁhā** منہا
deduct, subtract *v.t.* **miṁhā karnā** منہا کرنا
reduction, decrease *n.f.* **miṁhā'ī** منہائی
demolished, destroyed *adj.* **munhadim** منہدم
defeated *adj.* **munhazim** منہزم
absorbed, engrossed *adj.* **munhamik** منہمک
forbidden, prohibited, banned *adj.* **maṁhī** منہی
like, as if, as though *conj.* **manō** منو
mind, soul, life *n.m.* **manvā** منوا
satisfaction, reconciliation *n.f.* **manautī** منوتی
brilliant, splendid, illuminated, enlightened *adj.* **munavvar** منور
prohibiting, preventing *adj.* **manūᶜ** منوع
pleasing, lovely *adj.* **manōhar** منوہر
presumption, egoism *n.f.* **manī** منی
master, patron, agent *n.m.* **munīb** منیب
splendid, brilliant, shining, illuminating *adj.* **munīr** منیر
moon; month *n.m.* **mah** • chief, principal, great *adj.* **mih** مہ
great, high, supreme, extreme, illustrious *adj.* **mahā** مہا
emigrant, refugee *n.m.* **muhājir** مہاجر
separation, flight, desertion, migration *n.f.* **muhājarat** مہاجرت
sovereign, prince, king, emperor, maharaja *n.m.* **mahā rājah** مہاراجہ
practice, skill, experience, proficiency *n.f.* **mahārat** مہارت
pimple *n.m.* **muhāsā** مہاسا
beehive *n.f.* **muhāl** مہال

mahout (*elephant driver*) *n.m.* **mahāvat** مہاوت
landing place, place of descent *n.m.* **mahbat** مہبط
chief, headman (*of a village*); clerk, agent *n.m.* **mahtā** مہتا
moon, moonlight *n.m.* **mahtāb** مہتاب
directed, guided *adj.* **muhtadā** • leading, guiding *adj.* **muhtadī** مہتدی
superior, chief *adj.* **muhtar** • head man, chief, prince *n.m.* **mihtar** مہتر
manager, superintendent, inspector, supervisor *n.m.* **muhtamim** مہتمم
managership *n.f.* **muhtamimī** مہتممی
separated, cut off, rejected *adj.* **mahjūr** مہجور
separation, absence *n.f.* **mahjūrī** مہجوری
cradle, swing *n.m.* **mahd** مہد
cultured, civilized, polite, well-mannered *adj.* **muhazzab** مہذب
• dowry *n.m.* **mahr** • kindness, affection, favor *n.f.* / sun *n.m.* **mihr** مہر
seal, stamp; coin *n.f.* **muhr**
silent *adj.* **muhr balab** مہر بلب
asylum, place of refuge *n.m.* **mahrab** مہرب
kind, affectionate *adj.* **mihrbān** مہربان
kindness, affection, favor *n.f.* **mihrbānī** مہربانی
Please!, Do me a favor! *interj.* **mihrbānī karkē** مہربانی کرکے، ذرا
smell, fragrance *n.f.* **mahak** مہک
be fragrant *v.i.* **mahaknā** مہکنا
fragrant, aromatic *adj.* **mahkīlā** مہکیلا
postponement, delay, retarding, break, intermission; time; leisure *n.f.* **muhlat** مہلت
allow time; postpone *v.t.* **muhlat dēnā** مہلت دینا
fatal, mortal, destructive *adj.* **muhlik** مہلک
fatal injury *n.f.* **muhlik zaxm** مہلک زخم
urgent matter, important affair *n.f.* **muhimm** مہم
guest *n.m.* **mihmān** مہمان
guest-house *n.m.* **mihmān xānah** مہمان خانہ
hospitality, entertainment *n.f.* **mihmān dārī** مہمان داری
hospitable *adj.* **mihmān navāz** مہمان نواز
hospitality *n.f.* **mihmān navāzī** مہمان نوازی
host, entertainer *n.m.* **mihmān dār** مہماندار
entertainment, banquet, feast; hospitality *n.f.* **mihmānī** مہمانی
entertain *v.t.* **mihmānī karnā** مہمانی کرنا
meaningless *adj.* **muhmalah** مہملہ

مہمیز spur *n.f.* **mahmēz**
مہنا sarcasm, taunt, ridicule *n.m.* **mihnā**
مہنت monk, abbot, head of a religious order *n.m.* **mahant**
مہندس geometrician, mathematician; engineer *n.m.* **muhandis**
مہندی myrtle; henna *n.f.* **mahndī/mēhndī**
مہنگا expensive, dear *adj.* **mahngā**
مہنگائی expensiveness, dearness *n.f.* **mahngā'ī**
مہوس greedy, desirous *adj.* **muhavvis**
مہوسی greed *n.f.* **muhavvisī**
مہیا ready, prepared, arranged *adj.* **muhaiyyā**
مہیب tremendous, terrible, dreadful *adj.* **muhīb**
مہین fine, thin *adj.* **mahīn**
مہینہ month; salary, pay *n.m.* **mahīnah**
مہینہ بھر whole month *n.m.* **mahīnah bhar**
مہینے سے ہونا menstruate *v.i.* **mahīnē sē hōnā**
مہینے کے مہینے monthly, every month *adv.* **mahīnē kē mahīnē**
مو hair *n.m.* **mū** • perfection; pleasure *n.f.* **mau**
مو بہ مو hair by hair, minutely, exactly *adv.* **mū bah mū**
موتراش razor *n.m.* **mū tarāš**
موقلم hairbrush *n.m.* **mū qalam**
موا بادل sponge *n.m.* **mūā' bādal**
مواج waving *adj.* **mavvāj**
مواجہہ confronting, opposition; interview *n.m.* **muvājahah**
مواحنت enmity, dislike, hatred *n.f.* **mu'āḥanat**
مواخات fraternity, brotherhood *n.f.* **muvāxāt**
مواخذہ accountability, responsibility *n.m.* **mu'āxazah**
مواخذہ کرنا call to account, impeach *v.t.* **mu'āxazah karnā**
مواظبت assiduity, attention, carefulness *n.f.* **mavāzabat**
موافق fit, suitable, favorable *adj.* **muvāfiq**
موافق آنا agree, suit *v.i.* **muvāfiq ānā**
موافقت agreement, conformity, analogy *n.f.* **muvāfaqat**
موافقت رکھنا agree (with), suit *v.t.* **muvāfaqat rakhnā**
موالات friendship, cooperation *n.f.* **muvālāt**
موانست companionship, fellowship, familiarity, intimacy *n.f.* **muvānasat**
مواہنت idleness, laziness, indolence *n.f.* **mavāhnat**
مواء dead, lifeless *adj.* **mūā'**

doctor; philosopher; counselor *n.m.* **mūbad/mūbid** موبد
urine *n.m.* **mūt** • death, mortality *n.f.* **maut** موت
die *v.i.* **maut ānā** موت آنا
fear, be afraid of *v.i.* **maut paṛnā** موت پڑنا
be tired of life *v.t.* **maut cāhnā** موت چاہنا
urinate *v.i.* **mūtnā** موتنا
pearl *n.m.* **mōtī** موتی
fat, corpulent, bulky, thick, coarse, dense *adj.* **mōṭā** موٹا
motor, engine *n.m.* **mōṭar** موٹر
motorcycle *n.m.* **mōṭar sāikil** موٹر سائیکل
handle; fist; load *n.f.* **mūṭh** موٹھ
cast a spell, charm *v.t.* **mūṭh calānā** موٹھ چلانا
effective, striking, touching *adj.* **mu'assir** موثر
have an effect, be effective *v.i.* **mu'assir hōnā** موثر ہونا
steady, fixed, strong *adj.* **mu'assiq** موثق
wave, surge; whim; enjoyment, emotion *n.f.* **mauj** موج
waving, raging *adj.* **mauj zan** موج زن
enjoy oneself *v.t.* **mauj karnā** موج کرنا
billow, wave *v.t.* **mauj mārnā** موج مارنا
cause, reason, motive *n.m.* **mūjib** موجب
inventor; author *n.m.* **mūjid** موجد
agreeable, acceptable, valid, plausible *adj.* **muvajjah** موجہ
present, existing, available, ready *adj.* **maujūd** موجود
continue; attend, be present *v.i.* **maujūd rahnā** موجود رہنا
produce, bring before, apply *v.t.* **maujūd karnā** موجود کرنا
presence, existence *n.f.* **manjūdagī** موجودگی
present, existing, available, ready *adj.* **maujūdah** موجودہ
cheerful *adj.* **maujī** موجی
sprain, strain, twist *n.f.* **mōc** موچ
sprain, be sprained *v.i.* **mōc ānā** موچ آنا
shoemaker, cobbler *n.m.* **mōcī** موچی
moustache *n.f.* **mūch** موچھ
shocking, frightful *adj.* **muvaḥḥiš** موحش
posterior; consequent; delayed *adj.* **mu'axxar** موخر
last mentioned, latter *adj.* **mu'axxar-ul-zikr** موخر الذکر
civil, polite, disciplined, respectful, well-mannered *adj.* **mu'addab** مؤدب

friendship, love *n.f.* **muvaddat** مودت

grocer, shopkeeper, merchant *n.m.* **mōdī/mūdī** مودی

storehouse pantry *n.m.* **mōdī xānah** مودی خانہ

muezzin (*person in mosque who calls people to prayer*) *n.m.* **mu'azzin** موذن

noxious, troublesome *adj.* **mūzī** موذی

noxiousness, meanness *n.m.* **mūzi panā** موذی پنا

ant *n.f.* / peacock *n.m.* **mōr** مور

statue, idol *n.f.* **mūrtī/mūratī** مورتی

fortification, line of entrenchment *n.m.* **mōrcah** مورچہ

entrench *v.t.* **mōrcah bandī karnā** مورچہ بندی کرنا

swoon, stupefaction *n.f.* **mūrchā** مورچھا

swoon, faint *v.i.* **mūrchā ānā** مورچھا آنا

fainted, in swoon *adj.* **mūrchit** مورچھت

annalist, historian, biographer *n.m.* **mu'arrix** مورخ

dated *adj.* **mu'arraxah** مورخہ

place of arrival *n.m.* **maurid** مورد

illiterate, ignorant, foolish, stupid *adj.* **mūrakh** مورکھ

hereditary, ancestral *adj.* **maurūsī** موروثی

drain, gutter *n.f.* **mōrī** موری

twist, bend, turn, winding *n.f.* **mōṛ** موڑ

twist, bend, turn *v.t.* **mōṛnā** موڑنا

stool, chair *n.m.* **mōṛhā/mūṛhā** موڑھا

banana *n.m.* **mauz** موز

stocking, sock; glove *n.m.* **mōzah** موزہ

well-balanced, well-adjusted *adj.* **mauzūṁ** موزوں

correct, adjust *v.t.* **mauzūṁ karnā** موزوں کرنا

rat, mouse *n.m.* **mūsā** موسا

rod; bolt; root; pestle *n.m.* **mūslā** موسلا

season, weather, time *n.m.* **mausim/mausam** موسم

rainy season *n.m.* **mausim-ē-baršagāl** موسم برشگال

spring *n.m.* **mausim-ē-bahār** موسم بہار

autumn, fall *n.m.* **mausim-ē-xizāṁ** موسم خزاں

winter *n.m.* **mausim-ē-sarmā** موسم سرما

summer *n.m.* **mausim-ē-garmā** موسم گرما

green lime *n.f.* **mausambī** موسمبی

seasonal *adj.* **mausimī** موسمی

موسنا **mūsnā** *v.t.* pilfer, steal, rob, cheat, swindle
موسوم **mausūm** *adj.* called, named: marked, signed
موسیقی **mūsīqī** *n.f.* music
موش **mūš** *n.m.* mouse, rat
موصوف **mausūf** *adj.* praised, celebrated
موصول **mausūl** *adj.* joined, connected, related
موضع **mauzaᶜ** *n.m.* parcel (of land); place, district, village
موضوع **mauzūᶜ** *n.m.* object, subject / *adj.* placed, situated
موطن **mautin** *n.m.* birthplace, home
موظبت کرنا **mavāzabat karnā** *v.t.* take care of, do carefully
موظف **muvazzaf** *adj.* fixed, limited, allowed; paid
موعدت **mauᶜidat** *n.m.* promise
موعظت **mauᶜizat** *n.m.* lecture, sermon
موعود **mauᶜūd** *adj.* promised, predicted
موفور **maufūr** *adj.* copious, abundant, plentiful, numerous
موقت **muvaqqat** *adj.* fixed, restricted (*to a certain time*)
موقر **muvaqqar** *adj.* honored, revered, respected
موقع **mauqaᶜ** *n.m.* place, spot; situation, occasion, opportunity
موقع پر **mauqaᶜ par** *adv.* the proper time, the right place, on the spot
موقف **mauqif** *n.m.* halting place, station, stand, stop
موقوف **mauqūf** *adj.* fixed, dependent; stopped, ceased, abolished, dismissed
موقوف کرنا **mauqūf karnā** *v.t.* stop, abolish, dismiss
موقوفی **mauqūfī** *n.f.* abolition, suspension, dismissal
موکد **mu'akkad** *adj.* emphasized, confirmed, compelled, stressed
موکل **muvakkal** *n.m.* guardian, superintendent, trustee
موگرا **mōgrā** *n.m.* mallet, hammer
مول **mūl** *n.m.* • root, origin, source; generation; stock, capital
mōl *n.m.* purchase; price, value
مولانا **maulānā** *n.m.* sir, Mister (*a title for well-educated man*)
مولد **maulid** *n.m.* birthplace, nativeland
مؤلف **mu'allaf** *adj.* composed, edited, compiled • **mu'allif** *n.m.* compiler, editor
مولود **maulūd** *n.m.* baby; son / *adj.* born, generated
مولوی **maulavī** *n.m.* learned man, professor, doctor, priest
مولی **mūlī** *n.f.* radish
مولیٰ یا مولا **maulā** *n.m.* master, lord; God
موم **mōm** *n.m.* wax

candle *n.f.* **mōm battī** موم بتی
tender-hearted *adj.* **mōm dil** موم دل
make soft, soften, melt *v.t.* **mōm karnā** موم کرنا
/ true believer, follower, orthodox Muslim *n.m.* **mōmin** مومن
believing, faithful, orthodox *adj.*
waxen *adj.* **mōmī** مومی
mummy *n.f.* **mōmiyā** مومیا
mummify *v.i.* **mōmiyānā** مومیانہ
feminine *adj.* **mu'annas** مونث
moustache *n.f.* **mūṁch** مونچھ
close, shut; cover; imprison *v.t.* **mūndnā** موندنا
shave; make a disciple of; cheat *v.t.* **mūnḍnā** مونڈنا
friend, companion *n.m.* **mūnis** مونس
mung bean *n.m.* **mūng** مونگ
peanut *n.f.* **mūng phalī** مونگ پھلی
coral *n.m.* **mūngā** مونگا
fascination, charm, affection; sympathy, compassion *n.m.* **mōh** موہ
fascinate, charm, attract, allure *v.t.* **mōh lēnā** موہ لینا
fascinating, charming, alluring, seducing *adj.* **mōhan** موہن
fascinate, charm, enchant, allure *v.t.* **mōhnā** موہنا
fascination, charm; spell, magic *n.f.* **mōhnī** موہنی
conference, committee *n.m.* **mu'tamar** موتمر
raisin, dried grape *n.m.* **mavēz** مویز
strengthened, aided, reinforced *adj.* **mu'ayyad** موید
wine, liquor *n.f.* **mai** مے
drunkard; wine-drinker *n.m.* **mai parast** مے پرست
sir, master, gentleman *n.m.* **miyāṁ** میاں
among, between, in the center of *pp.* **miyān** میان
ready, prepared *adj.* **miyan bastah** میان بستہ
mediator, arbitrator; pedagogue schoolmaster *n.f./n.m.* **miyāṁ jī** میاں جی
sweet talker; parrot *n.m.* **miyāṁ miṭhū** میاں مٹھو
sedan, palanquin *n.m.* **miyānā** میانا
middling, moderate *adj.* **miyānah** میانہ
corpse, dead body *n.f.* **maiyyit** میت
friend, companion, lover *n.m.* **mīt** میت
fenugreek *n.f.* **mēthī** میتھی

meter *n.m.* **mīṭar** میٹر
sweet; light, slow, mild *adj.* **mīṭhā** میٹھا
speak mildy *v.t.* **mīṭhā bōlnā** میٹھا بولنا
light pain *n.m.* **mīṭhā dard** میٹھا درد
mild season, temperate season *n.m.* **mīṭhā mausim** میٹھا موسم
kiss *n.f.* **mīṭhī** میٹھی
sweet speech *n.f.* **mīṭhā bōlī** میٹھی بولی
sound sleep *n.f.* **mīṭhī nīnd** میٹھی نیند
agreement, promise, bargain *n.m.* **mīsāq** میثاق
close eyes, wink *v.t.* **mīcnā** میچنا
nail, wedge *n.f.* **mēx** میخ
nail, impale *v.t.* **mēx ṭhōnknā** میخ ٹھونکنا
mallet, hammer *n.f.* **mēx cū** میخ چو
plain, open field, large area *n.m.* **maidān** میدان
battlefield *n.m.* **maidān-ē-jang** میدان جنگ
make room (for) *v.t.* **maidān dēnā** میدان دینا
win a battle *v.t.* **maidān mārnā** میدان مارنا
flour, fine powder *n.m.* **maidah** میدہ
chief, leader *n.m.* **mīr** میر
admiral *n.m.* **mīr-ē-baḥr** میر بحر
head steward *n.m.* **mīr-ē-sāmān** میر سامان
eloquent speaker *n.m.* **mīr-ē-kalām** میر کلام
head of department *n.m.* **mīr-ē-maḥkamah** میر محکمہ
chief secretary, head clerk *n.m.* **mir munšī** میر منشی
my, mine *pron.* **mērā** میرا
patrimony *n.f.* **mirās** میراث
inherited *adj.* **mirāsī** میراثی
leadership, chiefship *n.f.* **mīrī** میری
table *n.f.* **mēz** میز
balance; Libra (*Zodiac*) *n.f.* **mīzān** میزان
grand total *n.f.* **mīzān-ē-kul** میزان کل
available, attained, obtained *adj.* **muyassar** میسر
sheep, ram; Aries (*Zodiac*) *n.m.* **mēš** میش
shy *adj.* **mēš cašm** میش چشم
time limit, term, duration, period *n.m.* **mīᶜād** میعاد
limited, terminable *adj.* **miyᶜādī** میعادی

mechanic *n.m.* **mēkanik** میکنک
cloud *n.m.* **mēgh** میگھ
• connection, relationship *n.m.* **mēl** • inclination, tendency; dirt, filth *n.m.* **mail** میل
mile; pencil *n.m.* **mīl**
connect, associate (with) *v.t.* **mēl karnā** میل رکھنا
unite, mix, accord *v.t.* **mēl khānā** میل کھانا
fair, trade fair; meeting *n.m.* **mēlā** • dirty, foul; nasty *adj.* / dirt, filth *n.m.* **mailā** میلا
dirtiness, filthiness *n.m.* **mailā pan** میلاپن
make dirty, foul *v.t.* **mailā karnā** میلا کرنا
birthday *n.m.* **mīlād** میلاد
inclination, bent *n.m.* **mailān** میلان
madam *n.f.* **mēm** میم
kid goat; ram *n.m.* **mēmnā** میمنا
fortune, prosperity *n.f.* **maimanat** میمنت
fortunate, prosperous, auspicious *adj.* **maimūn** میمون
in, within, at, between, among *pp.* **mēṁ** • I, me *pron.* **maiṁ** میں
fish; Pisces (*Zodiac*) *n.f.* **mīn** مین
myself *pron.* **maiṁ xūd** میں خود
I agree! *interj.* **maiṁ rāzī hūṁ!** میں راضی ہوں !
be an egotist *v.t.* **maiṁ maiṁ karnā** میں میں کرنا
bird, starling *n.f.* **mainā** مینا
fancy fair, fun fair *n.m.* **minā bāzār** مینا بازار
pillar, minaret, tall tower *n.m.* **mīnār** مینار
boundary, border; mound (of a field) *n.f.* **mēnḍ** مینڈ
frog *n.m.* **mēnḍak** مینڈک
ram *n.m.* **mēnḍhā** مینڈھا
rain *n.m.* **mēṁh** مینہہ
rain *v.i.* **mēṁh barasnā** مینہہ برسنا
paradise, heaven *n.m.* **minū** مینو
menu (*restaurant*) *n.m.* **mēnyū** مینیو
fruit *n.m.* **mēvah** میوہ
fruit-seller *n.m.* **mēvah farōš** میوہ فروش
May (*month*) *n.f.* **ma'iy** مئی

nūn ن

no, not *adj./adv.* **nā** نا
disagreement, discord *n.f.* **nā ittifāqi** نا اتفاقی
unknown, unacquainted, unfamiliar *adj.* / stranger *n.m.* **nā āšnā** نا آشنا
untrustworthy *adj.* **nā i^c^timād** نا اعتماد
untrustworthiness *n.f.* **nā i^c^timādī** نا اعتمادی
hopeless, despairing *adj.* **nā ummīd** نا امید
disappoint, despair *v.t.* **nā ummīd karnā** نا امید کرنا
be disappointed *v.i.* **nā ummīd hōnā** نا امید ہونا
hopelessly *adv.* **nā ummīdānah** نا امیدانہ
hopelessness *n.f.* **nā ummīdī** نا امیدی
shortsighted, thoughtless *adj.* **nā andēš** نا اندیش
unjust, unfair *adj.* **nā insāf** نا انصاف
injustice *n.f.* **nā insafī** نا انصافی
uselessness, worthlessness *n.f.* **nā bakārī** نا بکاری
foreigner, stranger *n.m.* **nā balad** نا بلد
nonexistent, extinct, annihilated *adj.* **nā būd** نابود
annihilate *v.t.* **nā būd karnā** نابود کرنا
impurity, uncleanliness, pollution *n.f.* **nā pākī** نا پاکی
frail, inconstant, unstable, passing, transitory *adj.* **nā pā'īdār** نا پائیدار
instability, inconstancy, frailty *n.f.* **nā pā'īdārī** نا پائیداری
invisible, concealed *adj.* **nā padīd** نا پدید
disapproved, rejected, offensive, disagreeable *adj.* **nā pasand** نا پسند
dislike, rejection, disapproval *n.f.* **nā pasandīdagī** نا پسندیدگی
rejected, disliked, unacceptable *adj.* **nā pasandīdah** نا پسندیدہ
not available, nonexistent, lost, missing *adj.* **nā paid** نا پید
vanish *v.i.* **nā paid hōnā** نا پید ہونا
inexperienced, untrained *adj.* **nā tajribah kār** نا تجربہ کار
impolite, uncivilized *adj.* **nā tarāšīdah** نا تراشیدہ
incomplete, imperfect *adj.* **nā tamām** نا تمام
weak, feeble, impotent, powerless *adj.* **nā tavān** نا تواں
weakness, impotence, inability *n.f.* **nā tavanī** نا توانی
unlawful, illegal *adj.* **nā jā'iz** نا جائز
helpless, distressed, destitute *adj.* **nā cār** نا چار

helplessness, distress, destitution, impotence *n.f.* **nā cārī** ناچاری

disagreement, indisposition, discord *n.f.* **nā cāqī** ناچاقی

undutiful; vicious, wicked *adj.* **nā xalaf** ناخلف

uneducated, illiterate *adj.* **nā xvāndah** ناخوانده

displeased, unhappy, sad *adj.* **nā xūš** ناخوش

unpleasant, disgusting, undesirable *adj.* **nā xūšgavār** ناخوشگوار

displeasure, disagreement *n.f.* **nā xūšī** ناخوشی

poor, insolvent, indigent *adj.* **nā dār** نادار

poverty, insolvency, indigence, pauperism *n.f.* **nā dārī** ناداری

ignorant, silly, foolish; innocent *adj.* **nā dān** نادان

ignorance *n.f.* **nā dānistagī** نادانستگی

unknowingly, unwillingly *adv.* **nā dānistah** نادانستہ

incorrect, wrong, false; unhealthy *adj.* **nā durust** نادرست

unseen, invisible *adj.* **nā dīdah** نادیده

dishonest, unfair; fake, false *adj.* **nā rāst** ناراست

dishonesty, unfairness, falseness *n.f.* **nā rāstī** ناراستی

dissatisfied, displeased *adj.* **nā rāz** ناراض

displeasure, discontent *n.f.* **nā rāzī** ناراضی

unworthy, unfit, unmannerly *adj.* **nā rasā** نارسا

inability, incapability, unskillfulness *n.f.* **nā rasā'ī** نارسائی

unripe, immature *adj.* **nā rasīdah** نارسیده

without strength, weak *adj.* **nā zōr** نازور

ungraceful, ugly, unsuitable *adj.* **nā zēbā** نازیبا

disagreeing, indisposed *adj.* **nā sāz** ناساز

unfavorable, unfortunate; out of tune; absurd *adj.* **nā saz gar** ناسازگار

ungrateful, unthankful *adj.* **nā sipās** ناسپاس

unworthy, improper, indecent *adj.* **nā sazā** ناسزا

pear *n.f.* **nāšpātī** ناشپاتی

impatience, restlessness *n.f.* **nā sabūrī** ناصبوری

useless, worthless *adj.* **nā bakār** نابکار

blind *adj.* **nā bīnā** نابینا

impure, unclean, dirty, polluted *adj.* **nā pāk** ناپاک

fearless; pitiless, merciless; severe *adj.* **nā tars** ناترس

heterogeneous, of another sort *adj.* **nā jins** ناجنس

dance *v.i.* **nācnā** ناچنا

trifle, worthless, insignificant *adj.* **nā cīz** ناچیز

unjust, improper, wrong *adj.* / improperly, falsely *adv.* **nā ḥaqq** ناحق

improper, unsuited, unlawful, prohibited *adj.* **nāravā** ناروا

thin, slender, delicate, tender, fine; tricky, critical, fastidious *adj.* **nāzuk** نازک

unbored, unstrung *adj.* **nā suftah** ناسفتہ

unintelligent, stupid, foolish *adj.* **nā samajh** ناسمجھ

breakfast; luncheon *n.m.* **nāštah** ناشتہ

adviser, counselor *n.m.* **nāsiḥ** ناصح

defender, helper, assistant *n.m.* / helping, assisting *adj.* **nāsir** ناصر

speaker *n.m.* **nātiq** ناطق

governor, ruler, administrator, manager, director *n.m.* **nāzim** ناظم

leave, absence *n.m.* **nāġah** ناغہ

navel *n.f.* **nāf** ناف

passed, issued, operative, in force *adj.* **nāfiz** نافذ

profitable, advantageous, beneficial *adj.* **nāfiᶜ** نافع

nose *n.f.* / full (of), affected (with) *adj.* **nāk** ناک

snake, cobra *n.m.* **nāg** ناگ

barrel, tube, pipe *n.f.* **nāl** نال

canal, brook, gutter *n.m.* **nālā** نالا

lamentation, moaning *n.m.* **nālāṁ** نالاں

lamentation, complaint *n.f.* **nāliš** نالش

drain, vein, tube *n.f.* **nālī** نالی

name *n.m.* **nām** نام

famous, celebrated *adj.* **nām dār** نام دار

letter; book; history *n.m.* **nāmah** نامہ

fame, reputation, respect *n.f.* **nāmūs** ناموس

famous, renowned *adj.* **nāmī** نامی

naan (*a kind of bread*) *n.f.* **nān** نان

grandfather (*maternal*) *n.m.* **nānā** نانا

grandmother (*maternal*) *n.f.* **nānī** نانی

boat, ship *n.f.* **nā'ō** ناؤ

arrow; tube; canal *n.m.* **nāvak** ناوک

assistant, deputy, delegate *n.m.* **nā'ib** نائب

chief, leader *n.m.* **nāyak** نایک

barber *n.m.* **nā'ī** نائی

vegetables, plants *n.f.* **nabātāt** نباتات

be settled, be concluded *v.i.* **nibaṭnā** نبٹنا

accomplishment, fulfillment, completion *n.m.* **nibah** نباہ

accomplish, complete, fulfill; support, maintain *v.t.* **nibāhnā** نباہنا

settle, conclude, decide *v.t.* **nibṭānā** نبٹانا

prophet *n.m.* **nabī** نبی

perform, accomplish, carry through, fulfill *v.t.* **nibhānā** نبھانا

always, ever, eternally *adv.* **nit** نِت

result, conclusion, issue, consequence *n.m.* **natījah** نتیجہ

nose-ring *n.f.* **nath** نتھ

juggler; actor; dancer *n.m.* **naṭ** نٹ

scattering, throwing; sacrifice *adj.* **nisār** نثار

scatter, throw; sacrifice *v.t.* **nisār karnā** نثار کرنا

prose *n.f.* **nasr** نثر

own, personal, individual, particular *adj.* **nij** نِج

private *adj.* **nij kā** نِج کا

nobleness, nobility *n.f.* **najābat** نجابت

liberation, salvation *n.f.* **najāt** نجات

carpenter *n.m.* **najjār** نجار

carpentry *n.f.* **najjārī** نجاری

dirty, impure *adj.* **najis/najs** نجس

star; planet; horoscope, prediction *n.m.* **najm** نجم

astrologer, fortune-teller *n.m.* **nujūmī** نجومی

private *adj.* **nijī** نجی

noble, excellent, generous, honorable *adj.* **najīb** نجیب

be squeezed, be pressed *v.i.* **nicuṛnā** نچڑنا

silent, calm, quiet *adj.* **niclā** نچلا

squeeze, wring *v.t.* **nicōṛnā** نچوڑنا

sacrifice *n.f.* **nichāvar** نچھاور

sacrifice *v.t.* **nichāvar karnā** نچھاور کرنا

unlucky, ill-fated, inauspicious *adj.* **naḥs** نحس

bee *n.f.* **naḥl** نحل

grammar, syntax *n.f.* **naḥv** نحو

weak; slender *adj.* **naḥīf** نحیف

palm-tree *n.m.* **naxl** نخل

نخلستان **naxlistān** oasis *n.m.*
نخوت **naxvat** pride, magnificence, pomp *n.f.*
نخود **nuxūd** gram, chickpea *n.m.*
ند **nad** ocean; river *n.m.*
ندا **nidā** voice, sound *n.f.*
ندامت **nadāmat** regret, repentance *n.f.*
ندی **nadī** river *n.f.*
ندیم **nadīm** courtier, friend, companion, fellow *n.m.*
نڈر **nidaṛ** fearless *adj.*
نذر **nazr** vow, offering, gift *n.f.*
نذرانہ **nazrānah** tribute, present, gift *n.m.*
نر **nar** male, man, mankind *n.m.* / male, masculine *adj.*
نرا **nirā** mere, pure, only *adj.*
نرالا **nirālā** odd, strange, rare, aloof *adj.*
نرخ **nirx** price, rate; tariff *n.m.*
نرخ نامہ **nirx nāmah** price list *n.m.*
نرخرا **narxarā** throat *n.m.*
نردبان **nirdbān** staircase, ladder *n.m.*
نرس **nars** nurse *n.f.*
نرسنگھا **nar singhā** horn *n.m.*
نرک **nark** hell *n.m.*
نرگس **nargis** narcissus *n.f.*
نرم **narm** smooth, soft, gentle, mild *adj.*
نرمی **narmī** softness, gentleness, mildness *n.f.*
نرینہ **narīnah** male, masculine *adj.*
نزار **nazār** thin, slim, slender, subtle *adj.*
نزاع **nizā**[c] quarrel, dispute, lawsuit *n.m.*
نزاکت **nazākat** elegance, politeness; delicacy *n.f.*
نزدیک **nazdīk** near, nearby, close *adj.*
نزلہ **nazlah** catarrh *n.m.*
نزول **nuzūl** descent, alighting; catarrh *n.m.*
نژاد **nažād** origin, root, race, family *n.f.*
نس **nis** night *n.f.*
نسب **nasab** genealogy, lineage, race, caste, family *n.m.*
نسب نامہ **nasab nāmah** pedigree *n.m.*
نسبت **nisbat** with reference (to) *adv.* / relation, connection, reference *n.f.*

related, with reference (to) *adj.* **nisbatī** نسبتی

nastaliq (*form of Persian writing*), Urdu writing *n.m.* **nastaᶜlīq** نستعلیق

abolition *n.m.* **nasx** نسخ

prescription, recipe; edition; copy, model *n.m.* **nusxah** نسخہ

arrangement, order *n.m.* **nasq** نسق

race, breed, caste, origin *n.m.* **nasl** نسل

by descent *adv.* **naslan** نسلاً

chewing tobacco *n.m.* **nasvār** نسوار

oblivion, forgetfulness *n.m.* **nisyān** نسیان

breeze, fresh air *n.f.* **nasīm** نسیم

starch, paste *n.m.* **nišāstah** نشاستہ

pleasure, joy, gladness, happiness *n.f.* **našāt** نشاط

sign, mark, signal, emblem *n.m.* **nišān** نشان

aim, target, mark *n.m.* **nišānah** نشانہ

token, sign, mark *n.f.* **nišānī** نشانی

lost, destroyed *adj.* **ništ** نشت

sitting; seat *n.f.* **nišast/našast** نشست

parlor, drawing room *n.f.* **nišast gah** نشست گاہ

intoxication *n.m.* **našah** نشہ

growth, vegetation *n.m.* **našv** نشو

growth, development *n.m.* **našv-ō-namā** نشو ونما

slope, descent *n.m.* **našēb** نشیب

intoxicating *adj.* **našīlā** نشیلا

sitting *adj.* **našīn** نشین

root, source, origin, principle *n.f.* **nisāb** نصاب

establishment, fixing, planting *n.m.* **nasb** نصب

ideal *n.m.* **nasb-ul-ᶜain** نصب العین

advice, counsel *n.m.* **nasḥ** نصح

assistance, support; victory *n.f.* **nasr** نصر

Christian *n.m.* **nasrānī** نصرانی

Christianity *n.f.* **nasrāniyat** نصرانیت

victory, triumph *n.f.* **nusrat** نصرت

half, middle *adj.* **nisf** نصف

midnight *n.m.* **nisf šab** نصف شب

sincere, honest *adj.* **nasūḥ** نصوح

fortune, luck, chance, lot *n.m.* **nasīb** نصیب

advice, counsel *n.m.* **nasīḥat** نصیحت

assistant, helper, defender, ally *n.m.* **nasīr** نصیر

freshness *n.f.* **nazārat** نضارت

semen, seed *n.m.* **nutfah** نطفہ

speech, language, articulation *n.m.* **nutq** نطق

sight, view; show scene *n.m.* **nazārah** نظارہ

order, arrangement, system *n.m.* **nizām** نظام

sight, look, glance, vision, view *n.f.* **nazar** نظر

confinement, arrest *n.f.* **nazar bandī** نظر بندی

review, revision *n.f.* **nazar-ē-sanī** نظرِ ثانی

order, arrangement *n.m.* / poetry, verse *n.f.* **nazm** نظم

organization, management, administration *n.m.* **nazm-ō-nasq** نظم و نسق

instance, example *n.f.* / alike, equal, resembling *adj.* **nazīr** نظیر

slogan, logo *n.m.* **naᶜrah** نعرہ

corpse; bier, coffin *n.f.* **naᶜš** نعش

shoe; hoof *n.m.* **naᶜl** نعل

blessing, favor, graciousness, benefit, delight, joy *n.f.* **niᶜmat** نعمت

song, melody, tone, note *n.m.* **naġm** نغم

song, melody, tone, note *n.m.* **naġmah** نغمہ

musician; singer *n.m.* **naġmah pardāz** نغمہ پرداز

music; singing *n.f.* **naġmah sarā'ī** نغمہ سرائی

refinement, purity *n.f.* **nafāsat** نفاست

disunity, disagreement; hypocrisy *n.m.* **nifāq** نفاق

individual, person *n.m.* **nafar** نفر

hatred, disgust, aversion, abhorrence; fright *n.f.* **nafrat** نفرت

curse *n.f.* **nafrīn** نفرین

respiration, breath *n.m.* **nafas** نفس

soul, spirit *n.m.* **nafs** نفس

sensual, lustful *adj.* **nafsānī** نفسانی

profit, gain, advantage *n.m.* **nafaᶜ** نفع

refusal, rejecting; prohibition *n.f.* **nafī** نفی

fine, decent; precious, exquisite *adj.* **nafīs** نفیس

veil *n.m.* **niqāb** نقاب

kettledrum, timpani *n.m.* **naqārah** نقارہ

painter *n.m.* **naqqāš** نقاش
painting *n.f.* **naqqāšī** نقاشی
actor, player; clown *n.m.* **naqqāl** نقال
acting *n.f.* **naqqālī** نقالی
weakness *n.f.* **naqāhat** نقاہت
burglary, housebreaking *n.f.* **naqb** نقب
burglar *n.m.* **naqb zan** نقب زن
burglary, housebreaking *n.f.* **naqb zanī** نقب زنی
cash *n.m.* **naqd** نقد
silver *n.m.* **nuqrah** نقرہ
made of silver *adj.* **nuqra'ī** نقرئی
painting, drawing *n.m.* **naqš** نقش
footprint *n.m.* **naqš-ē-pā** نقش پا
decoration *n.m.* **naqš-ō-nigār** نقش ونگار
map, plan, chart, model, pattern; portrait, sketch *n.m.* **naqšah** نقشہ
defect, fault; diminution *n.m.* **naqs** نقص
loss; defect, deficiency *n.m.* **nuqsān** نقصان
point, dot, spot *n.m.* **nuqtah** نقطہ
narrative, tale, story; mimic, copy, copying; transport, removal *n.f.* **naql** نقل
artificial, counterfeit *adj.* **naqlī** نقلی
pure, clean *adj.* **naqī** نقی
leader, chief, adjutant *n.m.* **naqīb** نقیب
marriage *n.m.* **nikāḥ** نکاح
bleach; strain *v.t.* **nikhārnā** نکھارنا
origin, source, outlet, issue; export; sale *n.m.* **nikās** نکاس
withdrawal, extradition, banishment *n.m.* **nikālā** نکالا
come out, take out, pull out, remove, drive out, expel *v.t.* **nikālnā** نکالنا
perfume, scent *n.f.* **nakhat** نکہت
worthless, idle *adj.* **nikhaṭṭū** نکھٹو
be bleached, be cleaned *v.i.* **nikharnā** نکھرنا
come out, be declared, be published, emerge *v.t.* **nikalnā** نکلنا
worthless, base, poor *adj.* **nikammā** نکما
good, fair *adj.* **nikō/nikū** نکو
goodness, beneficence *n.f.* **nikō kārī** نکو کاری
pointed, thorny *adj.* **nukīlā** نکیلا
precious stone *n.m.* **nag** نگ

painting, picture, portrait *n.m.* **nigār** نگار
art gallery *n.m.* **nigāristān** نگارستان
description *n.f.* **nigāriš** نگارش
look, glance; sight, view *n.f.* **nigāh** نگاہ
city, town *n.m.* **nagar** نگر
guard, supervisor; watching, guarding *n.m.* **nigarān** نگران
town, village *n.f.* **nagrī** نگری
swallow *v.t.* **nigalnā** نگلنا
care *n.m.* **nigahdāšt** نگہداشت
gem, jewel *n.m.* **nagīn** نگین
tube, pipe; barrel *n.m.* **nal** نل
tube, pipe *n.f.* **nalī** نلی
showing, exhibiting, resembling *adj.* **numā** نما
prayer (*by Muslims*) *n.f.* **namāz** نماز
devout *n.m.* **namāzī** نمازی
show, exhibition, display; vision, sight *n.f.* **numā'iš** نمائش
museum, gallery, exhibition place *n.f.* **numā'iš gāh** نمائش گاہ
representative, agent, deputy *n.m.* **numā'indah** نمائندہ
number *n.m.* **nambar** نمبر
salutation; adoration *n.m.* **namaskār** نمسکار
salt *n.m.* **namak** نمک
disloyal, disobedient *adj.* **namak ḥarām** نمک حرام
loyal, obedient *adj.* **namak ḥalāl** نمک حلال
servant *n.m.* **namak xvār** نمک خوار
salty *adj.* **namkīn** نمکین
show, display, appearance, sight *n.m.* **namūd** نمود
apparent, visible *adj.* **namūdār** نمودار
specimen, sample, pattern, model *n.m.* **namūnah** نمونہ
pneumonia *n.m.* **namūniyā** نمونیا
moisture, humidity, dampness *n.f.* **namī** نمی
ninety-nine *num.* **ninānavē** ننانوے
sister-in-law (*husband's sister*) *n.f.* **nand/nanad** نند
shame, disgrace; honor, esteem, grace, reputation *n.m.* **nang** ننگ
(*negative connotation is more common usage*)
naked, stark *adj.* **nang ḍharang** ننگ ڈھرنگ
honor, esteem; shame *n.m.* **nang-ō-nāmūs** ننگ و ناموس
(*positive connotation is more common usage*)

naked, bare *adj.* **nangā** ننگا
barefoot *adj.* **nangē pā'ōṁ** ننگے پاؤں
bareheaded *adj.* **nangē sar** ننگے سر
young, small, tiny *adj.* **nanhā** ننھا
no, not, neither, nor, any *adv.* **nah** نہ
day *n.m.* **nahār** نہار
pleased, happy *adj.* **nihāl** نہال
bathe, take a bath *v.i.* **nahānā** نہانا
/ very much, extreme, remarkable *adj.* / extremely *adv.* **nihāyat** نہایت
extreme, limit, end *n.f.*
stream, canal, channel *n.f.* **nahr** نہر
no, not *adj.* **nahīṁ** نہیں
No sir!, No madam! *interj.* **nahīṁ jī!** نہیں جی
new, fresh, young; raw *adj.* / nine *num.* **nau** نو
novice, beginner, apprentice *n.m.* **nau āmūz** نوآموز
young *adj.* **nau javān** نوجوان
youth *n.f.* **nau javānī** نوجوانی
writer, clerk, accountant *n.m.* **nōvīsandah** نویسنده
sound, voice; song, air *n.f.* **navā** نوا
nawab (*a Muslim governor*) *n.m.* **navvāb** نواب
cherishing, soothing, caressing *adj.* **navāz** نواز
kindness, politeness, courtesy *n.f.* **navāziš** نوازش
grandson (*daughter's son*) *n.m.* **navāsah** نواسہ
granddaughter (*daughter's daughter*) *n.f.* / eighty-nine *num.* **navāsī** نواسی
time, period; turn, opportunity, occasion *n.f.* **naubat** نوبت
pinch, scratch, pluck *v.t.* **nōcnā** نوچنا
lamentation, moaning *n.m.* **nauḥah** نوحہ
light, splendor *n.m.* **nūr** نور
light of the eye; child, son *n.m.* **nūr-ē-cašm** نورچشم
bright, luminous *adj.* **nūrānī** نورانی
drinking *adj.* **nōš** نوش
document, letter; writing *n.f.* **navišt** نوشت
written *adj.* / letter *n.m.* **navištah** نوشتہ
pleasant, agreeable *n.m.* **nōšīṁ** نوشیں
kind, sort *n.f.* **nau**[c] نوع
point, tip, end; angle *n.f.* **nōk** نوک

نوکر **naukar** servant *n.m.*
نوکری **naukarī** service, employment *n.f.*
نوم **naum** sleep *n.f.*
نومبر **navambar** November *n.m.*
نومید **naumīd** hopeless *adj.*
نوے **navvē** ninety *num.*
نویس **navis** writing *adj.*
نویسی **navīsī** writing *n.f.*
نیا **nayā** new, recent, modern *adj.*
نیا **naiyyā** boat *n.f.*
نیاز **niyāz** offering, supplication; desire *n.f.*
نیاز مند **niyaz mand** humble, obedient; indigent, needy *adj.*
نیام **niyām** sheath, case *n.m.*
نیبو **nībū** lime, lemon *n.m.*
نیت **niyyat** intention *n.f.*
نیچ **nīc** low, base, vile, vulgar, mean *adj.* / descent, slope; deepness *n.f.*
نیچا **nīcā** low, inferior *adj.*
نیمچہ **nīmcah** sword, dagger *n.m.*
نیچے **nīcē** below, beneath, down, downwards *adv.*
نیر **naiyyir** star *n.m.*
نیر **nīr** water *n.m.*
نیرنگ **nairang** miracle, magic; fascination; deceit, trick *n.m.*
نیز **nīz** also, likewise, again *conj.*
نیزہ **nēzah** spear, lance *n.m.*
نیزہ باز **nēzah bāz** spearman, lancer *n.m.*
نیش **nēš** sting, puncture *n.m.*
نیک **nēk** good, virtuous; lucky *adj.*
نیک نیت **nēk niyyat** honest, well-intentioned *adj.*
نیکی **nēkī** goodness, virtue *n.f.*
نیلا **nīlā** blue *adj.*
نیلا سا **nīlā sā** bluish *adj.*
نیلاہٹ **nīlāhaṭ** blueness *n.m.*
نیلم **nīlam** gem, sapphire *n.m.*
نیم **nīm** half, middle *adj.*
نیم پخت **nīm puxt** half-cooked, half-boiled *adj.*
نیم خوابدہ **nīm xvābidah** dozing, half-asleep *adj.*

half-satisfied *adj.* **nīm rāzī** نیم راضی
midnight *n.f.* **nīm šab** نیم شب
half-drawn; agonizing *adj.* **nīm kaš** نیم کش
half, middle *n.m.* **nīmah** نیمہ
eye *n.m.* **nain** نین
sleep *n.f.* **nīnd** نیند
feel sleepy *v.i.* **nīnd ānā** نیند آنا
sleep soundly *v.i.* **nīnd bhar sōnā** نیند بھر سونا
affection, kindness, love *n.m.* **nēhā** نیہا
foundation *n.f.* **nēō** نیو
invitation *n.m.* **niyōtā** نیوتا
hearing, listening *adj.* **nīyūš** نیوش
hearer, listener *n.m.* **nīyūšindah** نیوشندہ

chōṭī hē ہ

Alas!, Oh!; Shame! *interj.* **ha!** ہا

angel, oracle *n.m.* **hātif** ہاتف

hand; arm *n.m.* **hāth** ہاتھ

pray; salute *v.t.* **hāth uṭhānā** ہاتھ اٹھانا

help, lend a hand *v.t.* **hāth baṭānā** ہاتھ بٹانا

endeavor, gain possession *v.t.* **hāth baṛhānā** ہاتھ بڑھانا

hands and feet; someone who is working hard *n.m.* **hāth pā'ōṁ** ہاتھ پاؤں

be strong (*to work*) *v.i.* **hāth pā'ōṁ calnā** ہاتھ پاؤں چلنا

struggle, work hard *v.t.* **hāth pā'ōṁ hilānā** ہاتھ پاؤں ہلانا

get someone married *v.t.* **hāth pīlē karnā** ہاتھ پیلے کرنا

caress, coax; cheat *v.t.* **hāth phērnā** ہاتھ پھیرنا

depend on someone *v.t.* **hāth taknā** ہاتھ تکنا

be poor, be broke *v.i.* **hāth tang hōnā** ہاتھ تنگ ہونا

expertness, skillfulness *n.f.* **hāth cālākī** ہاتھ چالاکی

lose *v.i.* **hāth sē jānā** ہاتھ سے جانا

cash, money, wealth *n.m.* **hāth kā mail** ہاتھ کا میل

regret, repent, lament *v.t.* **hāth malnā** ہاتھ ملنا

fighting, quarreling *n.f.* **hāthā pā'ī** ہاتھا پائی

fight *v.t.* **hāthā pā'ī karnā** ہاتھا پائی کرنا

hand to hand, with hand; by, on account of *adv.* **hāthōṁ** ہاتھوں

elephant *n.m.* **hāthī** ہاتھی

mahout (*elephant-driver*) *n.m.* **hāthi bān** ہاتھی بان

ivory *n.m.* **hāthi dānt** ہاتھی دانت

satirist *n.m.* **hājī** ہاجی

director, leader, guide, spiritual guide *n.m.* **hādī** ہادی

loss, defeat *n.f.* / pearl necklace *n.m.* **hār** ہار

gambling, hazarding *n.f.* **hār jīt** ہار جیت

be overcome, be tired, be defeated *v.i.* / lose *v.t.* **hārnā** ہارنا

digestive, digestible *adj.* **hāzim** ہاضم

digestive system, digestion *n.m.* **hāzimah** ہاضمہ

tire; plow; rudder *n.f.* **hāl** ہال

desert; plain *n.m.* **hāmūn** ہامون

confirmation, assurance, guarantee *n.f.* **hāmī** ہامی

consent, confirm *v.t.* **hāmi bharnā** ہامی بھرنا

yes, indeed, sure *adv.* **hāṁ** ہاں

Yes sir!, Yes madam! *interj.* **hāṁ jī!** ہاں جی!

assent, agree *v.t.* **hāṁ kahnā** ہاں کہنا

be out of breath, puff, pant *v.i.* **hāmpnā** ہانپنا

pot, saucepan; small lamp *n.f.* **hānḍī** ہانڈی

cry, call *n.f.* **hānk** ہانک

uproar, outcry, shout *n.f.* **hānk pukār** ہانک پکار

call aloud, shout loudly *v.t.* **hānk mārnā** ہانک مارنا

shout, call; drive off, drive away, urge; utter *v.t.* **hānknā** ہانکنا

Alas!, Ah! *interj.* / sigh *n.f.* **hā'ē** ہائے

groan, moan *v.t.* **hā'ē hā'ē karnā** ہائے ہائے کرنا

gift, present; bequest, grant *n.m.* **hiba** ہبہ

descent, decline, decreasing, downfall *n.m.* **hubūt** ہبوط

gulp down, eat up, swallow *v.t.* **hap karnā** ہپ کرنا

disrespect, defamation *n.f.* **hatak** ہتک

disgrace, defame *v.t.* **hatak ᶜizzat karnā** ہتک عزت کرنا

murder, slaughter, killing *n.f.* **hattiyā** ہتیا

murderer, assassin *n.m.* **hattiyārā** ہتیارا

loan *n.m.* **hath udhār** ہتھ ادھار

handcuff *n.f.* **hath kaṛī** ہتھ کڑی

cunningness, cleverness *n.m.* / handmade *adj.* **hath kanḍā** ہتھ کنڈا

handle; shovel *n.m.* **hatthā** ہتھا

female elephant *n.f.* **hathnī** ہتھنی

sledgehammer *n.m.* **hathaurā** ہتھورا

small hammer *n.f.* **hathauṛī** ہتھوڑی

small handle *n.f.* **hatthī** ہتھی

gain power, gain control; get an opportunity *v.i.* **hatthē caṛhnā** ہتھے چڑھنا

be uprooted, be separated *v.i.* **hatthē sē ukhaṛnā** ہتھے سے اکھڑنا

tool, instrument; weapon, arms *n.m.* **hathiyār** ہتھیار

wear a weapon, arm *v.t.* **hathiyār bāndhnā** ہتھیار باندھنا

armed, equipped *adj.* **hathiyār band** ہتھیار بند

murder, slaughter; violence *n.f.* **hathiyā'ī** ہتھیائی

palm *n.f.* **hathēlī** ہتھیلی

obstinacy, stubbornness, perverseness *n.f.* **haṭ** ہٹ

obstinate, stubborn, tyrannical, dishonest, unjust *adj.* **haṭ dharm** ہٹ دھرم

injustice, obstinacy, dishonesty *n.f.* **haṭ dharmī** ہٹ دھرمی
resist, be obstinate, disobey *v.t.* **haṭ karnā** ہٹ کرنا
active; stout, strong, robust *adj.* **haṭṭā kaṭṭā** ہٹا کٹا
repel, foil, drive back, push back, put off, remove *v.t.* **haṭānā** ہٹانا
fall back, be driven back, retire, retreat *v.i.* **haṭnā** ہٹنا
obstinate, teasing *adj.* **haṭṭīlā** ہٹیلا
spelling *n.m.* **hijā** ہجا
separation, absence, desertion *n.m.* **hijr** ہجر
separation *n.m.* **hijrān** ہجراں
separated, absent, deserted *adj.* **hijrān zadah** ہجراں زدہ
(*escape of Mohammad to Medina, beginning of Islamic era*) hijrat *n.m.* **hijrat** ہجرت
belonging to the Islamic era *adj.* **hijrī** ہجری
satire; blame, infamy *n.f.* **hajv** ہجو
satirist *n.m.* **hajv gō** ہجو گو
crowd, mob; assault, attack *n.m.* **hujūm** ہجوم
rush upon, attack *v.t.* **hujūm karnā** ہجوم کرنا
spelling *n.m.* **hijē/hijjē** ہجے
dispute; excuse; hesitation *n.f.* **hicar micar** ہچر مچر
make excuses; hesitate *v.t.* **hicar micar karnā** ہچر مچر کرنا
jolt, shock, jerk *n.m.* **hickā** ہچکا
doubt, hesitate *v.i.* **hickicānā** ہچکچانا
doubt, hesitation *n.f.* **hickicāhāṭ** ہچکچاہٹ
doubt, hesitation *n.f.* **hickicī** ہچکچی
draw back, recoil, waver, decline *v.i.* **hicaknā** ہچکنا
jolt, shake *n.m.* **hackōlā** ہچکولا
hiccup *n.f.* **hickī** ہچکی
suffer from hiccups *v.i.* **hickī lagnā** ہچکی لگنا
guidance, instruction; righteous path, path to salvation *n.m.* **hudā** ہدا
guidance, instruction; righteousness *n.f.* **hidāyat** ہدایت
accept guidance, be guided *v.t.* **hidāyat pānā** ہدایت پانا
mark, target, aim, goal *n.m.* **hadaf** ہدف
hit the nail on the head *v.t.* **hadaf mārnā** ہدف مارنا
offering, gift, present *n.f.* **hadī** ہدی
offering, gift, present *n.m.* **hadiyah** ہدیہ
large bone *n.m.* **haḍḍā** ہڈا

small bone *n.f.* **haḍḍī** ہڈی

bony, hard *adj.* **haḍḍīlā** ہڈیلا

this *pron.* **hazā** ہذا

every, any, each, all *adj.* **har** ہر

every moment, constantly *adv.* **har ān** ہرآن

everyone, everybody, each *adj.* **har ēk** ہرایک

every time *adv.* **har bār** ہربار

at length, at last, after all, time and again *adv.* **hir phir kē** ہرپھرکے

popular *adj.* **har dil ʿazīz** ہردل عزیز

every moment *adv.* **har dam** ہردم

every day *adv.* **har rōz** ہرروز

in every way, anyhow *adv.* **har taraḥ** ہرطرح

everywhere *adv.* **har taraf** ہرطرف

everywhere *adv.* **har kahīṁ** ہرکہیں

doe, roe deer, hind *n.f.* **harnī** ہرنی

sound, voice, shout *n.m.* **harrā** • green, fresh *adj.* **harā** ہرا

fruitful, prosperous, lush *adj.* **harā bharā** ہرابھرا

fear, terror, confusion *n.m.* **hirās** ہراس

frightened, alarmed; disappointed *adj.* **hirāsāṁ** ہراساں

beat, defeat, foil; tire *v.t.* **harāna** ہرانا

greenness, freshness *n.f.* **harā'ī** ہرائی

trouble, loss; harm, injury *n.m.* **harj** ہرج

obstruct, harm, injure; waste *v.t.* **harj karnā** ہرج کرنا

trouble, bustle, tumult, disorder *n.m.* **harj marj** ہرج مرج

compensation *n.m.* **harjānah** ہرجانہ

damage *n.m.* **harjah** ہرجہ

although, even if, as often as *adv.* **har cand** ہرچند

whatever, whatsoever *pron.* **har cih** ہرچہ

nonsense, absurdity, babble, prate *n.f.* **harzagī** ہرزگی

absurd, frivolous, silly, idle *adj.* **harzah** ہرزہ

courier, messenger; spy *n.m.* **har kārah** ہرکارہ

ever, on any occasion *adv.* **hargiz** ہرگز

antelope *n.m.* **haran/hiran** ہرن

seize, take by force, remove *v.t.* **harnā** ہرنا

green, fresh *adj.* **haryālā** ہریالا

greenness, freshness *n.f.* **haryālī** ہریالی

become green, grow green *v.i.* **hariyānā** ہریانا
confusedly, hurriedly, hastily *adv.* **haṛbaṛā kar** ہڑبڑا کر
be confused, be in a hurry *v.i.* **haṛbaṛānā** ہڑبڑانا
hurry, alarm, uproar, tumult *n.f.* **haṛbaṛī** ہڑبڑی
agitated, hasty, nervous *adj.* **haṛbaṛiyā** ہڑبڑیا
disorder, confusion, uproar, tumult; anarchy *n.f.* **haṛbōng** ہڑبونگ
create an uproar, create a disturbance *v.t.* **haṛbōng macānā** ہڑبونگ مچانا
turbulent, tumultuous, troublesome *adj.* **huṛdangī** ہڑدنگی
heart disease *n.f.* **huṛak** ہڑک
swallowing *n.f.* **haṛap** ہڑپ
swallow, gulp down *v.t.* **haṛap karnā** ہڑپ کرنا
strike *n.f.* **haṛtāl** ہڑتال
thousand *num.* **hazār** ہزار
cancer *n.m.* **hazār cašmah** ہزار چشمہ
nightingale *n.m.* **hazār dāstān** ہزار داستان
flight, defeat *n.f.* **hazimat** ہزیمت
be defeated *v.t.* **hazimat uṭhānā** ہزیمت اٹھانا
existence, being *n.f.* **hast** ہست
life, existence; world *n.f.* **hastī** ہستی
digestion *n.m.* **hazm** ہضم
digest *v.t.* **hazm karnā** ہضم کرنا
week; Saturday *n.m.* **haftah** ہفتہ
confused, aghast *adj.* **hakkā bakkā** ہکا بکا
similarly *adv.* **hakazā** ہکذا
stammer, stutter *v.i.* **haklānā** ہکلانا
plow *n.m.* **hal** ہل
move, shake *v.i.* **hil jānā** ہل جانا
plow, cultivate *v.t..* **hal jōtnā** ہل جوتنا
motion; confusion, disorder, bustle, uproar *n.m.* **hal cal** ہل چل
assault, attack *n.m.* **hallā** ہلا
dead, killed; destroyed *adj.* **halāk** ہلاک
death, destruction *n.f.* **halākat** ہلاکت
new moon, crescent *n.m.* **hilāl** ہلال
move, shake, agitate *v.t.* **hilānā** ہلانا
turmeric *n.f.* **haldī** ہلدی
alarm, tumult, disturbance, row *n.m.* **hullaṛ** ہلڑ

ہلکا **halkā** light, easy, soft, gentle *adj.*
ہلکا پن **halkā pan** lightness *n.m.*
ہلکا کرنا **halkā karnā** lighten *v.t.*
ہلکورا **hilkōrā** wave, surge *n.m.*
ہلنا **hilnā** move, shake, tremble *v.i.*
ہم **ham** / we, us *pron.* / also, even, same, likewise, equally *adv.*
worry, care, grief, anxiety *n.m.*
ہم آغوشی **ham āġōš** embracing *adj.*
ہم آہنگ **ham āhang** harmonious, concordant *adj.*
ہم آہنگی **ham āhangī** harmony, agreement, tune *n.m.*
ہم آواز **ham āvāz** harmonious, concordant *adj.*
ہم بطن **ham batn** related by blood, akin *adj.* / blood relation *n.m.*
ہم پہلو **ham pahlū** adjacent *adj.*
ہم پیشہ **ham pēšah** of the same trade, of the same profession *n.m.*
ہم جولی **ham jōli** equal; playmate, friend *n.m./n.f.*
ہم چشم **ham cašm** equal, rival *adj.*
ہم درس **ham dars** classmate *n.m.*
ہم دست **ham dast** companion, accomplice *n.m.*
ہم دگر **ham digar** together *adv.*
ہم راہ **ham rāh** fellow-traveler, companion *n.m.* / with, along with, together *adv.*
ہم سایہ **ham sāyah** neighbor *n.m.*
ہم سخن **ham saxun** interlocutor *n.m.*
ہم سری **ham sarī** equality, matching, evenness *n.f.*
ہم شکل **ham šakl** alike (*same appearance*) *adj.*
ہم شیر **ham šīr** sister *n.f.*
ہم عصر **ham ᶜasr** contemporary *adj.*
ہم قدم **ham qadam** companion, attendant *n.m.*
ہم کلام **ham kalām** conversing (together) *adj.*
ہم کلامی **ham kalāmī** conversation *n.f.*
ہم کنار **ham kinār** embracing *adj.*
ہم نام **ham nām** namesake, of the same name *adj.*
ہم وار **ham vār** level, even, smooth *adj.*
ہما **humā** eagle; phoenix *n.m.*
ہمارا **hamārā** our *pron.*
ہمالیہ **himāliyah** Himalayas *n.m.*

lucky, fortunate *adj.* **humāyāṁ** ہمایوں
courage, bravery; spirit, mind; purpose *n.f.* **himmat** ہمت
courageous, brave, bold, daring *adj.* **himmatī** ہمتی
neighborhood *n.f.* **hamsāyagī** ہمسایگی
neighbor *n.m.* **hamsāyah** ہمسایہ
all, whole, every *adj.* **hamah** ہمہ
eternity *n.f.* **hamēšagī** ہمیشگی
always, ever, perpetually, continually *adv.* **hamēšah** ہمیشہ
us, to us *pron.* **hamēṁ** ہمیں
geometry *n.m.* **hindsah** ہندسہ
Hindu *adj.* **hindū** ہندو
India, Hindustan *n.m.* **hindūstān** ہندوستان
Indian, Hindustani *adj.* **hindūstānī** ہندوستانی
cradle, swing *n.m.* **hiṁḍōlā** ہنڈولا
check, bill *n.f.* **huṁḍī** ہنڈی
virtue, art, skill *n.m.* **hunar** ہنر
skillful, clever *adj.* **hunar mand** ہنر مند
skillfulness, cleverness *n.f.* **hunar mandī** ہنر مندی
swan, goose, duck *n.m.* **haṁs** ہنس
jolly, cheerful, merry, laughing *adj.* **haṁs mukh** ہنس مکھ
laugh *v.i.* **haṁsnā** ہنسنا
laughter, laugh, fun *n.f.* **haṁsī** ہنسی
disturbance, disorder, tumult, uproar, riot *n.m.* **hangāmah** ہنگامہ
yet, still, just now, not yet *adv.* **hanūz** ہنوز
are *v.i.* **hō** ہو
become *v.i.* **hō jānā** ہو جانا
air, wind, atmosphere, breeze *n.f.* **havā** ہوا
friend, well-wisher *n.m.* **hava xvāh** ہوا خواہ
airy, aerial; windy *adj.* **havā'ī** ہوائی
airport *n.m.* **havā'ī aḍḍah** ہوائی اڈہ
airplane, aircraft *n.m.* **havā'ī jahāz** ہوائی جہاز
airmail *n.f.* **havā'ī ḍāk** ہوائی ڈاک
exactly, perfectly *adv.* **hūbahū** ہوبہو
hotel *n.m.* **hōṭal** ہوٹل
become *v.i.* **hō jānā** ہوجانا

be finished, be completed *v.i.* **hō cuknā** ہوچکنا
litter (*an open seat*) *n.m.* **haudah** ہودہ
ambition, desire, lust, curiosity *n.f.* **havas** ہوس
lustful, curious, desirous *adj.* **havas nāk** ہوس ناک
sense, judgment, understanding, discretion; mind, soul *n.m.* **hōš** ہوش
careful, sensible; intelligent *adj.* **hōš mand** ہوش مند
wisdom, intelligence, understanding *n.f.* **hōš mandī** ہوشمندی
intelligent, attentive, discreet, careful, alert, accurate *adj.* **hōšiyār** ہوشیار
warn, give notice, caution *v.t.* **hōšiyār karnā** ہوشیار کرنا
cleverness, intelligence, skill, sense; carefulness *n.f.* **hōšiyārī** ہوشیاری
pain, ache; stitch, twitch *n.f.* **hūk** ہوک
greediness, cupidity *n.m.* **haukā** ہوکا
thrust, stab, attack *n.f.* **hūl** • terror, horror, fright *n.m.* **haul** ہول
melancholy *n.m.* **haul-ē-dil** ہول دل
terrified, frightened *adj.* **haul zadah** ہول زدہ
restless, nervous *adj.* **haulā** ہولا
thrust, goad; drive an elephant *v.t.* **haulnā** ہولنا
terrible, dreadful, fearful, frightful *adj.* **haul nāk** ہولناک
slowly, gradually *adv.* **haulē** ہولے
Holi (*a Hindu festival*) *n.f.* **hōlī** ہولی
patiently, gently, softly, slowly *adv.* **haulē haulē** ہولے ہولے
well, too, also, exactly *adv.* / am *v.i.* **hūṁ** ہوں
be, exist, belong, become; have *v.i.* **hōnā** ہونا
lip *n.m.* **hōnṭ** ہونٹ
be angry, disdain *v.t.* **hōnṭ nikālnā** ہونٹ نکالنا
desire, wish, want, ambition, envy, lust *n.f.* **hauṁs** ہونس
hopeful, promising, feasible, possible *adj.* **hōnhār** ہونہار
is, are *v.i.* **hai** ہے
exactly, even, indeed, only, mere, just, truly *adv.* **hī** ہی
rising (*of dust or anger*), tumult, war, commotion *n.m.* **haijān** ہیجان
eunuch *n.m.* **hījṛā** ہیجڑا
worthless, insignificant *adj.* / nothing, any, anything *pron.* **hēc** ہیچ
alternate *v.t.* **hēr phēr karnā** ہیر پھیر کرنا
diamond *n.m.* **hīrā** ہیرا
cholera *n.m.* **haizah** ہیضہ
strong, robust; wealthy *adj.* **hēkaṛ** ہیکڑ

building, palace, temple; face; form, figure, statue, shape *n.f.* **haikal** ہیکل

are *v.i.* **haiṁ** ہیں

asafoetida (*a spice*) *n.f.* **hing** ہینگ

astronomy *n.f.* **hai'at** ہیئت

vāū و

and *conj.* **va/ō/u** و
again; back, behind *adv.* / Ah!, Oh!, Ouch! *interj.* / open *adj.* **vā** وا
open *v.t.* **vā karnā** وا کرنا
tired; remaining behind *adj.* **vā mānda** واماندہ
become open, be opened, be freed *v.i.* **vā hōnā** وا ہونا
connections, relations *n.m.* **vābastagān** وابستگان
adherence, adhesion; connection, relation *n.f.* **vābastagī** وابستگی
bound, related, connected *adj.* **vābastah** وابستہ
behind, again, back, returning *adj.* **vāpas** واپس
obtain, get back, be restored (to) *v.i.* **vāpas milnā** واپس ملنا
withdrawal, return *n.f.* **vāpasī** واپسی
necessary, obligatory, proper, worthy, binding *adj.* **vājib** واجب
necessary, proper, expedient, admissible, allowable *adj.* **vājibī** واجبی
finder, possessor *adj.* **vājid** واجد
one, sole, individual, single, unique *adj.* **vāḥid** واحد
valley; perverseness, disobedience, obstinancy; habit *n.f.* **vādī** وادی
blow, stroke, wound; attack, assault *n.m.* / like, resembling *adj.* **vār** وار
attack, assault *v.t.* **vār karnā** وار کرنا
blessing, benefit; sacrifice, offering *n.m.* **vārā** وارا
heir, successor; master, lord, owner *n.m.* **vāris** وارث
inherit, become the heir (to) *v.i.* **vāris hōnā** وارث ہونا
inheritance, heritage *n.f.* **vārisī** وارثی
occurrence, event; accident, incident *n.f.* **vāridāt** واردات
relation, medium, connection; concern, sake *n.m.* **vāstah** واسطہ
for, for the sake of, on behalf of, on account of *pp.* **vāstē** واسطے
wide, spacious, large, extensive *adj.* **vāsiᶜ** واسع
connected, joined *adj.* **vāsil** واصل
clear, evident, obvious, apparent *adj.* **vāziḥ** واضح
preacher *n.m.* **vāᶜiz** واعظ
abundant, plentiful, much, many *adj.* **vāfir** وافر
happening, appearing *adj.* **vāqiᶜ** واقع
in fact, in reality, really, actually *adv.* **vāqiᶜ mēṁ** واقع میں
happen, appear *v.i.* **vāqiᶜ hōnā** واقع ہونا

event, incident, news, occurrence *n.m.* **vāqiᶜa** واقعہ
actually, truly, certainly, indeed *adv.* **vāqaᶜī** واقعی
aware, acquainted; experienced *adj.* **vāqif** واقف
acquaintance; knowledge *n.f.* **vāqifiyyat** واقفیت
keeping, possessing *adj.* / keeper, possessor *n.m.* **vālā** والا
father *n.m.* **vālid** والد
mother *n.f.* **vālidah** والدہ
parents *n.m.* **vāildain** والدین
By God! *interj.* **vallah!** واللہ
prince, ruler, chief *n.m.* **vālī** والی
debt, credit *n.m.* **vām** وام
vagrant; crazy *adj.* **vāhī** واہی
nonsense *n.f.* **vāhiyāt** واہیات
lamentation, bewailing *n.m.* **vāvailā** واویلا
plague, epidemic *n.f.* **vabā** وبا
misfortune, ruin, burden; plague, epidemic *n.m.* **vabāl** وبال
manner, habit, custom; way, path *n.m.* **vatīrah** وتیرہ
strength, firmness *n.m.* **vusūq** وثوق
enthusiasm, ecstasy, excessive love *n.m.* **vajd** وجد
intuitive *adj.* **vijdānī** وجدانی
pain, disease; complaint *n.m.* **vajaᶜ** وجع
reason, cause; face *n.f.* **vajh** وجہ
being, existence *n.m.* **vujūd** وجود
handsome, goodlooking *adj.* **vajīh** وجیہ
oneness, unity *n.f.* **vaḥdat** وحدت
beast *n.m.* **vaḥš** وحش
fear, abhorrence, dread; solitude; barbarism *n.f.* **vaḥšat** وحشت
savage, wild, ferocious; uncivilized *adj.* / beast, wild animal *n.m.* **vaḥšī** وحشی
inspiration, revelation *n.f.* **vaḥī** وحی
unique, matchless, unparalleled *adj.* **vaḥīd** وحید
goodbye, farewell *n.m.* **vidāᶜ** وداع
say goodbye, bid farewell *v.t.* **vidāᶜ karnā** وداع کرنا
science, learning, knowledge *n.f.* **vidyā/viddyā** ودیا
inheritance, heritage *n.f.* **virāsat** وراثت
heritage, bequest *n.m.* **virsah** ورثہ
uniform *n.f.* **vardī** وردی

ورزش exercise *n.f.* **varziš**
ورزشی athlete *n.m.* / athletic *adj.* **varzišī**
ورغلانا tempt, deceive, seduce *v.t.* **varġalānā**
ورق leaf; card; slice; foil *n.m.* **varaq**
ورم swelling, inflammation; tumor *n.m.* **varam**
ورم کرنا swell *v.t.* **varam karnā**
ورنہ although, otherwise, if not *conj.* **varnah**
وزارت ministry *n.f.* **vizārat**
وزارت امور خارجہ Ministry of Foreign Affairs *n.f.* **vizārat-ē-umūr-ē-xārijah**
وزارت تجارت Ministry of Trade and Commerce *n.f.* **vizārat-ē-tijārat**
وزارت تعلیم Ministry of Education *n.f.* **vizārat-ē-taᶜlīm**
وزارت داخلہ Ministry of the Interior *n.f.* **vizārat-ē-dāxilah**
وزارت دفاع Ministry of Defense *n.f.* **vizārat-ē-difāᶜ**
وزارت مالیات Ministry of Finance *n.f.* **vizārat-ē-māliyāt**
وزارت مواصلات Ministry of Communication *n.f.* **vizārat-ē-muvāsilāt**
وزن weight, weighing *n.m.* **vazn**
وزنی heavy, weighty *adj.* **vaznī**
وزیر minister *n.m.* **vazīr**
وزیر اعظم prime minister *n.m.* **vazīr-ē-aᶜazam**
وساطت medium, means *n.m.* **vasātat**
وسط center, middle *n.m.* **vast**
وسعت extent, space, wideness *n.m.* **vusᶜat**
وسواس whim, doubt, hesitation *n.m.* **vasvās**
وسوسہ temptation, evil idea *n.m.* **vasvasah**
وسیع spacious, extensive, large *adj.* **vasīᶜ**
وسیلہ means, support, relation, affinity *n.m.* **vasīlah**
وصال meeting, interview; connection, union *n.m.* **visāl**
وصف virtue, merit, praise *n.f.* **vasf**
وصل connection, conjunction, union, meeting *n.m.* **vasl**
وصل کرنا unite, attach *v.t.* **vasl karnā**
وصول arrival; conjunction, acquisition, collection; receipt *n.m.* **vusūl**
وصولی recovery *n.f.* **vusūlī**
وصیت legacy, bequest, testament, last will *n.f.* **vasiyyat**
وصیت نامہ testament, last will *n.m.* **vasiyyat nāmah**
وضاحت explanation, description *n.f.* **vazāḥat**
وضاحت کار explained, described, elaborated *adj.* **vazāḥat kār**

conduct; procedure; style, state, condition, manner; deduction *n.f.* **vaza^c** وضع
giving birth, delivery *n.m.* **vaza^c-ē-ḥaml** وضع حمل
stylish, elegant *adj.* **vaza^c dār** وضع دار
deduct, subtract *v.t.* **vaza^c karnā** وضع کرنا
ablution *n.m.* **vuzū** وضو
native country, home country *n.m.* **vatan** وطن
native, belonging to one's country *adj.* **vatanī** وطنی
pension, salary, stipend, scholarship *n.m.* **vazīfah** وظیفہ
promise *n.m.* **va^cdah** وعدہ
make a promise *v.t.* **va^cdah karnā** وعدہ کرنا
preaching, sermon *n.m.* **va^cz** وعظ
preach *v.t.* **va^cz karnā** وعظ کرنا
threat; denunciation *n.f.* **va^cīd** وعید
etcetera, and so on, and so forth *conj.* **va-ġairah** وغیرہ
fulfillment of a promise *n.f.* **vafā** وفا
faithful, sincere, loyal *adj.* **vafā dār** وفا دار
faithfully, sincerely *adv.* **vafā dārānah** وفا دارانہ
faithfulness, sincerity *n.f.* **vafā dārī** وفا داری
fulfill a promise, keep faith *v.t.* **vafā karnā** وفا کرنا
death, demise *n.f.* **vafāt** وفات
federation; harmony, concord *n.m.* **vifāq** وفاق
federal *adj.* **vifāqī** وفاقی
federalism *n.f.* **vifāqiyat** وفاقیت
deputation, commission, delegation *n.m.* **vafd** وفد
reputation, dignity, prestige *n.m.* **vaqār** وقار
time, term, duration; opportunity *n.m.* **vaqt** وقت
take time, last *v.i.* **vaqt lagnā** وقت لگنا
from time to time *adv.* **vaqtan fa-vaqtan** وقتاً فوقتاً
force, weight *n.m.* **vaqa^ct** وقعت
charitable fund, foundation, trust, endowment *n.m.* **vaqf** وقف
pause, intermission, delay, interval (*of time*) *n.m.* **vaqfah** وقفہ
contingency; accident, occurrence, event *n.m.* **vuqū^c** وقوع
pleadership, advocacy, attorneyship, deputation *n.f.* **vakālat** وکالت
pleader, commissioner, agent, ambassador, lawyer, counsellor *n.m.* **vakīl** وکیل
and if *conj.* **vagar** وگر
and if not *conj.* **vagar nah** وگرنہ

nearness, affinity, friendship *n.f.* **vilā** ولا
nativity, birth *n.f.* **vilādat** ولادت
country, dominion *n.f.* **vilāyat** ولایت
on behalf of *adv.* **vilāyatan** ولایتاً
foreign *adj.* **vilāyatī** ولایتی
son *n.m.* **valad** ولد
patronage, descent, pedigree *n.f.* **valadiyyat** ولدیت
ardor, fervor, enthusiasm, spirit *n.m.* **valvalah** ولولہ
but, yet, however *adv.* **valē** ولے
prince, lord, master; friend, mediator; saint, guardian *n.m.* **valī** ولی
son; child *n.m.* **valīd** ولید
girl *n.f.* **valīdah** ولیدہ
but, yet, however *conj.* **va-lēkin** و لیکن
that, those; he, she, it; they, them *pron.* **vah/vōh** وہ
Bravo!, Wonderful! *interj.* **vah vah!** وہ وہ
generous *adj.* **vahhāb** وھاب
Wahhabite (*follower of religious movement within Islam*) *n.m.* **vahhābī** وھابی
there, there to, yonder *adv.* **vahāṁ** وہاں
at that very place *adv.* **vahāṁ par** وہاں پر
imagination, illusion, idea, fancy *n.m.* **vahm** وہم
imaginary, illusionary, ideal, fanciful, visionary *adj.* **vahmī** وہمی
indolence, sluggishness *n.f.* **vahn** وہن
he, himself, that very *pron.* **vahī** وہی
then, there, that very time, that very place; immediately *adv.* **vahīṁ** وہیں
• knowledge, science; Veda (*sacred Hindu scriptures*) *n.m.* **vēd** وید
physician, doctor (*of Ayurveda*) *n.m.* **vaid**
heroic, brave *adj.* / hero *n.m.* **vīr** ویر
renouncing any worldly pleasure, austerity, penance *n.m.* **vairāg** ویراگ
desolate, ruined, unpopulated *adj.* **vīrān** ویران
ruin, lay waste *v.t.* **vīrān karnā** ویران کرنا
ruined place, desolate place *n.m.* **vīrānah** ویرانہ
desolation, destruction *n.f.* **vīrānī** ویرانی
visa *n.m.* **vīzā** ویزا
in that manner; though, thus *adv.* **vaisē** ویسے
like that, in that manner, so, such, similar *adv./adj.* **vaisā** ویسا
as before, the same as before *adv.* **vaisē kā vaisā** ویسے کا ویسا

yē ی

or, either *conj.* / Oh! *interj.* **yā** یا
My God! *interj.* **yā Allah!** یا اللہ
dry, arid *adj.* **yābis** یابس
recipient, finder *n.m.* **yābindah** یابندہ
departure, journey; pilgrimage (*of Hindus*) *n.f.* **yātrā** یاترا
memory, recollection, remembrance *n.f.* **yād** یاد
miss *v.i.* **yād ānā** یاد آنا
remind *v.t.* **yād dilānā** یاد دلانا
reminder, reminding *n.f.* **yād dihāni** یاد دہانی
send for, call *v.t.* **yād farmānā** یاد فرمانا
recollect, remember *v.t.* **yād karnā** یاد کرنا
monument, memorial *n.f.* **yād gār** یادگار
matchless, unparalleled *adj.* **yād gār-ē-zamānah** یادگار زمانہ
memorable *adj.* **yād gārī** یادگاری
learn by heart, remember *v.i.* **yād hōnā** یاد ہونا
friend, buddy, companion; lover *n.m.* **yār** یار
power, strength, courage *n.m.* **yārah** یارہ
friendship, assistance, love *n.f.* **yārī** یاری
despair; fear, terror *n.f.* **yās** یاس
jasmine *n.f.* **yāsamīn** یاسمین
grease, oil *n.m.* **yāġ** یاغ
rebel; enemy *n.m.* **yāġī** یاغی
earning, gain, income, profit *n.f.* **yāft** یافت
ruby, precious stone *n.m.* **yāqūt** یاقوت
aiding, friendly *adj.* / assistant, companion, friend *n.m.* **yāvar** یاور
friendship; aid, assistance, favor *n.f.* **yāvarī** یاوری
absurd, vain, futile; lost, ruined *adj.* **yāvah** یاوہ
dryness, aridity *n.f.* **yubūsat** یبوست
orphan *n.m.* **yatīm** یتیم
orphanage *n.m.* **yatīm xānah** یتیم خانہ
ice, snow *n.f.* / very cold *adj.* **yax** یخ
frozen *adj.* **yax bastah** یخ بستہ
hand; power, authority; aid, assistance *n.m.* **yad** ید

war, battle, fight *n.f.* **yuddh** یدھ
hostage *n.m.* **yarġamāl** یرغمال
God *n.m.* **yazdān** یزدان
divine *adj.* **yazdānī** یزدانی
left; left hand; plenty, affluence, opulence *n.m.* **yasār** یسار
prosperity, wealth *n.m.* **yusur** یسر
small, little; easy *adj.* **yasīr** یسیر
that is (i.e.), namely, it means; for, because *adv./pp.* **yaᶜnī** یعنی
plunder, pillage, spoil *n.m.* **yaġmān** یغمان
certainty, assurance, confidence, truth, trust *n.m.* **yaqīn** یقین
believe, ascertain *v.t.* **yaqīn karnā** یقین کرنا
believe, have faith (in) *v.t.* **yaqīn lānā** یقین لانا
certainly, indeed *adv.* **yaqīnan** یقیناً
true, indisputable, certain, definite *adj.* **yaqīnī** یقینی
one, a, an *adj.* **yak** یک
one by one; suddenly, successively *adv.* **yak bah yak** یک بہ یک
in one place, together *adv.* **yak jā** یک جا
unanimous *adj.* **yak dil** یک دل
of one color, uniform *adj.* **yak rang** یک رنگ
with one voice *adv.* **yak zabān** یک زبان
aside *adv.* **yak taraf** یک طرف
a handful, all at once *adv.* **yak mušt** یک مشت
single, unique, incomparable *adj.* **yaktā** یکتا
unity, uniqueness, matchlessness *n.f.* **yaktā'ī** یکتائی
equal, alike, even, same *adj.* **yak sān** یکساں
all at once, altogether *adv.* **yak sar** یکسر
full attention, one-sidedness *n.f.* **yak sū'ī** یکسوئی
singularity, union, unity, excellence, concord, uniqueness *n.f.* **yagāngat** یگانگت
singularity, union, unity, excellence, concord, uniqueness *n.f.* **yagāngi** یگانگی
/ unique, single, singular; unequaled, incomparable *adj.* **yagānah** یگانہ
kinsman, kindred *n.m.*
sea, ocean *n.m.* **yam** یم
felicity, prosperity, good luck *n.m.* **yumn** یمن
right (hand); oath *n.m.* **yamīn** یمین
this; he, she, it *pron.* **yēh** یہ

That's right!, That's correct! *interj.* **yēh sac hai!** یہ سچ ہے!
here *adv.* **yahāṁ** یہاں
from here *adv.* **yahāṁ sē** یہاں سے
Jewish, Hebrew *adj.* / Jew *n.m.* **yahūdī** یہودی
this very *adj.* **yahī** یہی
right here, in this place *adv.* **yahīṁ** یہیں
here about, in this very place, hither and thither *adv.* **yahīṁ kahīṁ** یہیں کہیں
assault, storm, invasion *n.f.* **yūriš** یورش
euro (*currency*) *n.m.* **yūrō** یورو
yoga *n.m.* **yōg** یوگ
yogi (*Hindu ascetic*) *n.m.* **yōgī** یوگی
day *n.m.* **yaum** یوم
doomsday, day of judgement *n.m.* **yaum-ul-ḥisāb** یوم الحساب
day of resurrection *n.m.* **yaum-ul-ḥašr** یومِ الحشر
per day, daily *adv.* **yauman** یوماً
daily *adv.* **yaumiyah** یومیہ
thus, in this manner *adv.* **yūṁ** یوں
thus, in this way; accidently, by chance, unintentionally *adv.* **yūṁ hī** یوں ہی
Greece *n.m.* **yūnān** یونان
Greek *adj.* **yūnānī** یونانی
university *n.f.* **yūnivarsiṭī** یونیورسٹی

ENGLISH-URDU DICTIONARY

A

a (an) *art.* yak/ēk یک
abandon *v.* chōṛnā چھوڑنا, chōṛ jānā چھوڑ جانا
abandoned *adj.* matrūk متروک, gum rāh گمراہ
abashed *adj.* šarm sār شرمسار, munfaᶜil منفعل
abate *v.* ghaṭnā گھٹنا
abbot *n.* mahant مہنت
abbreviate *v.* ixtisār karnā اِختصار کرنا, muxtasar karnā مختصر کرنا
abbreviation *n.* ixtisār اِختصار
abdication *n.* tiyāg تیاگ
abdomen *n.* batn بطن
abhorrence *n.* karāhat کراہت, nafrat نفرت
ability *n.* qābiliyyat قابلیت
ablaze *adj.* šuᶜlah-ē-zan شعلہ زن
able *adj.* tavālī توالی
ablution *n.* vuzū وضو, tahārat طہارت
abnormal *adj.* šāz-ō-nādir شاذونادر
abode *n.* iqāmat اقامت, ghar گھر
abolish *v.* mauqūf karnā موقوف کرنا, muᶜattal karnā معطل کرنا
abolition *n.* mansūxī منسوخی, mauqūfī موقوفی
abominable *adj.* laᶜīn لعین
abort *v.* ḥaml sāqit hōnā حمل ساقط ہونا, ḥaml girnā حمل گرنا
abortion *n.* isqāt اسقاط
about *adv.* lag bhag لگ بھگ, taqrīban تقریباً
above *adj.* zabar زبر / *adv.* ūpar اوپر / *prep.* par پر, bar بر ♦ **the one** ~ ūpar vālā اوپر والا
above-mentioned *adj.* mazkūrah bālā مذکورہ بالا, sābiq-uz-zikr سابق الذکر
abridge *v.* xulāsah karnā خلاصہ کرنا, muxtasar karnā مختصر کرنا
abroad *adv.* bāhar باہر / *n.* pardēs پردیس, ghair mulk غیر ملک
abscess *n.* phōṛā پھوڑا
abscond *v.* rafū cakkar hōnā رفو چکر ہونا, khisak jānā کھسک جانا
absence *n.* ġair ḥāzirī غیر حاضری

absent *adj.* ġair ḥāzir غیرحاضر, ġā'ib غائب
absolute *adj.* mutlaq مطلق, xālis خالص
absolutely *adv.* mutlaqan مطلقاً
absolution *n.* maġfirat مغفرت
absorb *v.* jazb karnā جذب کرنا, cūsnā چوسنا
absorbent *adj.* jāzib جاذب
absorption *n.* jazb جذب
abstain *v.* bāz ānā باز آنا, parhēz karnā پرہیز کرنا
abstinence *n.* parhēz پرہیز, iḥtirāz اِحتراز
abstinent *adj.* pārsā پارسا
abstract *v.* ixtisār karnā اِختصار کرنا
absurd *adj.* bēhūdah بیہودہ, xilāf qiyās خلافِ قیاس, muḥal محال
absurdity *n.* xarāfāt خرافات, bēhūdagī بیہودگی, harzagī ہرزگی
abundance *n.* bahutāt بہتات, ifrāt افراط, kasrat کثرت
abundant *adj.* kasīr کثیر, vāfir وافر
abundantly *adv.* kasrat sē کثرت سے, bakasrat بکثرت
abuse *n.* dušnām دشنام, gālī گالی, gālī gālōc گالی گلوچ / *v.* gālī dēnā گالی دینا
• ~ **verbally** zabān darāzī karnā زبان درازی کرنا
abusive *adj.* mumh phaṭ منہ پھٹ ♦ **verbally** ~ bad zabān بدزبان, zabān darāz زبان دراز ♦ ~ **language** *n.* muġallazāt مغلظات
abyss *n.* pātāl پاتال, athāh اتھاہ, qaᶜr قعر
Abyssinia *n.* ḥabaš حبش
Abyssinian *n.* ḥabašī حبشی
academy *n.* dars gāh درس گاہ, madrasah مدرسہ, akādamī اکادمی
accent *n.* laḥjah لہجہ
accept *v.* mānnā ماننا, rakh lēnā رکھ لینا ♦ ~ **guidance** hidāyat pānā ہدایت پانا
acceptable *adj.* qābil qabūl قابل قبول, pasandīdah پسندیدہ
acceptance *n.* pazīrā'ī پذیرائی
accepted *adj.* qabūl šudah قبول شدہ, manzūr kiyā hū'ā منظور کیا ہوا
access *n.* rasā'ī رسائی, mudāxalat مداخلت
accession *(to the throne) n.* taxt našīnī تخت نشینی
accident *n.* ḥādisah/ḥādsah حادثہ
accidental *adj.* ᶜārizī عارضی
accidentally *adv.* ittifāqan اتفاقاً

accommodations *n.* guṁjā'iš گنجائش
accompany *v.* pahuṁcānā پہنچانا, sāth sāth calnā ساتھ ساتھ چلنا
accomplice *n.* rafīq-ē-jurm رفیق جرم, sāthī ساتھی
accomplish *v.* anjām dēnā انجام دینا, kām tamām karnā کام تمام کرنا
accomplished *adj.* takmīl šudah تکمیل شدہ , mukammal مکمل
accomplishment *n.* itmām اِتمام, anjām dahī انجام دہی
accord *v.* mēl khānā میل کھانا , ham āhang hōnā ہم آہنگ ہونا
according to *adv.* bamūjab بموجب, bamutābiq بمطابق
account *n.* ḥisāb حساب, muḥāsabah محاسبہ ♦ ~ **book** *n.* ḥisāb kitāb حساب کتاب, khātah کھاتہ
accountability *n.* mu'āxazah مواخذہ, javāb dahī جواب دہی.
accountable *adj.* ḥisābī حسابی
accountancy *n.* muḥāsabah محاسبہ
accountant *n.* muḥāsib محاسب, ḥisāb likhnē vālā حساب لکھنے والا
accumulate *v.* jamaᶜ karnā جمع کرنا
accumulated *adj.* jamaᶜ šudah جمع شدہ
accumulation *n.* jamaᶜ جمع , ḍhēr ڈھیر
accuracy *n.* durustī درستی, barābarī برابری
accurate *adj.* ṭhīk ٹھیک
accurately *adv.* durustī درستی, qarār vaqā'ī قرارواقعی
accusation *n.* ilzām الزام, ittihām اِتہام
accuse *v.* ilzām lagānā الزام لگانا, tuhmat lagānā تہمت لگانا , qusūr vār ṭhahrānā قصوروار ٹھہرانا
accused *adj.* mulzam ملزم
accustom *v.* xū ḍālnā خوڈالنا , ᶜādat ḍālnā عادت ڈالنا
accustomed *adj.* ᶜādī عادی, mānūs مانوس
ache *n.* dard درد, dukh دکھ / *v.* dard karnā درد کرنا, dukhnā دکھنا
achieve *v.* sar karnā سر کرنا, ḥāsil karnā حاصل کرنا
acid *adj.* khaṭṭā کھٹا , turš ترش
acidity *n.* khaṭās کھٹاس , turšī ترشی
acknowledgment *n.* rasīd رسید, iᶜtirāf nāmah اعتراف نامہ
acquaintance *n.* jān pahcān جان پہچان, sūrat āšnā'ī صورت آشنائی
acquire *v.* ḥāsil karnā حاصل کرنا, kamānā کمانا
acquired *adj.* ḥāsil kardah حاصل کردہ, andōxtah اندوختہ

acquisition *n.* istiḥsāl استحصال , taḥsīl تحصیل
acrid *adj.* kaṛvā کڑوا
acridity *n.* kaṛvāhat کڑواہٹ
across *adj.* ārpār آرپار, tirchā ترچھا / *adv.* pār پار
act *n.* kāj کاج, kām کام, ᶜamal عمل / *v.* ḥarakat karnā حرکت کرنا, karnā کرنا
♦ ~ **in a play** *v.* kirdār nibhānā کردار نبھانا, tamāšā karnā تماشا کرنا
acting *n.* adākārī اداکاری, savāng سوانگ, naqqālī نقالی
action *n.* ḥarakat حرکت, kām کام, fiᶜil فعل
active *adj.* cālāk چالاک
activity *n.* sar garmī سرگرمی, phurtī پھرتی, cahal pahal چہل پہل, kām kāj کام کاج
actor *n.* adākār اداکار
actress *n.* ᶜaurat adākār عورت اداکار
actual *adj.* ḥaqīqī حقیقی aslī اصلی
actually *adv.* vāqaᶜī واقعی, vāqiᶜ mēṁ واقع میں
acute *adj.* tēz تیز, zakī ذکی
acuteness *n.* zēhn ذہن
add *v.* šāmil karnā شامل کرنا, jamaᶜ karnā جمع کرنا , jōṛnā جوڑنا.
added *adj.* šāmil kiyā hū'ā شامل کیاہوا
addicted *adj.* nashē mēṁ madhōš نشے میں مدہوش bādah parast بادہ پرست
♦ ~ **to opium** manšiyat kā ᶜādī منشیات کا عادی, afīmī افیمی, pōstī پوستی
addition *n.* zamīmah ضمیمہ , izāfah اضافہ ♦ **in** ~ *adv.* savā سوا, maᶜ hazā مع ہذا
♦ **in** ~ **(to)** *adv.* ᶜilāvah علاوہ
additional *adj.* izāfī اضافی, bālā'i بالائی, furūᶜī فروعی
address *n.* patā پتا, patah پتہ / *v.* muxātib karnā مخاطب کرنا, xitāb karnā خطاب کرنا
adequate *adj.* kāfī کافی, barābar برابر
adhere *v.* apnānā اپنانا, taᶜmīl karnā تعمیل کرنا , cipaknā چپکنا
adherence *n.* taᶜmīl تعمیل , vābastagī وابستگی, lagā'ō لگاؤ
adherent *n.* lais dār لیس دار , muᶜtaqid معتقد
adhesion *n.* vābastagī وابستگی, paivastgī پیوستگی
adhesive *adj.* cipaknē vālā چپکنے والا, caspāṁ چسپاں
adhesiveness *n.* cipcipāhaṭ چپچپاہٹ
adjacent *adj.* ās pās آس پاس, qarīb قریب

adjoining *adj.* muttasil متصل, mutavassil متوصل
adjournment *n.* iltivā' التواء
adjust *v.* cukānā چکانا, ṭhīk karnā ٹھیک کرنا
administration *n.* intizām انتظام, nazm-ō-nasq نظم ونسق
administrator *n.* mudīr مدیر, nāzim ناظم
admiral *n.* amīr-ul-baḥr امیرالبحر, mīr-ē-baḥr میر بحر
admiration *n.* iḥtirām اِحترام
admire *v.* sarāhnā سراہنا
admissible *adj.* vājibī واجبی
admission *n.* dāxilah داخلہ
admit *v.* dāxil karnā داخل کرنا, mānnā ماننا
admitted *adj.* daxīl دخیل, maqbūl مقبول
adolescence *n.* javānī جوانی, jōban جوبن
adolescent *adj.* javān جوان
adopt *v.* *(~ a child)* mutabannā karnā متبنی کرنا; *(~ a habit)* apnānā اپنانا, ᶜādat karnā عادت کرنا
adoration *n.* iḥtirām اِحترام, pābōsī پابوسی
adore *v.* pābōsī karnā پابوسی کرنا, ānkhēṁ bichānā آنکھیں بچھانا
adoring *n.* taᶜzīm تعظیم, taqdīs تقدیس
adorn *v.* sajānā سجانا, singār karnā سنگار کرنا
adult *adj.* bāliġ بالغ / *n.* javān جوان
adulteration *n.* khōṭ کھوٹ
adulterer *n.* zinā kār زنا کار
adultery *n.* zinā زنا, zinā kārī زنا کاری
advance *n.* udhār ادھار, pēšī پیشی
advanced *adj.* pēš پیش
advantage *n.* fā'idah فائدہ, nafaᶜ نفع
advantageous *adj.* fā'idah mand فائدہ مند, nāfiᶜ نافع
adversary *n.* ḥarīf حریف
adverse *adj.* muġāyar مغایر, muxālif مخالف
adversity *n.* bad qismatī بد قسمتی
advice *n.* nasīḥat نصیحت, mušvarah مشورہ ♦ **take** ~ *v.* mušvarah karnā مشورہ کرنا, salāḥ karnā صلاح کرنا
advise *v.* maslaḥat karnā مصلحت کرنا, salāḥ dēnā صلاح دینا, rā'ē dēnā رائے دینا

adviser *n.* nāsiḥ ناصح, salāḥ kār صلاح کار, mušīr مشیر
advocacy *n.* vakālat وکالت
advocate *n.* vakīl وکیل, šāfiᶜ شافع, šafīᶜ شفیع
aerial *adj.* havā'ī ہوائی
affair *n.* muᶜāmalah معاملہ
affect *v.* asar karnā اثر کرنا
affected *adj.* mutā'assir متاثر, nāk ناک
affecting *adj.* dil sōz دل سوز
affection *n.* šafaqat شفقت mihrbānī مہربانی, muḥabbat/maḥabbat محبت
affectionate *adj.* šafīq شفیق, mihrbān مہربان, muḥabbat āmēz محبت آمیز
affectionately *adv.* mušfiqānah مشفقانہ
affinity *n.* irtibāṭ ارتباط, vasīlah وسیلہ
affirmative *n.* musbat مثبت
affix *v.* caspāṁ karnā چسپاں کرنا
afflict *v.* kalpānā کلپانا
affliction *n.* kabīdagī کبیدگی, sōg سوگ, kasak کسک
affluence *n.* yasār یسار, sarvat ثروت
affront *v.* ihānat karnā اہانت کرنا
Afghani *adj.* afġānī افغانی
Afghanistan *n.* afġānistān افغانستان
aflame *adj.* šuᶜlah-ē-zan شعلہ زن
afloat *adv.* bahtā بہتا
afore-mentioned *adj.* sābiq-uz-zikr سابق الذکر
afraid *adj.* ḍarā hū'ā ڈرا ہوا, xā'if خائف, tarsāṁ ترساں
African *(dark-skinned person) n.* ābnūs آبنوس
after *prep.* ᶜaqab عقب / *adv.* baᶜd بعد, us kē baᶜd اُس کے بعد
afternoon *n.* tīsrā pahar تیسرا پہر • ~ **tea** *n.* ᶜasrānah عصرانہ
afterwards *adv.* baᶜd بعد, us kē baᶜd اُس کے بعد, phir پھر
again *adv.* dīgar دیگر, vāpas واپس, phir پھر, dōbārah دوبارہ, nīz نیز
♦ ~ **and** ~ *adv.* ka'ī bār کئی بار
age *n.* ᶜumr عمر, sinn سن
aged *adj.* buzurg بزرگ, sāl xūrdah سال خوردہ
agent *n.* pēškār پیشکار, gumāštah گماشتہ, fāᶜil فاعل
aggregate *adj.* majmūᶜī مجموعی

aggrieved *adj.* zār زار
aghast *adj.* bhauncakkā بھونچکا, hakkā bakkā ہکا بکا, ḥairān zadah حیرت زدہ
agility *n.* cābukī چابکی, jald bāzī جلد بازی
agitate *v.* hilānā ہلانا, māxūz ماخوذ
agitated *adj.* muztarib مضطرب, haṛbaṛiyā ہڑبڑیا مضطر
agitation *n.* khalbalī کھلبلی, ghabrāhaṭ گھبراہٹ, tazalzul تزلزل
agonizing *adj.* aziyat xēz اذیت خیز, dard angēz درد انگیز
agony *n.* tahlukah/tahalkah تہلکہ, ᶜazāb عذاب
agree *v.* mānnā ماننا, rāzī hōnā راضی ہونا
agree with *v.* ittifāq karnā اتفاق کرنا, muvāfaqat rakhnā موافقت رکھنا
agree upon *v.* muttafiq hōnā متفق ہونا
agreeable *adj.* muvajjah موجہ, suhānā سہانا, dil pazīr دل پذیر
agreement *n.* ittifāq اتفاق, ijmāᶜ اجماع, qarār قرار
agriculture *n.* khētī bāṛī کھیتی باڑی, zarāᶜat زراعت, kāšt kārī کاشت کاری
agriculturist *n.* muzāriᶜ مزارع, zarāᶜat pēšah زراعت پیشہ
ague *n.* tap-ē-larzah تپ لرزہ
ah! *interj.* vā وا, hā'ē ہائے
ahead *adv.* āgē آگے
aid *n.* madad مدد, sahārā سہارا, taqviyat تقویت / *v.* madad karnā مدد کرنا
ailment *n.* ᶜalālat علالت
aim *n.* murād مراد, hadaf ہدف, maqsūd مقصود / *v.* šast bāndhnā شست باندھنا
air *n.* havā ہوا, fizā' فضاء; *(musical)* dhun دھن ♦ **fresh** ~ *n.* nasīm نسیم
air conditioning (AC) *n.* ē sī اے سی
aircraft *n.* havā'ī jahāz ہوائی جہاز
airmail *n.* havā'ī ḍāk ہوائی ڈاک
airplane *n.* havā'ī jahāz ہوائی جہاز, tayyārah طیارہ
airport *n.* havā'ī aḍḍah ہوائی اڈہ
airy *adj.* havā'ī ہوائی, rangīlā رنگیلا
akin *adj.* qarīb قریب, ham batn ہم بطن, qarābatī قرابتی
alarm *n.* hullaṛ ہلڑ, khalbalī کھلبلی, haṛbaṛī ہڑبڑی
alas! *interj.* hā ہا, hā'ē ہائے
alchemist *n.* kīmiyā gar کیمیا گر
alchemy *n.* kīmiyā garī کیمیا گری, kīmiyā کیمیا
alcoholic drink *n.* dārū دارو

alert *adj.* caukas چوکس, caukannā چوکنا, hōšiyār ہوشیار
alertness *n.* pēš qadamī پیش قدمی, bēdārī بیداری, cābukī چابکی
algebra *n.* aljabrā الجبرا
alias *n.* ᶜurf عرف
alienation *n.* mufāraqat مفارقت
alight *v.* utarnā اترنا
alike *adj.* ēk sā ایک سا, mutašābih متشابہ, ham šakl ہم شکل; *(of the same tribe)* kufū کفو
alive *adj.* zindah زندہ, jītā جیتا, ḥaiyy حیّ
all *adj.* sārā سارا, sab سب
Allah *n.* Allāh اللہ
allegation *n.* ilzām الزام, bayān بیان
allegory *n.* tašbīh تشبیہ
alley *n.* galī گلی
alliance *n.* ittiḥād اِتحاد, irtibāt ارتباط, aḥdiyat احدیت
allied *adj.* mansūb منسوب
alligator *n.* magar مگر
all-knowing *adj.* ᶜallām علام, sab kuch jānnē vālā سب کچھ جاننے والا
allot *v.* dēnā دینا
allotment *n.* baxš بخش
allow *v.* ijāzat dēnā اجازت دینا
allowable *adj.* vājibī واجبی
allowance *(for food) n.* bhattah بھتہ
alloy *n.* khōṭ کھوٹ / *v.* khōṭ milānā کھوٹ ملانا
allure *v.* mōhnā موہنا, mōh lēnā موہ لینا, lubhānā لبھانا
allurement *n.* kašiš کشش
alluring *adj.* mōhan موہن, dil kaš دل کش
allusion *n.* manšā' منشاء, kināyah کنایہ
ally *n.* rafīq رفیق, muᶜāhid معاہد
almanac *n.* taqvīm تقویم
almond *n.* bādām بادام, lauz لوز
almost *adv.* lag bhag لگ بھگ, qarīb قریب, kuch kuch کچھ کچھ
alms *n.* sadqah صدقہ, dān دان, bhēkh بھیک
aloft *adj.* farāz فراز
alone *adj.* tanhā تنہا, akēlā اکیلا

aloof *adj.* nirālā نرالا
alphabet *n.* ḥurūf-ē-tahajjī حروف تہجی, alif bē الف بے ♦ **Arabic** ~ *n.* abjad ابجد
already *adv.* pahlē hī پہلے ہی
alright *adv.* ṭhīk ṭhāk ٹھیک ٹھاک
also *adv.* bhī بھی, ham ہم, hūṁ ہوں / *conj.* aur اور, nīz نیز
altar *n.* qurbān gāh قربان گاہ, mazbaḥ مذبح
alter *v.* badalnā بدلنا, tabdīl karnā تبدیل کرنا
alteration *n.* radd-ō-badal ردوبدل, adal badal ادل بدل, tabādalah تبادلہ
altercation *n.* jhamēlā جھمیلا
alternate *adj.* mutabādil متبادل / *v.* hēr phēr karnā ہیر پھیر کرنا
alternation *n.* badalnā بدلنا, taġayyur تغیر, phērā phērī پھیرا پھیری
alternative *adj.* mutabādil متبادل
although *adv.* gō kih گوکہ, har cand ہرچند / *conj.* agar cih اگرچہ, ḥālānkih حالانکہ, harcand ہرچند
altitude *n.* ūṁchā'ī اونچائی, irtifāᶜ ارتفاع
altogether *adj.* jamīᶜan جمیعاً, yak sar یکسر, mutlaqan مطلقاً
always *adv.* jāvīd جاوید, hamēšah ہمیشہ, sadā سدا
am (I ~) *v.* hūṁ ہوں
amateur *n.* ᶜatā'ī عطائی
amazement *n.* taᶜajjub تعجب, taḥayyur تحیر
ambassador *n.* safīr سفیر, ēlcī ایلچی
ambassadorship *n.* sifārat kārī سفارت کاری, ēlcī panā ایلچی پنا
ambiguity *n.* laġziš لغزش, ibhām اِبہام
ambiguous *adj.* muštabah مشتبہ, maškūk مشکوک
ambition *n.* ᶜazm عزم, ḥausalah حوصلہ, havas ہوس
ambitious *adj.* ḥarīs حریص, ḥausalah mand حوصلہ مند
ambush *n.* dā'ō khāt داؤگھات, dabkī دبکی
amen *adv.* āmīn آمین
amendment *n.* tarmīm ترمیم
America *n.* Amrīkā امریکا
American *adj.* amrīkī امریکی
amid *prep.* darmiyāṁ درمیان
amity *n.* ixtilāt اختلاط

among *prep.* miyān میان, bayn بین, fī فی, mēṁ میں / *adv.* bīc بیچ
amorous *adj.* ᶜāšiqānah عاشقانہ
amount *n.* miqdār مقدار
ample *adj.* munfarijah منفرجہ, farāx فراخ
amputate *v.* kāṭ ḍālnā کاٹ ڈالنا
amputation *n.* inqitāᶜ انقطاع
amulet *n.* taᶜvīz تعویذ
amuse *v.* dil xūš karnā دل خوش کرنا, bahlānā بہلانا ♦ ~ **oneself** *v.* jī bahlānā جی بہلانا
amusement *n.* dil lagī دل لگی, tafrīḥ تفریح, tamāšā تماشا
amusing *adj.* farḥat afzā' فرحت افزاء
analogy *n.* muvāfaqat موافقت, mutābaqat مطابقت, qarīnah قرینہ, tajnīs تجنیس
analysis *n.* tajzī تجزی
anarchy *n.* haṛbōng ہڑبونگ
anatomy *n.* ᶜilm-ul-ajsām علم الاجسام
ancestors *n.* bāp dādā باپ دادا, ābā-ō-ajdād آباؤاجداد,
ancestral *adj.* maurūsī موروثی
anchor *n.* langar لنگر
ancient *adj.* qadīm قدیم, purānā پرانا, ᶜatīq عتیق
and *conj.* aur اور, va/ō/u و
angel *n.* fariŝtah فرشتہ ♦ ~ **of death** *n.* dāᶜī ajal داعی اجل
anger *n.* ġussah غصہ, krōdh کرودھ
angle *n.* kōnā کونا, kōnah کونہ
angry *adj.* ġusīlā غصیلا, xašmgīṁ خشمگیں, jhunjhlā جزبز, lāl لال
anguish *n.* zīq ضیق, kōft کوفت, karb کرب
angular *adj.* zāviyah dār زاویہ دار, kōnē dār کونے دار
animal *n.* jānvar جانور, ḥaivān حیوان
animate *v.* jilānā جلانا, ḍhāras bandhānā ڈھارس بندھانا
anise seed *n.* saunf سونف
ankle joint *n.* ṭaxnah ٹخنہ
anklet *n.* kaṛā کڑا
annex *v.* ṭānknā ٹانکنا
annexation *n.* ilḥāq الحاق
annihilate *v.* maᶜdūm karnā معدوم کرنا, nā būd karnā نابود کرنا
annihilation *n.* inhidām انہدام

announce *v.* sunānā سنانا
announcement *n.* ḍhanḍhōrā ڈھنڈھورا
annoy *v.* īzā dēnā ایذا دینا, sir khānā سر کھانا, taklīf dēnā تکلیف دینا
annoyance *n.* īzā ایذا
annoying *adj.* īzā rasāṁ ایذا رساں, sōhān-ē-rūḥ سوہان روح
annual *adj.* sālānah سالانہ
another *adj.* ēk aur ایک اور, digar دگر, dīgar دیگر
answer *n.* uttar اتر, javāb جواب, javāb جواب / *v.* javāb dēnā جواب دینا
answering machine *n.* āṁsaring mašīn آنسرنگ مشین
ant *n. (large)* ciyūnṭā چیونٹا, makōṛā مکوڑا, *(small)* ciyūnṭī چیونٹی, mōr مور,
Antarctic *n.* qutb-ē-junūbī قطب جنوبی
antecedent *adj.* muqaddam مقدم
antelope *n.* haran/hiran ہرن
anterior *adj.* mutaqaddim متقدم
antibiotics *n.* anṭī bāyōṭik انٹی بایوٹک
anticipation *n.* pēš qadamī پیش قدمی
antiquity *n.* qadāmat قدامت
anxiety *n.* tašvīš تشویش, zīq ضیق, andōh اندوہ, intišār انتشار
anxious *adj.* mutafakkir متفکر, mutaraddid متردد, mutazabzib متذبذب
any *adj.* har ہر, hēc ہیچ, kō'ī کوئی, kuch کچھ / *adv.* nah نہ
anybody *pron.* kō'ī کوئی, kis کس
anyhow *adv.* kisī taraḥ کسی طرح, har taraḥ ہر طرح
anyone *pron.* kō'ī کوئی, kisī کسی
anything *pron* kuch کچھ, hēc ہیچ
anywhere *adv.* kahīṁ کہیں
apart *adj.* bartaraf برطرف, darkinār درکنار, ᶜalāḥidah علاحدہ
apartment *n.* kamrah کمرہ
ape *n.* bandar بندر, ban mānus بن مانس
apology *n.* ᶜuzr عذر, iᶜtizār اعتذار, maᶜzirat معذرت
apostle *n.* mursal مرسل
apparel *n.* libās لباس, raxt رخت
apparent *adj.* zāhir ظاہر, sariḥ صریح, namūdār نمودار
apparently *adv.* ġāliban غالبا, zāhir mēṁ ظاہر میں, zāhiran ظاہراً
appeal *n.* murāfaᶜah مرافعہ, rujūᶜ رجوع / *v.* rujūᶜ karnā رجوع کرنا

appear *v.* zāhir hōnā ظاہر ہونا, dikhā'ī dēnā دکھائی دینا, maᶜlūm hōnā معلوم ہونا
appearance *n.* zuhūr ظہور
appease *v.* taskīn dēnā تسکین دینا
appendix *n.* tatimmah تتمہ, zamīmah ضمیمہ
appetite *n.* ištiha اشتہا, bhūk بھوک, jūᶜ جوع
applaud *v.* taḥsīn karnā تحسین کرنا, tālī mārnā تالی مارنا, šābāš dēnā شاباش دینا
applause *n.* taḥsīn تحسین, sanā ثنا, šābāšī شاباشی
apple *n.* sēb سیب
applicant *n.* sā'il سائل, xvāstgār خواستگار, multajī ملتجی
application *n.* darxvāst درخواست, xvāstgārī خواستگاری
apply *v.* lagānā لگانا, darxvāst karnā درخواست کرنا, istiᶜmāl karnā استعمال کرنا
appoint *v.* mutaᶜaiyyan karnā متعین کرنا, lagānā لگانا, muᶜaiyyan karnā معین کرنا
appointment *n.* taqarrur تقرر
appraise *v.* ānknā آنکنا
appreciate *v.* tamīz karnā تمیز کرنا
apprentice *n.* talmīz تلمیذ
apprenticeship *n.* talammuz تلمذ, šāgirdī شاگردی
approach *n.* rasā'ī رسائی, āgman آگمن, taqarrub تقرب
approbation *n.* qabūl/qubūl قبول
appropriate *adj.* muxtass مختص
approval *n.* ravādārī رواداری, manzūrī منظوری, rizā رضا
approve *v.* ixtiyār karnā اختیار کرنا
approximate *adj.* muqarrab مقرب
approximately *adv.* lag bhag لگ بھگ, pās pās پاس پاس, taqrīban تقریباً
apricot *n.* zard ālū زرد آلو, xūbānī خوبانی
April *n.* aprail اپریل
aptitude *n.* ahliyat اہلیت
Aquarius *(Zodiac) n.* dalv دلو
aqueduct *n.* kārēz کاریز
Arab *n.* ᶜarab عرب
Arabia *n.* ᶜarab عرب
Arabian *adj.* ᶜarabī عربی
Arabic *adj.* ᶜarabī عربی
arbitration *n.* sālisī ثالثی, bīc bacā'ō بیچ بچاؤ, faislah فیصلہ

arbitrator *n.* sālis ثالث
arc *n.* qaus قوس
arch *n.* miḥrāb محراب, kamān کمان, ḍāt ڈاٹ / *v.* ḍāṭ lagānā ڈاٹ لگانا
arched *adj.* miḥrābī محرابی
archer *n.* kamān dār کمان دار, tīr andāz تیر انداز
archery *n.* tīr andāzī تیر اندازی
architect *n.* bānī بانی, miᶜmār معمار
architecture *n.* miᶜmārī معماری
Arctic *n.* qutb-ē-šimālī قطب شمالی
ardent *adj.* ḥārr حار, sar garm سرگرم
ardor *n.* šauq شوق, ḥamīt حمیت, šaġaf شغف, valvalah ولولہ
arduous *adj.* dušvār دشوار, kaṭhin کٹھن
area *n.* raqbah رقبہ, ᶜilāqah علاقہ
area code *(telephone) n.* ēriyā kōḍ ایریا کوڈ
argue *v.* ḥujjat karnā حجت کرنا, baḥas karnā بحث کرنا, jhagaṛnā جھگڑنا
argument *n.* ḥujjat حجت, javāb savāl جواب سوال, istidlāl استدلال
argumentative *adj.* taqrīrī تقریری, ḥujjatī حجتی
arid *adj.* yābis یابس
Aries *(Zodiac) n.* mēš میش
arithmetic *n.* siyāq سیاق
arm *n.* bāzū بازو, bāhū باہو / *v.* hathiyār bāndhnā ہتھیار باندھنا
armchair *n.* kōhnī dār kursī کوہنی دار کرسی
armed *adj.* musallaḥ مسلح, hathiyār band ہتھیار بند, kamar bastah کمر بستہ
armlet *n.* bāzū band بازوبند, jaušan جوشن
armor *n.* asliḥah اسلحہ, jaušan جوشن
armory *n.* asliḥah xānah اسلحہ خانہ
armpit *n.* baġal بغل
arms *n.* asliḥah اسلحہ, hathiyār ہتھیار
army *n.* fauj فوج, sipāh سپاہ, jaiš جیش, laškar لشکر ♦ ~ **camp** *n.* urdū-ē-mōᶜalla اردوئے معلیٰ, urdū اردو
aromatic *adj.* mahkīlā مہکیلا
arrange *v.* intizām dēnā انتظام دینا, intizām karnā انتظام کرنا, durust karnā درست کرنا
arrangement *n.* nasq نسق, nazm نظم، nizām نظام, taiyārī تیاری
arrears *n.* bāqiyāt باقیات

arrest *n.* ḥirāsat حراست, nazar bandī نظر بندی, giriftārī گرفتاری / *v.* pakaṛnā پکڑنا, giriftār karnā گرفتار کرنا
arrival *n.* pahuṁc پہنچ, āgman آگمن, āmad آمد, vusūl وصول
arrive *v.* pahuṁcnā پہنچنا, ānā آنا ♦ ~ **at** *v.* dar ānā در آنا
arrogance *n.* takabbur تکبر, maġrūrī مغروری, gustāxī گستاخی
arrogant *adj.* mutakabbir متکبر, maġrūr مغرور, gustāx گستاخ
arrow *n.* tīr تیر, nāvak ناوک
arsenal *n.* asliḥah xānah اسلحہ خانہ, tōp xānah توپ خانہ
art *n.* fann فن, sanā°t صناعت
art gallery *n.* nigāristān نگارستان
artery *n.* širyān شریان, rag رگ
artful *adj.* dam bāz دم باز, chalyā چھلیا, dilbāz دل باز
article *n.* maqālah مقالہ
articulation *n.* uccāran اچارن, nutq نطق
artificial *adj.* masnū°ī مصنوعی, naqlī نقلی, tarkībī ترکیبی
artillery *n.* tōp xānah توپ خانہ ♦ ~ **man** *n.* tōpcī توپچی
artisan *n.* dast kār دست کار, pēšah var پیشہ ور, mistarī مستری
artist *n.* *(male)* fann kār فن کار, kārīgar کاریگر, mutrib مطرب; *(female)* fann kārah فن کارہ
artistic *adj.* san°atī صنعتی
artless *n.* sādah dil سادہ دل
as *adv.* baḥaiysiyat بحیثیت, sā سا, cūṁ چوں / *adv./prep.* jūṁ جوں, bataur بطور, bamūjab بموجب / *conj.* kih/kē کہ
asafoetida *n.* hing ہینگ
ascend *v.* caṛhnā چڑھنا
ascension *n.* °urūj عروج
ascent *n.* irtifā° ارتفاع, su°ūd صعود, caṛhā'ō چڑھاؤ
ascertain *v.* ṭhīk karnā ٹھیک کرنا, yaqīn karnā یقین کرنا
ascetic *n.* zāhid زاہد, bairāgī بیراگی, jōg جوگ, sādhū سادھو
ascetic *(a Hindu monk)* *n.* sannyāsī سنیاسی
ashamed *adj.* munfa°il منفعل, xijl خجل, šarm sār شرم سار
ashes *n.* rākh راکھ, bhasm بھسم, xāk خاک
ashram *n.* āšram آشرم
ashtray *n.* rākh dānī راکھ دانی

aside *adv.* bartaraf برطرف, yak taraf یک طرف, darkinār درکنار
ask *v.* pūchnā پوچھنا, sū'āl karnā سوال کرنا ♦ ~ **for** māngnā مانگنا, talab karnā طلب کرنا, mangvānā منگوانا
asking *n.* pūchnā پوچھنا, pursiš پرسش
asleep *adj.* xvābīdah خوابیدہ
aspect *n.* talᶜat طلعت, ruxsār رخسار, tēvar تیور, manzar منظر
ass *n.* gadhā گدھا
assailant *n.* ḥamlah āvar حملہ آور
assassin *n.* qātil قاتل, hattiyārā ہتیارا
assault *n.* dhāvā دھاوا, ḥamlah حملہ, hujūm ہجوم, caṛhā'ī چڑھائی / *v.* dhāvā karnā دھاوا کرنا, dhāvā mārnā دھاوا مارنا, ḥamlah karnā حملہ کرنا
assemble *v.* jamaᶜ hōnā جمع ہونا
assembled *adj.* mujtamaᶜ مجتمع
assembly *n.* majlis مجلس, aṁjuman انجمن
assembly room *n.* baiṭhak xānah بیٹھک خانہ
assent *n.* qabūl/qubūl قبول, marzī مرضی
assert *v.* bayān karnā بیان کرنا, bāt rakhnā بات رکھنا, hāṁ kahnā ہاں کہنا
assertion *n.* bayān بیان, zaᶜm زعم
assessment *n.* bihrī بہری; *(of revenue)* māl guzārī مال گذاری
assiduity *n.* inhimāk انہماک, gahrī tavajjuh گہری توجہ
assign *v.* dilānā دلانا, tafvīz karnā تفویض کرنا
assignee *n.* zimmah dār ذمہ دار
assignment *n.* diyā gayā kām دیا گیا کام
assimilate *v.* pacānā پچانا
assassin *n.* xūnī خونی
assist *v.* muᶜāvanat karnā معاونت کرنا, madad karnā مدد کرنا, tā'īd karnā تائید کرنا
assistance *n.* taᶜāvun تعاون, tā'īd تائید, muᶜāvanat معاونت, madad مدد
associate *n.* sāthī ساتھی, zahīr ظہیر, šarīk شریک / *v.* (~ **with**) mēl karnā میل رکھنا
association *n.* majlis مجلس, maᶜiyyat معیت, samāj سماج, jamāᶜat جماعت
assume *v.* farz karnā فرض کرنا, dharnā دھرنا
assurance *n.* yaqīn یقین, bharōsah بھروسہ, bīmah بیمہ
asthma *n.* damah دمہ
astonished *adj.* mutaᶜajjib متعجب, mutḥaiyyir متحیر, bhauncakkā بھونچکا, mabhūt مبہوت

astonishing *adj.* ᶜajab عجب
astonishment *n.* taᶜajjub تعجب , ḥairat حیرت , acambhā اچمبھا
astray *adj.* gum rāh گم راہ
astrologer *n.* nujūmī نجومی , sitārah šinās ستارہ شناس
astrology *n.* sitārah šināsī ستارہ شناسی
astronomer *n.* munajjim منجم , sitārah šinās ستارہ شناس
astronomy *n.* hai'at ہیئت, sitārah šināsī ستارہ شناسی
asylum *n.* ḥirz حرز , mahrab مہرب , marjaᶜ مرجع
at *prep.* pās پاس , kō کو , mēṁ میں , par پر , sē سے
at first *phr.* pahlē پہلے, pahlē pahal پہلے پہل, avvalan اولاً, ibtidā mēṁ اِبتدا میں
at last *phr.* hir phir kē ہر پھر کے , āxir mēṁ آخر میں
at night *phr.* rāt kō رات کو
at once *phr.* barjastah برجستہ , fauran فوراً
atheism *n.* ilḥād الحاد , kufr کفر
atheist *n.* dhariyah دھریہ , munāfiq منافق , muᶜtazilī معتزلی
athlete *n.* kasratī کسرتی , pahlvān پہلوان, varzišī ورزشی
athletic *adj.* kasratī کسرتی , varzišī ورزشی
athleticism *n.* pahlvānī پہلوانی
ATM *n.* ē ṭī ēm اے ٹی ایم
atmosphere *n.* havā ہوا , fazā فضا
atone (for) *v.* kafārah dēnā کفارہ دینا
atonement *n.* kafārah کفارہ
attach *v.* vasl karnā وصل کرنا , lagānā لگانا , šāmil karnā شامل کرنا , milānā ملانا چپٹانا
attached *adj.* lāgū لاگو , marbūt مربوط , laff لف , girvīdah گرویدہ ♦ ~ **to** mutaᶜalliq متعلق , dāman gīr دامن گیر
attachment *n.* lagan لگن , girvīdagī گرویدگی
attack *n.* ḥamlah حملہ , *(by robbers)* ḍākā ڈاکا / *v.* ḥamlah karnā حملہ کرنا
attacker *n.* ḥamlah āvar حملہ آور
attain *v.* ḥāsil karnā حاصل کرنا
attained *adj.* muyassar میسر , dastiyāb دستیاب
attempt *n.* kōšiš کوشش , iqdām اقدام , saᶜī سعی / *v.* kōšiš karnā کوشش کرنا
attend *v.* ḥāzir rahnā حاضر رہنا , maujūd rahnā موجود رہنا , xidmat karnā خدمت کرنا
attend to *v.* mutavajjih hōnā متوجہ ہونا , rux karnā رخ کرنا
attendance *n.* xidmat gārī خدمت گاری , ḥāzrī حاضری , xidmat خدمت

attendant *n.* ḥuzūrī حضوری, mulāzim ملازم, xādim خادم
attending *adj.* manaᶜtif منعطف
attention *n.* tandihī تندہی, dhiyān دھیان, tavajjuh توجہ
attentive *adj.* mutavajjih متوجہ, xabar dār خبر دار, hōšiyār ہوشیار
attestation *n.* tasdīq تصدیق, maḥzar محضر
attitude *n.* dhaj دھج, uṭhān اُٹھان
attorney *n.* muxtār مختار, vakīl وکیل,
attract *v.* jazb karnā جذب کرنا, mōh lēnā موہ لینا, lubhānā لبھانا
attraction *n.* jazb جذب, girvīdagī گرویدگی, kašiš کشش
attractive *adj.* jāzib جاذب, dil band دل بند, dil kaš دل کش, dilbar دلبر
aubergine *n.* baingan بینگن
audible *adj.* sunnē kē qābil سننے کے قابل, masmūᶜ مسموع
audience *n.* ḥāzrīn حاضرین
augment *v.* ziyādah karnā زیادہ کرنا
August *n.* agast اگست
aunt *(father's brother's wife)* cacī چچی, tā'ī تائی; *(father's sister)* kākī کاکی; *(father's sister)* phūphū پھوپھو, phuptī پھپتی; *(maternal)* māmī مامی; *(mother's sister)* xālah خالہ; *(paternal)* cācī چاچی, phuptī پھپتی, phūphū پھوپھو
auspicious *adj.* maimūn میمون, mubārāk مبارک, xūš axtar خوش اختر
austerity *n.* vairāg ویراگ
authenticated *adj.* musaddaqah مصدقہ
author *n.* musannif مصنف, mūjid موجد
authoritatively *adv.* ḥākimānah حاکمانہ
authority *n.* ixtiyār اِختیار, ḥukūmat حکومت, qudrat قدرت
authorize *v.* muxtār karnā مختار کرنا
automobile *n.* kār کار
autumn *n.* xizāṁ خزاں, mausam-ē-xizāṁ موسم خزاں
autumnal *adj.* xizānī خزانی
auxiliary *adj.* madad gār مددگار
avail *v.* dāl galānā دال گلانا
available *adj.* muyassar میسر, maujūd موجود, maujūdah موجودہ
avarice *n.* lālac لالچ, lōbh لوبھ, tamaᶜ طمع, ḥirs حرص
avaricious *adj.* lālcī لالچی, ḥirsī حرصی, tammāᶜ طماع
avenge *v.* badlah lēnā بدلہ لینا, intiqām lēnā انتقام لینا

average *n.* bīc بیچ / *adj.* ausat اوسط, mutavassit متوسط
aversion *n.* karāhat کراہت, nafrat نفرت, khaiṁc کھینچ
avoid *v.* parhēz karnā پرہیز کرنا, ṭālnā ٹالنا
awaited *adj.* muntazar منتظر
awake *adj.* bēdār بیدار
awaken *v.* jagānā جگانا
aware *adj.* vāqif واقف, mutanabbah متنبہ, muttalaᶜ مطلع
away *adv.* bāhar باہر ♦ **take ~** *v.* uṭhā lēnā اُٹھا لینا
awe *n.* ruᶜab رعب, ḍar ڈر, dahšat دہشت
awe-inspiring *adj.* ruᶜab dār رعب دار
awful *adj.* ghōr گھور
awkward *adj.* bhaddā بھدا, anāṛī اناڑی
awkwardness *n.* anāṛī pan اناڑی پن
awry *adj.* ṭēṛhā ٹیڑھا
axe *n.* kulhāṛā کلہاڑا, kulhāṛī کلہاڑی
axis *n.* maḥvar محور, dhurā دھرا, kīlī کیلی
azure *adj.* kabūd کبود, lājvardī لاجوردی / *n.* lājvard لاجورد

B

babble *n.* harzagī ہرزگی / *v.* bākna بکنا
baboon *n.* bandar بندر
baby *n.* maulūd مولود
bachelor *n.* kuṁvārah کنوارہ
back *adj.* vāpas واپس, pichlā پچھلا / *adv.* vā وا / *n.* pīṭh پیٹھ zahr ظہر, pušt پشت
backbite *v.* pīṭh pīchē kahnā پیٹھ پیچھے کہنا cuġlī khānā چغلی کھانا
backbiter *n.* cuġl xōr چغل خور, ġammāz غماز
backbiting *n.* cuġlī چغلی, ġammāzī غمازی
backbone *n.* rīṛh ریڑھ
backpack *n.* baik paik بیک پیک
bad *adj.* bad بد, xarāb خراب, burā برا
badness *n.* badī بدی, xarābī خرابی, burā'ī برائی
bag *n.* thailā تھیلا, thailī تھیلی, baig بیگ, jhōlī جھولی
baggage *n.* sāmān سامان
bail *n.* zamānat ضمانت
bait *n.* cīnā چینا, kāṇṭā کانٹا
bake *v.* pakānā پکانا
baked *adj.* pakkā پکا
baker *n.* rōṭī pakānē vālā روٹی پکانے والا
balance *n.* mīzān میزان, pāsang پاسنگ, ḥāsil tafrīq حاصل تفریق
balcony *n.* chajjā چھجا, bar āmdah بر آمدہ, kāx کاخ
bald *adj.* gaṁjā گنجا, mucarrā معرا
baldness *n.* gaṁj گنج
ball *n.* gōlā گولا, gōlī گولی
balloon *n.* ġubārah غبارہ
balsam *n.* gul mahndī گل مہندی
bamboo *n.* bāṁs بانس
banana *n.* kēlā کیلا, mauz موز
band *n.* jhūmar جھومر
bandage *n.* paṭṭī پٹی, lapēṭ لپیٹ
band-aid *n.* baiṇḍ ēḍ بینڈ ایڈ, lēp لیپ

bandit *n.* ḍākū ڈاکو
Bangladesh *n.* Banglah Dēš بنگلہ دیش
bangle *n.* cūṛī چوڑی
banish *v.* ucāṭnā اچاٹنا, šahr badr karnā شہر بدر کرنا
banishment *n.* šahr badr شہر بدر, nikālā نکالا, istixrāj استخراج
bank *n. (financial)* baink بینک, sarrāfah صرافہ; *(of a canal or road)* paṭṛī پٹڑی; *(of a river)* šatt شط
banker *n.* sarrāf صراف, sēṭh سیٹھ, sāhūkār ساہوکار
banking *n.* sarrāfī صرافی
bankrupt *adj.* muflis مفلس, kangāl کنگال / *v.* dēvāliyah دیوالیہ
bankruptcy *n.* dēvālah دیوالہ, muflisī مفلسی, kangālī کنگالی
banner *n.* alam علم, jhanḍā جھنڈا, parcam پرچم
banquet *n.* mihmānī مہمانی, ziyāfat ضیافت, daᶜvat دعوت
banyan tree *n.* bāṛ بڑ
barat *(marriage procession) n.* barāt برات
barbarism *n.* vaḥšat وحشت
barber *n.* nā'ī نائی, ḥajjām حجام
bare *adj.* barahnah برہنہ / *v.* ughāṛnā اگھاڑنا
barefoot *adj.* nangē pā'ōṁ ننگے پاؤں
bareheaded *adj.* nangē sar ننگے سر
bargain *n.* mīsāq میثاق
bargaining *n.* saudā سودا
bark *v.* bhaunknā بھونکنا / *n. (of tree)* chilkā چھلکا
barn *n.* khalyān کھلیان, xurman خرمن
barrack *(for soldiers) n.* chā'ōnī چھاؤنی
barred *adj.* band بند
barrel *n.* nāl نال, pīpā پیپا, nal نل
barren *adj.* ᶜaqīm عقیم, bāṁjh بانجھ, kallar کلر
barrier *n.* sadd سد
base *adj.* zalīl ذلیل, nikammā نکما, nīc نیچ, kam zāt کم ذات / *n.* qāᶜidah قاعدہ, jarr جڑ, asās اساس
baseness *n.* qubḥ قبح, razālat رذالت
bashful *adj.* ġairat mand غیرت مند, bā ḥayā با حیا, šarmīlā شرمیلا
bashfulness *n.* lāj لاج, šarmindagī شرمندگی, šarm شرم, lajjā لجا
basil (sweet ~) *n.* tulsī تلسی

basin *n.* cilamcī چلمچی; *(large)* tašt طشت; *(of a river)* tās طاس
basis *n.* qāᶜidah قاعدہ, buniyād بنیاد
basket *n.* ṭōkrā ٹوکرا, ṭōkrī ٹوکری
basmati rice *n.* bāsmatī باسمتی
bastard *n.* ḥarāmī حرامی
bat *(animal) n.* cimgāḍar چمگاڈر, šappar شپر
bate *v.* ḥiqārat karnā حقارت کرنا
bath *n.* ḥammām حمام ♦ **take a ~** *v.* nahānā نہانا
bathe *v.* nahānā نہانا
bathing *n.* ġusl غسل, ašnān اشنان
bathroom *n.* ġusl xānah غسل خانہ, ḥammām حمام, saqāvah سقاوہ
battery *n.* baiṭrī بیٹری
battle *n.* jang جنگ, qitāl قتال, laṛā'ī لڑائی, muqātalah مقاتلہ
battlefield *n.* maidān-ē-jang میدان جنگ, laṛā'ī kā maidān لڑائی کا میدان
bay *n.* khāṛī کھاڑی, xalīj خلیج
bazaar *n.* bāzār بازار
be *v.* hōnā ہونا
beach *n.* sāḥil ساحل
bead *n.* saifī سیفی
beam *n.* lakkaṛ لکڑ, dharan دھرن, kiran کرن
bean *n.* chailā چھیلا
bear *n.* bhālū بھالو / *v.* bardāšt karnā برداشت کرنا
bearable *adj.* gavārā گوارا
beard *n.* dāṛhī داڑھی
beast *n.* ḥaivān حیوان, jānvar جانور
beastliness *n.* ḥaivāniyyat حیوانیت
beastly *adj.* ḥaivānī حیوانی
beat *v.* mārnā مارنا, jītnā جیتنا; *(~ someone up)* zarb lagānā ضرب لگانا, mārnā pīṭnā مارنا پیٹنا / *n. (musical)* tāl dēnā تال دینا
beaten *adj.* kōftah کوفتہ, zadah زدہ
beating *adj.* kōb کوب
beating *n.* mār مار, zarb ضرب,
beautiful *adj.* xūbsūrat خوبصورت sōhnā سوہنا, ḥasīn حسین,
beauty *n.* xūbsūratī خوبصورتی, ḥusn حسن, jamāl جمال

because *conj.* cūṁ چوں, yaᶜnī یعنی, kyōṁkih/kyōṁkē کیونکہ, kih/kē کہ
become *v.* hō jānā ہوجانا, hōnā ہونا, ban jānā بن جانا
bed *n.* bistar بستر, palang پلنگ; *(of a river)* rūd xānah رود خانہ
bedcover *n.* palang pōš پلنگ پوش
bedding *n.* bistār بستار, gadēlạ̄ گدیلا
bedouin *n.* saḥrā našīn صحرا نشین
bedroll *n.* bistār بستار
bedroom *n.* xvābgāh خوابگاہ, ārām gāh آرام گاہ
bedstead *n.* palang پلنگ
bee *n.* naḥl نحل, šahad kī makkhī شہد کی مکھی, *(black ~)* bhanvrā بھنورا
beef *n.* gā'ē kā gōšt گائے کا گوشت
beehive *n.* chattā چھتا, muhāl مہال
beet (~root) *n.* cuqandar چقندر
befall *v.* ᶜāriz hōnā عارض ہونا
before *adv.* pahlē پہلے, us sē pahlē اُس سے پہلے, mā qabl ماقبل
beforehand *adv.* qabl قبل
befriend *v.* rifāqat karnā رفاقت کرنا, sulūk karnā سلوک کرنا
beg *v.* māṅgnā مانگنا, phērī karnā پھیری کرنا; *(~ to)* muṁh ḍālnā منہ ڈالنا
beggar *n.* bhikārī بھکاری, faqīr فقیر, phērī vālā پھیری والا
beggary *n.* faqīrī فقیری
begging *n.* bhēkh بھیک, phērī پھیری
begin (to) *v.* lagnā لگنا, šurūᶜ karnā شروع کرنا
beginner *adj.* nau āmūz نوآموز / *n.* mubtadī مبتدی
beginning *n.* šurūᶜ شروع, ibtidā اِبتدا, mabdā مبدا
behave *v.* pēš ānā پیش آنا
behavior *n.* calan چلن, ravaiyah رویہ
behead *v.* qalam karnā قلم کرنا
behind *adj.* vāpas واپس, ᶜaqab عقب / *adv.* pīchē پیچھے pīchē pīchē پیچھے پیچھے
being *n.* vujūd وجود, būd بود, hast ہست
belch *v.* ḍakār lēnā ڈکار لینا
belief *n.* īmān ایمان, irādat ارادت, yaqīn یقین
believe *v.* yaqīn karnā یقین کرنا
believer *n.* muᶜtaqid معتقد, muḥaddis محدث
bell *n.* ghanṭā گھنٹا, ghanṭī گھنٹی

bellow *v.* ḍakār lēnā ڈکار لینا, *(~ as buffalo)* rēnknā رینکنا

bellows *n.* khāl کھال

belly *n.* pēṭ پیٹ, šikam شکم

belong *v.* hōnā ہونا

belonging *n.* milk ملک / *prep.* kā کا

beloved *adj.* piyārā پیارا, ᶜazīz عزیز, dil ārā دل آرا, dilbar دلبر / *n.* piyārā پیارا, piyārī پیاری, maḥbūb محبوب , maḥbūbah محبوبہ

below *adj.* farō/firō فرو, past پست / *adv./prep.* nīcē نیچے

belt *n.* mintaqah منطقہ

bend *n.* albēṭ البیٹ / *v.* mōṛnā موڑنا, muṛnā مڑنا

beneath *adv.* farōd فرود, pā'īṁ پائیں / *adv./prep.* nīcē نیچے talē تلے

benediction *n.* duᶜā دعا, barak برک

benefactor *n.* muḥsin محسن , dātā داتا

beneficence *n.* iḥsān اِحسان

beneficent *adj.* fā'iz فائض, munᶜim منعم

beneficial *adj.* nāfiᶜ نافع, mufīd مفید

benefit *n.* fā'idah فائدہ

benevolence *n.* ḥasnah حسنہ, muᶜātafat معاطفت

Bengali *n./adj.* bangālī بنگالی

bent *adj.* maᶜvajj معوج, juftah جفتہ, xamīdah خمیدہ / *n.* mōṛ موڑ, mailān میلان

bequest *n.* virsah ورثہ, vasiyyat وصیت

berry *n.* tūt-ē-siyāh توت سیاہ, ḥabbah حبہ

beseech *v.* giṛgiṛānā گڑگڑانا

beside *adv.* baġair بغیر / *prep./adv.* ġair غیر

besides *adv.* ᶜilāvah علاوہ, siyā سوا / *prep.* bajuz بجز, mā dūn ما دون

besiege *v.* maḥsūr karnā محصور کرنا , muḥāsarah karnā محاصرہ کرنا

besieged *adj.* maḥsūr محصور

besieging *adj.* muḥāsir محاصر

best *adj.* bihtarēṁ بہترین, aḥsan اَحسن

bestow *v.* marḥamat karnā مرحمت کرنا, ᶜatā karnā عطا کرنا

bet *v.* bāzī lagānā بازی لگانا

betel-leaf *n.* pān پان

betel-nut *n.* supārī سپاری, chālyah چھالیہ

betel-seller *n.* pān vālā پان والا

betroth *v.* mangnī karnā منگنی کرنا
betrothal *n.* mangnī منگنی , sagā'ī سگائی
betrothed *n.* mansūb منسوب
better *adj.* aur acchā اور اچھا, bihtar بہتر, aḥsan اَحسن
between *adv.* miyān میان, mābain مابین, bīc بیچ darmiyāṁ درمیان / *prep.* darmiyāṁ درمیان, bayn بین
beverage *n.* mašrūb مشروب; *(alcoholic)* šarāb شراب
bewildered *adj.* ḥairān حیران, bad ḥavās بد حواس
bewitched *adj.* masḥūr مسحور
beyond *adj./adv.* mā varā ما ورا, parē پرے
Bhagadvad Gita *n.* gītā گیتا
Bible *n.* iṁjīl انجیل
bicycle *n.* sā'ikil سائیکل
bid farewell *v.* vidāᶜ karnā وداع کرنا, ruxsat karnā رخصت کرنا
bier *n.* naᶜš نعش, kāṭh kī ghōṛī کاٹھ کی گھوڑی
bifold *n.* dō harā دوہرا
big *adj.* baṛā بڑا, ḍapōl ڈپول, kalāṁ کلاں
bigotry *n.* ᶜasabiyyat عصبیت
bile *n.* zahrah زہرہ
bill *n.* bil بل, ḥisāb حساب
billion *num.* kharab کھرب
billow *v.* mauj mārnā موج مارنا
bind *v.* bāndhnā باندھنا, kasnā کسنا
binding *adj.* vājib واجب
binding *n.* bandhātī بندھائی, bandhan بندھن; *(of a book)* juz bandī جز بندی
biographer *n.* mu'arrix مورخ
bird *n.* parindah پرندہ
birth *n.* paidā'iš پیدائش taulīd تولید, janam جنم ♦ **give** ~ *v.* janam dēnā جنم دینا; *(animals only)* biyānā بیانا
birthday *n.* sāl girah سال گرہ, janam din جنم دن
birthplace *n.* maulid مولد
biryani *n.* biryānī بریانی
bishop *(in chess)* *n.* pīl پیل
bit *n.* purzah پرزہ, luqmah لقمہ

bitch *n.* kuttī کتی, kuttiyā کتیا
bite *n.* ḍank ڈنک / *v.* kāṭnā کاٹنا
bitter *adj.* kaṛvā کڑوا
bitter gourd *n.* karēlā کریلا
bitterly *adv.* zār زار, zār zār زار زار
bitterness *n.* kaṛvāhat کڑواہٹ
black *adj.* siyāh سیاہ, kālā کالا
blackboard *n.* taxtah siyāh تختہ سیاہ
blackness *n.* siyahī سیاہی, kālak/kālik کالک
blacksmith *n.* lōhār لوہار
bladder *n.* masānah مثانہ
blade *(of grass)* *n.* tinkā تنکا
blame *n.* ilzām الزام, dōš دوش, mazammat مذمت / *v.* dōš lagānā دوش لگانا
blank *adj.* sādah سادہ, safēd سفید
blanket *n.* kambal کمبل
blaze *n.* šuᶜlah شعلہ / *v.* dahaknā دہکنا, lahaknā لہکنا
bleach *v.* safēd karnā سفید کرنا, nikhārnā نکھارنا
blend *v.* milānā ملانا
blended *adj.* maxlūt مخلوط
bless *v.* mubārāk bādī dēnā مبارک بادی دینا
blessed *adj.* mubārāk مبارک, faiz yāb فیض یاب; *(~ with a long life)* muᶜammar معمر
blessing *n.* barkat برکت, mubārākī مبارکی, mubārāk bādī مبارک بادی
blind *adj.* andhā اندھا / *n.* cilman چلمن
blindfold *v.* paṭṭī bāndhnā پٹی باندھنا
blindness *n.* andhāpan اندھاپن
blink *v.* mickānā مچکانا
blister *n.* āblah آبلہ
block *n.* kundā کندا / *v.* rōknā روکنا, ghērnā گھیرنا
blockade *n.* ḥasr حصر, ghērā گھیرا, muḥāsarah محاصرہ / *v.* muḥāsarah karnā محاصرہ کرنا
blood *n.* xūn خون, dam دم
bloodshed *n.* kušt-ō-xūn کشت و خون
bloody *adj.* xūnī خونی
bloom *n.* jōban جوبن, bahār بہار / *v.* lahlahānā لہلہانا, khilnā کھلنا
blossom *n.* phūl پھول / *v.* phūlnā پھولنا, phūl ānā پھول آنا

blossomed *adj.* phūlā پھولا
blot *n.* phuṭkī پھٹکی
blouse *n.* kurtī کرتی
blow *n.* phūnk پھونک / *v.* phūnknā پھونکنا; *(~ one's nose)* sinaknā سنکنا
blow up *v.* phūnk dēnā پھونک دینا
blue *adj.* nīlā نیلا / *n.* nīlāhaṭ نیلاہٹ
blunt *adj.* kund کند
boar *n.* bārāh باراہ, sū'ar سوَر
board *n.* taxtah تختہ, majlis مجلس
boast *n.* faxr فخر / *v.* ḍīng māṛnā ڈینگ مارنا
boastfully *adv.* faxriyyah فخریہ
boasting *n.* mufāxarat مفاخرت, tafāxur تفاخر, ḍīng ڈینگ
boat *n.* kištī/kaštī کشتی, nā'ō ناوَ
boatman *n.* kištī bān کشتی بان
bodice *n.* kurtī کرتی
body *n.* jism جسم, šarīr شریر ♦ **~ and soul** tan man تن من
bog *n.* daldal دلدل
boggy *adj.* daldalī دلدلی
boil *n.* phōṛā پھوڑا, phuṁsī پھنسی / *v.* ubalnā ابلنا, ubālnā اُبالنا
boiled *adj.* matbūx مطبوخ ♦ **~ water** *n.* ublā pānī ابلا پانی
boiling *adj.* jōšāṁ جوشاں
bold *adj.* dalēr دلیر, sūrmā سورما, himmatī ہمتی
boldly *adv.* dalērānah دلیرانہ
boldness *n.* dalērī دلیری, jasārat جسارت
bolster *v.* takiyah lagānā تکیہ لگانا
bolt *n.* dhabbah دھبہ, kāblah کابلہ, qufl قفل / *v.* dhabbah lagānā دھبہ لگانا
bomb *n.* bam بم
bombardment *n.* bambārī بمباری
bond *n.* mucalkah مچلکہ, tamassuk تمسک, rābitah رابطہ
bone *n.* *(big)* haḍḍā ہڈا, *(small)* haḍḍī ہڈی
bony *adj.* haḍḍīlā ہڈیلا, kaṛyal کڑیل
book *n.* kitāb کتاب / *v.* buking karnā بکنگ کرنا
bookworm *n.* kitāb kā kīṛā کتاب کا کیڑا
booking *n.* buking بکنگ

bookkeeping *n.* ḥisāb kitāb حساب کتاب
bookseller *n.* saḥāf صحاف, kutub farōš کتب فروش
boon *n.* bar بر, ġanīmat غنیمت
boorish *adj.* dahqānī دہقانی
booty *n.* lūṭ kā māl لوٹ کا مال
border *n.* sarḥadd سرحد, ḥāšiyah حاشیہ
bore *v.* surāx karnā سوراخ کرنا
bored *adj.* siftah سفتہ
boring *adj.* ġair dilcasp غیر دلچسپ
born *adj.* paidā پیدا, maulūd مولود ♦ ~ **of** zā زا, zādah زادہ
borrow *v.* māngnā مانگنا, māng lēnā مانگ لینا, udhār lēnā ادھار لینا
borrower *n.* mangtā منگتا
bosom *n.* jaib جیب, ankvār انکوار
boss *n.* dukāndār دکاندار
both *adj.* dōnōṁ دونوں
bother *v.* zaḥmat dēnā زحمت دینا, takalluf karnā تکلف کرنا
bottle *n.* bōtal بوتل, šīšah شیشہ
bottom *n.* qa^cr قعر, talā تلا, talī تلی
bough *n.* šāx شاخ
bounce *n.* lapak لپک / *v.* caunk paṛnā چونک پڑنا
bound *adj.* vābastah وابستہ, mujallad مجلد, pāband پابند; *(~ for)* bandiš بندش, pāband پابند / *n.* caukaṛī چوکڑی, chalāng چھلانگ, jast جست / *v.* uchalnā اچھلنا, ḥadd bāndhnā حد باندھنا
boundary *n.* sarḥadd سرحد ♦ ~ **line** ḥadd حد, ḥadd-ē-fāsil حدفاصل
boundless *adj.* ġair maḥdūd غیر محدود
bountiful *adj.* muxaiyyir مخیر, karīm کریم
bounty *n.* faiz فیض
bouquet *n.* gul dastah گل دستہ
bow *n.* kamān کمان, qaus قوس / *v.* jhukānā جھکانا ♦ ~ **one's head** sir jhukānā سر جھکانا
bowing *(while praying) adj.* sajjād سجاد
bowl *n.* piyālah پیالہ; *(as a measure)* paimānah پیمانہ / *v.* gēnd dēnā گیند دینا
bowman *n.* kamān dār کمان دار, tīr andāz تیر انداز
bow-shaped *adj.* qausī قوسی

box *n.* ḍibbā ڈبا, sandūq/sundūq صندوق
boy *n.* laṛkā لڑکا, chōkrā چھوکرا
boyhood *n.* laṛakpan لڑکپن
boyish *adj.* cibilā چبلا
bracelet *n.* bāzū band بازو بند, cūriyāṁ چوریاں
brackish *adj.* khārā کھارا
brag *v.* ḍīng mārnā ڈینگ مارنا, šēxī bhagārnā شیخی بھگارنا
Brahman *n.* panḍit پنڈت
brain *n.* dimāġ دماغ, bhējā بھیجا
brake *n.* brēk بریک
bramble *n.* jhāṛ جھاڑ, xār خار
bran *n.* cāpaṭ چاپٹ, bhūsī بھوسی
branch *n.* ḍāl ڈال, šuᶜbah شعبہ, ṭahnī ٹہنی
brand *n.* dāġ داغ, mārkah مارکہ / *v.* dāġ dēnā داغ دینا, jhulsānā جھلسانا
branded *adj.* tijāratī mārkah vālī masnūᶜāt تجارتی مارکہ والی مصنوعات, mutassam متسم
brass *n.* pītal پیتل
brave *adj.* himmatī ہمتی, bahādur بہادر
bravely *adv.* dalērānah دلیرانہ
bravery *n.* himmat ہمت, bahādrī بہادری
bravo! *interj.* vah yah وہ وہ, šābāš شاباش
brawl *n.* jhagṛā جھگڑا
bray *(as a donkey)* *v.* rēnknā رینکنا
breach *n.* ṭūṭ ٹوٹ, kasr کسر, phūṭ پھوٹ
bread *n.* rōṭī روٹی, capātī چپاتی
breadth *n.* cauṛā'ī چوڑائی
break *n.* tōṛ توڑ, phūṭ پھوٹ / *v.* ṭūṭnā ٹوٹنا, tōṛnā توڑنا, phūṭnā پھوٹنا ♦ **~ a fast** rōzah khōlnā روزہ کھولنا ♦ **~ out** bharaknā بھڑکنا, macnā مچنا
breakage *n.* šikastagī شکستگی
breakfast *n.* nāštah ناشتہ
breaking *n.* ṭūṭ ٹوٹ, takassur تکسر ♦ **~ the fast** *(during Ramadan)* iftār افطار
breast *n.* chātī چھاتی, pistān پستان
breath *n.* sāṁs سانس
breathe *v.* sāṁs lēnā سانس لینا

breathing *n.* tanaffus تنفس
breed *n.* nasl نسل / *v.* pālnā پالنا
breeding *n.* pālan پالن
breeze *n.* havā ہوا
brevity *n.* inxifāf انخفاف
bribe *n.* rišvat رشوت / *v.* rišvat dēnā رشوت دینا ♦ **take a** ~ *v.* paisā khānā پیسا کھانا
brick *n.* īnṭ اینٹ
bride *n.* dulhan دلہن ♦ **celestial** ~ *n.* ḥūr حور
bridegroom *n.* dulhā دلہا
bridge *n.* pul پل
bridle *n.* lagām لگام / *v.* lagām dēnā لگام دینا
brief *adj.* muxtasar مختصر
briefly *adv.* muxtasaran مختصراً, bil-ijmāl بالاجمال
brigade *n.* lām لام
bright *adj.* raušan/rōšan روشن, camak dār چمک دار
brighten *v.* camkānā چمکانا
brightness *n.* raušanā'ī/rōšnā'ī روشنائی, rōšnī روشنی, camak damak چمک دمک
brilliance *n.* camak damak چمک دمک
brilliant *adj.* camak dār چمک دار
bring *v.* lānā لانا, ā lānā آلانا, lē ānā لے آنا
brinjal *n.* baigan بیگن
brisk *adj.* šōx شوخ
briskness *n.* phurtī پھرتی
Britain *n.* Bartāniyah برطانیہ
British *adj.* angrēzī انگریزی
brittle *adj.* kurkurā کرکرا
broad *adj.* cauṛā چوڑا
broadcast *v.* šā'iᶜ karnā شائع کرنا
brocade *n.* tāš تاش, zar baft زربفت
broken *adj.* phūṭā پھوٹا, ṭūṭā hū'ā ٹوٹا ہوا
brokenhearted *adj.* xastah dil خستہ دل, dil šikastah دل شکستہ, dil figār دل فگار
broker *n.* dallāl دلال
brokerage *n.* dalālī دلالی

bronze *n.* pītal پیتل
brooch *n.* brūc بروچ
brook *n.* nālā نالا
broom *n.* jhāṛū جھاڑو
broth *n.* šōrbā شوربا
brother *n.* bhā'ī بھائی, bhayā بھیا, *(older ~)* kākā کاکا
brotherhood *n.* bhā'ī cārā بھائی چارا; barādarī برادری
brother-in-law *n.* *(husband's younger brother)* dēvār دیور; *(sister's husband / also an abuse)* sālā سالا
brotherly *adj.* birādarānah برادرانہ
brow *n.* pēšānī پیشانی
brown *adj.* bhūrā بھورا
bruise *n.* cīnṭ چینٹ, cōṭ چوٹ / *v.* pīsnā پیسنا, masalnā مسلنا
brush *n.* kūcī کوچی, kūṁcī کونچی
brutal *adj.* ḥaivānī حیوانی
brutality *n.* ḥaivāniyyat حیوانیت
bubble *n.* bulbulah بلبلہ / *v.* bhabaknā بھبکنا
bucket *n.* bālṭī بالٹی; *(made of leather)* carsah چرسہ
buckle *n.* qulābah قلابہ
bud *n.* kalī کلی
buddy *n.* yār یار
buffalo *n.* *(female)* bhaiṁs بھینس, *(male)* bhaiṁsā بھینسا
buffoon *n.* masxarah مسخرہ
buffoonery *n.* tamasxur تمسخر
build *v.* banānā بنانا
builder *n.* bānī بانی, mi^cmār معمار
building *n.* ^cimārat عمارت
bulkiness *n.* jasāmat جسامت, zaxāmat ضخامت
bulky *adj.* mōṭā موٹا, zaxīm ضخیم, jasīm جسیم
bull *n.* bail بیل, sāṇḍ سانڈ
bullet *n.* gōlī گولی
bullock cart *n.* bail gāṛī بیل گاڑی
bum *n.* cūtaṛ چوتڑ
bunch *n.* guchā گچھا

bundle *n.* guṭhaṛī گٹھڑی, pulandā پلندا / *v.* guṭhaṛī bāndhnā گٹھڑی باندھنا
bungalow *n.* bangalah بنگلہ
burden *n.* bōjh بوجھ
burglar *n.* naqb zan نقب زن, cōr چور
burglary *n.* naqb نقب, naqb zanī نقب زنی
burial *n.* tadfīn تدفین
burial place *n.* madfan مدفن
buried *adj.* madfūn مدفون
burn *v.* jalnā جلنا, jalānā جلانا; *(~ with iron)* dāġnā داغنا
burning *adj.* sōzāṁ سوزاں, muḥriq محرق, tābān تابان ♦ ~ **ground** *(for Hindu cremations) n.* marghaṭ مرگھٹ
burnish *v.* saiqal karnā صیقل کرنا
burnt *adj.* sōxtah سوختہ
burqa *n.* burqaᶜ برقع
burst *adj.* phūṭā پھوٹا / *v.* phaṭnā پھوٹنا, phūṭnā پھٹنا / *n. (~ of laughter)* qahqahah قہقہہ
bury *v.* dafn karnā دفن کرنا
bus *n.* bas بس, gāṛī گاڑی ♦ ~ **station** bas isṭēšan بس اسٹیشن ♦ ~ **stop** bas isṭāp بس اسٹاپ
bush *n.* jhāṛī جھاڑی, jhunḍ جھنڈ
business *n.* kārōbār کاروبار, dukāndārī دکانداری
businessman *n.* kārōbārī کاروباری
bustle *n.* gaṛbaṛ گڑبڑ, khalbalī کھلبلی, hal cal ہل چل / *v.* dauṛ dhūp karnā دوڑ دھوپ کرنا
busy *adj.* mašġūl مشغول / *v.* masrūf مصروف
but *adv.* balkih بلکہ, valē ولے / *conj.* magar مگر, par پر, lēkin لیکن, va-lēkin ولیکن
butcher *n.* qassāb قصاب
butler *n.* xānsāmāṁ خانساماں
butt *n.* pīpā پیپا
butter *n.* makkhan مکھن
buttered *adj.* rauġanī روغنی
butterfly *n.* titlī تتلی
buttermilk *n.* chāch چھاچھ
buttock *n.* cūtaṛ چوتڑ, juftah جفتہ

button *n.* ghunḍī گھنڈی
buy *v.* xarīdnā خریدنا
buyer *n.* xarīdār خریدار
buying *n.* xarīd خرید ♦ ~ **and selling** baiᶜ بیع
by *adv.* hāthōṁ ہاتھوں / *prep.* sē سے
bygone *adj.* guzaštah گزشتہ

C

cabin *n.* kōṭhṛī کوٹھڑی
cable *n.* rassā رسا, tār تار
cage *n.* piṁjrā پنجرا, qafas قفس
calamity *n.* idbār اِدبار, musībat مصیبت, āfat آفت
calculate *v.* ḥisāb karnā حساب کرنا
calculated *adj.* maḥsūb محسوب
calculation *n.* ḥisāb حساب, muḥāsabah محاسبہ
calendar *n.* sālnāmah سال نامہ, taqvīm تقویم
calf *n.* *(animal)* gā'ē kā bichṛā گائے کا بچھڑا; *(of leg)* pinḍlī پنڈلی
caliph *n.* xalīfah خلیفہ
call *n.* pukār پکار, hānk ہانک / *v.* pukārnā پکارنا ♦ ~ **for** mangvānā منگوانا ♦ ~ **names** zabān darāzī karnā زبان درازی کرنا, gālī dēnā گالی دینا ♦ ~ **out** āvāz dēnā آواز دینا
calligrapher *n.* kātib کاتب
calligraphy *n.* kitābat کتابت
calling *n.* lalkār للکار, byōhār بیوہار, balāvā بلاوا
calm *adj.* niclā نچلا / *v.* taskīn dēnā تسکین دینا
calmly *adv.* cup cāp چپ چاپ
camel *n.* ūnṭ اونٹ
camel-driver *n.* sār bān ساربان
camp *n.* laškar لشکر / *v.* xaimah karnā خیمہ کرنا
camping ground *n.* xaimah gāh خیمہ گاہ
can *v.* saknā سکنا
Canada *n.* Kainēḍā کینیڈا
Canadian *adj.* kainēḍiyan کینیڈین
canal *n.* nālā نالا, nahr نہر
cancellation *n.* mansūxī منسوخی, tansīx تنسیخ
cancer *n.* kēkṛā کیکڑا; *(disease)* rāj phōṛā راج پھوڑا, kainsar کینسر; *(Zodiac)* sartān سرطان
candidate *n.* tālib طالب
candle *n.* mōm battī موم بتی, šamaᶜ شمع

candlestick *n.* fānūs فانوس
candy *n.* miṭhā'ī مٹھائی
cane *n.* chaṛī چھڑی, bēd بید
canister *n.* kanistar کنستر
cannibal *n.* ādam xōr آدم خور, mardum xōr مردم خور
cannon *n.* tōp توپ
cannonball *n.* gōlā گولا
canoe *n.* ḍōngā ڈونگا
canopy *n.* sā'ibān سائبان, šāmiyānah شامیانہ
cantonment *n.* chā'ōnī چھاؤنی
canvas *n.* ṭāṭ ٹاٹ
cap *n.* ṭōpī ٹوپی
capability *n.* liyāqat لیاقت, qābiliyyat قابلیت
capable *adj.* lā'iq لائق, qābil قابل
capacity *n.* guṁjā'iš گنجائش, maqdūr مقدور
capital *n.* *(monetary)* sarmāyah سرمایہ, rās-ul-māl راس المال; *(city)* dār-ul-ḥukūmat دارالحکومت
capital crime *n.* sangīn jurm سنگین جرم
capitalist *n.* sarmāyah dār سرمایہ دار, māyah dār مایہ دار
Capricorn *(Zodiac) n.* jadī جدی
captivate *v.* qaid karnā قید کرنا
captive *n.* zindānī زندانی, maḥbūs محبوس, giriftār گرفتار
capture *n.* girift گرفت, giriftārī گرفتاری, pakaṛ پکڑ, / *v.* pakaṛnā پکڑنا, axaz karnā اخذ کرنا
car *n.* gāṛī گاڑی, kār کار
caravan *n.* kārvāṁ کارواں ♦ ~ **serai** kārvāṁ sarā'ē کارواں سرائے
card *n.* kārḍ کرڈ, pattā پتا
cardamom *n.* ilā'icī الائچی
cardboard *n.* gattā گتا
care *n.* rakhvālī رکھوالی, rakh rakhā'ō رکھ رکھاؤ, iḥtiyāt اِحتیاط / *v.* iḥtiyāt karnā اِحتیاط کرنا ♦ **take** ~ *v.* xabar gīrī karnā خبرگیری کرنا, xabar lēnā خبر لینا ♦ **take** ~ **of** *v.* mavāzabat karnā موظبت کرنا
careful *adj.* hōš mand ہوش مند, xabar dār خبردار, hōšiyār ہوشیار
carefully *adv.* iḥtiyāt sē اِحتیاط سے, iḥtiyātan اِحتیاطا, sambhal kar سنبھل کر

careless *adj.* bē parvā بے پروا, zāhil ذاہل, ġāfil غافل

carelessness *n.* ġaflat غفلت, rukhā'ī رکھائی

caress *v.* sahlānā سہلانا, piyār karnā پیار کرنا

caressing *adj.* navāz نواز / *n.* nāz bardār ناز بردار

caretaking *n.* rakh rakhā'ō رکھ رکھاؤ

cargo *n.* bār bardārī بار برداری

carnage *n.* muqātalah مقاتلہ

carnivorous *adj.* gōšt xōr گوشت خور

carpenter *n.* najjār نجار, mistarī مستری

carpentry *n.* najjārī نجاری

carpet *n.* darī دری, *(small) n.* ġālīcah غالیچہ; *(for praying)* musallā مصلیٰ

carpeted *adj.* mafrūš مفروش, farš bichā hū'ā فرش بچھا ہوا

carriage *n.* gāṛī گاڑی ; *(four-wheeled)* rath رتھ

carried *adj.* muntaqqal منتقل

carrier *n.* bār bardār بار بردار, ḥammāl حمال

carrot *n.* gājar گاجر

carry *v.* ḍhōnā ڈھونا ♦ ~ **on** jārī rakhnā جاری رکھنا

cart *n.* gāṛī گاڑی, chakṛā چھکڑا

carter *n.* gāṛī bān گاڑی بان

cartridge *n.* kārtūs کارتوس

carve *v.* khōdnā کھودنا, kandah karnā کندہ کرنا

carved *adj.* kandah کندہ, manqūš منقوش

carver *n.* kandah kār کندہ کار, but tarāš بت تراش

cascade *n.* jharnā جھرنا

case *n.* ġilāf غلاف, muqaddamah مقدمہ, ḥāl حال / *v.* maṛhnā مڑھنا

cash *n.* naqd نقد, rōkaṛ روکڑ

cash machine *n.* ē ṭī ēm اے ٹی ایم

cash-book *n.* rōkaṛ bahī روکڑ بہی

cashew *n.* kājū کاجو

cask *n.* pīpā پیپا phēnk پھینک

cast *v.* phēnknā پھینکنا ♦ ~ **a spell** *v.* mūṭh calānā موٹھ چلانا

caste *n.* jāt جات, qaum قوم

castle *n.* qilᶜah/qalᶜah قلعہ

castrated *adj.* zanxah زنخہ

casual *adj.* ᶜāriẓī عارضی
cat *n.* billī بلی, gurbah گربہ
catarrh *n.* zukām زکام
catch *v.* pakaṛnā پکڑنا ♦ ~ **a cold** zukām hōnā زکام ہونا ♦ ~ **fire** āg lagnā آگ لگنا
category *n.* qabīl قبیل
cathedral *n.* kalīsah کلیسہ
cattle *n.* pašū پشو, ḍhōr ڈھور
caught *adj.* giriftah گرفتہ
cauldron *n.* kaṛāh کڑاہ
cauliflower *n.* gōbhī گوبھی, phūl gōbhī پھول گوبھی
cause *n.* sabab سبب, vajh وجہ / *v.* macānā مچانا
caution *n.* xabar dār خبر دار, ḥazar حذر, iḥtiyāt اِحتیاط, / *v.* hōšiyār karnā ہوشیار کرنا
cautious *adj.* xabar dār خبر دار, hōšiyār ہوشیار
cautiously *adv.* iḥtiyāt sē اِحتیاط سے, iḥtiyātan اِحتیاطاً
cavalry *n.* risālah رسالہ
cave *n.* ġār غار
cavern *n.* ġār غار
cavity *n.* gaṛhā گڑھا, jauf جوف, khaḍḍā کھڈی
CD *n.* sī ḍī سی ڈی
cease *v.* xatm hōnā ختم ہونا, marnā مرنا, thamnā تھمنا
ceiling *n.* saqf سقف, chat چھت
celebrate *v.* taqrīb karnā تقریب کرنا, racānā رچانا ♦ ~ **a wedding** šādī karnā شادی کرنا
celebrated *adj.* nām dār نام دار, maᶜrūf معروف, munaᶜqid منعقد, mašhūr مشہور
celebrity *n.* šuhrat شہرت
celestial *adj.* āsmānī آسمانی, falkī فلکی ♦ ~ **bride** *n.* ḥūr حور
celibacy *n.* tajarrud تجرد
cell *n.* xaliyah خلیہ
cellar *n.* tah xānah تہ خانہ
cemetery *n.* qabristān قبرستان
censure *n.* taᶜzīr تعزیر, mazammat مذمت
census *n.* xānah šumārī خانہ شماری, mardum šumarī مردم شماری

centenary *n.* sadī صدی
center *n.* markaz مرکز / *adj.* ḥāq حاق
central *adj.* markazī مرکزی
century *n.* sadī صدی
ceremony *n.* taqrīb تقریب
certain *adv.* baᶜz بعض / *adj.* taḥqīqī تحقیقی, yaqīnī یقینی
certainly *adv.* vāqaᶜī واقعی, yaqīnan یقیناً
certainty *n.* yaqīn یقین
certificate *n.* sanad سند, dastāvēz دستاویز
certified *adj.* mustanad مستند
cession *n.* dast bardāri دست برداری
chaff *n.* bhūsī بھوسی
chai tea *n.* masālā cā'ē مسالا چائے
chain *n.* zanjīr زنجیر
chair *n.* kursī کرسی
chairman *n.* sar paṁc سرپنچ
chairmanship *n.* sadārat صدارت
challenge *n.* lalkār للکار / *v.* lalkārnā للکارنا, ṭōknā ٹوکنا
chamber *n.* kamrah کمرہ
chamber hall *n.* baiṭhak x̱ānah بیٹھک خانہ
chameleon *n.* girgaṭ گرگٹ
champion *n.* pahlvān پہلوان, ġazanfar غضنفر
chance *n.* nasīb نصیب, iḥtimāl اِحتمال / *v.* ittifāq paṛnā اِتفاق پڑنا
chancellorship *n.* sadārat صدارت
change *n.* badal بدل, tabdīl تبدیل; *(coins)* chūṭṭē چھوٹے / *v.* badalnā بدلنا, tabdīl karnā تبدیل کرنا
changeable *adj.* mutalavvin متلون
channel *n.* rūd/rōd رود, rūdbār رودبار, nahr نہر
chapati *(thin bread)* *n.* capātī چپاتی
chapter *n.* bāb باب
character *n.* calan چلن, cāl calan چال چلن
characteristic *n.* ixtisās اِختصاص
charcoal *n.* kō'ēlah کوئلہ
charge *n.* ilzām الزام / *v.* aparādh lagānā اپرادھ لگانا

chariot *n.* rath رتھ
charitable *adj.* xairātī خیراتی, muxaiyyir مخیّر ♦ ~ **fund** *n.* vaqf وقف
charity *n.* xairāt خیرات
charm *v.* lubhānā لبھانا; *(~ a snake)* kīlnā کیلنا
chart *n.* naqšah نقشہ
charter *n.* ᶜahd nāmah عہد نامہ, manšūr منشور
chase *n.* taᶜāqub تعاقب, šikār شکار / *v.* taᶜāqub karnā تعاقب کرنا; *(~ away)* bhagānā بھگانا
chaste *adj.* pārsā پارسا, pākīzah پاکیزہ
chasteness *n.* pākīzagī پاکیزگی
chastisement *n.* muᶜāqabat معاقبت
chastity *n.* pārsā'ī پارسائی, pākdāmnī پاکدامنی, pākbāzī پاکبازی
chat *v.* bāt cīt karnā بات چیت کرنا / *n.* taḥrīrī guftgū تحریری گفتگو, gap گپ
chatter *v.* bākna بکنا, ṭarrānā ٹرانا, cīṁ cīṁ karnā چیں چیں کرنا
cheap *adj.* sastā سستا
cheapness *n.* sastā'ī سستائی
cheat *n.* dhōkā bāzī دھوکا بازی, farēbī فریبی / *v.* dhōkā dēnā دھوکا دینا, farēb dēnā فریب دینا
cheating *n.* cakmah چکمہ, daġā bāzī دغا بازی
check *n.* ḥisāb حساب, cēk چیک, bil بل, huṁḍī ہنڈی / *v.* jāṁcnā جانچنا, lagām dēnā لگام دینا ♦ ~ **accounts** *v.* muḥasabah karnā محاسبہ کرنا
checkered *adj.* būqalmūn بوقلمون
cheek *n.* ruxsār رخسار
cheerful *adj.* zindah dil زندہ دل
cheerfulness *n.* zindah dilī زندہ دلی
cheers *n.* taḥsīn تحسین
cheese *n.* panīr پنیر
chemist *n.* kīmiyā gar کیمیا گر, māhir-ē-ᶜilm-ē-kīmiyā ماہر علم کیمیا
chemistry *n.* kīmiyā کیمیا, kīmiyā garī کیمیا گری, ᶜilm-ē-kīmiyā علم کیمیا
chess *n.* šatranj شطرنج ♦ ~ **board** *n.* taxtah-ē-šatranj تختۂ شطرنج ♦ ~ **player** *n.* šatranj bāz شطرنج باز
chest *n.* sadr صدر, chātī چھاتی, sīnah سینہ
chestnut tree *n.* balūt بلوط
chew *v.* cabānā چبانا, cābnā چابنا

chewing tobacco *n.* nasvār نسوار
chicken *n.* cūzah چوزہ, murġī مرغی
chickpea *n.* canā چنا, nuxūd نخود
chief *adj.* agra اگر, mih مہ, muhtar مہتر / *n.* amīr امیر, šaix شیخ, nāyak نایک, naqīb نقیب
chilam *(smoking pipe) n.* cilam چلم
child *n.* baccah بچہ; *(adopted ~)* mutabannā متبنی
childbirth *n.* zih زہ
childhood *n.* bacpan بچپن
childish *adj.* cibilā چبلا, backānah بچکانہ
childishness *n.* cibilāpan چبلاپن
childless *adj.* ʿaqīm عقیم, lā valad لاولد
chili pepper *n.* mirc مرچ
chill *n.* ṭhanḍ ٹھنڈ, sard سرد
chilliness *n.* sardī سردی
chime *v.* tāl dēnā تال دینا
chimney *n.* cimnī چمنی
chin *n.* ṭhōṛī ٹھوڑی
China *n.* cīn چین
Chinese *adj.* cīnī چینی
chirp *n.* cīṁ چیں / *v.* cīṁ cīṁ karnā چیں چیں کرنا, cahcahānā چہچانا
chisel *n.* basūlī بسولی, chēnī چھینی, ṭānkī ٹانکی
chit-chat *n.* gap šap گپ شپ, bāt cīt بات چیت
chocolate *n.* cāklēṭ چاکلیٹ
choice *n.* intixāb انتخاب
choke *v.* phāṁsnā پھانسنا, ṭēnṭū'ā dabānā ٹینٹوا دبانا
cholera *n.* haizah ہیضہ
choleric *adj.* maġlūb-ul-ġazab مغلوب الغضب
choose *v.* cunnā چننا, intixāb karnā انتخاب کرنا
choosing *n.* ijtibā اِجتبا
chord *n.* rassī رسی, tāgā تاگا
chosen *adj.* muntaxab منتخب, pasand پسند, pasandīdah پسندیدہ
Christ *n.* masīḥ مسیح, ʿīsā عیسی

Christian *n.* nasrānī نصرانی, ᶜīsā'ī عیسائی
Christian name *n.* pahlā nām پہلا نام
Christianity *n.* nasrāniyat نصرانیت
church *n.* girjā گرجا
churn *v.* mathnā متھنا, bilōnā بلونا
cigarette *n.* sigrēṭ سگریٹ
cinema *n.* sinēmā سنیما
cinnamon *n.* dāl cīnī دال چینی, dārcīnī دارچینی
circle *n.* ḥalqah حلقہ
circuit *n.* dā'irah دائرہ, ghēr گھیر, phērī پھیری, daur دور
circular *adj.* gōl گول / *n.* cakkā چکا
circulate *v.* ghumānā گھمانا, phirnā پھرنا
circulation *n.* daur دور
circumcision *n.* xatnah ختنہ
circumference *n.* madār مدار, muḥīt محیط
circumstance *n.* ḥālat حالت, kaifiyyat کیفیت
cistern *n.* ḥauz حوض
citadel *n.* qasr قصر
citizen *n.* ahl اہل, šahrī شہری
citizenship *n.* šahriyat شہریت, qaumiyat قومیت
citron *n.* galgal گلگل
city *n.* šahr/šahar شہر
civics *n.* šaharyāt شہریات
civil *adj.* mu'addab مؤدب, mulkī ملکی, šahrī شہری, majlisī مجلسی ♦ ~ **court** dīvānī دیوانی ♦ ~ **procedure code** zābitah-ē-dīvānī ضابطہ دیوانی ♦ ~ **war** xānah jangī خانہ جنگی
civility *n.* tavāzuᶜ تواضع, xulq خلق
civilization *n.* tahzīb تہذیب, tamaddun تمدن
civilize *v.* ādmī banānā آدمی بنانا
civilized *adj.* muhazzab مہذب, tahzīb yāftah تہذیب یافتہ
civility *n.* sulūk سلوک
claim *n.* daᶜvā دعوی, istiḥqāq استحقاق, ḥaqiyyat حقیت; *(financial)* taqāzā تقاضا
clan *n.* qabīlah قبیلہ

clandestine *adj.* cōrī cōrī چوری چوری
clap (hands) *v.* tālī bajānā تالی بجانا
clapping (of hands) *n.* tālī تالی
clarification *n.* tasrīḥ تصریح
clarion *n.* šahnā'ī شہنائی
clash *n.* tasādum تصادم / *v.* khaṭaknā کھٹکنا
class *n.* darjah درجہ
claw *n.* paṁjah پنجہ / *v.* paṁjah mārnā پنجہ مارنا
clay *n.* ciknī maṭṭī چکنی مٹی
clean *adj.* sāf صاف / *v.* sāf karnā صاف کرنا, safā'ī karnā صفائی کرنا
cleanliness *n.* safā'ī صفائی
cleanse *v.* sāf karnā صاف کرنا, safā'ī karnā صفائی کرنا
clear *adj.* vāzaḥ واضح / *v.* sāf karnā صاف کرنا
clearly *adv.* sarāḥatan صراحتا
clearness *n.* sarāḥat صراحت, suthrā'ī ستھرائی
cleave *v.* kāṭnā کاٹنا
clergyman *(Christian)* *n.* pādrī پادری
clerk *n.* munšī منشی
clever *adj.* cālāk چالاک
cleverness *n.* cālākī چالاکی
client *n.* gāhak گاہک, xarīdār خریدار
climate *n.* āb-ō-havā آب وہوا, kišvar کشور
climb *v.* caṛhnā چڑھنا
cling *v.* cimaṭnā چمٹنا, lipaṭnā لپٹنا
clinic *n.* šifā xānah شفاخانہ
clink *v.* khanaknā کھنکنا, ṭhinaknā ٹھنکنا, ṭhankānā ٹھنکانا
clip *n.* kāṭ کاٹ / *v.* kāṭnā کاٹنا, kāṭ chānṭ kārnā کاٹ چھانٹ کرنا
cloak *n.* cōlā چولا, cūġah چوغہ, ᶜabā عبا
clock *n.* ghanṭā گھنٹا, ghaṛī گھڑی
clocktower *n.* ghanṭā ghar گھنٹا گھر
clod *n.* ḍālā ڈالا; *(of earth)* ḍhēlā ڈھیلا, kulūx کلوخ
close *adj.* nazdīk نزدیک / *v.* band karnā بند کرنا
closed *adj.* band بند
closet *n.* kōṭhṛī کوٹھڑی, ḥujrah حجرہ

cloth *n.* kapṛā کپڑا
clothes *n.* kapṛē کپڑے ♦ **take off one's** ~ *v.* kapṛē utārnā کپڑے اتارنا
clothing *n.* pahnāvā پہناوا, pārcah پارچہ
cloth-printer *n.* chīpī چھیپی
cloud *n.* bādal بادل, ghaṭā گھٹا
cloudiness *n.* ghaṭā گھٹا
cloudy *adj.* abr ālūd ابر آلود
clove *n.* gaṭṭhā گٹھا, qaranfal قرنفل ♦ ~ **of garlic** pōthī پوتھی
clown *n.* ganvār گنوار
club *n.* aṁjuman انجمن, ḍanḍā ڈنڈا
clump (of trees) *n.* jhunḍ جھنڈ
clumsy *adj.* bhaddā بھدا
cluster *n.* guchā گچھا
coach *n.* bas بس, gāṛī گاڑی
coachman *n.* gāṛī bān گاڑی بان
coal *n.* kō'ēlah کوئلہ
coarse *adj.* mōṭā موٹا, gāṛhā گاڑھا
coast *n.* kinārā کنارا, sāḥil ساحل
coat *n.* kōṭ کوٹ, angā انگا / *v.* maṛhnā مڑھنا, mulammaᶜ karnā ملمع کرنا
coating *n.* lapēṭ لپیٹ
coax *v.* jhāṁsnā جھانسنا, phuslānā پھسلانا
cobble *v.* ṭānknā ٹانکنا
cobbler *n.* mōcī موچی, cammār چمار
cobra *n.* sānp سانپ, nāg ناگ
cobweb *n.* jālā جالا, makṛī kā jālā مکڑی کا جالا
cock *n.* murġā مرغا
cockroach *n.* til caṭṭā تل چٹا
cod *n.* phalī پھلی
code *n.* kōḍ کوڈ, zābitah ضابطہ
coffee *n.* kōfī کوفی, kāfī کافی, qahvah قہوہ
coffeehouse *n.* qahvah xānah قہوہ خانہ
coffin *n.* tābūt تابوت
cohabit *v.* suḥbat rakhnā صحبت رکھنا
coherent *adj.* caspāṁ چسپاں

cohesion *n.* sanjōg سنجوگ
coil *n.* kunḍal کنڈل, kunḍlī کنڈلی
coiled *adj.* pēcīdah پیچیدہ, pēc dār پیچ دار
coin *n.* sikkah سکہ, paisā پیسا
coincide *v.* mutābiq hōnā مطابق ہونا
coincidence *n.* mutābaqat مطابقت
cold *adj.* ṭhanḍā ٹھنڈا, sard سرد / *n.* ṭhanḍ ٹھنڈ, sardī سردی, zukām زکام
coldness *n.* sardī سردی, ṭhanḍak ٹھنڈک
collapse *v.* girnā گرنا
collar *n.* girēbān گریبان
collateral *adj.* zimnī ضمنی
colleague *n.* jalīs جلیس, šarīk شریک
collect *v.* jamaᶜ karnā جمع کرنا
collection *n.* jamaᶜ جمع, majmūᶜah مجموعہ, jamᶜiyat جمعیت
collective *adj.* jāmiᶜ جامع
college *n.* dars gāh درس گاہ, madrasah مدرسہ
collide *v.* ṭakkar mārnā ٹکر مارنا
collision *n.* ṭakkar ٹکر, tasādum تصادم
colonialism *n.* istiᶜmāriyat استعماریت
colonization *n.* istiᶜmār استعمار
colony *n.* bastī بستی
color *n.* rang رنگ / *v.* rang dēnā رنگ دینا
colored *adj.* rangīn رنگین, rangdār رنگدار
coloring *n.* rang āmēzī رنگ آمیزی
column *n.* sutūn/satūn ستون
comb *n.* kanghā کنگھا, kanghī کنگھی / *v.* kanghī karnā کنگھی کرنا
combat *n.* jang جنگ / *v.* jang karnā جنگ کرنا
combination *n.* ralā رلا
combine *v.* murakkab karnā مرکب کرنا
combustion *n.* sōxtagī سوختگی
come *v.* ānā آنا
comfort *n.* ārām آرام / *v.* ārām dēnā آرام دینا
comfortable *adj.* ārām dēh آرام دہ
comfortless *adj.* dil šikastah دل شکستہ

command *n.* amar امر, farmā'iš فرمائش, farmān فرمان / *v.* farmānā فرمانا, farmā'iš karnā فرمائش کرنا

commander *n.* sālār سالار; *(of an army)* sar xail سر خیل

commander-in-chief *n.* sipah sālār سپہ سالار

commence *v.* šurūᶜ karnā شروع کرنا

commencement *n.* šurūᶜ شروع, mubtadā مبتدا

commentary *n.* tafsīr تفسیر

commentator *n.* šāriḥ شارح, mufassir مفسر

commerce *n.* tijārat تجارت

commercial *adj.* tijāratī تجارتی

commission *n.* dastūrī دستوری, dalālī دلالی

commissioner *n.* vakīl وکیل

commit *v.* macānā مچانا ♦ ~ **a crime** jurm karnā جرم کرنا ♦ ~ **a sin** pāp karnā پاپ کرنا ♦ ~ **suicide** *v.* ḥarām maut marnā حرام موت مرنا, xūd kušī karnā خود کشی کرنا

committee *n.* majlis مجلس, mu'tamar موئتمر

common *adj.* ᶜumūmī عمومی, ᶜām عام

common man *n.* ᶜām ādmī عام آدمی

common people *n.* riᶜāyā رعایا, ᶜavām عوام

common sense *n.* faham-ē-ᶜāmmah فہم عامہ, ᶜaql-ē-salīm, عقل سلیم, sudh budh سدھ بدھ

commonly *adv.* bil-ᶜumūm بالعموم, ᶜumūman عموماً

commotion *n.* tazalzul تزلزل, haijān ہیجان, khalbalī کھلبلی

commutation *n.* bāham tabādalah karnā باہم تبادلہ کرنا, adal badal ادل بدل

commute *v.* adlā badlā karnā ادلا بدلا کرنا

compact *adj.* ṭhōs ٹھوس

companion *n.* sāthī ساتھی

companionship *n.* sāth ساتھ, suḥbat صحبت, musāḥabat مصاحبت

company *n.* suḥbat صحبت, musāḥabat مصاحبت, kampanī کمپنی, širkat شرکت ♦ **keep** ~ *v.* suḥbat rakhnā صحبت رکھنا

compare *v.* mavāznah karnā موازنہ کرنا

comparison *n.* mavāznah موازنہ

compartment *n.* xānah خانہ

compassion *n.* dard mandī درد مندی, raḥm رحم, marḥamat مرحمت

compassionate *adj.* dard mand درد مند, raḥm dil رحم دل, šafīq شفیق
compel *v.* majbūr karnā مجبور کرنا
compensation *n.* harjānah ہرجانہ, jazā جزا, muzd مزد
compete *v.* muqābalah karnā مقابلہ کرنا
competency *n.* ixtiyār اختیار
competent *adj.* ahl اہل, māhir ماہر, ḥāziq حاذق
competition *n.* muqābalah مقابلہ
competitor *n.* raqīb رقیب
compilation *n.* tālīf تالیف
compile *v.* tasnīf karnā تصنیف کرنا
compiler *(of a book) n.* mu'allif مؤلف
complain *v.* šikāyat karnā شکایت کرنا
complaint *n.* šikāyat شکایت
complete *adj.* kāmil کامل, mukammal مکمل, tamām تمام / *v.* takmīl karnā تکمیل کرنا, tamām karnā تمام کرنا
completely *adv.* pūrī taraḥ پوری طرح, tamām-ō-kamāl تمام وکمال
completion *n.* mukammal مکمل, takmīl تکمیل
complexion *n.* ruxsār رخسار, fām فام
compliance *n.* ta^cmīl تعمیل
complicate *v.* uljhānā الجھانا
complicated *adj.* pēcīdah پیچیدہ
complication *n.* pēc پیچ
compliment *n.* salām سلام
comply *v.* bāt rakhnā بات رکھنا
composer *n.* musannif مصنف, bānī بانی
composition *n.* tasnīf تصنیف, ᶜibārat عبارت
compound *n.* murakkab مرکب / *v.* murakkab karnā مرکب کرنا
comprehend *v.* samajhnā سمجھنا, būjhnā بوجھنا
comprehension *n.* samajh سمجھ, būjh بوجھ, samajh būjh سمجھ بوجھ
comprehensive *adj.* jāmiᶜ جامع
compromise *n.* musālaḥat مصالحت, rāzī nāmah راضی نامہ / *v.* musālaḥat karnā مصالحت کرنا
compulsion *n.* majbūrī مجبوری
compulsorily *adv.* majbūran مجبوراً

compulsory *adj.* jabrī جبری, lāzim لازم
compulsory labor *n.* bēgār بیگار
comrade *n.* sāthī ساتھی
conceal *v.* muxfī karnā مخفی کرنا , ixfā' karnā اِخفاء کرنا
concealment *n.* ixfā' اِخفاء, pardah dārī پردہ داری
conceited *adj.* mizaj dār مزاج دار, mudammiġ مدمغ
conceive *v.* būjhnā بوجھنا, qiyās karnā قیاس کرنا
concern *n.* taᶜalluq تعلق
conciliate *v.* manānā منانا
concise *adj.* muxtasar مختصر
conclude *v.* ixtitām karnā اِختتام کرنا, natījah karnā نتیجہ کرنا
conclusion *n.* ixtitām اِختتام, natījah نتیجہ, aṁjām انجام
conclusive *adj.* qataᶜī قطعی
concord *n.* milāp ملاپ, ixtilāt اختلاط
concordant *adj.* dam sāz دم ساز, ham āvāz ہم آواز, ham āhang ہم آہنگ
concubine *n.* dāštah داشتہ
condemn *v.* mazammat karnā مذمت کرنا
condensed milk *n.* māvā ماوا, murtakiz dūdh مرتکز دودھ
condition *n.* ḥālat حالت
conditionally *adv.* mašrūtan مشروطاً, šart kē sāth شرط کے ساتھ
condole *v.* taᶜziyat karnā تعزیت کرنا
condolence *n.* taᶜziyat تعزیت
conduct *n.* calan چلن, cāl calan چال چلن / *v.* pahuṁcānā پہنچانا
conductor *n.* rāhnumā راہنما
confection *n.* murabbā مربی
confectionery *n.* miṭhā'ī مٹھائی
confer *v.* ᶜatā karnā عطا کرنا, marḥamat karnā مرحمت کرنا
conference *n.* jalsah-ē-mušāvarat جلسہ مشاورت, mu'tamar موئتمر
confess *v.* mānnā ماننا
confession *n.* iᶜtirāf اعتراف
confessor *n.* iqbālī اقبالی, iqrārī اقراری
conflict *n.* satēz ستیز
confide (in) *v.* iᶜtibār karnā اعتبار کرنا
confidence *n.* yaqīn یقین, iᶜtimād اعتماد
confident *adj.* rāz dār رازدار

confidential *adj.* muᶜtabar معتبر, muᶜtamad معتمد
confine *v.* maḥdūd karnā محدود کرنا, iḥātah karnā اِحاطہ کرنا
confinement *n.* nazar bandī نظر بندی, qaid قید
confirm *v.* hāmi bhārnā ہامي بھرنا, sābit karnā ثابت کرنا
confirmation *n.* tasdīq تصدیق
confiscate *v.* zabt karnā ضبط کرنا
confiscation *n.* zabtī ضبطی
conflict *n.* tasādum تصادم, parxāš پرخاش, muqātalah مقاتلہ
confluence *(of rivers) n.* sangam سنگم
conform *v.* mutābiq hōnā مطابق ہونا
conformity *n.* mutābaqat مطابقت, muvāfaqat موافقت, zābitagī ضابطگی
confound *v.* māt dēnā مات دینا
confront *v.* sāmnā karnā سامنا کرنا, muqābalah karnā مقابلہ کرنا
confrontation *n.* muqābalah مقابلہ, muvājahah مواجہہ, sāmnā سامنا
confuse *v.* darham barham karnā درہم برہم کرنا, uljhānā الجھانا
confused *adj.* uljhā الجھا, darham barham درہم برہم
confusedly *adv.* haṛbaṛā kar ہڑبڑا کر, muztaribānah مضطربانہ
confusion *n.* uljhan الجھن, ghabrāhaṭ گھبراہٹ
congratulate *v.* mubārāk bādī dēnā مبارک بادی دینا, mubārāk bād kahnā مبارک باد کہنا
congratulations *n.* mubārāk bādī مبارک بادی, tahniyat تہنیت / *interj.* mubārāk مبارک, mubārāk bād مبارک باد
congregation *n.* ijtimāᶜ اِجتماع, aṁjuman انجمن
congress *n.* kāngrēs کانگریس, majlis ᶜāmilah مجلس عاملہ
conical *adj.* maxrūtī مخروطی
conjugate *v.* sīġah gardānnā صیغہ گردانںا
conjugation *n.* tasrīf تصریف
conjunction *n.* rābitah رابطہ, ittisāl اِتصال
conjurer *n.* šuᶜbadah bāz شعبدہ باز
connect *v.* mēl karnā میل رکھنا, jōṛnā جوڑنا.
connected *adj.* marbūt مربوط, vāsil واصل; *(~ with)* mutaᶜalliq متعلق
connection *n.* rabt ربط, taᶜalluq تعلق
conquer *v.* sar karnā سر کرنا, jītnā جیتنا
conqueror *n.* ġāzī غازی

conquest *n.* ġalabah غلبہ, fatḥ فتح
conscience *n.* jī جی, zamīr ضمیر
conscientious *adj.* raušan zamīr روشن ضمیر, īmāndār ایماندار
conscientiously *adv.* īmān sē ایمان سے
consciousness *n.* sudh سدھ
consecutive *adj.* mutarādif مترادف, silsilah vār سلسلہ وار
counsellor *n.* mantarī/mantrī منتری
consent *n.* iqrār اقرار, qabūl/qubūl قبول, ravādārī رواداری, qaul قول / *v.* iqrār karnā اقرار کرنا, muttafiq hōnā متفق ہونا
consenting *adj.* muttafiq متفق
consequence *n.* muzā'iqah مضائقہ, natījah نتیجہ
consequent *adj.* mu'axxar موخر
consequently *adv.* lihazā لہذا, pas پس
conservation *n.* taḥaffuz تحفظ
conservative *adj.* qadāmat pasand قدامت پسند
consider *v.* ġaur karnā غور کرنا, fikr karnā فکر کرنا
considerate *adj.* sanjīdah سنجیدہ, mutasavvar متصور
consideration *n.* mutālaᶜah مطالعہ, mulāḥazah ملاحظہ, murāᶜāt مراعات
consign *v.* supurd karnā سپرد کرنا
consistency *n.* munāsibat مناسبت
consolation *n.* dilāsā دلاسا
consolidation *n.* tašdīd تشدید
consort *n.* jōrū جورو
conspiracy *n.* sāz bāz سازباز, sāziš سازش
conspirator *adj.* sāzišī سازشی
conspire *v.* mansūbah bāndhnā منصوبہ باندھنا
constancy *n.* sabāt ثبات
constant *adj.* rāsix راسخ, sābit ثابت, māmūn مامون
constantly *adv.* har ān ہر آن, lagā tār لگاتار, jam jam جم جم
constellation *n.* kaukab کوکب
consternation *n.* sarāsīmagī سراسیمگی
constipation *n.* qabz قبض
constitution *n.* dastūr دستور, ā'īn آئین, tabīᶜat طبیعت
constitutional *adj.* dastūrī دستوری, tabaᶜī طبعی

constraint *n.* ijbār اِجبار
construct *v.* banānā بنانا
construction *n.* banāvaṭ بناوٹ, sāxt ساخت
consul *n.* qaunsal قونصل
consult *v.* maslaḥat karnā مصلحت کرنا, salāḥ karnā صلاح کرنا, mušvarah karnā مشورہ کرنا
consultation *n.* mušāvarat مشاورت, mušvarah مشورہ, mašvarat مشورت
consume *v.* khānā کھانا, cāṭnā چاٹنا
consumption *n.* khapat کھپت
contagion *n.* sirāyat سرایت
contain *v.* muštamil hōnā مشتمل ہونا
containing *adj.* muštamil مشتمل, ḥāvī حاوی
contamination *n.* chūt چھوت, laus لوث
contemplate *v.* ġōr karnā غور کرنا
contemplation *n.* tasavvuf تصوف; murāqabah مراقبہ
contemporary *adj.* ham ᶜasr ہم عصر
contempt *n.* ḥiqārat حقارت
contemptible *adj.* mubtazal مبتذل, mazmūm مذموم
contend *v.* ḍaṭnā ڈٹنا
content *n.* mazmūn مضمون, iktafā اکتفاء
contention *n.* xusūmat خصومت
contentious *adj.* futūrī فتوری
contentment *n.* qanāᶜat قناعت
contest *n.* mubāḥasah مباحثہ, munāzarah مناظرہ
contested *adj.* mutanāzaᶜ متنازع
context *n.* siyāq-ō-sabāq سیاق وسباق
continent *n.* barr aᶜzam برِاعظم
contingency *n.* vuqūᶜ وقوع
continual *adj.* muttasil متصل, dā'imī دائمی, istimrārī استمراری
continually *adv.* lagā tār لگاتار, hamēšah ہمیشہ
continuance *n.* tasalsul تسلسل, istimrār استمرار
continuation *n.* tavātur تواتر
continue *v.* jārī rahnā جاری رہنا
continuity *n.* ilḥāq الحاق

contortion *n.* pēcīdgī پیچیدگی
contract *n.* muᶜāmalah معاملہ, muᶜāhadah معاہدہ
contraction *n.* qabz قبض, inqibāz انقباض
contractor *n.* muᶜāhid معاہد, mustājir مستاجر
contradict *v.* kāṭ karnā کاٹ کرنا, zidd karnā ضد کرنا
contradiction *n.* takzīb تکذیب, muᶜārizah معارضہ
contrary *adj.* mutanāqis متناقص, mutazād متضاد, xilāf خلاف, muġāyar مغایر
contrast *n.* tazādd تضاد, tanāquz تناقض
contribution *n.* candah چندہ, bihrī بہری
contrivance *n.* ixtirāᶜ اختراع
contrive *v.* ixtirāᶜ karnā اختراع کرنا
control *n.* iḥtisāb احتساب, ixtiyār اختیار / *v.* ixtiyār karnā اختیار کرنا
controversy *n.* qīl-ō-qāl قیل وقال, takrār تکرار
convenience *n.* munāsibat مناسبت, maslaḥat مصلحت
convenient *adj.* munāsib مناسب
convent *n.* xānqāh خانقاہ
convention *n.* majlis مجلس
conversation *n.* bōl cāl بول چال, guftgū گفتگو
converse *v.* bāt cīt karnā بات چیت کرنا, bōlnā calnā بولنا چالنا.
convert *v.* dīn mēṁ milānā دین میں ملانا
convey *v.* pahuṁcānā پہنچانا
convict *v.* mujrim ṭhahrānā مجرم ٹھہرانا
convicted *adv.* mulzam ملزم
convince *v.* qā'il karnā قائل کرنا
convocation *n.* daᶜvat دعوت
cook *n.* bāvarcī باورچی / *v.* pakānā پکانا, paknā پکنا
cooked *adj.* pakkā پکا
cool *adj.* sard سرد, ṭhanḍā ٹھنڈا / *v.* ṭhanḍā karnā ٹھنڈا کرنا
coolie *n.* qulī قلی, bār bardār بار بردار
coolness *n.* ṭhanḍak ٹھنڈک
cooperate *v.* sāth dēnā ساتھ دینا
cooperation *n.* taᶜāvun تعاون, muvālāt موالات
copied *adj.* manqūl منقول
copious *adj.* maufūr موفور

copper *n.* tāmbā تانبا
copulation *n.* jimāᶜ جماع
copy *n.* naql نقل, taqlīd تقلید / *v.* taqlīd karnā تقلید کرنا
copyist *n.* kātib کاتب
coral *n.* mūngā مونگا
cord *n.* ḍōrī ڈوری
cordial *adj.* qalbī قلبی, jānī جانی
cordiality *n.* tapāk تپاک
coriander *n.* dhaniyā دھنیا, kašnīz کشنیز
cork *n.* ḍāt ڈاٹ / *v.* ḍāṭ lagānā ڈاٹ لگانا
corn *n.* anāj اناج
corner *n.* kōnah کونہ, kōnā کونا
coronation *n.* taxt našīnī تخت نشینی
corporeal *adj.* jismānī جسمانی
corpse *n.* maiyyit میت, naᶜš نعش, lāš لاش
corpulence *n.* zaxāmat ضخامت
corpulent *adj.* jasīm جسیم, mōṭā موٹا, zaxīm ضخیم
correct *adj.* durust درست, ṭhīk ٹھیک, saḥīḥ صحیح حسابی / *v.* durust karnā درست کرنا
correction *n.* durustī درستی, islāḥ اصلاح
correctness *n.* durustī درستی
correspondence *n.* byōhār بیوہار
correspondent *n.* rāqim راقم
corresponding *adj.* mutābiq مطابق
corrupt *adj.* fāsidah فاسدہ, luccā لچا ♦ ~ **person** ḥarām xōr حرام خور
cost *n.* xarcah خرچہ, qīmat قیمت / *v.* lagnā لگنا
costly *adj.* qīmatī قیمتی
costume *n.* libās لباس
cottage *n.* kulbah کلبہ
cotton *n.* kapās کپاس, rūʾī روئی
cotton cloth *n.* khādī کھادی
cotton seed *n.* binaulā بنولا
couch *n.* sēj سیج, khāṭ کھاٹ, cār bāliš چار بالش
cough *n.* khāṁsī کھانسی / *v.* khāṁsnā کھانسنا, khāṁsī ānā کھانسی آنا

council *n.* ijmāᶜ اجماع, majlis مجلس, paṁcāyat پنچایت
counsel *n.* mušvarah مشورہ, mašvarat مشورت / *v.* mušvarah dēnā مشورہ دینا
counsellor *n.* mušīr مشیر
count *v.* ginnā گننا, gintī karnā گنتی کرنا
counted *adj.* maḥsūb محسوب, muᶜaddad معدد, maᶜdūd معدود
countenance *n.* sūrat šakl صورت شکل, cēhrah چہرہ
counterfeit *adj.* jaᶜlī جعلی / *n.* jaᶜl جعل, jaᶜlsāzī جعلسازی / *v.* jaᶜlsāzī karnā جعلسازیکرنا
counterfeiting *n.* jaᶜl جعل, jaᶜlsāzī جعلسازی
counterpart *n.* javābī جوابی, jōṛā جوڑا
countless *adj.* arab kharab ارب کھرب
country *n.* mulk ملک, dēs دیس
countryman *n.* ganvār گنوار
countryside *n.* dēhāt دیہات
couple *n.* jōṛā جوڑا
couplet *n.* bayt بیت, šiᶜr شعر
courage *n.* himmat ہمت, jurāt جرات
courageous *adj.* bahādur بہادر, himmatī ہمتی
courageously *adv.* dalērānah دلیرانہ
courier *n.* har kārah ہرکارہ, ḍākiyā ڈاکیا
course *n.* path پتھ daur دور
court *n.* *(royal)* dīvān xānah دیوان خانہ, darbār دربار; *(of arbitration)* paṁcāyat پنچایت; *(of justice)* ᶜadālat عدالت; *(royal)* dīvān دیوان
courteous *adj.* latīf لطیف, šā'istah شائستہ
courtesy *n.* rmudārāt مدارات, navāziš نوازش, lutf لطف
courtier *n.* darbārī درباری, nadīm ندیم
courtship *n.* ᶜāšiqī عاشقی
courtyard *n.* āngan آنگن, angnā'ī انگنائی, saḥn صحن
cousin *n.* kazin کزن
cover *n.* ġilāf غلاف, xōl خول, sar pōš سرپوش, lifāfah لفافہ, tabaq طبق / *v.* ḍhānknā ڈھانکنا
covering *n.* satr ستر
coverlet *n.* razā'ī رضائی
covet *v.* lalcānā للچانا

cow *n.* gā'ē گائے
coward *n.* buz dil بز دل
cowardly *adj.* gīdī گیدی
cowherd *n.* gūjar گوجر, gvālā گوالا, ghōsī گھوسی
coxcomb *n.* chailā چھیلا
crab *n.* kēkṛā کیکڑا
crack *n.* khaḍ کھڈ, phūṭ پھوٹ, raxnah رخنہ / *v.* caṭakna چٹکنا, caṭaxnā چٹخنا, carcarānā چرچرانا
crackle *v.* caṭakna چٹکنا, caṭaxnā چٹخنا, carcarānā چرچرانا, kaṛaknā کڑکنا
crackling *adj.* bhurburā بھربھرا
cradle *n.* gahvārah گہوارہ
craft *n.* fann فن, ḥirfat حرفت
craftsman *n.* pēšah var پیشہ ور, dast kār دست کار
cram *v.* rēlnā ریلنا, khacā khac bharnā کھچا کھچ بھرنا, ghusēṛnā گھسیڑنا
crane *n.* sāras سارس, baglā بگلا
cranium *n.* khōpṛī کھوپڑی
crash *n.* dhamākah دھماکہ / *v.* phūṭnā پھوٹنا
crawl *v.* rēngnā/rīngnā رینگنا
craze *n.* lagan لگن
crazy *adj.* dīvānā دیوانا, pāgal پاگل
creak *v.* carcarānā چرچرانا
crease *n.* šikan شکن / *v.* šikan ḍālnā شکن ڈالنا
create *v.* paidā karnā پیدا کرنا, banānā بنانا
creation *n.* paidā'iš پیدائش, āfrīniš آفرینش
creator *n.* bārī باری, xāliq خالق, xudā خدا, xalāq خلاق
creature *n.* maxlūq مخلوق
credentials *n.* sanad سند
credible *adj.* qābil-ē-iᶜtibār قابل اعتبار, muᶜtabar معتبر
credit *n.* udhār ادھار, vām وام, sākh ساکھ
creditor *n.* qarz xvāh قرض خواہ
credulous *adj.* kān kā kaccā کان کا کچا
creed *n.* ᶜaqīdah عقیدہ
creek *n.* khāṛī کھاڑی, khāl کھال

creep *v.* rēngnā/rīngnā رینگنا, sarsarānā سرسرانا
crematorium *n.* masān مسان
crescent *n.* hilāl ہلال
crest *n.* mukaṭ مکٹ, kalġī کلغی
crime *n.* jurm جرم ♦ **capital** ~ sangīn jurm سنگین جرم ♦ **commit a** ~ jurm karnā جرم کرنا
criminal *adj.* mujrimānah مجرمانہ / *n.* mujrim مجرم, gunāh gār گناہ گار ♦ ~ **case** fauj dārī فوج داری ♦ ~ **court** fauj dārī فوج داری ♦ ~ **procedure code** zābitah-ē-fauj dāri ضابطہ فوج داری
crispy *adj.* kurkurā کرکرا, bhurburā بھربھرا
criteria *n.* miᶜyār معیار
critic *n.* saxun cīṁ سخن چیں
criticism *n.* tanqīd تنقید
criticize *v.* tanqīd karnā تنقید کرنا
croak *v.* ṭarrānā ٹرانا
crocodile *n.* magar مگر
crook *n.* bad mᶜāš بدمعاش
crooked *adj.* xamīdah خمیدہ, maᶜvajj معوج
crookedness *n.* xamīdagī خمیدگی
cross *n.* salīb صلیب / *v.* pār karnā پار کرنا
crossing *n.* ᶜubūr عبور
crossroads *n.* cauk چوک
crossword *n.* muᶜammah معمہ
crouch *v.* dubaknā دبکنا
crow *n.* kavvā کوا, kāg کاگ
crowd *n.* jamᶜiyat جمعیت, hujūm ہجوم
crowded *adj.* khacā khac کھچا کھچ
crown *n.* tāj تاج; *(of the head)* ṭāṛ ٹانٹ
crucified *adj.* maslūb مصلوب
crucifix *n.* salīb صلیب
crucifixion *n.* taslīb تصلیب
crude *adj.* xām خام
cruel *adj.* zālimānah ظالمانہ
cruelty *n.* bē raḥmī بے رحمی, saxtī سختی

crunch *v.* cābnā چابنا
crusade *n.* dīnī laṛā'ī دینی لڑائی
crusaders *n.* mujāhidīn مجاہدین
crush *v.* kucalnā کچلنا
crust *n.* chilkā چھلکا
cry *n.* pukār پکار / *v.* rōnā رونا
crystal *n.* billaur بلور, šīšah شیشہ
crystal palace *n.* šīš maḥal شیش محل
cubic *adj.* mukaᶜab مکعب
cubit *n.* zirāᶜ ذراع
cucumber *n.* xiyār خیار
cudgel *n.* gatkā گتکا, lāṭhī لاٹھی
culpable *adj.* zamīm ذمیم
culprit *n.* gunāh gār گناہ گار
cultivate *v.* kāšt karnā کاشت کرنا
cultivation *n.* kāšt کاشت, kāšt kārī کاشت کاری
cultivator *n.* kāšt kār کاشت کار, kisān کسان
cultural *adj.* saqāfatī ثقافتی
culture *n.* saqāfat ثقافت
cultured *adj.* muhazzab مہذب
cumin *n.* jīrā جیرا, zīrah زیرہ
cunning *adj.* ᶜayyār عیار, dil farēb دل فریب / *n.* ᶜayyārī عیاری
cup *n.* piyālah پیالہ
cupboard *n.* almārī الماری
cupidity *n.* haukā ہوکا
curative *adj.* siḥḥat baxš صحت بخش
curb *v.* lagām dēnā لگام دینا
curd *n.* dahī دہی, dōġ دوغ, māvā ماوا
cure *n.* ᶜilāj علاج
cure *v.* ᶜilāj karnā علاج کرنا, muᶜālajah karnā معالجہ کرنا, tandurust karnā تندرست کرنا
curiosity *n.* tajassus تجسس, havas ہوس
curious *adj.* havas nāk ہوس ناک
curl *n.* zulf زلف, kākul کاکل, xam خم, kunḍal کنڈل
currants *n.* kišmiš کشمش

current *adj.* jārī جاری, muravvaj مروج / *n.* dhār دھار, rau رو, rūd/rōd رود, sail سیل
curry *n.* kaṛhī کڑھی
curse *n.* laᶜnat لعنت / *v.* kōsnā کوسنا, phiṭkārnā پھٹکارنا
cursed *adj.* laᶜnatī لعنتی, malᶜūn ملعون
curtain *n.* pardah پردہ, ḥijāb حجاب
curve *n.* xam خم
cushion *n.* gaddī گدی, takiyah تکیہ
custard apple *n.* šarīfah شریفہ
custody *n.* phāṭak bandī پھاٹک بندی, ḥavālāt حوالات, muḥāfazat محافظت
custom *n.* rasm رسم, rivāj رواج, rasm-ō-rivāj رسم و رواج, ᶜādat عادت
customarily *adv.* badastūr بدستور
customary *adj.* rasmī رسمی, rivājī رواجی
customer *n.* xarīdār خریدار, gāhak گاہک
customs *n.* kasṭam کسٹم
cut *n.* kāṭ کاٹ, kaṭā'ō کٹاؤ / *v.* kāṭnā کاٹنا, kāṭ karnā کاٹ کرنا
cynic *n.* xušk خشک
cynical *adj.* turš rū ترش رو
cynicism *n.* xuškī خشکی

D

daddy *n.* pāpā پاپا, bābā بابا
dagger *n.* xanjar خنجر
daily *adj.* rōz ba-rōz روز بروز, rōzānah روزانہ ♦ ~ **wages** rōzīnah روزینہ
dam *n.* band بند, pāl پال
damage *n.* zarar ضرر, mazarrat مضرت, harjah ہرجہ, xasārah خسارہ / *v.* zarar pahuṁcānā ضرر پہنچانا
damp *adj.* martūb مرطوب, bhījā بھیجا, gīlā گیلا
dampness *n.* rutūḇat رطوبت, gīlāpan گیلاپن
dance *n.* raqs رقص / *v.* nācnā ناچنا
dancer *n.* raqqās رقاص
dancing *n.* raqs رقص
danger *n.* xatar خطر, xatrah خطرہ
dangerous *adj.* xatarnāk خطرناک
dangle *v.* laṭaknā لٹکنا, jhulānā جھلانا
dare *v.* dalērī karnā دلیری کرنا, jurāt karnā جرات کرنا
daring *adj.* himmatī ہمتی, dalēr دلیر, jān bāz جان باز
dark *adj.* andhērā اندھیرا, muzlim مظلم, tārīk تاریک; *(skin color)* ābnūsī آبنوسی
dark-colored *adj.* sānvlā سانولا
darken *v.* andhēr karnā اندھیر کرنا
darkness *n.* andhērā اندھیرا, andhērī اندھیری, tārīkī تاریکی
darling *n.* maḥbūbah محبوبہ, maḥbūb محبوب
darn *v.* rafū karnā رفو کرنا
dart *v.* phēnknā پھینکنا
dash *v.* paṭaknā پٹکنا
date *n.* *(calendar)* tārīx تاریخ; *(dried fruit)* chu'ārā چھوارا; *(fruit)* khajūr کھجور, xurmā خرما ♦ ~ **tree** khajūr کھجور
dated *adv.* mu'arraxah مورخہ
daughter *n.* bēṭī بیٹی
daughter-in-law *(son's wife)* *n.* bahū بہو
dawn *n.* fajr فجر, savērā سویرا, subḥ صبح / *v.* subḥ hōnā صبح ہونا
day *n.* din دن, rōz/rūz روز

daybreak *n.* savērā سویرا, subḥ صبح
daylight *n.* ujālā اجالا
dazzle *v.* jagmagānā جگمگانا
dead *adj.* murdah مردہ, marā مرا
dead body *n.* maiyyit میت, lāš لاش
deadlock *n.* jamūd جمود
deadly *adj.* qātil قاتل, kārī کاری
deaf *adj.* bahrā بہرا ♦ ~ **man/woman** bahrā
dealer *n.* byōpārī بیوپاری, bāyaᶜ بایع
dear *adj.* piyārā پیارا ᶜazīz عزیز, maḥbūb محبوب ♦ ~ **sir** *interj.* janāb-ē-man جناب من
dearth *n.* girānī گرانی
death *n.* maut موت
debate *n.* mubāḥasah مباحثہ
debauchery *n.* avbāšī اوباشی
debility *n.* kamzōrī کمزوری
debit *n.* uthā'ō اتھاو
debris *n.* malbah ملبہ
debt *n.* qarz قرض
debtor *n.* qarz dār قرض دار
decampment *n.* kūc کوچ
decay *n.* zavāl زوال, firsudagī فرسودگی / *v.* saṛnā سڑنا, chījnā چھیجنا
deceased *adj.* marḥūm مرحوم
deceit *n.* dhōkā دھوکا, farēb فریب
deceitful *adj.* farēbī فریبی
deceitfully *adv.* ḥīlatan حیلتاً
deceitfulness *n.* makkārī مکاری, daġā bāzī دغا بازی
deceive *v.* dhōkā dēnā دھوکا دینا, farēb dēnā فریب دینا
deceiver *n.* jhāṁsū جھانسو, kīmiyā gar کیمیا بنانا, dajjāl دجال
December *n.* disambar دسمبر
decency *n.* šā'istagī شائستگی
decent *adj.* nafīs نفیس
deception *n.* farēb فریب, dhōkā دھوکا
deceptive *adj.* dil farēb دل فریب

decide *v.* tē karnā طے کرنا, faisalah karnā فیصلہ کرنا
decided *adj.* tē šudah طے شدہ
decision *n.* faislah فیصلہ
decisive *adj.* faislah kun فیصلہ کن, qātiᶜ قاطع, qataᶜī قطعی
deck *n.* ᶜaršah عرشہ
declaration *n.* iᶜlān اعلان, bayān بیان
declare *v.* iᶜlān karnā اعلان کرنا, bayān karnā بیان کرنا ♦ ~ **war** laṛā'ī ṭhānnā لڑائی ٹھاننا
decline *n.* tanazzul تنزل, hubūt ہبوط, utār اُتار / *v.* hicaknā ہچکنا, tanazzul hōnā تنزل ہونا
decompose *v.* saṛnā سڑنا
decorate *v.* sajānā سجانا
decoration *n.* sajāvaṭ سجاوٹ
decrease *n.* kamī کمی, taxfīf تخفیف
decrease *v.* ghaṭnā گھٹنا, ghaṭānā گھٹانا, taxfīf karnā تخفیف کرنا
decree *n.* ḥukm nāmah حکم نامہ
dedicated *adj.* maᶜnūn معنون
dedication *n.* intisāb انتساب
deduct *v.* vazaᶜ karnā وضع کرنا, kam karnā کم کرنا
deduction *n.* kāṭ کاٹ, katar bēvant کتر بیونت, vazaᶜ وضع
deed *n.* kām کام, kartūt کرتوت, kirdār کردار ♦ **good** ~ iḥsān اِحسان
deep *adj.* gahrā گہرا
deer *n.* mirg مرگ, hiran ہرن, sābar سابر
deface *v.* bigāṛnā بگاڑنا
defamation *n.* tauhīn توہین, bad nāmī بد نامی
defame *v.* bad nām karnā بد نام کرنا
defeat *n.* šikast شکست / *v.* šikast dēnā شکست دینا
defect *n.* bigāṛ بگاڑ, qabāḥat قباحت, nuqsān نقصان / *v.* dušman sē jā milnā دشمن سے جا ملنا
defection *n.* maᶜsiyat معصیت
defective *adj.* khōṭā کھوٹا, maᶜyūb معیوب
defend *v.* ḥimāyat karnā حمایت کرنا
defendant *n.* muddaᶜā ᶜalaih مدعا علیہ
defender *n.* nāsir ناصر, ḥimāyatī حمایتی, ḥāmī حامی

defense *n.* ᶜismat عصمت , ḥimāyat حمایت
deficiency *n.* nuqsān نقصان, nuqs نقص
deficient *adj.* zā'il زائل, qāsir قاصر, manqūs منقوص
deficit *n.* kamī کمی
defilement *n.* chūt چھوت
definite *adj.* yaqīnī یقینی, qātiᶜ قاطع
definitely *adv.* lā maḥālah لا محالہ
definition *n.* taᶜrīf تعریف
deflect *v.* inḥirāf karnā انحراف کرنا
deflection *n.* inḥirāf انحراف
deformity *n.* qubḥ قبح
degrade *v.* maᶜzūl karnā معزول کرنا
degree *n.* ḍigrī ڈگری, darjah درجہ
degree-holder *n.* ḍigrī dār ڈگری دار
deity *n.* qahhār قہار
dejected *adj.* šōrīdah شوریدہ, matrūḥ مطروح, malūl ملول
delay *n.* dēr دیر, tā'axur تأخر / *v.* dēr lagānā دیر لگانا, tavaqquf karnā توقف کرنا
delegate *n.* nā'ib نائب, muxtār مختار
delegation *n.* vafd وفد
deliberately *adv.* irādatan ارادةً, bil-irādah بالارادہ
delicacy *n.* nazākat نزاکت, subkī سبکی
delicate *adj.* patlā پتلا, latīf لطیف, kōmal کومل
delicious *adj.* mazēdār مزیدار, xūšgavār خوشگوار
deliciousness *n.* mazah مزہ, latāfat لطافت
delight *n.* niᶜmat نعمت , xūšnūdī خوشنودی, šiguftagī شگفتگی / *v.* šād kārnā شاد کرنا
delightful *adj.* xurram خرم, bēš بیش
delirium *n.* sarsām سرسام
deliver *v.* farāham karnā فراہم کرنا, ḥavālē karnā حوالے کرنا; *(~ a child)* baccah jannā بچہ جننا, paidā karnā پیدا کرنا
deliverance *n.* falāḥ فلاح, maġfirat مغفرت
delivery *n.* vazaᶜ-ē-ḥaml وضع حمل
delude *v.* muġālatah dēnā مغالطہ دینا, muġālatah ḍālnā مغالطہ ڈالنا
delusion *n.* muġālatah مغالطہ

demand *n.* talab طلب, daᶜvā دعویٰ / *v.* māngnā مانگنا
demise *n.* vafāt وفات
democracy *n.* jumhūrī sultanat جمہوری سلطنت
demolish *v.* tōṛnā توڑنا, ujāṛnā اجاڑنا
demolition *n.* inhidām انہدام
demon *n.* bhūt بھوت, dē'ō دیو
demonstration *n.* burhān برہان, muzāharah مظاہرہ
den *n.* kahaf کہف
denial *n.* inkār انکار, ibā اِبا
denomination *n.* ism اسم
dense *adj.* guṁjān گنجان, ganghōr گھنگھور, kasīf کثیف
density *n.* taksīf تکثیف, kasāfat کثافت
dentist *n.* dāntōṁ kā ḍākṭar دانتوں کا ڈاکٹر, ḍēnṭisṭ ڈینٹسٹ
denunciation *n.* vaᶜīd وعید
deny *v.* inkār karnā انکار کرنا
depart *v.* ruxsat hōnā رخصت ہونا
departed *adj.* ravānah روانہ, raftah رفتہ
department *n.* daftar دفتر, šuᶜbah شعبہ
departure *n.* ravāngī روانگی, ruxsat رخصت
dependence *n.* madār مدار, iᶜtimād اعتماد
dependent *adj.* munḥasir منحصر, mauqūf موقوف, mā taḥat ماتحت
deposit *n.* amānī امانی
deposition *n.* maᶜzūlī معزولی
depravity *n.* gum rāhī گم راہی, avbāšī اوباشی
depressed *adj.* udās اداس
depression *n.* afsurdagī افسردگی, udāsī اداسی
depth *n.* gahrā'ī گہرائی
deputy *n.* nā'ib نائب
dervish *n.* darvēš درویش
descend *v.* utarnā اترنا, utarānā اُترانا
descendant *n.* aulād اولاد
descent *n.* hubūt ہبوط, utār اُتار, nuzūl نزول, tanazzul تنزل
describe *v.* bayān karnā بیان کرنا, samjhānā سمجھانا
description *n.* bayān بیان

desert *n.* rēgistān ریگستان / *v.* qataᶜ-ē-taᶜlluq karnā قطع تعلق کرنا
deserted *adj.* ujāṛ اجاڑ, barbād برباد, hijrān zadah ہجراں زدہ
desertion *n.* tark ترک, hijr ہجر, muhājarat مہاجرت
deserve *v.* qābil hōnā قابل ہونا
deserving *adj.* qābil قابل, mustaḥiqq مستحق
design *n.* mansūbah منصوبہ
designation *n.* ᶜuhdah عہدہ, ādāb-ō-alqāb آداب والقاب
desirable *adj.* marġūb مرغوب
desire *n.* irādah ارادہ, raġbat رغبت, xvāhiš خواہش / *v.* irādah karnā ارادہ کرنا, raġbat karnā رغبت کرنا
desist *v.* bas karnā بس کرنا
desolate *adj.* ujṛā اُجڑا
desolation *n.* vīrānī ویرانی
despair *n.* yās یاس, māyūsī مایوسی / *v.* nā ummīd karnā نا امید کرنا, paizār par marnā پیزار پر مرنا
desperate *adj.* māyūs مایوس
despicable *adj.* ḥaqīr حقیر
despot *n.* jābir جابر
despotic *adj.* jābir جابر, mutasallit متسلط
despotism *n.* istibdād استبداد, firᶜaunī فرعونی
destiny *n.* taqdīr تقدیر
destitute *adj.* maflūk مفلوک, nā cār نا چار
destitution *n.* nā cārī نا چاری
destroy *v.* barbād karnā برباد کرنا
destruction *n.* barbādī بربادی
destructive *adj.* muhlik مہلک, tabāh kun تباہ کن
detailed *adj.* mufassal مفصل
detain *v.* rōknā روکنا, muᶜattal karnā معطل کرنا
detective *n.* kāšif کاشف, surāġ rasāṛ سراغ رساں
deteriorate *v.* bigāṛnā بگاڑنا
deterioration *n.* bigāṛ بگاڑ
determination *n.* tahiyyah تہیہ, ᶜazīmat عزیمت, asālat اصالت, mansūbah منصوبہ
determine *v.* mansūbah bāndhnā منصوبہ باندھنا, tahiyyah karnā تہیہ کرنا
detestable *adj.* qabīḥ قبیح

dethrone *v.* gaddī sē utārnā گدی سے اتارنا
devastate *v.* ujāṛnā اجاڑنا, tārāj karnā تاراج کرنا
devastation *n.* pāmālī پامالی, tārāj تاراج
develop *v.* baṛhnā بڑھنا, baṛhānā بڑھانا
development *n.* taraqqī ترقی
deviate *v.* tajāvuz karnā تجاوز کرنا
deviation *n.* tajāvuz تجاوز
devil *n.* šaitān شیطان
devilish *adj.* šaitānī شیطانی
devote (oneself) *v.* fidā karnā فدا کرنا
devotee *n.* zāhid زاہد, sālik سالک,
devotion *n.* zāhidī زاہدی, zuhd زہد, fidā فدا, parastiš پرستش
devour *v.* bhasaknā بھسکنا, bhanbōṛnā بھنبوڑنا
devout *adj.* xudā parast خداپرست, taqī تقی, ᶜārif عارف
dew *n.* šabnam شبنم
diabolical *adj.* šaitānī شیطانی
diagnose *v.* tašxīs karnā تشخیص کرنا
diagnosis *n.* tašxīs تشخیص
diagonal *adj.* āṛā آڑا
dialect *n.* bōl cāl بول چال, bōlī بولی.
dialogue *n.* mukālamah مکالمہ
diamond *n.* hīrā ہیرا
diarrhea *n.* ishāl اسہال, pēciš پیچش
diary *n.* rōz nāmcah روزنامچہ, bahī بہی
dice *n.* pāsā پاسا, qimār قمار
dictate *v.* likhānā لکھانا
dictatorship *n.* āmiriyat آمریت
diction *n.* ᶜibārat عبارت
dictionary *n.* luġat لغت
die *v.* marnā مرنا, mar jānā مرجانا
diet *n.* ġizā غذا
difference *n.* farq فرق, ixtilāf اختلاف
different *adj.* muxtalif مختلف, alag الگ
difficult *adj.* muškil مشکل

difficulty *n.* dušvārī دشواری, muškil مشکل, taklīf تکلیف
dig *v.* khōdnā کھودنا
digest *v.* hazm karnā ہضم کرنا
digestible *adj.* hāzim ہاضم
digestion *n.* hāzimah ہاضمہ
digestive system *n.* nizām-ē-hāzimah نظام ہاضمہ
digger *n.* bēldār بیلدار
dignified *adj.* mufaxxar مفخر, ᶜazīm-ul-šān عظیم الشان
dignity *n.* vaqār وقار
dike *n.* band بند
dilemma *n.* šāxsānah شاخسانہ, maxmaṣah مخمصہ
diligence *n.* tandihī تندہی, jānfišānī جانفشانی
dim *adj.* mānd ماند, dhundlā دھندلا / *v.* andhēr karnā اندھیر کرنا
dimension *n.* misāhat مساحت, miqdār مقدار
diminish *v.* kam karnā کم کرنا, ghaṭānā گھٹانا
diminution *n.* kamī کمی, taxfīf تخفیف
dimness *n.* dhundlāpan دھندلاپن
dinner *n.* rāt kā khānā رات کا کھانا
dip *n.* ḍubkī ڈبکی / *v.* ḍubkī dēnā ڈبکی دینا
diploma *n.* manšūr منشور, tamġah تمغہ
direct *adj.* sīdhā سیدھا, mustaqīm مستقیم / *v.* patā dēnā پتا دینا
direction *n.* rux رخ, taraf طرف
directness *n.* sīdh سیدھ
director *n.* nāzim ناظم
directory *n.* ḍā'irēkṭrī ڈائریکٹری
dirt *n.* gandagī گندگی
dirtiness *n.* mailā pan میلاپن
dirty *adj.* gandah گندہ, mailā میلا
disabled *adj.* apāhaj اپاہج, lā cār لاچار
disagree *v.* muxālafat karnā مخالفت کرنا
disagreeable *adj.* nā pasand ناپسند
disagreement *n.* nā ittifāqi نا اتفاقی
disappear *v.* kāfūr hō jānā کافور ہوجانا, chupnā چھپنا
disappoint *v.* māyūs kārnā مایوس کرنا

disappointed *adj.* māyūs مایوس
disappointment *n.* māyūsī مایوسی
disapproval *n.* nā pasandīdagī ناپسندیدگی
disaster *n.* musībat مصیبت
disbelief *n.* ilḥād الحاد
discernment *n.* tamīz تمیز, imtiyāz امتیاز, firāsat فراست
discharge *n.* xulāsī خلاصی, xalās خلاص / *v.* xalās karnā خلاص کرنا, xārij karnā خارج کرنا
disciple *n.* šāgird شاگرد
discipline *n.* riyāzat ریاضت, tādīb تادیب
disciplined *adj.* mu'addab مؤدب
discomfort *n.* qalaq قلق
disconnect *v.* munqatiᶜ karnā منقطع کرنا
disconnection *n.* muqātaᶜah مقاطعہ
discontent *n.* nā rāzī ناراضی
discontinuance *n.* ᶜadam عدم
discord *n.* nā ittifāqi نااتفاقی
discount *n.* sarrāfī صرافی, kamīšan کمیشن
discourage *v.* kamar tōṛnā کمر توڑنا
discourse *n.* taqrīr تقریر, kalām کلام
discover *v.* daryāft karnā دریافت کرنا, maᶜlūm karnā معلوم کرنا
discovery *n.* daryāft دریافت
discreet *adj.* hōšmand ہوشمند
discrepancy *n.* tanāquz تناقض
discrete *adj.* salīqah dār سلیقہ دار
discretion *n.* tamīz تمیز, hōš ہوش
discriminate *v.* imtiyāz karnā امتیاز کرنا
discrimination *n.* imtiyāz امتیاز, tašaxxus تشخص
discuss *v.* baḥas karnā بحث کرنا, kalām karnā کلام کرنا
discussion *n.* baḥas بحث
disdain *n.* ḥiqārat حقارت, taḥqīr تحقیر
disdain *v.* hōnṭ nikālnā ہونٹ نکالنا, ihānat karnā اہانت کرنا
disdainful *adj.* mutakabbir متکبر
disease *n.* bimārī بیماری

diseased *adj.* maᶜlūl معلول
disentangle *v.* suljhānā سلجھانا
disfigure *v.* šakl bigāṛnā شکل بگاڑنا , rūp bigāṛnā روپ بگاڑنا
disgrace *n.* bē ᶜizzat بیعزت, šarmindagī شرمندگی / *v.* šakl bigāṛnā شکل بگاڑنا, hatak ᶜizzat karnā ہتک عزت کرنا, ᶜizzat bigāṛnā عزت بگاڑنا
disgraceful *adj.* zalīl ذلیل
disguise *n.* savāng سوانگ / *v.* bhēs badalnā بھیس بدلنا
disgust *n.* karāhat کراہت
disgusting *adj.* nā xūšgavār نا خوشگوار
dish *n.* qāb قاب, rakābī رکابی
dishearten *v.* dil tōṛnā دل توڑنا
dishonest *adj.* farēbī فریبی, bē imān بے ایمان
dishonesty *n.* bē imānī بے ایمانی, bē iᶜtibārī بے اعتباری
dishonor *n.* bē ᶜizzatī بے عزتی, rusvā'ī رسوائی / *v.* bē ᶜizzatī karnā بے عزتی کرنا
disinclination *n.* tāmmul تامل
dislike *n.* nā pasandīdagī ناپسندیدگی / *v.* nā pasand karnā ناپسند کرنا
dislocation *(of a bone) n.* haḍḍī kā utarnā ہڈی کا اترنا, infikāk انفکاک
dislodge *v.* ukhāṛna اکھاڑنا
disloyal *adj.* bāġī باغی, namak ḥarām نمک حرام, ġaddār غدار
disloyalty *n.* ġaddārī غداری
dismay *v.* kamar tōṛnā کمر توڑنا
dismiss *v.* barxāst karnā برخاست کرنا
dismissal *n.* barxāst برخاست, barxāstgī برخاستگی
disobedience *n.* maᶜsiyat معصیت, tamarrud تمرد, vādī وادی
disobedient *adj.* ᶜāqq عاق, namak ḥarām نمک حرام, muᶜānid معاند
disobey *v.* xilāf-ē-varzī karnā خلافِ ورزی کرنا, haṭ karnā ہٹ کرنا
disorder *n.* gaṛbaṛ گڑبڑ, hangāmah ہنگامہ, khalbalī کھلبلی
disown *v.* munkir hōnā منکر ہونا
dispatch *n.* ravāngī روانگی, cābukī چابکی / *v.* ravānah karnā روانہ کرنا, bhējnā بھیجنا
dispatched *adj.* ravānah روانہ
dispel *v.* dūr karnā دور کرنا
disperse *v.* bikhairnā بکھیرنا
dispersion *n.* intišār انتشار, namūd نمود, dikhāvaṭ دکھاوٹ, dikhāvah دکھاوہ

display *v.* dikhānā دکھانا, dikhlānā دکھلانا
displease *v.* ranjīdah karnā رنجیدہ کرنا, āzurdah karnā آزردہ کرنا
displeasure *n.* xafgī خفگی, nā rāzī نا راضی
disposal *n.* farōxt فروخت
dispose *v.* rafa^c dafa^c karnā رفع دفع کرنا, pattā kāṭnā پتا کاٹنا, bhugtānā بھگتانا
disposed *adj.* muntašir منتشر
disposition *n.* xū خو, tīnat طینت, mizāj مزاج
dispossess *v.* dūr karnā دور کرنا
dispute *n.* baḥas بحث, jhagṛā جھگڑا / *v.* baḥas karnā بحث کرنا, jhagaṛnā جھگڑنا
disputed *adj.* mutanāza^c متنازع
disregard *v.* phēnknā پھینکنا
disreputable *adj.* bad nām بدنام
disrespect *n.* ^cadam iḥtirām عدم احترام, gustāxī گستاخی, hatak ہتک / *v.* bē adabī karnā بے ادبی کرنا, gustāxī karnā گستاخی کرنا
disrespectful *adj.* bad liḥāz بد لحاظ, gustāx گستاخ
dissatisfied *adj.* ġair mutma'in غیر مطمئن,
dissect *v.* taqtī^c karnā تقطیع کرنا
dissection *n.* taqtī^c تقطیع
dissenter *n.* mu^ctazil معتزل
dissolute *n.* avbāš اوباش
dissolve *v.* ḥall karnā حل کرنا
dissolved *adj.* ḥall hō gayā حل ہوگیا
distance *n.* masāfat مسافت, dūrī دوری, fāsilah فاصلہ
distant *adj.* dūr دور
distill *v.* ṭapkānā ٹپکانا
distillation *n.* ṭapkā'ō ٹپکاؤ
distinct *adj.* lafzī لفظی, judā جدا
distinction *n.* imtiyāz امتیاز
distinctly *adv.* lafzan لفظاً
distinguish *v.* imtiyāz karnā امتیاز کرنا
distinguished *adj.* mumtāz ممتاز
distract *v.* maġz khānā مغز کھانا
distracted *adj.* figār فگار, bē ḥavās بے حواس
distractedly *adv.* muztaribānah مضطربانہ

distraction *n.* ḥairānā حیرانی, bē ḥavāsī بے حواسی
distress *n.* pēc-ō-tāb پیچ و تاب dukh دکھ, parēšānī پریشانی
distressed *adj.* xastah ḥāl خستہ حال, āšuftah ḥāl آشفتہ حال, parēšān پریشان
distribute *v.* bānṭnā بانٹنا
distributor *n.* taqsīm kunindah تقسیم کنندہ, qasīm قسیم
district *n.* mauzaᶜ موضع, zilaᶜ ضلع, muḥallah محلہ, xittah خطہ
distrust *n.* gumān گمان, ištibāh اشتباہ
distrustful *adj.* bad gumān بدگمانی
disturb *v.* xalal ḍālnā خلل ڈالنا
disturbance *n.* xalal خلل
disturbant *adj.* parēšān kun پریشان کن, dangalī دنگلی
disturbed *adj.* parāgandah پراگندہ
disturber *n.* muxill مخل
disunity *n.* nifāq نفاق
ditch *n.* xandaq خندق, khāʾī کھائی
dive *n.* ḍubkī ڈبکی, ġōtah غوطہ / *v.* ḍubkī lagānā ڈبکی لگانا, ġōtah mārnā غوطا مارنا
diverse *adj.* muxtalif مختلف
diversion *n.* kalōl کلول
diversity *n.* tanavvōᶜ تنوع
divert *v.* bahlānā بہلانا
divide *v.* taqsīm karnā تقسیم کرنا
divided *adj.* maqsūm مقسوم, munqasim منقسم, munfasil منفصل
divider *n.* qasīm قسیم
divine *adj.* muqaddas مقدس ♦ ~ **power** qudrat قدرت
divinity *n.* xudāʾī خدائی, ḥaqqāniyat حقانیت
division *n.* qism قسم, taqsīm تقسیم; *(of a province)* taᶜalluqah تعلقہ
divorce *n.* talāq طلاق, chūṭ چھوٹ / *v.* talāq dēnā طلاق دینا
Diwali *n.* dīvālī دیوالی
do *v.* karnā کرنا
dockyard *n.* ᶜaršah عرشہ
doctor *n.* ḍākṭar ڈاکٹر, tabīb طبیب; *(of Ayurveda)* vaid وید
doctrine *n.* ᶜaqīdah عقیدہ, usūl اصول
document *n.* dastāvēz دستاویز, navišt نوشت, taḥrīr تحریر / *v.* taḥrīr karnā تحریر کرنا
doe *n.* harnī ہرنی

doer *n.* fāᶜil فاعل
dog *n.* kuttā کتا
dogmatic *adj.* šaraᶜī شرعی
doll *n.* guṛiyā گڑیا
dollar *n.* ḍālar ڈالر
dome *n.* gumbad گنبد
domestic *adj.* gharēlū گھریلو ♦ ~ **quarrel** *n.* gharēlū jhagṛā گھریلو جھگڑا
dominant *adj.* mumtāz ممتاز, ammārah امارہ
domination *n.* tasallut تسلط
dominion *n.* vilāyat ولایت, siyādat سیادت, riyāsat ریاست
donation *n.* dān دان, bēlā بیلا
done *adj.* xatm ختم
donkey *n.* gadhā گدھا
donor *n.* baxšindah بخشندہ
doom *n.* ā'ī آئی
doomsday *n.* yaum-ul-ḥisāb یوم الحساب
door *n.* dar در, darvāzah دروازہ
dot *n.* nuqtah نقطہ
double *adj.* dūhrā/dōhrā/dō harā دوہرا, dugnā دگنا
doubt *n.* šakk شک / *v.* šakk karnā شک کرنا
doubtful *adj.* mutašakkī متشکی, maškūk مشکوک, šakkī شکی
doubtless *adv.* šakk kē baġair شک کے بغیر
dove *n.* fāxtah فاختہ
down *adj.* girā hū'ā گرا ہوا, farō/firō فرو / *adv.* nīcē نیچے talē تلے, farōd فرود
♦ **take** ~ *v.* utār lēnā اُتار لینا, utārnā اُتارنا
down payment *n.* naqd adā'ēgī نقد ادائیگی, amānī امانی
downfall *n.* zavāl زوال, hubūt ہبوط
downwards *adv.* nīcē نیچے
dowry *n.* jahēz جہیز, mahr مہر
doze *v.* jhapaknā جھپکنا, jhapkī lēnā جھپکی لینا
dozen *n.* darjan درجن
draft *n.* masavvadah مسودہ, xākah خاکہ
drag *v.* khaiṁcnā کھینچنا
drain *n.* parnālah پرنالہ, nālī نالی

draw *v.* khaiṁcnā کھینچنا
drawer *n.* musavvir مصور
drawing *n.* naqš نقش, musavvirī مصوری, khaiṁc کھینچ
drawing room *n.* nišast gah نشست گاہ
dread *n.* xauf خوف, ḍar ڈر
dreadful *adj.* xauf nāk خوف ناک, haul nāk ہول ناک
dream *n.* xvāb خواب, sapnā سپنا / *v.* xvāb dēkhnā خواب دیکھنا
dregs *n.* phōk پھوک
drench *v.* bhigō dēnā بھگو دینا, šarābōr Kar dēnā شرابور کر دینا
dress *n.* kapṛā کپڑا / *v.* pahnānā پہنانا, pahannā پہننا
dressed *adj.* malbūs ملبوس, lais لیس
dressmaker *n.* libās sāz لباس ساز, pārcāh dōz پارچہ دوز
drift *v.* bahnā بہنا
drink *n.* mašrūb مشروب / *v.* pīnā پینا
drip *v.* risnā رسنا, ṭapak paṛnā ٹپک پڑنا
drive *v.* calānā چلانا, dauṛānā دوڑانا; gāṛī calānā گاڑی چلانا, gāṛī hānknā گاڑی ہانکنا
  drive an elephant haulnā ہولنا
  drive away mār bhagānā مار بھگانا, hānknā ہانکنا
  drive back paspā karnā پسپا کرنا, haṭānā ہٹانا
  drive off bhagānā بھگانا, hānknā ہانکنا
  drive out nikālnā نکالنا
driver *n.* ḍrā'īvar ڈرائیور
drizzle *n.* phuvār پھوار
dromedary *n.* sānḍnī سانڈنی
drop *n.* būnd بوند, qatrah قطرہ / *v.* girna گرنا, girānā گرانا
dropsy *n.* istasqā استسقا, jalandar جلندر
drought *n.* xušk sālī خشک سالی, qaḥt sālī قحط سالی
drove *n.* galla گلہ
drown *v.* ḍūbnā ڈوبنا, ḍubōnā ڈبونا
drowned *adj.* ġarīq غریق, ġarq غرق
drowsiness *n.* ġanūdgī غنودگی, jhapkī جھپکی
drowsy *adj.* xvābīdah خوابیدہ
druggist *n.* davā farōš دوا فروش, ᶜattār عطار, pansārī پنساری
drugs *n.* davā'ēṁ دوائیں

drugstore *n.* davā xānah دوا خانہ
drum *n.* tabl/tabal طبل, dhaṛ دھڑ, kōs کوس; *(large)* ḍhōl ڈھول; *(small)* ḍhōlkī ڈھولکی, ḍhōlak ڈھولک
drumstick *n.* ḍankā ڈنکا
drunk/drunken *adj.* mast مست, mastānah مستانہ
drunkard *n.* šarābī شرابی, mai parast مے پرست
drunkenness *n.* mastī مستی
dry *adj.* sūkhā سوکھا, sukhā سکھا, xušk خشک / *v.* sūkhnā سوکھنا, sukhānā سکھانا
dryness *n.* xuškī خشکی
duck *n.* batax بطخ
duckling *n.* batax بطخ
due *adj.* rasadī رسدی
dull *adj.* kund کند, kund zihn کند ذہن
dumb *adj.* gūngā گونگا
duplicate *adj.* musannā مثنیٰ
duplicity *n.* alsēṭ السیٹ
durability *n.* pā'ēdārī پائیداری
durable *adj.* pā'ēdār پائیدار
duration *n.* muddat مدت
during *prep.* mābain مابین, darmiyāṁ درمیاں
dust *n.* gard گرد, ġubār غبار / *v.* pōṁchnā پونچھنا
dusty *adj.* gard ālūdah گرد آلودہ, ġubār ālūdah غبار آلودہ
dutiful *adj.* kār band کاربند, rašīd رشید
duty *n.* farz فرض
duty office *n.* ᶜuhdah عہدہ
dwarf *n.* baunā بونا
dwell *v.* basnā بسنا
dwelling *n.* iqāmat اقامت, xānah خانہ, maqām مقام ♦ ~ **place** thān تھان
dye *n.* rang رنگ / *v.* rang dēnā رنگ دینا
dyer *n.* rang rēz رنگ ریز
dyke *n.* puštah پشتہ
dynasty *n.* šāhī xāndān شاہی خاندان
dysentery *n.* pēciš پیچش

E

each *adj.* har ēk ہر ایک, har ہر ♦ ~ **one** apnā apnā اپنا اپنا
eager *adj.* šauqīn شوقین, ārzū mand آرزو مند
eagerly *adv.* šauqiyah شوقیہ
eagerness *n.* šauq شوق
eagle *n.* ʿuqāb عقاب
ear *n.* kān کان, gōš گوش
earlier *adj.* mā taqqadum ما تقدم
early *adv. (in the evening)* sar-ē-šām سر شام; *(in the morning)* subḥ dam صبح دم ♦ ~ **morning** fajr فجر
earn *v.* kamānā کمانا, kasab karnā کسب کرنا
earnestness *n.* sar garmī سرگرمی
earnings *n.* kamā'ī کمائی
earring *n.* bālī بالی
earth *n.* zamīn زمین, miṭṭī مٹی
earthenware *n.* sifāl سفال
earthly *adj.* arzī ارضی
earthquake *n.* zalzalah زلزلہ
earthy *adj.* xākī خاکی
ease *n.* suhūlat سہولت, rāhat راحت
easily *adv.* ba'āsanī باسانی, yūṁ hī یوں ہی
easiness *n.* āsānī آسانی
east *n.* mašriq مشرق, pūrab پورب
eastern *adj.* mašriqī مشرقی
easy *adj.* āsān آسان
eat *v.* khānā کھانا
ebb *n.* jazr جزر
echo *n.* gūṁj گونج / *v.* gūṁjnā گونجنا
eclipse *n.* girhan گرہن
economic *adj.* iqtisādī اقتصادی
economical *adj.* kam xarc کم خرچ, maʿašī معاشی
economically *adv.* kifāyat sē کفایت سے, sarfah sē صرفہ سے

economize *v.* kifāyat šiᶜārī karnā کفایت شعاری کرنا
economy *n.* iqtisādī nizām اقتصادی نظام, maᶜāšiyyāt معاشیات
ecstasy *n.* umang امنگ, vajd وجد
edge *n.* dhār دھار, kōr کور
edible *adj.* khānē kē qābil کھانے کے قابل / *n.* xōrdanī خوردنی
edifice *n.* ᶜimārat عمارت
edition *n.* tabaᶜ طبع, nusxah نسخہ, chapā'ī چھپائی
editor *n.* mu'allif مؤلف, mudīr مدیر; *(of a newspaper)* axbār navīs اخبار نویس
educate *v.* paṛhānā پڑھانا, taᶜlīm dēnā تعلیم دینا
educated *adj.* taᶜlīm yāftah تعلیم یافتہ
education *n.* taᶜlīm تعلیم, tarbiyat تربیت
educational *adj.* darsī درسی
efface *v.* maḥv karnā محو کرنا, miṭānā مٹانا
effect *n.* ᶜamal عمل, asar اثر / *v.* karnā کرنا
effective *adj.* mu'assir موثر, kār gar کارگر
effeminate *adj.* muxannas مخنث
efficient *adj.* kār gar کارگر
effort *n.* ijtihād اِجتہاد, kōšiš کوشش, jahd جہد
egg *n.* anḍā انڈا
eggplant *n.* baigan بیگن
egoism *n.* anā parastī انا پرستی, anāniyat انانیت
eight *num.* āṭh آٹھ
eighteen *num.* aṭhārah اٹھارہ
eighty *num.* assī اسی
eighty-one *num.* ikāsī اکاسی
eighty-two *num.* bayāsī بیاسی
eighty-three *num.* tirāsī تراسی
eighty-four *num.* caurāsī چوراسی
eighty-five *num.* pacāsī پچاسی
eighty-six *num.* chēyāsī چھیاسی
eighty-seven *num.* satāsī ستاسی
eighty-eight *num.* aṭhāsī اٹھاسی
eighty-nine *num.* navāsī نواسی
either *conj.* yā یا

elaborate *adj.* mufassal مفصل, vazāhat kār وضاحت کار
elapse *v.* bītnā بیتنا, guzarnā گزرنا
elastic *adj.* kamān کمان, lacak dār لچک دار
elasticity *n.* lacak لچک
elation *n.* umang امنگ
elbow *n.* kuhnī کہنی, kōhnī کوہنی
elder *n.* baṛā بڑا, āġā آغا
eldest *adj.* jēṭh جیٹھ, jēṭhā جیٹھا
elect *v.* intixāb karnā انتخاب کرنا
elected *adj.* muntaxab منتخب
election *n.* intixāb انتخاب
electricity *n.* bijlī بجلی
elegance *n.* ḥusn حسن, jamāl جمال
elegant *adj.* jamīl جمیل, ḥasīn حسین
element *n.* ᶜunsar عنصر
elementary *adj.* ᶜunṣurī عنصری
elephant *n.* hāthī ہاتھی, fīl فیل ♦ ~ **driver** fīl bān فیل بان ♦ **drive an** ~ haulnā ہولنا
elevated *adj.* ūṁca اونچا, buland بلند
elevation *n.* ūṁchā'ī اونچائی, bulandī بلندی
eleven *num.* gyārah گیارہ
eleventh *adj.* gyāravāṁ گیارھواں
eliminate *v.* xatm karnā ختم کرنا, xārij karnā خارج کرنا, kāṭnā کاٹنا
elk *n.* sābar سابر
ellipse *n.* anḍā kār انڈاکار
elliptical *adj.* anḍā kār انڈاکار
eloquence *n.* fasāḥat فصاحت, carb zabānī چرب زبانی
eloquent *adj.* faṣīḥ فصیح, xūš bayān خوش بیان
else *adj.* dīgar دیگر, dūsrā دوسرا
emaciated *adj.* lāġar لاغر, sūkhā سوکھا, zār-ō-nizār زارونزار
embankment *n.* puštah bandī پشتہ بندی, pāl پال
embargo *n.* tijāratī bandiš تجارتی بندش
embarrassed *adj.* šarmindah شرمندہ, muztarr مضطر
embassy *n.* sifārat سفارت, sifārat xānah سفارت خانہ

ember *n.* angārā انگارا, axgar اخگر
embezzle *v.* ġabn karnā غبن کرنا
embezzlement *n.* xiyānat خیانت, ġabn غبن
emblem *n.* nišān نشان, canvar چنور, ᶜalāmat علامت
embrace *n.* kaulī کولی, ankvār انکوار, gōd گود / *v.* lipaṭnā لپٹنا
embracing *adj.* ham āġōš ہم آغوشی, ham kinār ہم کنار
embroidered *adj.* bēl dār بیل دار ♦ ~ **cloth** *n.* cikan چکن
embroidery *n.* gul kārī گل کاری, zar dōzī زردوزی, kār cōbī کارچوبی
emerald *n.* zumurrud زمرد
emerge *v.* nikalnā نکلنا
emigrant *n.* muhājir مہاجر
emigration *n.* tark-ē-vatan ترک وطن
eminence *n.* sar bulandī سربلندی, rifᶜat رفعت, uṁcā'ī انچائی
eminent *adj.* muḥtašim محتشم, šarīf شریف
emission *n.* inzāl انزال
emotion *n.* jōš جوش, mauj موج, iḥsās احساس
emotional *adj.* ḥassās حساس
emperor *n.* šāhinšāh شاہنشاہ
emphasis *n.* tākīd تاکید
emphatic *adj.* tākīdī تاکیدی
emphatically *adv.* tākīdan تاکیداً
empire *n.* bādšāhat بادشاہت, saltanat سلطنت
employ *v.* lagānā لگانا, rakh lēnā رکھ لینا
employee *n.* mulāzim ملازم
employment *n.* kārōbār کاروبار, mulāzamat ملازمت, naukarī نوکری
empower *v.* muxtār karnā مختار کرنا
empress *n.* sultānah سلطانہ
emptiness *n.* xalā خلا
empty *adj.* xālī خالی / *v.* unḍēlnā انڈیلنا
encampment *n.* xaimah gāh خیمہ گاہ
enchant *v.* jādū karnā جادو کرنا
enchanted *adj.* masḥūr مسحور
enchanter *n.* sāḥir ساحر
enchantment *n.* saḥr سحر, sāḥirī ساحری

enchantress *n.* sāḥirah ساحرہ
encircle *v.* ghumānā گھمانا, muḥit ḥona محیط ہونا, ghērnā گھیرنا
encircling *adj.* dā'ir دائر, muḥīt محیط
enclose *v.* ghērnā گھیرنا, iḥātah karnā اِحاطہ کرنا
enclosed *adj.* laff لف
enclosure *n.* iḥātah اِحاطہ, ḥaram حرم
encounter *n.* āmnā sāmnā آمنا سامنا, muqābalah مقابلہ / *v.* sāmnā karnā سامنا کرنا
encourage *v.* šābāš dēnā شاباش دینا
encouragement *n.* ḍhāras ڈھارس
encyclopedia *n.* maxzan-ul-ᶜulūm مخزن العلوم
end *n.* āxar آخر, xatm ختم, xātimah خاتمہ / *v.* xatm hōnā ختم ہونا, xātimah hōnā خاتمہ ہونا
endeavor *n.* jahd جہد, kōšiš کوشش
endive *n.* kāsnī کاسنی
endless *adj.* lā yazāl لایزال, bē intihā بے انتہا
endowment *n.* vaqf وقف
endurance *n.* bardāšt برداشت, taḥammul تحمل, tāb تاب
endure *v.* jhēlnā جھیلنا, taḥammul karnā تحمل کرنا
enemy *n.* dušman دشمن, ᶜadū عدو
energetic *adj.* jafākaš جفاکش
energy *n.* jān جان, quvvat قوت
enforce *v.* rā'ij karnā رائج کرنا, ᶜamal dar āmad karnā عمل درآمد کرنا
engage *v.* rakh lēnā رکھ لینا
engaged *adj.* masrūf مصروف
engagement *n.* mašġalah مشغلہ, zimmah dārī ذمہ داری
engine *n.* injan انجن
engineer *n.* injīniyar انجینئر, muhandis مہندس
engineering *n.* handisiyāt ہندسیات
English *adj.* angrēzī انگریزی / *n.* angrēz انگریز
Englishman *n.* angrēz انگریز
engrave *v.* kandah karnā کندہ کرنا
engraver *n.* kandah kār کندہ کار
engraving *n.* khudā'ī کھدائی

enigma *n.* pahēlī پہیلی, cīstān چیستان
enjoy *v.* mazah lūṭnā مزہ لوٹنا, ḥazz uṭhānā حظ اٹھانا
enjoyment *n.* ᶜišrat عشرت, mauj موج
enlarge *v.* baṛhānā بڑھانا, azāfah karnā اضافہ کرنا
enlargement *n.* azāfah اضافہ, kušā'iš کشائش
enlightened *adj.* munavvar منور, raušan dil روشن دل, raušan zamīr روشن ضمیر
enlightenment *n.* ujlāpan اجلاپن, tanvīr تنویر
enlist *v.* dāxil karnā داخل کرنا
enmity *n.* ᶜadāvat عداوت, dušmanī دشمنی
enough *adj.* kāfī کافی, bas بس / *interj.* **(that's ~!)** bas! ! بس
enquire *v.* talab karnā طلب کرنا, khōjnā کھوجنا
enquirer *n.* tālib طالب
enquiry *n.* talab طلب, khōj کھوج
enrage *v.* bhabkānā بھبکانا
enrich v. mālā māl karnā مالا مال کرنا
enroll *v.* bhartī karnā بھرتی کرنا
ensign *n.* ᶜalam علم; *(military)* parcam پرچم
entangle *v.* lapēṭna لپیٹنا, phandā lagānā پھندا لگانا
entanglement *n.* jhamēlā جھمیلا, lapēṭ لپیٹ
enter *v.* andar jānā اندر جانا, dāxil hōnā داخل ہونا
entertain *v.* bahlānā بہلانا, mihmānī karnā مہمانی کرنا
entertainer *n.* mihmān dār مہماندار
entertaining *adj.* farḥat afzā' فرحت افزاء
entertainment *n.* mihmānī مہمانی, tafrīḥ تفریح, tamāšā تماشا
enthrone *v.* taxt par biṭhānā تخت پر بٹھانا
enthronement *n.* rāj gaddī راج گدی
enthusiasm *n.* jōš جوش, šaġaf شغف, vajd وجد, valvalah ولولہ
entire *adj.* tamām تمام, pūrā پورا, sārā سارا
entirely *adv.* tamām-ō-kamāl تمام وکمال, bil-kul بالکل, mutlaqan مطلقاً
entitled *adj.* musammā مسمی, mulaqqab ملقب
entrance *n.* dāxilah داخلہ
entrap *v.* phāṁsnā پھانسنا, phaṁsānā پھنسانا
entreaty *n.* šafāᶜt شفاعت, samājat سماجت
entrench *v.* mōrcah bandī karnā مورچہ بندی کرنا

entrust *v.* saunpnā سونپنا, supurd karnā سپرد کرنا
entry *n.* dāxilah داخلہ
enumeration *n.* šumārī شماری, taᶜdād تعداد
envelope *n.* lifāfah لفافہ
envious *adj.* ḥāsid حاسد, ḥasūd حسود
environment *n.* mā ḥaul ما حول
envoy *n.* safīr سفیر, qāsid قاصد
envy *n.* ḥasad حسد, rašk رشک / *v.* jalnā جلنا, kuṛhnā کڑھنا, rašk karnā رشک کرنا
epidemic *n.* vabāl وبال, vabā وبا
epitaph *n.* lauḥ-ē-qabar لوح قبر
epoch *n.* tārīx تاریخ, jug جگ
equal *adj.* barābar برابر, معادل, musāvī مساوی
equality *n.* barābarī برابری, musāvāt مساوات
equally *adv.* ham ہم
equation *n.* musāvāt مساوات
equator *n.* xatt-ē-istivā خط استوا
equipment *n.* kīl kānṭā کیل کانٹا
equipped *adj.* hathiyār band ہتھیار بند
equity *n.* insāf انصاف, maᶜdalat معدلت
equivalent *adj.* muᶜādal معادل, ᶜadīl عدیل
era *n.* tārīx تاریخ, sanh سنہ
eradication *n.* bēx kanī بیخ کنی
erase *v.* mēṭnā میٹنا, miṭānā مٹانا مٹانا
erect *adj.* qā'im قائم, khaṛā کھڑا
ermine *n.* sanjāb سنجاب
err *v.* ġalatī karnā غلطی کرنا
erroneously *adv.* sahvan سہواً
error *n.* ġalatī/ġaltī غلطی ♦ **make an** ~ *v.* phisalnā پھسلنا
eruption *n.* phōṛā phuṁsī پھوڑا پھنسی
escape *n.* bacāō بچاؤ / *v.* bacnā بچنا, bac nikalnā بچ نکلنا
especially *adv.* xas kar خاص کر, xusūsan خصوصاً
espionage *n.* jāsūsī جاسوسی
essay *n.* inšā' انشاء
essence *n.* jauhar جوہر.

essential *adj.* lā budī لا بدی, zātī ذاتی, maᶜnavī معنوی
essentially *adv.* zarūratan ضرورتاً
establish *v.* muᶜaiyyan karnā معین کرنا
establishment *n.* nasb نصب
estate *n.* jā'ēdād جائداد
esteem *n.* iḥtarām احترام / *v.* ānkhēṁ bichānā آنکھیں بچھانا
estimate *n.* andāzah اندازہ, taxmīnah تخمینہ ♦ **rough** ~ kaccā taxmīnah کچا تخمینہ / *v.* andāzah karnā اندازہ کرنا, tōlnā تولنا
estimated *adj.* taxmīni تخمینی
etcetera (etc.) *n.* va-ġairah وغیرہ
eternal *adj.* jāvīd جاوید, dā'imī دائمی
eternally *adv.* mudām مدام, jāvidāṁ جاوداں
eternity *n.* jāvdānī جاودانی, hamēšagī ہمیشگی , dvām دوام
ethics *n.* ᶜilm-ē-adab علم ادب
Ethiopia *n.* ḥabaš حبش
Ethiopian *n.* ḥabašī حبشی
etiquette *n.* takalluf تکلف, ādāb-ē-maḥfil آداب محفل
eunuch *n.* hījṛā ہیجڑا
euro *(currency)* *n.* yūrō یورو
Europe *n.* yūrōp یوروپ, farang فرنگ, farangistān فرنگستان
European *adj.* yūrōpī یوروپی, farangī فرنگی
evade *v.* āj kal karnā آج کل کرنا, ṭāl maṭōl karnā ٹال مٹول کرنا
evaporate *v.* bhāp banānā بھاپ بنانا, kāfūr hō jānā کافور ہوجانا
evasion *n.* ṭālā ٹالا, ṭāl maṭōl ٹال مٹول, bacā'ō بچاؤ
even *adj.* ham vār ہم وار / *adv.* ham ہم, bhī بھی, hī ہی
evening *n.* šām شام, sāṁjh سانجھ
evenness *n.* musāvāt مساوات, ham sarī ہم سری
event *n.* vāqiᶜa واقعہ
eventual *adj.* imkānī امکانی
eventuality *n.* imkān امکان
ever *adv.* hamēšah ہمیشہ, kabhī کبھی
everlasting *adj.* dā'imī دائمی, bāqī باقی, xālid خالد
every *adj.* har ہر, sab سب

everybody *pron.* har ēk ہر ایک
everyone *pron.* har ēk ہر ایک
everything *pron.* sab kuch سب کچھ
everywhere *adv.* har taraf ہر طرف, har kahīṁ ہر کہیں, jagah jagah جگہ جگہ
evidence *n.* šahādat شہادت, subūt-ē-taḥrīrī ثبوت تحریری
evident *adj.* zāhir ظاہر, maᶜlūm معلوم
evidently *adv.* zāhiran ظاہراً, zāhir mēṁ ظاہر میں
evil *adj.* burā برا / *n.* šarr شر
exact *adj.* tamām تمام, ṭhīk ٹھیک, barjastah برجستہ
exactly *adv.* bil-kul ṭhīk بالکل ٹھیک
exaggerate *v.* mubālaġah karnā مبالغہ کرنا
exaggeration *n.* mubālaġah مبالغہ, ġulū غلو
exalt *v.* mušarraf karnā مشرف کرنا
exaltation *n.* caṛhā'ī چڑھائی, farāzī فرازی, sar bulandī سربلندی
examination *n.* imtiḥān امتحان
examine *v.* imtiḥān lēnā امتحان لینا, muᶜāyanah karnā معاینہ کرنا
examiner *n.* mumtaḥin ممتحن
example *n.* misāl مثال ♦ **for** ~ *adv.* masalan مثلاً
excavate *v.* khōdnā کھودنا
exceeding *adj.* zā'id زائد
excel *v.* sabqat lē jānā سبقت لے جانا
excellence *n.* šaraf شرف, kamāl کمال, ᶜumdagī عمدگی, bartarī برتری, sabqat سبقت
excellent *adj.* baṛhiyā بڑھیا, bihtar بہتر, najīb نجیب, fāxir فاخر / *interj.* šābāš شاباش, kyā xūb کیا خوب, kyā bāt hai کیا بات ہے
except *prep.* sivā سوا, bajuz بجز, baġair بغیر
exception *n.* istisnā' استثناء
excess *n.* ziyādatī زیادتی, bahutāt بہتات
excessive *adj.* mufrit مفرط, ziyādah زیادہ
exchange *n.* badal بدل, mubādalah مبادلہ, tabādalah تبادلہ; (~ *of foreign currency)* sarrāfah صرافہ / *v.* badalnā بدلنا, tabdīl karnā تبدیل کرنا
excite *v.* lalcānā للچانا, macānā مچانا, tarġīb dēnā ترغیب دینا
excitement *n.* jōš جوش, jōš-ō-xarōš جوش وخروش
exclaim *v.* bōl uṭhnā بول اٹھنا

exclude *v.* xārij karnā خارج کرنا
exclusively *adv.* sirf صرف
excrement *n.* chī chī چھی چھی, gū گو
excursion *n.* sair سیر
excusable *adj.* maᶜzūr معذور
excuse *n.* maᶜzirat معذرت / *v.* muᶜāf karnā معاف کرنا, maᶜzūr rakhnā معذور رکھنا
♦ **make an ~** *v.* bahānah karṇā بہانہ کرنا
execute *v.* phāṁsī dēnā پھانسی دینا, sūlī caṛhānā سولی چڑھانا، sūlī dēnā سولی دینا
execution *n.* taᶜmīl تعمیل
executioner *n.* jallād جلاد
exemplary *adj.* ᶜibrat numā عبرت نما
exemption *n.* istisnā' استثناء
exercise *n.* mašq مشق / *v.* mašq karnā مشق کرنا
exertion *n.* jatan جتن
exhale *v.* sāṁs nikālnā سانس نکالنا
exhaust *v.* khapānā کھپانا
exhausted *adj.* thakā تھکا, muzmaḥill مضمحل
exhaustion *n.* thakāvaṭ تھکاوٹ
exhibit *v.* numā'iš karnā نمائش کرنا
exhibition *n.* numā'iš نمائش
exhibitor *n.* numā'iš kunindah نمائش کنندہ, muzhir مظہر
exhilaration *n.* šiguftagī شگفتگی, kaif کیف
exile *n.* šahr badr شہر بدر / *v.* šahr badr karnā شہربدر کرنا
exist *v.* hōnā ہونا, jīnā جینا, rahnā رہنا
existence *n.* vujūd وجود, hastī ہستی
exit *n.* bāhar jānē kā rāstā باہر جانے کا رستا / *v.* bāhar jānā باہر جانا
exorcise *v.* bhūt utārnā بھوت اتارنا
exorcism *n.* mantar jantar منتر جنتر
expand *v.* pasārnā پسارنا, phailānā پھیلانا
expansion *n.* phailā'ō پھیلاؤ
expect *v.* tavaqqaᶜ karnā توقع کرنا, intizār karnā انتظار کرنا
expectation *n.* tavaqqaᶜ توقع, intizār انتظار, intizārī انتظاری
expedience *n.* maslaḥat مصلحت
expedient *adj.* mōzūṁ موزوں

expediently *adv.* maslaḥatan مصلحتاً
expedition *n.* jald bāzī جلد بازی
expeditious *adj.* jald bāz جلد باز
expel *v.* xārij karnā خارج کرنا, nikālnā نکالنا
expend *v.* xarc karnā خرچ کرنا
expenditure *n.* xarc خرچ
expense *n.* xarc خرچ
expensive *adj.* mahngā مہنگا
experience *n.* mahārat مہارت, tajurbah kārī تجربہ کاری / *v.* tajurbah karnā تجربہ کرنا
experienced *adj.* vāqif واقف, jahāṁdīdah جہاندیدہ
experiment *n.* tajurbah تجربہ / *v.* tajurbah karnā تجربہ کرنا
expert *adj.* māhir ماہر / *n.* ustād اُستاد
expertise *n.* hāth cālākī ہاتھ چالاکی
expiration *n.* inqizā انقضاء
expire *v.* muddat xatm hōnā مدت ختم ہونا, bītnā بیتنا, binasnā بنسنا
explain *v.* tašrīḥ karnā تشریح کرنا, maᶜnī dēnā معنی دینا, samjhānā سمجھانا
explanation *n.* tašrīḥ تشریح, taᶜrīf تعریف
explicit *adj.* lafzī لفظی
explicitly *adv.* bil-tafsīl بالتفصیل, lafzan لفظاً
exploitation *n.* istiḥsāl استحصال
exploration *n.* justjū جستجو
explorer *n.* mutalāšī متلاشی
explosion *n.* dhamākah دھماکہ
export *n.* nikās نکاس
express mail *n.* iksprēs ḍāk ایکسپریس ڈاک
expulsion *n.* ixrāj اِخراج, istixrāj استخراج
exquisite *adj.* nafīs نفیس
extend *v.* pasārnā پسارنا, vasīᶜ karnā وسیع کرنا
extension *n.* cauṛā'ī چوڑائی, darāzī درازی
extensive *adj.* farāx فراخ, vasīᶜ وسیع
extent *n.* vusᶜat وسعت
extermination *n.* inhidām انہدام, bēx kanī بیخ کنی

exterminator *n.* bēx kan بیخ کن
external *adj.* bērūni بیرونی
externally *adv.* xārijan خارجاً
extinct *adj.* munaᶜdim منعدم, munqatiᶜ منقطع, maᶜdūm معدوم
extinguish *v.* bujhānā بجھانا
extort *v.* dhamkī sē kām lēnā دھمکی سے کام لینا
extra *adj.* zā'id زائد, fāltu فالتو
extract *n.* xulāsah خلاصہ / *v.* ~ **a tooth** dānt ukhāṛnā دانت اکھاڑنا
extraction *n.* nasl نسل, chānṭ چھانٹ
extradition *n.* ixrāj اِخراج, nikālā نکالا
extraordinary *adj.* anōkhā انوکھا, ġair maᶜmūlī غیر معمولی, turfah طرفہ
extravagant *adj.* fuzūl xarc فضول خرچ
extravagance *n.* fuzūl xarcī فضول خرچی ,isrāf اصراف
extreme *adj.* intihā'ī انتہائی, qiyāmat قیامت, ġāyat غایت, nihāyat نہایت /
n. nihāyat نہایت
extremely *adv.* ḥad darjah حد درجہ, ēk dām ایک دام
extremity *n.* āxrī darjah آخری درجہ, pāyāṁ پایاں
exuberant *adj.* pur jōš پرجوش, zindah dil زندہ دل, kasrat sē کثرت سے
eye *n.* ānkh آنکھ, ᶜain عین
eyebrow *n.* abrū ابرو, qāš قاش
eyelash *n.* palak پلک
eyelid *n.* papōṭā پپوٹا
eyesight *n.* basārat بصارت, rōšnī روشنی
eyewitness *n.* ᶜainī šāhid عینی شاہد , gavāh-ē-cašm dīd گواہ چشم دید

F

fable *n.* kahānī کہانی, afsānah افسانہ
fabricate *v.* gharnā گھڑنا, taškīl karnā تشکیل کرنا
fabrication *n.* sāxt ساخت, taškīl تشکیل
face *n.* cēhrah چہرہ, muṁh منہ, vajh وجہ
facilitate *v.* āsān karnā آسان کرنا
facilitation *n.* tashīl تسہیل
facility *n.* suhūlat سہولت
facing *n.* sāmnā سامنا
fact *n.* ḥaqīqat حقیقت
factory *n.* kār xānah کارخانہ
fade *v.* murjhānā مرجھانا, rang uṛnā رنگ اڑنا
fail *v.* cūknā چوکنا, xatā karnā خطا کرنا, xatā hōnā خطا ہونا
failing *adj.* zā'il زائل, qāsir قاصر
failure *n.* nākāmī ناکامی, kōtāhī کوتاہی
faint *adj.* mānd ماند, phīkā پھیکا / *v.* bē hōš hōnā بے ہوش ہونا, ġāš khānā غش کھانا
fair *adj.* gōrā گورا / *n.* mēlā میلا
fairly *adv.* munsifānah منصفانہ
fairy *n.* farzī فرضی
fairyland *n.* paristān پرستان
faith *n.* *(mainly Hinduism)* dharma/dharm دھرم, bharōsah بھروسہ; *(mainly Islam)* *n.* mazhab مذہب, īmān ایمان, iᶜtimād اعتماد ♦ **keep** ~ *v.* vafā karnā وفا کرنا
faithful *adj.* īmāndār ایماندار, vafā dār وفا دار, bharōsah mand بھروسہ مند
faithfully *adv.* vafā dārānah وفا دارانہ, muxlisānah مخلصانہ
faithfulness *n.* īmāndārī ایمانداری, vafā dārī وفا داری
faithless *adj.* bē vafā بے وفا, bē imān بے ایمان
fake *adj.* masnūᶜī مصنوعی, jaᶜlī جعلی
falcon *n.* bāz باز
fall *n.* zavāl زوال, tanazzul تنزل; *(season)* xarīf خریف, fasl-ē-xarīf فصل خریف, xizāṁ خزاں, mausam-ē-xizāṁ موسم خزاں / *v.* girna گرنا

fallacy *n.* muġālatah مغالطہ
false *adj.* ġalat غلط, jhūṭā جھوٹا
falsehood *n.* jhūṭ جھوٹ
falsely *adv.* nā ḥaqq ناحق
falseness *n.* nā rāstī ناراستی
falsify *v.* jhuṭlānā جھٹلانا
fame *n.* šuhrat شہرت
familiar *adj.* šināsā شناسا, vāqif واقف; *(~ with)* māhir ماہر
familiarity *n.* āšnā'ī آشنائی, muvānasat موانست
family *n.* xāndān خاندان
famine *n.* qaḥt قحط, qaḥt sālī قحط سالی
famous *adj.* mašhūr مشہور ♦ ~ **person** *n.* mušāhīr مشاہیر
fan *n.* pankhā پنکھا / *v.* jhalnā جھلنا
fanciful *adj.* vahmī وہمی
fancy *adj.* taxayyul تخیل, vahm وہم
fantastic *adj.* ajīb-ō-ġarīb عجیب و غریب, lahrī لہری
far *adj.* dūr دور
faraway *adj.* sāt samundar pār سات سمندر پار, kōsōṁ dūr کوسوں دور
farce *n.* ḍhōng ڈھونگ, svāng سوانگ
fare *n.* kirāyah کرایہ, bhāṛā بھاڑا
farewell *interj.* xudā ḥāfiz خدا حافظ / *n.* vidā' وداع
farm *n.* khēt کھیت / *v.* zamīn ṭhīk par dēnā زمین ٹھیک پر دینا
farmer *n.* kisān کسان
farsighted *adj.* dūr andēš دور اندیش
farsightedness *n.* dūr andēšī دور اندیشی
fascinate *v.* mōhnā موہنا, mōh lēnā موہ لینا
fascination *n.* mōh موہ, mōhnī موہنی, dilkašī دلکشی
fashion *n.* faišan فیشن, tōr-ō-tarīq طور و طریق
fast *adj.* tēz تیز, šōx شوخ / *v.* fāqah karnā فاقہ کرنا / *n.* rōzah روزہ ♦ **break a ~** rōzah khōlnā روزہ کھولنا ♦ **breaking the ~** *(during Ramadan)* iftār افطار ♦ **keep a ~** *v.* rōzah rakhnā روزہ رکھنا
fasten *v.* bāndhnā باندھنا
fastening *n.* bandhan بندھن, bandhātī بندھائی
fastidious *adj.* nāzuk نازک, nāzuk pasand نازک پسند

fat *adj.* mōṭā موٹا, carb چرب / *n.* ciknā'ī چکنائی, carbī چربی
fatal *adj.* muhlik مہلک
fate *n.* qismat قسمت, taqdīr تقدیر
father *n.* vālid والد, pitā پتا, bāp باپ, bābā بابا
father-in-law *n.* sasur سسر
fatherly *adj.* pidarī پدری
fatigue *n.* takān تکان, xastagī خستگی, māndagī ماندگی
fatness *n.* mōṭāpā موٹاپا
fatten *v.* phulānā پھلانا
fatwa *n.* fatvā فتوی
fault *n.* ġaltī غلطی, xatā خطا
faultless *adj.* bē taqsīr بے تقصیر, bē qusūr بے قصور
faulty *adj.* xarāb خراب, xatā kār خطا کار
favor *n.* hamdardī ہمدردی, mihrbānī مہربانی / *v.* mutavajjih hōnā متوجہ ہونا
favorable *adj.* mutavajjih متوجہ, muvāfiq موافق
favorite *adj.* pasandīdah پسندیدہ
fax *n.* faiks فیکس
fear *n.* xauf, خوف, ḍar ڈر / *v.* ḍarnā ڈرنا
fearful *adj.* xauf nāk خوف ناک
fearless *adj.* bē xauf بے خوف, nidaṛ نڈر
fearlessly *adv.* bē andēšah بے اندیشہ
fearlessness *n.* bē xaufī بے خوفی
feasible *adj.* qābil-ē-ᶜamal قابل عمل, mumkin ممکن
feast *n.* daᶜvat دعوت, ziyāfat ضیافت / *v.* ziyāfat karnā ضیافت کرنا
feather *n.* pankh پنکھ
feature *n.* rūp روپ, cēhrah mōhrah چہرہ مہرہ
February *n.* farvarī فروری
federal *adj.* vifāqī وفاقی
federalism *n.* vifāqiyat وفاقیت
federation *n.* vifāq وفاق
fee *n.* fīs فیس, ujrat اجرت
feeble *adj.* kamzōr کمزور
feebleness *n.* kamzōrī کمزوری
feed *v.* khilānā کھلانا ♦ ~ **birds** cugnā چگنا

feel *v.* maḥsūs karnā محسوس کرنا , lagnā لگنا
feeling *n.* iḥsās احساس
felicity *n.* xūšī خوشی
fell *v.* girānā گرانا
fellow *n.* nadīm ندیم, sāthī ساتھی
fellowship *n.* suḥbat صحبت , muvānasat موانست
felon *n.* mujrim مجرم
female *adj.* zanānah زنانہ / *n.* ᶜaurat عورت
feminine *adj.* zanānah زنانہ
fence *n.* bēṛā بیڑا, janglā جنگلا / *v.* iḥātah karnā احاطہ کرنا
fennel *n.* saunf سونف
fenugreek *n.* mēthī میتھی
ferment *v.* xamīr uṭhānā خمیر اٹھانا
ferocious *adj.* darindah درندہ, vaḥšī وحشی
fertile *adj.* zarxēz زرخیز
fervor *n.* garam jōšī گرم جوشی
festival *n.* tē'ōhār تیوہار
festivity *n.* jašn جشن
fetch *v.* lānā لانا, lē ānā لے آنا
fetter *n.* bēṛī بیڑی, zanjīr زنجیر
fever *n.* buxār بخار
few *adj.* kuch کچھ, ka'ī ēk کئی ایک, kam کم, thōṛā تھوڑا
fiber *n.* rēšah ریشہ
fibrous *adj.* rēšah dār ریشہ دار
fiction *n.* afsānah افسانہ
fidelity *n.* vāfadārī وفاداری
fidget *v.* kulbalānā کلبلانا
field *n.* khēt کھیت , mēdān میدان
field map *n.* šujarah شجرہ
fierce *adj.* tund تند
fifteen *num.* pandrah پندرہ, pandrah پندرہ
fifteenth *adj.* pandrahvāṁ پندرھواں
fifth *adj.* pāṁcvāṁ پانچواں

fifty *num.* pacās پچاس
fifty-one *num.* ikāvan اکاون
fifty-two *num.* bāvan باون
fifty-three *num.* tirēpan ترپن
fifty-four *num.* cavvan چون
fifty-five *num.* pacpan پچپن
fifty-six *num.* chappan چھپن
fifty-seven *num.* sattāvan ستاون
fifty-eight *num.* aṭhāvan اٹھاون
fifty-nine *num.* unsaṭh انسٹھ
fig *n.* aṁjīr انجیر
fig tree *n.* cīṛ چیڑ
fight *n.* laṛā'ī لڑائی, jang جنگ / *v.* laṛnā لڑنا, jang karnā جنگ کرنا
fighter *n.* muḥārib محارب
figurative *adj.* majāzī مجازی
figure *n.* šakl شکل, sūrat صورت
file *n.* fā'il فائل / *v.* dāxil dāftar karnā داخل دفتر کرنا
fill *v.* bharnā بھرنا; *(~ up)* pūrā karnā پورا کرنا
film *n.* film/filim فلم, jhillī جھلی / *v.* film/filim karnā فلم کرنا, jhillī karnā جھلی کرنا
filter *v.* chānnā چھاننا
filth *n.* mail میل, gandagī گندگی, gand گند
filthiness *n.* mailāpan میلاپن
filthy *adj.* mailā میلا, gandah گندہ, ġalīz غلیظ
final *adj.* āxirī آخری
finance *n.* āmdanī آمدنی
financial *adj.* mālī مالی ♦ ~ **examiner** muḥāsib محاسب ♦ ~ **year** *n.* mālī sāl مالی سال
find *v.* pānā پانا ♦ ~ **guilty** mujrim ṭhahrānā مجرم ٹھہرانا ♦ ~ **out** *v.* maᶜlūm karnā معلوم کرنا, ṭōh lagānā ٹوہ لگانا
finder *n.* vājid واجد, yābindah یابندہ
fine *adj.* ᶜumdah عمدہ, baṛhiyā بڑھیا, nafīs نفیس, latīf لطیف / *n.* tāvān تاوان, jurmānah جرمانہ / *v.* tāvān lagānā تاوان لگانا, jurmānah karnā جرمانہ کرنا ♦ **pay a** ~ *v.* ḍanḍ bharnā ڈنڈ بھرنا
finger *n.* unglī انگلی, ankušt انگشت

finish *v.* xatm karnā ختم کرنا, tamām karnā تمام کرنا, cukānā چکانا

fire *n.* āg آگ, ātaš آتش / *v.* gōlī calānā گولی چلانا, bandūq calānā بندوق چلانا, bandūq chōṛnā بندوق چھوڑنا ♦ **set on ~** *v.* phūnk dēnā پھونک دینا, āg sulgānā آگ سلگانا, phūnknā پھونکنا

firefly *n.* jugnū جگنو

fireplace *n.* ātaš dān آتش دان

firewood *n.* indhan ایندھن

fireworks *n.* ātaš bāzī آتش بازی

firm *adj.* mazbūt مضبوط

firmament *n.* āsmān آسمان

firmness *n.* mazbūtī مضبوطی, istiqlāl استقلال,

first *adj.* pahlā پہلا, avval اول / *adv.* *(~ of all)* pahlē پہلے ♦ **~ class** *n.* pahlā darjah پہلا درجہ ♦ **~ name** *n.* pahlā nām پہلا نام ♦ **at** *~ phr.* pahlē پہلے, pahlē pahal پہلے پہل, avvalan اولاً, ibtidā mēṁ اِبتدا میں

first-born *adj.* jēṭhā جیٹھا

fish *n.* machlī مچھلی / *v.* machlī pakaṛnā مچھلی پکڑنا, machlī kā šikār karnā مچھلی کا شکار کرنا

fisherman *n.* māhī gīr ماہی گیر, machvā مچھوا

fishhook *n.* baṁsī بنسی

fishing *n.* māhī gīrī ماہی گیری

fishmonger *n.* machvā مچھوا

fissure *n.* šigāf شگاف

fist *n.* muṭṭhī مٹھی

fit *adj.* muvāfiq موافق, munāsib مناسب / *v.* phabnā پھبنا

five *num.* pāṁc پانچ

fix *v.* jaṛnā جڑنا, lagānā لگانا ♦ **~ a price** qīmat lagānā قیمت لگانا

fixation *n.* taᶜiyun تعین

fixed abode *n.* mā'ab مآب

flabbiness *n.* pilpilāhaṭ پلپلاہٹ

flabby *adj.* pilpilā پلپلا, ḍhīlā ڈھیلا

flag *n.* jhanḍā جھنڈا

flake *n.* chilkā چھلکا

flame *n.* šuᶜlah شعلہ

flank *n.* pahlū پہلو

flannel *n.* falālīn فلالین
flap *v.* phaṛphaṛānā پھڑپھڑانا
flash *n.* lahak لہک, camak چمک, damak دمک, bhaṛak بھڑک
flash *v.* kaundnā کوندنا, lahaknā لہکنا, dhamaknā دھمکنا ♦ ~ **of lightning** *n.* kaund کوند
flashing *adj.* barrāq براق
flask *n.* bōtal بوتل, šīšah شیشہ
flat *adj.* sathī سطحی
flatten *v.* mānḍnā مانڈنا
flatter *v.* cāplūsī karnā چاپلوسی کرنا
flatterer *n.* cāplūs چاپلوس, xūšāmdī خوشامدی
flattery *n.* cāplūsī چاپلوسی, xūšāmad خوشامد
flavor *n.* mazah مزہ, lazzat لذت
flavorful *adj.* zā'iqah dār ذائقہ دار, mazēdār مزیدار
flaw *n.* darz درز, suqm سقم
flax *n.* tīsī تیسی
flea *n.* pissū پسو
flee *v.* bhāgnā بھاگنا
fleet *n.* jangī bēṛah جنگی بیڑہ
flesh *n.* mās ماس, gōšt گوشت
flexibility *n.* lacak لچک
flexible *adj.* lacak dār لچک دار
flicker *v.* jhilmilānā جھلملانا
flight *n.* uṛān اڑان, parvāz پرواز
fling *n.* phēnk پھینک / *v.* paṭaxnā پٹخنا
flint *n.* caqmāq چقماق
flirt *v.* nāz naxrē karnā ناز نخرے کرنا, maṭak karnā مٹک کرنا
flirtation *n.* nāz naxrē ناز نخرے, maṭak مٹک
flirting *n.* ᶜišvah عشوہ, ᶜišvah garī عشوہ گری
float *v.* tairnā تیرنا
flock *n.* jhunḍ جھنڈ, galla گلہ, ḍār ڈار
flock *n.* *(of cotton)* pahal پہل; *(of sheep or goats)* rēvaṛ ریوڑ
flood *n.* sailāb سیلاب / *v.* ḍubōnā ڈبونا
flood-tide *n.* jivār bhāṭā جوار بھاٹا, sailābī lahar سیلابی لہر

floor *n.* manzil منزل
flora *n.* banāspatī بناسپتی
florist *n.* gul farōš گل فروش
flour *n.* āṭā آٹا
flour mill *n.* āṭē kī cakkī آٹے کی چکی, xarās خراس
flourish *v.* phūlnā پھولنا, phalnā پھلنا
flow *n.* bahā'ō بہاؤ, sail سیل, ravānī روانی, rau رو / *v.* bahnā بہنا
flower *n.* phūl پھول, gul گل / *v.* khilnā کھلنا
flower bed *n.* kyārī کیاری, caman چمن, camnistān چمنستان
flower garden *n.* bustān بستان, gulšan گلشن
flowerpot *n.* gul dān گل دان, gamlah گملہ
flowing *adj.* sayyāl سیال, caltā چلتا, mutrid مطرد, jārī جاری / *n.* sail سیل
fluency *n.* ravānī روانی
fluent *adj.* ravān روان, lassān لسان, zabān āvar زبان آور
fluently *adv.* farfar فرفر
fluid *adj.* sayyāl سیال / *n.* mā'i[c] مائع
flush *n.* hamvār ہموار
flute *n.* bānsurī بانسوری
flutter *n.* pharpharāhaṭ پھڑپھڑاہٹ / *v.* pharpharānā پھڑپھڑانا
fly *n.* makhnī مکھی / *v.* uṛnā اڑنا, jhapaṭnā جھپٹنا; *(~ an aircraft or kite)* uṛānā اڑانا
flying *adj.* uṛan اڑن
foam *n.* jhāg جھاگ
focus *n.* māsikah ماسکہ; *(~ of)* mā'ab مآب
foe *n.* dušman دشمن
fog *n.* kuhr کہر
foggy *adj.* kuhr dār کہر دار
foil *n.* varaq ورق
fold *n.* tah تہ
fold up *v.* tah karnā تہ کرنا
follow *v.* pīchā karnā پیچھا کرنا
follower *n.* mu[c]taqid معتقد, muttabi[c] متبع, mōmin مومن
following *n.* tābi[c] تابع, pīchā پیچھا
fond *adj.* šā'iq شائق; *(~ of)* šauqīn شوقین
fondly *adv.* šauqiyah شوقیہ

fondness *n.* šauq شوق
food *n.* ġizā غذا ♦ ~ **supply** *n.* ann ان
fool *n.* bē vaqūf بے وقوف, gadhā گدھا, bakrā بکرا, ullū الو
foolish *adj.* bē vaqūf بے وقوف, kam ᶜaql کم عقل
foolishly *adv.* aḥmaqānah احمقانہ
foolishness *n.* ḥamāqat حماقت, bēhūdagī بیہودگی, ullūpan الوپن, gadhā pan گدھاپن
foot *n.* pā'ōṁ پاؤں ♦ **on** ~ *adj./adv.* paidal پیدل pā'ōṁ pā'ōṁ پاؤں پاؤں
footpath *n.* pēdal rāstah پیدل راستہ
footprint *n.* naqš-ē-pā نقش پا
footstep *n.* qadam قدم
fop *n.* chailā چھیلا
for *prep./conj.* kē li'ē کے لئے
for example *adv.* masalan مثلاً
forbear *v.* parhēz karnā پرہیز کرنا
forbearance *n.* bardāšt برداشت, parhēz پرہیز, sabr صبر
forbid *v.* manaᶜ karnā منع کرنا
forbidden *adj.* maḥjūr محجور, mamnūᶜ ممنوع; *(~ by Islam)* ḥarām حرام
forbidding *n.* zajar زجر
force *n.* tāqat طاقت, majbūrī مجبوری, qudrat قدرت, zōr زور / *v.* majbūr karnā مجبور کرنا, zōr dēnā زور دینا ♦ **take by** ~ *v.* harnā ہرنا
forceful *adj.* tāqatvar طاقتور
forceps *n.* cimṭā چمٹا
forcibly *adv.* zabardastī sē زبردستی سے, jabran جبراً, bil-jabr بالجبر
forefathers *n.* ābā-ō-ajdād آباؤاجداد
forehead *n.* pēšānī پیشانی
foreign *adj.* ajnabī اجنبی, pardēsī پردیسی, ġair mulkī غیر ملکی
foreign country *n.* pardēs پردیس
foreigner *n.* pardēsī پردیسی, ġair mulkī غیر ملکی
foremost *adj.* avval اول, aglā اگلا
forepart *n.* āgā آگا, pēš پیش
foresight *n.* dūr andēš دور اندیش,
forest *n.* ban بن, jangal جنگل
foretelling *n.* pēšingō'ī پیشنگوئی

forge *v.* gharṛnā گھڑنا
forgery *n.* jaᶜl جعل, jaᶜl sāzī جعل سازی
forget *v.* bhūlnā بھولنا
forgetful *adj.* bhulakkaṛ بھلکڑ
forgetfulness *n.* bhūl بھول
forgive *v.* muᶜāf karnā معاف کرنا
forgiveness *n.* muᶜāfī معافی
forgotten *adj.* farāmōš فراموش
fork *n.* kānṭā کانٹا
form *n.* šakl شکل / *v.* gharṛnā گھڑنا, banānā بنانا, šakl banānā شکل بنانا
formal *adj.* rasmī رسمی
formality *n.* takalluf تکلف
former *adj.* pēšin پیشن, pēšīnah پیشینہ, sābiq سابق, qadīmī قدیمی
formerly *adv.* pēš azīṁ پیش ازیں, pēštar پیشتر, sābiqan سابقا, sābiq mēṁ سابق میں
formula *n.* qāᶜidah قاعدہ
fornication *n.* zinā زنا, zinā kārī زناکاری
fornicator *n.* zinā kār زناکار
fort *n.* qilᶜah/qalᶜah قلعہ
fortification *n.* qilᶜah bandī قلعہ بندی
fortified *adj.* muḥkam محکم
fortress *n.* qilᶜah band šahr قلعہ بند شہر
fortunate *adj.* xūš qismat خوش قسمت xūš nasīb خوش نصیب
fortunately *adv.* qismat sē قسمت سے
fortune *n.* qismat قسمت, nasīb نصیب, baxt بخت
fortune-teller *n.* najūmī/nujūmī نجومی, rammāl رمال
fortune-telling *n.* mustaqbil gōʾī مستقبل گوئی, ramal رمل
forty *num.* cālīs چالیس
forty-one *num.* iktālīs اکتالیس
forty-two *num.* bayālīs بیالیس
forty-three *num.* taintālīs تینتالیس
forty-four *num.* cavālīs چوالیس
forty-five *num.* paiṃtālīs پینتالیس
forty-six *num.* chēyālīs چھیالیس
forty-seven *num.* saiṁtālīs سینتالیس

forty-eight *num.* arṭālīs اڑتالیس
forty-nine *num.* uṁcās انچاس
forward *adj.* sīdhā سیدھا
foster *v.* pālnā پالنا
foul *adj.* mailā میلا, gadlā گدلا, gandah گندہ / *v.* mailā karnā میلا کرنا
foulness *n.* kudūrat کدورت
foundation *n.* buniyād بنیاد
founder *n.* bānī بانی
fountain *n.* favvārah فوارہ, manbaᶜ منبع, cašmah چشمہ
four *num.* cār چار
fourteen *num.* caudah چودہ
fourteenth *adj.* caudhavāṁ چودھواں
fourth *adj.* cauthā چوتھا
fowl *n.* ciṛī mār چڑی مار
fowler *n.* saiyyād صیاد
fox *n.* lōmaṛ لومڑ, lōmaṛī لومڑی
fraction *n.* kasr کسر
fracture *n.* ṭūṭ ٹوٹ, šikastagī شکستگی
fragile *adj.* nāzuk نازک
fragment *n.* ṭukṛā ٹکڑا
fragrance *n.* xūšbū خوشبو, mahak مہک
fragrant *adj.* xūšbūdār خوشبودار, mahkīlā مہکیلا
frail *adj.* nā pāʿīdār نا پائیدار, kamzōr کمزور
frailty *n.* nā pāʾīdārī نا پائیداری
frame *n.* ḍhāncah ڈھانچہ
frank *adj.* kušādah dil کشادہ دل, daryā dil دریا دل, sāf dil صاف دل
fraternal *adj.* birādarānah برادرانہ
fraternity *n.* barādarī برادری, bhāʾī cārā بھائی چارا
fraud *n.* dhōkā دھوکا, daġā دغا, farēb فریب
fraudulent *adj.* daġā bāz دغا باز
fraudulently *adv.* ḥīlatan حیلتاً
free *adj.* āzād آزاد, ḥurr حر; *(~ from)* ᶜārī عاری / *v.* churānā چھڑانا, rihā karnā رہا کرنا ♦ **set ~** *v.* āzād karnā آزاد کرنا, churānā چھڑانا, rihā karnā رہا کرنا
freedom *n.* āzādī آزادی, ḥuriyyat حریت

freeze *v.* jamnā جمنا, jamānā جمانا
freight *n.* bhāṛā بھاڑا, bār bardārī بار برداری
frenzy *n.* sarsām سرسام, saudā سودا
frequently *adv.* aksar اکثر
fresh *adj.* tāzah تازہ, harā ہرا, haryālā ہریالا ♦ ~ **air** *n.* nasīm نسیم
freshness *n.* tāzgī تازگی, harā'ī ہرائی, haryālī ہریالی
friction *n.* ragaṛ رگڑ
Friday *n.* jumᶜah جمعہ
friend *n.* dōst دوست, yār یار ♦ **make ~s with** *v.* ulfat karnā الفت کرنا
friendless *adj.* bē kas بے کس
friendly *adj.* dōstānah دوستانہ, yāvar یاور
friendship *n.* dōstī دوستی
fright *n.* saxt xauf سخت خوف, haul ہول
frighten *v.* bhaṛkānā بھڑکانا, ḍarānā ڈرانا
frightful *adj.* bhayānak بھیانک, xaufnāk خوفناک
frigid *adj.* munjamid منجمد, jamā hū'ā جما ہوا, bārid بارد
frill *n.* jhālar جھالر
fringe *n.* jhālar جھالر, sanjāf سنجاف
frivolous *adj.* harzah ہرزہ, fuḥš فحش
frog *n.* mēnḍak مینڈک
from *prep.* az از, sē سے, min من
front *adj.* sāmnē سامنے, āgē آگے / *n.* pēš پیش, sāmnā سامنا ♦ **in** ~ *adv.* sāmnē سامنے, āgē آگے
frontier *n.* sarḥadd سرحد
frost *n.* pālā پالا, žālah ژالہ
froth *n.* jhāg جھاگ, kaf کف / *v.* jhāg paidā karnā جھاگ پیدا کرنا, phēnānā پھینانا
frown *n.* ghaṛkī گھڑکی / *v.* tēvarī caṛhānā تیوری چڑھانا
frozen *adj.* jamā hū'ā جما ہوا, yax bastah یخ بستہ
frugal *adj.* kifāyat šiᶜār کفایت شعار, kifāyatī کفایتی, kam xarc کم خرچ
frugality *n.* kifāyat šiᶜārī کفایت شعاری
frugally *adv.* kifāyat sē کفایت سے
fruit *n.* phal پھل, mēvah میوہ
fruit seller *n.* mēvah farōš میوہ فروش, kuṁjṛā کنجڑا
fruitful *adj.* phalit پھلت, harā bharā ہرا بھرا

fruitless *adj.* bē bar بے بر, bē fā'idah بے فائدہ, lā ḥāsil لاحاصل
frustration *n.* māyūsī مایوسی
fry *v.* talnā تلنا, bhunānā بھنانا, bhūnnā بھوننا
frying pan *n.* karāhī کڑاہی
fuel *n.* indhan ایندھن
fugitive *adj.* mafrūr مفرور / *n.* bhigōṛā بھگوڑا
fulfill *v.* pūrā karnā پورا کرنا
fulfillment *n.* nibāh نباہ, īfā' ایفاء
full *adj.* bharā بھرا, pūrā پورا; *(~ of)* nāk ناک; *(with food)* pēṭ bhar پیٹ بھر
♦ ~ **moon** *n.* badr بدر
fullness *n.* maᶜmūrī معموری
fully *adv.* muṁh bhar kē منہ بھر کے, mufassal مفصل, tamām-ō-kamāl تمام وکمال
fume *v.* bhabaknā بھبکنا
fun *n.* mazāq مذاق, mazḥakah مضحکہ, tafrīḥ تفریح, khēl کھیل
function *n.* kār کار, taqrīb تقریب
fund *n.* zaxīrah ذخیرہ
funds *n.* pūṁjī پونجی
funeral *n.* tajhīz تجہیز
funnel *n.* cōngā چونگا
funny *adj.* mazāqiyah مذاقیہ, muzḥik مضحک
fur *n.* samūr سمور
furious *adj.* ġusīlā غصیلا, ġazab nāk غضب ناک, xašmnāk خشمناک
furniture *n.* cīz bast چیزبست, raxt رخت, sāmān سامان
further *adj.* mazīd مزید, abᶜad ابعد / *adv.* kē alāvah کے علاوہ, parē پرے
fury *n.* ġussah غصہ, jazbah جذبہ, qahr قہر
fuse *n.* falītah فلیتہ
futile *adj.* fuzūl فضول
future *n.* mustaqbil مستقبل

G

gain *n.* kamā'ī کمائی, fā'idah فائدہ, ḥāsil حاصل, nafaᶜ نفع, bacat بچت / *v.* kamānā کمانا, ḥāsil karnā حاصل کرنا

gait *n.* xarām خرام

galaxy *n.* kahkašāṁ کہکشاں

gall-bladder *n.* pittā پتا, zahrah زہرہ

gallery *n.* chajjā چھجا, aivān ایوان, numā'iš gāh نمائش گاہ

gallop *v.* ḍapṭānā ڈپٹانا, ḍapaṭnā ڈپٹنا

gallows *n.* sūlī سولی

gamble *v.* jū'ā khēlnā جوا کھیلنا, bāzī lagānā بازی لگانا

gambler *n.* jū'ā bāz جواباز, jō'āṛī جواری, qimār bāz قمارباز

game *n.* bāzī بازی, khēl کھیل, laᶜb لعب

gang *n.* ġōl غول; *(of robbers)* dhāṛ دھاڑ

Ganges *n.* gangā گنگا

gangster *n.* luṭērā لٹیرا

gap *n.* raxnah رخنہ

gape *v.* jamā'ī lēnā جمائی لینا

garage *n.* kār xānah کارخانہ, gāṛī xānah گاڑی خانہ

garam masala *n.* garm masālā گرم مسالا

garden *n.* bāġ باغ

garden *n.* *(full of flowers)* gul zār گل زار, phulvāṛī پھلواڑی; *(full of trees)* šāxsār شاخسار

gardener *n.* mālī مالی, mālan/mālin مالن, bāġbān باغبان

gardening *n.* bāġbānī باغبانی

gargle *v.* ġarārah karnā غرارہ کرنا, ācaman karnā آچمن کرنا

garland *n.* gajrā گجرا, mālā مالا, māl مال; *(worn during a wedding ceremony)* sēhrā سہرا

garlic *n.* lahsan/lahsun لہسن

garment *n.* pōšāk پوشاک, malbūs ملبوس; *(made of fur or leather)* pōstīn پوستین

gas *n.* gais گیس, paiṭrōl پیٹرول

gas station *n.* paiṭrōl pamp پیٹرول پمپ

gasp *v.* dam phūlnā دم پھولنا, sisaknā سسکنا

gate *n.* dar در, darvāzah دروازه, bāb باب
gatekeeper *n.* phāṭak dār پھاٹک دار
gather *v.* jamaᶜ karnā جمع کرنا, farāham karnā فراہم کرنا, ijtimāᶜ karnā اجتماع کرنا
gathering *n.* ḥašr حشر, majmaᶜ مجمع
gaudy *adj.* zarq barq زرق برق
gay *adj.* šādmāṛ شادماں
gaze *v.* ṭak bāndhnā ٹک باندھنا, taknā تکنا
gazelle *n.* ġazāl غزال
gem *n.* gauhar گوہر, jauhar جوہر
Gemini *(Zodiac) n.* jauzā جوزا, dō paikar دوپیکر
gender *n.* jins جنس
genealogy *n.* nasab نسب, pīṛhī پیڑھی
general *adj.* ᶜāmmah عامہ, ᶜumūm عموم, kullī کلی, cām عام / *n.* sipah sālār سپہ سالار, sar xail سر خیل, baxšī بخشی
general manager *n.* muxtār-ē-ᶜām مختار عام
generally *adv.* bil-ᶜumūm بالعموم, ᶜumūman عموماً
generation *n.* taulīd تولید
generic *adj.* jinsī جنسی
generosity *n.* faizān فیضان, fayyāzī فیاضی
generous *adj.* fayyāz فیاض
gentle *adj.* asīl اصیل, šarīf شریف, ḥalīm حلیم
gentleman *n.* xvājah خواجہ, mardum مردم, miyāṁ میاں
gentleness *n.* zill ذل, ḥilm حلم, āhistagī آہستگی, narmī نرمی
gently *adv.* āhistah آہستہ, haulē haulē ہولے ہولے, dhīmē dhīmē دھیمے دھیمے
genuine *adj.* aslī اصلی, xālis خالص, kharā کھرا, sac سچ
geographer *n.* māhir-ē-ᶜilm-ē-juġrāfiyah ماہر علم جغرافیہ
geography *n.* juġrāfiyah جغرافیہ
geologist *n.* māhir-ē-arziyāt ماہر علم ارضیات
geomancy *n.* ramal رمل
geometrician *n.* muhandis مہندس
geometry *n.* ᶜilm-ē-hindsah علم ہندسہ, hindsah ہندسہ, misāhat مساحت
germ *n.* bīj بیج
gesture *n.* junbiš جنبش
get *v.* kamānā کمانا, pānā پانا

get up *v.* uṭhnā اُٹھنا, jāgnā جاگنا
get used to *v.* ᶜādat paṛnā عادت پڑنا
ghee *n.* ghī گھی
ghost *n.* bhūt بھوت, bhutnā بھتنا
giant *n.* dē'ō دیو
gibbet *n.* sūlī سولی
gift *n.* tōḥfah تحفہ
ginger *n.* adrak ادرک
girl *n.* laṛkī لڑکی, chōrī چھوری, chōkrī چھوکری
girlfriend *n.* sahēlī سہیلی
give *v.* dēnā دینا
give birth *v.* janam dēnā جنم دینا; *(animals only)* *v.* biyānā بیانا
give up *v.* bāz ānā باز آنا, chōṛnā چھوڑنا, tiyāgnā تیاگنا, chōṛ dēnā چھوڑ دینا
giver *n.* baxšindah بخشندہ
glad *adj.* xūš خوش, masrūr مسرور
gladly *adv.* bāxūšī بخوشی
gladness *n.* našāt نشاط
glance *n.* nigāh نگاہ, nazar نظر
glare *n.* camak چمک / *v.* kaundnā کوندنا
glass *n.* zujāj زجاج, kāṁc کانچ, gilās گلاس, šīšah شیشہ
glasses (eyeglasses) *n.* ᶜainak عینک, cašmah چشمہ
glimmer *v.* jhilmilānā جھلملانا
glimpse *n.* jhalak جھلک
glitter *n.* jhamak جھمک, jagmagāhaṭ جگمگاہٹ, camak چمک, / *v.* jagmagānā جگمگانا, camaknā چمکنا
global *adj.* ᶜālimī عالمی
globe *n.* kurrah کرہ
gloominess *n.* murdanī مردنی
glorification *n.* iᶜzāz اعزاز
glorified *adj.* muftaxar مفتخر
glorious *adj.* jalīl جلیل, majīd مجید, zū-ul-jalāl ذوالجلال
glory *n.* jalāl جلال
glossary *n.* farhang فرہنگ
glossy *adj.* ciknā چکنا

glove *n.* dastānah دستانہ, mōzah موزہ
glow *n.* camak چمک, tamtamāhaṭ تمتماہٹ, lapaṭ لپٹ / *v.* damaknā دمکنا
glow-worm *n.* jugnū جگنو
glue *n.* sarēš سریش, gōnd گوند / *v.* cipkānā چپکانا, cipṭānā چپٹانا
glutinous *adj.* lais dār لیس دار
gnash (teeth) *v.* pīsnā پیسنا
gnaw *v.* cabānā چبانا, cābnā چابنا, bhanbōṛnā بھنبوڑنا
go *v.* jānā جانا, calnā چلنا
  go along with *v.* sāth jānā ساتھ جانا
  go away *v.* calā jānā چلا جانا, ṭalnā ٹلنا
  go back *v.* lauṭ jānā لوٹ جانا, lauṭnā لوٹنا
  go shopping *v.* xarīdārī karnā خریداری کرنا
  go to war *v.* laṛā'ī par jānā لڑائی پر جانا
goad *v.* haulnā ہولنا
goal *n.* hadaf ہدف
goat *n.* buz بز
goblet *n.* sāġar ساغر
God *n.* Allāh اللہ, ilāh الاہ, xudā خدا, bhagvān بھگوان; *(mainly in Hinduism)* dēv دیو
  God be blessed! *interj.* subḥān Allah سبحان اللہ
  God be praised! *interj.* al-ḥamdu-lillah الحمد للہ
  God forbid *phr.* mubādā مبادا / *interj.* ḥāšā Allah حاشا اللہ
  God willing *phr.* inšā' allah انشاء اللہ
Goddess *(in Hinduism) n.* Dēvī دیوی
godhead *n.* xudā'ī خدائی
godly *adj* rabbānī ربانی
god-worshipping *adj.* xudā parast خداپرست
goggles *n.* ᶜainak عینک
gold *n.* sōnā سونا, tilā طلا, zar زر
golden *adj.* zarrīṁ زریں, sōnahlā سونہلا, talā'ī طلائی
goldsmith *n.* zar gar زرگر, sunār سنار
gone *adj.* raftah رفتہ, faqq فق, guzaštah گزشتہ
gong *n.* ghanṭī گھنٹی
good *adj.* acchā اچھا, xūb خوب, xair خیر, tayyib طیب
good luck *n.* xūš qismatī خوش قسمتی

good wishes! *interj.* mubārāk bād مبارک باد
goodbye! *interj.* vidā^c وداع, xudā ḥāfiz خدا حافظ ♦ **say** ~ *v.* vidā^c karnā وداع کرنا
good-looking *adj.* vajīh وجیہ
goodness *n.* nikō kārī نکو کاری, nēkī نیکی
goods *n.* matā^c متاع, cīz چیز, māl مال
goodwill *n.* sākh ساکھ, nēk nāmī نیک نامی, irādat ارادت
goose *n.* haṁs ہنس, rāj haṁs راج ہنس, qāz قاز
gossip *n.* gap گپ, bakvās بکواس / *v.* zaṭal mārnā زٹل مارنا, gap šap karnā گپ شپ کرنا
gossiper *adj.* bakvāsī بکواسی
gossiper *n.* zaṭallī زٹلی
gourd *n.* ghiyā گھیا; *(sweet)* pēṭhā پیٹھا
govern *v.* ḥukūmat karnā حکومت کرنا, rāj karnā راج کرنا
governed *adj.* ma^cmūl معمول
government *n.* ḥukūmat حکومت, rāj راج, sarkār سرکار ♦ **national** ~ qaumī ḥukūmat قومی حکومت
government house *n.* qasr-ē-ḥukūmat قصر حکومت
government post *n.* mansab-ē-sarkārī منصب سرکاری
governor *n.* nāzim ناظم, ḥākim حاکم, ḥāfiz حافظ
gown *n.* jubbah جبہ
grace *n.* jamāl جمال, šān شان, karam کرم, lutf لطف
graceful *adj.* xūš aslūb خوش اسلوب
gracefulness *n.* sabāḥat صباحت
gracious *adj.* karīm کریم
graciousness *n.* taufīq توفیق, ni^cmat نعمت
grade *n.* darjah درجہ
gradual *adj.* rasadī رسدی
gradually *adv.* raftah raftah رفتہ رفتہ, haulē ہولے
grafted *adj.* paivandī پیوندی
grain *n.* ġallah غلہ, anāj اناج, dānah دانہ
grain merchant *n.* baqqāl بقال
grainseller *n.* baniyā بنیا
gram *n.* grām گرام, canā چنا
gram flour *n.* bēsan بیسن

grammar *n.* qavāᶜid قواعد, naḥv نحو, sarf-ō-naḥū صرف و نحو
grammarian *n.* sarfī صرفی
granary *n.* khalyān کھلیان, gaṁj گنج, maxzan مخزن
grand *adj.* šān dār شان دار
grand total *n.* mīzān-ē-kul میزان کل
granddaughter *n.* navāsī نواسی
grandeur *n.* jalāl جلال, buzurgī بزرگی, kibr کبر
grandfather *n.* jadd جد; *(maternal)* nānā نانا; *(paternal)* dādā دادا, ājā آجا
grandmother *n.* jaddah جده; *(maternal)* nānī نانی; *(paternal)* dādī دادی
grandson *n.* *(son's son)* pōtā پوتا; *(daughter's son)* navāsah نواسہ
grant *n.* hiba ہبہ, ᶜatiyyah عطیہ / *v.* dēnā دینا, marḥamat karnā مرحمت کرنا
grape *n.* angūr انگور, ᶜinab عنب ♦ **dried** ~ kišmiš کشمش, mavēz مویز
grasp *n.* girift گرفت
grasp *v.* axaz karnā اخذ کرنا, dharnā دھرنا
grass *n.* ghās گھاس, giyāh گیاہ ♦ **dried** ~ payāl پیال
grasshopper *n.* ṭiḍḍā ٹڈا, phangā پھنگا
grate *v.* ragaṛnā رگڑنا
grateful *adj.* maškūr مشکور, šukr guzār شکر گزار, mamnūn ممنون
gratefulness *n.m* šukr شکر
gratis *adj.* muft مفت / *adv.* muft mēṁ مفت میں
gratitude *n.* šukr شکر
grave *n.* qabr قبر, laḥad لحد, mazār مزار, gōr گور / *adj.* sanjīdah سنجیدہ
gravel *n.* bajrī بجری, pathrī پتھری, kankar کنکر
graveyard *n.* qabristān قبرستان
gravity *n.* kašiš-ē-siql کشش ثقل, sanjīdagī سنجیدگی
graze *v.* carnā چرنا, carānā چرانا
grease *n.* ciknā'ī چکنائی, carbī چربی, yāġ یاغ, rauġan روغن
greasy *adj.* carb چرب, rauġanī روغنی, cupṛī چپڑی, ciknā چکنا
great *adj.* baṛhiyā بڑھیا, ᶜazīm عظیم, buzurg بزرگ
Great Britain *n.* Bartāniyah برطانیہ
great grandfather *n.* *(maternal)* parnānā پرنانا; *(paternal)* pardādā پردادا
great grandmother *n.* *(maternal)* parnānī پرنانی; *(paternal)* *n.* pardādī پردادی

greater *adj.* zabar زبر
greatest *adj.* akbar اکبر
greatness *n.* baṛā'ī بڑائی, kibr کبر, ᶜazmat عظمت
Greece *n.* yūnān یونان
greed *n.* lālac لالچ, muhavvisī مہوسی
greediness *n.* ḥirs حرص, tamaᶜ طمع
greedy *adj.* tammāᶜ طماع, tāmiᶜ طامع, ḥarīs حریص
Greek *adj.* yūnānī یونانی
green *adj.* harā ہرا, haryālā ہریالا, sabz سبز
greenery *n.* sabzah سبزہ
greengrocer *n.* sabzī farōš سبزی فروش, kuṁjṛā کنجڑا
greenish *adj.* sabz sā سبز سا
greens *n.* bhājī بھاجی
greet *v.* salām karnā سلام کرنا
greeting *n.* ādāb آداب
grey *adj.* xākistarī خاکستری, bhūrā بھورا
grey-haired *adj.* bhūrē bāl vālā بھورے بال والا, zāl زال
grief *n.* ġam/ġamm غم, ḥazn/ḥuzn حزن
grieve *v.* kalapnā کلپنا, kuṛhnā کڑھنا, jhīnknā جھینکنا
grieved *adj.* ġam zadah غم زدہ, ḥasrat zadah حسرت زدہ, ranjīdah رنجیدہ
grin *n.* muskurāhaṭ مسکراہٹ / *v.* muskurānā مسکرانا
grind *v.* pīsnā پیسنا, dulnā دلنا, pērnā پیرنا, ragaṛnā رگڑنا ♦ ~ **powder** safūf banānā سفوف بنانا, cūrā cūrā karnā چورا چورا کرنا
grinder *n.* sanān سنان, ḍāṛh ڈاڑھ, xarās خراس
grindstone *n.* sān سان, cakkī چکی
grip *n.* qabzah قبضہ
grit *n.* pathrī پتھری
gritty *adj.* kirkirā کرکرا, patthrīlā پتھریلا
groan *n.* zār زار / *v.* karāhnā کراہنا, hā'ē hā'ē karnā ہائے ہائے کرنا
grocer *n.* baqqāl بقال, mōdī/mūdī مودی
grocery *n.* kiryānah کریانہ
groom *n.* sā'is سائیس
ground *adj.* kōftah کوفتہ / *n.* zamīn زمین, turāb تراب, maidān میدان
group *n.* ḥazb حزب, jamāᶜat جماعت

grow *v.* lahlahānā لہلہانا, phailnā پھیلنا, baṛhnā بڑھنا, ubharnā ابھرنا
growl *v.* ġurrānā غرانا
growth *n.* rō'īdagī روئیدگی, bālīdagī بالیدگی, našv-ō-namā نشوونما
grudge *n.* lāg لاگ, kīnah کینہ
gruel *n.* māṛī ماڑی
grumble *v.* cīṁ cīṁ karnā چیں چیں کرنا, kulbalānā کلبلانا, baṛbaṛānā بڑبڑانا
guarantee *n.* hāmī ہامی, zamānat ضمانت, kafīl کفیل
guard *n.* darbān دربان, rakhvālā رکھوالا, caukī dār چوکی دار
guardian *n.* muḥāfiz محافظ, amīn امین
guardianship *n.* tavaqī توقی
guava *n.* amrūd امرود
guess *n.* taxmīnah تخمینہ, andāzah اندازہ, qiyās قیاس / *v.* andāzah karnā اندازہ کرنا, iḥtimāl karnā اِحتمال کرنا, qiyās karnā قیاس کرنا
guest *n.* mihmān مہمان, zaif ضیف
guest-house *n.* mihmān xānah مہمان خانہ
guidance *n.* rāhnumā'ī راہنمائی, hudā ہدا, hidāyat ہدایت ♦ **divine** ~ taufīq توفیق
guide *n.* hādī ہادی, rāhnumā راہنما / *v.* rāstah dikhānā راستہ دکھانا, rāh batānā راہ بتانا
guilt *n.* jurm جرم, pāp پاپ
guilty *adj.* taqsīr vār تقصیروار, qusūr vār قصور دار, murtakib مرتکب
guise *n.* bhēs بھیس
gulf *n.* xalīj خلیج, baḥr بحر
gulp *n.* ghūnṭ گھونٹ / *v.* ḍakār jānā ڈکار جانا
gum *n.* gōnd گوند, lēs لیس
gumbo *n.* bhinḍī بھنڈی
gun *n.* tōp توپ, bandūq بندوق
gunner *n.* tōpcī توپچی
gunpowder *n.* bārūd بارود
guru *n.* panḍit پنڈت; *(spiritual guide)* gurū گرو
gust *n.* thapēṛā تھپیڑا
gutter *n.* mōrī موری, parnālah پرنالہ, nālā نالا
gypsy *n.* kaṁjar کنجر, xānah badōš خانہ بدوش

H

habit *n.* ᶜādat عادت, xū خو, xāssah خاصہ

habitual *adj.* ᶜādī عادی, šiᶜārī شعاری

habitually *adv.* ᶜādatan عادتاً

habituate *v.* xū ḍālnā خو ڈالنا

hadith *n.* ḥadīs حدیث

hail *n.* žālah ژالہ / *v.* patthar barasnā پتھر برسنا, žālah bārī hōnā ژالہ باری ہونا

hailstorm *n.* žālah bārī ژالہ باری

hair *n.* bāl بال, mū مو; *(on body)* rō'āṁ رواں; *(on head)* kēs کیس

hairdresser *n.* ḥajjām حجام

half *adj./n.* ādhā آدھا, nisf نصف, nīm نیم

hall *n.* aivān ایوان, darbār دربار

halt *v.* qiyām karnā قیام کرنا

halva *n.* ḥalvā حلوا

hammer *n.* hathauṛī ہتھوڑی, mōgrā موگرا, mēx cū میخ چو / *v.* ṭhōknā ٹھوکنا, ṭhōknā ٹھوکنا

hand *n.* hāth ہاتھ, dast دست

hand over *v.* saunpnā سونپنا

handbook *n.* dastī kitābcah دستی کتابچہ

handcuff *n.* hathkaṛī ہتھکڑی, kaṛī کڑی

handful (a ~ of) *n.* muṭṭhī bhar مٹھی بھر, yak mušt یک مشت

handful *n.* muṭṭhī مٹھی, mušt مشت,

handicraft *n.* dast kārī دست کاری

handkerchief *n.* rūmāl رومال, dast māl دست مال

handle *n.* mūṭh موٹھ, hatthā ہتھا, dastah دستہ

handmade *adj.* hath sē banā hū'ā ہاتھ سے بنا ہوا

hands and feet *n.* hāth pā'ōṁ ہاتھ پاؤں

handsome *adj.* xūbsūrat خوبصورت, ḥasīn حسین, sōhnā سوہنا, sundar سندر

handwork *n.* dast kārī دست کاری

handwriting *n.* xatt خط

hang *v.* laṭaknā لٹکنا, laṭkānā لٹکانا, phāṁsī پھانسی

hang up *v.* ṭāng dēnā ٹانگ دینا, ṭāngnā ٹانگنا, phāṁsī dēnā پھانسی دینا

hanging *adj.* laṭaktā hū'ā لٹکتا ہوا, muᶜallāq معلق
happen *v.* paṛnā پڑنا, hōnā ہونا
happily *adv.* baxūšī بخوشی, bil-xair بالخیر
happiness *n.* xairiyat خیریت, xūšī خوشی, xūšḥālī خوشحالی; *(in a marriage)* suhāg سہاگ
happy *adj.* mubārāk مبارک, masrūr مسرور, xūš خوش / *adv.* xūš خوش
harass *v.* hirāsāṁ karnā ہراساں کرنا
harbor *n.* bandar بندر, bandargāh بندرگاہ
hard *adj.* saxt سخت, muškil مشکل, ṭhōs ٹھوس,
hardness *n.* saxtī سختی, salābat صلابت
hardship *n.* xvārī خواری, taklīf تکلیف, saᶜūbat صعوبت, tašaddud تشدد
hardworking *adj.* miḥnat kaš محنت کش, miḥnatī محنتی
hare *n.* xargōš خرگوش
harm *n.* ziyāṁ زیاں, īzā ایذا, muzā'iqah مضائقہ, mazarrat مضرت / *v.* aziyat dēnā اذیت دینا, harj karnā ہرج کرنا, satānā ستانا
harmful *adj.* zarar rasāṁ ضرر رساں
harmonious *adj.* ham āhang ہم آہنگ
harmonize *v.* ittifāq bannā اِتفاق بننا
harmony *n.* ham āhangī ہم آہنگی
harsh *adj.* durušt درشت, saxt سخت
harshness *n.* duruštī درشتی
harvest *n.* fasl kaṭā'ī فصل کٹائی, xurman خرمن / *v.* fasl kāṭnā فصل کاٹنا
harvesttime *n.* kaṭā'ī کٹائی, fasl kaṭā'ī فصل کٹائی
hashish *n.* ḥašīš حشیش
haste *n.* jaldī جلدی, ᶜujlat عجلت ♦ **make** ~ *v.* jaldī karnā جلدی کرنا
hastily *adv.* haṛbaṛā kar ہڑبڑا کر
hasty *adj.* jald bāz جلدباز, haṛbaṛiyā ہڑبڑیا, ᶜājil عاجل
hat *n.* ṭōp ٹوپ, ṭōpī ٹوپی, kulāh کلاہ
hatchet *n.* tabar تبر, kulhāṛā کلہاڑا
hate *v.* ḥiqārat karnā حقارت کرنا, nafrat karnā نفرت کرنا
hateful *adj.* makrūh مکروہ
hatred *n.* nafrat نفرت
haughtiness *n.* raᶜūnat رعونت, maġrūrī مغروری, ġarūr غرور

haughty *adj.* dimāġ dār دماغ دار, maġrūr مغرور
haul *v.* ghasīṭnā گھسیٹنا
have *v.* kē pās hōnā کے پاس ہونا
hawk *n.* bāz باز, šikrah شکرہ / *v.* phērī karnā پھیری کرنا
hawker *n.* phērī vālā پھیری والا, xurdah farōš خردہ فروش
hay *n.* kāh کاہ, ḥašīš حشیش
hazard *n.* xatar خطر
hazardous *adj.* xatarnāk خطرناک
haze *n.* dhund دھند, dūd دود
haziness *n.* andhērā اندھیرا
hazy *adj.* andhērā اندھیرا
he *pron.* vah/vōh وہ, yēh یہ, vahī وہی
head *n.* sar سر, sir سر; *(of an arrow)* sirā سرا, paikān پیکان; *(of an organization or group)* sarġanah سرغنہ; *(of a bed or tomb)* sarhānah سرہانہ; *(of a religious order)* mahant مہنت; *(of a department)* sadr-ē-šu^c^bah صدر شعبہ, mīr-ē-maḥkamah میر محکمہ, sarbarāh سربراہ
headache *n.* dard-ē-sar درد سر, xumār خمار
heading *n.* ^c^unvān عنوان
headlights *(of a car) n.* battiyāṁ بتیاں
headman *n.* mukhiyā مکھیا; *(of a village)* mahtā مہتا, caudharī چودھری
headmaster *n.* mudīr مدیر
headstrong *adj.* muṁh zōr منہ زور
heal *v.* mu^c^ālajah karnā معالجہ کرنا, šifā dēnā شفا دینا, ārām dēnā آرام دینا
healer *n.* dāfa^c^ دافع, šāfī شافی
health *n.* tabī^c^at طبیعت, tandurustī تندرستی
healthy *adj.* tandurust تندرست
heap *n.* ambār انبار, ṭāl ٹال, ḍhēr ڈھیر, gaṁj گنج / *v.* lādna لادنا, thōpnā تھوپنا
hear *v.* sunnā سننا
hearing *n.* sāmi^c^ah سامعہ, sama^c^ سمع
hearsay *n.* avā'ī اوائی
heart *n.* dil دل, qalb قلب
heart disease *n.* dil kā maraz دل کا مرض, qalb kī bīmārī قلب کی بیماری
heartless *adj.* bē dil بے دل
hearty *adj.* qalbī قلبی, dilī دلی, jānī جانی

heat *n.* garmī گرمی, ḥarārat حرارت, jalan جلن, tāb تاب / *v.* garmānā گرمانا, tānā تانا, tapānā تپانا

heaven *n.* āsmān آسمان, falak فلک, firdaus فردوس ♦ ~**s be praised!** *interj.* subḥān Allah! سبحان الله

heavenly *adj.* āsmānī آسمانی, falakī فلکی

heaviness *n.* saqālat ثقالت

heavy *adj.* bhārī بھاری, vaznī وزنی

Hebrew *adj.* yahūdī یہودی

hedge *n.* bāṛā باڑا

hedgehog *n.* xār pušt خارپشت

heel *n.* ēṛī ایڑی

height *n.* bulandī بلندی, ūṁchā'ī اونچائی, irtifāᶜ ارتفاع

heir *n.* vāris وارث, xalaf خلف

held *adj.* munaᶜqid منعقد

hell *n.* pātāl پاتال, jahannum جہنم, dōzax دوزخ

hellish *adj.* jahannumī جہنمی, dōzaxī دوزخی

hello! *interj.* marḥabā مرحبا

helmet *n.* xōd خود, ḥadīd حدید

help *n.* madad مدد, sahārā سہارا; *(from God)* taufīq توفیق / *v.* madad karnā مدد کرنا, sahārā dēnā سہارا دینا

helper *n.* dast gīr دست گیر, madad gār مددگار, nāsir ناصر, nasīr نصیر

helpless *adj.* bē bas بے بس, bē cārah بے چارہ, bicārah بچارہ, majbūr مجبور

helplessly *adv.* ᶜājzānah عاجزانہ

helplessness *n.* bē axtiyārī بے اختیاری, ᶜājizī عاجزی, majbūrī مجبوری

hem *n.* maġzī مغزی, kinārī کناری

hemp *n.* bhang بھنگ

hemp-addicted *n.* bhangaṛ بھنگڑ

hen *n.* murġī مرغی, kukṛī ککڑی

hence *adv.* is li'ē اس لئے, is par اس پر, pas پس, sō سو

henna *n.* mahndī/mēhndī مہندی

hen-sparrow *n.* ciṛī چڑی

her *pron.* us اس

herb *n.* sāg ساگ

herd *n.* dal دل, galla گلہ, jhunḍ جھنڈ; *(of horses)* risālah رسالہ

herdsman *n.* ahīr اہیر, carvāhā چرواہا
here *adv.* yahāṁ یہاں, idhar اِدھر
hereafter *adv.* ā'īndah آئیندہ
hereditary *adj.* maurūsī موروثی
hereupon *adv.* is par اس پر
heritage *n.* virsah ورثہ, vārisī وارثی, virāsat وراثت
hermaphrodite *n.* xvājah sirā خواجہ سرا
hermit *n.* zāhid زاہد, qalandar قلندر, tiyāgī تیاگی,
hero *n.* bahādur بہادر, ġāzī غازی, rustam رستم
heroic *adj.* vīr ویر, sar bāz سرباز
heroism *n.* bahādrī بہادری, mardānagī مردانگی
heron *n.* baglā بگلا, sāras سارس
hesitate *v.* hickicānā ہچکچانا, tāmmul karnā تامل کرنا
hesitation *n.* hickicāhāṭ ہچکچاہٹ, tāmmul تامل
heterogeneous *adj.* nā jins ناجنس, anmēl اَمیل
hew *v.* kāṭ ḍālnā کاٹ ڈالنا
hexagon *n.* šaš pahlū شش پہلو
hiccup *n.* hickī ہچکی
hidden *adj.* chuppā/chippā چھپا, maġlūq مغلوق, mastūr مستور, maxfī مخفی
♦ ~ **treasure** dafīnah دفینہ
hide *n.* camṛā چمڑا, carm چرم khāl کھال / *v.* chupānā/chipānā چھپانا ♦ ~ **oneself** pardah karnā پردہ کرنا
hideout *n.* ōṭ اوٹ
high *adj.* buland بلند, ᶜazīm عظیم, ūṁca اونچا, ᶜālī عالی / *adv.* ūpar اوپر / *n.* muᶜallā معلی
higher *adj.* bartar برتر
highest *adj.* jēṭhā جیٹھا, uttam اُتم, ġāyat غایت
highland *n.* kōhistān کوہستان, ḍāng ڈانگ
highlander *n.* kōhistānī کوہستانی
highway *n.* šāh-ē-rāh شاہ راہ, šāriᶜ شارع
highwayman *n.* rāh zan راہ زن
hike *v.* pahāṛōṁ par caṛhnā پہاڑوں پر چڑھنا
hilarious *adj.* zindah dil زندہ دل, zarāf ظراف
hill *n.* kōh کوہ, pahāṛ پہاڑ, pahāṛī پہاڑی, jabal جبل

hill-man *n.* kōhistānī کوہستانی
hilly *adj.* kōhistānī کوہستانی
him *pron.* us اس
Himalayas *n.* himāliyah ہمالیہ
himself *pron.* xūd خود, vahī وہی
hind *n.* harnī ہرنی
hinder *v.* mānīᶜ hōnā مانع ہونا, aṭkānā اٹکانا, ruknā رکنا
hindrance *n.* ixtilāl اختلال, rōk ṭōk روک ٹوک, rukāvaṭ رکاوٹ
Hindu *adj.* hindū ہندو
Hindustan *n.* hindūstān ہندوستان
Hindustani *adj.* hindūstānī ہندوستانی
hint *n.* išārah اشارہ, kināyah کنایہ, ramz رمز / *v.* išārah karnā اشارہ کرنا
hip *n.* cūtaṛ چوتڑ
hire *n.* bhāṛā بھاڑا, ijārah اجارہ, kirāyah کرایہ / *v.* kirāyah par caṛhānā کرایہ پرچڑھانا, kirāyah par lēnā کرایہ پر لینا
hirer *n.* kirāyah dār کرایہ دار
hiss *(as a snake) v.* phunkārnā پھنکارنا
hissing *n.* phūṁ پھوں, saṁsanāhaṭ سنسناہٹ; *(of a snake)* phunkār پھنکار
historian *n.* mu'arrix مورخ, māhir-ē-ᶜilm-ē-tārīx ماہر علم تاریخ
history *n.* tārīx تاریخ, nāmah نامہ
hoe *n.* kudāl کدال, bēlak بیلک, phā'ōṛā پھاوڑا
hog *n.* sū'ar سوَر, xanzīr خنزیر
hold *n.* girift گرفت, pakaṛ پکڑ, qabzah قبضہ / *v.* dharnā دھرنا, pakaṛnā پکڑنا, rakhnā رکھنا
hold up *v.* sambhālnā سنبھالنا
hole *n.* chēd چھید, sūrāx سوراخ, rōzan/rauzan روزن, raxnah رخنہ
holiday *n.* chuṭṭī چھٹی, taᶜṭīl تعطیل, ᶜīd عید
holiness *n.* pārsā'ī پارسائی, taqaddus تقدس, ittiqā' اتقاء
hollow *adj.* mujavvaf مجوف, pūlā پولا / *n.* jauf جوف.
holy *adj.* muqaddas مقدس, mutabarrak متبرک, pāk پاک
holy crusade *n.* jihād جہاد
holy man *n.* pīr پیر
Holy Quran *n.* qur'ān šarīf قرآن شریف
holy spot *n.* mutabarrak maqām متبرک مقام, tīrath تیرتھ

holy war *n.* dīnī laṛā'ī دینی لڑائی
home *n.* ghar گھر, makān مکان
homeless *adj.* lā makān لا مکان, ḍānvāṁ ḍōl ڈانواں ڈول, bē ghar بے گھر
homemade *adj.* dēsī دیسی
homicide *n.* mardum kašī مردم کشی, qatl قتل
honest *adj.* īmān dār ایمان دار, nasūḥ نصوح, ḥaqq pasand حق پسند
honestly *adv.* īmān sē ایمان سے
honesty *n.* īmāndārī ایمانداری
honey *n.*šahd شہد, mad مد
honor *n.* ᶜizzat عزت, šaraf شرف / *v.* mān rākhnā مان رکھنا, mušarraf karnā مشرف کرنا, taᶜzīm karnā تعظیم کرنا ; *(~ somebody)* pā'ōṁ cūmnā پاؤں چومنا
honorable *adj.* fāxir فاخر, mājid ماجد, muᶜazzaz معزز, šarīf شریف
hoof *n.* khur کھر, naᶜl نعل, sum سم
hook *n.* kānṭā کانٹا, kunḍā کنڈا, qulābah قلابہ; *(for reaping)* darāntī درانتی
hop *n.* phudkī پھدکی / *v.* phudaknā پھدکنا
hope *n.* ās آس, ummīd امید / *v.* ummid hōnā امید ہونا, ummīd rakhnā امید رکھنا
hopeful *adj.* ummīdvār امیدوار, hōnhār ہونہار, mutavaqqiᶜ متوقع
hopeless *adj.* māyūs مایوس, murdah dil مردہ دل, nā ummīd نا امید
hopelessly *adv.* nā ummīdānah نا امیدانہ
hopelessness *n.* māyūsī مایوسی, nā ummīdī نا امیدی
horizon *n.* āfāq آفاق, ufaq افق, matlaᶜ مطلع
horizontal *adj.* āṛā آڑا
horn *n.* šāx شاخ, sīng سینگ, nar singhā نر سنگھا
horned *adj.* šāx dār شاخ دار
hornet *n.* zambūr زنبور, bhiṛ بھڑ
horoscope *n.* janam pattrī جنم پتری, zā'icah زائچہ, najm نجم
horrible *adj.* ghōr گھور, , dahšat angēz دہشت انگیز, ḍarā'ōnā ڈراؤنا
horror *n.* haul ہول
horse *n.* ghōṛā گھوڑا
horse race *n.* ghuṛ dauṛ گھڑ دوڑ
horse rider *n.* cābuk savār چابک سوار
horseman *n.* fāris فارس, savār سوار
horsewhip *n.* cābuk چابک
hospitable *adj.* mihmān navāz مہمان نواز

hospital *n.* aspatāl اسپتال, bimār xānah بیمار خانہ, šifā xānah شفا خانہ
hospitality *n.* mihmānī مہمانی, mihmān navāzī مہمان نوازی
host *n.* mihmān dār مہماندار, sāḥib-ē-xānah صاحب خانہ
hostage *n.* yarġamāl یرغمال
hostile *adj.* mutaxāsim متخاصم, muᶜānid معاند
hostility *n.* bair بیر, dušmanī دشمنی, ᶜadāvat عداوت, muxāsamat مخاصمت
hot *adj.* garm/garam گرم ♦ ~ **season** *n.* garmī گرمی, garmā گرما ♦ ~ **wind** *n.* lū لو
hotel *n.* hōṭal ہوٹل, musāfir xānah مسافر خانہ
hound *n.* sag-ē-šikārī سگ شکاری, šikārī kuttā شکاری کتا
house *n.* ghar گھر, makān مکان; *(of one's father-in-law) n.* susrāl سسرال
house-breaking *n.* naqb نقب, naqb zanī نقب زنی
household *n.* ᶜayāl عیال, ghar bār گھربار, gharānā گھرانا, xānumāṁ خانماں
household items *n.* gharēlū sāmān گھریلو سامان, gharēlū āšyā' گھریلو اشیاء
how *adv.* kaisē کیسے kis taraḥ کس طرح / *pron.* kyōṁkar کیونکر / *pron./adj.* kaisā کیسا
how many *adj.* cand چند / *pron.* kaē کے / *adv.* kitnā کتنا, kitnē کتنے
how much *adj./adv.* kitnā کتنا
however *adv.* gō kih گوکہ, phir bhī پھر بھی, valē ولے / *conj.* lēkin لیکن, magar مگر, par پر
hue *n.* rangat رنگت
huge *adj.* kāfī ziyādah کافی زیادہ, ᶜazīm عظیم
hum *n.* bhanak بھنک / *v.* gunganānā گنگنانا
human *adj.* ḥalīm حلیم
human being *n.* insān انسان, mānus/mānas مانس, banī ādam بنی آدم
human nature *n.* bašariat بشریت, insāniyat انسانیت
humanity *n.* ādmiyat آدمیت, insāniyat انسانیت
humble *adj.* xāksār خاکسار, ġarīb غریب, niyaz mand نیاز مند
humbleness *n.* inkisār انکسار
humbly *adv.* ġarībānah غریبانہ, ᶜājzānah عاجزانہ
humidity *n.* tarāvaṭ تراوٹ, rutūbat رطوبت, gīlāpan گیلاپن
humiliate *v.* zak dēnā زک دینا
humiliated *adj.* khisyānā کھسیانا
humiliation *n.* xušūᶜ خشوع

humility *n.* firōtī فروتی, ġarībī غریبی, ġurbat غربت; *(in a religious way)* faqīrī فقیری

humor *n.* mazḥakah مضحکہ, mizāj مزاج

humorous *adj.* zarāf ظراف, mazāqiyah مذاقیہ

hump *n.* kub کب, kūz کوز, kōhān کوہان

humpbacked *adj.* kubā کبا

hundred *num.* sau سو, sad صد

hundred thousand *num.* lākh لاکھ

hunger *n.* bhūk بھوک

hungry *adj.* bhūkā بھوکا

hunt *v.* šikār karnā شکار کرنا, šikār khēlnā شکار کھیلنا

hunter *n.* šikārī شکاری, said afgan صید افگن, saiyyād صیاد

hunting *n.* ahēr اہیر, šikār شکار

hunting dog *n.* sag-ē-šikārī سگ شکاری, šikārī kuttā شکاری کتا

hurricane *n.* kālī āndhī کالی اندھی, tūfān طوفان, jhakkaṛ جھکڑ

hurriedly *adv.* haṛbaṛā kar ہڑبڑا کر

hurry *n.* haṛbaṛī ہڑبڑی, jaldī جلدی, khalbalī کھلبلی, khalbalī کھلبلی / *v.* jaldī karnā جلدی کرنا

hurt *adj.* ghā'il گھائل, majrūḥ مجروح, mazrūb مضروب / *n.* cōṭ چوٹ, mazarrat مضرت / *v.* cōṭ karnā چوٹ کرنا, dukh dēnā دکھ دینا, dukhānā دکھانا

hurtful *adj.* taklīf dēh تکلیف دہ, muzir مضر

husband *n.* šauhar شوہر

husk *n.* cāpaṭ چاپٹ, chilkā چھلکا, cōkar چوکر / *v.* chilkā utārnā چھلکا اتارنا

hut *n.* kulbah کلبہ, jhōnpṛā جھونپڑا, maṭṭh مٹھ

hymn *n.* bhajan بھجن, gīt گیت, ḥamd حمد

hypocrisy *n.* munāfaqat منافقت, riyā ریا, riyākārī ریاکاری

hypocrite *n.* baglā bhagat بگلا بھگت, munāfiq منافق

hypocritical *adj.* pākhanḍī پاکھنڈی, riyākār ریاکار

hypothesis *n.* mafrūzah مفروضہ

I

I *pron.* maiṁ میں
ice *n.* yax یخ barf برف, salj ثلج
iced *adj.* barfīlā برفیلا
iconoclast *n.* but šikan بت شکن
icy *adj.* barfīlā برفیلا, barfānī برفانی
ID card *n.* šināxtī kārḍ شناختی کارڈ
idea *n.* xayāl خیال, fikr فکر
ideal *adj.* xayālī خیالی, vahmī وہمی / *n.* nasb-ul-ᶜain نصب العین
identical *adj.* mutābiq مطابق, ēk sā ایک سا
identification *n.* šināxt شناخت
identify *v.* šināxt karnā شناخت کرنا
identity *n.* ḥulyah حلیہ
idiom *n.* muḥāvarah محاورہ, mustalaḥ مصطلح
idiomatic *adj.* mustalaḥ مصطلح, istilāḥī اصطلاحی, ṭhēṭh ٹھیٹھ
idiomatic language *n.* ṭiksālī zabān ٹکسالی زبان
idiot *n.* pāgal پاگل, ullū الو, cuġad چغد, jullāha جلاہا
idiotically *adv.* aḥmaqānah احمقانہ
idle *adj.* bēhūdah بیہودہ, majhūl مجہول, sust سست, muzmaḥill مضمحل
idle talk *n.* gap šap گپ شپ, bēhūdagī بیہودگی
idleness *n.* taᶜattul تعطل, mavāhnat مواہنت
idol *n.* but بت, mūrtī/mūratī مورتی, sanam صنم
idolater *n.* kāfir کافر
if *conj.* agar اگر / *n./conj.* kih/kē کہ
if not *conj.* varnah ورنہ
ignoble *adj.* siflah سفلہ
ignorance *n.* nā dānistagī نا دانستگی, jihālat جہالت
ignorant *adj.* jāhil جاہل, bē vaqūf بے وقوف, kam ᶜaql کم عقل
ignorantly *adv.* aṁjānē انجانے
ill *adj.* bimār بیمار, zabūn زبون, rōgī روگی
illegal *adj.* nā jā'iz نا جائز, ḥarāmī حرامی
illegitimacy *n.* ḥarām zadgī حرام زدگی

illegitimate *adj.* ḥarāmī حرامی, ḥarām zādah حرام زاده
illiteracy *n.* jihālat جہالت, jāhlīt جاہلیت
illiterate *adj.* nā xvāndah نا خوانده, mūrakh مورکھ, jāhil جاہل
illness *n.* bimārī بیماری, āzār آزار, rōg روگ
ill-tempered *adj.* talx mizāj تلخ مزاج, bad mizāj بد مزاج, bē dimāġ بیدماغ, kaj xulq کج خلق
illuminate *v.* farōġ dēnā فروغ دینا, raušan karnā روشن کرنا
illumination *n.* farōġ فروغ, tanvīr تنویر, rōšnī روشنی
illusion *n.* māyā مایا, sarāb سراب, vahm وہم
illusory *adj.* majāzī مجازی
illustrated *adj.* munkašif منکشف, musavvar مصور
illustration *n.* tauzīḥ توضیح
illustrious *adj.* mumtāz ممتاز, jalālī جلالی, jalvah gar جلوه گر
image *n.* but بت, šabīh شبیہ
imaginary *adj.* xayālī خیالی, qiyāsī قیاسی, vahmī وہمی
imagination *n.* taxayyul تخیل, tasavvur تصور, tavahhum توہم
imagine *v.* xayāl bāndhnā خیال باندھنا, tasavvur karnā تصور کرنا
imitate *v.* taqlīd karnā تقلید کرنا
imitation *n.* savāng سوانگ, taqlīd تقلید, svāng سوانگ
imitator *n.* savāngī سوانگی
immature *adj.* kaccā کچا, nā rasīdah نا رسیده
immaturity *n.* xāmī خامی
immediately *adv.* fauran فوراً, ēk dām ایک دام
immense *adj.* baikrāṁ بیکراں, kabīr کبیر
immerse *v.* ḍubkī dēnā ڈبکی دینا, ḍōb dēnā ڈوب دینا, ḍubōnā ڈبونا
immersion *n.* ḍōb ڈوب
immoderate *adj.* bē andāzah بے اندازه
immodest *adj.* bē ḥijāb بے حجاب, bē ḥayā بے حیا, bē pardah بے پرده
immoral *adj.* adharmī اِدھرمی
immorality *n.* baqā بقا
immortal *adj.* lā yamūt لایموت, jāvidāṁ جاوداں
immovable *adj.* acal اچل, sābit qadam ثابت قدم, aṭal اٹل
immunity *n.* amān امان
impale *v.* mēx ṭhōnknā میخ ٹھونکنا

impartiality *n.* insāf انصاف
impassable *adj.* aughat اوگھٹ
impatience *n.* tilmalī تلملی, nā sabūrī نا صبوری
impatient *adj.* bē dimāġ بیدماغ, bē tāb بے تاب, bē sabr بے صبر
impeach *v.* mu'āxazah karnā مواخذہ کرنا
impede *v.* muᶜtariz hōnā معترض ہونا, aṭkānā اٹکانا
impediment *n.* māniᶜ مانع, muzāḥamat مزاحمت, ᶜārizah عارضہ
impel *v.* calānā چلانا, dauṛānā دوڑانا
imperative *adj.* farzī فرضی
imperceptible *adj.* xafī خفی
imperfect *adj.* ġair mukammal غیر مکمل, manqūs منقوص, nā tamām ناتمام
imperfection *n.* xāmī خامی
imperial *adj.* bādšāhānah بادشاہانہ, šāhinšāhī شاہنشاہی, šāhānah شاہانہ, ᶜāmirah عامرہ
impertinent *adj.* bad zabān بدزبان
impetuosity *n.* ḥamīt حمیت, saulat صولت
impious *adj.* fāsiq فاسق, kāfir کافر
implore *v.* ᶜājizī karnā عاجزی کرنا
imply *v.* maᶜni rakhnā معنی رکھنا
impolite *adj.* cibilā چبلا, bē adab بے ادب, nā tarāšīdah ناتراشیدہ
impoliteness *n.* bē adabī بے ادبی
import *n.* dar āmad درآمد / *v.* dar āmad karnā درآمد کرنا
important *adj.* aham/ahm اہم
importunity *n.* lajājat لجاجت
impose (a duty) *v.* farz karnā فرض کرنا
impossible *adj.* muḥāl محال, ġair mumkin غیر ممکن
imposter *n.* farēbī فریبی
impotence *n.* nā cārī ناچاری, nā tavanī ناتوانی
impotent *adj.* nā tavān ناتواں
impoverish *v.* muflis karnā مفلس کرنا, muḥtāj karnā محتاج کرنا
impoverished *adj.* ġurbat zadah غربت زدہ
impressed *adj.* mutā'assir متاثر
impression *n.* chāp چھاپ, tabaᶜ طبع, tā'asur تأثر, dāb داب
impressively *adv.* mutā'assifānah متاسفانہ

imprison *v.* mūndnā موندنا, qaid karnā قید کرنا
imprisoned *adj.* muqaiyyad مقید
imprisonment *n.* bandhan بندھن, qaid قید, bandī بندی, ḥabs حبس
improper *adj.* nā ḥaqq ناحق, bē jā بے جا, ġair vājib غیر واجب
improperly *adv.* nā ḥaqq ناحق
improvement *n.* tarmīm ترمیم, bihtarī بہتری
imprudent *adj.* ġabī غبی, kōtāh bīn کوتاہ بین
impudence *n.* ḍhiṭā'ī ڈھٹائی
impudent *adj.* bad liḥāz بد لحاظ, fāḥiš فاحش
impure *adj.* najis/najs نجس, nā pāk ناپاک
impurity *n.* nā pākī ناپاکی, kudūrat کدورت
in *prep.* mēṁ میں, bīc بیچ, dar در, fī فی
  in addition *adv.* savā سوا, maᶜ hazā مع ہذا
  in addition (to) *adv.* ᶜilāvah علاوہ
  in front *adv.* sāmnē سامنے, āgē آگے
  in love *adj.* dil bastah دل بستہ, šēftah شیفتہ / *adv.* farēftah فریفتہ
  in order to *prep.* tākih تاکہ, tā تا
  in person *adv.* bil-mušāfah بالمشافہ
inability *n.* nā tavanī ناتوانی
inaccessible *adj.* agam اگم, aughat اوگھٹ
inaccurate *adj.* bē jā بے جا
inactive *adj.* ālasī آلسی
inactivity *n.* jamūd جمود
inanimate *adj.* sāmit صامت
inattentive *adj.* ġāfil غافل
inauguration *n.* iftitāḥ افتتاح
inauspicious *adj.* kālā zabān کالی زبان, naḥs نحس
inborn *adj.* mādar zād مادر زاد, paidā'išī پیدائشی
incantation *n.* mantar jantar منتر جنتر
incapability *n.* nā rasā'ī نارسائی
incapable *adj.* ᶜājiz عاجز
inch *n.* iṁc انچ
incident *n.* vāqiᶜa واقعہ, ḥādisah/ḥādsah حادثہ, ᶜāriz عارض
incidental *adj.* ittifāqī اتفاقی

incidentally *adv.* zimnan ضمناً, ḥasb-ē-ittēfāq حسب اتفاق
incision *n.* kāṭ کاٹ
incite *v.* bhaṛkānā بھڑکانا, uksānā اکسانا
inclination *n.* raġbat رغبت, rujūᶜ رجوع, mailān میلان
incline *v.* jhuknā جھکنا,, jhukānā جھکانا, rujūᶜ karnā رجوع کرنا
inclined *adj.* mā'il مائل, rāġib راغب, maᶜṭūf معطوف
include *v.* dāxil karnā داخل کرنا, šāmil karnā شامل کرنا, šarīk karnā شریک کرنا
inclusion *n.* šamūliyat شمولیت, ištimāl اشتمال
inclusive *adj.* mutazarrib متضرب, dāxilī داخلی
income *n.* dar āmad درآمد, kamā'ī کمائی ♦ ~ **and expenditure** darāmad barāmad درآمد برآمد ♦ ~ **and expenses** āmad-ō-xarc آمد و خرچ
incomparable *adj.* farīd فرید, lā sānī لاثانی, yagānah یگانہ
incomplete *adj.* ġair mukammal غیر مکمل, nā tamām ناتمام
inconceivable *adj.* baᶜīd-ul-qiyās بعید القیاس
inconsiderate *adj.* bē tāmmul بے تامل
inconsistent *adj.* ġair mustaqil غیر مستقل, fānī فانی
inconstancy *n.* nā pā'īdārī ناپائیداری
inconstant *adj.* nā pā'īdār ناپائیدار, mutalavvin متلون
incorrect *adj.* ġalat غلط, nā durust نا درست
increase *n.* ziyādatī زیادتی, mazīd مزید, baṛhā'ī بڑھائی, baṛhtī بڑھتی / *v.* ziyādah karnā زیادہ کرنا, baṛhānā بڑھانا, baṛhnā بڑھنا
incredible *adj.* bē asal بے اصل, ġair muᶜatabir غیر معتبر
incumbent *adj.* farzī فرضی
incurable *adj.* lā ᶜilāj لاعلاج, lā davā لا دوا
incursion *n.* dauṛ دوڑ
indebted *adj.* qarz dār قرض دار, madyūn مدیون
indecent *adj.* bad zabān بدزبان, fuḥš فحش, maᶜyūb معیوب, fāḥiš فاحش
indecision *n.* taradud تردد
indeed *adj.* acchā اچھا / *adv.* hī ہی, vāqaᶜī واقعی, bil-faᶜil بالفعل
indefinite *adj.* ġair maḥdūd غیر محدود
independence *n.* xūd muxtārī خود مختاری, āzādī آزادی
independent *adj.* muxtār مختار, āzād آزاد
indestructible *adj.* lā zavāl لازوال, lā fānī لافانی, amiṭ امٹ
index *n.* kalīd کلید, fihrist فہرست

India *n.* inḍiyā انڈیا, hindūstān ہندوستان
Indian *adj.* hindūstānī ہندوستانی
indication *n.* dalālat دلالت, maᶜnī/maᶜnā معنی
indifference *n.* rukhā'ī رکھائی, bē iᶜtinā'ī بے اِعتنائی, bē tavajhī بے توجہی
indigence *n.* nā dārī ناداری
indigenous *adj.* dēsī دیسی
indigent *adj.* maflūk مفلوک, niyaz mand نیاز مند, nā dār نادار
indigestible *adj.* nāqābil hazm ناقابل ہضم
indigestion *n.* bad hazmī بد ہضمی
indirect *adj.* furūᶜī فروعی, bil-vāstah بالواسطہ
indirectly *adv.* kināyitan کنایتاً, bil-vāstah taur par بالواسطہ طور پر
indiscreet *adj.* kōtāh bīn کوتاہ بین
indispensable *adj.* zarūrī ضروری, lāzimī لازمی
indisposition *n.* nā cāqī ناچاقی, kasal کسل, kasālat کسالت
indisputable *adj.* ġair mutanāzaᶜ غیر متنازع, yaqīnī یقینی
indistinct *adj.* ġair vāziḥ غیر واضح, mubham مبہم
individual *adj.* fard فرد, vāḥid واحد, nij نج / *n.* nafar نفر, mutanaffis متنفس, šaxs شخص
individuality *n.* aḥdiyat احدیت, šaxsiyyat شخصیت
individually *adv.* infirādītaur par انفرادی طور پر, alag alag الگ الگ
indolence *n.* ārām talbī آرام طلبی, mavāhnat مواہنت, vahn وہن, kāhilī کاہلی
indolent *adj.* kāhil کاہل
induce *v.* bhaṛkānā بھڑکانا
indulgence *n.* jī bhar جی بھر, šauq شوق, xū خو
industrial *adj.* sanᶜatī صنعتی
industrious *adj.* miḥnatī محنتی
industry *n.* sanāᶜt صنعت
ineffective *adj.* ġair mutā'ssir غیر متأثر
inefficient *adj.* nākārah ناکارہ, bē asar بے اثر
inequality *n.* ᶜadam musāvāt عدم مساوات
inequity *n.* nā insāfī ناانصافی
inestimable *adj.* anmōl انمول, bē andāzah بے اندازہ
inevitable *adj.* aṭal اٹل, mubram مبرم, lā budī لابدی, lāzimī لازمی
inevitably *adv.* cār-ō-nācār چاروناچار

inexperience *n.* bhōlāpan بھولاپن
inexpressible *adj.* mā lā kalām مالا کلام
inextricable *adj.* nā qābil ḥall نا قابل حل, mā lā yanḥal مالاینحل
infamous *adj.* bad nām بدنام, rusvā رسوا
infamy *n.* xizzī خزی, rusvā'ī رسوائی, hajv ہجو
infancy *n.* bacpan بچپن, saġīrī صغیری
infant *n.* baccah بچہ, tifl طفل
infantile *adj.* tiflānah طفلانہ
infection *n.* chūt چھوت, sirāyat سرایت, ᶜafūnat عفونت
inferior *adj.* nīcā نیچا, siflī سفلی, radī/raddī ردی, ghaṭiyā گھٹیا, mā taḥat ماتحت
♦ ~ **to** *prep./adj.* zēr زیر
inferiority *n.* pastī پستی
infernal *adj.* jahannumī جہنمی, dōzaxī دوزخی
inferno *n.* dōzax دوزخ
infidel *n.* kāfir کافر, bē imān بے ایمان, zimmī ذمی
infidelity *n.* kufr کفر, bē imānī بے ایمانی, kufrān کفران
infinite *adj.* bē intihā بے انتہا, bē ḥadd بے حد
inflame *v.* jalānā جلانا, bhaṛkānā بھڑکانا
inflamed *adj.* jaltā hū'ā جلتا ہوا, muḥriq محرق, barāfruxtah برافروختہ, muštaᶜil مشتعل
inflammation *n.* jalan جلن, varam ورم
inflate *v.* phulānā پھلانا
inflection *n.* tasrīf تصریف
influence *n.* asar اثر / *v.* asar karnā اثر کرنا
inform *v.* muttalaᶜ karnā مطلع کرنا, xabar dēnā خبر دینا, janānā جتانا
information *n.* maᶜlūmāt معلومات, xabar خبر, itlāᶜ اطلاع
informed *adj.* bā xabar باخبر, muttalaᶜ مطلع
informer *n.* muxbir مخبر, xabar gīr خبر گیر
ingenius *adj.* zahīn ذہین
ingenuity *n.* ہنر مندی hunar mandī, hōšiyārī ہوشیاری
ingratitude *n.* kufrān کفران, kufrān-ē-niᶜmat کفران نعمت
ingredient *n.* juz جز, juzū جزو
inhabitant *n.* rahnē vālā رہنے والا, bāšindah باشندہ
inhabited *adj.* basā hū'ā بسا ہوا, maᶜmūr معمور

inhale *v.* sūnghnā سونگھنا, sāṁs lēnā سانس لینا
inharmonious *adj.* بے آہنگ bē āhang, bē mēl بے میل
inherent *adj.* xilqī خلقی
inherit *v.* vāris hōnā وارث ہونا
inheritance *n.* irs ارث, vārisī وارثی, virāsat وراثت
inhuman *adj.* bē murauvat بے مروت
injure *v.* īzā dēnā ایذا دینا, majrūḥ karnā مجروح کرنا
injurious *adj.* nuqsān dēh نقصان دہ, zarar rasāṁ ضرررساں
injury *n.* zarar ضرر, mazarrat مضرت, cōṭ چوٹ
injustice *n.* bē insāfī بے انصافی
ink *n.* siyahī سیاہی, raušanā'ī/rōšnā'ī روشنائی
inkpot *n.* davāt دوات
inky *adj.* ḥamat حمت
inn *n.* musāfir xānah مسافر خانہ, kārvāṁ sarā'ē کارواں سرائے
innate *adj.* mādar zād مادرزاد, paidā'išī پیدائشی tabīcī طبیعی
innocence *n.* maᶜsūmiyat معصومیت, pākdāmnī پاکدامنی, bhōlāpan بھولاپن
innocent *adj.* maᶜsūm معصوم, pākdāman پاکدامن, bē gunāh بے گناہ, bhōlā بھولا
inquire *v.* pūchnā پوچھنا, taftīš karnā تفتیش کرنا, taḥqīq karnā تحقیق کرنا
inquirer *n.* mutalāšī متلاشی, jō'indah جوئندہ, jōyā جویا
inquiry *n.* mabḥas مبحث, taftīš تفتیش, taḥqīq تحقیق, taḥqīqāt تحقیقات
insane *adj.* junūnī جنونی, dīvānā دیوانا, pāgal پاگل
insanity *n.* junūn جنون, xabt خبط, dīvānagī دیوانگی
inscribe *v.* sabt karnā ثبت کرنا
inscription *n.* kandah kārī کندہ کاری, katbah کتبہ, kitābah کتابہ
insect *n.* kīṛī کیڑی, kīṛā کیڑا, ḥašrah حشرہ; *(flying ~)* patangā پتنگا
insensibility *n.* bē ḥavāsī بے حواسی, madhōšī مدہوشی
insensible *adj.* sun سن, karaxt کرخت
insert *v.* darj karnā درج کرنا, ghusēṛnā گھسیڑنا, utār lēnā اُتارلینا
inside *adv.* andar اندر / *n.* bātin باطن / *prep.* andar اندر, darōṁ دروں
insight *n.* basīrat بصیرت, basar بصر
insignificant *adj.* lā yaᶜnī لایعنی, hēc ہیچ, xafīf خفیف, nā cīz ناچیز
insincere *adj.* farēbī فریبی, daġā bāz دغاباز, kīnah var کینہ ور
insolent *adj.* bē adab بے ادب, šōx شوخ

insoluble *adj.* lā ḥal لا حل, mā lā yanḥal مالاینحل
insolvency *n.* nā dārī نا داری
insolvent *adj.* muflis مفلس, nā dār نا دار
inspect *v.* muᶜāyanah karnā معاینہ کرنا, parakhnā پرکھنا, dēkhnā bhālnā دیکھنا بھالنا
inspection *n.* iḥtisāb اِحتساب, mulāḥazah ملاحظہ, muᶜāyanah معاینہ, parakh پرکھ
inspector *n.* muᶜāyanah kār معاینہ کار
inspiration *n.* ilhām الہام, vaḥī وحی
instability *n.* nā pā'īdārī نا پائیداری
install *v.* biṭhānā بٹھانا
instance *n.* nazīr نظیر, misāl مثال
instantly *adv.* fauran فوراً, ēk dām ایک دام, ab hī اب ہی, turt ترت
instead *adv.* bajā'ē بجائے
instead of *prep./adv.* li'ē لئے
institute *n.* dars gāh درس گاہ
instruct *v.* samjhānā سمجھانا, paṛhānā پڑھانا, sikhānā سکھانا, taᶜlīm karnā تعلیم کرنا
instruction *n.* hidāyat ہدایت, fahmā'iš فہمائش, paṛhā'ī پڑھائی, taᶜlīm تعلیم
instructor *n.* muršid مرشد, muᶜallim معلم, ustād اُستاد
instrument *n.* ālah آلہ, hathiyār ہتھیار
insult *n.* zillat ذلت, ihānat اہانت / *v.* bē ᶜizzati karnā بے عزتی کرنا, ᶜizzat bigāṛnā عزت بگاڑنا, latāṛnā لتاڑنا
insurance *n.* bīmah بیمہ
insurrection *n.* sarkašī سرکشی
integrity *n.* salāḥiyyat صلاحیت
intellect *n.* ᶜaql عقل, dimāġ دماغ
intellectual *adj.* ᶜaqlī عقلی, zahīn ذہین, dimāġī دماغی
intelligence *n.* hōšiyārī ہوشیاری, ᶜaql mandī عقل مندی, hōš mandī ہوشمندی
intelligent *adj.* hōš mand ہوش مند, tēz faham تیز فہم, hōšiyār ہوشیار, ᶜaql mand عقل مند
intend *v.* irādah karnā ارادہ کرنا, qasd karnā قصد کرنا
intended *adj.* matlūb مطلوب, maqsūd مقصود
intent *n.* maqsad مقصد, matlab مطلب
intention *n.* irādah ارادہ, maqsad مقصد, mansūbah منصوبہ
intentionally *adv.* irādatan ارادۃً, bil-irādah بالارادہ, ᶜamadan عمداً
interchange *n.* bāhm tabādalah باہم تبادلہ, phērā phērī پھیرا پھیری / *v.* adlā badlā karnā ادلا بدلا کرنا

interest *n.* dil caspī دل چسپی, matlab مطلب, lābh لابھ; *(on money)* sūd سود, ribā ربا
interesting *adj.* dil casp دلچسپ
interference *n.* mudāxalat مداخلت, ḥarj حرج
interim *n.* asnā' اثناء
interlocutor *n.* ham saxun ہم سخن, kalīm کلیم
intermediate *adj.* ausaṭī اوسطی
interment *n.* tadfīn تدفین
intermission *n.* muhlat مہلت, vaqfah وقفہ
internal *adj.* dāxilī داخلی, bātinī باطنی, bhītarī بھیتری
internally *adv.* andar sē اندر سے
international *adj.* bayn-al-āqvāmī بین الاقوامی
interpretation *n.* tašrīḥ تشریح, tāvīl تاویل, taᶜbīr تعبیر
interpret *v.* maᶜnī dēnā معنی دینا
interpreter *n.* tarjumān ترجمان, mutarjim مترجم
interrupt *v.* bāt kāṭnā بات کاٹنا, ḥā'il hōnā حائل ہونا, rōknā روکنا
interruption *n.* mudāxalat مداخلت, ṭōk ٹوک, xalaš خلش, xalal خلل
interval *n.* fāsilah فاصلہ, qāb قاب, muddat مدت; *(~ of time)* vaqfah وقفہ
intervention *n.* mudāxalat مداخلت, bīc bacā'ō بیچ بچاؤ
interview *n.* muvājahah مواجہہ, rū ba-rū sū'āl-ō-javāb رو برو سوال و جواب
intimacy *n.* qurbat قربت, ixtilāt اختلاط, muvānasat موانست, xullat خلت, ulfat الفت
intimate *adj.* mānūs مانوس, qarībī قریبی
intimidation *n.* dhamkī دھمکی, taxvīf تخویف
into *adv.* bīc بیچ / *prep.* is mēṁ اس میں, dar در, fī فی
intolerable *adj.* nā qābil bardāšt نا قابل برداشت
intoxicated *adj.* sar mast سر مست, maxmūr مخمور, matvālā متوالا, mast مست
intoxicating *adj.* našīlā نشیلا
intoxication *n.* našah نشہ, mastī مستی, xumār خمار
intricacy *n.* muškil مشکل
intricate *adj.* pēc dār پیچ دار muškil مشکل, muġlaq مغلق
intrigue *n.* sāz bāz سازباز, sāziš سازش
introduce *v.* jārī karnā جاری کرنا, rivāj dēnā رواج دینا
introduction *n.* taᶜāruf تعارف, tamhīd تمہید, dībācah/dēbācah دیباچہ
intruder *n.* daxl andāz دخل انداز, muxill مخل
intuition *n.* āgāhī آگاہی

intuitive *adj.* vijdānī وجدانی
inundation *n.* tuġyānī طغیانی, sailāb سیلاب
invaluable *adj.* bē bahā بے بہا, anmōl انمول, anmōl انمول
invasion *n.* tāxt تاخت, yūriš یورش, caṛhā'ī چڑھائی
invent *v.* paidā karnā پیدا کرنا īījād karnā ایجاد کرنا, ixtirāᶜ karnā اِختراع کرنا, ghaṛnā گھڑنا
invented *adj.* paidā پیدا
invention *n.* īījād ایجاد, ixtirāᶜ اِختراع, ghaṛat گھڑت
inventor *n.* mūjid موجد
inventory *n.* fihrist فہرست
inverse *adj.* ulṭā الٹا, munaᶜkis منعکس
inversion *n.* ulaṭ الٹ
investigate *v.* daryāft karnā دریافت کرنا, taftīš karnā تفتیش کرنا , taḥqīq karnā تحقیق کرنا
investigation *n.* daryāft دریافت, tajassus تجس , taftīš تفتیش , taḥqīq تحقیق
invincible *adj.* nā qābil tasxīr نا قابل تسخیر
invisible *adj.* alōp الوپ, ġā'ib غائب, ġaib غیب , nā dīdah نا دیده
invitation *n.* niyōtā نیوتا, daᶜvat دعوت
invite *v.* bulānā بلانا, daᶜvat dēnā دعوت دینا
invoice *n.* bil بل
involved *adj.* šāmil شامل, mubtalā مبتلا, māxūz ماخوذ
inward *adj.* andarūnī اندرونی, bhītarī بھیتری
Iran *n.* īrān ایران
Iranian *adj.* īrānī ایرانی
irascibility *n.* tāmas تامس
iron *n.* lōhā/lauhā لوہا, āhan آہن, ḥadīd حدید
ironically *adv.* tanzan طنزاً
ironsmith *n.* lōhār لوہار
irony *n.* taᶜn zanī طعن زنی
irrational *adj.* nā maᶜqūl نا معقول, bē dalīl بے دلیل
irregular *adj.* xilāf qāᶜidah خلافِ قاعده, kaj raftār کج رفتار
irreligious *adj.* lā mazhab لا مذہب
irresolution *n.* bē istiqlāl بے استقلالی, tāmmul تامل
irresponsibility *n.* ġair zimmah dārī غیر ذمہ داری, kōtāhī کوتاہی

irrigate *v.* sīṁcnā سینچنا , pānī dēnā پانی دینا
irrigation *n.* sīṁc سینچ , ābyārī آبیاری, āb pāšī آب پاشی
irritate *v.* chēṛnā چھیڑنا, khujānā کھجانا
irritation *n.* chēṛ چھیڑ
Islam *n.* islām اسلام
Islamic *adj.* islāmī اسلامی, musalmānī مسلمانی
Islamic fighters *n.* mujāhidīn مجاہدین
island *n.* jazīrah جزیرہ; *(small ~)* ṭāpū ٹاپو
isolated *adj.* ēkānt ایکانت, munfarid منفرد
issue *n.* amar امر, xurūj خروج, ijrā' اِجراء, nikās نکاس / *v.* jārī karnā جاری کرنا, ijrā' karnā اِجراء کرنا, sādir karnā صادر کرنا, šā'iᶜ karnā شائع کرنا
it *pron.* vah/vōh وہ, is اس, yēh یہ
itch *n.* xāriš خارش, khāj کھاج / *v.* khujānā کھجانا , kulbalānā کلبلانا
itchiness *n.* kulbalāhaṭ کلبلاہٹ
itchy *adj.* xārišī خارشی
item *n.* xurdah خردہ
ivory *n.* ᶜāj عاج, hāthi dānt ہاتھی دانت

J

jackal *n.* šaġāl شغال, gīdaṛ گیدڑ
jacket *n.* cōlī چولی
jail *n.* jēl جیل, maḥbas محبس, qaid xānah قید خانہ, zindān زندان
jalebi *(deep-fried sweet) n.* jalēbī جلیبی
January *n.* janvarī جنوری
jar *n.* ghaṛā گھڑا, martabān مرتبان, māṭ ماٹ, sabū سبو; *(large ~)* xum خم
jasmine *n.* jūhī جوہی, cambīlī چنبیلی, saman سمن, yāsamīn یاسمین
jasmine flower *n.* cambēlī چمبیلی
jaw *n.* jabṛā جبڑا, kallā کلا
jealous *adj.* ḥāsid حاسد, ḥasūd حسود
jealousy *n.* ḍāh ڈاہ, ḥasad حسد, rašk رشک, xār خار
jerk *n.* hickā ہچکا, jhaṭkā جھٹکا / *v.* jhaṭaknā جھٹکنا
jest *n.* ṭhaṭā ٹھٹا
jester *n.* laṭīfah gō لطیفہ گو, ṭhaṭhē bāz ٹھٹھے باز
Jesus *n.* ᶜīsā عیسی
Jew *n.* yahūdī یہودی
jewel *n.* jauhar جوہر, zēvar زیور
jeweler *n.* jauharī جوہری
jewelry *n.* zēvrāt زیورات
Jewish *adj.* yahūdī یہودی
jihad *n.* jihād جہاد
jingle *n.* jhankār جھنکار, ṭhan ṭhan ٹھن ٹھن / *v.* jhanjhanānā جھنجھنانا, khanaknā کھنکنا
jobless *adj.* bē ḥāl بے حال, muᶜattal معطل
jockey *n.* cābuk savār چابک سوار
join *v.* gāṁṭhnā گانٹھنا, jōṛnā جوڑنا, juṛnā جڑنا, milānā ملانا
joint *adj.* girah dār گرہ دار / *n.* band بند, ᶜuzū عضو, gāṁṭh گانٹھ, jōṛ جوڑ
joke *n.* laṭīfah لطیفہ, mazāq مذاق, ṭhaṭā ٹھٹا ♦ **tell ~s** *v.* mazḥakah uṛānā مضحکہ اڑانا
joker *n.* laṭīfah gō لطیفہ گو, masxarah مسخرہ, ṭhaṭhē bāz ٹھٹھے باز
jolly *adj.* haṁs mukh ہنس مکھ

jolt *n.* dhakkā دھکا, hackōlā ہچکولا, hickā ہچکا
jostle *n.* dhakkā دھکا / *v.* dhakēlnā دھکیلنا
journalist *n.* saḥāfī صحافی
journey *n.* musāfirī مسافری, safar سفر, siyāḥat سیاحت
joy *n.* farḥat فرحت, xūšī خوشی
joyful *adj.* farḥaṁ فرحاں, ḥašāš bašāš حشاش بشاش, bašāš بشاش
joyfulness *n.* bašāšat بشاشت
jubilee *n.* jašn جشن
judge *n.* munsif منصف, qāzī قاضی / *v.* rā'ē dēnā رائے دینا
judgment *n.* tamīz تمیز, rā'ē رائے, hōš ہوش
judicial *adj.* ᶜadālatī عدالتی
judicial decision *n.* faislah-ē-ᶜadālat فیصلہ عدالت
judicially *adv.* ḥākimānah حاکمانہ
judicious *adj.* tamīzdār تمیزدار
jug *n.* kūzah کوزہ
juggler *n.* bāzī gar بازی گر, šuᶜbadah bāz شعبدہ باز
juggling *n.* šuᶜbadah شعبدہ
juice *n.* ᶜaraq عرق, ras رس, šīrah شیرہ
juicy *adj.* ras bharā رس بھرا, rasīlā رسیلا, tar تر
July *n.* jūlā'ī جولائی
jump *n.* chalāng چھلانگ, jast جست / *v.* kūdnā کودنا
junction *n.* paivand پیوند, paivastgī پیوستگی, sangam سنگم
June *n.* jūn جون
jungle *n.* dašt دشت, jangal جنگل
Jupiter *n.* muštarī مشتری
jurisdiction *n.* ᶜilāqah علاقہ, ḥukm حکم, qalam rau قلم رو, taᶜalluqah تعلقہ
jury *n.* paṁcāyat پنچایت
just *adj.* ᶜādil عادل, ḥaqīqī حقیقی, jā'iz جائز, munsif منصف / *adv.* hī ہی
justice *n.* ᶜadālat عدالت, ᶜadl عدل, insāf انصاف
justly *adv.* munsifānah منصفانہ

K

Kaaba *n.* xānah-ē-kaᶜbah خانہ کعبہ, xānah-ē-xudā خانہ خدا
kebab *n.* kabāb کباب
keen *adj.* tēz تیز
keep *v.* dharnā دھرنا, rakhnā رکھنا
  keep a fast *v.* rōzah rakhnā روزہ رکھنا
  keep back *v.* pīchē rahnā پیچھے رہنا
  keep company *v.* suḥbat rakhnā صحبت رکھنا
  keep faith *v.* vafā karnā وفا کرنا
  keep in custody *v.* qaid rakhnā قید رکھنا
  keep order *v.* intizām rakhnā انتظام رکھنا
  keep something secret *v.* dil mēṁ rakhnā دل میں رکھنا
  keep watch *v.* caukasī karnā چوکسی کرنا
keeper *n.* ḥārris حارس, muḥāfiz محافظ, rakhvālā رکھوالا
kernel *n.* maġz مغز, gūdah گودہ
kettle *n.* kētlī کیتلی; *(small ~)* patīlī پتیلی
kettledrum *n.* naqārah نقارہ, ḍankā ڈنکا, kōs کوس
key *n.* cābī چابی, kalīd کلید, miftāḥ مفتاح
keynote *n.* dhun دھن, ḍāt ڈاٹ
kick *n.* lāt لات, ṭhuḍḍā ٹھڈا / *v.* lāt mārnā لات مارنا, ṭhukrānā ٹھکرانا
kid *n.* mēmnā میمنا
kidney *n.* gurdah گردہ
kill *v.* mārnā مارنا
kilogram *n.* kilōgrām کلوگرام
kilometer *n.* kilūmīṭar کلومیٹر
kin *n.* kufū کفو
kind *adj.* mihrbān مہربان, raḥīm رحیم, šafīq شفیق / *n.* jins جنس, nauᶜ نوع, qism قسم
kindhearted *adj.* raḥm dil رحم دل, raqīq-ul-qalb رقیق القلب
kindle *v.* bhaṛkānā بھڑکانا, sulgānā سلگانا
kindly *adv.* mušfiqānah مشفقانہ
kindness *n.* karam کرم, mihrbānī مہربانی, navāziš نوازش, raḥmat رحمت
kindred *n.* yagānah یگانہ

king *n.* bādšāh بادشاہ, mahā rāj مہاراج, malik ملک, rājah راجہ, šāh شاہ
king's court *n.* bādšāhī ᶜadālat بادشاہی عدالت
kingdom *n.* bādšāhat بادشاہت, mamlakat مملکت, rāj راج, saltanat سلطنت
kingly *adj.* šāhānah شاہانہ
kinship *n.* apnāyat اپنائیت, rištah رشتہ
kinsman *n.* mutavallī متولی, rištah dār رشتہ دار, yagānah یگانہ, zāt bhā'ī ذات بھائی
kiss *n.* bōsah بوسہ, cūmā چوما, cummā چما, cummī چمی / *v.* bōsah dēnā بوسہ دینا, bōsah lēnā بوسہ لینا, cūmnā چومنا
kitchen *n.* bāvarcī xānah باورچی خانہ, matbax مطبخ, rasō'ī رسوئی
kite *n.* patang پتنگ, cīl چیل
knead *v.* mathnā متھنا, māndnā مانڈنا
knee *n.* ghuṭnā گھٹنا, zānū زانو
kneel down *v.* dō zānū hōnā دو زانو ہونا
knife *n.* cāqū چاقو; *(long ~)* churī چھری
knit *v.* bināvaṭ بناوٹ
knock *n.* ṭhēs ٹھیس
knock *v.* kharkharānā کھڑکھڑانا, ṭakkar mārnā ٹکر مارنا; *(~ at the door)* khaṭkhaṭānā کھٹکھٹانا
knock down *v.* mār girānā مار گرانا, paṭaknā پٹکنا
knot *n.* ᶜaqd عقد, ᶜuqdah عقدہ, gāṁṭh گانٹھ, girah گرہ / *v.* ᶜaqd karnā عقد کرنا, phandā lagānā پھندا لگانا
knotty *adj.* gaṭhīlā گٹھیلا
know *v.* maᶜlūm karnā معلوم کرنا, jānnā جاننا
knowingly *adv.* dānistah دانستہ
knowledge *n.* maᶜlūmāt معلومات, jānkārī جانکاری, ᶜilm علم, dāniš دانش, maᶜrifat معرفت
known *adj.* rūšināš روشناس, maᶜlūm معلوم
knuckle *n.* girah گرہ, band بند
kohl *(black eye cosmetic) n.* kājal کاجل

L

labor *n.* jad-ō-jahad جدوجہد , kār کار , kām kāj کام کاج , mazdūrī/muzdūrī مزدوری
laboratory *n.* kār xānah کارخانہ
laborer *n.* qulī قلی , kārīgar کاریگر , mazdūr/muzdūr مزدور
laborious *adj.* kamā'ū کماؤ
labyrinth *n.* bhūl bulaiyāṁ بھول بھلیاں
lace *n.* kinārī کناری
lad *n.* launḍā لونڈا
ladder *n.* nirdbān نردبان , sīṛhī سیڑھی
ladle *n.* palī پلی
lady *n.* ᶜaurat عورت , bēgam بیگم , saḥibah صاحبہ , xānum خانم
lake *n.* ḍābar ڈابر , jhīl جھیل , tāl تال
lamb *n.* lēlā لیلا
lame *adj.* langṛā لنگڑا
lameness *n.* langṛā'ī لنگڑائی
lament *v.* bilāpnā بلاپنا , giryah-ō-zārī karnā گریہ وزاری کرنا , jhīnknā جھینکنا , sir pīṭnā سرپیٹنا
lamentation *n.* bilāp بلاپ , kuhrām کہرام , nālāṁ نالاں , nāliš نالش , zār زار
lamp *n.* cirāġ چراغ , dīpak دیپک , diyā دیا , laimp لیمپ
lance *n.* nēzah نیزہ
lancer *n.* bhālā bardār بھالا بردار , nēzah bāz نیزہ باز
land *n.* zamīn زمین
landholder *n.* māl guzār مال گذار
landlord *n.* milkī ملکی , zamīndār زمیندار , māl guzār مال گذار
landmark *n.* ḍānḍā ڈانڈا
landscape *n.* manzar منظر
lane *n.* galī گلی , kūcah کوچہ
language *n.* zabān زبان , bōlī بولی , lisān لسان
lantern *n.* fānūs فانوس , lālṭain لالٹین , mašᶜal مشعل , šamaᶜ شمع
lap *n.* gōd گود , zānū زانو / *v.* cāṭnā چاٹنا
lapse *n.* bhūl بھول
large *adj.* baṛā بڑا , farāx فراخ , kalāṁ کلاں , vasīᶜ وسیع

largeness *n.* farāxī فراخی
lash *n.* kōṛā کوڑا / *v.* cābuk mārnā چابک مارنا, kōṛā mārnā کوڑا مارنا
lassi *n.* lassī لسی
last *adj.* āxir آخر, āxirī آخری, pichlā پچھلا / *v.* vaqt lagnā وقت لگنا ♦ **at** ~ *phr.* hir phir kē ہر پھر کے, āxir mēṁ آخر میں
late *adj.* marḥūm مرحوم, pichlā پچھلا
lateness *n.* avēr اویر
latitude *n.* kušādagī کشادگی
latter *adj.* mu'axxar-ul-zikr موخر الذکر
lattice *n.* qafas قفس
laudable *adj.* mustaḥsan مستحسن
laugh *n.* haṁsī ہنسی, xandah خندہ / *v.* haṁsnā ہنسنا, khilnā کھلنا
laughter *n.* xandah خندہ, xandāṁ خنداں
lavatory *n.* paixānah پیخانہ
law *n.* ā'īn آئین, qānūn قانون, zābitah ضابطہ
lawful *adj.* ḥalāl حلال, jā'iz جائز, qānūnī قانونی, šaraᶜī شرعی
lawfully *adv.* majāzan مجازاً, qānūnan قانوناً
lawfulness *n.* javāz جواز.
lawlessness *n.* andhēr اندھیر
lawn *n.* sabzah zār سبزہ زار
lawsuit *n.* muqaddamah مقدمہ, nizāᶜ نزاع
lawyer *n.* qānūn dān قانون دان, vakīl وکیل
laxative *n.* mushil مسہل
laxity *n.* kasal کسل
lay *v.* bichānā بچھانا
layer *n.* parat پرت, pōst پوست, tabaq طبق, tah تہ
layman *n.* bāzārī ādmī بازاری آدمی
laziness *n.* kāhilī کاہلی, kasālat کسالت, tasāhul تساہل
lazy *adj.* bē himmat بے ہمت, kāhil کاہل, sust سست
lead *n.* sīsah سیسہ
leader *n.* naqīb نقیب, pēšvā پیشوا, qā'id قائد, rāhnumā راہنما
leadership *n.* pēšvā'ī پیشوائی, sarvarī سروری
leaf *n.* barg برگ, kāġaz کاغذ, pāt پات, pattā پتا, varaq ورق; *(of a flower)* pankhṛī پنکھڑی

league *n.* farsang فرسنگ
leak *v.* pānī nikalnā پانی نکلنا, risnā رسنا, ṭapakna ٹپکنا
leaky *adj.* jhāṁjhar جھانجھر
lean *adj.* dublā دبلا, lāġar لاغر, patlā پتلا / *v.* takiyah lagānā تکیہ لگانا
leanness *n.* lāġarī لاغری
leap *n.* chalāng چھلانگ, phalāng پھلانگ, phānd پھاند / *v.* kūdnā کودنا, uchalnā اچھلنا
learn *v.* sīkhnā سیکھنا, maᶜlūm karnā معلوم کرنا, paṛhnā پڑھنا
learned *adj.* ᶜālim عالم, dānišmand دانشمند, xabīr خبیر
lease *n.* ijārah اِجارہ, mustājirī مستاجری
least *adj.* kam tarīn کم ترین
leather *n.* camṛā چمڑا, carm چرم, jild جلد
leave *v.* cal dēnā چل دینا, chōṛnā چھوڑنا / *n.* chuṭṭī چھٹی, fursat فرصت, ijāzat اِجازت ♦ **take** ~ *v.* ruxsat hōnā رخصت ہونا
leaven *n.* xamīr خمیر
lecture *n.* dars درس, sabaq سبق, xitāb خطاب, xatīb خطیب
ledger *n.* bahī khātā بہی کھاتا, bahī بہی, khataunī کھتونی
leech *n.* jōnk جونک, kīṛī کیڑی
left *adj.* bāyāṁ بایاں, guzaštah گزشتہ, chōṛā چھوڑا
leg *n.* pā'ē پائے, pā'ōṁ پاؤں, ṭāng ٹانگ
legacy *n.* tarkah ترکہ, vasiyyat وصیت
legal *adj.* ḥalāl حلال, jā'iz جائز, mašrūᶜ مشروع, qānūnī قانونی
legally *adv.* qānūnan قانوناً, šarᶜan شرعاً
legend *n.* rivāyat روایت
legislate *v.* qānūn banānā قانون بنانا
legislator *n.* qānūn gō قانون گو, šāriᶜ شارع
legitimacy *n.* javāz جواز
legitimate *adj.* mašrūᶜ مشروع, sulbī صلبی
leisure *n.* farāġat فراغت, fursat فرصت, muhlat مہلت
lemon *n.* līmūṁ لیموں, nībū نیبو
lemonade *n.* šarbat شربت
lend *v.* mustaᶜār dēnā مستعار دینا
length *n.* lambā'ī لمبائی, tūl طول
lengthen *v.* lambā karnā لمبا کرنا, tūl dēnā طول دینا

lengthy *adj.* tavīl طویل, bahut hī lambā بہت ہی لمبا
lent *adj.* ᶜāriyyatī عاریتی, qarz diyā قرض دیا
Leo *(Zodiac) n.* asad اسد
leopard *n.* tēndū'ā تیندوا
leper *n.* juzāmī جذامی, kōṛhī کوڑھی
leprosy *n.* juzām جذام, kōṛh کوڑھ
leprous *adj.* kōṛhī کوڑھی
less *adj.* kam tar کم تر, kam کم, kamtī کمتی, thōṛā تھوڑا
lessen *v.* ghaṭānā گھٹانا, kam karnā کم کرنا, thōṛā karnā تھوڑا کرنا
lesson *n.* dars درس, sabaq سبق
let *v.* chōṛnā چھوڑنا
let's go! *interj.* ā'īē calēṁ آئیے چلیں, calō چلو
letter *n.* nāmah نامہ, navišt نوشت, navištah نوشتہ, xatt خط; *(of the alphabet)* ḥarf حرف
level *adj.* ham vār ہم وار, musattaḥ مسطح / *v.* ḍhalānā ڈھلانا, randah phērnā رندہ پھیرنا
levy *n.* bhāṛā بھاڑا / *v.* ᶜā'id karnā عائد کرنا ♦ ~ **a tax** *v.* maḥsūl lagānā محصول لگانا
liability *n.* zimmah dārī ذمہ داری
liable *adj.* mustaujib مستوجب, sazā vār سزا وار
liaison *n.* rābitah رابطہ
liar *n.* jhūṭ bōlnē vālā جھوٹ بولنے والا, kāzib کاذب, darōġ-ē-gō دروغ گو
liberal *adj.* daryā dil دریا دل, fā'iz فائض, karīm کریم, saxī سخی
liberation *n.* āzādī آزادی, ḥuriyyat حریت
liberty *n.* āzādī آزادی, ḥuriyyat حریت
Libra *(Zodiac) n.* mīzān میزان
librarian *n.* saḥāf صحاف
library *n.* kutub xānah کتب خانہ
licence *n.* parvānah پروانہ, ruxsat رخصت
lick *v.* cāṭnā چاٹنا
lid *n.* sar pōš سرپوش
lie *n.* darōġ دروغ, jhūṭ جھوٹ, kizb کذب / *v.* jhūṭ bōlnā جھوٹ بولنا; *(~ down)* paṛnā پڑنا ♦ **tell a** ~ *v.* jhūṭ bōlnā جھوٹ بولنا
life *n.* ᶜumr عمر, ḥayāt حیات, zindagānī زندگانی, zindagī زندگی
lifeless *adj.* bē jān بے جان, mūā' مواء, murdah dil مردہ دل

lifetime *n.* daur-ē-ḥayāt دور حیات, ḥīn-ē-ḥayāt حین حیات
lift *v.* caṛhānā چڑھانا, ubhārna ابھارنا, uṭhānā اُٹھانا ♦ ~ **up** *v.* uckānā اچکانا
light *adj.* āsān آسان, halkā ہلکا, mīṭhā میٹھا, xafīf خفیف / *n.* nūr نور, rōšnī روشنی, zau ضو, ziyā ضیا / *v.* jalānā جلانا, raušan karnā روشن کرنا, sulgānā سلگانا
lighten *v.* halkā karnā ہلکا کرنا, kaundnā کوندنا
lighthouse *n.* manārah منارہ
lighting *n.* daraxiš درخش
lightness *n.* āsānī آسانی, halkā pan ہلکاپن, inxifāf انخفاف, subkī سبکی
lightning *n.* barq برق, sā^ciqah صاعقہ
like *adj.* misl مثل, mutābiq مطابق, sā سا, vār وار / *adv./prep.* jūṁ جوں, bataur بطور, cūṁ چوں / *conj.* manō منو / *v.* jī lagnā جی لگنا, pasand karnā پسند کرنا
likely *adj.* iḥtimālī اِحتمالی
likened *adj.* mušabbah مشبہ
likeness *n.* misāl مثال, qiyāfah قیافہ
likewise *adv.* ham ہم
limb *n.* ank انگ, ᶜuzū عضو
lime *n.* līmūṁ لیموں, nībū نیبو, mausambī موسمبی
limit *n.* ḥadd حد, intihā انتہا, nihāyat نہایت / *v.* ḥadd bāndhnā حد باندھنا, iḥātah karnā اِحاطہ کرنا, maḥdūd karnā محدود کرنا
limitless *adj.* az ḥadd از حد, bē ḥadd بے حد
line *n.* qitār; qatār قطار, rēkhā ریکھا, rištah رشتہ, satar سطر, xatt خط
lineage *n.* ḥasb nasab حسب نسب, nasab نسب, tanāsul تناسل, zurriyat ذریت
linen *n.* katān/kattān کتان
linguist *n.* māhir-ē-lisāniyāt ماہر لسانیات, zabān dān زبان دان
link *n.* jōṛ جوڑ, laṛī لڑی
linseed *n.* tīsī تیسی
lion *n.* šēr babar شیر ببر, šēr شیر
lioness *n.* šērnī شیرنی
lip *n.* hōnṭ ہونٹ, lab لب
liquid *adj.* raqīq رقیق, sayyāl سیال / *n.* mā'iᶜ مائع
liquidation *n.* bē bāqī بیباقی
liquor *n.* mai مے, šarāb شراب
lisp *v.* tutlānā تتلانا, zabān tutlānā زبان تتلانا
list *n.* fard فرد, fihrist فہرست

listen *v.* sunnā سننا
listener *n.* nīyūšindah نیوشندہ, sāmiᶜ سامع
liter *n.* līṭar لیٹر
literal *adj.* lafzī لفظی, luġvī لغوی
literally *adv.* lafzan لفظاً
literary *adj.* ᶜilmī علمی
literate *adj.* xvāndah خواندہ
literature *n.* ᶜilm-ē-adab علم ادب
litter *n.* kacrā کچرا, pīnas پینس; *(an open seat) n.* haudah ہودہ
little *adj.* chōṭā چھوٹا, thōṛā تھوڑا, kam کم
live *v.* jīnā جینا, jītē rahnā جیتے رہنا, rahnā رہنا, zindah rahnā زندہ رہنا
livelihood *n.* maᶜāš معاش, maᶜišat معیشت, qūt قوت
liveliness *n.* zindah dilī زندہ دلی
lively *adj.* rangīlā رنگیلا, zindah dil زندہ دل
liver *n.* jigar جگر, kabid کبد, kalējah کلیجہ
living *adj.* ḥaiyy حیّ, jītā جیتا, zindah زندہ / *n.* guzārah گزارہ, jīnā جینا, zindagānī زندگانی, zindagī زندگی
lizard *n.* chupkalī چھپکلی, girgaṭ گرگٹ, gōh گوہ
load *n.* bhār بھار, bōjh بوجھ, lād لاد / *v.* bharnā بھرنا, bhartī karnā بھرتی کرنا, lādna لادنا ♦ ~ **a gun** bandūq bharnā بندوق بھرنا
loaf *n.* rōṭī روٹی / *v.* āvārah phirnā آوارہ پھرنا
loan *n.* qarz قرض, udhār ادھار
local *adj.* dēsī دیسی, maqāmī مقامی
locality *n.* thān تھان, jā جا
lock *n.* qufl قفل, tālā تالا
lock of hair *n.* laṭ لٹ; *(as worn by Hindus)* cuṭīyā چٹیا
lock up *v.* bhēṛnā بھیڑنا, tālā lagānā تالا لگانا
lockup *n.* ḥavālāt حوالات
locust *n.* ṭiḍḍī ٹڈی
lodge *v.* basērā karnā بسیرا کرنا, ṭikānā ٹکانا, ṭiknā ٹکنا
lodging *n.* basērā بسیرا, manzil منزل, ṭikā'ō ٹکاؤ
loftiness *n.* fauq فوق
lofty *adj.* nihāyat buland نہایت بلند
log *n.* kundā کندا, lakkaṛ لکڑ

logic *n.* mantiq/mantaq منطق
logo *n.* naᶜrah نعرہ
loins *n.* kamar کمر, pīṭh پیٹھ
loneliness *n.* tanhā'ī تنہائی
lonely *adj.* alag الگ, ēkānt ایکانت
long *adj.* lambā لمبا, tavīl طویل, darāz دراز / *n.* muddat مدت
long for *v.* jī tarasnā جی ترسنا, lalcānā للچانا, xvāhiš karnā خواہش کرنا
longing *n.* armān ارمان, cāhat چاہت, lagan لگن, tišnagī تشنگی
longitude *n.* tūl-ul-balad طول البلد
look *n.* cašm چشم, nazar نظر, nigāh نگاہ / *v.* dēkhnā دیکھنا, taknā تکنا
look after *v.* caukasī karnā چوکسی کرنا, xabar gīrī karnā خبر گیری کرنا, xabar lēnā خبر لینا
look at *v.* dēkhnā bhālnā دیکھنا بھالنا, ghūrnā گھورنا, tāknā تاکنا
look for *v.* ḍhūnḍnā ڈھونڈنا, talāš karnā تلاش کرنا
loom *n.* kargah کرگہ
loop *n.* phalī پھلی, phāṁsī پھانسی / *v.* phandā lagānā پھندا لگانا
loose *adj.* khulā کھلا
loosen *v.* khōlnā کھولنا, phaskānā پھسکانا
looseness *n.* ḍhēlāpan ڈھیلاپن
loot *n.* lūṭ لوٹ / *v.* lūṭnā لوٹنا
lord *n.* maulā مولیٰ یا مولا, rabb رب, sāḥib صاحب, saiyyid سید, xvājah خواجہ
lordship *n.* imārāt امارات
lose *v.* khōnā کھونا
loseness *n.* ḍhīl ڈھیل
loss *n.* nuqsān نقصان, ṭōṭā ٹوٹا, xasārah خسارہ, zarar ضرر
lost *adj.* gumrāh گمراہ, gum گم
lot *n.* taqdīr تقدیر, nasīb نصیب, qismat قسمت
lotus *n.* kaṁval کنول
lotus flower *n.* kamal کمل, padam پدم
loud *adj.* zōr sē زور سے
loudly *adv.* zōr sē زور سے
louse *n.* jūṁ جوں
love *n.* ᶜišq عشق, muḥabbat/ maḥabbat, piyār پیار / *v.* muḥabbat karna محبت کرنا, piyār karnā پیار کرنا cāhnā چاہنا ♦ **in** ~ *adj.* dil bastah دل بستہ, šēftah شیفتہ / *adv.* farēftah فریفتہ

loveliness *n.* maᶜšūqī معشوقی, maḥbūbī محبوبی, raᶜnā'ī رعنائی
lovely *adj.* dilbar دلبر, manōhar منوہر, sōhnā سوہنا, dil kaš دل کش
lovemaking *n.* suhāg سہاگ
lover *n.* ᶜāšiq عاشق, muḥibb محب, piyā پیا sajan سجن
loving *adj.* kāmnī کامنی, muḥabbat āmēz محبت آمیز, piyārā پیارا
low *adj.* nīcā نیچا
low tide *n.* bhāṭā بھاٹا
lower *adv.* pā'īṁ پائیں / *prep./adj.* zēr زیر / *v.* nīcē karnā نیچے کرنا
lowly *adj.* kam tar کم تر, siflī سفلی
lowness *n.* pastī پستی
loyal *adj.* vafā dār وفا دار, namak ḥalāl نمک حلال, tābiᶜdār تابعدار
lucid *adj.* bayyin بیّن, duraxšandah درخشندہ
luck *n.* baxt بخت, iqbāl اقبال, nasīb نصیب, qismat قسمت ♦ **good** ~ xūš qismatī خوش قسمتی
luckily *adv.* qismat sē قسمت سے
lucky *adj.* baxtāvar بختاور, qismat vālā قسمت والا, xūš nasīb خوش نصیب
luggage *n.* sāmān سامان
lukewarm *adj.* garm sard گرم سرد
lull *v.* sulānā سلانا
lullaby *n.* lōrī لوری
luminous *adj.* nūrānī نورانی, tāb dār تاب دار, ujlā اجلا
lump *n.* pinḍ پنڈ
lunacy *n.* dīvānagī دیوانگی
lunar *adj.* qamarī قمری
lunar month *n.* māh-ē-qamrī ماہ قمری
lunatic *adj.* dīvānī دیوانی / *n.* dīvānah دیوانہ
lunatic asylum *n.* pāgal xānah پاگل خانہ
luncheon *n.* nāštah ناشتہ
lung *n.* phēpṛā پھیپڑا
lurk *v.* chupnā چھپنا, ghāt mēṁ baiṭhnā گھات میں بیٹھنا
lush *adj.* harā bharā ہرا بھرا
lust *n.* hauṁs ہونس, havas ہوس, mastī مستی, šahvat شہوت / *v. (sexually)* bāh باہ
lustful *adj.* havas nāk ہوس ناک, nafsānī نفسانی, šahvat parast شہوت پرست

lustre *n.* damak دمک, duraxšandagī درخشندگی, jalvah جلوه, jilā جلا
luxurious *adj.* ᶜayyāš عیاش, rasīlā رسیلا
luxury *n.* ᶜayyāšī عیاشی

M

machine *n.* mašīn مشین, kal کل
mad *adj.* dīvānā دیوانا, pāgal پاگل, junūnī جنونی / *n.* dīvānah دیوانہ
madam *n.* mēm میم, bībī بی بی, xātūn خاتون / *interj. (madam!)* jī جی
made *adj.* maᶜmūl معمول, banā بنا; *(~ of)* sāxtah ساختہ
madhouse *n.* pāgal xānah پاگل خانہ
madman *n.* šaidā شیدا
madness *n.* dīvānagī دیوانگی, junūn جنون
madwoman *n.* dīvānī دیوانی
magazine *n.* risālah رسالہ, gaṁjīnah گنجینہ, maxzan مخزن, xazīnah خزینہ
magic *n.* saḥr سحر, jādū جادو
magical *adj.* tilismātī طلسماتی, talismī طلسمی
magically *adv.* sāḥir sē ساحر سے
magician *n.* sāḥir ساحر, jādūgar جادوگر
magistrate *n.* qāẓī قاضی
magnificence *n.* ᶜazmat عظمت, šaukat شوکت
magnificent *adj.* ᶜazīm عظیم, ᶜālī šān عالی شان
maharaja *n.* mahā rājah مہاراجہ
mahout *(elephant-driver) n.* mahāvat مہاوت, hāthi bān ہاتھی بان
maid *n.* dāyah دایہ, dā'ī دائی, kuṁvārī کنواری
mail *n.* ḍāk ڈاک
mailbox *n.* ḍāk kā ḍibbā ڈاک کا ڈبا
mailman *n.* ḍāk vālā ڈاک والا, ḍākiyā ڈاکیا
maintain *v.* nibāhnā نباہنا, baḥāl rakhnā بحال رکھنا, thāmnā تھامنا, sambhālnā سنبھالنا
maize *n.* maka'ī مکئی, kukṛī ککڑی
majestic *adj.* jalālī جلالی
majesty *n.* ḥazrat حضرت, tamkanat تمکنت, jalāl جلال
majority *n.* kasrat کثرت
make *v.* karnā کرنا, banānā بنانا
  make a mistake *v.* cūknā چوکنا, ġalatī karnā غلطی کرنا
  make a promise *v.* vaᶜdah karnā وعدہ کرنا

make an error *v.* phisalnā پھسلنا
make an excuse *v.* bahānah karnā بہانہ کرنا
make friends with *v.* ulfat karnā الفت کرنا
make fun of *v.* tamāšā karnā تماشا کرنا, chēṛnā چھیڑنا
make haste *v.* jaldī karnā جلدی کرنا
make peace *v.* musālaḥat karnā مصالحت کرنا
maker *n.* banānē vālā بنانے والا, gar گر
male *adj.* nar نر, muzakkar مذکر / *n.* nar نر, narīnah نرینہ, mard مرد
malediction *n.* phiṭ پھٹ
malevolent *adj.* bad tīnat بد طینت
malice *n.* kīnah کینہ, buġz بغض
malicious *adj.* tīrah dil تیرہ دل, kīnah var کینہ ور, qallāš قلاش
malignant *adj.* xabīs خبیث
mallet *n.* mōgrā موگرا, mēx cū میخ چو
man *n.* ādmī آدمی, ādam آدم, bašar بشر, mard مرد
manage *v.* intizām karnā انتظام کرنا
management *n.* intizām انتظام, ihtimām اہتمام, nazm-ō-nasq نظم و نسق
manager *n.* pēškār پیشکار, muntazim منتظم, muhtamim مہتمم
mandate *n.* manšūr منشور, cahd عہد
mango *n.* ām آم
manhood *n.* javānī جوانی
manifest *adj.* sariḥ صریح, kašfī کشفی, jalvah gar جلوہ گر / *n.* fāš فاش
manifestation *n.* tasrīḥ تصریح, kašf کشف, zuhūr ظہور
mankind *n.* xalq خلق, xalqat خلقت, ᶜavām-ul-nās عوام الناس
manliness *n.* javān mardī جوان مردی, mardānagī مردانگی
manner *n.* xāssah خاصہ, tarīqah طریقہ, taur طور, uslūb اسلوب, tarīq طریق
mansion *n.* ḥavēlī حویلی, maḥall محل
manual *n.* guṭkā گٹکا
manufacture *n.* sāxt ساخت
manufacturer *n.* dast kār دست کار
manuscript *n.* masavvadah مسودہ
many *adj.* kasīr کثیر, ka'ī کئی, bahutērā بہیترا
map *n.* naqšah نقشہ, bīrang بیرنگ ♦ **field** ~ šujarah شجرہ
marble *n.* sang-ē-marmar سنگ مرمر, marmar مرمر

march *n.* kūc کوچ, mārc مارچ, sapāṭā سپاٹا / *v.* kūc karnā کوچ کرنا
mare *n.* ghōṛī گھوڑی, mādiyān مادیان
margin *n.* ḥāšiyah حاشیہ, kōr کور, taraf طرف
marijuana *n.* ḥašīš حشیش
mariner *n.* mallāḥ ملاح
mark *n.* asar اثر, ᶜalāmat علامت, nišān نشان / *v.* raqm karnā رقم کرنا, asar karnā اثر کرنا, dāġ dēnā داغ دینا
market *n.* bāzār بازار, manḍī منڈی, gaṁj گنج
marketing *n.* saudā سودا
marriage *n.* šādī شادی, nikāḥ نکاح, biyāh بیاہ
married woman *n.* māng bharī مانگ بھری
marrow *n.* maġz مغز
marry *v.* šādī karnā شادی کرنا, biyāh karnā بیاہ کرنا
Mars *(planet) n.* mangal منگل
marsh *n.* daldal دلدل
marshy *adj.* daldalī دلدلی
mart *n.* manḍī منڈی
martial *adj.* jangī جنگی
martyr *n.* šahīd شہید
martyrdom *n.* šahādat شہادت
marvel *n.* acambhā اچنبھا, ᶜajūbah عجوبہ
masculine *adj.* nar نر, muzakkar مذکر
mason *n.* miᶜmār معمار, mistarī مستری
masonry *n.* miᶜmārī معماری
mass *n.* thōk تھوک
massacre *n.* kušt-ō-xūn کشت و خون, qatl قتل
massage *n.* cappī چپی, māliš مالش / *v.* māliš kārnā مالش کرنا
master *n.* āġā آغا, āqā آقا, sāḥib صاحب, maulā مولیٰ یا مولا
masterpiece *n.* šāh kār شاہ کار
mat *n.* caṭā'ī چٹائی
match *n.* sānī ثانی, battī بتی, jōṛ جوڑ
matches *n.* mācis ماچس
matchstick *n.* diyā salā'ī دیا سلائی
mate *n.* jōṛī جوڑی

material *adj.* māddī مادی, zātī ذاتی
materialism *n.* māddah parastī مادہ پرستی, māddıyat مادیت
materialist *n.* māddah parast مادہ پرست
maternal *adj.* mādrī مادری ♦ ~ **affection** māmtā مامتا, pēṭ kī āg پیٹ کی آگ
mathematician *n.* riyāzī dāṁ ریاضی داں, māhir-ē-riyāziyāt ماہر ریاضیات, muhandis مہندس
mathematics *n.* riyāzī ریاضی
matter *n.* muᶜāmalah معاملہ, māddah مادہ, pīp پیپ
mattock *n.* phā'ōṛā پھاوڑا
mattress *n.* tōšak توشک
mature *adj.* bāliġ بالغ, rasīdah رسیدہ, pakkā پکا
maturity *n.* rasīdagī رسیدگی, bulūġ بلوغ, puxtagī پختگی
mausoleum *n.* rauzah روضہ, maqbarah مقبرہ
maxim *n.* guftah گفتہ, maqūlah مقولہ
May *(month) n.* ma'iy مئی
may be! (It ~) *interj.* kyā jānē کیا جانے
may God bless you! *interj.* bārak Allah بارک اللہ
may it so happen! *interj.* kāš کاش
maybe *adv.* šāyad شاید, inšā' allah انشاء اللہ
me *pron.* maiṁ میں, mujhē مجھے mujh sē مجھ سے
meadow *n.* sabzah zār سبزہ زار, carāgāh چراگاہ, murġazar مرغزار
meal *n.* bhōjan بھوجن
mean *adj.* bad kār بد کار, mubtazal مبتذل, zalīl ذلیل, kamīn کمین / *v.* maᶜni rakhnā معنی رکھنا , matlab hōna مطلب ہونا
meaning *n.* mafhūm مفہوم , maᶜnī/maᶜnā معنی , matlab مطلب
meaningless *adj.* lā yaᶜnī لایعنی, muhmalah مہملہ, lacar لچر
meanness *n.* razālat رذالت, pājīpan پاجیپن, mūzi panā موذی پنا
means *n.* vasīlah وسیلہ, vasātat وساطت, maqdūr مقدور
meanwhile *adj.* itnē mēṁ اتنے میں
measles *n.* khasrā کھسرا
measure *n.* upā'ē اپائے, miqdār مقدار
measurement *n.* pajmā'iš پیمائش misāhat مساحت
meat *n.* gōšt گوشت, laḥm لحم , mās ماس
mechanic *n.* mēkanik میکنک

mechanical *adj.* mašīnī مشینی
medal *n.* tamġah تمغہ
meddle (with) *v.* chūnā چھونا
mediate *v.* murāqabah karnā مراقبہ کرنا, šafā^ct karnā شفاعت کرنا
mediation *n.* sālisī ثالثی, bīc baçā'ō بیچ بچاؤ
mediator *n.* musliḥ مصلح, šāfi^c شافع, sālis ثالث
medical *adj.* tibbī طبی
medical practice *n.* tabābat/tibābat طبابت
medical treatment *n.* tibbī ^cilāj طبی علاج, davā dārū دوادارو
medicine *n.* davā دوا, darmāṁ درماں, dārū دارو; *(the science)* tibb طب
♦ **take** ~ *v.* davā khānā دوا کھانا
meditate *v.* riyāzat karnā ریاضت کرنا, tasavvur karnā تصور کرنا
meditation *n.* ġaur غور, murāqabah مراقبہ, tafakkur تفکر
meditative *adj.* mutā'ammil متامل, andēš mand اندیش مند
medium *adj.* ausat اوسط, maddham مدھم / *n.* vasātat وساطت, vāstah واسطہ
meet *v.* milnā ملنا, bhīṭnā بھیٹنا
meeting *n.* vasl وصل, milnī ملنی, mulāqāt ملاقات
meeting place *n.* baiṭhak xānah بیٹھک خانہ, ma^criz معرض
melancholic *adj.* dil figār دل فگار, saudā'ī سودائی
melancholy *n.* afsurdagī افسردگی, zīq ضیق, haul-ē-dil ہول دل, murdanī مردنی
melodious *adj.* surīlā سریلا, mutarannim مترنم, madhur مدھر
melody *n.* rāg راگ, naġmah نغمہ, tarānah ترانہ
melon *n.* xarbūzah خربوزہ
melt *v.* ghulnā گھلنا, galnā گلنا, ghōlnā گھولنا
member *(of a family) n.* ahl اہل
memoir *n.* tazkirah تذکرہ
memorable *adj.* yād gārī یاد گاری
memorial *n.* yād gār یاد گار
memorize *v.* raṭnā رٹنا
memory *n.* ḥāfizah حافظہ, yād یاد, zikr ذکر
menace *n.* tahdīd تہدید, ḍānṭ ڈانٹ, dhamkī دھمکی
menace *v.* dhamkānā دھمکانا, ḍānṭnā ڈانٹنا
mend *v.* rafū karnā رفو کرنا, murammat karnā مرمت کرنا
menstruate *v.* mahīnē sē hōnā مہینے سے ہونا

menstruation *n.* māhvārī ماہواری, maᶜmūl kē din معمول کے دن
mental *adj.* dimāġī دماغی, ᶜaqlī عقلی
mental power *n.* quvvat-ē-ḥāfizah قوت حافظہ
mention *n.* zikr ذکر / *v.* zikr karnā ذکر کرنا ♦ **don't ~ it!** *interj.* kō'ī bāt nahīṁ! کوئی بات نہیں
menu *n.* mēnyū مینیو
mercantile *adj.* tijāratī تجارتی
merchandise *n.* māl مال
merchant *n.* tājir تاجر, saudāgar سوداگر
merciful *adj.* karīm کریم, raḥm dil رحم دل, raḥīm رحیم, ġafūr غفور
merciless *adj.* sang dil سنگ دل, kaṭṭar کٹر, nā tars ناترس
mercury *n.* pārā پارا
Mercury *(planet) n.* ᶜattārad عطارد
mercy *n.* raḥm رحم, raḥmat رحمت, marḥamat مرحمت
mere *adj.* maḥz محض , nirā نرا
merely *adv.* sirf صرف, hī ہی, faqat فقط
merit *n.* qadr قدر, vasf وصف
merriment *n.* šādmānī شادمانی, dil lagī دل لگی
merry *adj.* rangīlā رنگیلا, farḥaṁ فرحاں, haṁs mukh ہنس مکھ, lahrī لہری / *n.* rangīn mizāj رنگین مزاج
message *n.* payām پیام paiġām پیغام
messenger *n.* har kārah ہرکارہ, qāsid قاصد, paiġāmbar پیغامبر rasūl رسول
metal *n.* dhāt دھات
metaphor *n.* kināyah کنایہ, tašbīh تشبیہ
metaphorically *adv.* kināyitan کنایتاً
meter *n.* mīṭar میٹر
method *n.* salīqah سلیقہ, uslūb اسلوب, tartīb ترتیب
methodically *adv.* tartīb vār ترتیب وار
metropolis *n.* dār-ul-imārāt دارالامارات, rāj dhānī راج دھانی
mid *adj.* ḥāq حاق
midday *n.* dōpahar دوپہر, zuhr ظہر
middle *adj.* nisf نصف, nīm نیم, ḥāq حاق / *n.* nīmah نیمہ, markaz مرکز, vast وسط, bīc بیچ
middling *adj.* miyānah میانہ

midnight *n.* rāt kē bārah bajē رات کے بارہ بجے, nisf šab نصف شب, nīm šab نیم شب
midwife *n.* janā'ī جنائی, qābilah قابلہ, dā'ī دائی ۔ دایہ
might *n.* šaukat شوکت, tāqat طاقت
mighty *adj.* bīr بیر, jabbār جبار
migration *n.* muhājarat مہاجرت
mild *adj.* ḥalīm حلیم, salīm سلیم, narm نرم, mulā'im ملائم
mild season *n.* mīṭhā mausim میٹھا موسم
mildness *n.* ḥilm حلم, narmī نرمی, mulā'imat ملائمت
mile *n.* mīl میل
military *adj.* faujī فوجی, laškarī لشکری, sipāhiyānah سپاہیانہ
milk *n.* dūdh دودھ, šīr شیر, *(fresh and unboiled)* ḥalīb حلیب; *(thick ~)* dahī دہی / *v.* dūdh dōhnā دودھ دوہنا, dōhnā دوہنا, duhnā دہنا
milkmaid *n.* gvālan گوالن
milkman *n.* gvālā گوالا, ghōsī گھوسی
milky *adj.* dūdhyā دودھیا
Milky Way *n.* kahkašāṁ کہکشاں
mill *n.* cakkī چکی
millet *n.* jō'ār جوار, bājrā باجرا, kangnī کنگنی
millionaire *n.* karōṛ patī کروڑپتی, lakh pati لکھ پتی
millstone *n.* cakkī چکی, xarās خراس
mimic *v.* naql utārnā نقل اتارنا, naqqālī karnā نقالی کرنا, bhagat khēlnā بھگت کھیلنا / *n.* savāngī سوانگی
minaret *n.* manārah منارہ, mīnār مینار
mind *n.* man من, dil دل, qalb قلب, hōš ہوش
mine *n.* ma^cdan/ma^cdin معدن, kān کان, surang سرنگ / *pron.* mērā میرا
miner *n.* kān kan کان کن
mineral *adj.* ma^cdanī معدنی
mineral *n.* dhāt دھات
mineralogy *n.* ^cilm-ē-jamādāt علم جمادات, ^cilm-ē-ma^cdaniyāt علم معدنیات
mining *n.* kān kanī کان کنی
minister *n.* vazīr وزیر, mantarī/mantrī منتری
ministry *n.* vizārat وزارت
Ministry of Communication *n.* vizārat-ē-muvāsilāt وزارت مواصلات

Ministry of Defense *n.* vizārat-ē-difāᶜ وزارت دفاع
Ministry of Education *n.* vizārat-ē-taᶜlīm وزارت تعلیم
Ministry of Finance *n.* vizārat-ē-māliyāt وزارت مالیات
Ministry of Foreign Affairs *n.* vizārat-ē-umūr-ē-xārijah وزارت امور خارجہ
Ministry of the Interior *n.* vizārat-ē-dāxilah وزارت داخلہ
Ministry of Trade and Commerce *n.* vizārat-ē-tijārat وزارت تجارت
minor *adj.* kam san کم سن, kam ᶜumr کم عمر / *n.* saġīr san صغر سن
minority *n.* saġīr sanī صغر سنی, kam sinī کم سنی
mint *n.* pōdīnah پودینہ, ṭaksāl ٹکسال
minute *n.* minaṭ منٹ, daqīqah دقیقہ, lamḥah لمحہ
minutely *adv.* mū bah mū مو بہ مو
miracle *n.* ᶜajūbah عجوبہ, muᶜjizah معجزہ, iᶜjāz اعجاز
mirage *n.* māyā مایا, sarāb سراب
mirror *n.* ā'īnah آئینہ, ārsī آرسی
misappropriate *v.* xūrdburd karnā خوردبرد کرنا
misbehavior *n.* bad sulūkī بد سلوکی
miscarry *v.* pēṭ girnā پیٹ گرنا, ḥaml girānā حمل گرانا
miscellaneous *adj.* mutafarraq متفرق, phuṭkal پھٹکل
mischief *n.* xarābī خرابی, burā'ī برائی, šarārat شرارت, šaitānī شیطانی
mischievous *adj.* šōx شوخ, mufsid مفسد, fitnah angēz فتنہ انگیز, šarīr شریر
mischievously *adv.* mufsidānah مفسدانہ
miser *n.* kaṁjūs کنجوس, makhnī cūs مکھی چوس
miserable *adj.* munaġaz منغض, munkasir منکسر, musībat zadah مصیبت زدہ
miserly *adj.* baxīl بخیل
misery *n.* xvārī خواری, musībat مصیبت, āzārī آزاری
misfortune *n.* bad baxtī بد بختی, kōr baxtī کور بختی, musībat مصیبت, kam baxtī کم بختی
mishap *n.* kam baxtī کم بختی
mislead *v.* bhaṭkānā بھٹکانا, bahkānā بہکانا, muġālatah dēnā مغالطہ دینا
mismanagement *n.* bē intizāmī بے انتظامی
misplaced *adj.* bē jā بے جا
miss *n.* kuṁvārī کنواری; *(form of address/ Miss)* bībī بی بی / *v.* yād ānā یاد آنا, bhūlnā بھولنا
mission *n.* paiġām پیغام paiġāmbarī پیغامبری ♦ **divine** ~ risālat رسالت

mist *n.* dhund دھند, kuhr کہر
mistake *n.* ġalatī/ġaltī غلطی, xatā خطا ♦ **make a ~** *v.* cūknā چوکنا, ġalatī karnā غلطی کرنا
Mister (Mr.) *n.* sāḥib صاحب; *(title for well-instructed person) n.* maulānā مولانا
mistiness *n.* dhundlāpan دھندلاپن
mistress *n.* jānāṁ جاناں
mistrust *n.* bad gumānī بدگمانی
misty *adj.* dhundlā دھندلا
misunderstanding *n.* ġalat fahmī غلط فہمی
mix *v.* mēl khānā میل کھانا, murakkab karnā مرکب کرنا, milānā ملانا
mixed *adj.* maxlūt مخلوط, ralā milā رلا ملا, murakkab مرکب
mixing *n.* imtizāj امتزاج
mixture *n.* ralā رلا, murakkab مرکب, ghulāvaṭ گھلاوٹ
moan *v.* karāhnā کراہنا, hā'ē hā'ē karnā ہائے ہائے کرنا
moat *n.* xandaq خندق
mob *n.* dangal دنگل, ġōl غول, hujūm ہجوم
mockery *n.* svāṅg سوانگ, mazāq مذاق, ṭhaṭhōl ٹھٹھول
mode *n.* taur طور, tarḥ طرح, dastūr دستور, tarīqat طریقت
model *n.* naqšah نقشہ, rasm رسم, qālib قالب, nusxah نسخہ, namūnah نمونہ
moderate *adj.* maddham مدھم, mutavassit متوسط, iᶜtidāl pasand اعتدال پسند, muᶜtadil معتدل
moderate *v.* maddham karnā مدھم کرنا, muᶜtadil karnā معتدل کرنا
moderation *n.* iᶜtidāl اعتدال, salāmat ravī سلامت روی
modern *adj.* jadīd جدید, nayā نیا, mujaddid مجدد
modest *adj.* ġairat mand غیرت مند, pākdāman پاکدامن, bā ḥayā با حیا, šarmīlā شرمیلا
modesty *n.* ḥayā حیا, inkisār انکسار, ġairat غیرت, šarm شرم
modification *n.* tarmīm ترمیم, tabdīl تبدیل
moist *adj.* tar تر, gīlā گیلا
moisture *n.* sīl سیل, namī نمی, tarī تری
molasses *n.* rāb راب, šīrah شیرہ
mold *n.* qālib قالب, sāṁcah سانچہ / *v.* sāṁcah mēṁ ḍhālnā سانچہ میں ڈھالنا, ḍhālnā ڈھالنا
molest *v.* chēṛnā چھیڑنا

mom *n.* ammā اما, mā'ī مائی, māmā ماما, ammāṁ اماں
moment *n.* dam دم, laḥzah لحظہ, lamḥah لمحہ, pal پل
mommy *n.* mā'ī مائی, māmā ماما, mōmiyā مومیا
monarch *n.* rājah راجہ, malik ملک, šāh شاہ, sultān سلطان
monastery *n.* xānqāh خانقاہ, dargāh درگاہ
Monday *n.* sōmvār سوموار, pīr پیر
money *n.* paisā پیسا, paisē پیسے rūpayah/rūpiyah روپیہ
money *n.* *(especially coins)* sikkē سکے; *(for charity)* bēlā بیلا
money changer *n.* sarrāf صراف
money changing *n.* sarrāfī صرافی
moneylender *n.* sāhūkār ساہوکار
monk *n.* mahant مہنت, rāhib راہب, sant سنت, qalandar قلندر
monkey *n.* bandar بندر
monkey-dancer *n.* madārī مداری
monsoon *n.* barsāt برسات
monster *n.* dē'ō دیو
monstrous *adj.* ḍapōl ڈپول
month *n.* šahr شہر, mahīnah مہینہ, māh ماہ
monthly *adj./adv.* māhvārī ماہواری, māh ba-māh ماہ بماہ, mahīnē kē mahīnē مہینے کے مہینے ♦ ~ **pay** *n.* māhiyānah ماہیانہ
monument *n.* yād gār یادگار
mood *n.* mizāj مزاج, tarang ترنگ
moon *n.* cānd چاند, qamar قمر, mahtāb مہتاب ♦ **full** ~ badr بدر ♦ **new** ~ cānd rāt چاند رات, hilāl ہلال
moon-faced *adj.* māh jabīṁ ماہ جبیں
moonlight *n.* cāndnī چاندنی, qamrā قمرا
moonshine *n.* māh tāb ماہ تاب
more *adj.* ziyādah زیادہ, ziyādah tar زیادہ تر / *adv.* aur اور, savā سوا
moreover *adv.* mazīd مزید, ziyādah زیادہ, ʿilāvah azīṁ علاوہ ازیں, balkih بلکہ / *conj.* magar مگر
morning *n.* sabāḥ صباح, savērā سویرا, subḥ صبح; *(early ~)* bhōr بھور, subḥ kāzib صبح کاذب
morsel *n.* luqmah لقمہ
mortal *adj.* muhlik مہلک, fānī فانی

mortality *n.* maut موت, fanā فنا
mortar *n.* kharal کھرل, chōṭī tōp چھوٹی توپ
mortgage *n.* rihn/rahn رہن, girau گرو
mortgage *v.* rahin rakhnā رہن رکھنا
mortgaged *adj.* girvī گروی
mosaic *n.* pacī kārī پچی کاری
mosque *n.* masjid مسجد ; *(for Friday's prayers)* jāmiᶜ masjid جامع مسجد
mosquito *n.* macchar مچھر
mosquito net *n.* masahrī مسہری
most *adj.* ziyādah tar زیادہ تر
motel *n.* musāfir xānah مسافر خانہ
moth *n.* patangā پتنگا
mother *n.* māṁ ماں, vālidah والدہ, ammāṁ اماں
mother tongue *n.* mādrī zabān مادری زبان
mother-in-law *n.* sās ساس, *(husband's mother)* xāš خاش, *(term also used as an abuse)* susrī سسری
motherly *adj.* mādrī مادری
motion *n.* junbiš جنبش, ḥarakat حرکت, hal cal ہل چل, cāl چال
motionless *adj.* acal اچل
motive *n.* mūjib موجب, matlab مطلب, jihat جہت
motor *n.* mōṭar موٹر
motorcycle *n.* mōṭar sāikil موٹر سائیکل
motto *n.* usūl اصول, maqūlah مقولہ
mound *(of a field)* *n.* mēnḍ مینڈ
mount *v.* caṛhnā چڑھنا
mountain *n.* pahāṛ پہاڑ, jabal جبل
mountain pass *n.* ghāṭ گھاٹ
mountain range *n.* pahāṛī silsilah پہاڑی سلسلہ
mountaineer *n.* pahāṛī پہاڑی, kōhistānī کوہستانی
mountainous *adj.* kōhistānī کوہستانی
mountains *n.* kōhistān کوہستان
mourn *v.* sōg karnā سوگ کرنا, mātam karnā ماتم کرنا
mourner *n.* mātam dār ماتم دار
mournful *adj.* mātamī ماتمی, maġmūm مغموم

mourning *n.* ġamī غمی , mātam ماتم, sōg سوگ
mouse *n.* cūhā چوہا, mūsā موسا
mouse trap *n.* cūhē dān چوہیدان
moustache *n.* mūṁch مونچھ
mouth *n.* dahan دہن, mukh مکھ, muṁh منہ
mouthful *n.* luqmah لقمہ
move *v.* taḥrīk karnā تحریک کرنا, ḥarakat karnā حرکت کرنا, calnā چلنا
moveable *adj.* mutaḥarrik متحرک
moved *adj.* mutaḥarrik متحرک
movement *n.* ḥarakat حرکت, taḥrīk تحریک, cāl چال
moving *adj.* mutaḥarrik متحرک , muḥarrik محرک, caltā چلتا, dil sōz دل سوز
much *adj.* qiyāmat قیامت, kasīr کثیر, vāfir وافر / *adv.* bisyār بسیار, bahut بہت
mud *n.* gil گل , kīcaṛ کیچڑ, gārā گارا
muddiness *n.* gadlā pan گدلاپن, kudūrat کدورت
muddy *adj.* gadlā گدلا
muezzin *n.* mu'azzin موذن
mufti *n.* muftī مفتی
Mughal *adj.* muġliyyah مغلیہ / *n.* muġal مغل
mulberry *n.* tūt توت
mule *n.* xacar خچر
mullah *n.* mullā ملا
multiply *v.* zarb dēnā ضرب دینا, phailānā پھیلانا
multitude *n.* kasrat کثرت, jamᶜiyat جمعیت , majmaᶜ مجمع
mummify *adv.* mōmiyānā مومیانہ
mummy *n.* mōmiyā مومیا
murder *n.* qatl قتل , xūn خون / *v.* mārnā مارنا, xūn karnā خون کرنا, mār ḍālnā مار ڈالنا
murderer *n.* qātil قاتل, xūnī خونی, saffāk سفاک
murmur *v.* baṛbaṛānā بڑبڑانا, cīṁ cīṁ karnā چیں چیں کرنا
muscle *n.* ᶜuzlah عضلہ, ᶜasab عصب
muscular *adj.* kaṛyal کڑیل
museum *n.* ᶜajā'ib ghar عجائب گھر , numā'iš gāh نمائش گاہ
mushroom *n.* dhartī kā phūl دھرتی کا پھول
music *n.* mūsīqī موسیقی

musical instrument *n.* bājā باجا
musician *n.* muġannī مغنی, mutrib مطرب
musk *n.* kastūrī کستوری, mušk مشک
musky *adj.* mušk bār مشک بار, muškiṁ مشکیں
Muslim *adj.* musalmānī مسلمانی / *n.* muslim مسلم, musalmān مسلمان
must *v. (inv.)* cāhī'ē چاہیے
mustard *n.* xardal خردل, sarsōṁ سرسوں
mustard seed *n.* rā'ī رائی
mute *adj.* gūngā گونگا, bē zabān بے زبان, sākit ساکت
muteness *n.* xamōšī خموشی
mutiny *n.* ġadar غدر, fitnah فتنہ, balvā بلوا
mutual *adj.* dō tarfah دوطرفہ, mutabādilah متبادلہ
mutual care *n.* bāhmī nigahdāšt باہمی نگہداشت
mutually *adv.* bāham باہم
my *pron.* mērā میرا
my God! *interj.* yā Allah یا اللہ
myrtle *n.* mahndī/mēhndī مہندی
myself *pron.* maiṁ xūd میں خود
mysterious *adj.* ġaib غیب, muzlim مظلم
mystery *n.* bhēd بھید, rāz راز, sirr سر
mystical *adj.* tilismātī طلسماتی, talismī طلسمی
mysticism *n.* tasavvuf تصوف

N

naan *n.* nān نان
nail *n.* kīl کیل, mēx میخ, khūnṭā کھونٹا / *v.* mēx ṭhōnknā میخ ٹھونکنا, kīlnā کیلنا
naked *adj.* nangā ننگا, ᶜuryān عریان, barahnah برہنہ
nakedness *n.* barahangī برہنگی, ᶜuryānī عریانی
name *n.* nām نام, ism اسم ♦ **first** ~ pahlā nām پہلا نام
named *adj.* mausūm موسوم, musammā مسمی, mulaqqab ملقب
namely *adv.* yaᶜnī یعنی
namesake *n.* ham nām ہم نام
nap *n.* jhapkī جھپکی, aungh اونگھ / *v.* jhapaknā جھپکنا ♦ **take a** ~ *v.* jhapkī lēnā جھپکی لینا
napkin *n.* rūmāl رومال
narcissus *n.* nargis نرگس
narcotic plant *n.* dhatūrā دھتورا
narrative *n.* ḥikāyat حکایت, rivāyat روایت
narrator *n.* rāvī راوی, muḥaddis محدث
narrow *adj.* patlā پتلا, tang تنگ
narrow-minded *adj.* aisā taisā ایسا تیسا
narrowness *n.* tangī تنگی
nasty *adj.* mailā میلا
nation *n.* qaum قوم
national *adj.* mallī ملی, mulkī ملکی, qaumī قومی
national assembly *n.* qaumī majlis قومی مجلس
national government *n.* qaumī ḥukūmat قومی حکومت
nationality *n.* šahriyat شہریت, qaumiyat قومیت
native *adj.* vatanī وطنی, dēsī دیسی / *n.* mutavattin متوطن
native country *n.* vatan وطن
native land *n.* maulid مولد, mādar vatan مادر وطن
nativity *n.* vilādat ولادت, mīlād-ē-masīḥ میلاد مسیح
natural *adj.* qudratī قدرتی, tabaᶜī طبعی, fitratī فطرتی, zātī ذاتی
nature *n.* fitrat فطرت, tabīᶜat طبیعت, mizāj مزاج, jauhar جوہر.
naughty *adj.* šarīr شریر, ziddī ضدی

nausea *n.* ghin گھن , ubkā'ī ابکائی, matlī متلی
nautical *adj.* baḥrī بحری, jahāzī جہازی
naval *adj.* jahāzī جہازی
navel *n.* nāf ناف, dharan دھرن
navy *n.* fauj-ē-baḥrī فوج بحری
nawab *(a Muslim governor) n.* navvāb نواب
near *adj.* nazdīk نزدیک, ās pās آس پاس, qarīb قریب / *adv.* qarīb قریب, pās پاس
nearby *adj.* qarīb قریب, nazdīk نزدیک
nearly *adv.* lag bhag لگ بھگ, taqrīban تقریباً
nearness *n.* nazdīkī نزدیکی, taqarrub تقرب, qurb قرب
neat *adj.* suthrā ستھرا , pākīzah پاکیزہ
neatness *n.* pākīzagī پاکیزگی, safā'ī صفائی
necessarily *adv.* majbūran مجبوراً
necessary *adj.* zarūrī ضروری, lāzimī لازمی, vājib واجب
necessity *n.* zarūrat ضرورت, iḥtiyāj اِحتیاج, ḥājat حاجت
neck *n.* gardan گردن
necklace *n.* kanṭh mālā کنٹھ مالا, tauq طوق, gajrā گجرا
necktie *n.* gulū band گلوبند
nectar *n.* amrit امرت
need *n.* iḥtiyāj اِحتیاج, zarūrat ضرورت, ḥājat حاجت
needle *n.* abrah ابرہ, sū'ī سوئی
needless *adj.* fuzūl فضول
needy *adj.* muḥtāj محتاج, ḥājat mand حاجت مند, niyaz mand نیاز مند
negative *adj.* manfī منفی
neglect *n.* taḥqīr تحقیر / *v.* kōtāhī karnā کوتاہی کرنا
neglectful *adj.* ġāfil غافل
negligence *n.* ġaflat غفلت , tasāhul تساہل, kōtāhī کوتاہی
negligent *adj.* ġāfil غافل
negotiate *v.* byōhār karnā بیوہار کرنا
negotiation *n.* mu^cāmalah معاملہ
neighbor *n.* paṛōsī پڑوسی, hamsāyah ہمسایہ
neighborhood *n.* hamsāyagī ہمسایگی, paṛōs پڑوس
neither *adv.* nah نہ

nephew *n. (brother's son)* bhatījā بھتیجا, *(sister's son)* bhāṁjā بھانجا
nerve *n.* ᶜasab عصب
nervous *adj.* haṛbaṛiyā ہڑبڑیا, haulā ہولا
nest *n.* ghōṁslah گھونسلہ; *(of a bird)* jhōṁjh جھونجھ
net *n.* dām دام, jāl جال, phandā پھندا
network *n.* qafas قفس, jālī جالی
neutral *adj.* musāvī مساوی
never *adv.* kabhī nahīṁ کبھی نہیں, ziṁhār زنہار
nevertheless *adv.* tab bhī تب بھی
new *adj.* nau نو, nayā نیا, tāzah تازہ
New Testament *(of the Bible) n.* iṁjīl انجیل
news *n.* xabar خبر
newspaper *n.* axbār اخبار, jarīdah جریدہ
news-writer *n.* axbār navīs اخبار نویس
next *adj.* ā'īndah آئندہ, aglā اگلا, dūsrā دوسرا
next to *adj.* qarīb قریب / *adv.* sāth ساتھ
nice *adj.* baṛhiyā بڑھیا
niche *n.* tāq طاق, miḥrāb محراب
niece *n. (brother's daughter)* bhatījī بھتیجی, *(sister's daughter)* bhāṁjī بھانجی
night *n.* rāt رات, šab شب, lailat لیلۃ ♦ **at** ~ *phr.* rāt kō رات کو
nightfall *n.* sāṁjh سانجھ
nightingale *n.* bulbul بلبل, gul dam گل دم, hazār dāstān ہزار داستان
nightly *adj.* šabānah شبانہ
nightmare *n.* kābūs کابوس
nimble *adj.* cābuk dast چابک دست, sarīc سریع
nine *num.* nau نو
nineteen *num.* unnīs انیس
ninety *num.* navvē نوے
  ninety-one *num.* ikānavē اکانوے
  ninety-two *num.* bānavē بانوے
  ninety-three *num.* tirānavē ترانوے
  ninety-four *num.* caurānavē چورانوے
  ninety-five *num.* pacānavē پچانوے
  ninety-six *num.* chēyānavē چھیانوے
  ninety-seven *num.* satānavē ستانوے

ninety-eight *num.* aṭhānavē اٹھانوے
ninety-nine *num.* ninānavē ننانوے
nitre *n.* šōrah شورہ
no *adj./adv./prep.* nahīṁ نہیں, nā نا, nah نہ, lā لا
no more *adj.* bas بس
no one *pron.* kō'ī nahīṁ کوئی نہیں
nobility *n.* karāmat کرامت, šarāfat شرافت, najābat نجابت
noble *adj.* ašrāf اشرف, najīb نجیب, majīd مجید, šarīf شریف / *n.* asīl اثیل
nobleman *n.* amīr امیر
nobleness *n.* buzurgī بزرگی, najābat نجابت
nobody *pron.* kō'ī nahīṁ کوئی نہیں
nocturnal *adj.* šabānah شبانہ
noise *n.* šōr شور, ġul غل, tantanah طنطنہ
noisy *adj.* ġauġā'ī غوغائی
nomad *n.* xānah badōš خانہ بدوش
nominal *adj.* farzī فرضی
nomination *n.* tasmiyah تسمیہ, taqarrur تقرر
nonetheless *conj.* ḥālānkih حالانکہ
non-Muslim *(living in an Islamic country)* *n.* zimmī ذمی
nonperishable *adj.* lā zavāl لازوال
nonsense *n.* vāhiyāt واہیات, harzagī ہرزگی, bāṛ بڑ, zaṭal زٹل
noon *n.* dōpahar دوپہر, zuhr ظہر
noose *n.* phandā پھندا, phāṁsī پھانسی
nor *conj.* nah نہ
normal *adj.* ᶜumūmī عمومی
north *n.* uttar اتر, šamāl/šimāl شمال
North Pole *n.* qutb-ē-šimālī قطب شمالی
northern *adj.* uttarāhā اتراہا, šamālī شمالی
nose *n.* nāk ناک
nose-ring *n.* nath نتھ
not *adj./adv./prep.* nahīṁ نہیں, nā نا, nah نہ
notch *n.* ṭānkī ٹانکی, raxnah رخنہ
note *n.* mucalkah مچلکہ, tamassuk تمسک, ruqᶜah رقعہ, naġmah نغمہ; *(in music)* tān تان / *v.* raqm karnā رقم کرنا

notebook *n.* bayāz بیاض
nothing *pron.* hēc ہیچ / *adv.* kuch nahīṁ کچھ نہیں
notice *n.* itlāc اطلاع
notoriety *n.* mašhūrī مشہوری
notorious *adj.* macrūf معروف
notwithstanding *conj.* bā vujūd با وجود
noun *n.* macrifah معرفہ
nourish *v.* pālnā پالنا, parvariš karnā پرورش کرنا
nourishment *n.* taġziah تغذیہ, parvariš پرورش
November *n.* navambar نومبر
novice *adj.* nau āmūz نوآموز / *n.* mubtadī مبتدی
now *adv.* ab اب, fīl-ḥāl فی الحال, ḥālī حالی,
now and then *adv.* jab tab جب تب, ab tab اب تب, kabhī kabhī کبھی کبھی
nowadays *adv.* āj kal آج کل, fī zamānah فی زمانہ, in dinōṁ اِن دنوں
nowhere *adv.* kahīṁ nahīṁ کہیں نہیں
noxious *adj.* mūzī موذی, muzir مضر
noxiousness *n.* mūzi panā موذی پنا
nude *adj.* curyān عریاں, barahnah برہنہ
nudity *n.* curyānī عریانی
numb *adj.* sun سن
number *n.* cadad عدد, nambar نمبر, raqm رقم / *v.* ginnā گننا, šumār karnā شمار کرنا, gintī karnā گنتی کرنا
numerous *adj.* kasīr کثیر, maufūr موفور
nurse *n.* nars نرس, dā'ī دائی
nut *n.* jauz جوز, ḍhibrī ڈھبری
nutmeg *n.* jauz جوز, jā'ē phal جائے پھل
nutrition *n.* ġizā'iyat غذائیت
nymph *n.* ḥūr حور

O

oak *n.* balūt بلوط

oar *n.* cappū چپو, ḍānḍ ڈانڈ

oasis *n.* naxlistān نخلستان

oath *n.* saugand سوگند, qasam قسم, ḥalaf حلف ♦ **take an** ~ *v.* ḥalaf uṭhānā حلف اٹھانا, qasam khānā قسم کھانا, saugand khānā سوگند کھانا

obedience *n.* tābiᶜdārī تابعداری, itāᶜat اطاعت; *(~ to God)* qanūt قنوت

obedient *adj.* ḥukm bardār حکم بردار, mutīᶜ مطیع, tābiᶜdār تابعدار

obey *v.* mānnā ماننا ♦ ~ **an order** kahnā mānnā کہنا ماننا

object *n.* ġaraz غرض, maqsad مقصد, murād مراد / *v.* muᶜtariz hōnā معترض ہونا

object to *v.* māniᶜ hōnā مانع ہونا

objection *n.* taᶜarruz تعرض, iᶜtirāz اعتراض

objector *n.* muᶜtazir معتذر

obligation *n.* zimmah ذمہ, qaid قید, minnat منت

obligatory *adj.* vājib واجب

oblige *v.* talattuf karnā تلطف کرنا

oblivion *n.* nisyān نسیان

oblivious *adj.* bhulakkaṛ بھلکڑ

obscene *adj.* ġalīz غلیظ, fāḥiš فاحش, fuḥš فحش

obscure *adj.* tārīk تاریک, tīrah تیرہ, muġlaq مغلق

obscured *adj.* maġlūq مغلوق

obscurity *n.* tārīkī تاریکی, tīragī تیرگی, andhāpan اندھاپن

observance *n.* pās پاس

observation *n.* mušāhadah مشاہدہ, murāqabah مراقبہ, liḥāz لحاظ

observe *v.* pāband hōnā پابند ہونا, murāqabah karnā مراقبہ کرنا, dēkhnā دیکھنا

observer *n.* mubassir مبصر, mušāhid مشاہد

obsolete *adj.* matrūk متروک, matrūk-ul-istiᶜmāl متروک الاستعمال

obstacle *n.* taᶜarruz تعرض, rukāvaṭ رکاوٹ, rōk روک, aṭak اٹک

obstinacy *n.* ᶜinād عناد, haṭ ہٹ, tamarrud تمرد

obstinate *adj.* musirr مصر, muᶜānid معاند, haṭṭilā ہٹیلا

obstruct *v.* muᶜtariz hōnā معترض ہونا, harj karnā ہرج کرنا, aṭkānā اٹکانا

obstruction *n.* rōk ṭōk روک ٹوک, aṛangā اڑنگا, ḥārij حارج, ixtilāl اختلال

obsure *adj.* ghup گھپ
obtain *v.* vāpas milnā واپس ملنا, pānā پانا
obvious *adj.* vāziḥ واضح
occasion *n.* maqām مقام, mauqaᶜ موقع, naubat نوبت
occasionally *adv.* kabhī kabhī کبھی کبھی, aḥyānan احیانا, ab tab اب تب
occidental *adj.* maġribī مغربی
occult *adj.* mubham مبہم
occupant *n.* qābiz قابض, daxīl kār دخیل کار
occupation *n.* šuġl/šaġl شغل, kārōbār کاروبار, kām کام
occupier *n.* qābiz قابض
occur *v.* sarzad hōnā سرزد ہونا
occurrence *n.* vuqūᶜ وقوع, vāridāt واردات, maᶜriz معرض, mājrā ماجرا, vāqiᶜa واقعہ
ocean *n.* samundar سمندر, baḥr بحر
October *n.* aktūbar اکتوبر
odd *adj.* munfarid منفرد, phuṭkal پھٹکل, nirālā نرالا
oddly *adv.* lahrī لہری
ode *n.* qasīdah قصیدہ
odor *n.* bās باس, šamīm شمیم, tīb طیب, bū بو.
of *prep.* kā کا, sē سے, min من
offend *v.* ranjīdah karnā رنجیدہ کرنا
offender *n.* mujrim مجرم
offense *n.* jurm جرم, taqsīr تقصیر ♦ **take** ~ *v.* jī burā karnā جی براکرنا
offensive *adj.* nā pasand ناپسند, mutanaffir متنفر
offer *v.* pēš karnā پیش کرنا, bhēṭ dēnā بھیٹ دینا
offering *n.* niyāz نیاز, qurbānī قربانی, nazr نذر, pēškaš پیشکش
office *n.* daftar دفتر, maktab مکتب
office manager *n.* daftarī دفتری
office worker *n.* daftarī دفتری
officer *n.* afsar افسر
official *adj.* ᶜuhdah dār عہدہ دار, daftarī دفتری, sarkārī سرکاری
official position *n.* mansab-ē-sarkārī منصب سرکاری
offspring *n.* zād زاد, phulvāṛī پھلواڑی
often *adj.* aksar اکثر / *adv.* ka'ī bār کئی بار, baᶜz auqāt بعض اوقات
oh! *interj.* vā وا, ha ہا, yā یا

oil *n.* tēl تیل, rauġan روغن
oil press *n.* ghānī گھانی
oiliness *n.* ciknāhaṭ چکناہٹ
oily *adj.* carb چرب, ciknā چکنا
ointment *n.* lēp لیپ
OK *adv.* ṭhīk ṭhāk ٹھیک ٹھاک
okra *n.* bhinḍī بھنڈی
old *adj.* būṛhā بوڑھا, pāstān پاستان, purānā پرانا; *(for persons)* buzurg بزرگ ♦ ~ **lady** *n.* buṛhiyā بڑھیا ♦ ~ **man** *n.* buzurg بزرگ
old age *n.* pīrī پیری, kibar کبر, zaᶜīfī ضعیفی
olive *n.* zaitūn زیتون
olive tree *n.* zaitūn kā pēṛ زیتون کا پیڑ
omelet *n.* āmlēṭ آملیٹ
omen *n.* fāl فال, šugun شگن, šagūn شگون
omission *n.* farō guzāšt فروگزاشت, xatā خطا
omit *v.* farō guzāštī karnā فروگزاشتی کرنا
omnipotence *n.* jabrūt جبروت
omnipotent *adj.* jabbār جبار
omnipresent *adj.* ḥāzir-ō-nāzir حاضروناظر
omniscient *adj.* ᶜallām علام, sab kuch jānnē vālā سب کچھ جاننے والا
on *adv.* ūpar اوپر / *prep.* ba بہ, bar بر, bar بر, kō کو, par پر, min من
  on foot *adj./adv.* paidal پیدل pā'ōṁ pā'ōṁ پاؤں پاؤں
  on purpose *adv.* ᶜamadan عمداً
  on the other hand *adv.* bil-ᶜaks بالعکس
once *adv.* gāhē گاہے ♦ ~ **upon a time** *phr.* ēk bār ایک بار ♦ **at** ~ *phr.* barjastah برجستہ, fauran فوراً
one *adj.* vāḥid واحد, yak یک / *adj./num.* ēk ایک / *num.* aḥad اَحد, ik اک / *num. (as a prefix / one-)* ik اک
one-way ticket *n.* ēk tarfah ṭikaṭ ایک طرفہ ٹکٹ
onion *n.* piyāz پیاز
only *adj.* nirā نرا / *adj./adv.* sirf صرف / *adv.* faqat فقط, hī ہی
ooze *v.* risnā رسنا, pānī nikalnā پانی نکلنا
open *adj.* caupaṭ چوپٹ, khulā کھلا, vā وا / *v.* khōlnā کھولنا, khul jānā کھل جانا, vā karnā وا کرنا

opening *n.* chēd چھید, iftitāḥ افتتاح, kašf کشف
openly *adv.* sar-ē-bāzār سر بازار, bar milā بر ملا, ᶜalāniyah علانیہ
openness *n.* kušādagī کشادگی
operation *n.* kār کار
operative *adj.* nāfiz نافذ
operator *n.* fāᶜil فاعل, āpērēṭar آپریٹر
opinion *n.* bicār بچار, rā'ē رائے, tadbīr تدبیر
opium *n.* afīm افیم ♦ **addicted to ~** manšiyat kā ᶜādī منشیات کا عادی, afīmī افیمی, pōstī پوستی
opponent *n.* dušman دشمن, muxālif مخالف, muᶜāriz معارض
opportunity *n.* maqām مقام, mauqaᶜ موقع, naubat نوبت, dā'ō داؤ
oppose *v.* muqābalah karnā مقابلہ کرنا, muxālafat karnā مخالفت کرنا
opposing *adj.* muᶜtariz معترض / *adj./prep.* muqābil مقابل
opposite *adj.* mutanāqis متناقص, mutazād متضاد, muxālif مخالف / *adj./prep.* muqābil مقابل / *adv.* āgē آگے, bil-muqābil بالمقابل, sāmnē سامنے / *n.* sāmnā سامنا, zidd ضد
opposition *n.* muzāḥamat مزاحمت, muvājahah مواجہہ, muxālafat مخالفت, muᶜārizah معارضہ / *adv.* **(in ~ to)** baxilāf بخلاف
oppress *v.* jabr karnā جبر کرنا, zulm karnā ظلم کرنا
oppressed *adj.* maᶜtūb معتوب, mazlūm مظلوم, maqhūr مقہور, majbūr مجبور
oppression *n.* darāz dastī دراز دستی, jabr جبر, tazallum تظلم, sitam ستم
oppressor *n.* zālim ظالم, sitam gar ستم گر, jafāšiᶜār جفاشعار
optimism *n.* rajā'iyat رجائیت
option *n.* ixtiyār اِختیار
optional *adj.* ixtiyārī اختیاری
opulence *n.* yasār یسار
opulent *adj.* farāvāṁ فراواں, tavangar تونگر
or *conj.* yā یا
oracle *n.* hātif ہاتف
oral *adj.* muṁh zabānī منہ زبانی, zabānī زبانی
orange *(fruit) n.* rangtarā رنگترا, sangtarah سنگترہ
orator *n.* saxun sāz سخن ساز
orbit *n.* madār مدار
orchard *n.* bāġīcah باغیچہ, phulvāṛī پھلواڑی, bāġ باغ

order *n.* ḥukm حکم, amar امر, farmā'iš فرمائش, nizām نظام, tartīb ترتیب / *v.* ārḍar dēnā آرڈر دینا, farmā'iš karnā فرمائشی کرنا, mangvānā منگوانا
ordinance *n.* zābitah ضابطہ
ordinary *adj.* maᶜmūlī معمولی , rasmī رسمی
organ *n.* ank انگ
organization *n.* tanzīm تنظیم , intizām انتظام, nazm-ō-nasq نظم ونسق
organize *v.* intizām dēnā انتظام دینا, intizām karnā انتظام کرنا
organized *adj.* munnazzam منتظم
oriental *adj.* mašriqī مشرقی, šarqī شرقی
origin *n.* āġāz آغاز, ᶜunsar عنصر , buniyād بنیاد, asl اصل
original *adj.* ᶜunsurī عنصری , aslī اصلی
originally *adv.* ḥaqīqat mēṁ حقیقت میں , asālatan اصالتاً
ornament *n.* singār سنگار, zēbā'iš زیبائش, gahnā گہنا, zēvar زیور
ornamental *adj.* zēbā'išī زیبائشی, ārā'išī آرائشی
ornamentation *n.* saj dhaj سج دھج
orphan *n.* yatīm یتیم
orphanage *n.* yatīm xānah یتیم خانہ
orthodox *adj.* mutašarriᶜ متشرع, rāšid راشد, mutadaiyyin متدین
orthodox Muslim *n.* mōmin مومن
orthography *n.* tahajjī تہجی
oscillate *v.* jhūlnā جھولنا
other *adj.* digar دگر, dīgar دیگر, dūsrā دوسرا
otherwise *conj.* varnah ورنہ
ouch! *interj.* vā وا
our *pron.* hamārā ہمارا
out *adv.* bāhar باہر
outcast *adj.* xārij خارج, rajīm رجیم
outcry *n.* šōr شور, ġul غل , hānk pukār ہانک پکار
outdo *v.* māt karnā مات کرنا
outer *adj.* bērūni بیرونی
outlet *n.* nikās نکاس; *(of water)* parnālah پرنالہ
outrageousness *n.* taṛap تڑپ
outside *adv.* bāhar باہر, badar بدر
outskirts *n.* muzāfāt-ē-šahr مضافات شہر

outwardly *adv.* xārijan خارجاً
oval *adj.* baizavī بیضوی, anḍā kār انڈاکار
oven *n.* tandūr تندور, tanūr تنور, bhaṭṭhah بھٹھہ
over *adv.* pār پار
overcoat *n.* cūġah چوغہ
overcome *adj.* maġlūb مغلوب / *v.* ġālib karnā غالب کرنا, maġlūb karnā مغلوب کرنا
overflow *n.* chalak چھلک, tuġyānī طغیانی / *v.* chalaknā چھلکنا, chalaknā چھلکنا
overlook *v.* farō guzāštī karnā فروگزاشتی کرنا
overpower *v.* ġālib karnā غالب کرنا, pachāṛnā پچھاڑنا
overshadow *v.* tārī hōnā طاری ہونا
overturn *v.* aundhānā اوندھانا; ulaṭnā الٹنا, lunḍhānā لنڈھانا
overwork *n.* kasrat kām کثرت کام
owl *n.* ullū الو, cuġad چغد
own *adj.* nij نج sagā سگا, xūd خود
owner n. mālik مالک, vāris وارث
ownership *n.* ḥaqiyyat حقیت
ox *n.* gā'ō گاؤ, bail بیل

P

pace *n.* qadam قدم, gām گام, raftār رفتار
pacification *n.* musālaḥat مصالحت
pacify *v.* taskīn dēnā تسکین دینا
pack (up) *v.* guṭharī bāndhnā گٹھڑی باندھنا
package *n.* gaṭṭhā گٹھا, pulandā پلندا
packet *n.* guṭharī گٹھڑی, paikiṭ پیکٹ
paddle *n.* cappū چپو
paddy *n.* dhān دھان
padlock *n.* kalaf کلف
paganism *n.* širk شرک, kufr کفر
page *n.* musḥaf مصحف, saḥīfah صحیفہ, safḥah صفحہ
pagoda *n.* but xānah بت خانہ, but kadah بت کدہ
paid *adj.* muvazzaf موظف
pain *n.* dard درد, zaḥmat زحمت / *v.* īzā dēnā ایذا دینا, dukhānā دکھانا ♦ **take ~s** *v.* takalluf karnā تکلف کرنا
painful *adj.* dard nāk دردناک, dard āmēz درد آمیز, sōhān-ē-rūḥ سوہان روح
painkiller *n.* dard kī davā درد کی دوا
paint *n.* rang رنگ / *v.* tasvīr banānā تصویر بنانا, tasvīr kaiṁcnā تصویر کھینچنا, rang bharnā رنگ بھرنا
painter *n.* naqqāš نقاش, rang āmēz رنگ آمیز, musavvir مصور, sūrat gar صورت گر
painting *n.* naqqāšī نقاشی, rang āmēzī رنگ آمیزی, tasvīr تصویر
pair *n.* zauj زوج, juft جفت, jōṛī جوڑی, jōṛā جوڑا. ♦ **~ of shoes** *n.* jōtī جوتی.
Pakistan *n.* Pākistān پاکستان
Pakistani *adj.* Pākistānī پاکستانی
pakora *(deep-fried vegetables) n.* pakōṛā پکوڑا
palace *n.* maḥall محل, aivān ایوان, qasr قصر, dargāh درگاہ
palanquin *n.* pīnas پینس, pālkī پالکی, miyānā میانا, ḍōlī ڈولی
palatable *adj.* gavārā گوارا
palate *n.* tālū تالو
pale *adj.* pīlā پیلا zard زرد
paleness *n.* zardī زردی, pīlāpan پیلاپن

palm *n.* hathēlī ہتھیلی; *(of the hand)* kaf-ē-dast کف دست
palm tree *n.* naxl نخل
palpitate *v.* dhamaknā دھمکنا, tinaknā تنکنا, phaṛaknā پھڑکنا
palpitation *n.* phaṛak پھڑک
pamphlet *n.* risālah رسالہ
pan *n.* patīlā پتیلا
panic *n.* khalbalī کھلبلی, tahlukah/tahalkah تہلکہ, afrātafrī افراتفری
pant *v.* hāmpnā ہانپنا, dam phūlnā دم پھولنا
pants *n.* patlūn پتلون, painṭ پینٹ
pap *n.* gūdah گودہ
papadum *(flatbread) n.* pāpaṛ پاپڑ
papaya *n.* papītā پپیتا
papaya tree *n.* papītā پپیتا
paper *n.* qirtās قرطاس, kāġaz کاغذ
paradise *n.* firdaus فردوس, rizvān رضوان, jannat جنت, bihišt بہشت
parallel *adj.* musāvī مساوی, mutasāvī متساوی, mutavāzī متوازی
paralysis *n.* laqvah لقوہ
paralytic *adj.* laqvah zadah لقوہ زدہ, maflūj مفلوج
parasite *n.* tufailī طفیلی, muft xōr مفت خور
paratha *(flatbread) n.* parāṭhā پراٹھا
parcel *n.* pārsal پارسل, pulandā پلندا
parcel of land *n.* mauzaᶜ موضع
pardon *n.* muᶜāfī معافی, ġafr غفر, ᶜafū عفو / *v.* muᶜāf karnā معاف کرنا, ᶜafū karnā عفو کرنا
pardonable *adj.* qābil-ē-muᶜāfī قابل معافی
pardoner *n.* baxšindah بخشندہ
pare *v.* chīlnā چھیلنا, chōlnā چھولنا
parents *n.* vāildain والدین, māṁ bāp ماں باپ,
park *n.* pārk پارک, bāġ باغ
parlor *n.* nišast gah نشست گاہ
parrot *n.* miṭṭhū مٹھو, tōtā طوطا, miyāṁ miṭhū میاں مٹھو
part *n.* qism قسم, ḥissah حصہ, juzū جزو, ṭukṛā ٹکڑا
partial *adj.* tarafdār طرفدار, mutaᶜassib متعصب
partiality *n.* rū riᶜāyat رورعایت, taraf dārī طرف داری, riᶜāyat رعایت
participant *n.* šarīk شریک

participate *v.* šarākat karnā شراکت کرنا

particle *n.* šōšah شوشہ, rēzah ریزہ, ḥarf حرف

particular *adj.* xas خاص, nij نج maxsūs مخصوص

particularity *n.* taxsīs تخصیص

particularly *adv.* xas kar خاص کر, xusūsan خصوصاً

parting *(of hair on head) n.* māng مانگ

partition *n.* inqisām انقسام, taqsīm تقسیم

partner *n.* jōṛī جوڑی, šarīk شریک, qasīm قسیم ; *(in trade)* jār جار

partnership *n.* šarākat شراکت, sājhā ساجھا

party *n.* majlis مجلس , ḥazb حزب, jalsah جلسہ, bēram بیرم

pasha *(governor or nobleman) n.* pāšā پاشا

pashmina *(woolen shawl) n.* pašmīnah پشمینہ

pass *n.* guzar گزر, ghāṭī گھاٹی / *v.* tajāvuz karnā تجاوز کرنا , bītnā بیتنا, bitānā بتانا

pass away *v.* cal basnā چل بسنا, bīt jānā بیت جانا

passage *n.* guzar گزر, guzārah گزارہ

passenger *n.* musāfir مسافر, rāhī راہی

passenger boat *(on a river) n.* bajrā بجرا

passing *n.* murūr مرور

passion *n.* xvāhiš خواہش, jazbah جذبہ, jōš-ō-xarōš جوش و خروش, ḥiddat حدت

passionate *adj.* tīkhā تیکھا, jhakkī جھکی , ātaš mizāj آتش مزاج

passive *adj.* mutaḥammil متحمل , majhūl مجہول

passive resistance *n.* sattiyah girah ستیہ گرہ

passport *n.* pāspōrṭ پاسپورٹ, safar nāmah سفر نامہ , guzar nāmah گزر نامہ

passport number *n.* pāspōrṭ nambar پاسپورٹ نمبر

past *n.* māzī ماضی, salaf سلف / *adj.* mazā مضی , guzaštah گزشتہ, pāstān پاستان

paste *n.* mānḍ مانڈ, nišāstah نشاستہ / *v.* cēpnā چیپنا, cipaknā چپکنا, cipṭānā چپٹانا

pastime *n.* tafannun تفنن, lahv-ō-laᶜb لہو ولعب

pastry *n.* pakvān پکوان

pasture *v.* carānā چرانا / *n.* carāgāh چراگاہ, murġazar مرغزار, sabzah zār سبزہ زار

patch *n.* paivand پیوند jōṛ جوڑ / *v.* paivand lagānā پیوند لگانا jōṛ lagānā جوڑ لگانا, jōṛnā جوڑنا

paternal *adj.* abvī ابوی, pidrānah پدرانہ, jaddī جدی

path *n.* rāstah راستہ, rāh راہ, tarīq طریق, tarīqat طریقت; *(~ to salvation)* hudā ہدا

pathway *n.* gail گیل
patience *n.* bardāšt برداشت, taḥammul تحمل , sabr صبر
patient *adj.* sābir صابر, burdbār بردبار, šikēbā شکیبا, mutaḥammil متحمل / *n.* marīz مریض
patiently *adv.* haulē haulē ہولے ہولے
patrimonial *adj.* pidarī پدری
patrimony *n.* mirās میراث
patriot *n.* ḥubb-ul-vatan حب الوطن, muḥibb-ul-vatan محب الوطن
patriotism *n.* ḥubb-ul-vatanī حب الوطنی
patron *n.* sar parast سرپرست, murabbī مربی
patronage *n.* dāšt داشت, valadiyyat ولدیت
pattern *n.* tartīb ترتیب, naqšah نقشہ, namūnah نمونہ
paunch *n.* miᶜdah معدہ, pēṭ پیٹ , šikam شکم
pauper *n.* nā dār نادار
pause *v.* tavaqquf karnā توقف کرنا, tavaqquf توقف, vaqfah وقفہ
pavement *n.* farš فرش
pavilion *n.* šāmiyānah شامیانہ, xargāh خرگاہ, xaimah خیمہ
pawn *n.* girau گرو, kafālat کفالت, gahnā گہنا
pay *n.* tanxvāh تنخواہ , mahīnah مہینہ, mazdūrī/muzdūrī مزدوری / *v.* paisē dēnā پیسے دینا , dēnā دینا
  pay a fine *v.* ḍanḍ bharnā ڈنڈ بھرنا
  pay attention *v.* dhiyān dēnā دھیان دینا
  pay off (debt) *v.* cukānā چکانا
  pay respect *v.* kōrniš bajānā کورنش بجانا
  pay the price *v.* dām dēnā دام دینا
paymaster *n.* baxšī بخشی
pea *n.* maṭar مٹر
peace *n.* camn امن, salām سلام, sulḥ صلح ♦ **make** ~ *v.* musālaḥat karnā مصالحت کرنا
peach *n.* āṛū آڑو, šaftālū شفتالو
peacock *n.* tā'ūs طاؤس, mōr مور
peak *n.* qullah قلہ, rās راس, kalas کلس , cōṭī چوٹی
peanut *n.* mūng phalī مونگ پھلی
pear *n.* nāšpātī ناشپاتی
pearl *n.* mōtī موتی, lō' lō' لؤلؤ

peasant *n.* kisān کسان, rōstā'ī روستائی
pebble *n.* kankar کنکر
peck *v.* ṭhōṁsnā ٹھونسنا, cugnā چگنا
peculiar *adj.* xusūsī خصوصی, muxtass مختص
peculiarity *n.* xāsiyyat خاصیت, xusūsiyyat خصوصیت
pedigree *n.* valadiyyat ولدیت, nasab nāmah نسب نامہ, ḥasb nasab حسب نسب
peel *v.* chīlnā چھیلنا, chilkā utārnā چھلکا اتارنا / *n.* chāl چھال
peep *n.* jhānk جھانک / *v.* jhānknā جھانکنا, ujhaknā اُجھکنا, tāknā تاکنا
peevish *adj.* ciṛciṛā چڑچڑا
peevishness *n.* ciṛciṛāhaṭ چڑچڑاہٹ
peg *n.* kīlā کیلا, kīl کیل, khūnṭā کھونٹا
pen *n.* pēn پین, qalam قلم, xāmah خامہ
penalty *n.* tāvān تاوان, jurmānah جرمانہ, ḍanḍ ڈنڈ
penance *n.* kafārah کفارہ, taubah توبہ
pencil *n.* pansil پنسل
pendant *n.* āvēzah آویزہ, laṭkan لٹکن
pending *adj.* mu^callāq معلق
pendulum *n.* laṭkan لٹکن
penetrate *v.* gaṛnā گڑنا, ghusnā گھسنا
penetration *n.* tā'asur تأثر, firāsat فراست
peninsula *n.* jazīrah numā جزیرہ نما
penitence *n.* kafārah کفارہ, taubah توبہ, pašēmānī پشیمانی
penitent *adj.* pašēmān پشیمان
penniless *adj.* xālī hāth خالی ہاتھ, muflis مفلس
pension *n.* vazīfah وظیفہ, rātib راتب
people *n.* lōg لوگ, ahl اہل
pepper *n.* pilpil پلپل, filfil فلفل, mirc مرچ
peppermint *n.* pōdīnah kā sat پودینہ کا ست
per *adv.* bamūjab بموجب / *prep.* fī فی
perceive *v.* samajhnā سمجھنا, sūjhnā سوجھنا, maḥsūs karnā محسوس کرنا
perception *n.* samajh سمجھ, firāsat فراست, iḥsās احساس, sūjh سوجھ
perfect *adj.* kāmil کامل, mukammal مکمل, ḥaqqānī حقانی
perfection *n.* fazīlat فضیلت, kamāl کمال, takmilah تکملہ
perfectly *adv.* hūbahū ہوبہو

perforate *v.* chidānā چھدانا, bēdhnā بیدھنا, chēdnā چھیدنا
perform *v.* khēlnā کھیلنا, nibhānā نبھانا, bhugtanā بھگتانا
performance *n.* kamā'ī کمائی, pardāzī پردازی, insirām انصرام, taqdīm تقدیم
perfume *n.* ᶜitr/ᶜatr عطر, nakhat نکہت, xūšbū خوشبو
perfumer *n.* ᶜattār عطار, gandhī گندھی, gāndhī گاندھی
perfume-seller *n.* gāndhī گاندھی
perhaps *adv.* šāyad شاید, inšā' allah انشاء اللہ
peril *n.* khaṭkā کھٹکا
period (of time) *n.* daurān دوران, zamānah زمانہ, ᶜarsah عرصہ
perish *v.* fanā hōnā فنا ہونا, binasnā بنسنا
perishable *adj.* fānī فانی
perjury *n.* darōġ-ē-xalfī دروغ خلفی
permanence *n.* sabāt ثبات, davām دوام
permanent *adj.* pā'ēdār پائیدار, qayūm قیوم
permissible *adj.* mubāḥ مباح
permission *n.* manzūrī منظوری, ijāzat اِجازت, ruxsat رخصت
permit *n.* javāz جواز / *v.* ruxsat dēnā رخصت دینا, ijāzat dēnā اجازت دینا
pernicious *adj.* muzir مضر
perpetual *adj.* mudāmī مدامی, istimrārī استمراری, dā'im دائم
perpetually *adv.* jāvidāṁ جاوداں, hamēšah ہمیشہ
perpetuity *n.* baqā بقا, istimrār استمرار, davām دوام
perplex *v.* diqq karnā دق کرنا
perplexity *n.* tazabzub تذبذب, maxmasah مخمصہ, sarāsīmagī سراسیمگی, žōlīdagī ژولیدگی
persecute *v.* pīchē paṛnā پیچھے پڑنا
persevere *v.* zidd karnā ضد کرنا
perseverence *n.* istiqlāl استقلال
Persia *n.* fārs فارس, mulk-ē-fars ملکِ فرس
Persian *n./adj.* fārsī فارسی, pārsī پارسی
persist *v.* zidd karnā ضد کرنا
persistence *n.* zidd ضد, isrār اصرار
person *n.* šaxs شخص, insān انسان, mutanaffis متنفس ♦ **in** ~ *adv.* bil-mušāfah بالمشافہ
personal *adj.* šaxsī شخصی, zātī ذاتی, nij نج xusūsī خصوصی, apnā اپنا

personality *n.* šaxsiyyat شخصیت
personally *adv.* asālatan اصالتاً
personnel *n.* camalah عملہ
persuade *v.* mā'il karnā مائل کرنا, manānā منانا
perverse *adj.* kaj کج kaj raftār کج رفتار ziddī ضدی
perverseness *n.* haṭ ہٹ, vādī وادی
pessimism *n.* qunūtiyyat قنوطیت
pestle *n.* dastah دستہ, mūslā موسلا
pet *n.* munnā منا
petal *n.* pankhṛī پنکھڑی
petition *n.* darxvāst درخواست, ᶜarzī عرضی, maᶜrūz معروض
petitioner *n.* xvāstgār خواستگار
petrol *n.* paiṭrōl پیٹرول
petrol station *n.* paiṭrōl pamp پیٹرول پمپ
petticoat *n.* ghāghrā گھاگھرا, lahangā لہنگا
petty *adj.* chachōrā چھچھورا
pharmacy *n.* davā xānah دوا خانہ
philologist *n.* māhir-ē-lisāniyāt ماہر لسانیات
philosopher *n.* failsūf فیلسوف, falsafī فلسفی, ḥakīm حکیم
philosophical *adj.* ḥakīmānah حکیمانہ, falsafiyānah فلسفیانہ
philosophy *n.* falsafah فلسفہ, ḥikmat حکمت, ᶜilm-ē-ḥikmat علم حکمت
phlegm *n.* balġam بلغم
phlegmatic *adj.* balaġmī بلغمی
phoenix *n.* humā ہما
phone *n.* fōn فون / *v.* fōn karnā فون کرنا
photo *n.* fōṭō فوٹو, tasvīr تصویر ♦ **take a ~** *v.* fōṭō khaiṁcnā فوٹو کھینچنا, fōṭō lēnā فوٹو لینا
photograph *v.* tasvīr kaiṁcnā تصویر کھینچنا
photographer *n.* musavvir مصور, fōṭōgrāfar فوٹوگرافر
photography *n.* musavvirī مصوری
phrase *n.* jumlah جملہ, fiqrah فقرہ
phraseological *adj.* mustalaḥ مصطلح
phraseology *n.* ᶜibārat عبارت
physical *adj.* jismānī جسمانی, tabaᶜī طبعی

physical strength *n.* quvvat-ē-jismānī قوت جسمانی
physician *n.* ḍākṭar ڈاکٹر, tabīb طبیب, vaid وید
physicist *n.* māhir-ē-tabiᶜyāt ماہر طبعیات
physique *n.* jussah جثہ
pick *n.* kudāl کدال / *v.* cunnā چننا ♦ ~ **holes** *v.* raxnah nikālnā رخنہ نکالنا
pickaxe *n.* gēntī گنتی
pickle *n.* acār اچار; *(made of mango)* kacūmar کچومر
pickpocket *n.* cōṭṭā چوٹا
picture *n.* nigār نگار, rūp روپ, šabīh شبیہ, tasvīr تصویر
piece *n.* purzah پرزہ, pārah پارہ, ṭukṛā ٹکڑا, qitᶜah/qatᶜah قطعہ
piece of bread *n.* ṭikkī ٹکی
piece of cloth *n.* pārcah پارچہ
piece of paper *n.* parcah پرچہ, ruqᶜah رقعہ
pierce *v.* bēdhnā بیدھنا, chēdnā چھیدنا, bhōnknā بھونکنا
piety *n.* diyānat دیانت, taqvā تقویٰ, dīndārī دینداری, tavvaruᶜ تورع
pig *n.* sū'ar سوَر, xanzīr خنزیر
pigeon *n.* ḥammāmah حمامہ, kabūtar کبوتر
pigeon-house *n.* kābuk کابک
pigment *n.* rang رنگ
pigtail *n.* cuṭīyā چٹیا
pile *n.* ḍhēr ڈھیر, ambār انبار / *v.* thōpnā تھوپنا, lādna لادنا
pilfer *v.* mūsnā موسنا
pilgrim *n.* jātrī جاتری, zā'ir زائر, sayyāḥ سیاح; *(to Mecca)* ḥājah حاجہ, ḥājī حاجی
pilgrimage *n.* jātrā جاترا, ziyārat زیارت, siyāḥat سیاحت; *(in Hinduism)* tīrath jātrā تیرتھ جاتا, yātrā یاترا; *(to Mecca)* ḥajj حج
pill *n.* gōlī گولی
pillage *n.* ġārat garī غارتگری, yaġmān یغمان
pillar *n.* sutūn/satūn ستون, mīnār مینار, lāṭ لاٹ
pillow *n.* takiyah تکیہ, bāliš بالش
pimple *n.* muhāsā مہاسا, phuṁsī پھنسی
pin *n.* khūnṭā کھونٹا, kīl کیل / *v.* kīlnā کیلنا
pincers *n.* cimṭī چمٹی, cimṭā چمٹا
pinch *n.* cimṭī چمٹی, cuṭkī چٹکی / *v.* cimṭī kānṭā چمٹی کانٹا, nōcnā نوچنا
pine *v.* murjhānā مرجھانا

pine tree *n.* cīṛ چیڑ, sanōbar صنوبر
pineapple *n.* anannās اناناس
pinnacle *n.* kalas کلس
pious *adj.* xudā parast خداپرست, mutadaiyyin متدین, dīndār دیندار
pious man *n.* sāḥib-ē-dil صاحب دل, bhagat بھگت
pipe *n.* šahnā'ī شہنائی, nalī نلی, nal نل
pirate *n.* jahāzī ḍākū جہازی ڈاکو, qazzāq قزاق
Pisces *(Zodiac) n.* samak سمک, mīn مین
pistachio *n.* pistah پستہ
pistol *n.* tamancah تمنچہ, tamancah طمنچہ
pit *n.* gaṛhā گڑھا
pitch *v.* gāṛnā گاڑنا
pitcher *n.* ghaṛā گھڑا, sabū سبو, gāgar گاگر
pith *n.* maġz مغز
pitiable *adj.* dard āmēz دردآمیز, qābil-ē-afsōs قابلِ افسوس
pitiful *adj.* dard mand دردمند, mutaraḥḥim مترحم
pitiless *adj.* kaṭṭar کٹر, nā tars ناترس
pity *n.* raḥm رحم, afsōs افسوس / *v.* kuṛhnā کڑھنا
pivot *n.* qutb قطب, kīlī کیلی
place *n.* jā جا, maqām مقام, jagah جگہ, mauqaᶜ موقع / *v.* dharnā دھرنا, rakhnā رکھنا, biṭhānā بٹھانا ♦ **take ~** *v.* baratnā برتنا
plague *n.* marī مری, vabā وبا, vabāl وبال
plain *adj.* sādah سادہ, musattaḥ مسطح, sādī سادی / *n.* hāmūn ہامون, maidān میدان
plainness *n.* sādagī سادگی, salāsat سلاست
plait *v.* tah jamānā تہ جمانا / *n.* šikan شکن
plan *n.* ḍhāncah ڈھانچہ, naqšah نقشہ, maqṣad مقصد, xākah خاکہ / *v.* mansūbah bāndhnā منصوبہ باندھنا, irādah karnā ارادہ کرنا
plane *v.* randah phērnā رندہ پھیرنا
planet *n.* sayyārah سیارہ, najm نجم
plank *n.* taxtah تختہ, paṭṛī پٹڑی, lauḥ لوح
planning *n.* mansūbah bandī منصوبہ بندی
plant *v.* gāṛnā گاڑنا, paudā lagānā پودا لگانا / *n.* šajar شجر, pēṛ پیڑ
plaster *n.* lēp لیپ, rēxtah ریختہ, lēs لیس / *v.* thōpnā تھوپنا

plate *v.* mulammaᶜ karnā ملمع کرنا / *n.* kāsah کاسہ, plēṭ پلیٹ
platform *n.* macān مچان, sataḥ سطح, cauntrah چونترہ
platter *n.* thālī تھالی
plausibility *n.* maᶜqūliyat معقولیت
plausible *adj.* muvajjah موجہ, maᶜqūl معقول
play *v.* khēlnā کھیلنا; *(an instrument)* bajānā بجانا / *n.* khēl کھیل, lahv-ō-laᶜb لہو ولعب, bāzī بازی ♦ **~ a trick** *v.* farēb karnā فریب کرنا
player *n.* muzhir مظہر, naqqāl نقال
playful *adj.* khilāṛī کھلاڑی, tannāz طناز, aṭkhēl اٹکھیل
playfulness *n.* aṭkhēlī اٹکھیلی, šōxī شوخی
playmate *n.* ham jōli ہم جولی
plea *n.* maᶜzirat معذرت, bahānah بہانہ
pleasant *adj.* suhānā سہانا, piyārī پیاری xūšgavār خوشگوار, farḥat baxš فرحت بخش
pleasantness *n.* maṭhās مٹھاس
pleasantry *n.* latīfah لطیفہ, mazḥakah مضحکہ, mazāq مذاق
please *v.* xūš karnā خوش کرنا / *interj.* mihrbānī karkē مہربانی کرکے، ذرا
pleasure *n.* farḥat فرحت, xūšī خوشی, surūr سرور, lazzat لذت
pledge *n.* girau گرو, iqrār اقرار, paimān پیمان, rihn/rahn رہن / *v.* rakhnā رکھنا, iqrār karnā اقرار کرنا, rahin rakhnā رہن رکھنا
plentiful *adj.* vāfir وافر, maufūr موفور
plentifully *adv.* bakasrat بکثرت, kasrat sē کثرت سے
plenty *adv.* bisyār بسیار / *n.* bahutāt بہتات
plight *n.* gat گت
plot *n.* sāz bāz سازباز, sāziš سازش, qitᶜah/qatᶜah قطعہ
plow *n.* hal ہل, hāl ہال / *v.* hal jōtnā ہل جوتنا, jōtnā جوتنا
plowing *n.* jutā'ī جتائی
plowshare *n.* phāl پھال
pluck *v.* nōcnā نوچنا, cunnā چننا, khasōṭnā کھسوٹنا, chīnnā چھیننا; *(~ flowers)* tōṛ lēnā توڑلینا
plug *n.* ṭhēpī ٹھیپی
plum *n.* ālū buxārā آلو بخارا
plume *n.* kalġī کلغی
plummet *n.* laṭṭū لٹو
plump *adj.* farbah فربہ, gudgudā گدگدا

plumpness *n.* farbahī فربہی
plunder *n.* tārāj تاراج, lūṭ لوٹ / *v.* tārāj karnā تاراج کرنا, luṭānā لٹانا, lūṭnā لوٹنا
plunderer *n.* luṭērā لٹیرا, ġārat gar غارت گر, sāriq سارق, ġāzib غاصب
plunge *n.* ḍubkī ڈبکی, ḍōb ڈوب, ġōtah غوطہ / *v.* ḍubkī lagānā ڈبکی لگانا, ġōtah mārnā غوطا مارنا
ply *n.* parat پرت
pneumonia *n.* namūniyā نمونیا
pocket *n.* jēb جیب, kīsah کیسہ
pocket money *n.* jēb xarc جیب خرچ
pod *n.* phalī پھلی
poem *n.* qasīdah قصیدہ, kavītā کویتا
poet *n.* šāᶜir شاعر
poetess *n.* šāᶜirah شاعرہ
poetic *adj.* manzūm منظوم
poetry *n.* šāᶜirī شاعری, kavītā کویتا, nazm نظم
point *n.* sirā سرا, nuqtah نقطہ, nōk نوک; *(of an arrow)* bhāl بھال / *v.* patā dēnā پتا دینا
point out *v.* sujhānā سجھانا, išārah karnā اشارہ کرنا, jatānā جتانا
poison *n.* zahr زہر, samm سم, dhatūrā دھتورا / *v.* zahr dēnā زہر دینا
poisonous *adj.* zahrīlā زہریلا
polar *adj.* qutbī قطبی
polar star *n.* qutb قطب, jadī جدی
pole *n.* qutb قطب, kēndr کیندر
police *n.* pōlīs پولیس
police inspector *n.* muḥtasib محتسب
police officer *n.* thānah dār تھانہ دار
police post *n.* pōlīs caukī پولیس چوکی
police station *n.* thānah تھانہ
policy *n.* maslaḥat مصلحت, kārastānī کارستانی, ḥikmat ᶜamalī حکمت عملی
polish *n.* jilā جلا / *v.* jilā dēnā جلا دینا, jhalkānā جھلکانا, camkānā چمکانا
polisher *n.* jilā kār جلا کار, xarādī خرادی
polite *adj.* šā'istah شائستہ
politely *adv.* zarīf ظریف
politeness *n.* šā'istagī شائستگی
political *adj.* mulkī ملکی

politician *n.* siyāsat dān سیاست دان
politics *n.* ḥikmat ᶜamalī حکمت عملی, siyāsat سیاست
pollen *n.* zar-ē-gul زرِ گل
poll-tax *n.* jiziyah جزیہ
polluted *adj.* ālūdah آلودہ, mardār مردار, nā pāk ناپاک, palīd پلید
pollution *n.* ālūdagī آلودگی, ālā'iš آلائش, laus لوث, nā pākī ناپاکی
polo *n.* caugān چوگان
polytheism *n.* širk شرک
pomegranate *n.* anār انار, rummān رمان
pomp *n.* dhūm دھوم, tamtarāq طمطراق, šān-ō-šaukat شان و شوکت
pompous *adj.* šān dār شان دار
pond *n.* āb gīr آب گیر, tāl تال, ḍābar ڈابر, tālāb تالاب
pony *n.* ṭaṭṭū ٹٹو
pool *n.* jhīl جھیل, kunḍ کنڈ
poor *adj.* ġarīb غریب, muḥtāj محتاج, muflis مفلس, bicārah بچارہ māyah فرومایہ / *n.* tank dast تنگ دست
Pope *n.* pāpā پاپا
poppy *n.* pōst پوست
poppy flower *n.* lālah لالہ
popular *adj.* maqbūl-ē-ᶜām مقبول عام, har dil ᶜazīz ہر دل عزیز
population *n.* maᶜmūrī معموری, ābādī آبادی, jumhūr جمہور
porch *n.* ḍē'ōṛhī ڈیوڑھی, dahlēz دہلیز
pore *n.* masām مسام
port *n.* bandar gāh بندرگاہ, bandar بندر
porter *n.* qulī قلی, ḥammāl حمال, mazdūr/muzdūr مزدور
portico *n.* dahlēz دہلیز
portion *n.* ḥissah حصہ, juz جز, maqsūm مقسوم
portmanteau *n.* jāmdānī جامدانی
portrait *n.* šabīh شبیہ, tasvīr تصویر
portray *v.* tasvīr banānā تصویر بنانا, tasvīr kaiṁcnā تصویر کھینچنا
position *n.* šān شان, ḍhab ڈھب
positive *adj.* tākīdī تاکیدی
positively *adv.* tākīdan تاکیداً, qarār vaqā'ī قرار واقعی
possessing (something) *adj.* vājid واجد
possession *n.* qabzah قبضہ, mālkiyat مالکیت, tasarruf تصرف, milk ملک

possessor *n.* vālā والا, dārā دارا
possibility *n.* qābiliyyat قابلیت, imkān امکان, iḥtimāl اِحتمال
possible *adj.* imkānī امکانی, mumkin ممکن , hōnhār ہونہار
possibly *adv.* šāyad شاید,
post *n.* khambā کھمبا , ᶜuhdah عہدہ, ḍāk ڈاک, caukī چوکی
post office *n.* ḍāk xānah ڈاک خانہ
postage *n.* ḍāk kā xarc ڈاک کا خرچ, isṭāmp اسٹامپ, ḍāk ṭikaṭ ڈاک ٹکٹ
postal charges *n.* ḍāk kā xarc ڈاک کا خرچ
postbox *n.* ḍāk kā ḍibbā ڈاک کا ڈبا
postcard *n.* pōsṭ kārḍ پوسٹ کارڈ
posterior *adj.* mu'axxar موخر
postman *n.* ciṭhī rasāṁ چٹھی رساں, ḍāk vālā ڈاک والا, ḍākiyā ڈاکیا
postpone *v.* dēr lagānā دیر لگانا, muhlat dēnā مہلت دینا , ṭālnā ٹالنا
postponement *n.* tā'axur تاخر, muhlat مہلت , iltivā' التواء
posture *n.* dhaj دھج, baiṭhak بیٹھک, qadd-ō-qāmat قدوقامت
pot *n.* gharạ̄ گھڑا, bartan برتن, hānḍī ہانڈی
potato *n.* ālū آلو
potent *adj.* qādir قادر
potter *n.* kumhār کمہار
pouch *n.* jhōlī جھولی
poultry *n.* murġī مرغی
pounce *v.* jhapaṭnā جھپٹنا
pounce upon *v.* paṁjah mārnā پنجہ مارنا dabōcnā دبوچنا, jhapaṭ lēnā جھپٹ لینا
pound *v.* kūṭnā کوٹنا, būknā بوکنا.
pound sterling (money) *n.* pā'ūnḍ پاؤنڈ
pour *v.* lunḍhānā لنڈھانا, ḍālnā ڈالنا
pour out *v.* unḍēlnā انڈیلنا, ḍhālnā ڈھالنا, phēnknā پھینکنا
poverty *n.* muflisī مفلسی , faqīrī فقیری, tankdastī تنگدستی
powder *v.* pīsnā پیسنا, cūrā cūrā karnā چوراچوا کرنا / *n.* burādah برادہ, safūf سفوف, cūrā چورا, būrā بورا.
power *n.* tāqat طاقت, bal بل, quvvat قوت, zōr زور
power of attorney *n.* muxtār nāmah مختارنامہ
powerful *adj.* tāqatvar طاقتور, zōr āvar زور آور, qavī قوی, zabardast زبردست
powerless *adj.* nā tavān ناتواں, kamzōr کمزور

practical *adj.* ᶜamlī عملی, mašqī مشقی
practical knowledge *n.* tajribah kārī تجربہ کاری
practically *adv.* fiᶜilan فعلاً
practice *n.* mašq مشق, ᶜādat عادت, maᶜmūl معمول, maslak مسلک / *v.* mašq karnā مشق کرنا
praise *n.* taᶜrīf تعریف, sitā'iš/satā'iš ستائش; *(of God)* taḥmīd تحمید / *v.* taᶜrīf karnā تعریف کرنا; *(~ God)* ḥamd karnā حمد کرنا
praiseworthy *adj.* qābil-ē-taᶜrīf قابل تعریف, maḥmūd محمود
prawn *n.* jhīngā جھینگا
pray *v.* māngnā مانگنا, ᶜibādat karnā عبادت کرنا
prayer *n.* duᶜā دعا, pūjā پوجا, ᶜibādat عبادت; *(by Muslims)* salāt صلوٰۃ, namāz نماز
prayer rug *n.* sajjādah سجادہ
preach *v.* vaᶜz karnā وعظ کرنا
preacher *n.* vāᶜiz واعظ, xatīb خطیب
preaching *n.* vaᶜz وعظ
preamble *n.* muqaddamah مقدمہ, dībācah/dēbācah دیباچہ, tamhīd تمہید
precaution *n.* iḥtiyāṭ اِحتیاط, ḥifz-ē-mātaqaddum حفظ ماتقدم, ḥazm حزم ♦ **take ~s** *v.* iḥtiyāṭ karnā اِحتیاط کرنا
precedent *adj.* mutaqaddim متقدم
preceding *adj.* mā qabl ماقبل, mā sabaq ماسبق, sābiq سابق, muqaddam مقدم
precious *adj.* ᶜazīz عزیز, bēš qīmat بیش قیمت anmōl انمول, nafīs نفیس
precious stone *n.* nag نگ, ratan رتن, yāqūt یاقوت
prediction *n.* pēšingō'ī پیشنگوئی, najm نجم
predominance *n.* fart فرط
preface *n.* muqaddamah مقدمہ, dībācah/dēbācah دیباچہ, tamhīd تمہید
prefer *v.* tarjīḥ dēnā ترجیح دینا, pasand karnā پسند کرنا
preference *n.* pasand پسند, tarjīḥ ترجیح, fauqiyyat فوقیت
pregnancy *n.* pēṭ پیٹ, ḥaml حمل
pregnant *adj.* pēṭ sē پیٹ سے, ḥāmilah/ḥāmla حاملہ; *(used just for animals)* gābhan گابھن
prejudice *n.* ᶜasabiyyat عصبیت
prejudiced *adj.* mutaᶜassib متعصب
preliminary *adj.* qabl قبل
premier *n.* dīvān-ē-aᶜlā دیوان اعلی

preparation *n.* taiyārī تیاری, banā'ō بناؤ
prepare *v.* taiyār karnā تیار کرنا
prepare food *v.* khānā taiyār karnā کھانا تیار کرنا
prescribed *adj.* mujavvazah مجوزہ
prescription *n.* nusxah نسخہ
presence *n.* ḥuzūrī حضوری, ḥāzrī حاضری, manjūdagī موجودگی
presence of mind *n.* ausān اوسان, sudh budh سدھ بدھ
present *adj.* maujūd موجود, maujūdah موجودہ, ḥāzir حاضر / *n.* pēškaš پیشکش, tōḥfah تحفہ, nazrānah نذرانہ / *v.* pēš karnā پیش کرنا, ḥāzir karnā حاضر کرنا
presentation *n.* taqdīm تقدیم
presently *adv.* ab اب, fil-ḥāl فی الحال
preservation *n.* muḥāfazat محافظت, ḥifz حفظ
preserve *n.* murabbā مربی / *v.* ḥifāzat karnā حفاظت کرنا, sāt pardōṁ mēṁ rakhnā سات پردوں میں رکھنا
preserver *n.* bēlī بیلی, ḥāfiz حافظ
presidency *n.* sadārat صدارت
president *n.* sadr-ē-majlis صدر مجلس, sadr našīn صدر نشین
press *n.* matbaᶜ مطبع, chāpah xānah چھاپہ خانہ / *v.* dabā'ō ḍālnā دباؤڈالنا, dābnā دابنا, dabānā دبانا
press down *v.* dabkānā دبکانا
pressure *n.* dāb داب, dabā'ō دباؤ
prestige *n.* vaqār وقار
presume *v.* jurāt karnā جرات کرنا, zann karnā ظن کرنا, iḥtimāl karnā اِحتمال کرنا
presumption *n.* zaᶜm زعم, zann ظن, qiyās قیاس
pretend *v.* zāhir dārī baratnā ظاہر داری برتنا, zāhir karnā ظاہر کرنا
pretty *adj.* saḍaul سڈول
prevail *v.* rā'ij hōnā رائج ہونا
prevent *v.* manaᶜ karnā منع کرنا, rōknā روکنا
prevention *n.* imtināᶜ امتناع, rōk روک, muzāḥamat مزاحمت
previous *adj.* qabl قبل, pichlā پچھلا
previously *adv.* sābiqan سابقا, sābiq mēṁ سابق میں
prey *n.* said صید
price *n.* dām دام, qīmat قیمت ♦ **pay the ~** *phr.* dām dēnā دام دینا
price list *n.* nirx nāmah نرخ نامہ

priceless *adj.* anmōl انمول, anmōl انمول
pride *n.* takabbur تکبر, maġrūrī مغروری, ġarūr غرور
priest *n.* kāhan کاہن, pīr پیر, pēšvā پیشوا, maulavī مولوی; *(Catholic)* pādrī پادری; *(Christian)* rāhib راہب; *(Hindu)* pujārī پجاری, gusā'īṁ گسائیں
priesthood *n.* ruhbāniyyat رہبانیت
primary *adj.* ibtidā'ī اِبتدائی
primary education *n.* ibtidā'ī taᶜlīm ابتدائی تعلیم
prime minister *n.* vazīr-ē-aᶜazam وزیر اعظم
primitive *adj.* dahqānī دہقانی
prince *n.* bādšāh zādah بادشاہ زادہ, šāh zādah شاہ زادہ
princess *n.* bādšāh zādī بادشاہزادی, rāj dulārī راج دلاری, šāh zādī شاہزادی
principal *adj.* mih مہ
principle *n.* mudīr مدیر, manšā' منشاء, mubtadā مبتدا, nisāb نصاب
print *n.* chāp چھاپ, tabaᶜ طبع / *v.* tabaᶜ karnā طبع کرنا, chāpnā چھاپنا
printer *n.* chāpnē vālā چھاپنے والا, tābiᶜ طابع
printing *n.* chapā'ī چھپائی, intibāᶜ انطباع
printing house *n.* matbaᶜ مطبع
printing press *n.* matbaᶜ مطبع, chāpah xānah چھاپہ خانہ
prior *adj.* muqaddam مقدم, mā qabl ماقبل, sābiq سابق
priority *n.* taqaddum تقدم, taqdīm تقدیم
prison *n.* qaid xānah قید خانہ, jēl جیل, jēl xānah جیل خانہ
prisoner *n.* asīr اسیر, qaidī قیدی, zindānī زندانی, maḥbūs محبوس
privacy *n.* taxliyah تخلیہ, gōšah našīnī گوشہ نشینی
private *adj.* xas خاص, xāngī خانگی, nijī نجی, zātī ذاتی
prize *n.* ġanīmat غنیمت, inᶜām انعام
probability *n.* gumān-ē-ġālib گمان غالب, iḥtimāl اِحتمال, maᶜqūliyat معقولیت
probable *adj.* iḥtimālī اِحتمالی, maᶜqūl معقول
probably *adv.* šāyad شاید, ġāliban غالبا
problem *n.* ᶜuqdah عقدہ, masa'lah مسئلہ
procedure *n.* vazaᶜ وضع
proceed *v.* sādir hōnā صادر ہونا, baṛhnā بڑھنا
process *n.* ᶜamal dar āmad عمل در آمد
procession *n.* jalūs جلوس
proclaim *v.* sunānā سنانا, manādī karnā منادی کرنا

proclamation *n.* iᶜlān اعلان, manādī منادی, ḍhanḍhōrā ڈھنڈھورا

prodigal *adj.* musrif مصرف

produce *v.* ḥāzir karnā حاضر کرنا, pēš karnā پیش کرنا; *(~ crops)* ugānā اگانا / *n.* paidā'iš پیدائش ḥāsil حاصل, samar ثمر, phal پھل; *(in agriculture)* paidāvār پیداوار

product *n.* ḥāsil حاصل

productive *adj.* zarxēz زرخیز

profession *n.* kār کار, kām کام, ḥirfah حرفہ, pēšah پیشہ

professor *n.* mudarris مدرس, maulavī مولوی

professorship *n.* mudarrisī مدرسی

proficiency *n.* mahārat مہارت

proficient *adj.* muššāq مشاق

profit *n.* fā'idah فائدہ, manfaᶜat منفعت, nafaᶜ نفع, sūd سود ♦ ~ **and loss** *n.* kamī bēšī کمی بیشی

profitable *adj.* fā'idah mand فائدہ مند, sūd mand سود مند, mufīd مفید

profound *adj.* ᶜamīq عمیق, gahrā گہرا

program *n.* mansūbah منصوبہ, prōgrām پروگرام

progress *n.* taraqqī ترقی

prohibit *v.* manaᶜ karnā منع کرنا

prohibition *n.* imtināᶜ امتناع, mumānaᶜat ممانعت, manaᶜ منع

prohibitive *adj.* imtināᶜī امتناعی

project *n.* mansūbah منصوبہ

prolong *v.* lambā karnā لمبا کرنا

prolongation *n.* abkā ابکا, imtidād امتداد

promise *n.* vaᶜdah وعدہ, iqrār اقرار, paimān پیمان / *v.* vaᶜdah karnā وعدہ کرنا, iqrār karnā اقرار کرنا ♦ **make a** ~ *v.* vaᶜdah karnā وعدہ کرنا

promising *adj.* hōnhār ہونہار

promote *v.* farōġ dēnā فروغ دینا

promotion *n.* taraqqī ترقی

prompt *adj.* mustaᶜidd مستعد, muᶜajjal معجل

promptness *n.* mustaᶜiddī مستعدی

pronounce *v.* uccāran karnā اچارن کرنا

pronunciation *n.* talaffuz تلفظ, uccāran اچارن, qirāt قرات

proof *n.* burhān برہان, dalīl دلیل, subūt ثبوت

prop *v.* ṭēknā ٹیکنا, thāmnā تھامنا / *n.* ṭēk ٹیک
proper *adj.* xas خاص, munāsib مناسب, ucit اچت, vājib واجب
properly *adv.* kamā ḥaqqah کما حقہ
property *n.* ḥaqiyyat حقیت, milk ملک, māl مال
prophecy *n.* pēšingō'ī پیشنگوئی
prophet *n.* nabī نبی, mursal مرسل, rasūl رسول
proportion *n.* tanāsub تناسب
proportionate *adj.* rasadī رسدی
proposal *n.* tajvīz تجویز, tadbīr تدبیر
propose *v.* tajvīz karnā تجویز کرنا
proprietary *adj.* milkī ملکی
proprietor *n.* mālik مالک
proprietorship *n.* mālkiyat مالکیت
prose *n.* nasr نثر
prosper *v.* phalnā پھلنا
prosperity *n.* iqbāl اقبال, kāmyābī کامیابی, daulat mandī دولت مندی, kalyān کلیان, farāxī فراخی
prosperous *adj.* kāmyāb کامیاب, harā bharā ہرا بھرا, daulat mand دولت مند, sar sabz سر سبز
prostitute *n.* tavā'if طوائف, randī رنڈی, fāḥišah فاحشہ, rānḍ رانڈ
prostrate *adj.* cit چت, sājid ساجد
protect *v.* pālnā پالنا, bacānā بچانا, ḥimāyat karnā حمایت کرنا
protection *n.* amān امان, ḥifāzat حفاظت, panāh پناہ, ḥimāyat حمایت
protector *n.* muḥāfiz محافظ, ḥāmī حامی
protest *n.* iḥtijāj اِحتجاج, i'tirāz اعتراض
protraction *n.* imtidād امتداد
proud *adj.* mutakabbir متکبر, maġrūr مغرور, mudammiġ مدمغ
proudly *adv.* faxriyyah فخریہ
prove *v.* sābit karnā ثابت کرنا, kasvaṭī par parakhnā کسوٹی پر کھنا, mutaḥaqqaq karnā متحقق کرنا
proverb *n.* zarb-ul-masal ضرب المثل, kahāvat کہاوت
proverbial *adj.* istilāḥī اصطلاحی
provide *v.* sar anjām dēnā سر انجام دینا, baham pahuṁcānā بہم پہنچانا
provident *adj.* pēš bīn پیش بین

province *n.* sūbah صوبہ, dīyār دیار
provision *n.* ġizā'iyat غذائیت, zaxīrah ذخیرہ, rasad رسد
provisions *n.* xōrāk خوراک, zād زاد; *(for a journey)* zād-ē-rāh زادراہ
provoke *v.* bhabkānā بھبکانا, uksānā اکسانا
proximity *n.* taqarrub تقرب
prudence *n.* ḥazm حزم, tadabbur تدبر
prudent *adj.* maslaḥat bīṁ مصلحت بیں, pēš bīṉ پیش بیں
prune *v.* qalam karnā قلم کرنا, qaiṁcī karṇā قینچی کرنا
psychologist *n.* māhir-ē-nafsiyāt ماہر نفسیات
puberty *n.* bulūġ بلوغ
public *n.* riᶜāyā رعایا, ᶜavām عوام, ᶜavām-ul-nās عوام الناس / *adj.* ᶜām عام
public bath *n.* saqāvah سقاوہ
public good *n.* faiz-ē-ᶜām فیض عام, rifāh xalā'iq رفاہ خلائق, rifāh ᶜām رفاہ عام
public hall *n.* dīvān xānah دیوان خانہ
public road *n.* šāh-ē-rāh شاہ راہ, guzar-ē-ᶜām گزر عام
public speaker *n.* saxun sāz سخن ساز
public welfare *n.* rifāh xalā'iq رفاہ خلائق, rifāh ᶜām رفاہ عام
publication *n.* išāᶜat اشاعت, ibdāᶜ اِبداع
publicly *adv.* bar milā برملا, ᶜalāniyah علانیہ
publish *v.* chāpnā چھاپنا, šā'iᶜ karnā شائع کرنا
puff *v.* hāmpnā ہانپنا / *n.* phūnk پھونک
pulao *(rice dish) n.* pulā'ō پلاؤ
pull *n.* khicā'ō کھچاؤ, khaiṁc کھینچ / *v.* khaiṁcnā کھینچنا, aiṁcnā اینچنا, ghasīṭnā گھسیٹنا
  pull down *v.* ḍhānā ڈھانا
  pull out *v.* nikālnā نکالنا
pulley *n.* ghirnī گھرنی
pulp *n.* gūdah گودہ
pulpit *n.* minbar منبر
pulse *(legume) n.* dāl دال
pumpkin *n.* ghiyā گھیا
pun *n.* mazḥakah مضحکہ, jugat جگت
punctual *adj.* zābit ضابط
puncture *n.* nēš نیش
pungent *adj.* tīkhā تیکھا, talx تلخ, kasēlā کسیلا, tēz تیز

punish *v.* mārnā مارنا, sazā dēnā سزا دینا

punishment *n.* taᶜzīr تعزیر, sazā سزا, ᶜuqūbat عقوبت

Punjab *n.* paṁjāb پنجاب

Punjabi *adj.* paṁjābī پنجابی

punt *v.* khēnā کھینا

pupil *n.* cailā چیلا, šāgird شاگرد; *(of the eye)* putlī پتلی, tārā تارا

puppet *n.* putlā پتلا, kaṭh putlī کٹھ پتلی

puppy *n.* pillā پلا

purchase *n.* xarīd خرید, mōl مول

purchaser *n.* muštarī مشتری

pure *adj.* sāf صاف, pāk پاک, xālis خالص, muxlis مخلص

purely *adv.* sirf صرف

pureness *n.* sarāḥat صراحت

purgative *n.* dast āvar دست آور, jullāb جلاب

purgative *adj.* mushil مسہل

purge *n.* jullāb جلاب, dast دست, jhāṛā جھاڑا

purification *n.* tazkiyah تزکیہ, tasfiyah تصفیہ, tathīr تطہیر

purify *v.* safā'ī karnā صفائی کرنا, pāk karnā پاک کرنا

purity *n.* safā'ī صفائی, pākī پاکی, pākbāzī پاکبازی

purple *adj.* ūdā اودا, arġavānī ارغوانی

purpose *n.* matlab مطلب, maqsad مقصد ♦ **on ~** *adv.* ᶜamadan عمداً

purse *n.* thailī تھیلی, pars پرس, kīsah کیسہ, baṭvā بٹوا

pursue *v.* taᶜāqub karnā تعاقب کرنا, pīchā karnā پیچھا کرنا

pursuit *n.* taᶜāqub تعاقب, pai پے, pīchā پیچھا

pus *n.* cirk چرک, pīp پیپ

pusillanimous *adj.* buzdil بزدل

push *n.* ṭhēs ٹھیس, dhakkā دھکا / *v.* dhakēlnā دھکیلنا, rēlnā ریلنا, pēlnā پیلنا

push back *v.* haṭānā ہٹانا

pushcart *n.* ṭhēlah ٹھیلہ

pustule *n.* chālah چھالہ

put *v.* rakhnā رکھنا, ḍālnā ڈالنا ♦ **~ on clothes** kapṛē pahannā کپڑے پہننا, paharnā پہرنا

putrid *adj.* saṛā سڑا, mutaᶜaffin متعفن

puzzle *n.* bhūl bulaiyāṁ بھول بھلیاں, gutthī گتھی, muᶜammah معمہ

Q

qawwali *(a music style) n.* qavvālī قوالی
quadrilateral *adj.* caukōr چوکور
quadruped *n.* carind چرند
quadruple *adj.* caugunā چوگنا
quake *v.* laraznā لرزنا
quality *n.* xūbī خوبی, xulq خلق, kaifiyyat کیفیت
quantity *n.* miqdār مقدار, kammiyyat کمیت, mablaġ مبلغ
quarrel *n.* jhagṛā جھگڑا, laṛā'ī لڑائی / *v.* jhagaṛnā جھگڑنا, jhagṛā karnā جھگڑا کرنا
quarrelsome *adj.* laṛākā لڑاکا, fasādī فسادی, fitnah angēz فتنہ انگیز
quarry *n.* kān کان, said صید
quarter *n.* pā'ō پاؤ, cauthā'ī چوتھائی, ruba^c ربع; *(of town)* muḥallah محلہ, ṭōlā ٹولا
quartz *n.* billaur بلور
quay *n.* ghāṭ گھاٹ
queen *n.* sultānah سلطانہ, malikah ملکہ, rānī رانی
quest *n.* talāš تلاش, justjū جستجو , khōj کھوج
question *n.* sū'āl/savāl سوال / *v.* pūchnā پوچھنا, sū'āl karnā سوال کرنا
questioning *n.* purs پرس, pursiš پرسش
quick *adj.* phurtīlā پھرتیلا, jhap جھپ, cābuk dast چابک دست, šitāb شتاب
quickly *adv.* jald جلد, jaldī sē جلدی سے
quickness *n.* phurtī پھرتی, jaldī جلدی
quicksilver *n.* āb-ē-naqrah اب نقرہ, pārā پارا
quiet *adj.* xāmōš خاموش,, sākit ساکت
quieted *adj.* musammat مصمت
quietly *adv.* cupkē cupkē چپکے چپکے cup cāp چپ چاپ
quietness *n.* xāmōšī خاموشی, sukūt سکوت, cup چپ
quilt *n.* dulā'ī دلائی, razā'ī رضائی
quire *(of paper) n.* dastah دستہ
quiver *n.* tarkaš ترکش / *v.* tharrānā تھرانا
quotation *n.* iqtibās اقتباس
quote *v.* misāl dēnā مثال دینا, ḥavālah dēnā حوالہ دینا
Quran *n.* qur'ān قرآن, qur'ān šarīf قرآن شریف

R

rabbit *n.* xargōš خرگوش
race *n.* jāt جات, nasl نسل, qaum قوم, nasab نسب
racial *adj.* qaumī قومی
radial *adj.* šuᶜāᶜī شعاعی
radiance *n.* jyōtī جیوتی
radiant *adj.* šuᶜāᶜī شعاعی
radiator *n.* rēḍiyēṭar ریڈییٹر
radio *n.* rēḍiyō ریڈیو
radish *n.* mūlī مولی
rafter *n.* kaṛī کڑی
rag *n.* cithṛā چتھڑا, dhajjī دھجی
raga *(a musical tune) n.* rāg راگ
rage *n.* ġussah غصہ, krōdh کرودھ, jazbah جذبہ / *v.* buxār nikālnā بخار نکالنا
rags *(old clothes) n.* gūdaṛ گودڑ
raid *n.* dhāvā دھاوا / *v.* dhāvā karnā دھاوا کرنا, dhāvā mārnā دھاوا مارنا
raider *n.* ġārat gar غارت گر
railway *n.* rēl ریل, rēlgāṛī ریل گاڑی, ṭrēn ٹرین
rain *n.* bāriš بارش; *(a small amount)* būndā bāndī بوندا باندی; *(continuous)* jhaṛī جھڑی; *(fine ~)* phuvār پھوار; *(heavy ~)* bauchāṛ بوچھاڑ / *v.* barasnā برسنا; *(continuously)* jhaṛī lagnā جھڑی لگنا
rainbow *n.* dhanak دھنک, qaus-ē-quzaḥ قوس قزح
rainwater *n.* āb-ē-bārāṁ آب باراں
rainy *adj.* barsātī برساتی
rainy season *n.* barsāt برسات
raise *v.* uṭhānā اُٹھانا ◆ ~ **funds** *v.* ugāhnā اگاہنا, candah karnā چندہ کرنا
raisin *n.* kišmiš کشمش, mavēz مویز
ram *n.* bhēṛā بھیڑا, mēnḍhā مینڈھا
rampart *n.* cār dīvārī چار دیواری, šahr-ē-panāh شہرپناہ, fasīl فصیل
range *n.* zad زد
rank *n.* qitār; qatār قطار, saff صف / *adj.* *(of high ~)* ᶜālī jah عالی جاہ
rape *n.* zinā bil-jabr زنا بالجبر

rapid *adj.* tund تند
rapidity *n.* suraᶜt سرعت
rare *adj.* anūṭhā انوٹھا, birlā برلا, nirālā نرالا
rarely *adv.* šāz-ō-nādir شاذونادر
rarity *n.* sūġāt سوغات, kam yābī کم یابی
rascal *n.* ḥarāmī حرامی, gunḍā گنڈا, ġunḍah غنڈہ
rasgulla *(cheese-based sweet dish) n.* ras gullā رس گلا
rat *n.* cūhā چوہا, mūš موش
rate *n.* dām دام, nirx نرخ, bhā'ō بھاؤ
rather *adj.* zarā ذرا
rational *adj.* ᶜaqlī عقلی
rattle *n.* kharkharāhaṭ کھڑکھڑاہٹ, jhankār جھنکار / *v.* jhanjhanānā جھنجھنانا, kharkharānā کھڑکھڑانا, khaṭaknā کھٹکنا
ravage *n.* ġārat غارت / *v.* ġārat karnā غارت کرنا
raven *n.* kāg کاگ, pahāṛī kavvā پہاڑی کوا
ravishing *adj.* rubā ربا
raw *adj.* xām خام, dūdhyā دودھیا, kaccā کچا
raw sugar *n.* guṛ گڑ
rawness *n.* xāmī خامی
ray *n.* kiran کرن
rays *n. (of light)* raxš رخش; *(of the sun)* šuᶜaᶜ شعاع
raze *v.* ujāṛnā اجاڑنا
razor *n.* mū tarāš موتراش
reach *v.* pahuṁcnā پہنچنا, pās ānā پاس آنا
read *v.* paṛhnā پڑھنا
readiness *n.* taiyārī تیاری, mustaᶜiddī مستعدی
reading *n.* mutālaᶜah مطالعہ, qirāt قرات; *(of the Quran)* tilāvat تلاوت
ready *adj.* taiyār تیار, ḥāzir حاضر, mustaᶜidd مستعد
real *adj.* aslī اصلی, saccā سچا
reality *n.* asliyat اصلیت, saccā'ī سچائی, ḥaqīqat حقیقت
really *adj.* vāqaᶜī واقعی, acchā اچھا, ḥaqqā حقا / *adv.* sac muc سچ مچ, vāqiᶜ mēṁ واقع میں, sac سچ
reap *v. (a field)* khēt kāṭnā کھیت کاٹنا ♦ ~ **the reward of** *phr.* phal pānā پھل پانا

reaping season *n.* kaṭā'ī کٹائی
rear *n.* pīchā پیچھا / *v.* pōsnā پوسنا
reason *n.* sabab سبب, vajh وجہ / *v.* **(~ with)** manānā منانا
reasonable *adj.* munāsib مناسب, maᶜqūl معقول, mudallal مدلل
reasonableness *n.* maᶜqūliyat معقولیت
reasoning *n.* istidlāl استدلال, mantiq/mantaq منطق
reassure *v.* bharōsah dēnā بھروسہ دینا
rebel *n.* yāġī یاغی, bāġī باغی / *v.* muxālafat karnā مخالفت کرنا
rebellion *n.* sarkašī سرکشی, baġāvat بغاوت, tamarrud تمرد
rebellious *adj.* bāġī باغی, sarkaš سرکش
rebuke *n.* ḍapaṭ ڈپٹ, jhiṛkī جھڑکی, ḍānṭ ڈانٹ / *v.* jhiṛaknā جھڑکنا, ḍapaṭnā ڈپٹنا, ḍānṭnā ڈانٹنا
receipt *n.* rasīd رسید, qabz-ul-vasūl قبض الوصول
receive *v.* qarār pānā قرار پانا, lēnā لینا, istiqbāl karnā استقبال کرنا ♦ **~ a penalty** *v.* ḍanḍ bharnā ڈنڈ بھرنا
recent *adj.* mujaddid مجدد, ḥādis حادث, nayā نیا
reception *n.* pazīrā'ī پذیرائی, salāmī سلامی, istiqbāl استقبال
recipe *n.* nusxah نسخہ
recipient *n.* yābindah یابندہ
reciprocal *adj.* mutabādilah متبادلہ
recitation *n.* qirāt قرات, tilāvat تلاوت
recite *v.* ḥifz karnā حفظ کرنا, zikr karnā ذکر کرنا, raṭnā رٹنا
reciter *(especially of the Quran)* *n.* ḥāfiz حافظ
recklessly *adv.* bē taḥāšā بے تحاشا
reckon *v.* ginnā گننا
recluse *adj.* gōšah našīn گوشہ نشین
recognise *v.* šināxt karnā شناخت کرنا, jānnā جاننا
recognition *n.* šināxt شناخت
recoil *v.* hicaknā ہچکنا
recollect *v.* yād karnā یاد کرنا
recollection *n.* yād یاد
recommend *v.* sifāriš karnā سفارش کرنا, šafāᶜt karnā شفاعت کرنا
recommendation *n.* sifāriš سفارش, šafāᶜt شفاعت
recompense *n.* ᶜivaz عوض, silah صلہ, pādāš پاداش / *v.* ajr dēnā اجر دینا

reconcile *v.* musālaḥat karnā مصالحت کرنا
reconciliation *n.* musālaḥat مصالحت
record *n.* taḥrīr تحریر, daftar دفتر / *v.* darj karnā درج کرنا, taḥrīr karnā تحریر کرنا
recourse *n.* mā'ab مآب, murāja^cat مراجعت
recover *v.* sambhalnā سنبھلنا, acchā karnā اچھا کرنا, siḥḥat pānā صحت پانا
recovery *n.* vusūlī وصولی, šifā/šafā شفا
recruit *v.* bhartī karnā بھرتی کرنا
rectify *v.* saḥīḥ karnā صحیح کرنا, durust karnā درست کرنا
rectitude *n.* rušd رشد, ma^cdalat معدلت
red *adj.* lāl لال, surx سرخ, aḥmar احمر
red lead *n.* sēndūr سیندور
reddish *adj.* surxī mā'il سرخی مائل
redness *n.* surxī سرخی, lālī لالی
reduce *v.* kam karnā کم کرنا, ghaṭānā گھٹانا, taxfīf karnā تخفیف کرنا,
reduction *n.* kamī کمی, ghaṭā'ō گھٹاؤ, taxfīf تخفیف
redundance *n.* fuzlah فضلہ
redundant *adj.* zā'id زائد
reed *n.* kalk کلک, qalam قلم
reel *n.* carxā چرخا
refer *v.* ḥavālah dēnā حوالہ دینا
refer to *v.* rujū^c karnā رجوع کرنا
reference *n.* ḥavālah حوالہ, nisbat نسبت, rujū^c رجوع
referendum *n.* istisvāb استصواب
refinement *n.* nafāsat نفاست
reflect *v.* tāmmul karnā تامل کرنا, ^caks ḍālnā عکس ڈالنا
reflected *adj.* mutasavvar متصور
reflection *n.* tafakkur تفکر, ^caks عکس, murā^cāt مراعات, in^cikās انعکاس
reflective *adj.* ^caksī عکسی, andēš mand اندیش مند
reform *n.* islāḥ اصلاح / *v.* islāḥ karnā اصلاح کرنا
reformer *n.* musliḥ مصلح
refractory *adj.* sarkaš سرکش
refrain *v.* bāz rēhnā باز رہنا
refresh *v.* tāzah karnā تازہ کرنا
refreshing *adj.* mufarriḥ مفرح, farḥat baxš فرحت بخش

refrigerator *n.* frij فرج
refuge *n.* ḥirz حرز, marjaᶜ مرجع, panāh پناہ
refugee *n.* muhājir مہاجر, panāh gīr پناہ گیر
refusal *n.* inkār انکار, nafī نفی, manaᶜ منع
refuse *n.* chānṭ چھانٹ, fuzlah فضلہ, ibā ابا / *v.* chānṭnā چھانٹنا, manaᶜ karnā منع کرنا, mukarnā مکرنا, inkār karnā انکار کرنا
refutation *n.* tardīd تردید
refute *v.* tardīd karnā تردید کرنا
regal *adj.* sultānī سلطانی
regard *n.* liḥāz لحاظ, mulāḥazah ملاحظہ / *v.* muṁh karnā منہ کرنا, xayāl karnā خیال کرنا
region *n.* ᶜilāqah علاقہ
regional *adj.* arzī ارضی
register *n.* daftar دفتر, jarīdah جریدہ / *v.* darj karnā درج کرنا
registration *n.* rajisṭarī رجسٹری
regret *n.* darēġ دریغ, ḥasrat حسرت, nadāmat ندامت / *v.* pachtānā پچھتانا, pašēmān hōnā پشیمان ہونا
regretful *adj.* mutā'assif متاسف
regretfully *adv.* mutā'assifānah متاسفانہ
regular *adj.* ḥāzir baš حاضر باش, munnazzam منتظم, bā qāᶜēdah باقاعدہ
regularity *n.* zābitagī ضابطگی
regularly *adv.* tartīb vār ترتیب وار, bilā nāġah بلاناغہ
regulation *n.* ā'īn آئین, qānūn قانون
reign *n.* šāhī شاہی, daur دور, rāj راج / *v.* rāj karnā راج کرنا
rein *n.* lagām لگام, zamām زمام; *(for a horse)* bāg باگ
reinforce *v.* mazbūt banānā مضبوط بنانا
reinforced *adj.* mazbūt banā hū'ā مضبوط بنا ہوا, bāz taqviyat باز تقویت
reinstate *v.* baḥāl karnā بحال کرنا
reinstatement *n.* baḥālī بحالی
reiterate *v.* raṭnā رٹنا
reject *v.* radd karnā رد کرنا
rejection *n.* nā pasandīdagī ناپسندیدگی, radd رد
rejoice *v.* xūš hōnā خوش ہونا
rejoicing *n.* tafrīḥ تفریح, šādmānī شادمانی

related *adj.* mansūb منسوب, vābastah وابستہ, mutavassil متوصل; *(by blood)* ham batn ہم بطن

related to *adj.* qarābatī قرابتی

relating to *n.* bābat بابت / *prep.* darbāb درباب

relation *n.* taᶜalluq تعلق, rištah dār رشتہ دار

relationship *n.* rištah رشتہ, qarābat قرابت

relative *adj.* qarābatī قرابتی, qarīb قریب / *n.* muqarrab مقرب

relator *n.* muḥaddis محدث

relax *v.* sust karnā سست کرنا, ārām karnā آرام کرنا

release *n.* rihā'ī رہائی, xalās خلاص / *v.* rihā karnā رہا کرنا, xalās karnā خلاص کرنا

relevancy *n.* munāsibat مناسبت

reliable *adj.* muᶜtabar معتبر, iᶜtibārī اعتباری, muᶜtamad معتمد

reliance *n.* muᶜtabarī معتبری, iᶜtimād اعتماد, bharōsah بھروسہ, tavaqquᶜ توقع

relief *n.* taxfīf تخفیف, sukh سکھ, ārām آرام, kal کل

relieve *v.* taxfīf karnā تخفیف کرنا, ārām dēnā آرام دینا

religion *n.* mazhab مذہب, dīn دین

religiosity *n.* dīndārī دینداری

religious *adj.* mazhabī مذہبی, dīndār دیندار, dīnī دینی

religious division *n.* panth پنتھ

religious instruction *n.* talqīn تلقین

religious person *(among Hindus) n.* rišī رشی; *(among Muslims)* mazhabī ādmī مذہبی آدمی

religious teacher *n.* muršid مرشد

religiousness *n.* mazhabiyat مذہبیت

relinquishment *n.* tiyāg تیاگ

relish *n.* cāšnī چاشنی, mazāq مذاق, zā'iqah ذائقہ / *v.* cakhnā چکھنا, zā'iqah lēnā ذائقہ لینا

reluctance *n.* bē dilī بے دلی

reluctant *adj.* bē dil بے دل

rely *v.* takiyah lagānā تکیہ لگانا

rely upon *v.* iᶜtibār karnā اعتبار کرنا

rely on *v.* ummīd rakhnā امید رکھنا

remain *v.* bāqī rahnā باقی رہنا, rahnā رہنا, ṭiknā ٹکنا

remainder *n.* bāqī māndah باقی ماندہ, ḥāsil tafrīq حاصل تفریق, mā baqā ما بقا

remark *n.* kaifiyyat کیفیت
remarkable *adj.* nihāyat نہایت
remedy *n.* davā دوا, muᶜālajah معالجہ
remember *v.* yād karnā یاد کرنا, yād hōnā یاد ہونا
remembrance *n.* zikr ذکر, yād یاد
remind *v.* yād dilānā یاد دلانا
reminder *n.* yād dihāni یاد دہانی, fuzlah فضلہ
remission *n.* muᶜāfī معافی, chūṭ چھوٹ, maġfirat مغفرت, riᶜāyat رعایت
remittance *n.* cālān چالان
remnant *n.* bāqiyāt باقیات
remote *adj.* dūr دور, baᶜīd بعید
remoteness *n.* dūrī دوری
removal *n.* barxāst برخاست, barxāstgī برخاستگی, naql نقل
remove *v.* nikālnā نکالنا, dūr karnā دور کرنا, rafaᶜ karnā رفع کرنا
remuneration *n.* muᶜāvazah معاوضہ
rend *v.* cīrnā چیرنا, cāk karnā چاک کرنا
renew *v.* tāzah karnā تازہ کرنا
renewal *n.* tajdīd تجدید
renowned *adj.* rōšnās روشناس, zabān zadah زبان زدہ, nāmī نامی
renowned person *n.* mušāhīr مشاہیر
rent *n.* kirāyah کرایہ / *v.* *(~ land)* māl guzāri مال گذاری
rent-free *adj.* lā xirāj لاخراج
rental *n.* ijārah اِجارہ
renunciation *n.* dast bardāri دست برداری
repair *n.* murammat مرمت / *v.* murammat karnā مرمت کرنا
repeat *v.* takrār karnā تکرار کرنا, raṭnā رٹنا, dōhrānā/dūhrānā دوہرانا
repeatedly *adv.* mukarrar مکرر, ka'ī bār کئی بار, mutavātir متواتر
repel *v.* haṭānā ہٹانا, dafaᶜ karnā دفع کرنا, tardīd karnā تردید کرنا
repent *v.* pactānā پچتانا, pachtānā پچھتانا, pašēmān hōnā پشیمان ہونا
repentance *n.* pactāvā پچتاوا, pašēmānī پشیمانی
repentant *adj.* pašēmān پشیمان, mutā'assif متاسف
repetition *n.* takrār تکرار, raṭ رٹ
replace *v.* baḥāl karnā بحال کرنا
replete *adj.* mālā māl مالا مال

reply *n.* uttar اُتّر, javāb جواب / *v.* javāb dēnā جواب دینا
report *n.* bayān بیان, itlāᶜ اطلاع, xabar خبر / *v.* bayān karnā بیان کرنا, muxbirī karnā مخبری کرنا, xabar dēnā خبر دینا
reporter *n.* muxbir مخبر
repose *n.* tamāniyat طمانیت, farāġat فراغت, istirāḥat استراحت, rāḥat راحت
represent *v.* guzāriš karnā گزارش کرنا
representation *n.* maᶜrūz معروض, guzāriš گزارش, maᶜrūzah معروضہ
representative *n.* gumāštah گماشتہ, numā'indah نمائندہ, kārindah کارندہ
reproach *n.* taᶜnah طعنہ, taᶜn-ō-tašnīᶜ طعن و تشنیع / *v.* taᶜnah mārnā طعنہ مارنا
reproof *n.* ᶜitāb عتاب
reptile *n.* rēngnē vālā jānvar رینگنے والا جانور, ḥašrah حشرہ
republic *n.* jumhūrī sultanat جمہوری سلطنت
repugnance *n.* muġāyarat مغایرت
repulsion *n.* dafaᶜ دفع, mudāfaᶜat مدافعت
repulsive *adj.* dafᶜiyyah دفعیہ
reputation *n.* nāmūs ناموس, šuhrah شہرہ, mašhūrī مشہوری
reputed *adj.* mašhūr مشہور
request *n.* ārzū آرزو, ᶜarz عرض, darxvāst درخواست, guzāriš گزارش / *v.* ārzū karnā آرزو کرنا, darxvāst karnā درخواست کرنا, guzāriš karnā گزارش کرنا; *(humbly)* giṛgiṛānā گڑگڑانا
require *v.* māngnā مانگنا
required *adj.* matlūb مطلوب, darkār درکار
research *n.* kāviš کاوش, taftīš تفتیش / *v.* taftīš karnā تفتیش کرنا
researcher *n.* muḥaqqiq محقق, mutaḥaqqiq متحقق
resemblance *n.* tamsīl تمثیل, timsāl تمثال, mušābahat مشابہت, tašābuh تشابہ
resentment *n.* kašīdagī کشیدگی, kudūrat کدورت; krōdh کرودھ
reservation *n.* buking بکنگ
reserve *v.* buking karnā بکنگ کرنا
reservoir *n.* ḥauz حوض, kunḍ کنڈ; *(of water)* tālāb تالاب
residence *n.* būd-ō-bāš بودوباش, qiyām قیام, sukūnat سکونت
resident *n.* bāšindah باشندہ, rahnē vālā رہنے والا; *(of the same district)* muḥallah dār محلہ دار
resign *v.* tiyāgnā تیاگنا

resignation *n.* isti^cfā' استعفاء
resigned *adj.* mufavvazah مفوضہ, musta^cfī مستعفی , mutavakkil متوکل
resist *v.* muxālafat karnā مخالفت کرنا
resolution *n.* ^cazm عزم, ^cazīmat عزیمت, musammam irādah مصمم ارادہ , iqdām اقدام
resolve *v.* qasd karnā قصد کرنا; mansūbah bāndhnā منصوبہ باندھنا
resound *v.* gūṁjnā گونجنا, ṭhinaknā ٹھنکنا
resource *n.* cārah چارہ, maqdūr مقدور
respect *n.* ^cizzat عزت, iḥtirām احترام, ta^czīm تعظیم / *v.* ḥurmat karnā حرمت کرنا, mān rākhnā مان رکھنا, mānnā ماننا ♦ **pay** ~ *v.* kōrniš bajānā کورنش بجانا
respectable *adj.* girāmī گرامی
respected *adj.* mutaḥarrim متحرم, mukarram مکرم, mu^cazzam معظم
respected sir! *interj.* janāb-ē-^cālī جناب عالی
respectful *adj.* mu'addab مؤدب, bā adab با ادب
respective *adj.* apnā apnā اپنا اپنا
respiration *n.* tanaffus تنفس, nafas نفس
respondent *n.* javābī جوابی
responsibility *n.* farz فرض, mu'āxazah مواخذہ, zimmah dārī ذمہ داری
rest *n.* ārām آرام, fursat فرصت, istirāḥat استراحت / *v.* ārām karnā آرام کرنا
restaurant *n.* rēstōrān ریستوران
restless *adj.* bē cain بے چین, bē tāb بے تاب, bē sabr بے صبر
restlessness *n.* bē tābī بے تابی, iztirāb اضطراب, nā sabūrī نا صبوری
restoration *n.* baḥālī بحالی; *(of health)* šifā/šafā شفا
restraint *n.* qaid قید, pābandī پابندی, rōk روک
restricted *adj.* munḥasir منحصر ; *(to a certain time)* muvaqqat موقت
restriction *n.* pābandī پابندی, imtinā^c امتناع, mumāna^cat ممانعت
result *n.* natījah نتیجہ
resurrection *n.* rustaxēz رستخیز, ḥāqah حاقہ, qiyāmat قیامت
resurrection day *n.* maḥšar محشر
retail *v.* xūdah bēcnā خوردہ بیچنا
retaliate *v.* intiqām lēnā انتقام لینا, bair lēnā بیر لینا, bair nikālnā بیر نکالنا
retaliation *n.* ^civaz عوض, mubādalah مبادلہ, mu^cāvazah معاوضہ, jazā جزا
retention *n.* ḥabs حبس
retire *v.* haṭnā ہٹنا, kinārā kaš hōnā کنارا کش ہونا

retired *adj.* gōšah našīn گوشہ نشین, gōšah gīr گوشہ گیر
retirement *n.* ᶜuzlat عزلت, gōšah našīnī گوشہ نشینی
retract *v.* phir jānā پھر جانا
retreat *n.* baz gašt باز گشت, iḥtijāb احتجاب, paspā'ī پسپائی / *v.* haṭnā ہٹنا, paspā hōnā پسپا ہونا
retribution *n.* xamyāzah خمیازہ
return *n.* dar āmad در آمد, murājaᶜat مراجعت, rujūᶜ رجوع, vāpasī واپسی / *v.* lauṭānā لوٹانا, lauṭnā لوٹنا, phir ānā پھر آنا
reveal *v.* azhār karnā اظہار کرنا, zāhir karnā ظاہر کرنا
revealer *n.* kāšif کاشف
revel *v.* mazah lūṭnā مزہ لوٹنا
revelation *n.* azhār اظہار, kašf کشف, ilhām الہام
revenge *n.* badlā بدلا, intiqām انتقام ♦ **take** ~ *v.* badlā lēnā بدلا لینا, intiqām lēnā انتقام لینا
revenue *n.* ḥāsil حاصل, fōtah فوطہ
revered *adj.* mutaḥarrim متحرم, mukarram مکرم, muᶜazzaz معزز, muvaqqar موقر
reverence *n.* takrīm تکریم, buzurgī بزرگی
reversal *n.* ulaṭ الٹ
reverse *adj.* muġāyar مغایر / *n.* ulṭī taraf الٹی طرف
reversed *adj.* ulṭā الٹا, maᶜkūs معکوس, munaᶜkis منعکس
reverted *adj.* bargaštah برگشتہ
review *n.* tanqīd تنقید, jā'izah جائزہ, nazar-ē-sanī نظر ثانی
revise *v.* dōhrānā/dūhrānā دوہرانا
revision *n.* nazar-ē-sanī نظر ثانی, tarmīm ترمیم, islāḥ اصلاح
revive *v.* jiyānā جیانا, jilānā جلانا
revocation *n.* tansīx تنسیخ
revoke *v.* phir jānā پھر جانا
revolt *n.* fitnah فتنہ
revolution *n.* inqilāb انقلاب, gardiš گردش
revolve *v.* gardānnā گردانتا, phirnā پھرنا, ghūmnā گھومنا
reward *n.* jazā جزا, pādāš پاداش, silah صلہ / *v.* ajr dēnā اجر دینا
rhetoric *n.* balāġat بلاغت
rheum *n.* zukām زکام
rhinoceros *n.* gēṇḍā گینڈا

rhubarb *n.* rēvand ریوند
rhyme *n.* qāfiyah قافیہ, tuk تک / *v.* qāfiyah lagānā قافیہ لگانا, tuk mēṁ tuk milānā تک میں تک ملانا
rib *n.* paslī پسلی, paṁjar/piṁjar پنجر
ribbon *n.* fītah فیتہ
rice *n.* cāval چاول
rice plant *n.* dhān دھان
rice pudding *n.* khīr کھیر
rich *adj.* amīr امیر, daulat mand دولت مند, paisē vālā پیسے والا; *(soil)* zarxēz زرخیز
rickshaw *n.* āṭō rikšā آٹو رکشا, rikšā رکشا
riddle *n.* pahēlī پہیلی,
rider *n.* rākib راکب, savār سوار
ridicule *n.* mihnā مہنا / *v.* bōl mārnā بول مارنا.
ridiculous *adj.* mazḥakah xēz مضحکہ خیز, muzḥik مضحک
rifle *n.* bandūq بندوق
rift *n.* phūṭ پھوٹ
right *adj.* ḥaqq حق, mustaqīm مستقیم, sac سچ, saḥīḥ صحیح; *(hand or side)* dāyāṁ دایاں, dāhnā داہنا / *n.* ḥaqiyyat حقیت, istiḥqāq استحقاق
righteous *adj.* rāst bāz راست باز, sāliḥ صالح ♦ ~ **path** *n.* hudā ہدا ♦ ~ **people** *n.* axyār اخیار
righteousness *n.* hidāyat ہدایت
rightful *adj.* mustaḥiqq مستحق ♦ ~ **heir** *n.* vāris-ē- ḥaqīqī وارث حقیقی, xalaf-ul-sidq خلف الصدق
rightly *adv.* qarār vaqā'ī قرار واقعی
rigid *adj.* durušt درشت, karārā کرارا, lōhā laṭh لوہا لٹھ
rigorous *adj.* muġallaz مغلظ
rind *n.* chilkā چھلکا, pōst پوست, chāl چھال
ring *n.* challā چھلا, dā'irah دائرہ; *(jewelry)* angūṭhī انگوٹھی / *v.* bajānā بجانا, ṭhinaknā ٹھنکنا
ringleader *n.* sarġanah سرغنہ, sar dār سردار, sar garōh سرگروہ
ringlet *n.* kunḍlī کنڈلی
ringworm *n.* dād داد
rinse *v.* ghanghōlnā گھنگولنا, khangālnā کھنگالنا, phīṁchā پھینچنا; *(~ one's mouth)* acānā اچانا, ācaman karnā آچمن کرنا

riot *n.* fasād فساد, futūr فتور, balvā بلوا
riotous *adj.* futūrī فتوری
ripe *adj.* pakkā پکا
ripen *v.* pakānā پکانا, paknā پکنا
ripeness *n.* rasīdagī رسیدگی, puxtagī پختگی
rise *n.* caṛhā'ī چڑھائی, uṭhān اُٹھان / *v.* caṛhnā چڑھنا, uṭhnā اُٹھنا
risk *n.* xatar خطر, jōkhōṁ جوکھوں, bīm بیم ♦ ~ **one's life** *v.* jān par khēlnā جان پر کھیلنا
rite *n.* rīt ریت, tarīqah طریقہ
rival *adj.* ham cašm ہم چشم / *n.* ḥarīf حریف, dušman دشمن, raqīb رقیب
rivalry *n.* dušmanī دشمنی, raqābat رقابت, muʿārizah معارضہ
river *n.* daryā دریا, nadī ندی
road *n.* rāstah راستہ, rāh راہ, path پتھ, saṛak سڑک
roam *v.* ramnā رمنا, xāk uṛānā خاک اڑانا
roar *n.* dhāṛ دھاڑ, dhaṛākā دھڑاکا, jōš-ō-xarōš جوش و خروش / *v.* cillānā چلانا, dhāṛnā دھاڑنا, garajnā گرجنا
roast *v.* kabāb karnā کباب کرنا, bhūnnā بھوننا
rob *v.* dhāṛnā دھاڑنا, ṭhagnā ٹھگنا, lūṭnā لوٹنا, cōrī karnā چوری کرنا
robber *n.* ḍākū ڈاکو, ḍakait ڈکیت, cōr چور, ṭhag ٹھگ
robbery *n.* ṭhagī ٹھگی, ḍakaitī ڈکیتی, lūṭ لوٹ, cōrī چوری
robe *n.* saub ثوب, jubbah جبہ, pairāhan پیراہن
robust *adj.* gaṭhīlā گٹھیلا, haṭṭā kaṭṭā ہٹا کٹا, hēkaṛ ہیکڑ, kaṛyal کڑیل
rock *n.* caṭān چٹان, pahāṛ پہاڑ, patthar پتھر / *v.* jhūmnā جھومنا; *(~ a cradle)* jhulānā جھلانا
rocky *adj.* patthrīlā پتھریلا
rod *n.* ḍanḍā ڈنڈا, mūslā موسلا, cōb dastī چوب دستی, qamcī قمچی
roe *n.* harnī ہرنی
rogue *n.* šaix cillī شیخ چلی
roll *n.* phērā پھیرا / *v.* lōṭnā لوٹنا
roll over *v.* luṛhaknā لڑھکنا
roll up *v.* tai karnā طے کرنا
Roman *adj.* rūmī رومی
romance *n.* fasānah فسانہ
roof *n.* bām بام, chat چھت, saqf سقف; *(thatched ~)* sā'ibān سائبان

room *n.* kamrah کمرہ, xānah خانہ
root *n.* jaṛ جڑ, bēx بیخ asās اساس ♦ **take ~** *v.* jamnā جمنا
rope *n.* rassā رسا, ḍōr ڈور
rope dancer *n.* rasan bāz رسن باز
rosary *n.* saifī سیفی, mālā مالا, tasbīḥ تسبیح
rose *n.* gulāb گلاب, gul گل
rose-apple *n.* jambū جمبو
rosebud *n.* ġuncah غنچہ
rose-colored *adj.* gulābī گلابی
rosy *adj.* gulābī گلابی
rot *v.* saṛnā سڑنا
rotate *v.* ghūmnā گھومنا
rotation *n.* ghūm گھوم, phirā'ō پھراؤ
roti *(traditional bread) n.* rōṭī روٹی
rotten *adj.* bōsīdah بوسیدہ, saṛā سڑا, mutaᶜaffin متعفن
rottenness *n.* saṛānd سڑاند, bōsīdagī بوسیدگی, gandagī گندگی
rough *adj.* khurdarā کھردرا, khurkhurā کھرکھرا ♦ **~ estimate** *n.* kaccā taxmīnah کچا تخمینہ
roughly *adj.* andāzan اندازاً
roughness *n.* rukhā'ī رکھائی, duruštī درشتی
round *adj.* gōl گول, mudavvar مدور, caklā چکلا
round about *adv.* pās pās پاس پاس
roundness *n.* gōlā'ī گولائی
rouse (from sleep) *v.* jagānā جگانا
routine *n.* maslak مسلک
rove *v.* ramnā رمنا
row *n.* qitār; qatār قطار, satar سطر, šāxsānah شاخسانہ / *v.* khēnā کھینا
rower *n.* ḍānḍī ڈانڈی
royal *adj.* bādšāhānah بادشاہانہ, mālkī مالکی, šāhinšāhī شاہنشاہی, sultānī سلطانی
royal camp *n.* urdū-ē-mōᶜalla اردوئے معلیٰ
royal court *n.* rāj darbār راج دربار
royal grant *n.* tamġah تمغہ
royalty *n.* tājvarī تاجوری, rāj راج
rub *v.* ragaṛnā رگڑنا, malnā ملنا

rubbish *n.* kūṛā karkaṭ کوڑا کرکٹ, malbah ملبہ, kacrā کچرا
ruby *n.* laᶜl لعل, yāqūt یاقوت
rudder *n.* hāl ہال
rude *adj.* bad zabān بدزبان, gustāx گستاخ, dahqānī دہقانی, bē adab بے ادب
rudeness *n.* gustāxī گستاخی, bē adabī بے ادبی
rugged *adj.* khurdarā کھردرا
ruin *n.* tabāhī تباہی, pāmālī پامالی, barbādī بربادی, xānah xarābī خانہ خرابی / *v.* abtar karnā ابتر کرنا, talaf karnā تلف کرنا, tārāj karnā تاراج کرنا, vīrān karnā ویران کرنا
rule *n.* dastūr دستور, ḥukm rānī حکم رانی, qāᶜidah قاعدہ, qānūn قانون, tarīqat طریقت / *v.* ḥukūmat karnā حکومت کرنا, rāj karnā راج کرنا
ruler *n.* amīr امیر, ḥākim حاکم, nāzim ناظم
rules *n.* ā'īn آئین
rumble *n.* dhaṛākā دھڑاکا
rumor *n.* afvāh افواہ
run *n.* dauṛ دوڑ / *v.* dauṛnā دوڑنا, jhapaṭnā جھپٹنا
run away *v.* dūr bhāgnā دور بھاگنا, bhāgnā بھاگنا
runaway *n.* bhigōṛā بھگوڑا
rupee *n.* rūpayah/rūpiyah روپیہ
rupture *n.* tōṛ توڑ
rural *adj.* dēhātī دیہاتی
rush *v.* jaldī mēṁ hōnā جلدی میں ہونا, ḍapaṭnā ڈپٹنا, lapakna لپکنا
rust *n.* zang زنگ
rust-colored *adj.* zangārī زنگاری
rustic *adj.* dahqānī دہقانی
rustle *v.* sarsarānā سرسرانا, kharkharānā کھڑکھڑانا
rustling *n.* kharkharāhaṭ کھڑکھڑاہٹ
rusty *adj.* zang ālūdah زنگ آلودہ, zangārī زنگاری

S

sable *n.* samūr سمور
sack *n.* jhōlī جھولی, thailā تھیلا
sackcloth *n.* ṭāṭ ٹاٹ
sacred *adj.* ḥaram حرم, muqaddas مقدس, mutabarrak متبرک
sacred place (of pilgrimage) *n.* mutabarrak maqām متبرک مقام, tīrath تیرتھ
sacrifice *n.* qurbānī قربانی / *v.* qurbānī dēnā قربانی دینا
sad *adj.* fikr mand فکر مند, ġam gīn غم گین, ḥazīn حزین
saddle *n.* kāṭhī کاٹھی, zīn زین
sadhu *(Hindu monk) n.* sādhū سادھو
sadness *n.* ḥazn/ḥuzn حزن, malāl ملال
safe *adj.* maḥfūz محفوظ / *n.* mahfūz lākar محفوظ لاکر
safely *adv.* baxairiyat بخیریت
safety *n.* amn امن, ḥifāzat حفاظت
saffron *n.* kēsar کیسر, zaᶜfarān زعفران
saffron-colored *adj.* zaᶜfarānī زعفرانی
sagacity *n.* zēhn ذہن
sage *adj.* dānā دانا / *n.* buzurg بزرگ, giyāni گیانی, ḥakīm حکیم, rišī رشی
Sagittarius *(Zodiac) n.* kamān کمان, qaus قوس
sago *n.* sāgū dānah ساگودانہ
sail *n.* bādbān بادبان
sailor *n.* jahāzī جہازی
saint *n.* gusā'īṁ گسائیں, rišī رشی, sant سنت, valī ولی
sake *n.* vāstah واسطہ
salary *n.* tanxvāh تنخواہ
sale *n.* baiᶜ بیع, farōxt فروخت, khapat کھپت, nikās نکاس
salesman *n.* dallāl دلال
saliva *n.* luᶜāb لعاب, rāl رال
salt *n.* lūn/lavan لون, namak نمک
saltpeter *n.* šōrah شورہ
salty *adj.* malīḥ ملیح
salutation *n.* ādāb آداب, salām سلام, taslīm تسلیم

salute *v.* salām karnā سلام کرنا
salvation *n.* muxlis مخلص, najāt نجات
same *adj.* yaksān یکساں / *adv.* ham ہم
samosa *(savory filled pie) n.* samōsā سموسا
sample *n.* namūnah نمونہ
sanctification *n.* tathīr تطہیر
sanctuary *n.* ḥaram حرم
sand *n.* rēg ریگ, rēt ریت
sandal tree *n.* candan چندن
sandals *n.* cappal چپل
sandalwood *n.* candan چندن, jandal جندل, sandal صندل
sandbank *n.* ṭabbah ٹبہ
sandy *adj.* kirkirā کرکرا, rēgistānī رگستانی, rētlā ریتلا
sanguinary *adj.* xūnī خونی
sapphire *n.* nīlam نیلم
sarcasm *n.* taᶜn zanī طعن زنی
sarcastically *adv.* tanzan طنزا
sari *n.* sāṛī ساڑی
Satan *n.* iblīs اِبلیس, šaitān شیطان
satin *n.* atlas اطلس
satire *n.* hajv ہجو, mazammat مذمت
satirist *n.* hājī ہاجی, hajv gō ہجو گو
satisfaction *n.* itmīnān اطمینان, taskīn تسکین, xātir jamaᶜ خاطر جمع
satisfactory *adj.* xātir xavāh خاطر خواہ
satisfied *adj.* āsūdah آسودہ, mutma'in مطمئن, rāzī راضی
satisfy *v.* itmīnān karnā اطوار, rāzī karnā راضی کرنا
saturated *adj.* sēr سیر
Saturday *n.* haftah ہفتہ, sanīcar سنیچر
Saturn *n.* zuḥal زحل
saucepan *n.* hānḍī ہانڈی
savage *adj.* vaḥšī وحشی, janglī جنگلی
save *v.* bacānā بچانا; *(~ money)* raqm bacānā رقم بچانا
savings *n.* bacat بچت
savor *n.* taᶜam طعم

savory *adj.* lazīz لذیذ, zā'iqah dār ذائقہ دار
saw *v.* kāṭnā کاٹنا / *n.* ārah آرہ, ārī آری
say *v.* farmānā فرمانا, kahnā کہنا ♦ ~ **goodbye** vidā^c karnā وداع کرنا ♦ ~ **prayers** bhajan karnā بھجن کرنا
saying *n.* kahāvat کہاوت, maqūlah مقولہ, qaul قول
saz *(a musical instrument) n.* sāz ساز
scale *n.* tadrīj تدریج
scandal *n.* kalank کلنک
scanty *adj.* kamtī کمتی
scarce *adj.* birlā برلا, thōṛā تھوڑا, xāl xāl خال خال
scarcity *n.* girānī گرانی, kam yābī کم یابی, qaḥt قحط
scare *v.* ḍarānā ڈرانا
scatter *v.* bikhairnā بکھیرنا, nisār karnā نثار کرنا
scene *n.* manzar منظر
scent *n.* bās باس, lapaṭ لپٹ, nakhat نکہت
scented oil *n.* xūšbūdār tēl خوشبودار تیل
scepter *n.* ^casā عصا
scheme *n.* iskīm اسکیم, mansūbah منصوبہ, upā'ē اُپائے
schism *n.* bida^cat بدعت
scholar *n.* muta^callim متعلم, šāgird شاگرد
scholarship *n.* ^cilmiyyat علمیت, vazīfah وظیفہ
school *n.* iskūl اسکول, madrasah مدرسہ
schoolmaster *n.* pānḍē پانڈے
science *n.* ^cilm علم, ^cirfān عرفان
scientific *adj.* ^cilmī علمی, sā'insdāṁ سائنسداں
scissors *n.* miqrāz مقراض, qaiṁcī قینچی
scold *v.* ḍānṭnā ڈانٹنا, jhiṛaknā جھڑکنا, phiṭkārnā پھٹکارنا
scooter *n.* kā'inēṭik کائینیٹک, skūṭar سکوٹر
scorch *v.* jhulsānā جھلسانا
score *n.* kōṛī کوڑی
scorn *n.* ḥiqārat حقارت, ihānat اہانت, taḥqīr تحقیر
Scorpio *(Zodiac) n.* ^caqrab عقرب
scorpion *n.* bicchū بچھو, ^caqrab عقرب, kuzdum کزدم
scoundrel *n.* gunḍā گنڈا

scour *v.* ragaṛnā رگڑنا
scrap *v.* chīlnā چھیلنا / *n.* pārah پارہ, rēzah ریزہ, rēzgī ریزگی; *(of cloth)* lattā لتا; *(of paper)* purzah پرزہ
scrape *v.* chōlnā چھولنا, khuracnā کھرچنا
scraper *n.* chōlnī چھولنی
scratch *n.* carkā چرکا, xarāš خراش / *v.* chīlnā چھیلنا, khuracnā کھرچنا, nōcnā نوچنا
scream *n.* cinghāṛ چنگھاڑ, cīx چیخ / *v.* cillānā چلانا
scream out *v.* cinghāṛnā چنگھاڑنا
screech *n.* cinghāṛ چنگھاڑ, cīx چیخ
screen *n.* cilman چلمن, ciq چق, ōjhal اوجھل / *v.* jhānpnā جھانپنا, ōjhal karnā اوجھل کرنا
screw *n.* ḍhibrī ڈھبری, kīlī کیلی
scribble *v.* bē iḥtiyātī sē likhnā بے احتیاطی سے لکھنا
script *n.* taḥrīr تحریر, xatt خط
scrub *v.* ragaṛnā رگڑنا
sculptor *n.* but tarāš بت تراش, sang tarāš سنگتراش
scum *n.* jhāg جھاگ, kaf کف, phēn پھین
sea *n.* baḥr بحر, samundar سمندر
seal *(emblem/stamp) n.* muhr مہر, tābiᶜ طابع
seam *n.* darz درز, sīvan سیون
search *n.* ḍhūnḍ ڈھونڈ, taḥqīq تحقیق, talāš تلاش / *v.* ḍhūnḍnā ڈھونڈنا, talāš karnā تلاش کرنا
searcher *n.* mutalāšī متلاشی
seashore *n.* sāḥil ساحل
season *n.* mausim/mausam موسم, fasl فصل
seasonal *adj.* mausimī موسمی
seasoning *n.* garm masālā گرم مسالا
seat *n.* baiṭhak بیٹھک, gaddī گدی, kursī کرسی, sīṭ سیٹ
secluded *adj.* tanhā'ī pasand تنہائی پسند, gōšah gīr گوشہ گیر
seclusion *n.* bairāg بیراگ, iḥtijāb احتجاب
second *adj.* dūsrā دوسرا, musannā مثنیٰ, sānī ثانی / *n.* pal پل, sēkanḍ سیکنڈ
secrecy *n.* pōšīdagī پوشیدگی
secret *adj.* xufyah خفیہ, maxfī مخفی, xafī خفی / *n.* jauhar جوہر, rāz راز, sirr سر
♦ **keep something** ~ *v.* dil mēṁ rakhnā دل میں رکھنا

secretary *n.* dīvān دیوان, munšī منشی
secretly *adv.* cōrī cōrī چوری چوری, dar pardah در پردہ
sect *n.* firqah فرقہ
section *n.* bāb باب, kāṭ کاٹ, šuᶜbah شعبہ
secular *adj.* lā mazhab لا مذہب
secure *adj.* māmūn مامون, mutma'in مطمئن
security *n.* amān امان, amn امن
sedan *n.* ḍōlī ڈولی, miyānā میانا, pālkī پالکی
sediment *n.* gād گاد, phōk پھوک, talchaṭ تلچھٹ
seduce *v.* bahkānā بہکانا, varġalānā ورغلانا
seducing *adj.* bahkānē vālā بہکانے والا
seduction *n.* gum rāhī گم راہی
see *v.* dēkhnā دیکھنا
seed *n.* bīj بیج tuxm تخم
seek *v.* ḍhūnḍnā ڈھونڈنا, talāš karnā تلاش کرنا
seeker *n.* jō'indah جوئندہ, jōyā جویا, tālib طالب
seem *v.* jān paṛnā جان پڑنا, lagnā لگنا, maᶜlūm hōnā معلوم ہونا
seemingly *adv.* zāhir mēṁ ظاہر میں
segment *n.* qataᶜ قطع
seize *v.* harnā ہرنا, pakaṛnā پکڑنا, zabt karnā ضبط کرنا
seizure *(arrest / taking possession of) n.* giriftārī گرفتاری, pakaṛ پکڑ, qabz قبض, zabt ضبط; *(by force) n.* tasxīr تسخیر
seldom *adv.* šāz-ō-nādir شاذونادر
select *v.* chānṭnā چھانٹنا, cunnā چننا, intixāb karnā انتخاب کرنا
selection *n.* chānṭ چھانٹ, intixāb انتخاب, iqtibās اقتباس
self *adj.* xūd خود / *n.* zāt ذات / *pron.* āppas آپس
self-defense *n.* mudāfaᶜat مدافعت
selfish *adj.* matlabī مطلبی, xūd ġarz خود غرض
selfishness *n.* lālac لالچ, tan parvarī تن پروری, xūdī خودی
selflessness *n.* ēsār ایثار
self-made *adj.* tabaᶜ zād طبع زاد
self-respect *n.* xūdī خودی
sell *v.* bēcnā بیچنا
seller *n.* bāyaᶜ بایع, farōšindah فروشندہ

semen *n.* nutfah نطفہ
senator *n.* mušīr مشیر
send *v.* bhējnā بھیجنا
send back *v.* lauṭānā لوٹانا
send for *v.* mangvānā منگوانا, yād farmānā یاد فرمانا
sense *n.* ᶜaql عقل, ḥiss حس, maᶜnī/maᶜnā معنی, mafhūm مفہوم, matlab مطلب
senseless *adj.* bē hōš بے ہوش, bē xabar بے خبر, bē xūd بے خود, madhōš مدہوش
senselessness *n.* bē hōšī بے ہوشی, bē xūdī بے خودی, madhōšī مدہوشی
sensibility *n.* ḥiss حس
sensible *adj.* bā tamīz باتمیز, ᶜāqil عاقل, ḥassās حساس, hōš mand ہوش مند
sensitive *adj.* ḥassās حساس
sensual *adj.* nafsānī نفسانی
sentence *n.* fiqrah فقرہ
sentiment *n.* ḥiss حس
sentinel *n.* santrī سنتری
separate *adj.* alag الگ / *v.* alag karnā الگ کرنا
separately *adv.* alag alag الگ الگ
separation *n.* firāq فراق, judā'ī جدائی, muhājarat مہاجرت, tajrīd تجرید
separatist *n.* muᶜtazil معتزل
September *n.* sitambar ستمبر
sequence *n.* tasalsul تسلسل
seraglio *(women's living place)* *n.* ḥaram sarā'ē حرم سرائے
serai *(inn, caravan)* *n.* sarā'ī سرائے
serial *adj.* musalsal مسلسل, silsilah vār سلسلہ وار
series *n.* silsilah سلسلہ, tasalsul تسلسل
serious *adj.* gambhīr گمبھیر, mutafakkir متفکر, sanjīdah سنجیدہ
sermon *n.* mauᶜizat موعظت, vaᶜz وعظ
serpent *n.* mār مار
servant *n.* cākar چاکر, naukar نوکر, xādim خادم, xidmat gār خدمت گار
serve *v.* ṭahal karnā ٹہل کرنا, xidmat karnā خدمت کرنا
service *n.* cākrī چاکری, mulāzamat ملازمت, naukarī نوکری, xidmat خدمت
serviceable *adj.* kār āmad کارآمد
sesame seed *n.* til تل

set *v.* biṭhānā بٹھانا; *(the sun)* ġurūb hōnā غروب ہونا
set on fire *v.* phūnk dēnā پھونک دینا, āg sulgāna آگ سلگانا, phūnknā پھونکنا
set foot in/on *v.* pā'ōṁ dharnā پاؤں دھرنا
set free *v.* āzād karnā آزاد کرنا, chuṛānā چھڑانا, rihā karnā رہا کرنا
set out *v.* ravānah hōnā روانہ ہونا, sidhārnā سدھارنا
settle *v.* basānā بسانا, cukānā چکانا, faisalah karnā فیصلہ کرنا, nibṭānā نبٹانا
settlement *n.* band-ō-basat بندوبست, isti^c^mār استعمار, istiqrār استقرار, qiyām قیام
seven *num.* sāt سات
seventeen *num.* satrah سترہ
seventeenth *adj.* satrahvāṁ سترھواں
seventh *adj.* sātvāṁ ساتواں
seventy *num.* sattar ستر
seventy-one *num.* ikhattar اکہتر
seventy-two *num.* bahattar بہتر
seventy-three *num.* tēhattar تہتر
seventy-four *num.* cauhattar چوہتر
seventy-five *num.* pachattar پچھتر
seventy-six *num.* chēhattar چھہتر
seventy-seven *num.* satattar ستتر
seventy-eight *num.* aṭhattar اٹھتر
seventy-nine *num.* unāsī اناسی
sever *v.* kāṭnā کاٹنا
several *adj.* ka'ī کئی, muta^c^addad متعدد / *adv.* cand ēk چند ایک
severe *adj.* muġallaz مغلظ, nā tars ناترس, saxt سخت
severity *n.* duruštī درشتی, šiddat شدت, tašaddud تشدد
sew *v.* sīnā سینا, ṭānkē lagānā ٹانکے لگانا
sewer *n.* badarraū بدرو
sex *n.* jins جنس
sexual *adj.* jinsī جنسی
sexual desire *n.* šahvat شہوت
sexual intercourse *n.* jimā^c^ جماع
sexuality *n.* jinsiyat جنسیت
shade *n.* chā'ōṁ چھاؤں, chāyā چھایا, sāyah سایہ / *v.* chānā چھانا
shadow *n.* chā'ōṁ چھاؤں, sāyah سایہ

shady *adj.* sāyah dār سایہ دار
shah *n.* šāh شاہ
shake *n.* hackōlā ہچکولا, jhaṭkā جھٹکا / *v.* hilānā ہلانا, hilnā ہلنا, jhaṭaknā جھٹکنا
♦ ~ **hands** musāfaḥah karnā مصافحہ کرنا
shaken *adj.* mutazalzal متزلزل
shaky *adj.* mutazalzal متزلزل
shallow *adj.* chachōrā چھچھورا , uthlā اتھلا
shame *n.* ḥayā حیا , lāj لاج, lajjā لجا , šarm شرم, šarmindagī شرمندگی / *interj.* ha ہا
shameful *adj.* qabīḥ قبیح
shamefulness *n.* xift خفت
shameless *adj.* bē ġairat بے غیرت , bē ḥayā بے حیا , bē ḥijāb بے حجاب
shamelessness *n.* ḍhiṭā'ī ڈھٹائی, xīrgī خیرگی
shampoo v. māliš kārnā مالش کرنا / *n.* māliš مالش
shape *n.* šakl شکل , sūrat صورت, tarāš تراش / *v.* šakl banānā شکل بنانا, tarāšnā تراشنا
share *n.* bānṭ بانٹ, ḥissah حصہ, sahm سہم / *v.* taqsīm karnā تقسیم کرنا
shareholder *n.* ḥissah dār حصہ دار
sharer *n.* qasīm قسیم
Sharia *(Islamic law) n.* šarīᶜat شریعت
sharp *adj.* dhār dār دھار دار, tēz تیز
sharpness *n.* dhār دھار, tēzī تیزی; *(of mind)* zihānat ذہانت, zakā ذکا
sharp-witted *adj.* ᶜālī dimāġ عالی دماغ
shatter *v.* cuknā cūr karnā چکنا چور کرنا
shave *v.* mūnḍnā مونڈنا, tarāšnā تراشنا, xatt banānā خط بنانا
shaver *n.* ḥajjām حجام
shawl *n.* gulū band گلوبند , šāl شال
she *pron.* vah/vōh وہ, yēh یہ
sheath *n.* niyām نیام
shed *v.* ḍālnā ڈالنا, girānā گرانا
shed tears *v.* āb dīdah hōnā آب دیدہ ہونا, āṁsū bhar ānā آنسو بھر آنا, rōnā رونا
sheep *n.* bhēṛ بھیڑ, bhēṛī بھیڑی , mēš میش
sheet *n.* cādar چادر; *(of paper)* fard فرد, taxtah تختہ
she-goat *n.* bakrī بکری
sheikh *n.* šaix شیخ

shelf *n.* miḥrāb محراب
shell *n.* chilkā چھلکا, pōst پوست
shelter *n.* āṛ آڑ, panāh پناہ
shelve *v.* dāxil dāftar karnā داخل دفتر کرنا
she-monkey *n.* bandariyā بندریا
shepherd *n.* gaḍaryā گڈریا
Shia *(an Islamic sect) n.* šīᶜah شیعہ
shield *n.* sipar سپر
Shiite *adj.* šiᶜī شعی
shimmer *v.* jhilmilānā جھلملانا
shin *n.* pinḍlī پنڈلی
shine *v.* camaknā چمکنا
shining *adj.* camak dār چمک دار, daraxšāṁ درخشاں, raušan/rōšan روشن / *n.* jhamak جھمک
ship *n.* jahāz جہاز, nā'ō ناؤ, safīnah سفینہ
shirker *n.* kām cōr کام چور
shirt *n.* kurtah کرتہ, qamīz قمیض ; *(long)* pairāhan پیراہن
shisha *(water-pipe/hookah) n.* ḥuqqah حقہ
shiver *v.* kāṁpnā کانپنا, kapkapānā کپکپانا
shock *n.* dhakkā دھکا, hickā ہچکا, sadmah صدمہ
shocking *adj.* muvaḥḥiš موحش
shoe *n.* cappal چپل, jūtā جوتا ♦ **pair of ~s** *n.* jōtī جوتی
shoemaker *n.* mōcī موچی, cammār چمار, kafiš dōz کفش دوز
shoot *n.* ankūrā انکورا, ṭappā ٹپا / *v.* bandūq calānā بندوق چلانا, bandūq chōṛnā بندوق چھوڑنا
shoot at *v.* gōlī mārnā گولی مارنا
shooter *n.* bandūqcī بندوقچی
shop *v.* xarīdārī karnā خریداری کرنا / *n.* dukān/dukkān دکان; *(small)* dukāncah دکانچہ
shopkeeper *n.* dukāndār دکاندار, baqqāl بقال, mōdī/mūdī مودی
shopkeeping *n.* dukāndārī دکانداری
shore *n.* kinārā کنارا
short *adj.* chōṭā چھوٹا, kōtāh کوتاہ
shortening *n.* inqibāz انقباض

shortly *adv.* qarīban قریباً
shortness *n.* kōtāhī کوتاہی
short-sighted *adj.* kōtāh bīn کوتاہ بین, kōtāh nazar کوتاہ نظر, nā andēš نا اندیش
should *v. (inv.)* cāhī'ē چاہیئے
shoulder *n.* kandhā کندھا, khavvā کھوا, šānah شانہ
shout *n.* āvāz آواز, bāng بانگ, pukār پکار / *v.* cillānā چلانا, hānknā ہانکنا, pukārnā پکارنا
shout at ḍapaṭnā ڈپٹنا
shout loudly hānk mārnā ہانک مارنا
shout out *v.* āvāz dēnā آواز دینا
shove *v.* dhakēlnā دھکیلنا, pēlnā پیلنا, rēlnā ریلنا, ṭhēlnā ٹھیلنا
shovel *n.* bēl بیل, hatthā ہتھا, phā'ōṛī پھاوڑی
show *n.* dikhāvā دکھاوا, dikhāvaṭ دکھاوٹ, numā'iš نمائش, tamāšā تماشا / *v.* dikhānā دکھانا, dikhlānā دکھلانا
shower *n.* šāvar شاور
showy *adj.* zāhir dār ظاہر دار
shred *n.* dhajjī دھجی
shrewd *adj.* aṭkal bāz اٹکل باز, qallāš قلاش
shriek *n.* cīx چیخ / *v.* kūknā کوکنا
shrimp *n.* jhīngā جھینگا
shrine *n.* dargāh درگاہ, mazār مزار, ziyārat gāh زیارت گاہ
shrink *v.* simaṭnā سمٹنا, sukaṛnā سکیڑنا
shrivel *v.* sukaṛnā سکیڑنا
shroud *n.* kafan کفن
shrub *n.* jhāṛ جھاڑ, pēṛ پیڑ
shut *adj.* band بند, bandhā بندھا / *v.* band karnā بند کرنا
shutter *n.* kivāṛ کواڑ
shy *adj.* ḥayā dār حیادار, mēš cašm میش چشم
shyness *n.* ḥayā حیا, jhijhak جھجھک
sick *adj.* bimār بیمار ♦ ~ **person** *n.* marīz مریض
sickle *n.* darāntī درانتی, ganḍāsā گنڈاسا
sickness *n.* bimārī بیماری, maraz مرض
side *n.* kinārā کنارا, simt/samt سمت, taraf طرف ♦ **by the ~ of** *adv.* kinārē kinārē کنارے کنارے ♦ **take ~s** *v.* taraf dārī karnā طرف داری کرنا
side with *v.* tarafdārī karnā طرفداری کرنا

sideways *adv./adj.* karvaṭ کروٹ
siege *n.* bēṛā بیڑا, ghērā گھیرا, muḥāsarah محاصرہ
siesta *n.* qāilūlah قیلولہ
sieve *n.* chalnī چھلنی, chalnī چھلنی
sift *v.* chānnā چھاننا
sigh *n.* darēġ دریغ, hā'ē ہائے, sāṁs سانس / *v.* karāhnā کراہنا, sisaknā سسکنا
sight *n.* basārat بصارت, manzar منظر, nazārah نظارہ, nigāh نگاہ
sign *n.* asar اثر, ᶜalāmat علامت, išārah اشارہ, nišān نشان / *v.* dastaxat karnā دستخط کرنا
signal *n.* nišān نشان
signature *n.* dastāvēz دستاویز, dastaxat دستخط
signed *adj.* mausūm موسوم
significance *n.* muzā'iqah مضائقہ
significant *adj.* maᶜnavī معنوی
signification *n.* maᶜnī/maᶜnā معنی
Sikh *(disciple of Guru Nanak) n.* sikh سکھ
silence *n.* cup چپ, xāmōšī خاموشی / *v.* jibh pakaṛnā جیبھ پکڑنا, lā javāb karnā لاجواب کرنا, muṁh mārnā منہ مارنا
silent *adj.* sākit ساکت, xāmōš خاموش
silently *adv.* cup cāp چپ چاپ, cupkē cupkē چپکے چپکے dabē pā'ōṁ دبے پاؤں
silk *n.* rēšam ریشم; *(raw ~)* abrēšam ابریشم ♦ ~ **cloth** ḥarīr حریر
silken *adj.* ḥarīrī حریری, rēšmī ریشمی
silkworm *n.* kirm pīlah کرم پیلہ
silliness *n.* sādah lauḥī سادہ لوحی, bē vaqūfī بے وقوفی, ullūpan الوپن
silly *adj.* ablah ابلہ, bē tamīz بے تمیز, gēglā گیگلا
silver *n.* cāndī چاندی
silvery *adj.* rūpahlā روپہلا
similar *adj.* misl مثل, mumāsil مماثل, mutanāsib متناسب,
similarity *n.* mušābahat مشابہت, mutābaqat مطابقت, šabāhat شباہت
similarly *adv.* hakazā ہکذا
similitude *n.* tamsīl تمثیل, tašābuh تشابہ, tašbīh تشبیہ
simple *adj.* āsān آسان, mufrad مفرد, sādah سادہ
simpleminded *adj.* ᶜaql rasāsē xālī عقل رسا سے خالی, gēglā گیگلا
simplemindedness *n.* sādah dalī سادہ دلی, gēglāpan گیگلاپن

simpleton *adj.* anāṛī اناڑی, bhōndū بھوندو, sādah lauḥ سادہ لوح
simplicity *n.* anāṛpan اناڑپن, āsānī آسانی, sīdhā pan سیدھاپن
simply *adv.* faqat فقط
sin *n.* ᶜisyān عصیان, gunāh گناہ, pāp پاپ ♦ **commit a** ~ pāp karnā پاپ کرنا
since *adv.* cūnkēh چونکہ, ḥais حیث, jab sē جب سے / *conj.* kyōṁkih/kyōṁkē کیونکہ / *prep.* sē سے
sincere *adj.* muxlis مخلص, sādiq صادق, xālis خالص
sincerely *adv.* muxlisānah مخلصانہ
sincerity *n.* ixlās اخلاص, sidq صدق, xulūs خلوص
sinful *adj.* ᶜāsī عاصی, fājir فاجر, kālā muṁh کالا منہ
sing *v.* gāna گانا
singe *v.* jhulsānā جھلسانا
singer *n.* gavayyā گویا, mutrib مطرب, qavvāl قوال
singing *adj.* mutarannim مترنم / *n.* naġmah sarā'ī نغمہ سرائی
single *adj.* akēlā اکیلا, mufrad مفرد, tanhā تنہا, vāḥid واحد; ēk ایک ♦ ~ **group** *n.* ikā'ī اکائی
singular *adj.* farīd فرید, yagānah یگانہ
singularity *n.* yagāngat یگانگت, yagāngi یگانگی
sink *n.* cilamcī چلمچی / *v.* ḍūbnā ڈوبنا, ḍubōnā ڈبونا, gāṛnā گاڑنا; *(~ money into)* paisā ḍubōnā پیسا ڈبونا
sinner *n.* gunāh gār گناہ گار, pāpī پاپی
sip *v.* cūsnā چوسنا
sir *interj.* janāb جناب, jī جی / *n.* maulānā مولانا, miyāṁ میاں, sāḥib صاحب, sar سر
sister *n.* bahan/bahin/bēhn بہن; *(elder ~)* bāji باجی, āpā آپا; *(adopted ~)* razāᶜī bahan رضاعی بہن, bhanēlī بھنیلی
sister-in-law *n.* *(elder brother's wife)* bhābhī بھابھی, bhaujī بھوجی, bhāvaj بھاوج; *(husband's sister)* nand/nanad نند; *(husband's younger brother's wife)* dēvarānī دیورانی; *(wife's sister)* sālī سالی
sit *v.* baiṭhnā بیٹھنا
  sit down baiṭhnā بیٹھنا, tašrīf rakhnā تشریف رکھنا
  sit near *v.* pās baiṭhnā پاس بیٹھنا
  sit on the throne *v.* taxt par baiṭhnā تخت پر بیٹھنا
sitar *(a musical instrument)* *n.* sitār ستار
sitar player *n.* sitār navāz ستار نواز

site *n.* jagah جگہ, maqām مقام, thal تھل
situated *adj.* mauzū^c موضوع
situation *n.* ḥālat حالت, mauqa^c موقع
six *num.* chē چھ
sixteen *num.* sōlah سولہ
sixteenth *adj.* sōlhavāṁ سولھواں
sixth *adj.* chaṭā چھٹا
sixty *num.* sāṭh ساٹھ
  sixty-one *num.* iksaṭh اکسٹھ
  sixty-two *num.* bāsaṭh باسٹھ
  sixty-three *num.* tirēsaṭh تریسٹھ
  sixty-four *num.* caunsaṭh چونسٹھ
  sixty-five *num.* paiṃsaṭh پینسٹھ
  sixty-six *num.* chēyāsaṭh چھیاسٹھ
  sixty-seven *num.* saṛsaṭh سڑسٹھ
  sixty-eight *num.* aṛsaṭh اڑسٹھ
  sixty-nine *num.* unhattar انہتر
size *n.* miqdār مقدار, qadd قد, sā'iz سائیز
skeleton *n.* paṁjar/piṁjar پنجر
skeptic *n.* munkir منکر, rind رند
skeptical *adj.* šakkī شکی
sketch *n.* ḍhāncah ڈھانچہ, xākah خاکہ
skewer *n.* sīx سیخ
skill *n.* fann فن, ḥirfat حرفت, ma^crifat معرفت, mahārat مہارت
skilled (in) *adj.* māhir ماہر; *(~ in language)* saxun dān سخن دان
skillful *adj.* saḥib kamāl صاحب کمال, sannā^c صناع, cātur چاتر, gunī گنی, hunar mand ہنر مند
skillfulness *n.* hāth cālākī ہاتھ چالاکی
skim *v.* chōlnā چھولنا
skin *n.* camṛā چمڑا, jild جلد, khāl کھال / *v.* khāl utārnā کھال اتارنا
skirmish *n.* jhaṛap جھڑپ
skirt *n.* lahangā لہنگا
skull *n.* khōpṛī کھوپڑی, sir سر, ṭāṛṭ ٹانٹ
sky *n.* āsmān آسمان

sky-blue *adj.* lājvardī لاجوردی
skylight *n.* raušan dān روشن دان
slack *adj.* sust سست / *n.* ḍhīl ڈھیل
slacken *v.* phaskānā پھسکانا
slackness *n.* ḍhēlāpan ڈھیلاپن
slain *adj.* kuštah کشتہ
slander *n.* ġībat غیبت / *v.* ġībat karnā غیبت کرنا
slant *n.* ḍhalvān ڈھلوان
slanting *adj.* tirchā ترچھا
slap *n.* lappaṛ لپڑ, thāp تھاپ, thappaṛ تھپڑ / *v.* dhūl lagānā دھول لگانا, dhūl mārnā دھول مارنا
slaughter *n.* muqātalah مقاتلہ, qatl قتل, zabaḥ ذبح / *v.* mārnā مارنا, zabaḥ karnā ذبح کرنا; *(in a religious way)* ḥalāl karnā حلال کرنا
slaughterhouse *n.* mazbaḥ مزبح
slaughtered *adj.* zabīḥ ذبیح
slaughterer *n.* zābiḥ ذابح
slave *n.* ġulām غلام
slavery *n.* ġulāmī غلامی
slay *v.* mār rakhnā مار رکھنا
sledgehammer *n.* hathauṛā ہتھوڑا
sleep *n.* naum نوم, nīnd نیند, xvāb خواب / *v.* sōnā سونا
sleeping *adj.* xvābīdah خوابیدہ
sleepy *adj.* xvābīdah خوابیدہ
slender *adj.* diqq دق, naḥīf نحیف , nazār نزار
slice *n.* phānk پھانک, qāš قاش, ṭukṛā ٹکڑا; *(of meat)* bōṭī بوٹی.
slight *n.* nazar نظر
slim *adj.* charērā چھریرا, nazār نزار
slimy *adj.* lucāb dār لعاب دار
slip *n.* laġziš لغزش, pālaġz پالغز; *(of paper)* parcah پرچہ / *v.* phisalnā پھسلنا
slip away *v.* khisak jānā کھسک جانا
slipper *n.* cappal چپل, jōtī جوتی.
slippery *adj.* ciknā چکنا
slipping *n.* phislāhaṭ پھسلاہٹ
slit *adj.* cāk چاک / *n.* raxnah رخنہ / *v.* cāk karnā چاک کرنا

slogan *n.* naᶜrah نعره
slope *n.* ḍhāl ڈھال, ḍhalān ڈھلان
slow *adj.* dhīmā دھیما
slow down *v.* sust karnā سست کرنا
slowly *adv.* āhistah آہستہ, dhīmē dhīmē دھیمے دھیمے, haulē haulē ہولے ہولے
slowness *n.* āhistagī آہستگی, dēr دیر
sluggish *adj.* maṭṭhā مٹھا
sluggishness *n.* vahn وہن
sly *adj.* ᶜayyār عیار, šātir شاطر
slyness *n.* ᶜayyārī عیاری
small *adj.* chōṭā چھوٹا, nanhā ننھا
smaller *adj.* kam tar کم تر
smallness *n.* chōṭā'ī چھوٹائی, kōtāhī کوتاہی, saġir صغر
smallpox *n.* cēcak چیچک, mātā ماتا
smart *adj.* cālāk چالاک, phurtīlā پھرتیلا
smartness *n.* cālākī چالاکی
smear *v.* dhabbah lagānā دھبہ لگانا
smell *n.* bū بو / *v.* sūnghnā سونگھنا
smile *n.* ibtisām اِبتسام, muskurāhaṭ مسکراہٹ, tabassum تبسم / *v.* muskurānā مسکرانا
smiling *adj.* mutabassim متبسم
smoke *n.* dhū'āṁ دھواں, dūd دود, duxān دخان / *v.* pīnā پینا, sigrēṭ pīnā سگریٹ پینا,, ḥuqqah pīnā حقہ پینا
smoking *adj.* duxānī دخانی
smoky *adj.* dhū'āṁ dhār دھواں دھار
smolder *v.* kajlānā کجلانا
smooth *adj.* ham vār ہموار, narm نرم
snake *n.* mār مار, nāg ناگ, sānp سانپ
snake charmer *n.* sānp vālā سانپ والا
snake-catcher *n.* sapērā سپیرا
snare *n.* dām دام, jāl جال, phandā پھندا
snare *v.* phaṁsānā پھنسانا
snatch *v.* chīnnā چھیننا, jhapaṭ lēnā جھپٹ لینا, jhapaṭṭā mārnā جھپٹا مارنا; *(~ at)* lapakna لپکنا

sneeze *n.* chīnk چھینک / *v.* chīnk mārnā چھینک مارنا, chīnknā چھینکنا
snore *v.* xarrāṭā bharnā خراٹا بھرنا, xarrāṭā mārnā خراٹا مارنا, xarxarānā خرخرانا
snoring *adj.* xar xarāhaṭ خرخراہٹ / *n.* xar xar خرخر, xarrāṭā خراٹا
snorting *(of a dog) n.* phūṁ پھوں
snow *n.* barf برف, salj ثلج, yax یخ / *v.* barf girnā برف گرنا
snowy *adj.* barfānī برفانی
snub *v.* dābnā دابنا
so *adj.* aisā ایسا, sā سا / *adj./adv.* taisā تیسا, vaisā ویسا / *conj./adv.* sō سو
  so and so *adj.* aisā taisā ایسا تیسا / *n.* fulān فلان
  so many *adj.* itnā اِتنا, utnā اُتنا / *adv.* candāṁ چنداں, jitnā جتنا, utnē اُتنے
  so much *adj.* itnā اِتنا, utnā اُتنا / *adv.* candāṁ چنداں, jitnā جتنا
  so that *conj.* ḥattā حتیٰ, tākih تاکہ / *conj./adv.* sō سو
soak *v.* bhigānā بھگانا, bhigōnā بھگونا
soaked *adj.* lat pat لت پت
soap *n.* sāban/sābun صابن, sābūn صابون
sob *v.* siskī bharnā سسکی بھرنا, subkiyāṁ lēnā سبکیاں لینا
sober *adj.* muttaqī متقی
social *adj.* majlisī مجلسی, mu'ašarti معاشرتی, muᶜāšaratī معاشرتی
society *n.* jamāᶜat جماعت, millat ملت, samāj سماج, aṁjuman انجمن
sock *n.* jurrāb جراب, mōzah موزہ
soda *n.* sōḍā سوڈا
sofa *n.* cār bāliš چار بالش, khāṭ کھاٹ
soft *adj.* halkā ہلکا, mulā'im ملائم, narm نرم, gudgudā گدگدا
soften *v.* mōm karnā موم کرنا
softly *adv.* dhīmē dhīmē دھیمے دھیمے, haulē haulē ہولے ہولے
softness *n.* mulā'imat ملائمت, narmī نرمی
soil *n.* dhartī دھرتی, zamīn زمین, miṭṭī مٹھی; *(hard and stony)* cāpaṛ چاپڑ
soiled *adj.* ālūdah آلودہ
solar *adj.* šamsī شمسی ♦ ~ **eclipse** *n.* kusūf کسوف ♦ ~ **month** *n.* māh-ē-šamsī ماہ شمسی
sold *adj.* farūxtah فروختہ
solder *n.* ṭānkā ٹانکا / *v.* ṭānkē lagānā ٹانکے لگانا, ṭānknā ٹانکنا
soldier *n.* ᶜaskarī عسکری, faujī فوجی, sipāhī سپاہی; *(infantry)* paidal پیدل
soldier-like *adj.* sipāhiyānah سپاہیانہ

sole *adj.* vāḥid واحد, ēk ایک / *n.* *(of a shoe)* talā تلا, talī تلی; *(of the foot)* talvā تلوا

solemnity *n.* sanjīdagī سنجیدگی

solicitation *n.* samājat سماجت

solid *adj.* mujassam مجسم, qavī قوی, ustuvārī استواری / *n.* karaxt کرخت

solidity *n.* matānat متانت, mazbūtī مضبوطی

solitary *adj.* mufrad مفرد, tanhā تنہا

solitude *n.* tanhā'ī تنہائی, gōšah našīnī گوشہ نشینی

soluble *adj.* galā'ū گلاؤ

solution *n.* ḥall حل, kašf کشف

solve *v.* ḥall karnā حل کرنا ♦ **~ a mystery** *v.* bhēd pānā بھید پانا ♦ **~ a puzzle** *v.* muᶜammah ḥal karnā معمہ حل کرنا

some *adj.* ka'ī کئی, kō'ī کوئی, kuch کچھ / *adv.* baᶜz بعض, cand ēk چند ایک

somebody *pron.* kō'ī کوئی / *n.* kas کس

somehow *adv.* kisī tarah کسی طرح

someone *pron.* kisī کسی

something *pron.* kō'ī کوئی, kuch کچھ / *adv.* cīzē چیزے

sometime *adv.* candē چندے

sometimes *adv.* baᶜz auqāt بعض اوقات, kabhī kabhī کبھی کبھی / *n.* kabhī کبھی

somewhat *adv.* cīzē چیزے, kuch kuch کچھ کچھ, qadrē قدرے

somewhere *adv.* kahīṁ کہیں

son *n.* bēṭā بیٹا, ibn ابن

song *n.* gānā گانا, gīt گیت, naġmah نغمہ, rāg راگ

son-in-law *n.* dāmād داماد

soon *adj./adv.* phir پھر / *adv.* jaldī جلدی

sooner *adv.* pahlē پہلے

soothe *v.* cumkārnā چمکارنا, taskīn dēnā تسکین دینا

soothing *adj.* navāz نواز

sorcerer *n.* jādūgar جادوگر

sorcery *n.* jādū جادو, saḥr سحر, tasxīr تسخیر

sore *adj.* figār فگار / *n.* phōṛā پھوڑا, qarḥah قرحہ, zaxm زخم, ghā'ō گھاؤ

sorrow *n.* afsōs افسوس, ġam/ ġamm غم, ranj رنج

sorrowful *adj.* fikr mand فکرمند, ġam gīn غمگین

sorry! *interj.* muᶜāf kījiē معاف کیجئے

sort *n.* jāt جات, nau^c نوع, qism قسم
sort out *v.* chānṭnā چھانٹنا
soul *n.* rūḥ روح, jān جان, nafs نفس
sound *adj.* cangā چنگا, salāmat سلامت, sālim سالم / *n.* āvāz آواز, saut صوت / *v.* bajānā بجانا, bajnā بجنا; *(as a musical instrument)* bājnā باجنا
soundness *n.* durustī درستی
soup *n.* šōrbā شوربا
sour *adj.* khaṭṭā کھٹا, turš ترش
source *n.* manba^c منبع, maṣdar مصدر, zarī^cah ذریعہ
sourness *n.* khaṭās کھٹاس, turšī ترشی
south *n.* janūb جنوب, dakkhin دکھن
South Pole *n.* qutb-ē-junūbī قطب جنوبی
southern *adj.* janūbī جنوبی, dakkhinī دکھنی
sovereign *n.* bādšāh بادشاہ, mahā rāj مہاراج, sultān سلطان
sovereignty *n.* ḥukm rānī حکمرانی, ḥukūmat حکومت, rāj راج
sow discord *v.* phūṭ ḍālnā پھوٹ ڈالنا
sow seeds *v.* bīj bōnā بیج بونا, bīj ḍālnā بیج ڈالنا
sowing *n.* bivā'ī بوائی, ḥars حرث
space *n.* fāsilah فاصلہ, masāfat مسافت, vus^cat وسعت
spacious *adj.* kušādah کشادہ, vāsi^c واسع, vasī^c وسیع
spade *n.* kudāl کدال, phā'ōṛā پھاوڑا
span *n.* bālišt بالشت
spare *adj.* fāltu فالتو
spark *n.* parkālah پرکالہ, šarārah شرارہ; *(of fire)* cingārī چنگاری, patangā پتنگا
sparkle *v.* camaknā چمکنا, jhilmilānā جھلملانا
sparrow *n.* ciṛiyā چڑیا, kuṁjašk کنجشک
speak *v.* bōlnā بولنا, bāt karnā بات کرنا, kalām karnā کلام کرنا, sunānā سنانا
speaker *n.* kalīm کلیم, muxātib مخاطب, nātiq ناطق
spear *n.* ballam بلم, nēzah نیزہ
spearman *n.* bhālā bardār بھالا بردار, nēzah bāz نیزہ باز
special *adj.* maxsūs مخصوص, xusūsī خصوصی
speciality *n.* taxsīs تخصیص, xuṣūsiyyat خصوصیت
specially *adv.* bi-ltaxsīs بالتخصیص
specialty *n.* ixtisās اِختصاص

species *n.* jins جنس, qabīl قبیل, sinf صنف
specific *adj.* muxtass مختص
specified *adj.* maxsūs مخصوص
specimen *n.* namūnah نمونہ
speckled *adj.* cītal چیتل, cittī dār چتی دار
spectacles *n.* ᶜainak عینک, cašmah چشمہ, cašmak چشمک
speech *n.* bāt بات, bōl بول, kalām کلام, bōlī بولی; *(mode of ~)* bōl cāl بول چال
speechless *adj.* gūngā گونگا, lā javāb لاجواب, lā kalām لا کلام
speed *n.* bēg بیگ, ᶜujlat عجلت, raftār رفتار / *v.* dauṛānā دوڑانا
speedy *adj.* ᶜājil عاجل, šitāb شتاب
spell *n.* mōhnī موہنی, ṭōṭkā ٹوٹکا / *v.* hijē/hijjē karnā ہجے کرنا
spelling *n.* hijā ہجا, hijē/hijjē ہجے tahajjī تہجی
spend *v.* xarc karnā خرچ کرنا ♦ ~ **money extravagantly** paisā uṛāna پیسا اُڑانا
sperm *n.* tuxm تخم
sphere *n.* kurrah کرہ, manḍal منڈل, sipahr سپہر
spice *n.* masālā مسالا
spicy *adj.* caṭpaṭā چٹپٹا, mirch مرچ, tīkhā تیکھا
spider *n.* ᶜankabūt عنکبوت, makṛī مکڑی
spiderweb *n.* jālā جالا, makṛī kā jālā مکڑی کا جالا
spike *n.* kīl کیل
spill *v.* chalkānā چھلکانا, ḍhālnā ڈھالنا, lunḍhānā لنڈھانا, phēnknā پھینکنا
spin *v.* ainṭhnā اینٹھنا, kātnā کاتنا
spinach *n.* pālak پالک
spine *n.* xār خار
spinning wheel *n.* carxah چرخہ
spiral *adj.* pēc dār پیچ دار
spire *n.* kalas کلس
spirit *n.* himmat ہمت, man من, nafs نفس, rūḥ روح,
spirited *adj.* jāndār جاندار
spirits *n.* bādah بادہ
spiritual *adj.* rūḥānī روحانی
spiritual guide *n.* hādī ہادی, muršid مرشد; *(especially in Islam)* imām امام
spiritual leader *n.* imām امام
spirituality *n.* rūḥāniyyat روحانیت

spit *n.* sīx سیخ , thūk تھوک / *v.* thūknā تھوکنا
spitting pot *n.* pīkdān پیکدان
spittle *n.* kaf کف, luᶜāb لعاب, rāl رال
spittoon *n.* pīkdān پیکدان
splash *n.* chīṇṭā چھینٹا
spleen *n.* tillī تلی
splendid *adj.* ᶜālī šān عالی شان, ᶜazīm-ul-šān عظیم الشان , fāxrah فاخرہ, šān dār شان دار
splendor *n.* camak damak چمک دمک, duraxšandagī درخشندگی, jilā جلا , jilā'ō جلاؤ
split *n.* phūṭ پھوٹ / *v.* cāk karnā چاک کرنا, caṭakna چٹکنا
spoil *n.* lūṭ لوٹ, munāfiᶜ منافع / *v.* bigāṛnā بگاڑنا, barbād karnā برباد کرنا, ġārat karnā غارت کرنا
sponge *n.* isfanj اسفنج
spongy *adj.* phusphusā پھسپھسا , pūlā پولا
sponsor *n.* zāmin ضامن
spontaneously *adv.* āp hī āp آپ ہی آپ
spoon *n.* camcah چمچہ, cammac چمچ, ḍōngā ڈونگا
spoonful *n.* camcah bhar چمچہ بھر
sport *n.* laᶜb لعب, līlā لیلا, khēl کھیل
sportive *adj.* culbulā چلبلا, khilāṛī کھلاڑی
sportiveness *n.* culbulāhaṭ چلبلاہٹ, culbulāpan چلبلاپن
sports *n.* lahv لہو, lahv-ō-laᶜb لہو ولعب
spot *n.* cittī چتی, dāġ داغ, dhabbah دھبہ; ṭhaur ٹھور; (black ~) kālak kā ṭīkā کالک کا ٹیکا
spotted *adj.* cītal چیتل, cittī dār چتی دار, dāġ dār داغ دار, manqūtah منقوطہ
spouse *n.* maḥram محروم
sprain *n.* mōc موچ / *v.* mōc ānā موچ آنا
sprawl *v.* lōṭnā لوٹنا
spread *adj.* phailā hū'ā پھیلا ہوا, mafrūš مفروش / *n.* phailā'ō پھیلاؤ / *v.* bichānā بچھانا, phailānā پھیلانا ♦ **~ a rumor** *v.* carcā karnā چرچا کرنا, afvāh uṛānā افواہ اڑانا
spread out *v.* phailā hū'ā پھیلا ہوا
spring *v.* jhapaṭ lēnā جھپٹ لینا, jhapaṭnā جھپٹنا, phalāngnā پھلانگنا, phāndnā پھاندنا / *n. (season)* bahār بہار, mausim-ē-bahār موسم بہار, basant بسنت

sprinkle *v.* chīnṭnā چھینٹنا, chīnṭā dēnā چھینٹا دینا
sprout *n.* ankūrā انکورا, kōnpal کونپل
spur *v.* ēṛ lagānā ایڑ لگانا / *n.* mahmēz مہمیز; *(for a horse)* ēṛ ایڑ
spurn *v.* lāt mārnā لات مارنا, latāṛnā لتاڑنا
spy *n.* jāsūs جاسوس, muxbir مخبر / *v.* bhēd lēnā بھید لینا, jhānknā جھانکنا, ujhaknā اُجھکنا
spyglass *n.* dūr bīn دور بین
spying *n.* jāsūsī جاسوسی, jhānk جھانک, ṭōh ٹوہ
squabbling *n.* takrār تکرار, jhagṛā جھگڑا
squadron *n.* munazzam girōh منظم گروہ ,dastah دستہ
squander *v.* zā'i^c karnā ضائع کرنا, ganvānā گنوانا, luṭānā لٹانا
square *adj.* murabba^c مربع / *n.* cār xānah چارخانہ, cauk چوک
squat *v.* cār zānūṁ baiṭhnā چارزانوں بیٹھنا
squeak *n.* cīṁ چیں / *v.* cīṁ bōlnā چیں بولنا
squeeze *v.* cāmpnā چانپنا, dabānā دبانا, nicōṛnā نچوڑنا
squeeze out *v.* duhnā دہنا
squint-eyed *adj.* bhēnkā بھینگا
squirrel *n.* gulahrī گلہری, sanjāb سنجاب
squirt *n.* pickārī پچکاری / *v.* pickārī mārnā پچکاری مارنا
stab *n.* hūl ہول / *v.* bēdhnā بیدھنا, bhōnknā بھونکنا, kaṭār mārnā کٹار مارنا; *(with a knife)* churī mārnā چھری مارنا
stability *n.* pā'ēdārī پائیداری, istiḥkām استحکام
stable *n.* astabal اصطبل, ghuṛ sāl گھڑسال / *adj.* mustaḥkam مستحکام
stack (of wood) *n.* ṭāl ٹال
staff *n.* ^camalah عملہ, lāṭh لاٹھ
stage *n.* manzil منزل, marḥalah مرحلہ
stagger *v.* ḍagmagānā ڈگمگانا, laṛkhaṛānā لڑکھڑانا
stain *n.* dāġ داغ, dhabbah دھبہ / *v.* dāġ lagānā داغ لگانا, dhabbah lagānā دھبہ لگانا; *(with henna)* racānā رچانا
stair *n.* zīnah زینہ, rutbah رتبہ
staircase *n.* sīṛhī سیڑھی
stake *v.* bāzī lagānā بازی لگانا
stale *adj.* bāsī باسی
stalk *n.* ṭāl maṭōl ٹال مٹول

stallion *n.* sānḍ ghōṛā سانڈ گھوڑا
stammer *v.* haklānā ہکلانا, tutlānā تتلانا
stamp *n.* chāp چھاپ, ḍāk ṭikaṭ ڈاک ٹکٹ, muhr مہر / *v.* chāp lagānā چھاپ لگانا, chāpnā چھاپنا, ṭhappā lagānā ٹھپا لگانا
stand *n.* isṭāp اسٹاپ, mauqif موقف / *v.* kharā hōnā کھڑا ہونا ♦ ~ **in a line** qatār bāndhnā قطار باندھنا
stand up *v.* uṭhnā اُٹھنا
standard *n.* micyār معیار, ᶜalam علم, pharairā پھریرا
stanza *n.* ašlōk اشلوک
star *n.* sitārah ستارہ, tārā تارا
starch *n.* kalaf کلف, nišāstah نشاستہ, sarēš سریش; *(made of rice flour)* mānḍ مانڈ, mānḍī مانڈی
starchy *adj.* lōc dār لوچ دار
stare *v.* ṭak bāndhnā ٹک باندھنا, tāk lagānā تاک لگانا, taknā تکنا
stare at *v.* ghūrnā گھورنا, tāknā تاکنا
stark *adj.* nang ḍharang ننگ ڈھرنگ
starling *n.* mainā مینا
start *n.* ᶜunfuvān عنفوان, šurūᶜ شروع / *v.* šurūᶜ karnā شروع کرنا, āġāz karnā آغاز کرنا, jārī karnā جاری کرنا
start up *v.* caunk paṛnā چونک پڑنا
starvation *n.* fāqah فاقہ
starve *v.* bhūkōṁ marnā بھوکوں مرنا, fāqah karnā فاقہ کرنا ♦ ~ **one's self** pēṭ kāṭnā پیٹ کاٹنا
state *n.* daulat دولت, ḥālat حالت, kaifiyyat کیفیت / *v.* bayān karnā بیان کرنا, raqm karnā رقم کرنا
stated *adj.* mutazakkirah متذکرہ
statement *n.* bayān بیان, ḥāl حال
station *v.* ṭikānā ٹکانا / *n.* mauqif موقف; *(bus or railway)* isṭēšan اسٹیشن
stationed *adj.* muqīm مقیم
statue *n.* haikal ہیکل, mūrtī/mūratī مورتی
stature *n.* qadd قد, qāmat قامت, uṁcā'ī انچائی
status *n.* ᶜuhdah عہدہ
statute *n.* but بت
staunch *adj.* rāsix راسخ

stay *n.* qiyām قیام / *v.* qiyām karnā قیام کرنا, rahnā رہنا
steadiness *n.* istiqāmat استقامت
steady *adj.* mu'assiq موثق, rakīn رکین, sābit qadam ثابت قدم
steal *v.* cōrī karnā چوری کرنا, curānā چرانا, mūsnā موسنا
stealth *n.* cōrī چوری
steam *n.* duxān دخان
steamer *n.* duxānī jahāz دخانی جہاز
steed *n.* tausan توسن
steel *n.* faulād فولاد, ispāt اسپات
step *n.* gām گام, sīṛhī سیڑھی / *v.* pair dharnā پیر دھرنا
step-brother *n.* sautēlā bhā'ī سوتیلا بھائی
step-sister *n.* sautēlā bahan/bahin/bēhn سوتیلا بہن
steward *n.* bhanḍārī بھنڈاری
stick *n.* ḍānḍ ڈانڈ, lakṛī لکڑی, lāṭhī لاٹھی / *v.* cipaknā چپکنا, cipṭānā چپٹانا, phaṁsnā پھنسنا
stick into *v.* cubhōnā چبھونا
stick to *v.* cimaṭnā چمٹنا
stick together *v.* cēpnā چیپنا
stickiness *n.* cēp چیپ, cipcipāhaṭ چپچپاہٹ, las لس
sticky *adj.* caspāṁ چسپاں, cipcipā چپچپا, las dār لس دار
stiff *adj.* kaṛā کڑا, saxt سخت
stigma *n.* kalank کلنک
stigmatize *v.* dāġnā داغنا
stigmatized *adj.* mutassam متسم
still *adv.* ab bhī اب بھی, hanūz ہنوز, phir bhī پھر بھی / *adj.* xamōš خموش, cup چپ / *conj.* lēkin لیکن, magar مگر, par پر
stillness *n.* cup چپ
stimulate *v.* tarġīb dēnā ترغیب دینا
stimulation *n.* tarġīb ترغیب
sting *n.* ḍank ڈنک, nēš نیش / *v.* ḍank mārnā ڈنک مارنا, ḍasnā ڈسنا
stinginess *n.* baxīlī بخیلی, buxl بخل, kaṁjūsī کنجوسی
stingy *adj.* baxīl بخیل, kā'iyāṁ کائیاں, līcaṛ لیچڑ, mumsik ممسک ♦ ~ **person** *n.* makhnī cūs مکھی چوس
stink *n.* gand گند, gandagī گندگی

stipend *n.* rātib راتب, vazīfah وظیفہ
stipulated *adj.* maᶜhūd معہود
stir *v.* calānā چلانا, hilānā ہلانا
stir up *v.* macānā مچانا
stirrup *n.* rakāb رکاب
stitch *n.* hūk ہوک, ṭānkā ٹانکا / *v.* sīnā سینا, ṭānknā ٹانکنا
stitched *adj.* dō xatah دوختہ
stitching *n.* silā'ī سلائی, ṭīs ٹیس; *(of a book)* šīrāzah شیرازہ
stock *n.* māl مال, zaxīrah ذخیرہ / *v.* zaxīrah karnā ذخیرہ کرنا
stocking *n.* jurrāb جراب, mōzah موزہ
stolen *adj.* masrūqah مسروقہ
stomach *n.* miᶜdah معدہ, ōjh اوجھ, pēṭ پیٹ
stone *n.* patthar پتھر
stony *adj.* patthrīlā پتھریلا, sangīn سنگین
stool *n.* kursī کرسی, mōṛhā/mūṛhā موڑھا
stoop *v.* jhuknā جھکنا
stop *n.* mauqif موقف, ṭhahrā'ō ٹھہراؤ; *(for a bus or taxi)* isṭāp اسٹاپ / *v.* rōknā روکنا, ruknā رکنا
stop at *v.* ṭikānā ٹکانا, ṭiknā ٹکنا
stopped *adj.* band بند, mauqūf موقوف
stopper *n.* ḍāṭ ڈاٹ, ḍaṭṭā ڈٹا, ṭhēpī ٹھیپی
stopping *n.* farōd فرود
store *n.* zaxīrah ذخیرہ / *v.* zaxīrah karnā ذخیرہ کرنا
storehouse *n.* gūdām گودام, maxzan مخزن ♦ ~ **pantry** *n.* mōdī xānah مودی خانہ
storekeeper *n.* bhanḍārī بھنڈاری
storey *n.* manzilah منزلہ, tabaqah طبقہ; *(of a house)* manzil منزل
storm *n.* tūfān طوفان
stormy *adj.* tūfānī طوفانی ♦ ~ **day** *n.* ᶜāsif عاصف
story *n.* afsānah افسانہ, ḥikāyat حکایت, kahānī کہانی, qissah قصہ
storyteller *n.* dāstān-ē-gō داستان گو
stout *adj.* farbah فربہ, haṭṭā kaṭṭā ہٹا کٹا, sanḍar سنڈر
stove *n.* tābdān تابدان
stow away *v.* dabkānā دبکانا
straight *adj.* mustaqīm مستقیم, mustavī مستوی, sīdhā سیدھا; *(~ to the point)* sā'ib صائب

straighten *v.* sīdhā karnā سیدھا کرنا
straightforward *adj.* kharā کھرا
straightness *n.* sīdh سیدھ, sīdhā pan سیدھاپن
strain *n.* mōc موچ / *v.* nikhārnā نکھارنا
strainer *n.* chalnī چھلنی
strange *adj.* ᶜajīb عجیب, ġarīb غریب
strangeness *n.* ġairiyyat غیریت
stranger *n.* pardēsī پردیسی
strangle *v.* phāṁsī dēnā پھانسی دینا
strangulation *n.* phāṁsī پھانسی
strap *(leather ~) n.* tasmah تسمہ
stratagem *n.* cāl چال, ghāt گھات, dāōṁ داوں, rōbāh bāzī روباہ بازی
straw *n.* ghās phūs گھاس پھوس, payāl پیال
stray *v.* bhaṭaknā بھٹکنا, bhūlnā بھولنا
straying *adj.* sar gardāṁ سرگرداں
streak *n.* dhārī دھاری, lakīr لکیر, xatt خط
stream *n.* dhār دھار, nahr نہر, rau رو, rūd/rōd رود
street *n.* galī گلی, kū کو, saṛak سڑک
strength *n.* mazbūtī مضبوطی, quvvat قوت, tāqat طاقت, zōr زور, dabā'ō دباؤ; *(of mind or body)* jaulānī جولانی
stress *n.* tākīd تاکید
stressed *adj.* tanā'ō zadah تناؤزدہ
stretch *v.* phailānā پھیلانا, tānnā تاننا
stretch out *v.* pasārnā پسارنا
stretched *adj.* mabsūt مبسوط
stretching *n.* xamyāzah خمیازہ
strict *adj.* mutašaddid متشدد, saxt سخت, zābit ضابط
strictly *adv.* tākīdan تاکیداً
strictness *n.* saxtī سختی
strife *n.* cax چخ, jhagṛā جھگڑا, xusūmat خصومت
strike *n.* haṛtāl ہڑتال / *v.* bajnā بجنا, mārnā مارنا
striking *adj.* mu'assir موثر / *n.* mār مار, ṭakkar ٹکر
string *v. (~ pearls)* pirōnā پرونا / *n.* ḍōr ڈور, jē'ōṛī جیوڑی, laṛī لڑی; *(~ of beads)* tasbīḥ تسبیح

strip (of cloth) *n.* dhajjī دھجی
stripe *n.* dhārī دھاری, lakīr لکیر
striped *adj.* lahriyā لہریا
striving *adj.* mujāhid مجاہد
stroke *n.* mār مار, vār وار
stroll *n.* gašt گشت, maṭar gašt مٹر گشت, sair سیر / *v.* sair karnā سیر کرنا
strong *adj.* mazbūt مضبوط, tāqatvar طاقتور, zabardast زبردست, zōr mand زور مند / *adj./adv.* zōr sē زور سے
stronger *adj.* zabar زبر
strong-hearted *adj.* qavī dil قوی دل
strongly *adj./adv.* zōr sē زور سے
strong-minded *adj.* qavī dil قوی دل
struck *adj.* zadah زدہ
structure *n.* ḍhāncah ڈھانچہ, kāṭhī کاٹھی
struggle *n.* dauṛ دوڑ, jahd جہد / *v.* laṛnā لڑنا
stubborn *adj.* ziddī ضدی
stubbornness *n.* isrār اصرار, tamarrud تمرد, zidd ضد
student *n.* talabah طلبہ, tālib-ē-ᶜilm طالب علم, talmīz تلمیذ
studious person *n.* kitāb kā kīṛā کتاب کا کیڑا
study *n.* taᶜallum تعلم, muṭālaᶜah مطالعہ / *v.* paṛhnā پڑھنا
studying *n.* šāgirdī شاگردی
stuff *v.* khacā khac bharnā کھچا کھچ بھرنا
stuffed *adj.* ṭhas ٹھس
stuffing *n.* bhartī بھرتی, ḥašv حشو
stumble *n.* ṭhōkar khānā ٹھوکر کھانا, cūknā چوکنا
stupefaction *n.* ḥairat zadagī حیرت زدگی, bē hōšī بے ہوشی, mūrchā مورچھا
stupefied *adj.* bad ḥavās بد حواس, mabhūt مبہوت
stupid *adj.* aḥmaq احمق, bē ᶜaql بے عقل, bē vaqūf بے وقوف, xar dimāġ خردماغ ♦ ~ **person** *n.* buddhū بدھو, kāṭh kā ullū کاٹھ کا الو
stupidity *n.* bē vaqūfī بے وقوفی, gadhā pan گدھاپن
stutter *v.* haklānā ہکلانا, zabān tutlānā زبان تتلانا
stuttering *n.* luknat لکنت
style *n.* ᶜibārat عبارت, rang ḍhang رنگ ڈھنگ, uslūb اسلوب
stylish *adj.* vazaᶜ dār وضع دار

subdivision *(of a district) n.* parganah پرگنہ
subdue *v.* maglūb karnā مغلوب کرنا
subdued *adj.* maġlūb مغلوب, musaxxar مسخر
subject *n.* fāᶜil فاعل, mauzūᶜ موضوع
sublime *adj.* buland بلند, ᶜalī علی, mutaᶜāl متعال, sāmī سامی / *n.* muᶜallā معلیٰ
sublimity *n.* ᶜuluv علو
submarine *n.* āb dōz آب دوز
submission *n.* itāᶜat اطاعت, izᶜān اذعان, mutābaᶜat متابعت, tāᶜat طاعت
submissive *adj.* munqād منقاد, mutīᶜ مطیع
submit *v.* pēš karnā پیش کرنا
subordinate *adj.* mā taḥat ما تحت / *n.* maḥkūm محکوم
subscribe *v.* candah dēnā چندہ دینا, sabt karnā ثبت کرنا
subscription *n.* candah چندہ
subsequent *adj.* ā'īndah آئندہ, mutaᶜāqib متعاقب
subside *v.* farō hōnā فرو ہونا
subsist *v.* auqat basarī karnā اوقات بسری کرنا
subsistence *n.* auqāt basarī اوقات بسری, maᶜāš معاش, maᶜišat معیشت
substance *n.* māddah مادہ, māddiyat مادیت
substitution *n.* ibdāl اِبدال, muᶜāvazah معاوضہ
subtle *adj.* bārik باریک, daqīq دقیق
subtleness *n.* riqqat رقت
subtract *v.* ghaṭānā گھٹانا, miṁhā karnā منہا کرنا, vazaᶜ karnā وضع کرنا
subtracted *adj.* manfī منفی, miṁhā منہا
subtraction *n.* tafrīq تفریق
suburbs *n.* muzāfāt-ē-šahr مضافات شہر
succeed *v.* fatḥ pānā فتح پانا
success *n.* kāmyābī کامیابی
successful *adj.* kāmyāb کامیاب
succession *n.* jā našīnī جانشینی, silsilah سلسلہ, tasalsul تسلسل, tavātur تواتر
successive *adj.* musalsal مسلسل, mutaᶜāqib متعاقب, mutarādif مترادف, muttasil متصل
successively *adv.* dhaṛā dhaṛ دھڑا دھڑ, lagā tār لگاتار, yak bah yak یک بہ یک
successor *n.* jā našīn جانشین, vāris وارث, xalaf خلف
succulence *n.* šādābī شادابی

succulent *adj.* šādāb شاداب
such *adj.* aisā ایسا / *adj./adv.* taisā تیسا, vaisā ویسا / *adv.* cūṁ چوں
suck *v.* cacōṛnā چچوڑنا, cūsnā چوسنا
suckle *v.* cacōṛnā چچوڑنا
sudden *adj.* jhap جھپ
suddenly *adv.* acānak اچانک, dafaᶜtan دفعتاً, yak bah yak یک بہ یک
sue *v.* faryād karnā فریاد کرنا
suffer *v.* bhūgnā بھوگنا, bardāšt karnā برداشت کرنا
suffer a blow *v.* sadmah uṭhānā صدمہ اٹھانا
suffer a loss *v.* ghāṭ uṭhānā گھاٹا اٹھانا, zak uṭhānā زک اٹھانا
suffer a shock *v.* sadmah uṭhānā صدمہ اٹھانا
suffer an injury *v.* cōṭ khānā چوٹ کھانا
suffer disgrace *v.* ḥarf ānā حرف آنا
suffer pain *v.* dukh uṭhānā دکھ اٹھانا
suffering *n.* dard درد, dukh دکھ, pīṛ پیڑ
sufficiency *n.* iktafā اکتفاء, kifāyat کفایت
sufficient *adj.* bas بس, kāfī کافی, kifāyah کفایہ
suffocation *n.* ḥabs-ul-nafas حبس النفس, ucchū اچھو
sufi *(a Muslim mystic) n.* sūfī صوفی
sugar *n.* šakar/šakkar شکر ♦ **raw** ~ guṛ گڑ
sugar mill *n.* ghānī گھانی
sugarcane *n.* gannā گنا
suggest *v.* tajvīz karnā تجویز کرنا
suggestion *n.* tajvīz تجویز
suicide *n.* xūd kušī خودکشی ♦ **commit** ~ *v.* ḥarām maut marnā حرام موت مرنا, xūd kušī karnā خودکشی کرنا
suit *n.* faryād فریاد, malbūs ملبوس, muᶜāmalah معاملہ / *v.* mutābiq hōnā مطابق ہونا, muvāfaqat rakhnā موافقت رکھنا, muvāfiq ānā موافق آنا
suitability *n.* munāsibat مناسبت, rās راس
suitable *adj.* lā'iq لائق, munāsib مناسب, mutābiq مطابق, muvāfiq موافق
suitcase *n.* sūṭkēs سوٹ کیس
sulphur *n.* gandhak گندھک, kibrīt کبریت
sultan *n.* sultān سلطان
sultanate *n.* saltanat سلطنت

sum *n.* jamaᶜ جمع, mablaġ مبلغ
sum up *v.* jōṛ lagānā جوڑ لگانا, xulāsah karnā خلاصہ کرنا
summary *n.* ijmāl اِجمال
summer *n.* ggarmī گرمی, mausim-ē-garmā موسم گرما, tābistān تابستان
summer-house *n.* bangalạh بنگلہ
summit *n.* auj اوج, cōṭī چوٹی, rās راس; *(of a mountain)* ḍāng ڈانگ, qullah قلہ
summon *v.* bulānā بلانا
summoning *n.* balạ̄vā بلاوا
sun *n.* āftab آفتاب, sūraj سورج
sunbathe *v.* dhūp khānạ̄ دھوپ کھانا
sunbeam *n.* kiran کرن
Sunday *n.* itvār اتوار
sunk *adj.* muġarraq مغرق
sunlight *n.* dhūp دھوپ, zau ضو
Sunna *(religious practice according to prophet Muhammed) n.* sunnat سنت
Sunni *adj.* sunnī سنی
sunrise *n.* tulūᶜ-ē-āftāb طلوع آفتاب
sunset *n.* ġurūb غروب, ġurūb-ē āftāb غروب آفتاب
sunshine *n.* dhūp دھوپ, šuᶜaᶜ شعاع, ujālā اجالا
superficial *adj.* sathị̄ سطحی
superfluous *adj.* fāzil فاضل, zā'id زائد
superintendent *n.* muhtamim مہتمم, muntazim منتظم, muvakkal موکل
superior *adj.* bihtar بہتر, fā'iq فائق, ucc اُچ
superiority *n.* fauqiyyat فوقیت, sabqat سبقت, tarjīḥ ترجیح
superscription *n.* sar nāmah سرنامہ
superstitious *adj.* mutaᶜassib متعصب
supervise *v.* murāqabah karnā مراقبہ کرنا
supervision *n.* ihtimām اہتمام, sar barāhī سربراہی
supervisor *n.* muhtamim مہتمم, nigarān نگران
supper *n.* rāt kā khānā رات کا کھانا, šām kā khānā شام کا کھانا
supplement *n.* tatimmah تتمہ
supplicate *v.* ᶜājizī karnā عاجزی کرنا, dāman phailānā دامن پھیلانا
supplication *n.* iltimās التماس, niyāz نیاز
supply *n.* rasad رسد / *v.* baham pahuṁcānā بہم پہنچانا

support *n.* ḥimāyat حمایت, madad مدد, sahārā سہارا , pāyah پایہ / *v.* ḥimāyat karnā حمایت کرنا, madad karnā مدد کرنا, sahārā dēnā سہارا دینا
supported *adj.* mustanad مستند
supporter *n.* ḥāmī حامی, piṭhū پٹھو
suppose *v.* farz karnā فرض کرنا, mānnā ماننا
supposition *n.* aṭkal اٹکل, qiyās قیاس, taxayyul تخیل
suppress *v.* dabānā دبانا, dābnā دابنا, farō karnā فرو کرنا
supremacy *n.* pēšvā'ī پیشوائی
supreme *adj.* mahā مہا
supreme being *n.* bhagvān بھگوان
supreme court *n.* sadr ᶜadālat صدر عدالت
sure *adv.* hāṁ ہاں / *interj.* zarūr ضرور / *adj.* taḥqīqī تحقیقی
surely *adv.* bil-zurūr بالضرور, lā maḥālah لا محالہ
surety *n.* kafīl کفیل , zamānat ضمانت, zāminī ضامنی
surface *n.* rū رو, safḥah صفحہ , sataḥ سطح , tah تہ
surge *n.* hilkōrā ہلکورا, mauj موج
surgeon *n.* jarrāḥ جراح
surname *n.* laqab لقب
surpass *v.* pīchē ḍālnā پیچھے ڈالنا sabqat lē jānā سبقت لے جانا
surpassing *n.* tajāvuz تجاوز
surplus *adj.* fāltu فالتو / *n.* bacat بچت, bēšī بیشی, taufīr توفیر, ziyādatī زیادتی
surprise *n.* istiᶜjāb استعجاب / *v.* ḥairān karnā حیران کرنا
surprised *adj.* dang دنگ, mutaᶜajjib متعجب
surrender *v.* ḥavālah karnā حوالہ کرنا
surround *v.* ghērnā گھیرنا, iḥātah karnā اِحاطہ کرنا, muḥit ḥōna محیط ہونا
surrounding *n.* ghēr گھیر, mā ḥaul ما حول
survey *n.* misāhat مساحت, paimā'iš پیمائش
survivor *n.* pas māndah پس ماندہ
suspect *adj.* muštabah مشتبہ / *v.* šakk karnā شک کرنا, gumān karnā گمان کرنا
suspend *v.* laṭkānā لٹکانا, muᶜattal karnā معطل کرنا , ṭāng dēnā ٹانگ دینا, ṭāngnā ٹانگنا
suspended *adj.* muᶜallāq معلق , muᶜattal معطل , mutaᶜalliq متعلق
suspense *n.* dubdhā دبدھا
suspension *n.* mauqūfī موقوفی, muᶜattalī معطلی , tavaqquf توقف

suspicion *n.* bad gumānī بدگمانی, gumān گمان, šubah شبہ
suspicious *adj.* bad gumān بدگمانی, šakkī شکی
sustain *v.* sambhālnā سنبھالنا
sustainer *n.* barqarār rakhnē vālā برقرار رکھنے والا, rāziq رازق
swallow *v.* nigalnā نگلنا
swamp *n.* daldal دلدل
swampy *adj.* daldalī دلدلی
swan *n.* haṁs ہنس
swarm *n.* ḍār ڈار, jhunḍ جھنڈ / *v.* chā jānā چھاجانا
sway *n.* tasallut تسلط / *v.* ḍōlnā ڈولنا, jhūlnā جھولنا, jhūmnā جھومنا
swear *v.* ḥalaf uṭhānā حلف اٹھانا, qasam khānā قسم کھانا, saugand khānā سوگند کھانا
sweat *n.* pasīnah پسینہ / *v.* pasīnah ānā پسینہ آنا
sweep *v.* buhārnā بہارنا, jhāṛū dēnā جھاڑودینا
sweeper *n.* cūṛhā چوڑھا, jārōb kaš جاروب کش, xākrōb خاکروب
sweeping *n.* karkaṭ کرکٹ
sweet *adj.* mīṭhā میٹھا
sweet and sour *adj.* cāšnī dār چاشنی دار
sweet potato *n.* šakar qandī شکرقندی
sweet talker *n.* miyāṁ miṭhū میاں مٹھو
sweetheart *adj.* dulārā دلارا / *n.* dil rubā دل ربا, maḥbūbah محبوبہ, piyā پیا, sājan ساجن
sweetness *n.* ḥalāvat حلاوت, maṭhās مٹھاس, šīrīnī شیرینی
swell *v.* apharnā اپھرنا, phūl jānā پھول جانا, sūjnā سوجنا, varam karnā ورم کرنا
swim *v.* pairnā پیرنا, tairnā تیرنا
swimmer *n.* pairāk پیراک, pairākī پیراکی, tairāk تیراک
swimming *n.* pairākī پیراکی, tairākī تیراکی
swindle *v.* māl mārnā مال مارنا, mūsnā موسنا
swindler *n.* ṭhag ٹھگ, ucakkā اچکا
swine *n.* sū'ar سوَر, xanzīr خنزیر
swing *n.* jhūlā جھولا, gahvārah گہوارہ, hiṁḍōlā ہنڈولا / *v.* ḍōlnā ڈولنا, jhulānā جھلانا, jhūlnā جھولنا
switch off a lamp *v.* cirāġ bujhānā چراغ بجھانا
switch on a lamp *v.* cirāġ rōšan karnā چراغ روشن کرنا
swollen *adj.* phūlā پھولا

swoon *n.* ġaš غش , ġašī غشی , mūrchā مورچھا / *v.* mūrchā ānā مورچھا آنا
sword *n.* talvār تلوار
swordsman *n.* šamšēr zan شمشیر زن , tēġ zan تیغ زن
symbol *n.* pattā پتا, ramz رمز
sympathy *n.* dard mandī درد مندی, ġam xvārī غم خواری , mōh موہ, uṁs اُنس
symphony *n.* tarānah ترانہ
symptom *n.* ᶜalāmat علامت, patā پتا, patah پتہ
synonymous *adj.* murādif مرادف
synopsis *n.* ixtisār اِختصار
syntax *n.* naḥv نحو
syringe *n.* pickārī پچکاری
syrup *n.* šarbat شربت, šīrah شیرہ
system *n.* nizām نظام, qāᶜidah قاعدہ

T

table *n.* mēz میز
tablecloth *n.* cādar چادر
tablet *n.* taxtī تختی , ṭikyā ٹکیا
tackle *v.* muṁh karnā منہ کرنا
tag *n.* ghunḍī گھنڈی
tail *n.* dum دم, pūṁch پونچھ
tailor *n.* darzī درزی, pārcāh dōz پارچہ دوز, xaiyāt خیاط
take *v.* lēnā لینا, rakh lēnā رکھ لینا
take a bath *v.* nahānā نہانا
take a bribe *v.* paisā khānā پیسا کھانا
take a nap *v.* jhapkī lēnā جھپکی لینا
take a photo *v.* fōṭō khaiṁcnā فوٹو کھینچنا, fōṭō lēnā فوٹو لینا
take a vow *v.* murād mānnā مراد ماننا
take advice *v.* mušvarah karnā مشورہ کرنا, salāḥ karnā صلاح کرنا
take an oath *v.* ḥalaf uṭhānā حلف اٹھانا, qasam khānā قسم کھانا, saugand khānā سوگند کھانا
take away *v.* uṭhā lēnā اُٹھا لینا
take back *v.* lē lēnā لے لینا
take by force *v.* harnā ہرنا
take care *v.* xabar gīrī karnā خبر گیری کرنا, xabar lēnā خبر لینا
take care of *v.* mavāzabat karnā موظبت کرنا
take down *v.* utār lēnā اُتار لینا, utārnā اُتارنا
take leave *v.* ruxsat hōnā رخصت ہونا
take medicine *v.* davā khānā دوا کھانا
take off one's clothes *v.* kapṛē utārnā کپڑے اتارنا
take offense *v.* jī burā karnā جی برا کرنا
take out *v.* nikālnā نکالنا
take pains *v.* takalluf karnā تکلف کرنا
take place *v.* baratnā برتنا
take precautions *v.* iḥtiyāt karnā اِحتیاط کرنا
take revenge *v.* badlā lēnā بدلا لینا, intiqām lēnā انتقام لینا

take root *v.* jamnā جمنا
take sides *v.* taraf dārī karnā طرف داری کرنا
take someone's life *v.* jī lēnā جی لینا
take time *v.* vaqt lagnā وقت لگنا
take the trouble *v.* taklīf karnā تکلیف کرنا
take upon oneself *v.* zimmah lēnā ذمہ لینا
tale *n.* dāstān داستان, ḥikāyat حکایت, kahānī کہانی, naql نقل, qissah قصہ
talebearer *n.* cuġl xōr چغل خور
talebearing *n.* cuġlī چغلی
talented *adj.* fāzil-ē-ajall فاضل اجل, gunī گنی
talisman *n.* tilism طلسم
talk *n.* carcā چرچا, guft-ō-šunīd گفت و شنید, maqāl مقال, saxun/suxan سخن / *v.* bāt karnā بات کرنا, bōlnā بولنا, kalām karnā کلام کرنا
talk about *v.* carcā karnā چرچا کرنا
talk face to face *v.* dō ba-dō kēhnā دو بدو کہنا
talk nonsense *v.* xarāfāt buknā خرافات بکنا, zaṭal mārnā زٹل مارنا
talk stupidly *v.* bhaunknā بھونکنا
talkative *adj.* jhakkī جھکی, lassān لسان, maġz caṭ مغزچٹ, taqrīrī تقریری
talkative person *n.* bātūnī باتونی, bhangaṛ بھنگڑ
talking *adj.* saxun pardāz سخن پرداز
tall *adj.* darāz دراز, lambā لمبا, qadd āvar قدآور, ūṁca اونچا
tall tower *n.* mīnār مینار
tallness *n.* darāzī درازی, ūṁchā'ī اونچائی
tamarind *n.* imlī املی
tamarind tree *n.* imlī املی
tambour *n.* tambūr طنبور
tambourine *n.* tablah طبلہ, tanbūrā تنبورا
tame *adj.* gharēlū گھریلو / *v.* pōsnā پوسنا, sadhānā سدھانا
tangent *n.* mamās مماس
tangled hair *n.* laṭ لٹ
tank *n.* kunḍ کنڈ, tālāb تالاب
tap *n.* thāp تھاپ / *v.* thāpnā تھاپنا
tape *n.* fītah فیتہ
taper *adj.* maxrūtī مخروطی

tapestry *n.* qālī bāft قالی بافت, qālīcah قلیچہ
target *n.* cānd چاند, hadaf ہدف, nišānah نشانہ, zad زد
tariff *n.* dar در, nirx نرخ
task *n.* kām کام
taste *n.* lazzat لذت, mazah مزہ, savād سواد, zā'iqah ذائقہ / *v.* cakhnā چکھنا, cāṭnā چاٹنا, zā'iqah lēnā ذائقہ لینا
tasteful *adj.* lazīz لذیذ, mazēdār مزیدار
tasteless *adj.* bē zauq بے ذوق, māsax ماسخ, phīkā پھیکا
tastelessness *n.* bad mazgī بدمزگی
tasty *adj.* lazīz لذیذ, zā'iqah dār ذائقہ دار
tatter *n.* cithṛā چھتڑا
taunt *n.* kināyah کنایہ, mihnā مہنا, taᶜn-ō-tašnīᶜ طعن و تشنیع / *v.* bōl mārnā بول مارنا, taᶜnah mārnā طعنہ مارنا
taunting *n.* taᶜn zanī طعن زنی
Taurus *(Zodiac) n.* saur ثور
tavern *n.* šarāb xānah شراب خانہ
tax *n.* fōtah فوطہ, xirāj خراج, maḥsūl محصول / *v.* xirāj lagānā خراج لگانا
taxable *adj.* maḥsūlī محصولی
taxi *n.* ṭaiksī ٹیکسی
tea *n.* cā'ē چائے ♦ ~ **with milk** dūdh vālī cā'ē دودھ والی چائے
teach *v.* dars dēnā درس دینا, paṛhānā پڑھانا, sikhānā سکھانا, sikhlānā سکھلانا
teacher *n.* gurū گرو, muᶜallim معلم, mudarris مدرس, ustād اُستاد
teaching *n.* muᶜallimī معلمی, paṛhā'ī پڑھائی, taᶜlīm تعلیم
teacup *n.* piyālī پیالی
teak tree *n.* sāgvān ساگوان
teakwood *n.* sāgvān ساگوان
teapot *n.* cā'ē dānī چائے دانی
tear *n.* *(rip)* āṁsū آنسو, ašk اشک / *v.* cāk karnā چاک کرنا, cīrnā چیرنا, khasōṭnā کھسوٹنا, tōṛnā توڑنا ♦ ~ **into pieces** *v.* dhajjī uṛānā دھجی اڑانا
tears *n.* āb-ē-cašm آبِ چشم ♦ **false** ~ *n.* ṭisvē ٹسوے
tease *v.* chēṛnā چھیڑنا, diqq karnā دق کرنا, satānā ستانا, sir khānā سر کھانا
teased *adj* zic زچ
teasing *adj.* haṭṭilā ہٹیلا

teat *n.* than تھن
technical term *n.* istilāḥ اصطلاح, mustalaḥ مصطلح
telephone *n.* fōn فون, ṭailīfōn ٹیلیفون
telescope *n.* dūrbīn دوربین
television/TV *n.* ṭailīvižan ٹیلیویژن, ṭī vī ٹی وی
tell *v.* batānā بتانا, batlānā بتلانا, kahnā کہنا, sunānā سنانا
tell jokes *v.* mazḥakah uṛānā مضحکہ اڑانا
tell a lie *v.* jhūṭ bōlnā جھوٹ بولنا
telling *adj.* gō گو
temper *n.* jabillat جبلت, tabaᶜ طبع / *v.* muᶜtadil karnā معتدل کرنا
temperament *n.* mizāj مزاج, tabīᶜat طبیعت
temperate *adj.* maddham مدھم, muᶜtadil معتدل, muttaqī متقی
temperate season *n.* mīṭhā mausim میٹھا موسم
temple *n.* mandir مندر, xānah-ē-xudā خانہ خدا; *(any place of worship)* muᶜabad معبد; *(where idols are kept)* sanam kadah صنم کدہ
temporary *adj.* cand rōzah چند روزہ
tempt *v.* tamaᶜ dēnā طمع دینا, tarġīb dēnā ترغیب دینا, varġalānā ورغلانا
temptation *n.* ibtilā ابتلا, tarġīb ترغیب, vasvasah وسوسہ
tempted *adj.* maftūn مفتون
ten *num.* dah دہ, das دس
tenant *n.* kirāyah dār کرایہ دار, māl guzār مال گذار, mustājir مستاجر
tendency *n.* mail میل
tender *adj.* kōmal کومل, mulā'im ملائم, ratb رطب
tenderhearted *adj.* mōm dil موم دل
tenderness *n.* kōmalnā کوملنا, mamtā ممتا, mulā'imat ملائمت
tennis *n.* ṭainis ٹینس
tenon *n.* cūl چول
tenseness *n.* khicā'ō کھچاؤ
tension *n.* ainṭhan اینٹھن, kaşīdagī کشیدگی
tent *n.* xaimah خیمہ, tambū تمبو
tenth *adj.* dahum دہم, dasvāṁ دسواں
term *n.* mīᶜād میعاد, šart شرط, vaqt وقت
terminable *adj.* miyᶜādī میعادی
termination *n.* aṁjām انجام, ᶜāqibat عاقبت, mā'al مآل, intihā انتہا

terrace *n.* bām بام, cabutrah چبوترہ
terrestrial *adj.* arzī ارضی
terrible *adj.* ḍarā'ōnā ڈراؤنا, haul nāk ہولناک, muhīb مہیب
terrified *adj.* xauf zadah خوف زدہ, haul zadah ہول زدہ
terrify *v.* ḍarānā ڈرانا
terrifying *adj.* dahšat angēz دہشت انگیز, ḍarā'ōnā ڈراؤنا
territory *n.* kišvar کشور, mulk ملک, dēs دیس, dēš دیش, sar zamīn سرزمین, xittah خطہ
terror *n.* dahšat دہشت
terrorist *n.* dahšat gurū دہشت گرو
test *n.* āzmā'iš آزمائش, imtiḥān امتحان, jāṁc جانچ, tajribah تجربہ / *v.* āzmānā آزمانا, jāṁcnā جانچنا, parakhnā پرکھنا
testament *n.* vasiyyat nāmah وصیت نامہ, vasiyyat وصیت
tested *adj.* cakhā hū'ā چکھا ہوا
tester *n.* mumtaḥin ممتحن
testicle *n.* baizah بیضہ
testimonial *n.* sanad سند
testimony *n.* gavāhī گواہی, subūt ثبوت
text *n.* inšā' انشاء; *(sacred)* mantar منتر
than *prep.* sē سے
thank *v.* šukr karnā شکر کرنا
thank you *interj.* šukriyā شکریا
thanked *adj.* maškūr مشکور
thankful *adj.* mamnūn ممنون, maškūr مشکور, šukr guzār شکرگزار
thankfulness *n.* iḥsān mandī اِحسان مندی
thanklessness *n.* kufrān-ē-niᶜmat کفران نعمت
thanks *interj.* šukriyā شکریا / *n.* šukr شکر
that *adv.* cūnkēh چونکہ / *prep.* mā ما / *pron.* jō جو, jis جس, us اس, vah/vōh وہ / *pron./conj.* kih/kē کہ
thatch *v.* chānā چھانا
thatched roof *n.* chān چھان
theater *n.* tamāša gāh تماشا گاہ, thiyēṭar تھیٹر
thee *pron.* tum , tujh تجھ تم
theft *n.* cōrī چوری, sarqah سرقہ
them *pron.* in اِن, inhēṁ, unhēṁ انہیں, un اُن, vah/vōh وہ

then *adj./adv.* phir پھر / *adv.* pas پس, tab تب, vahīṁ وہیں / *pron.* tō تو
theology *n.* ᶜilm-ē-ilahī علم الٰہی, fiqah/fiqh فقہ
there *adv.* udhar ادھر, vahāṁ وہاں
there to *adv.* tahāṁ تہاں, vahāṁ وہاں
thereafter *adv.* tab sē تب سے
therefore *adv.* is li'ē اس لئے, lihazā لہذا / *conj./adv.* sō سو / *pron.* tō تو
thereupon *adv.* us par اس پر
these *pron.* in اِن
these days *adv.* in dinōṁ اِن دنوں
they *pron.* vah/vōh وہ
thick *adj.* gāṛhā گاڑھا, guṁjān گنجان, kasīf کسیف, mōṭā موٹا
thickness *n.* taksīf تکثیف, kasāfat کثافت, zaxāmat ضخامت
thief *n.* cōr چور
thigh *n.* rān ران, zānū زانو
thin *adj.* bārik باریک, mahīn مہین, patlā پتلا
thing *n.* cīz چیز
think *v.* sōcnā سوچنا, andēšah karnā اندیشہ کرنا, fikr karnā فکر کرنا, xayāl karnā خیال کرنا
thinking *adj.* mufakkir مفکر
thinness *n.* lāġarī لاغری, riqqat رقت
third *adj.* tīsrā تیسرا
third person *n.* s̱ālis ثالث
thirst *n.* ᶜataš عطش, piyās پیاس tišnagī تشنگی
thirsty *adj.* piyāsā پیاسا tišnah تشنہ
thirteen *num.* tērah تیرہ
thirteenth *adj.* tērhavāṁ تیرھواں
thirtieth *adj.* tīsvāṁ تیسواں
thirty *num.* tīs تیس
thirty-one *num.* iktīs اکتیس
thirty-two *num.* battīs بتیس
thirty-three *num.* taiṇtīs تینتیس
thirty-four *num.* cauntīs چونتیس
thirty-five *num.* paiṃtīs پینتیس
thirty-six *num.* chattīs چھتیس
thirty-seven *num.* saiṁtīs سینتیس

thirty-eight *num.* aṛtīs اڑتیں
thirty-nine *num.* untālīs انتالیں
this *pron.* hazā ہذا, is اس, yēh یہ
this day *adv.* āj tak آج تک
this place *adv.* idhar اِدھر
this year *adv.* imsāl امسال
thorn *n.* kānṭā کانٹا, xār خار
thorny *adj.* nukīlā نکیلا, xār dār خاردار
thoroughfare *n.* guzar-ē-ᶜām گزر عام, šāriᶜ-ē-ᶜām شارع عام
thoroughly *adv.* bạxūbī بخوبی, tamām-ō-kamāl تمام وکمال
those *pron.* un اُن, vah/vōh وہ
though *adv.* gōyā گویا, vaisē ویسے / *conj.* agar cih اگرچہ
thought *n.* andēšah اندیشہ, sōc سوچ, xayāl خیال, fikr فکر
thoughtful *adj.* andēš mand اندیش مند, fikr mand فکر مند, gambhīr گمبھیر
thoughtless *adj.* bē fikr بے فکر, bē parvā بے پروا, nā andēš نا اندیش
thoughtlessly *adv.* bē andēšah بے اندیشہ
thousand *num.* alf الف, hazār ہزار
thrash *v.* kūṭnā کوٹنا
thrashing *n.* zad-ō-kōb زدوکوب
thread *n.* dhāgā دھاگا, ḍōrī ڈوری, sūt سوت, tār تار / *v.* tāgnā تاگنا; *(~ a needle)* dhāgā ḍālnā دھاگا ڈالنا, sū'ī pirōnā سوئی پرونا
threaded *adj.* munsalik منسلک
threat *n.* dhamkī دھمکی, tahdīd تہدید, taxvīf تخویف
threaten *v.* ḍānṭnā ڈانٹنا, dhamkānā دھمکانا, dabkī mārnā دبکی مارنا
three *num.* tīn تین
threshold *n.* caukhaṭ چوکھٹ, dahlēz دہلیز, ḍē'ōṛhī ڈیوڑھی
thrift *n.* kifāyat šiᶜārī کفایت شعاری, kifāyat کفایت
thrifty *adj.* kifāyat šiᶜār کفایت شعار, kam xarc کم خرچ, kifāyatī کفایتی
thrive *v.* phalnā پھلنا
throat *n.* galā گلا, gulū گلو, ḥalq حلق
throb *n.* ṭīs ٹیس / *v.* dhamaknā دھمکنا, ṭīs mārnā ٹیس مارنا
throbbing *n.* dhamak دھمک, ṭīs ٹیس
throne *n.* rāj gaddī راج گدی, taxt تخت ♦ **sit on the ~** *v.* taxt par baiṭhnā تخت پر بیٹھنا

throttle *n.* ḥanjarah خنجره / *v.* ṭēnṭū'ā dabānā ٹینٹوا دبانا
through *adv.* badaulat بدولت, pār پار / *prep.* kē zarīᶜah کے ذریعہ, sē سے
throw *n.* phēnk پھینک / *v.* ḍālnā ڈالنا, jhōnknā جھونکنا, phēnknā پھینکنا
throw away *v.* ḍāl dēnā ڈال دینا, ganvānā گنوانا, phēnk dēnā پھینک دینا
throw up *v.* uchālnā اچھالنا
thrust *n.* hūl ہول / *v.* bhōnknā بھونکنا, ghusēṛnā گھسیڑنا, haulnā ہولنا
thumb *n.* angūṭhā انگوٹھا, dhaul دھول / *v.* dhūl lagānā دھول لگانا, dhūl mārnā دھول مارنا
thump *n.* mukkā مکا
thumping *n.* dhamak دھمک
thunder *n.* raᶜd رعد / *v.* garajnā گرجنا, kaṛaknā کڑکنا
thunderbolt *n.* sāᶜiqah صاعقہ
thundering *n.* dhāṛ دھاڑ, garaj گرج
Thursday *n.* jumiᶜrāt جمعرات
thus *adv.* vaisē ویسے, yūṁ hī یوں ہی, yūṁ یوں
thy *pron.* tērā تیرا
tick *n.* cīcṛī چیچڑی
ticket *n./v.* ṭikaṭ ٹکٹ
tickle *v.* sahlānā سہلانا
tidiness *n.* suthrā'ī ستھرائی
tidy *adj.* suthrā ستھرا
tie *v.* bāndhnā باندھنا, jakaṛnā جکڑنا, kasnā کسنا; *(~ a knot)* gāṁṭhnā گانٹھنا
tied *adj.* bandhā بندھا
tiger *n.* šēr شیر
tight *adj.* jakaṛband جکڑبند, mubram مبرم, tank تنگ
tighten *v.* jakaṛnā جکڑنا, kasnā کسنا, sukaṛnā سکیڑنا, khaiṁcnā کھینچنا
tightening *n.* ainṭh اینٹھ
tightness *n.* kas کس, khicā'ō کھچاؤ, tankī تنگی
tigress *n.* šērnī شیرنی
tile *n.* sifāl سفال
till *v.* zarāᶜat karnā زراعت کرنا
timber *n.* kāṭh کاٹھ, cōb چوب, lakṛī لکڑی
time *n.* muddat مدت, sāᶜat ساعت, vaqt وقت, zamān زمان ♦ **take** ~ *v.* vaqt lagnā وقت لگنا

timid *adj.* bōdā بودا, buz dil بزدل, ḍarpōk ڈرپوک

tin *n.* kanistar کنستر, qalaᶜī قلعی, xum خم

tinkle *n.* ṭhan ṭhan ٹھن ٹھن

tinkling *n.* jhankār جھنکار

tinner *n.* qalaᶜī gar قلعی گر

tinsmith *n.* qalaᶜī gar قلعی گر

tint *n.* gūṁ گوں

tiny *adj.* nanhā ننھا

tip *n.* nōk نوک, sirā سرا; *(in a restaurant)* baxšiš بخشش

tipsy *adj.* sar karāṁ سرگراں

tire *n.* hāl ہال, ṭāyar ٹائر / *v.* harāna ہرانا

tired *adj.* malūl ملول, thakā تھکا, vā mānda وا ماندہ

tiredness *n.* takān تکان, thakāvaṭ تھکاوٹ

title *n.* ᶜunvān عنوان, ādāb-ō-alqāb آداب والقاب, laqab لقب, xitāb خطاب

to *adv.* tak تک, tā تا / *prep.* bah nisbat بہ نسبت, kō کو, sē سے

tobacco *n.* tambākū تمباکو

today *adv.* āj آج, imrōz امروز

together *adv./adj.* bāham باہم, ham rāh ہم راہ, maᶜan معاً, sāth sāth ساتھ ساتھ

together with *adj.* samēt سمیت

togetherness (with) *n.* ham rāh ہم راہ

toil *n.* mašaqqat مشقت, miḥnat محنت, taᶜab تعب / *v.* mārā mār karnā مارامار کرنا

toilet *n.* ġusl xānah غسل خانہ

toilet paper *n.* ṭā'ilēṭ pēpar ٹائلیٹ پیپر

token *n.* nišānī نشانی

tolerable *adj.* muᶜtadil معتدل

tolerance *n.* bardāšt برداشت, burdbārī بردباری, šikēb شکیب

tolerant *adj.* burdbār بردبار, šikēbā شکیبا

tolerate *v.* gavārā karnā گوارا کرنا, jhēlnā جھیلنا, sahnā سہنا, sahārnā سہارنا

toleration *n.* ravādārī رواداری

toll *n.* guzārah گزارہ, maḥsūl محصول, rāh dārī راہ داری

toll duty *n.* rāh dārī راہ داری

tomato *n.* ṭamāṭar ٹماٹر

tomb *n.* gōr گور, maqbarah مقبرہ, marqad مرقد

tomorrow *n.* kal کل
tone *n.* dhun دھن, laḥjah لہجہ, naġm نغم, sadā صدا
tongs *n.* cimṭā چمٹا
tongue *n.* jibh جیبھ, lisān لسان, zabān زبان
tonight *adv.* imšab امشب
too *adv.* bhī بھی, hūṁ ہوں
too late *adv.* dēr sē دیر سے
too much *adv.* ziyādah زیادہ
tool *n.* ālah آلہ, hathiyār ہتھیار
tools *n.* kīl kānṭā کیل کانٹا
tooth *n.* dandān دندان, dānt دانت
toothbrush *n.* dāntan دانتن, dātan داتن; *(used in the countryside)* misvāk مسواک
toothless *adj.* pōplā پوپلا
toothpick *n.* xilāl خلال
top *n.* cōṭī چوٹی, laṭṭū لٹو
topaz *n.* pukhrāj پکھراج
topple (over) *v.* luṛhaknā لڑھکنا
topsy-turvy *adj.* munaᶜkis منعکس, ulṭā الٹا, zēr-ō-zabar زیر وزبر
torch *n.* falītah فلیتہ, mašᶜal مشعل
torment *n.* aziyat اذیت, tā'alum تالم
torment *v.* bhūnnā بھوننا, pīchē paṛnā پیچھے پڑنا satānā ستانا
torn *adj.* cāk چاک, farsūdah فرسودہ, phaṭā پھٹا
torrent *n.* sailāb سیلاب
torture *n.* ᶜuqūbat عقوبت, aziyyat اذیت, kōft کوفت / *v.* taklīf dēnā تکلیف دینا
toss *v.* jhōnknā جھونکنا, lōṭnā لوٹنا
toss up *v.* uchālnā اچھالنا
total *adj.* mutlaq مطلق, sab سب, tamām تمام / *n.* ḥāsil jamaᶜ حاصل جمع, jamaᶜ جمع, jōṛ جوڑ
totally *adv.* min jumlah من جملہ
totter *v.* ḍagmagānā ڈگمگانا, laṛkhaṛānā لڑکھڑانا
touch *n.* chūṭ چھوٹ, lāmisah لامسہ, mas مس / *v.* chūnā چھونا, lagnā لگنا
touched *adj.* mutā'assir متاثر
touching *adj.* dil sōz دل سوز, lāḥiq لاحق, mu'assir موثر / *n.* mamās مماس

touchstone *n.* kasauṭī کسوٹی, miʿyār معیار
tour *n.* daurah دورہ, gašt گشت
towards *adv.* jānib جانب
towel *n.* tauliyā تولیا
tower *n.* burj برج, kāx کاخ ♦ **tall** ~ *n.* mīnār مینار
town *n.* šahr/šahar شہر, nagar نگر, qaryah قریہ
town hall *n.* majlis xānah مجلس خانہ
townsman *n.* šahrī شہری
toy *n.* kāṭh putlī کاٹھ پتلی, khilaunā کھلونا
trace *n.* asar اثر, khōj کھوج, surāġ سراغ / *v.* ṭōh lagānā ٹوہ لگانا, xākah utārnā خاکہ اتارنا
track *n.* maslak مسلک, surāġ سراغ
track (down) *v.* khōj nikālnā کھوج نکالنا
trade *n.* byōpār بیوپار, kārōbār کاروبار, lēn dēn لین دین, saudāgarī سوداگری, tijārat تجارت / *v.* lēn dēn karnā لین دین کرنا, tijārat karnā تجارت کرنا
trade fair *n.* mēlā میلا
trader *n.* byōpārī بیوپاری, dukāndār دکاندار, kārōbārī کاروباری, tājir تاجر
tradesman *n.* pēšah var پیشہ ور, saudāgar سوداگر
tradition *n.* ḥadīs حدیث, tadāvul تداول
traditional *adj.* rivājī رواجی, rivāyatī روایتی
traffic *n.* āmad-ō-raft آمد و رفت, byōpār بیوپار, lēn dēn لین دین, murūr مرور
traffic light *n.* signal سگنل
tragic *adj.* šāqq شاق
train *n.* rēl ریل, rēlgāṛī ریل گاڑی, ṭrēn ٹرین, gāṛī گاڑی / *v.* sadhānā سدھانا, tarbiyat karnā تربیت کرنا
training *n.* riyāzat ریاضت, tarbiyat تربیت
traitor *n.* bāġī باغی
trample *v.* kucalnā کچلنا, malnā ملنا, raundnā روندنا
tranquil *adj.* sākin ساکن, xātir xavāh خاطر خواہ
tranquility *n.* ārām آرام, qanāʿat قناعت, xātir jamaʿ خاطر جمع
transaction *n.* muʿāmalah معاملہ
transcendent *adj.* mufrit مفرط
transfer *n.* intiqāl انتقال, tabādalah تبادلہ, tahvīl تحویل / *v.* bēcn بیچنا, intiqāl karnā انتقال کرنا, tabdīl karnā تبدیل کرنا

transferable *adj.* qābil-ē-intiqāl قابل انتقال
transformation *n.* tanāsux تناسخ, ulaṭ الٹ
transgression *n.* tajāvuz تجاوز
transit *v.* pahuṁcānā پہنچانا
transition *n.* murūr مرور
transitory *adj.* cand rōzah چند روزہ, fānī فانی, nā pā'īdār ناپائیدار
translate *v.* tarjumah karnā ترجمہ کرنا
translation *n.* tarjumah ترجمہ
translator *n.* mutarjim مترجم, tarjumān ترجمان
transmigration *n.* tanāsux تناسخ
transparent *adj.* sāf ṣaffāf صاف شفاف, šaffāf شفاف
transport *n.* naql نقل / *v.* ḍhōnā ڈھونا, intiqāl karnā انتقال کرنا
transported *adj.* muntaqqal منتقل
trap *n.* jāl جال, piṁjrā پنجرا
trash *n.* kacrā کچرا, karkaṭ کرکٹ
travel *n.* safar سفر / *v.* ghūmnā گھومنا, safar karnā سفر کرنا
traveler *n.* sālik سالک, musāfir مسافر, rāh gīr راہ گیر, rāhī راہی, sayyāḥ سیاح
traveler's check *n.* ṭraivalars cēk ٹریولرس چیک
traveling *n.* musāfirī مسافری
traveling expenses *n.* safar xarc سفر خرچ, zād-ē-rāh زاد راہ
tray *n.* khāṁcā کھانچا, tabaq طبق, thāl تھال, xvān خوان
treacherous *adj.* bē vafā بے وفا, daġā bāz دغا باز, ġaddār غدار
treachery *n.* daġā bāzī دغا بازی
tread *v.* malnā ملنا, pair dharnā پیر دھرنا
treasure *n.* gaṁjīnah گنجینہ, xazānah خزانہ, kōš کوش, zaxīrah ذخیرہ ♦ **hidden ~** dafīnah دفینہ
treasurer *n.* gaṁjūr گنجور, taḥvīldār تحویلدار, xāzan خازن
treasury *n.* bayt-ul-māl بیت المال, maxzan مخزن, xazānah خزانہ
treat *v.* davā dārū karnā دوا دارو کرنا, muᶜālajah karnā معالجہ کرنا; *(~ a disease)* ᶜilāj karnā علاج کرنا
treatment *n.* ᶜilāj علاج, muᶜālajah معالجہ, mudāvā مداوا۔ مداومت, mudāvāt مداوات
treaty *n.* ᶜahd nāmah عہد نامہ, ᶜahd-ō-paimān عہد وپیمان
tree *n.* daraxt درخت, pēṛ پیڑ, šajar شجر

tremble *v.* ḍagmagānā ڈگمگانا, kāṁpnā کانپنا, laraznā لرزنا, tharrānā تھرانا
trembling *adj.* ḍagmag ڈگمگ, larzāṁ لرزاں / *n.* kapkapī کپکپی, larziš لرزش, phurairī پھریری
tremendous *adj.* muhīb مہیب
tremor *n.* raᶜšah رعشہ
trench *n.* khā'ī کھائی
trespass *v.* tajāvuz karnā تجاوز کرنا
trial *n.* āzmā'iš آزمائش, imtiḥān امتحان, jāṁc جانچ, tajribah تجربہ
triangle *n.* sēh gōšah سہ گوشہ
triangular *adj.* musallas مثلث, sēh gōšah سہ گوشہ
tribal *adj.* qaumī قومی
tribe *n.* jāt جات, qabīlah قبیلہ, qaum قوم
tribunal *n.* dīvān دیوان, maḥkamah محکمہ
tribute *n.* jiziyah جزیہ, nazrānah نذرانہ, pēškaš پیشکش, xirāj خراج
trick *n.* chal چھل, ḍhōng ڈھونگ, farēb فریب / *v.* jhāṁsnā جھانسنا
trickery *n.* cakmah چکمہ, chal bal چھل بل
trickle *v.* būnd ṭapaknā بوند ٹپکنا
tricks *n.* sāt pāṁc سات پانچ
tricky *adj.* ḍhōngyā ڈھونگیا, dil farēb دل فریب, muftarī مفتری, pharphandī پھرپھندی
tried *adj.* jacā جچا
trifle *adj.* nā cīz ناچیز
trigger *n.* kal کل
trilateral *adj.* musallas مثلث
trim *v.* katarnā کترنا, qaiṁcī karnā قینچی کرنا, xatt banānā خط بنانا
trinity *n.* sālūs ثالوث; *(in religion or astrology)* taslīs تثلیث
triple *adj.* musallas مثلث, tihrā تہرا
triumph *n.* fatḥ mandī فتح مندی, jai جے, nusrat نصرت, umang امنگ, zafar ظفر
triumphant *adj.* fatḥ mand فتح مند, mansūr منصور
trivial *adj.* xafīf خفیف
trolley *n.* ṭhēlah ٹھیلہ
troop *n.* ġōl غول, tuman تمن, zumrah زمرہ
trot *(of a horse) n.* dulkī دلکی

trouble *n.* āzurdagī آزردگی, parēšānī پریشانی, taklīf تکلیف, zaḥmat زحمت / *v.* īzā dēnā ایذا دینا, satānā ستانا, taklīf dēnā تکلیف دینا ♦ **take the ~** *v.* taklīf karnā تکلیف کرنا
troubled *adj.* āzurdah آزردہ, diqq دق, muztarib مضطرب, parēšān پریشان
troublesome *adj.* huṛdangī ہڑدنگی, šāqq شاق
trousers *n.* painṭ پینٹ, patlūn پتلون, šalvār شلوار
truce *n.* iltivā'-ē-jang التوائے جنگ, sulḥ صلح
true *adj.* bā vafā با وفا, ḥaqīqī حقیقی, sac سچ, saccā سچا, masdūr مصدور
true believer *n.* mōmin مومن
truly *adj.* ḥaqqā حقا / *adv.* ḥaqīqatan حقیقتاً, sac muc سچ مچ, vāqaᶜī واقعی
trumpet *n.* qarnā'ī قرنائی / *v. (like an elephant)* cinghāṛnā چنگھاڑنا
trunk *n.* dhaṛ دھڑ, sandūq/sundūq صندوق; *(of a tree)* tanah تنہ; *(of an elephant)* sūnḍ سونڈ
trust *n.* ᶜimād عماد, iᶜtibār اعتبار, yaqīn یقین, zimmah dārī ذمہ داری / *v.* iᶜtibār karnā اعتبار کرنا, ummīd rakhnā امید رکھنا
trustee *n.* amīn امین, mutavallī متولی, zimmah dār ذمہ دار
trusting *adj.* mutavakkil متوکل
trustworthiness *n.* muᶜtabarī معتبری
trustworthy *adj.* iᶜtibārī اعتباری, muᶜtabar معتبر, qābil-ē-iᶜtibār قابل اعتبار
trusty *adj.* rāz dār رازدار
truth *n.* ḥaqīqat حقیقت, ḥaqq حق, sac سچ, saccā'ī سچائی
truth-loving *adj.* ḥaqq pasand حق پسند
truthful *adj.* rāst bāz راست باز, sādiq-ul-qaul صادق القول
try *v.* kōšiš karnā کوشش کرنا, parakhnā پرکھنا; *(~ food)* cakhnā چکھنا
  try one's best *v.* mārā mār karnā مارامار کرنا
  try to forget *v.* bhulānā بھلانا
tub *n.* taġār تغار
tube *n.* nāl نال, nālī نالی
Tuesday *n.* mangal منگل
tuition *n.* atāliqī اتالیقی
tulip *n.* gul-ē-lālah گل لالہ, lālah لالہ
tumble *v.* girna گرنا
tumor *n.* rasaulī رسولی, varam ورم

tumult *n.* afrātafrī افراتفری, hangāmah ہنگامہ, khalbalī کھلبلی, šōriš شورش
tumultuous *adj.* huṛdangī ہڑدنگی
tune *n.* gat گت, la'ē لے, ham āhangī ہم آہنگی, tān تان
tunic *n.* kurtah کرتہ
tunnel *n.* surang سرنگ
turban *n.* ᶜimāmah عمامہ, dastār دستار, pagṛī پگڑی
turbulance *n.* šōr-ō-ġul شوروغل
turbulent *adj.* fitnah angēz فتنہ انگیز, huṛdangī ہڑدنگی
Turk *n.* turk ترک, turkī ترکی
turkey *(fowl) n.* fīl murġ فیل مرغ, pērū پیرو
Turkish *adj.* turkī ترکی, rūmī رومی
Turkish bath *n.* ḥammām حمام
turmeric *n.* haldī ہلدی
turn *n.* daur دور, mōṛ موڑ, phēr پھیر / *v.* ghūmnā گھومنا, marōṛnā مروڑنا, mōṛnā موڑنا, muṛnā مڑنا, phirnā پھرنا
  turn around *v.* ulaṭnā الٹنا
  turn back *v.* muṛnā مڑنا, pīṭh phērnā پیٹھ پھیرنا
  turn over *v.* lauṭnā لوٹنا, phērnā پھیرنا; ulaṭnā الٹنا
  turn pale *v.* zard hō jānā زرد ہو جانا
turned *adj.* maᶜṭūf معطوف
turned down *adj.* mustaradd مسترد
turner *n.* xarādī خرادی
turning *n.* gardān گردان, palṭā پلٹا, phēr پھیر
turquoise *n. (gem)* fīrōzah فیروزہ / *adj. (color)* fīrōzī فیروزی
turtledove *n.* qumrī قمری
tusk *n.* dānt دانت
tutor *n.* atālīq اتالیق, gurū گرو, muᶜallim معلم
tutorship *n.* muᶜallimī معلمی
TV *n.* ṭī vī ٹی وی
twelfth *adj.* bārhavāṁ بارھواں
twelve *num.* bārah بارہ
twentieth *adj.* bisvāṁ بیسواں
twenty *num.* bīs بیس
  twenty-one *num.* ikkīs اکیس

twenty-two *num.* bā'īs بائیس
twenty-three *num.* tē'īs تئیس
twenty-four *num.* caubīs چوبیس
twenty-five *num.* paccīs پچیس
twenty-six *num.* chabbīs چھبیس
twenty-seven *num.* sattā'is ستائیس
twenty-eight *num.* aṭhā'īs اٹھائیس
twenty-nine *num.* untīs انتیس
twice *adv.* dōbārah دوبارہ
twig *n.* šāx شاخ, ṭahnī ٹہنی qamcī قمچی, ; *(used to brush one's teeth)* dāntan دانتن, dātan داتن
twilight *n.* šafaq شفق
twin *n.* tavām توام
twinkle *v.* maṭaknā مٹکنا, maṭkānā مٹکانا, ṭimṭimānā ٹمٹمانا
twinkling *n.* saṁsanāhaṭ سنسناہٹ; *(of an eye)* palak پلک
twins *n.* juṛvāṁ جڑواں
twist *n.* pēc پیچ, ainṭhan اینٹھن, albēṭ البیٹ / *v.* ainṭhnā اینٹھنا, baṭnā بٹنا, pēc dēnā پیچ دینا
twisted *adj.* pēc dār پیچ دار pēcīdah پیچیدہ
twisting *n.* ainṭh اینٹھ, pēcīdgī پیچیدگی
twitch *n.* hūk ہوک, jhaṭkā جھٹکا / *v.* jhaṭaknā جھٹکنا, phaṛaknā پھڑکنا
two *num.* dō دو
tyrannical *adj.* siyāh kār سیاہ کار
tyrannize *v.* zulm karnā ظلم کرنا
tyranny *n.* jaur جور, muzlimah مظلمہ, zulm ظلم, sitam ستم
tyrant *adj.* haṭ dharm ہٹ دھرم / *n.* jābir جابر, zālim ظالم

U

udder *n.* than تھن
ugliness *n.* bad sūratī بد صورتی, zištī زشتی
ugly *adj.* bad sūrat بد صورت, bad šakl بد شکل, zišt زشت
umbrella *n.* chātā چھاتا, chatr/chattar چھتر
unable *adj.* ᶜājiz عاجز, qāsir قاصر
unacceptable *adj.* nā pasandīdah ناپسندیده
unacquainted *adj.* nā āšnā نا آشنا
unambitious *adj.* bē himmat بے ہمت
unanimous *adj.* yak dil یک دل
unanimously *adv.* bil-ittēfāq بالاتفاق
unarmed *adj.* xālī hāth خالی ہاتھ
unattainable *adj.* agam اگم
unavoidable *adj.* lā bud لابد, zarūr ضرور
unaware *adj.* lā ᶜilm لا علم / *adv.* aṁjānē انجانے
unbearable *adj.* mā lā yutāq مالا یطاق
uncertain *adj.* maškūk مشکوک
uncertainty *n.* dubdhā دبدھا, dugdā دگدا, šubah شبہ, tazabzub تذبذب
unchaste *adj.* fājir فاجر
uncivilized *adj.* nā tarāšīdah ناتراشیده, vaḥšī وحشی
uncle *n.* *(father's brother)* cacā چچا, ᶜamm عم, kākā کاکا; *(husband of mother's sister)* xālū خالو; *(maternal)* māmā ماما, māmūṁ ماموں; *(paternal)* cācā چاچا
unclean *adj.* nā pāk ناپاک, palīd پلید
uncleanliness *n.* janābat جنابت, nā pākī ناپاکی
uncommon *adj.* anōkhā انوکھا, ġair maᶜmūlī غیر معمولی
unconditional *adj.* ġair mašrūt غیر مشروط
unconquered *adj.* ajīt اجیت
unconscious *adj.* madhōš مدہوش
unconsciously *adv.* aṁjānē انجانے
uncover *v.* ughāṛnā اگھاڑنا
undefiled *adj.* pākbāz پاکباز
under *adj.* farō/firō فرو / *adv.* pā'īṁ پائیں, talē تلے / *adv./prep.* taḥt تحت / *prep./adj.* zēr زیر

undergo *v.* jhēlnā جھیلنا
undergo an examination *v.* imtiḥān dēnā امتحان دینا
undergo medical treatment *v.* davā karnā دوا کرنا
underground *n.* zamīn dōz زمین دوز
understand *v.* samajhnā سمجھنا , maᶜlūm karnā معلوم کرنا
understandable *adj.* maᶜqūl معقول
understanding *adj.* dān دان / *n.* fahm فہم, samajh سمجھ , tafahhum تفہم ; *(mutual ~)* samjhautā سمجھوتا
understood *adj.* fahmīdah فہمیدہ, mafhūm مفہوم , murādī مرادی
underwear *n.* kurtī کرتی
undesirable *adj.* ġair matlub غیر مطلب, nā xūšgavār نا خوشگوار
undisciplined *adj.* phūhaṛ پھوہڑ
undo *v.* udhēṛnā ادھیڑنا
undoubtedly *adv.* bē šak بے شک, bē šā'ibah بے شائبہ, lā raib لاریب
undutiful *adj.* nā xalaf نا خلف
uneasily *adv.* muztaribānah مضطربانہ
uneasiness *n.* xalijān خلجان; *(of the mind)* zaḥmat زحمت
uneasy *adj.* bē cain بے چین, mušavvaš مشوش, muztarib مضطرب , zaḥmatī زحمتی
uneducated *adj.* jāhil جاہل, nā xvāndah نا خواندہ, phūhaṛ پھوہڑ / *n.* sādah dil سادہ دل
unemployed *adj.* bē kār بے کار, bē rōzgār بے روزگار
unequaled *adj.* yagānah یگانہ
uneven *adj.* khurdarā کھردرا, xar xarā خرخرا
unexpectedly *adv.* ittifāq sē اِتفاق سے
unfair *adj.* nā insāf نا انصاف, nā rāst نا راست
unfairness *n.* nā rāstī نا راستی
unfaithful *adj.* xā'in خائن
unfamiliar *adj.* nā āšnā نا آشنا
unfavorable *adj.* nā sāz gār نا سازگار
unfinished *adj.* manqūs منقوص
unfit *adj.* nā rasā نا رسا
unfold *v.* suljhānā سلجھانا
unfortunate *adj.* bad baxt بدبخت, bad nasīb بدنصیب, bē nasīb بے نصیب, kam baxt کم بخت
unfortunately *adv.* bad qismatī sē بد قسمتی سے

ungraceful *adj.* nā zēbā نازیبا, iḥsān farāmōš اِحسان فراموش, kafūr کفور, nā sipās ناسپاس
unhappy *adj.* nā xūš ناخوش
unhealthy *adj.* nā durust نادرست, rōgī روگی
uniform *adj.* yak rang یک رنگ / *n.* vardī وردی
uninhabited *adj.* ġair ābād غیرآباد
unintelligent *adj.* nā samajh ناسمجھ
unintentionally *adv.* yūṁ hī یوں ہی
union *n.* ittiḥād اِتحاد, ittisāl اِتصال, yagāngat یگانگت, yagāngi یگانگی
unique *adj.* faqīd-ul-misāl فقید المثال, yaktā یکتا, ēk ایک
uniqueness *n.* yagāngat یگانگت, yagāngi یگانگی, yaktā'ī یکتائی
unit *n.* ikā'ī اکائی, sabaq سبق
unite *v.* jōṛnā جوڑنا, , milānā ملانا, muttaḥid karnā متحد کرنا
united *adj.* munzam منضم , muttaḥid متحد
United Nations (U.N.) *n.* aqvām-ē-muttaḥidah اقوام متحدہ
unity *n.* aḥdiyat احدیت, vaḥdat وحدت, yaktā'ī یکتائی; *(of God)* tauḥīd توحید
universal *adj.* ᶜālimī عالمی, ᶜamīm عمیم , jamīᶜ جمیع مطلق
universally *adv.* jamīᶜan جمیعا
universe *n.* ᶜālam عالم, jahāṁ جہاں, kā'ināt کائنات, saṁsār سنسار
university *n.* jāmiᶜah جامعہ, madrasah مدرسہ, yūnivarsiṭī یونورسٹی
unjust *adj.* bē insāf بے انصاف, nā ḥaqq ناحق, nā insāf ناانصاف
unjustice *n.* haṭ dharmī ہٹ دھرمی
unknowingly *adv.* aṁjānē انجانے, nā dānistah نادانستہ
unknown *adj.* aṁjān انجان, ġair maᶜlūm غیر معلوم
unlawful *adj.* bē jā بے جا, ḥarām حرام, nā jā'iz ناجائز, nā ravā ناروا
unless *conj.* magar مگر
unlimited *adj.* ġair maḥdūd غیر محدود, ġair maḥdūd غیر محدود
unlock *v.* khōlnā کھولنا
unlucky *adj.* bad baxt بدبخت, bad nasīb بدنصیب, kam baxt کم بخت
unmannerly *adj.* nā rasā نارسا
unmarried girl *n.* bākirah باکرہ, kuṁvārī کنواری
unoccupied *adj.* fāriġ فارغ
unpalatable *adj.* talx تلخ
unparalleled *adj.* vaḥīd وحید, yād gār-ē-zamānah یادگار زمانہ

unperishable *adj.* lā zavāl لازوال
unpleasant *adj.* nā xūšgavār ناخوشگوار
unpolluted *adj.* pāk sāf پاک صاف
unpopulated *adj.* vīrān ویران, bairan بیرن
unprincipled *adj.* kaj raftār کج رفتار
unproductive *adj.* bāṁjh بانجھ, kallar کلر, lā ḥāsil لاحاصل
unprofitable *adj.* lā ḥāsil لاحاصل
unproportional *adj.* ġair mutanāsib غیر متناسب
unquestionably *adv.* lā raib لاریب
unravel *v.* khulnā کھلنا, suljhānā سلجھانا, udhēṛnā ادھیڑنا
unraveling *n.* udhēṛ ادھیڑ
unreasonable *adj.* bē jā بے جا, ġair vājib غیر واجب
unreliable *adj.* ġair muᶜatabir غیر معتبر
unripe *adj.* kaccā کچا, nā rasīdah نارسیدہ, sabz سبز, xām خام
unseen *adj.* nā dīdah نادیدہ
unsettled *adj.* ḍānvāṁ ḍōl ڈانواں ڈول
unstable *adj.* nā pāʾīdār ناپائیدار
unsteady *adj.* cancal چنچل, ḍānvāṁ ḍōl ڈانواں ڈول
unsuitable *adj.* ġair munāsib غیر مناسب, nā zēbā نازیبا
unsuited *adj.* nāravā ناروا
unthankful *adj.* iḥsān farāmōš اِحسان فراموش, nā sipās ناسپاس
untie *v.* khōlnā کھولنا
until *prep.* jab tak جب تک, lag لگ, mā dām مادام, ḥattā حتیٰ / *conj.* tak تک, tā تا
untouched *adj.* achūtā اچھوتا
untrained *adj.* nā tajribah kār ناتجربہ کار
untrustworthiness *n.* bē iᶜtibārī بے اعتباری, nā iᶜtimādī نااعتمادی
untrustworthy *adj.* cār cašm چارچشم, nā iᶜtimād نااعتماد
unused *adj.* kōrā کورا, matrūk-ul-istiᶜmāl متروک الاستعمال
unusual *adj.* anōkhā انوکھا, ġair maᶜmūlī غیر معمولی
unveil *v.* ughāṛnā اگھاڑنا
unveiled *adj.* bē pardah بے پردہ
unwanted *adj.* ġair matlub غیر مطلب
unwell *adj.* bīmār بیمار

unwillingly *adv.* nā dānistah نا دانستہ
unwise *adj.* bē ᶜaql بے عقل, xām raiš خام ریش
unworthy *adj.* nā rasā نا رسا, nā sazā نا سزا
up *adv.* ūpar اوپر
up to *adj.* bhar بھر
update *v.* xabar dēnā خبر دینا
uphold *v.* baḥāl rakhnā بحال رکھنا
uplift *v.* caṛhānā چڑھانا
upon *adv.* ūpar اوپر / *prep.* bar بر, par پر
upper storey *n.* bām بام, kāx کاخ
upper-arm *n.* ḍanḍ ڈنڈ
upright *adj.* ᶜādil عادل, īmāndār ایماندار, rāst bāz راست باز
uprightness *n.* īmāndārī ایمانداری, istiqāmat استقامت, rāstī راستی
uproar *n.* cax چخ ġauġā غوغا, hangāmah ہنگامہ, šōr-ō-ġul شوروغل
uproot *v.* ukhāṛna اکھاڑنا
upset *adj.* darham barham درہم برہم, uthal puthal اُتھل پتھل / *v.* aundhānā اوندھانا, darham barham karnā درہم برہم کرنا, ulaṭnā الٹنا
upside-down *adj.* ulṭā الٹا, darham barham درہم برہم
upto *adv.* lag لگ, laġāyat لغایت, tak تک / *conj.* ḥattā حتیٰ
urad *(a legume)* *n.* uṛad اڑد
urbanization *n.* tamaddun تمدن
Urdu *(language)* *n.* urdū اردو, rēxtah ریختہ
Urdu writing *n.* nastaᶜlīq
urge *v.* hānknā ہانکنا, tākīd karnā تاکید کرنا
urgency *n.* iḥtiyāj اِحتیاج
urgent *adj.* mubram مبرم, tākīdī تاکیدی, zarūr ضرور
urgent matter *n.* muhimm مہم
urgently *adv.* jaldī sē جلدی سے
urinate *v.* mūtnā موتنا, pēšāb karnā پیشاب کرنا
urine *n.* mūt موت, pīšāb/pēšāb پیشاب
urn *n.* dalv دلو
us *pron.* ham ہم, hamēṁ ہمیں
USA (United States of America) *n.* Amērikā امیریکا
usage *n.* atlāq اطلاق, dastūr دستور, istiᶜmāl استعمال, rasm-ō-rivāj رسم ورواج

use *n.* isticmāl استعمال, kām کام / *adj. (in ~)* mutadāval متداول / *v.* isticmāl karnā استعمال کرنا

use force *v.* saxtī karnā سختی کرنا

use up *v.* khapānā کھپانا

used *adj.* mustacmal مستعمل

useful *adj.* kār āmad کار آمد, mufīd مفید

usefulness *n.* ifādiyat افادیت

useless *adj.* bē kār بے کار, nā bakār نابکار

uselessness *n.* nā bakārī نابکاری

usual *adj.* rā'ij رائج, rasmī رسمی

usually *adv.* camūman عموماً, cām taur sē عام طور سے

usurer *n.* sūd xōr سود خور

usurp *v.* dabānā دبانا, mār rakhnā مار رکھنا

usurper *n.* ġāzib غاصب

utmost *adj./adv.* ġāyat غایت

utter *v.* hānknā ہانکنا, uccāran karnā اچارن کرنا, bōlnā بولنا. ♦ ~ **a word** dam mārnā دم مارنا

utterance *n.* bōl بول, qirāt قرات, talaffuz تلفظ, uccāran اچارن

V

vacancy *n.* xalā خلا
vacant *adj.* xālī خالی
vacation *n.* chuṭṭī چھٹی, taᶜṭīl تعطیل
vagabond *n.* āvārah آوارہ
vagrant *adj.* sailānī سیلانی, xānah badōš خانہ بدوش
vain *adj.* ᶜabas عبث, bē kār بے کار
valiant *adj.* bahādur بہادر, dalēr دلیر
valid *adj.* maᶜqūl معقول, muvajjah موجہ
valley *n.* ghāṭī گھاٹی, vādī وادی
valor *n.* dil āvarī دل اوری, jurāt جرات
valuable *adj.* qīmatī قیمتی
valuables *n.* matāᶜ متاع
valuation *n.* ṭānk ٹانک
value *n.* māliyat مالیت, mōl مول, qadr قدر, qīmat قیمت / *v.* qīmat lagānā قیمت لگانا, ānknā آنکنا
vanish *v.* nā paid hōnā ناپید ہونا
vanity *n.* ġarūr غرور, lāf لاف, xūdī خودی
vapor *n.* buxārāt بخارات, dūd دود
variable *adj.* taġayyur pazīr تغیر پزیر، mutalavvin متلون
varied *adj.* gūnā gūṁ گوناگوں
variety *n.* tanavvōᶜ تنوع
various *adj.* mutaᶜaddad متعدد, muxtalif مختلف
varnish *n.* luk لک / *v.* rang bharnā رنگ بھرنا, rang dēnā رنگ دینا
vase *n.* zarf ظرف
vast *adj.* vasīᶜ وسیع, mufriṭ مفرط
vast multitude *n.* jam-ē-ġafīr جم غفیر
vat *n.* māṭ ماٹ
vaunting *n.* ḍīng ڈینگ
Veda *(the sacred Hindu scriptures) n.* vēd وید
vegetable *n.* sabzī سبزی
vegetable market *n.* sabzī manḍī سبزی منڈی

vegetable seller *n.* kuṁjṛā کنجڑا
vegetation *n.* nabātāt نباتات, rō'īdagī روئیدگی, našv نشو
vehicle *n.* gāṛī گاڑی
veil *n.* niqāb نقاب, burqaᶜ برقع, dōpaṭṭah دوپٹہ, ḥijāb حجاب
vein *n.* nālī نالی, rag رگ
velvet *n.* maxmal مخمل
vendor *n.* farōšindah فروشندہ, bēcnē vālā بیچنےوالا
venerable *adj.* muḥtaram محترم, mukarram مکرم
vengeance *n.* intiqām انتقام
vent (one's) spleen *v./phr.* buxār nikālnā بخار نکالنا
ventilator *n.* pankhā پنکھا, raušan dān روشن دان
venture *v.* dalērī karnā دلیری کرنا
venturesome *adj.* jānbāz جانباز
Venus *(planet) n.* zuhrah زہرہ
veranda *n.* barāmdah برآمدہ, dālān دالان
verb *n.* fiᶜil فعل
verbal *adj.* luġvī لغوی, muṁh zabānī منہ زبانی, zabānī زبانی
verbal meaning *n.* laġvī maᶜnī لغوی معنی
verdant *adj.* harā bharā ہرا بھرا, sar sabz سرسبز
verification *n.* taḥaqquq تحقق, tasdīq تصدیق
verified *adj.* musaddaqah مصدقہ, mutaḥaqqaq متحقق
verifier *n.* mutaḥaqqiq متحقق
verify *v.* tasdīq karnā تصدیق کرنا, taḥqīq karnā تحقیق کرنا
vermilion *n.* sēndūr سیندور
verse *n.* nazm نظم; *(of the Quran)* āyat آیت; *(sacred)* mantar منتر
very *adv./adj.* bahut بہت
vessel *n.* jahāz جہاز, safīnah سفینہ
vest *n.* vāskaṭ واسکٹ, pairāhan پیراہن
vestige *n.* sūrat سورت
veteran *adj.* tajurbah kār تجربہ کار, gurg-ē-bārāṁ dīdah گرگ باراں دیدہ
vex *v.* diqq karnā دق کرنا, zic karnā زچ کرنا
vibrate *v.* phaṛaknā پھڑکنا
vicinity *n.* gird-ē-navāḥ گردنواح, paṛōs پڑوس

vicious *adj.* fāsidah فاسده, nā xalaf نا خلف
victorious *adj.* fātiḥ فاتح, fatḥ mand فتح مند, fīrōz mand فیروز مند
victorious; *(as a person)* zafar yāb ظفریاب; *(in war)* zafar mauj ظفر موج
victory *n.* fatḥ mandī فتح مندی, fatḥ فتح
view *n.* manzar منظر
viewpoint *n.* ᶜindiyah عندیہ
vigilance *n.* cōkasī چوکسی, tavaqī توقی
vigilant *adj.* cōkas چوکس, bēdār بیدار
vigor *n.* bal بل, jān جان, quvvat قوت
vigorous *adj.* zabardast زبردست
vile *adj.* kam zāt کم ذات, pājī پاجی, qabīḥ قبیح, razīl رذیل
villa *n.* kāx کاخ
village *n.* dēhāt دیہات, gā'ōṁ گاؤں, pinḍ پنڈ
village chief *n.* caudharī چودھری
villager *n.* dēhātī دیہاتی, ganvār گنوار
villain *n.* ḥarāmī حرامی
vine *n.* angūr kī bēl انگور کی بیل, raz رز
vinegar *n.* sirkah سرکہ
vineyard *n.* angūr kā xānah انگور کا خانہ, raz رز
violation (of law) *n.* ᶜisyān عصیان
violence *n.* tašaddud تشدد, dast darāzī دست درازی, zarb ضرب
violent *adj.* ḥašrī حشری, mutašaddid متشدد, zabardast زبردست
violently *adv.* bil-jabr بالجبر, zabardastī sē زبردستی سے
violet *adj.* banafšī rang بنفشی رنگ, arġavānī ارغوانی
viper *(snake) n.* afaᶜī افعی
virgin *n.* dōšīzah دوشیزہ, bākirah باکرہ
virgin of paradise *n.* ḥūr حور
virginity *n.* dōšīzagī دوشیزگی
Virgo *(Zodiac) n.* ᶜazrā عذرا
virtue *n.* hunar ہنر, manqabat منقبت, nēkī نیکی, gun گن
virtuous *adj.* pākdāman پاکدامن, nēk نیک
visa *n.* vīzā ویزا
viscious *adj.* caspāṁ چسپاں

viscosity *n.* cēp چیپ, luᶜāb لعاب
viscous *adj.* luᶜāb dār لعاب دار
visibility *n.* zuhūr ظہور
visible *adj.* dīdānī دیدنی, manzūr منظور, namūdār نمودار
visibly *adv.* zāhiran ظاہراً
vision *n.* basārat بصارت, bīnā'ī بینائی, nazar نظر
visionary *adj.* xayālī خیالی, vahmī وہمی
visit *n.* mulāqāt ملاقات / *v.* mulāqāt karnā ملاقات کرنا
visiting *adj.* mulāqātī ملاقاتی
visitor *n.* mulāqātī ملاقاتی
vital *adj.* dam dār دم دار
vitality *n.* dam دم
vixen *n.* lōmaṛī لومڑی
vocabulary *n.* farhang فرہنگ
voice *n.* āvāz آواز; *(from heaven)* sarōš سروش
void (of) *adj.* ᶜārī عاری, xalā خلا
volcano *n.* ātaš fišāṁ pahāṛ آتش فشاں پہاڑ, kōh-ē-ātaš fišāṁ کوہ آتش فشاں
volume *n.* jasāmat جسامت, saḥīfah صحیفہ
voluntary *adj.* rizā kārānah رضاکارانہ, ixtiyārī اختیاری
volunteer *n.* rizā kār رضاکار
vomit *n.* qai قے / *v.* qai karnā قے کرنا
vote *n.* rā'iē رائے, mat مت / *v.* intixāb karnā انتخاب کرنا
vow *n.* ḥalaf حلف, mannat منت, nazr نذر ♦ **take a** ~ *v.* murād mānnā مرادماننا
vowel *n.* ḥarf-ē-ᶜillat حرف علت, kasrah کسرہ
voyage *n.* safar سفر, siyāḥat سیاحت
vulgar *adj.* bazārī بازاری, nīc نیچ
vulture *n.* gidh گدھ

W

wag tail *(a dog)* *v.* dum hilānā دم ہلانا
wage war *v.* jang karnā جنگ کرنا
wages *n.* mazdūrī/muzdūrī مزدوری ♦ **daily** ~ rōzīnah روزینہ
wail *v.* bilāpnā بلاپنا, kūknā کوکنا
wailing *n.* alāp الاپ, zārī زاری
waist *n.* kamar کمر
waistcoat *n.* kurtah کرتہ, banḍī بنڈی, cōlī چولی
wait *v.* intizār karnā انتظار کرنا
wait for *v.* rāstah dēkhnā راستہ دیکھنا
wait on *v.* ḥāzir rahnā حاضر رہنا
waiter *n.* bērā بیرا
wake up *v.* jāgnā جاگنا
wakeful *adj.* bēdār بیدار, mutanabbah متنبہ
wakefulness *n.* bēdārī بیداری
walk *n.* gašt گشت, sair سیر / *v.* calnā چلنا, sair karnā سیر کرنا
walking stick *n.* chaṛī چھڑی, cōb dastī چوب دستی
wall *n.* dīvār دیوار
wallet *n.* baṭvā بٹوا, jhōlī جھولی, zanbīl زنبیل
walnut *n.* axrōṭ اخروٹ
wander *v.* āvārah hōnā آوارہ ہونا, ghūmnā گھومنا, phirnā پھرنا
wander around *v.* ḍānvāṁ ḍōl phirnā ڈانواں ڈول پھرنا
wanderer *n.* āvārah آوارہ, sayyār سیار, xānah badōš خانہ بدوش
wandering *adj.* ḍānvāṁ ḍōl ڈانواں ڈول
want *n.* hauṁs ہونس, iḥtiyāj اِحتیاج, muḥtājī محتاجی / *v.* cāhnā چاہنا
wanted *adj.* darkār درکار
wantonness *n.* kalōl کلول
war *n.* jang جنگ ♦ **go to** ~ *v.* laṛā'ī par jānā لڑائی پر جانا
warble *v.* cahcahānā چہچہانا
ward *n.* gārad گارد mubārazat مبارزت, paikār پیکار, parxāš پرخاش
ward off *v.* dafaᶜ karnā دفع کرنا
ware *n.* saudā sulf سودا سلف

warehouse *n.* gūdām گودام, māl xānah مال خانہ
warlike *adj.* jangī جنگی
warm *adj.* garm/garam گرم / *v.* tapānā تپانا
warm oneself *v.* tāpnā تاپنا
warmth *n.* garmī گرمی
warn *v.* fahmā'iš karnā فہمائش, hōšiyār karnā ہوشیار کرنا
warrant *n.* ḥukm nāmah حکم نامہ, parvānah پروانہ
warrior *n.* mubāriz مبارز, muḥārib محارب, sūr سور
warship *n.* jangī jahāz جنگی جہاز
was *v.* thā تھا
wash *v.* dhōnā دھونا
wash basin *n.* cilamcī چلمچی
washed *adj.* maġsūl مغسول, šustah شستہ
washerman *n.* dhōbī دھوبی
washerwoman *n.* dhōban دھوبن
washing *(prior to praying) n.* masḥ مسح
wasp *n.* bhiṛ بھڑ
wastage *n.* tazīᶜ تضیع
waste *n.* kūṛā karkaṭ کوڑا کرکٹ, kacrā کچرا, ālā'iš آلائش / *v.* zā'iᶜ karnā ضائع کرنا
  waste money *v.* paisā khānā پیسا کھانا
  waste time *v.* din ginvānā دن گنوانا
wasted *adj.* barbād برباد, xarb خرب
wasteful *adj.* musrif مصرف
wasteland *n.* banjar بنجر
watch *n.* ghaṛī گھڑی, jēb ghaṛī جیب گھڑی / *v.* dēkhnā دیکھنا ♦ **keep** ~ *v.* caukasī karnā چوکسی کرنا
watchful *adj.* caukannā چکنا
watchfully *adv.* baġaur بغور
watchfulness *n.* caukasī چوکسی
watchman *n.* caukī dār چوکی دار
watchtower *n.* manārah منارہ
water *n.* pānī پانی, āb آب / *v.* chiṛaknā چھڑکنا, pānī dēnā پانی دینا, piyānā پیانا
water carrier *n.* saqqah سقہ

water course *n.* kārēz کاریز
water fowl *n.* murġābī مرغابی
water mill *n.* pan cakkī پن چکی
water pipe *(hookah) n.* ḥuqqah حقہ
water pot *n.* pānī kā bartan پانی کا برتن, abrīq اِبریق, garvā گڑوا
water vessel *n.* gāgar گاگر
watered *adj.* sērāb سیراب
waterfall *n.* ābšār آبشار, jharnā جھرنا
watering *n.* chiṛkā'ō چھڑکاؤ, sīṁc سینچ
watermelon *n.* tarbūz تربوز
watery *adj.* pacpacā پچپچا
wave *n.* lahar/lahr لہر, mauj موج / *v.* jhūmnā جھومنا, mauj mārnā موج مارنا
waver *v.* tharthatānā تھرتھرانا, hicaknā ہچکنا
waving *adj.* mauj zan موج زن, mavvāj مواج
wax *n.* mōm موم
waxen *adj.* mōmī مومی
way *n.* rāh راہ, rāstah راستہ, tarīq طریق, tarīqat طریقت
we *pron.* ham ہم
weak *adj.* kamzōr کمزور, nā zōr نا زور, zaᶜīf ضعیف; *(in mind)* ġabī غبی
weakly *adv.* ᶜalīl علیل
weakness *n.* kamzōrī کمزوری
wealth *n.* daulat mandī دولت مندی
wealthy *adj.* daulat mand دولت مند, amīr امیر, paisē vālā پیسے والا
weapon *n.* hathiyār ہتھیار
weaponry *n.* silāḥ سلاح
weapons *n.* asliḥah اسلحہ
wear *v.* pahannā پہننا
weariness *n.* thakāvaṭ تھکاوٹ
weary *adj.* thakā تھکا
weasel *n.* nēvlā نیولا, samūr سمور
weather *n.* mausim/mausam موسم
weaver *n.* jullāha جلاہا
wed *v.* šādī karnā شادی کرنا
wedding *n.* šādī شادی ♦ **celebrate a** ~ šādī karnā شادی کرنا

wedding dress *n.* cōlā چولا
wedding night *n.* suhāg rāt سہاگ رات
wedge *n.* kīl کیل, mēx میخ
wedlock *n.* šādī شادی, bēṛī بیڑی
Wednesday *n.* budh بدھ
weed *n.* ghās phūs گھاس پھوس
week *n.* haftah ہفتہ
weep *v.* rōnā رونا; *(~ bitterly)* rōnā pīṭnā رونا پیٹنا
weeping *adj.* āb dīdah آب دیدہ, giriyāṁ گریاں / *n.* bilāp بلاپ, kuhrām کہرام
weeping lamentation *n.* giryah گریہ
weigh *v.* tōlnā تولنا
weighing *n.* tōl تول, vazn وزن
weight *n.* bhār بھار, vazn وزن
weighty *adj.* bhārī بھاری, vaznī وزنی
welcome *n.* istiqbāl استقبال / *v.* istiqbāl karnā استقبال کرنا, xūš āmdēd kēhnā خوش آمدید کہنا / *interj.* xūš āmdēd خوش آمدید
welcoming (a person) *n.* istiqbāl استقبال
welfare *n.* ᶜāfiyat عافیت, xairiyat خیریت, xair-ō-ᶜāfiyat خیروعافیت
well *adj.* acchā اچھا, xair خیر / *adv.* acchī taraḥ اچھی طرح, bil-xair بالخیر / *n.* cāh چاہ, kuṁvāṁ کنواں
well done! *interj.* kyā xūb کیا خوب, šābāš شاباش
well-acquainted (with an art) *adj.* māhir ماہر
well-adjusted *adj.* acchī taraḥ mutābaqat pazīr اچھی طرح مطابقت پذیر, mauzūṁ موزوں
well-aimed *adj.* sā'ib صائب
well-argued *adj.* mudallal مدلل
well-balanced *adj.* acchī taraḥ mutavāzzin اچھی طرح متوازن
well-being *n.* salāmatī سلامتی, bahbūdi بہبودی
well-born *adj.* ḥurr حر / *n.* najīb نجیب, ᶜālī nažād عالی نژاد
well-done *adj.* dhan dhan دھن دھن
well-instructed *adj.* xabīr خبیر, acchī taraḥ hidāyat yāftah اچھی طرح ہدایت یافتہ
well-intentioned *adj.* nēk niyyat نیک نیت
well-known *adj.* mašhūr مشہور, zabān zad xalā'iq زبان زد خلائق
well-mannered *adj.* mu'addab مؤدب, muhazzab مہذب, salīqah dār سلیقہ دار

well-shaped *adj.* saḍaul سڈول, šakīl شکیل, tarḥ dār طرح دار
well-tempered *adj.* šā'istah mizāj شائستہ مزاج
well-wisher *n.* hava xvāh ہوا خواہ, xair xvāh خیر خواہ
went *v.* gayā گیا
west *n.* maġrib مغرب, pachham/pacchim پچھم
western *adj.* maġribī مغربی
westernization *n.* maġribiyyat مغربیت
westernized *adj.* maġrib zadah مغرب زدہ
wet *adj.* bhīgā hū'ā بھیگا ہوا, gīlā گیلا / *v.* bhigānā بھگانا, bhigōnā بھگونا, gīlā karnā گیلا کرنا
wetness *n.* gīlāpan گیلاپن, tarī تری
wharf *n.* māl gōdī مال گودی, ghāṭ گھاٹ
what *prep.* kā کا, mā ما / *pron.* jis جس, jō جو / *pron./conj.* kih/kē کہ
whatever *pron.* har cih ہرچہ
whatsoever *prep.* jō kuch bhī hō جو کچھ بھی ہو, mā ما / *pron.* har cih ہرچہ
wheat *n.* gandum گندم, gēhūṁ گیہوں
wheaten *adj.* gēhvāṁ گیہواں
wheel *v.* phirānā پھرانا / *n.* cakkā چکا, pahiyah پہیہ; *(potter's ~)* cakkar چکر
whelp *n.* pillā پلا
when *adv.* jab جب, kab کب
whenever *adv.* jab jab جب جب, jab kabhī جب کبھی
where *adj.* jahāṁ جہاں / *adv.* ḥais حیث, jidhar جدھر, jis jagah جس جگہ
where to? *adv.* kahāṁ کہاں, kidhar کدھر
whereabouts *n.* ṭhikānā ٹھکانا
whereas *adv.* cūnkēh چونکہ, jaisā kēh جیسا کہ
wheresoever *adv.* jahīṁ جہیں
whereupon *adv.* jis par جس پر
wherever *adv.* kahīṁ کہیں, jahīṁ جہیں, jidhar جدھر, jis jagah جس جگہ
whether *pron./conj.* kih/kē کہ
whey *n.* chāch چھاچھ
which *adv.* cūṁ چوں, jaisā جیسا / *prep.* kaun sā کون سا / *pron.* jis جس, jō جو / *pron./conj.* kaun sā کون سا, kaun کون, kin کن, kis کس, kih/kē کہ
while *adv.* jab kih جب کہ, kē dauran کے دوران
whim *n.* tarang ترنگ, mauj موج, vasvās وسواس

whimper *v.* ṭhinaknā ٹھنکنا
whip *n.* cābuk چابک / *v.* cābuk mārnā چابک مارنا
whirl *v.* phirānā پھرانا
whirlwind *n.* āndhī آندھی, bād gard باد گرد, bavanḍar بونڈر.
whirpool *n.* bhanvar بھنور
whisk *n.* jhāṛū جھاڑو.
whisper *v.* kānā phūsī karnā کانا پھوسی کرنا
whistle *n.* sīṭī سیٹی / *v.* sīṭī bajānā سیٹی بجانا
white *adj.* safēd سفید; *(skin color)* farangī فرنگی, gōrā گورا
whiten *v.* safēdī karnā سفیدی کرنا
whiteness *n.* safēdī سفیدی
whitewash *v.* safēdī karnā سفیدی کرنا
whitish *adj.* safēd sā سفید سا
whiz *n.* saṁsanāhaṭ سنسناہٹ
who *pron.* jō جو., jis جس., kaun کون, kin کن, kis کس / *pron./conj.* kih/kē کہ
who knows *interj.* kyā jānē کیا جانے
whole *adj.* mukammil مکمل pūrā پورا, sab سب, sārā سارا / *adv.* tamām-ō-kamāl تمام وکمال / *n.* jumlah جملہ
wholesale dealer *(in a village)* *n.* thōkdār تھوکدار
wholly *adv.* sar ba-sar سر بسر
whom *pron.* jis جس., kin کن, kis کس
whore *n.* tavā'if طوائف, ranḍī رنڈی
why *adv.* kāhē kō کاہے کو / *pron.* kyōṁ کیوں, kyōṁkar کیونکر / *pron./adj.* kaisā کیسا
why not *pron.* kyōṁ nahīṁ کیوں نہیں
wick *n.* battī بتی, falītah فلیتہ, fatīlah فتیلہ
wicked *adj.* burā برا, šarīr شریر ♦ ~ **person** *n.* luccā لچا ♦ ~ **woman** *n.* pāpan پاپن
wickedness *n.* badī بدی, burā'ī برائی, šaitānī شیطانی, šarārat شرارت
wide *adj.* cauṛā چوڑا
wide open *adj.* caupaṭ چوپٹ
widow *n.* bēvah بیوہ
width *n.* cauṛā'ī چوڑائی
wife *n.* bīvī بیوی, ghar vālī گھروالی, patnī پتنی
wifehood *n.* suhāg سہاگ
wild *adj.* janglī جنگلی

wild animal *n.* vaḥšī وحشی
wilderness *n.* bayābān بیابان, bēšah بیشہ, saḥrā صحرا
will *n.* irādah ارادہ, vasiyyat وصیت
willing *adj.* rizā mand رضامند, xvāhišmand خواہشمند
willingly *adv.* baxūšī بخوشی, bāxūšī بخوشی, šauq sē شوق سے
willow *n.* bēd بید
win *v.* jītnā جیتنا
  win a battle *v.* maidān mārnā میدان مارنا
  win influence *v.* rasūx ḥāsil karnā رسوخ حاصل کرنا
wind *n.* havā ہوا, tūfān طوفان / *v.* ainṭhnā اینٹھنا
winding *adj.* cakr dār چکر دار, pēc dār پیچ دار / *n.* mōṛ موڑ, pēcīdgī پیچیدگی phēr پھیر
window *n.* khiṛkī کھڑکی
windpipe *n.* ṭēnṭū'ā ٹینٹوا
windy *adj.* havā'ī ہوائی, tūfānī طوفانی
wine *n.* dārū دارو, šarāb شراب
wine cup *n.* sātgīn ساتگین, sāġar ساغر
wine drinker *n.* bādah nōš بادہ نوش, mai parast مے پرست
wing *n.* pahlū پہلو, pankh پنکھ, par پر
wink *n.* cašmak چشمک / *v.* ānkh jhapaknā آنکھ جھپکنا
winking *n.* cašmak چشمک
winter *n.* mausim-ē-sarmā موسم سرما, sardī سردی, zamistān/zamastān زمستان
wintery *adj.* sarmā'ī سرمائی
wipe *v.* pōṁchnā پونچھنا
wire *n.* tār تار, silk سلک, sūt سوت
wisdom *n.* ᶜaql mandī عقل مندی
wise *adj.* ᶜaql mand عقل مند
wise man *n.* luqmān لقمان, giyāni گیانی
wisely *adj.* ᶜālimānah عالمانہ, ᶜāqilānah عاقلانہ
wish *n.* icchā اچھا, xvāhiš خواہش / *v.* ārzū karnā آرزو کرنا, xvāhiš karnā خواہش کرنا
wit *n.* hōšmandī ہشمندی, jugat جگت, zarāfat ظرافت
witch *n.* afsūṁ sāz افسوں ساز, cuṛēl چڑیل
with *adv.* ᶜind عند, ham rāh ہم راہ, sāth ساتھ / *n.* ham rāh ہم راہ / *prep.* sē سے, kē sāth کے ساتھ
withdraw *v.* phir jānā پھر جانا, pīṭh phērnā پیٹھ پھیرنا, ṭalnā ٹلنا

withdraw from *v.* dast bardār hōnā دست بردار ہونا
withdrawal *n.* dast bardāri دست برداری, nikālā نکالا, vāpasī واپسی
wither *v.* murjhānā مرجھانا, sūkhnā سوکھنا
withered *adj.* sūkhā سوکھا, xušk خشک
withhold *v.* rōknā روکنا
within *prep.* dar در, mēṁ میں
without *adv.* baġair بغیر, bin بن, binā بنا, lā لا / *prep.* bē بے, bērūn بیرون, bilā بلا / *prep./adv.* ġair غیر
witness *n.* gavāh گواہ
witty *adj.* zarīf ظریف, mazāqiyah مذاقیہ, xām raiš خام ریش / *n.* bazlah sanj بذلہ سنج zarāf ظراف
witty person *n.* latīfah gō لطیفہ گو
wizard *n.* jādūgar جادوگر, kāhan کاہن
woe *n.* āzurdagī آزردگی
woeful *adj.* ġam nāk غم ناک
wolf *n.* bhēṛiyā بھیڑیا
woman *n.* ᶜaurat عورت
womb *n.* riḥm رحم, pēṭ پیٹ
wonder *n.* ḥairat حیرت
wonderful *adj.* ḥairat angēz حیرت انگیز / *interj.* kyā xūb کیا خوب, vah vah وہ وہ
wondering *adj.* mutḥaiyyir متحیر
wonderstruck *adj.* dang دنگ, ḥairān zadah حیرت زدہ
wood *n.* lakṛī لکڑی
wooden *adj.* lakṛī kā لکڑی کا, cōbī چوبی
wool *n.* ūn اون
woolen *adj.* ūnī اونی
woolen carpet *n.* qālīn قالین
word *n.* bāt بات, lafz لفظ, šabd شبد , kalām کلام
word by word *adv.* lafz bah lafz لفظ بہ لفظ, ḥarf baḥarf حرف بحرف
work *n.* kām کام, mazdūrī/muzdūrī مزدوری; *(done by contract)* ṭhēkah ٹھیکہ / *v.* kām karnā کام کرنا, kamānā کمانا
work hard *v.* hāth pā'ōṁ hilānā ہاتھ پاؤں ہلانا, mārā mār karnā مارامارکرنا
worker *n.* kār kun کارکن, mazdūr/muzdūr مزدور
working *adj.* kamā'ū کماؤ

workman *n.* mazdūr/muzdūr مزدور, kārīgar کاریگر, pēšah var پیشہ ور
workmanship *n.* gharat گھڑت, kārastānī کارستانی, kārī garī کاری گری
workshop *n.* kār gāh کارگاہ, kār xānah کارخانہ
world *n.* dunyā دنیا, jahāṁ جہاں, ᶜālam عالم ♦ **belonging to the ~** *adj.* dunyavī دنیوی
world-conquering *adj.* jahāngīr جہانگیر
worldliness *n.* dunyā dārī دنیا داری
worldly *adj.* dunyāvī دنیاوی, māddī مادی, dunyā dār دنیا دار
world-subduing *adj.* jahāngīr جہانگیر
worm *n.* kīṛā کیڑا, kīṛī کیڑی
worried *adj.* parēšān پریشان, fikar mand متفکر مند
worry *n.* parēšānī پریشانی / *v.* ghabrānā گھبرانا, parēšān karnā پریشان کرنا ♦ **don't ~!** *interj.* ghabrā'ō mat! گھبراؤ مت
worse *adj.* bad tar بدتر
worship *n.* ᶜibādat عبادت, parastiš پرستش / *v.* ᶜibādat karnā عبادت کرنا, parastiš karnā پرستش کرنا
worshipped *adj.* masjūd مسجود
worshipper *n.* ᶜābid عابد, parastār پرستار
worshipping *adj.* parast پرست, riyāzatī ریاضتی / *n.* but parastī بت پرستی
worth *n.* ahliyat اہلیت, liyāqat لیاقت, qīmat قیمت
worthless *adj.* bē bakār بے بکار, nā bakār نابکار
worthless stuff *n.* gājar mūlī گاجر مولی
worthlessness *n.* nā bakārī نابکاری
worthy *adj.* lā'iq لائق, qābil قابل, mustaḥiqq مستحق
wound *n.* zaxm زخم / *v.* cōṭ karnā چوٹ کرنا, majrūḥ karnā مجروح کرنا
wounded *adj.* majrūḥ مجروح, zaxmī زخمی, jarīḥ جریح
wrangle *n.* jhagṛā جھگڑا, kal کل / *v.* jhagṛā karnā جھگڑا کرنا, kalkal karnā کلکل کرنا
wrangling *n.* jhagṛā جھگڑا, kalkal کلکل
wrap *v.* lapēṭna لپیٹنا
wrapped *adj.* laff لف
wrapper *n.* dōpaṭṭah دوپٹہ
wrapping *n.* lapēṭ لپیٹ
wrathful *adj.* jhakkī جھکی

wrench *v.* jhukā dēnā جھکا دینا, chīnnā چھینا

wrestle *v.* kuštī laṛnā کشتی لڑنا

wrestler *n.* pahlvān پہلوان, kuštī bāz کشتی باز

wrestling *n.* kuštī کشتی, pahlvānī پہلوانی

wretched *adj.* adham ادھم, kam baxtī kā mārā کم بختی کا مارا

wring *v.* marōṛnā مروڑنا, nicōṛnā نچوڑنا

wring out *v.* phīṁchā پھینچنا

wrinkle *n.* juftah جفتہ, jhurrī جھری

wrinkled *adj.* juftah جفتہ, khurdarā کھردرا, khurkhurā کھرکھرا

wrist *n.* kalā'ī کلائی

write *v.* likhnā لکھنا

writer *n.* kātib کاتب, munšī منشی, musannif مصنف

writhe *v.* kulbalānā کلبلانا, marōṛnā مروڑنا

writing *adj.* navīs نویس / *n.* likhā'ī لکھائی, kitābat کتابت, navišt نوشت; darj درج

written *adj.* maktūb مکتوب, musannaf مصنف, navištah نوشتہ

wrong *adj.* ġalat غلط, nā ḥaqq نا حق

Y

yard *n.* āngan آنگن, gaz گز, zirāᶜ ذراع
yarn *n.* sūt سوت
yawn *v.* jamā'ī lēnā جمائی لینا
yawning *n.* jamā'ī جمائی
year *n.* sāl سال, baras برس
yearly *adj.* sālānah سالانہ
yearn *v.* muštāq hōnā مشتاق ہونا
yearn for *v.* jī tarasnā جی ترسنا
yeast *n.* xamīr خمیر
yellow *adj.* pīlā پیلا, zard زرد, zaᶜfarānī زعفرانی / *n. (color)* zard rang زرد رنگ
yellowish *adj.* zard sā زرد سا, pīlā sā پیلا سا
yellowness *n.* zardī زردی, pīlāpan پیلاپن
yes *adv.* hāṁ ہاں
yes madam! *interj.* hāṁ jī ہاں جی
yes sir! *interj.* hāṁ jī ہاں جی
yesterday *n.* kal کل
yet *adv.* ab bhī اب بھی, ab tak اب تک, hanūz ہنوز / *conj.* lēkin لیکن, va-lēkin ولیکن
yoga *n.* yōg یوگ, jōg جوگ
yogi *n. (a Hindu ascetic)* yōgī یوگی, jōgī جوگی; *(female)* jōgin جوگن
yogurt *n.* dahī دہی
yoke *n.* bandhan بندھن, šāxah شاخہ / *v.* gāṛī hānknā گاڑی ہانکنا, jōtnā جوتنا
yonder *adv.* sāmnē سامنے, vahāṁ وہاں
you *pron. (plural)* āp آپ, tum تم; *(singular)* āp آپ, tum تم, tū تو
you're welcome! *interj.* kō'ī bāt nahīṁ! کوئی بات نہیں
young *adj.* nau javān نوجوان, nanhā ننھا
youngster *n.* kam sin کم سن
your *pron.* tumhārā تمہارا, āp kā آپ کا, tērā تیرا
your excellency! *interj.* janāb جناب, janāb-ē-ᶜālī جناب عالی
your highness! *interj.* janāb جناب
your honor! *interj.* ḥuzūr حضور

youth *n.* nau javānī نوجوانی, šabāb شباب
youthful *n.* nau javān نوجوان

Z

zeal *n.* sar garmī سرگرمی, šauq شوق
zealous *adj.* sar garm سرگرم, šā'iq شائق
zenith *n.* nuqtah-ē-mintahā نقطۂ منتہا
zero *n.* sifar/sifr صفر
Zion *n.* saihūn صیہون
Zionism *n.* saihūniyat صیہونیت
Zionist *adj.* saihūnī صیہونی
Zodiac *n.* rās manḍal راس منڈل, mintaqat-ul-burūj منطقۃ البروج
zone *n.* mintaqah منطقہ, xittah خطہ
zoo *n.* ciṛiyā ghar چڑیا گھر
zoologist n. māhir-ē-ḥaivānāt ماہر حیوانات
zoology *n.* ḥaivāniyāt حیوانات, ᶜilm-ē-ḥaivānāt علم حیوانات
Zoroastrian *n./adj.* pārsī پارسی

Months of the Islamic Calendar

مُحَرَّمٌ	muḥarram	1st month
صَفَرٌ	safar	2nd month
رَبِيعُ الأَوَّلُ	rabī-ul-avval	3rd month
رَبِيعُ الثَّانِي	rabī-as-sāni	4th month
جُمَادىَ الأُولَى	jamādī-ul-avval	5th month
جُمَادىَ الثَّانِي	jamādī-us-sānī	6th month
رَجَبٌ	rajab	7th month
شَعْبَانُ	šābān	8th month
رَمَضَانُ	ramzān	9th month
شَوَّالٌ	šavvāl	10th month
ذُو الْقَعْدَةِ	zīqād	11th month
ذُو الْحِجَّةِ	zil-ḥidjdja	12th month